Braving

the

New World

Readings in Contemporary Politics

Braving

the
New World

Readings in Contemporary Politics

FOURTH EDITION

Edited by

Thomas M.J. Bateman
St. Thomas University

Richard M. Myers
St. Thomas University

Roger Epp
Augustana Faculty, University of Alberta

Australia   Canada   Mexico   Singapore   Spain   United Kingdom   United States

THOMSON
★
NELSON

Braving the New World: Readings in Contemporary Politics, Fourth Edition
by Thomas M.J. Bateman, Richard M. Myers, and Roger Epp

**Associate Vice President,
Editorial Director:**
Evelyn Veitch

**Editor-in-Chief,
Higher Education:**
Anne Williams

Executive Editor:
Cara Yarzab

Acquisitions Editor:
Bram Sepers

Executive Marketing Manager:
Lenore Taylor-Atkins

Developmental Editor:
Linda Sparks

Photo Researcher:
Sheila Hall

**Senior Content Production
Manager:**
Natalia Denesiuk Harris

**Copy Editor and
Proofreader:**
Karen Rolfe

Production Coordinator:
Ferial Suleman

Design Director:
Ken Phipps

Interior Design:
Ken Phipps

Cover Design:
Dianna Little

Cover Image:
MedioImages/Getty Images

Compositor:
ICC Macmillan Inc.

Printer:
Webcom

**Library and Archives Canada
Cataloguing in Publication Data**

Braving the new world : readings
in contemporary politics / edited
by Thomas M.J. Bateman, Richard
Myers, Roger Ivan Epp. — 4th ed.

Includes bibliographical
references.
ISBN 978-0-17-642415-2

1. Political science—Textbooks.
2. World politics—Textbooks.
I. Bateman, Thomas Michael
Joseph, 1962– II. Myers, Richard M.
(Richard Morley), 1957–
III. Epp, Roger Ivan, 1958–

JA83.B72 2008   320.9
C2007-903172-2

ISBN-13: 978-0-17-642415-2
ISBN-10: 0-17-642415-6

Contents

Unit 1
Global Challenges

Unit 2
Ideas and Ideologies

Unit 3
Citizenship and Democracy

Unit 4
Contemporary Politics at Home

Unit 5
Contemporary Politics Abroad

Preface

Preparing a revised and updated edition of a collection of readings in contemporary politics poses two challenges. The first is to select articles that create the right balance between topicality and enduring merit. Issues and events come and go; for students of politics the articles' value is in what they illuminate about the larger, permanent questions of politics. Topical articles retain value to the extent that they link a particular event or issue to these larger themes. Particular events of the U.S. occupation of Iraq, for example, will preoccupy only specialists as time passes. But if an article can put those events in a larger context of political development, regime change, and the conditions under which liberal democracy can or cannot take root, then it will have lasting merit.

The second challenge is to predict with some accuracy what issues will either have staying power over time or emerge as more important than they currently appear to be. At the time of writing, according to polls, environmental concern leads Canadians' estimates of the most important political issue. Is this a spike of interest produced by Al Gore's *An Inconvenient Truth* and a warm winter, or do deep anxieties about energy security, climate change, and the disappearance of unspoiled nature combine with postmaterialist value orientations to drive a basic, enduring shift in political priorities? It's hard to say. Political scientists are better at explaining why things have happened than at predicting what will happen.

These two challenges are as daunting as ever. Just when the market was glutted with books proclaiming the Liberals as Canada's natural governing party, the Conservative Party of Canada emerged from disorder on Canada's right to win the 2006 election—and under the leadership of a man most thought had neither the talent, flexibility, nor interest to be prime minister. Many observers concluded that the era of institutional reform in Canada died with the Charlottetown Accord of 1992 and Western Canadian populism, but the Harper government has taken action to reform the Senate by incremental means. Electoral reform continues to move up the political agenda, even in provinces historically resistant to institutional change, despite decades of talk but no action. Just when many court-watchers thought that the Supreme Court of Canada was irremediably the agent of a liberal-left political agenda, the Court in 2005 issued a decision casting constitutional doubt on Canada's single-payer health care system.

This fourth edition attempts to take stock of such changes in Canada and around the world. Of course, we were beset at every turn by questions as to what themes and developments to omit rather than what to include. We hope our choices roughly comport with what others see as important and engaging themes for introductory students of political science.

While each edition of *Braving the New World* is a substantial revision of the preceding volume, the influence of earlier co-editors, most recently Roger Epp, continues. We also acknowledge the able assistance and good humour of Linda Sparks of Thomson Nelson.

Contributors

▶ Gerald Baier is Assistant Professor in the Department of Political Science at the University of British Columbia. His research interests include federalism, the Constitution, and public law. He is the author of *Courts and Federalism: Judicial Doctrine in the United States, Australia and Canada* (2006).

▶ Benjamin R. Barber is the Gershon and Carol Kekst Professor of Civil Society and Distinguished University Professor at the University of Maryland, as well as president and director of the international NGO CivWorld. He is the author of the widely read *Jihad Versus McWorld*, and his most recent book is entitled *Consumed: How Markets Corrupt Children, Infantilize Adults, and Swallow Citizens Whole* (2007).

▶ Thomas M. J. Bateman is Associate Professor and Chair of Political Science at St. Thomas University. His teaching and research interests include Canadian politics, the *Charter of Rights and Freedoms,* and constitutionalism.

▶ Katherine Boothe is a Ph.D. candidate in the Department of Political Science at the University of British Columbia. Her special area of interest is comparative public policy.

▶ Ed Broadbent was leader of the federal New Democratic Party from 1974 to 1989. A one-time Professor of Political Science at York University, he has served, since retiring from electoral politics, as director of the International Centre for Human Rights and Democratic Development, visiting professor at several Canadian universities, and a member of task forces on the volunteer nonprofit sector and on corporate responsibility.

▶ David R. Cameron is Professor of Political Science at the University of Toronto. He has also had a significant career in public service at both the federal and provincial levels. His interests in Canadian government and politics include, in particular, questions of federalism, Quebec nationalism, French–English relations, constitutional renewal, and national unity. He is coauthor of *Cycling into Saigon: The 1995 Conservative Transition in Ontario* (2000).

▶ Jorge Castañeda was Foreign Minister of Mexico from 2000 to 2003 and is currently Global Distinguished Professor of Politics and Latin American Studies at New York University. His most recent book is *Perpetuating Power: How Mexican Presidents Were Chosen* (2000).

▶ William Cross is Associate Professor of Political Science at Carleton University and specializes in the study of political parties and party systems in Canada and around the world. Most recently he is the author of *Political Parties* (2004).

▶ Larry Diamond is a senior fellow at the Hoover Institution at Stanford University. He is the author of *Squandered Victory: The American Occupation and the Bungled Effort to Bring Democracy to Iraq* (2005).

▶ John Ibbitson is a political affairs columnist at *The Globe and Mail*. He is the author of several books on politics, the most recent of which is *The Polite Revolution: Perfecting the Canadian Dream* (2005).

▶ Michael Ignatieff is a Member of Parliament, federal Liberal leadership contender, and internationally renowned human rights scholar. His latest book is entitled *The Lesser Evil: Political Ethics in an Age of Terror* (2004).

▶ Harold Jansen is Associate Professor of Political Science at the University of Lethbridge and one of Canada's leaders in the study of electoral systems. He is senior editor of Mapleleafweb.com and is currently working on a major project tracing the effects of 2003 changes to Canada's political financing regime.

▶ Wenran Jiang is acting director of the China Institute and Associate Professor of Political Science at the University of Alberta. He is twice a Japan Foundation Fellow, a senior fellow at the Asia Pacific Foundation of Canada, President of the Canadian Consortium for Asia Pacific Security, special adviser on China to the United States– and Canada-based Energy Council, and a frequent contributor to media around the world on Asia Pacific affairs. His research interests include East Asia as an emerging region in world politics, and in particular Japanese and Chinese political economy and foreign policy.

▶ Loren Lomasky is Cory Professor of Political Philosophy, Policy and Law in the Department of Philosophy at the University of Virginia. He is best known for his work in moral and political philosophy. His book *Persons, Rights, and the Moral Community* (1987) established his reputation as a leading advocate of a rights-based approach to moral and social issues.

▶ Joseph Masciulli is Assistant Professor of Political Science at St. Thomas University. His most recent book is *Globalization and Political Ethics* (2006), (edited with Richard B. Day). He has also published on human rights and a culture of peace; democracy and technology; the Vatican, global politics, and ethics; and political leadership.

▶ Gordon McCord is a doctoral student in sustainable development and special assistant to Jeffrey Sachs at the Earth Institute at Columbia University.

▶ Mikhail Molchanov is Associate Professor of Political Science at St. Thomas University. He is the author of *Political Culture and National Identity in Russian–Ukrainian Relations* (2002) and co-author/editor of *Ukrainian Foreign and Security Policy: Theoretical and Comparative Perspectives* (2002).

▶ Richard Myers is Professor of Political Science at St. Thomas University. He is co-author of *The Canadian Regime* (2005).

▶ Shaun Narine is Associate Professor of Political Science at St. Thomas University. He teaches in the areas of international relations and the politics of the Asia-Pacific region and is author of *Explaining ASEAN: Regionalism in Southeast Asia* (2002).

▶ Neil Nevitte is Professor of Political Science at the University of Toronto. He is co-investigator of the 1997 and 2000 Canadian Election Studies, and principal investigator of the World Values Survey (Canada). His research interests include political

participation and value change. He has published a number of books and most recently edited *Value Change and Governance* (2002).

▶ Kenneth Newton is Professor of Comparative Politics at the University of Southampton. Formerly Executive Director of the European Consortium for Political Research, his most recent book is titled *Trust in People, Confidence in Political Institutions, and Satisfaction with Democracy: Citizenship and Involvement in European Democracies* (2007).

▶ John O'Sullivan is a writer, a political commentator, and an editor of *The National Review*. His most recent book is *The President, the Pope, and the Prime Minister: Three Who Changed the World* (2006).

▶ Ian Urquhart is Professor and Graduate Chair in the Department of Political Science at the University of Alberta. His interests are in Canadian politics, natural resources and environmental policy, and public administration.

▶ Robert D. Putnam is the Peter and Isabel Malkin Professor of Public Policy at Harvard University and author of *Bowling Alone: The Collapse and Revival of American Community* (2000). More recently he has co-authored, with Lewis Feldstein and Don Cohen, *Better Together: Restoring the American Community* (2003).

▶ Jeffrey Sachs is Director, Earth Institute at Columbia University, as well as Quetelet Professor of Sustainable Development and Professor of Health Policy and Management at the same institution. His most recent book is *The End of Poverty: Economic Possibilities for Our Time* (2005).

▶ Donald Savoie holds a Canada Research Chair in Governance and Public Administration at the University of Moncton. He has considerable experience in government and is also the author of numerous books on Canadian politics, economics, and public administration. He is currently conducting research on central agencies and the democratic deficit.

▶ Janice Gross Stein is the Belzberg Professor of Conflict Management in the Department of Political Science and the Director of the Munk Centre for International Studies at the University of Toronto. She is a Fellow of the Royal Society of Canada, member of the Order of Canada, and winner of the Molson Prize by the Canada Council for an outstanding contribution by a social scientist to public debate. Most recently, she is co-author of *The Unexpected War: Canada in Kandahar* (2007). She was the Massey Lecturer in 2001 and a Trudeau Fellow.

▶ Cass R. Sunstein is Karl N. Llewellyn Distinguished Service Professor of Jurisprudence at the University of Chicago Law School and Department of Political Science, and is author of scores of publications on law, politics, and human behaviour. His most recent book is *Laws of Fear: Beyond the Precautionary Principle* (2005).

▶ Linda Trimble is Professor and Chair in the Department of Political Science at the University of Alberta. She has most recently co-edited, with Marian Sawer and Manon Tremblay, *Representing Women in Parliament: A Comparative Study* (2006).

▶ Reg Whitaker is Distinguished Research Professor Emeritus at York University and Adjunct Professor of Political Science at the University of Victoria. He is the author, most recently, of *Canada's Cold War* (with Steve Hewitt) and *The End of Privacy: How Total Surveillance is Becoming a Reality*. He was a member of the Advisory Panel to Mr. Justice Dennis O'Connor for the Maher Arar Commission of Inquiry, and was Chair of the Advisory Panel on the review of the *Canadian Air Transport Security Authority Act* that reported to Parliament in December 2006 (*Flight Plan: Managing the Risks in Aviation Security*).

▶ Wing Thye Woo is Professor of Economics at the University of California-Davis and a Senior Fellow at the Brookings Institution. He has written extensively on the economics of international development, particularly in the Asian context.

▶ Lisa Young is Associate Professor of Political Science at the University of Calgary and specializes in the study of women and politics, political parties, and social movements. She is the co-author, with Joanna Everitt, most recently of *Advocacy Groups* (2004).

"O brave new world / that has such people in't!" So exclaims Miranda, in Shakespeare's *The Tempest*, when she first discovers that there are other human beings in the world besides herself and her father. Miranda has grown up on the deserted island to which her father Prospero was banished while she was still an infant. A violent storm has blown a ship bearing other Europeans onto her island and this shipwreck provides her with her first contact with outsiders. The castaways constitute a very political group. One is a legitimate king. Another is a usurper—the very man who has stolen the throne of Miranda's father and banished the two of them to this island. Other members of the group now seek to exploit the shipwreck to seize political power for themselves and rule the island tyrannically. Miranda's enthusiastic reaction to her fellow humans (the word "brave," in Elizabethan times, was synonymous with "wonderful") indicates a complete political naiveté on her part. The action of the play makes it clear that such naiveté would have led to grave consequences had it not been for the great political wisdom of Prospero.

It is very rare for a new college or university student to be as naive about political life as Miranda. Still, politics is a relatively unfamiliar world to new undergraduates, most of whom have never voted—or paid taxes! And what is true of politics is even more true of "political science." Most of the courses undergraduates will take are in subjects that have been familiar to them for many years—history, biology, mathematics, literature, and so on. In contrast, relatively few students come to college or university with any background in political science. Most students in an introductory political science course are thus in a situation that is at least somewhat similar to Miranda's. The study of politics is a new world, one that is intriguing, but at the same time, somewhat bewildering.

Politics can be bewildering for at least five reasons. First, the boundary defining political things from other things is unclear. How is political life different from, say, business life or family life? Second, it seems obvious that politics is a human activity, but who exactly counts as a political actor? Third, the language of politics can be frustratingly contentious. Definitions of political words are almost always in dispute. An education in politics involves learning not only the words but also how and why political actors use and redefine words. Fourth, political life in Canada and elsewhere is subject to new forces that are altering the terms of political activity. And fifth, politics seems to require an understanding of so much more than just politics. It appears that one also needs to be familiar with history, human nature, economics, law, and the biographies of influential people. Each of these reasons will be discussed in turn.

Politics is a distinctive human activity tied to matters of state and government. The word "politics" itself comes from the ancient Greek word, *polis,* for city-state. Yet we casually call all sorts of human conflict political, wherever conflict arises. If a friend of the boss gets the job in a company, we may call the decision a "political" one. Awkward moments around the table at a family holiday dinner are said to be rooted in "family politics." The word usually refers to shadowy issues with long histories that few can clearly explain. And "political" issues like these are almost always contentious. The problem is that we casually associate politics with conflict. Life contains a lot of conflict, but it is also true that much human conflict is not political. Two drunken brawlers exchanging blows outside a pub are not engaging in politics—though a political disagreement inside the pub may have produced the violence outside it. A World Cup soccer match between England and Germany may be hard fought, but this is not politics—though again, for fans, it may represent a contest between two states, two ideologies, or two nationalisms.[1]

Politics is associated with affairs of the political community. As the ancient Greek political philosopher Aristotle wrote, many animals are sociable and live in communities, but only humans debate with one another the nature and purposes of the communities in which they live.[2] Bees live in complex societies and perform their distinct functions without rancour. A bee colony is a type of monarchy, "ruled," as it were, by the queen bee. But other bees do not grumble about their subordinate status. They accept their position in the order of things. Aristotle's point is that bees are *unable* to complain. They are governed by instinct. Humans are animal-like in that they do many things by instinct, but they are also free to think about the nature of their communities. This makes them political. So politics involves reasoned debate about the nature and direction of communities—who is in or out, who gets what resources, who rules and on what terms—but those who debate are all committed to the welfare of the political community.

If we accept that politics is linked with the affairs of the polity, that still leaves lots of room for debate about what things advance the welfare of the polity. What are the boundaries of political life? What issues and problems should we assign to governments for their attention? Basic state functions are to provide military security to their populations and to keep domestic order. This latter job includes enforcing criminal law; providing access to basic services like water, sewage, and roads; and seeing to it that citizens have the basic means of participating in social and economic life—health and education pre-eminently.

In some states, even these functions are difficult to deliver. Such "failed states" do not deliver what we consider the minimal services associated with "stateness." The question in these cases is what can be done to strengthen states so they can provide the basics expected of any government.

In other cases, governments are asked to deal with emerging problems like climate change and energy self-sufficiency. They are asked to correct maldistributions of income and other forms of social power. They are asked to pass laws to alter relationships in civil society. Consider, for example, the debate in Canada about the legal definition of marriage. Supporters of the traditional definition argue that heterosexual marriage is rooted in tradition, nature, or fundamental theological principle, and that the state should not involve itself in redefining it. Supporters of the more expansive definition argue that it is entirely appropriate for the state to correct discrimination and injustice in society, whether or not these evils are enforced by law. This latter perspective stems from the view that the boundary between what is political and what is not is either blurry or nonexistent. For some, every part of life is fair game for political debate and public policy consideration. For others, not everything is political. Whatever the truth in this debate, it is clear that more and more things are on the public agenda. The sphere of the political is expanding; few parts of life are unaffected by some public policy or another.

A second source of confusion about politics concerns who is to be counted as a political actor. Of course those in political office are political actors: presidents, prime ministers, members of legislative assemblies. And when citizens in democratic countries engage the political process, they are properly considered political actors. But as soon as we consider the place of citizens in democracies, we come to realize that citizens themselves rarely participate fully in the political life of their countries. Citizens are often intermittent participants who limit their political engagement to voting in general elections, occasionally talking about politics with family and friends, answering pollsters' questions, and very occasionally donating money to parties or political causes. They depend to a great extent on other types of actors for informing them and for acting on their behalf. Democratic citizens rely heavily on communications media to inform them about what politicians are saying and doing. They also take cues from the media about what they should think about. As a result, the media have an important role to play in organizing and channelling information.

In addition, groups of people form to influence the political process. These groups are called interest groups because the members and activists in these groups have a particular interest or objective to advance in the public realm. An interest group may be after a change in foreign policy, an amendment to a law, or more favourable treatment in a government's budget. The group may have a continuing institutional existence with paid staff (think of Greenpeace), or it may have sprung up quickly to protest a certain decision and will dissipate soon after the issue has been addressed, or when members lose hope of change (think of a neighbourhood group formed to have traffic lights installed on a busy corner). An interest group may not necessarily have a strong relationship to its constituency. Interest groups often claim to speak for people who have no direct say in their activities or their policy positions.

In contemporary politics, a new type of actor, the terrorist organization, defies conventional categories. The terrorist organization usually has a political objective of some sort—the purging of a religious or ethnic group, the expulsion of an imperial power from a country or region, or the pursuit of a political ideology. It has a leadership—usually self-proclaimed—and a network of advisers, supporters, militants, and sympathizers. But terrorist groups are also notoriously decentralized, with cells that act autonomously. Some organizations possess military power greater than that of many recognized nation-states. Yet these organizations are not states. They do not assert a monopoly on the legitimate use of coercion over a defined population over a defined territory and are certainly not recognized by the international community as legitimate states. Yet they perform some functions associated with states. Hamas and Hezbollah are complex organizations operating, respectively, in the West Bank and Lebanon. They have political wings with representatives in legislative assemblies. They sometimes deliver social services to constituent populations. And they provide security against perceived threats from their enemies. Is Hezbollah a political party, a state, a social service provider, an army, a terrorist outfit, or a state within a state? In some ways it is all these things and none of them.

In the international realm, the student of politics is confronted with a welter of international organizations (IOs) reflecting a dizzying array of mandates, memberships, influence, and legitimacy. Chief among them is the United Nations, but the complete list would be pages in length. IOs are constituted by representatives of states, but they also stand above states in important ways, trying to order and regulate affairs within, between, and among them. Observers differ on the degree of influence IOs can exert. Some assert that organizations like the UN have impressive symbolic value and do provide a forum for the airing of issues of global interest, but that the interests of the stronger world powers will always prevail. Others consider that IOs form the institutional bedrock of an international society of shared norms and rules. In support of this view is evidence that levels of interstate violence as well as civil war have receded appreciably as the prominence of UN diplomatic and peacekeeping activity has increased.[3] In any event, IOs—and the alphabet soup of global nongovernment organizations (NGOs) that interact with state governments and societies as well as IOs—add to the bewilderment beginning students of politics surely experience.

The student of politics must cope also with the language of politics, a third source of confusion. Every academic discipline, every human activity, has its language, its key principles and terms, its names for the things being studied. Mathematics, biology, computer science, music, and chemistry are all examples. Political language is like these in that students of politics strive for descriptive accuracy as they attempt to explain political events and the forces and principles behind them. But humans are complex beings; they do not behave predictably, as do bees, microbes, or chemicals. So the object of the study of politics makes the job of description difficult. In addition, those who comment on politics often hold political views of their own. In their attempt to describe, they seek also to persuade.

For example, consider the word "dictator." In ancient Rome, a "dictator" was an interim ruler exercising political authority in emergency situations. Nowadays "dictator" is a bad word, used for rulers who refuse to share power or account to others for its use; it is synonymous with arbitrary rule and the violation of human rights. So the question in contemporary politics is who is properly labelled a dictator. Canada's former Prime Minister Jean Chrétien has been called a "friendly dictator"[4] for his allegedly undemocratic concentration of political power in the Prime Minister's Office. Opponents of Cuba's Fidel Castro unhesitatingly label him a dictator, but his supporters see a benevolent revolutionary leader without whom Cuba would be unable to resist the rapacious United States. The point is that when we describe, we often really intend to evaluate or judge. Judgment is an integral feature of the practice and study of politics. Politics is an ethical activity. But we sometimes hide our evaluations behind the cloak of description. Clarity of political language suffers.

In contests for political power, political actors often consider clarity and candour their enemy. Of course, politicians want their listeners to think the best of them. They want to be popular, especially when their continuation in office depends on popular support. Accordingly, they sometimes cannot afford to be totally honest. As George Orwell noticed a long time ago, political language is often the defence of the indefensible.[5] Politicians hide behind euphemism, equivocation, and long, bureaucratic-sounding phrases instead of making their meaning clear with direct, simple language.

Sometimes ambiguities have innocent-enough causes. Take the political ideology of conservatism. Conservatives are generally associated with resistance to political change, not because they are essentially dull people, but because they suspect that humans are not smart or wise enough to be able to engineer better worlds. They fear that more harm than good is likely to flow from grand visions of social and political reform. This disposition made them averse to bold experiments supported by socialist and fascist visionaries of the 19th and 20th centuries, all of whom sought to use state power to transform the conditions of human existence. This antisocialism inclines conservatives to liberal market economies in which the state plays a modest, order-keeping role. Conservatives end up supporting an economic production system that is the most dynamic and transformative in history. Change, development, and social upheaval are practically the touchstones of the market. Meanwhile, "progressive" critics of the minimal state defend welfare programs like unemployment insurance, regional development, social assistance, state-run health care, and state-owned enterprises, against efforts by contemporary conservatives to scale back these programs. In much contemporary political debate, then, it is usually the "conservatives" who stand for change, and the "progressives" who resist it.

Sometimes the ambiguity of political language emanates from the nature of the thing itself. Consider the word "democracy." Democracy is indisputably considered the best regime by most people around the world.[6] But widespread support for democracy is not the same as widespread agreement on what it is. Literally, the word refers to political rule by the people. It can be taken as a statement of the source of sovereign political power in the great body of the citizens of a state. In this way democracy is to be distinguished from monarchy, say, or from other contemporary regimes in which sovereign power resides in a "party" guiding a revolution. The Communist Party of the People's Republic of China or the Communist Party of Cuba are examples.

But is democracy fundamentally a commitment to a set of procedures for making decisions about the regime, or is it about a set of principles guiding political

decisions, regardless of the procedures used to make them? The first view would consider a democracy to be any regime in which the great body of citizens voted either directly on public policy questions or elected deputies to sit in assemblies and make laws on their behalf. For those who take this "procedural" view of democratic life, free and fair elections become the litmus test of democracy. It is the integrity of the procedures for law making, not the outcome of the process, that counts as democratic.

According to the second view, decision-making procedures are not primary; it is crucial instead that the regime enacts policies that advance the interests of the people. Advocates of the second view maintain that democratic procedures can produce antidemocratic results. If a legislative assembly passes a law that deprives classes of persons of civil liberties (for example, the right to a fair trial, the right of freedom of speech, or the right to vote), can that law be said to be democratic? If a terrorist organization runs candidates in a parliamentary election and wins, has it become a legitimate political party in government? Does it cease to be a terrorist organization? Should other states recognize its legitimacy? These are not idle questions. Countries like Algeria, Morocco, Iraq, Lebanon, and Afghanistan have faced them. Others surely will. If we were sure about our definition of democracy, we would have a clearer course of action to deal with groups that win elections and then implement programs that Western democrats find undemocratic. Alas, precise definitions elude us.

There is a fourth reason for the beginning student's bewilderment. New forces are reshaping political life. Chief among these is globalization, a blanket term describing changes in technology, communication, mobility, identity, and governance that call into question many assumptions on the basis of which we once understood politics and government.

New York Times columnist Thomas Friedman in a recent book refers to the "flattening" effect of these globalizing forces.[7] Prior to the current tide of globalizing forces, national borders were tall and rigid. What occurred inside nation-states concerned primarily the domestic populations themselves. Administrative structures in government and business were hierarchical. Ethnic differences were sharp. People had a strong sense of place. Travel and communication over time and distance were inconvenient and expensive. As Friedman points out, in a "flat" world, individuals are empowered by access to a wealth of information on Google. They have cell phones, enabling them to talk to almost anyone at little cost. Corporations spread their manufacturing processes over the globe. Businesses find they do better if they adopt flatter, more collaborative management styles that allow them to exploit more opportunities more quickly and make use of the knowledge, creativity, and talents of more people. In all, communication has conquered space and time and, increasingly, the local is affected by the global.

This "global intimacy"[8] is potent. We now can know so much about how others live. The rich are shocked at the poverty of the poor. But the poor understand how poor they really are by learning on the Web and Al-Jazeera about the fabulous wealth of the wealthy. Resentment and humiliation become powerful influences in the rise of anti-Western politics and terrorist activity. In Friedman's view, terrorists are a species of entrepreneur, using the communications and organizational techniques of business to run effective global operations. The flat world, he writes, "is a friend of both Infosys and al-Qaeda."[9]

In this global era, the international stage is filled with a dizzying variety of actors, including large global firms whose annual revenues far exceed those of many states. International organizations regulate trade flows, enforce standards in communication and travel, and promote equitable development and environmental sustainability. Electronic media attune us to the most local issues in otherwise obscure places. Nongovernment organizations advocate for myriad issues and groups, and in many cases deliver services more quickly and efficiently than government or international organizations. The nation-state is now one among a diverse array of players, and many have argued that the state has lost much of its sovereign power: not only are other global actors considered legitimate players, but also the state has lost its freedom to order domestic conditions as local areas are increasingly subject to forces originating beyond their borders. It has long been argued that globalization has at once thrust political authority upward to international organizations and global corporations, and downward to regional governments, political associations, small businesses, and empowered individuals.[10]

There is much truth to this but the complete picture is more complex. Out of the collapse of the Soviet Union in the late 1980s, the United States emerged as the lone superpower, not only an economic and military titan but also a vibrant, confident democracy. The "self-evident truths" held to found the American Constitution have formed the basis for American interest in global democratization. This has led the United States (with different coalitions of allies depending on the particular mission) into humanitarian and regime-building enterprises around the world. The country became a sort of global policeman. But one person's global policeman is another's imperial power.[11] To date, the more significant American interventions in Iraq and Afghanistan have attracted much more criticism than praise. As the United States continues to engage in an expensive, long-term operation to promote democracy in Iraq, its global reputation has suffered, its allies have become disillusioned, and its domestic population is becoming more isolationist. Meanwhile, countries like China and India are gathering economic and political strength. We are entering a period of multidimensional multipolarity: there is more than one global power, and the new powers compete on military, economic, and political fields of play. Observers worry about the stability of global order as these trends unfold.[12]

The state is not withering. It is, however changing shape and focusing on different functions as it engages and reacts to the global order. Canada, for instance, is highly dependent on the global economy as a source of imports and as a market for exports. Increasingly, economic value is found not in the price of materials exports but in the skills of the labour force. Education and labour market development is emerging as a key state role. States increasingly must engage actors beyond their borders to influence those trends and forces that affect them. Canadian politicians pay increasing attention to the quality of social infrastructure to attract capable workers to this country and to help them function effectively in the dynamic global economy. Globalization does not reduce the state to irrelevance, but it does force the state to adjust to new conditions. States need to be strong—that is, they need to be effective in performing the functions they set for themselves. The debate now is what exactly the state ought to be doing.[13]

The fifth reason for students' bewilderment: to understand politics one needs to understand history, human nature, and current events. A course in political science is also a crash course in history and the study of institutions. And the study of institutions is also the study of how people interact with one another in structured environments. We begin to understand political problems as we acquire a knowledge of particular countries, particular institutions, and the lives of particular people. From an understanding of these "particulars" we can see patterns and then form generalizations. Others with knowledge of other events, countries, and political actors may challenge our generalizations. Thus we move from elementary understandings of politics to more refined and general understandings. Yet particular events always unfold to test our own generalizations. And so an interest in genuine understanding should always make us interested in new events and issues, and also open to revising our settled views of how the political world operates.

This fourth edition presents essays that will engage all these issues. The essays contained in this collection provide particular accounts of aspects of political life. They do not pretend to be comprehensive treatments of a particular question or area of the world. In many cases they make an argument in support of a position, challenging us to think through the steps of the argument and to bring contrary evidence to bear on the author's position. Sometimes the editors' introductions help in this regard.

The essays also discuss key political actors in the contemporary world, from the United Nations to Canadian political parties. They also engage some of the big forces shaping the contemporary political world, from globalization and terrorism to the decline of deference in political cultures of liberal democracies like Canada's. The essays also attempt to grapple with the ambiguity of political language, making important but at times subtle distinctions. The goal throughout is to help students of politics confront this brave new world with interest and critical appreciation.

Unit One examines the large forces of globalization that simultaneously integrate and divide the diverse peoples of the world. Essays in this section also explore a subset of globalization, namely Canada's complex and ambivalent relationship to its continental neighbour, the United States.

Unit Two contains essays that deal with some of the big ideological categories of our time. The dominant political ideology in this country is undoubtedly liberalism. Very few people would challenge liberalism's central tenets—constitutional government; limits on the use of political power, individual rights and freedoms; and the use of reason to settle disagreements and formulate public policy. Yet these broad principles admit many different interpretations, and so liberalism itself is a very big tent housing a wide range of views. In this collection we present a trenchant account of an older, classical version of liberal political thought, bearing in mind that more recent variants take issue with certain parts of the classical view.

Political observers casually speak of the political "right" and the political "left" but rarely describe exactly what they mean by these words. In fact, "right" and "left" each have multiple meanings, and it is important to sort these multiple meaning out if political discussion is to be at all fruitful. Words like "conservatism" and "feminism" have undergone several changes of definition. Some ideological categories have nearly lapsed into disuse. For example, socialism claims very few partisans anymore. In this edition we include essays on the principal ideological categories influencing Canadian political life.

Unit Three is concerned with citizenship and people's involvement in the civic life of democratic regimes. Essays here explore the forces encouraging citizen activism and those tending to suppress such engagement. Information technologies are important parts of this puzzle and two essays explore the effects of new forms of media on political interest and participation.

Democratic citizens are not what they once were. Citizens in the developed world are more highly educated, wealthy, more independent in their political thinking, less deferential to political elites, and interested in different political issues than their parents and grandparents. Canadians' trust in politicians continues to slide. According to a 2006 survey, 14 percent of respondents say they trust politicians, putting members of this profession at the bottom of a list of 22.[14]

These changes are having all sorts of implications for the nature and extent of citizen participation in institutions of democratic government. In a nutshell, citizens fully support the ideals of democracy, but have many reservations about the practical functioning of Canadian democracy. Voters are shifting their voting allegiances. Political parties have undergone extraordinary reversals of fortune. In the 1993 election the Progressive Conservative Party went from majority government status down to a humiliating two seats, with the party leader and Prime Minister Kim Campbell losing her own seat. And just when pundits were concluding that Canada was becoming a one-party state under the Liberals, a new "Conservative Party of Canada" under Stephen Harper surprised everyone and eked out a minority government in early 2006. Voter volatility is coupled with voter dissatisfaction regarding the institutional rules of the game. This edition explores the new agenda for institutional reform that includes changing Canada's electoral system, fixing election dates, and allowing citizens more direct roles in public policy development—ideas that were unheard of two generations ago.

Unit Four examines political institutions within which political life unfolds. Institutions are legitimate rules that structure (and to an extent confine) relationships among the people working within them. They define acceptable and unacceptable conduct. But institutions themselves undergo change and are themselves sometimes the object of political dispute. For example, federalism in Canada is a way of organizing and accommodating diverse regional populations within one large united polity. Federalism in this sense conditions political life. But in Canada many of our debates are *about* federalism.

Unit Five contains articles that examine political themes in different regions around the world. The study of politics is often an exercise in comparison. We learn about our own polity by comparing it to other polities. Why did Canada enact same-sex marriage with countries like the Netherlands, Denmark, and Spain? What do we have in common with them? On the other hand, why does Canada not have labour market training policies like Denmark and Germany? If the root cause of terrorism, as many have said, is poverty, why is Haiti, the poorest country in the

Western hemisphere, not a hotbed of terrorist agitation? Why are some countries stable democracies and others not? Unit Five is concerned with political themes in different regions of the world, and invites readers to begin to ask questions like these.

The objective set for the first edition of this collection remains for the fourth: a well-educated university student must have an acquaintance with political life and the issues and forces that shape governments and public policies. This collection is designed to help the novice student of politics "brave" this intriguing yet bewildering new world. It is guided by the conviction that even if you are not interested in politics, politics is interested in you. We are all members of polities, whether we like it or not. We can take an active interest in the public affairs that shape our lives, or we can leave it to others who will shape them for us. We hope this collection will kindle an interest in active, responsible, and informed citizenship.

Notes

1. On the nature of political versus other types of human conflict, see Bernard Crick, *In Defence of Politics*, 2nd ed. (New York: Penguin, 1964).
2. Aristotle, *Politics*, Bk I.
3. See for example, Human Security Centre, *Human Security Report, 2005: War and Peace in the 21st Century*. (New York: Oxford University Press, 2005). Retrieved March 23, 2007, from www.humansecurityreport.info.
4. Jeffrey Simpson, *The Friendly Dictatorship* (Toronto: McClelland & Stewart, 2002).
5. Orwell's famous essay, "Politics and the English Language" was published in 1946 in the wake of World War II. The essay can be found in George Orwell, *A Collection of Essays* [1946] (New York: Harcourt Brace 1981), pp. 156–71. It can also be found at www.orwell.ru/library/essays/politics/english/e_polit (retrieved March 23, 2007).
6. See, for example, Ronald Inglehart and Christian Welzel, *Modernization, Cultural Change, and Democracy: The Human Development Sequence* (New York: Cambridge University Press, 2005). For more information on the global spread of democracy, see www.freedomhouse.org/template.cfm?page=1 (retrieved March 23, 2007).
7. Thomas L. Friedman, *The World is Flat: A Brief History of the Twenty-First Century* (New York: Farrar, Strauss and Giroux, 2005).

8. Ibid., p. 392.
9. Ibid., p. 429.
10. Daniel Bell, "The World and United States in 2013" *Daedelus* 116:3 (Summer, 1987): 1–32.
11. Michael Ignatieff, *Empire Lite: Nation-Building in Bosnia, Kosovo, and Afghanistan* (Toronto: Penguin, 2003).
12. Niall Ferguson, Sinking Globalization. *Foreign Affairs* (March/April 2005): 64–77.
13. For a discussion of strong states, weak states, and failed states, see Francis Fukuyama, *State-Building: Governance and World Order in the 21st Century* (Ithaca: Cornell University Press, 2004).
14. Leger Marketing, *Profession Barometer 2006* (March 2006). Retrieved March 23, 2007, from www.legermarketing.com/eng/Tencan.asp?p=2.

Braving
the
New World
Readings in Contemporary Politics

Unit One

Introduction: Global Challenges

◆ ◆ ◆

For most of us, politics in the contemporary world are most basically organized around the national state, a territorially defined political community whose borders are clear, whose government has the capacity to maintain order and provide for the welfare of its citizens, and whose permanent population is accorded rights and obligations of citizenship. Political life is largely carried on within these borders. Of course there are relations among states—diplomatic, economic, and military. And these relations influence and are influenced by domestic political factors. But, generally, we have proceeded on the assumption that national political life unfolds according to the rhythms and imperatives of national political communities and their histories.

Such an assumption is less tenable as time goes on. Information and transportation technologies are collapsing space and time at bewildering rates, making the distinction between the domestic and the global difficult to sustain. National economies exist only in name, and countries like Canada are profoundly exposed to international economic variables. Interdependence is rapidly outpacing national independence. Security threats, once arising from within the state system, now come from nonstate actors like terrorist organizations fuelled by quasi-religious ideologies that cannot be shoehorned into our received categories of conservatism, liberalism, and socialism. And, increasingly, problems demanding attention in one country have their roots outside its borders. Environmental pollution and climate change, for example, can be tackled only by concerted, international effort.

"Globalization" is the word commonly used to describe these trends. Canadians live in an economy deeply integrated into the global economy, and they import most of the goods they wear, eat, use, and drive every day. Eighteen percent of Canada's population was born in another country, making Canada one of the world's most multicultural countries. Canadians are famous for their historical commitment to internationalism that both causes and stems from a weak sense of national identity.

However, our era cannot simply be understood as the transition from national to global political identity and organization. Instead, global problems, imperatives, and solutions overlap and combine dynamically with existing,

© Ali Abbas/epa/Corbis

Since 2003, the United States has come to appreciate how difficult foreign sponsorship of democratization can be.

historic national identities and modes of political organization. This makes the contemporary political world both interesting and complicated. National identities are not necessarily weakening; they exist alongside gathering global awareness and obligation. Increasingly, people feel links to others in lands far afield. "Human rights" is now a staple of national and international political discourse, having acquired a universal, global appeal that even dictators feel constrained to cite in defence of their conduct.

The essays in Unit One engage some of the challenges arising from the interaction of national and global political forces. Among them is the question of terrorism—what it means and how it can be resisted. Is Islamist terrorism a response to a lack of democracy or to the existence of Western regime principles in the Arab world? Will democratization of the Middle East marginalize or legitimize terrorist organizations? How should liberal democracies protect themselves against terrorist threats? In addition, how should the international community respond to economic inequality, said by some to be the root cause of terrorism? How should Canada engage the international order? Should it stand by its traditional allies in a muscular posture or continue to support the UN, peacekeeping, and international development?

The State as Place amid Shifting Spaces

David R. Cameron and Janice Gross Stein

Editors' Note

Several articles in this book have considered the effect of globalization on political life. A recurrent theme is the withering of the territorial nation-state in the face of globalizing economic, communications, and political forces. Another theme is that globalization is inevitable; we are powerless before it.

In this essay, David R. Cameron and Janice Gross Stein argue that while some processes of globalization are inevitable, the directions of globalizing change are by no means foreordained. No one can say that it will deliver us to some perpetual peace as a global village or plunge us into a lawless condition of violence, insecurity, and material deprivation. Furthermore, while global forces influence local events and decisions, we still need institutions to staff schools,

fix the sewers, pave the roads, and set regulations for safety standards regarding food, buildings, and automobiles. Is it realistic to say that the state can no longer do these things, and that it should no longer do these things? If the state is not the political unit to attend to these public priorities, what is?

Cameron and Stein glimpse into the future and imagine two scenarios. Globalization can propel us into a condition of greater economic and political integration. Or globalization can sputter in the face of economic and terrorist shocks, allowing for a resurgence of the national state as a primary political unit. In either scenario, Cameron and Stein suggest, the state has choices. It can surrender to forces buffeting it from

without, or it can skilfully adjust itself to them and prepare its citizens to manage change. Indeed, they understand the idea of security to mean "building the capacity to change."

For all their emphasis on the freedom still accorded the state, they seem to concede a lot to the inevitability thesis. Economic language creeps into their description of the socially responsible state. "Social investment" replaces the older term "social security" or "welfare." Investment refers to the placing of money in an asset to make it more productive. Is the purpose of the social investment state to make people more productive?

◆ ◆ ◆

THE GLOBAL CHALLENGE

◆ ◆ ◆

For at least the last 200 years, the nation-state has been the dominant form of political organization, and, since the Second World War, the dominant economic force on the globe. Citizens in the industrialized world forced social contracts with their

governments and held these governments accountable not only for their security, but also for their well-being. However, the continuing economic and political pre-eminence of the state is no longer accepted conventional wisdom. Indeed, some argue that the state may be involuntarily retreating from its position of unchallenged control of the economic and political space within its territorial boundaries. This retreat may have

David R. Cameron and Janice Gross Stein, "The State as Place amid Shifting Spaces," in David R. Cameron and Janice Gross Stein, eds., *Street Protests and Fantasy Parks: Globalization, Culture, and the State* (Vancouver: UBC Press, 2002), pp. 141–159. Reprinted with permission.

profound implications for the social contract with its citizens, for accountable governance, and more broadly, for configurations of political identity. The state, it is argued, may lose its pre-eminence as the principal focus of political identity and become one among many actors bidding for the loyalty of its members in a competitive political marketplace.[1]

... the continuing economic and political pre-eminence of the state is no longer accepted conventional wisdom.

As processes of globalization accelerate, the state, some argue, is increasingly "hollow," because its borders no longer correspond broadly to the relevant economic, cultural, and social spaces.[2] As globalization proceeds, borders become more permeable and fluid, and identities multiply and reorder as structures of governance change. For a good part of this last century, the authoritative reach of the state overlapped almost entirely with the economic, cultural, and social spaces of its citizenry; cultural, social, and economic borders largely converged with the political. At the beginning of the twenty-first century, however, the reach of the state has retreated from a portion of the economic and cultural spaces that are important to citizens, and is shrinking from some of the social and even the security spaces.[3] The disjunction is clear: political boundaries continue to remain largely fixed, while cultural and economic spaces are reconfiguring.[4] Mathematicians would represent this changing configuration as sets that overlap less and less. Some see a continuing retreat of the state in the face of these changing configurations as both inevitable and irreversible, with disturbing consequences for national identities, legitimate and accountable governance, and the redress of social inequalities.

... political boundaries continue to remain largely fixed, while cultural and economic spaces are reconfiguring.

While we agree that globalization is having a profound impact on politics and society, we do not accept the proposition that the processes of globalization are inevitable. Nor do we accept the corollary argument that the state is largely hollowed out and increasingly irrelevant....

In this chapter, we advance four central arguments. First, the uncertainties in the pace and trajectory of globalization are very large. The future is contingent rather than determined, and even the parameters of future development are unknown. The processes of globalization are neither irreversible nor linear; rather there is a range of outcomes that are possible when we imagine the future.[5] Thinking about globalization needs to stretch to accommodate several possible futures.

Second, globalization is a "layered" process. Some of the threads of globalization may thicken more quickly than others, and, indeed, some may thin out. It is highly unlikely, for example, that the connections among societies that have been facilitated by the revolution in information and communication technologies will be reversed, but the density of economic integration among societies could well be.

Third, the nation-state remains an indispensable institution, under virtually all foreseeable contingencies. It is still the primary provider of social justice, and uniquely accountable to its citizens for their governance. The state will not continue to function, however, with its established roles and responsibilities unchanged from the last half-century; it faces new and powerful challenges to its core mandates.

The state will not continue to function ... with its established roles and responsibilities unchanged from the last half-century; it faces new and powerful challenges to its core mandates.

Finally, the state has the capacity and the opportunity to make important strategic choices about what roles it will play and what kinds of economic, social, and cultural investments it will make. These choices will differ depending in part on the pace and intensity of globalization, in part on the specific impact of globalization on a particular state and particular sectors, in part on the institutional capacity of the state, and in part on the quality of political leadership and the resilience and vibrancy of society.[6]

We will develop these arguments, acknowledging the reality of an uncertain future, by fashioning alternative scenarios.

CONTINGENT SCENARIOS: GLOBALIZATION TRIUMPHANT AND GLOBALIZATION IN RETREAT

◆ ◆ ◆

Is Globalization Inevitable?

The powerful effects of the revolution in information and communication technologies suggest that the current phase of "globalization," while not new, is qualitatively different from previous phases in some respects: its scope is unprecedented—it reaches literally around the globe—and the nature of technological development appears to make it irreversible. This argument needs qualification, however.

This is not the first time in history that economies have been integrated and culture spread broadly across the globe. In earlier phases of globalization, however, cultural homogeneity occurred largely through force, as religious proselytization swept through large swaths of population and as imperial powers imposed cultural idioms and languages on the peoples they conquered. The imperial powers were typically rooted in place: Rome, Constantinople, Madrid, Paris, and London.[7] Currently, culture spreads globally as economic product, pushed by the market or pulled by consumer demand. The contemporary equivalent of imperial power, the market, is everywhere and nowhere. The pace of the spread and the depth of the penetration of global culture are certainly unprecedented, but dependent in large part on thriving global markets. In the past, global markets have slowed and even collapsed.

... culture spreads globally as economic product, pushed by the market or pulled by consumer demand ...

Could such a reversal occur again? Shocks are not difficult to imagine, and the capacity of the current global system to brake and insulate against shocks is clearly limited. Historically, unexpected exogenous shocks to the system have always occurred, and we have no reason to think that these kinds of unanticipated "wildcards" will not continue to occur in the future.

War among the major powers in 1914 was an unexpected and dramatic shock to the system. While war among the great powers is unthinkable today, a nuclear conflict between India and Pakistan is certainly conceivable. Nor it is difficult to construct a path to regional war in the Middle East. These conflicts would shock the global economic system. It is not only interstate wars that threaten the global economy. In 1973, the dramatic increase in the price of oil was anticipated by very few, yet it severely jolted stock markets around the world. Even more dramatically, the attacks on the World Trade Center in New York and the Pentagon in Washington created an unprecedented crisis of confidence for the global travel and tourist industries. More generally, the vivid example of global terrorism gave pause to optimistic forecasters of uninterrupted global economic integration.

The current phase of economic globalization is perhaps more vulnerable to shocks precisely because of the broad base of the investment pool. Unlike the system a century ago, where a relatively small group of knowledgeable investors accounted for the bulk of global capital, current investments are far more likely to be short term, widely held, leveraged, and speculative. They are able to move far more quickly in and out of vulnerable economies and, indeed, to exacerbate the very vulnerabilities that then provoke further capital flight.[8] The international institutions designed to manage the global economy are lagging far behind the electronic flows of capital and investment. Even if current reforms are implemented, the capacity of global institutions to break real-time capital flows and to regulate capital markets will remain questionable.

A slowing or reversal of globalization is one among several plausible futures. Scenarios of possible contingent futures are appropriate when the uncertainties are large and exogenous shocks are a credible possibility. We develop only two contingent scenarios of globalization, each at opposite ends of a spectrum of possible futures, and consider the plausible impact of each of these on Canada in 2010. We do so fully conscious that these are stylized narratives, designed to highlight different tendencies. In 2010, Canada will likely find itself somewhere along the spectrum between these extremes.

GLOBALIZATION TRIUMPHANT

◆ ◆ ◆

It is easy to imagine the quickening and deepening of processes that are currently in play. Global capital markets, direct foreign investment, and trade continue to expand more rapidly than national economic flows. International institutions lag behind global economic flows, but nevertheless extend their capacity to monitor and regulate.

Processes of globalization reward innovation, analytic thinking, independence, and the capacity to "lead" flexible networks rather than command hierarchically organized, bureaucratic organizations. Those without the analytic skills to participate become further marginalized as global economic activity generates an increasing share of gross domestic product measured nationally.

Population movements continue to grow as people migrate in search of economic opportunities. A global underclass of the unskilled and their families moves from village to metropolitan center seeking a better life. It is more difficult, and getting harder all the time, for the unskilled to cross national borders. For the skilled, barriers to mobility decrease and "transilient citizens" move back and forth among multiple centers. They live "somewhere" but work "everywhere." Legal jurisdictions blur as projects and people become increasingly global, endowed with global identities and sharing a global culture.

"Global cities"—in Canada: Vancouver, Toronto and Montreal—grow in dynamism, in their attractiveness to new immigrants, and in their capacity to create wealth. They become the "hubs" connecting diverse populations to hubs worldwide. These cities become powerful global players, generating resources that dwarf those of provincial and federal governments. They become primary producers of cultural products that play directly in global markets. Cities invest their tax revenues primarily in infrastructure, safety, and tourism to increase their attractiveness as hubs. That these cities do not have an adequate tax base to meet the needs of those marginalized by new forms of wealth creation becomes a growing problem. In the cities social inequalities grow.

Control, but not always authority, continues to migrate up to a vibrant global economy and to international institutions, out to non-governmental organizations and global associations, and down to local communities. Local communities become more important as a haven from global pressures and as an arena of effective political action. The state, an authoritative voice increasingly disconnected from capacity and control, becomes the referee that seeks to enforce fair practices. It retreats as the commanding focus of political loyalty and identity for many, and extracts less revenue from its citizens through taxation as mobility and global market pressures grow. Nevertheless, the state remains central to the marginalized population who seek to mobilize political resources to press the state to honour the pre-existing social contract.

GLOBALIZATION IN RETREAT

◆ ◆ ◆

Processes of globalization could be slowed, stopped for a considerable period, or even reversed, as they have been in the past. It is unlikely that the growth of global production through intrafirm trade could be stopped for very long, and difficult to foresee how interlocking networks of information could be stopped at all, but the pace of expansion could be significantly slowed and processes of economic integration could be reversed. It is, unfortunately, not difficult to build a credible scenario.

A fresh wave of attacks by a global network of terror targets economic and civilian infrastructure in Los Angeles, Chicago, and London. Unconventional weapons are used to spread panic, destroy confidence, and limit global mobility. Stock markets around the world drop sharply, responding to the threat to global commerce and mobility. The market contraction is exacerbated by a significant and prolonged decline in commercial as well as tourist travel, and by a decline in foreign investment. Vulnerable economies sink quickly into recession and several default on payments of their debt. International financial institutions are unable to manage the cascading series of defaults, and political leaders of vulnerable economies, reacting to enraged populations, impose temporary currency controls in an effort to halt the devaluation of their currencies. In the wake of declining economic confidence and heightened fears about security, widespread restrictions on the mobility of people are put in place. Global economic activity—trade and direct foreign investment—declines significantly as a proportion of gross domestic product. The "global cities" experience real declines in housing prices, increasing unemployment and intense pressure on a social infrastructure that is already inadequate to meet social and economic needs.

Under these conditions, the state moves prominently to the foreground of the political landscape. Only the state can address the requirement for heightened security, the primary demand of frightened publics everywhere. The public also presses governments to rescue industries and sectors at risk of bankruptcy, to shore up currencies where devaluation would threaten life savings, and to reignite engines of economic growth and fulfil social contracts. The state again becomes the focal point of both political loyalty and public demand.

THE STATE IN THE TWO SCENARIOS

◆ ◆ ◆

Clearly, globalization sets different constraints for the state in each of these two scenarios. Equally important, however, is the fact that states have strategic choices under each set of constraints. Before we examine these pairs of constraints and choices, we will make four general points.

First, states can and do follow noticeably different paths in their response to globalization. Consider, for example, how differently Japan and the United States, Singapore and Hong Kong, have addressed the challenges of globalization. Consider as well the distinctive responses of the countries of Southeast Asia to the regional economic crisis which all experienced in the last few years. It is apparent that "one size" does not "fit all." The neoliberal policies allegedly necessary for participation in the global economy permit more degrees of freedom than is commonly thought.[9] Indeed, mounting evidence demonstrates significant differences in the way in which countries have been adjusting or protecting their welfare systems in response to the pressures of globalization.[10]

> *... states can and do follow noticeably different paths in their response to globalization.*

Second, countries do not start from similar terrain when they respond to globalization. Globalization does not level the past. States and societies bring with them their own territorial space, population, and resource base, as well as the traditions, culture, and political institutions of their community, built up over long periods of time. These shape their response to globalization as they have shaped earlier stages of their national development. A major reason for the "biodiversity" of global states lies

precisely in these deeply rooted historical traditions and institutional resources.[11]

Income inequality in the United States, for example, has grown much more dramatically than in Canada in the last twenty-five years. Indeed, income inequality among families in Canada after taxes and transfers does not appear to have grown between 1980 and 1995, the years of intensifying exposure to American and global markets.[12] Canada has spent more than the United States on social programs and the gap has widened since 1980.[13] Canadian programs have also been more strongly redistributive than equivalent programs in the United States. It appears that the Canadian state, rooted in its political values, culture, and institutions, has in the past mediated the impact of global market forces more aggressively than has its counterpart in the United States, although less so than many of the states in Europe.

Third, large chunks of the social policy field have not migrated out into the global system as have, for example, the formerly national dimensions of the economy, culture, information, and communications. Most social needs and demands, and consequently most social policy, remain domestic, not global, in character. For better or for worse, the state remains the principal, at times exclusive, repository of demands for social benefits. If states are able to generate budgetary surpluses as deficits recede in a period of expanding growth, they may have additional resources to meet these demands. Assuming that they do and that they choose to allocate resources in response to these pressures, they may recapture some of their centrality as focal points of loyalty, especially among that part of the population that is marginalized by globalization.

> *For better or for worse, the state remains the principal, at times exclusive, repository of demands for social benefits.*

Fourth, inequality, exclusion, and marginalization on a global level have become increasingly acute in the last two decades and show evidence of deepening.[14] In fact, if states do not respond by reducing inequalities, and globalization deepens, two societies may develop: one composed of "global citizens"—skilled, mobile, urban, autonomous of government, capable of exploiting the opportunities the global economy presents; and an unfortunate underclass—impoverished and poorly educated, whose status as economic refugees in their own country encourages them to look to their government as their only source of support.

With these four caveats, we develop four models of the state, two under the "Globalization Triumphant" scenario and two under the "Globalization in Retreat" scenario.[15] Drawing on our analyses of these pairs, we argue that the choices open to the state, should globalization retreat, are significantly affected by the choices it makes when globalization is moving forward. Path dependence limits the trajectory of the state should the parametric condition of globalization change. We examine the consequences of these restrictions in our conclusion.

GLOBALIZATION TRIUMPHANT: THE POSITION OF THE STATE

◆ ◆ ◆

Should globalization triumph, we can imagine two models of the state. We label the first the "handmaiden state" and the second the "social investment state."

In both models, state capacity decreases relative to the growing power of other institutions. The state attempts to mediate between the forces of globalization and its citizenry. It supports the efforts of its citizens, corporations, and private organizations to participate and compete successfully in global markets. Within its borders, it becomes the referee that seeks to ensure fair practices and compliance with international norms and regulations. The state defines its role as mediator, referee, and facilitator.

The state retreats as the commanding force of political loyalty and identity for many of its citizens, particularly those capable of participating successfully in global markets. Nationalism declines as a source of identity for these globalizing elites. In Canada, both Canadian patriotism and Quebec nationalism recede. As globalization triumphs, the state faces a fundamental challenge: How can the state address the increasingly acute problems of social and economic inequality and secure the inclusion of the marginalized and excluded population into the global community? We present two different stylized responses to this challenge.

The Handmaiden State

State leaders define as their central mission securing the "competitiveness" of their population. They seek to create and maintain the conditions generally understood

within a neoliberal framework as critical requisites for an adaptive and attractive response to globalization: a balanced budget, low taxes, a skilled and literate work force, an accommodating regulatory environment, and a climate conducive to research and innovation. Public policy concentrates on building the economic infrastructure and the trained human resources required for participation in the global economy.

The state's capacity and willingness to support the weakest and most vulnerable members of society are limited by two factors. First, social justice is not at the core of the neoliberal state's mandate in a global economy; at best, it is secondary and instrumental. Second, the discipline imposed by global markets reduces government revenues as a proportion of domestic earnings and, consequently, its capacity to meet social needs, either directly, by spending, or indirectly, through taxation and redistribution. Governments, for example, are pressed to lower taxes to satisfy mobile corporations and retain the talented professionals and innovators who participate effectively in the global economy, but doing so limits the capacity of the government to address the growing social inequality that accompanies deepening globalization when it is unmediated. Although economic growth continues as globalization deepens, redistribution in the service of social justice becomes more difficult.

Mark Neufeld calls this state, which seeks to adjust its society to the exigencies of the global economy rather than adjust the impact of the global economy on its society, the "national competitiveness/forced-adjustment state."[16] In this kind of state, the space for political and economic policy choices shrinks, and state capacity to make the choices in the space that remains declines.

The Social Investment State

States need not choose to be handmaidens of globalization, even when it triumphs. Globalization sets the parameters of policy, but the range of choices within these constraints is still large. Especially as publics begin to focus on the unacceptable social consequences of the handmaiden state, the space for leaders to choose different priorities grows.

The social investment state recognizes that effective participation in the global economy and engagement with the revolution in information and communications [technologies] are necessary to generate wealth. It has a more expansive view, however, of the requisites of global competitiveness than the neo-liberal handmaiden state. Crime, social disorder, disease, and poverty all reduce a country's competitiveness; other things being equal, people and firms will prefer to locate in areas where the quality of life is good. Cities that work—where pollution is low, where crime is not a threat to safety, where neighbourhoods thrive, where communities cohere, where schools teach—make good economic sense and, they are good places in which to live. A strong economic case can be made for an attempt to reduce the social inequalities that breed poverty and social disorder, for seeking to include the excluded.

The social investment state recognizes that effective participation in the global economy and engagement with the revolution in information and communications are necessary to generate wealth.

The case for including the socially excluded is more than economic. Leaders of the social investment state continue to feel a responsibility toward their citizens and their citizens' needs. In a social investment state, policy is justified in social as well as economic terms, and leaders seek to balance needs. Much of what the handmaiden state does the social investment state will do, too: balance the books, reduce taxation, and seek efficiencies in government and innovation in the delivery of public services. Both will probably want to provide high-quality economic infrastructure and equip talented citizens with the capacity to participate in the global economy. Their reasons for doing so, however, are different.

The generation of wealth is not the sole priority of the social investment state. The state is accountable to the whole community and the community encompasses not only those who are agile in the global marketplace, but also those who are excluded from it. Some of the resources generated by the expanding economy are dedicated to support those unable to participate directly in its functioning. We observed earlier that, unlike economies and cultures that have partly migrated out into the global world, societies have remained largely, though not exclusively, at home. The social investment state responds to the needs of its national community and invests broadly in the needs of its society.

The Standing Senate Committee on Social Affairs has observed that, in the era of the welfare state, security

used to mean protection from change, but that it now means building the capacity to change.[17] The Committee argues that the new concept of security implies a shift from an emphasis on social expenditure to social investment, a shift away from the traditional welfare state, based on direct provision of social services, to a new social investment state. Yet it acknowledges and accepts the limits to that approach. It recognizes that "the need for insulating or providing a social insurance for those in the country who suffer from the socially corrosive forces of globalization and technology has not diminished. If anything, the need has become greater as a consequence of globalization."[18] The Committee argues that Canada has not yet responded adequately to the challenge: "We have not yet found or agreed on a solution on how to achieve a more sustainable balance between economic globalization and social cohesion. Canada lacks a social consensus on this question. There has been no comprehensive blueprint of a social contract for the new global era."[19]

... the new concept of security implies a shift from an emphasis on social expenditure to social investment ...

The Committee identifies the central challenge for those who wish to construct a social investment state rather than a handmaiden state in response to the challenges of globalization. In an earlier era, the welfare state achieved a rough balance between economic productivity and social justice. That balance, along with the welfare state, is gone.[20] The challenge is to develop policies of social investment to rebalance economic and social needs, not only because a vibrant and functioning society enhances competitiveness, but also because the state has a responsibility to all of its citizens.

GLOBALIZATION IN RETREAT: THE REPOSITIONING OF THE STATE

◆ ◆ ◆

Processes of globalization do not necessarily march forward in an uninterrupted, smooth, linear sequence. As we argued earlier, globalization has proceeded historically in uneven, bumpy sequences. The scenario we described is a narrative of a bumpy reversal of some of the processes of economic globalization. It is only one of several plausible scenarios of globalization reversed.

Citizens, seeking security and protection, reinvest national governments with enhanced responsibilities. As concerns about public safety and security deepen and economic uncertainties intensify, citizens come "back home" to the state, which has a real if diminished capacity to act and retains substantial democratic legitimacy. National governments are reinvested with authority as well as control.

In a climate of enhanced insecurity, borders begin to matter more. The state promises protection as it restricts the mobility of people, goods, and services, its role as referee becomes less relevant, and government becomes an active player in national security and the national economy, in some cases challenging the dominance of international regulations and institutions. The global entrepreneurs and professionals, who worked everywhere and lived nowhere, are now being shed by retrenching multinational corporations as global trade and foreign investment declines and states begin to erect barriers to protect their domestic markets. These global entrepreneurs return "home" and look to the state as an engine of protection and economic recovery.

Social inequality remains an acute problem, although for reasons dramatically different from those related to scenarios of globalization triumphant. The political authority to redistribute income expands, but so does unemployment and social dislocation. The fiscal capacity necessary to act is limited by the shrinking economy that accompanies globalization's retreat, as well as by the low-tax regime put in place to remain competitive when the global economy was expanding and creating significant new wealth.

As the nation-state regains some of its prominence, loyalty to it and its institutions grows. Both patriotism in Canada and nationalism in Quebec intensify. In Canada, as in many industrialized countries, hostility to immigration grows, flexible migration and multiple citizenship decline, and citizens demand tighter control of entry into the country. When globalization retreats, the central question facing the state becomes: How can the state reignite the engines of economic growth in a "postglobal" world of re-emergent national economies and national communities and, at the same time, address the social dislocation that is the consequence of a contracting global economy?

We develop two prototypes of the state under the condition of a retreat of globalization. Each responds differently to the central question we have identified. The first we call "the state of unrequited dreams," and the second "the state as guardian."

THE STATE OF UNREQUITED DREAMS
◆ ◆ ◆

Weakened and diminished during the period of globalization, the state is shorn of some of the critical capacities it needs in order to respond proactively to retreating processes of globalization. Its logical precursor is the handmaiden state, which put its faith in the power and utility of now retrenching global markets. During the state's relative lack of concern for social cohesion as globalization moved forward, important institutions and policy capacities decayed, leaving the state of unrequited dreams ill equipped to address the painful social dislocations that are part of a retrenching global economy. What is more, its capacity to serve as a focal point not only for the rising demands of its citizens, but also for their loyalty, has been crippled. Captured by neoliberal ideology, the state has shrunk not only in size, but in its ambition. Conceptualizing a positive and proactive role for government is unfamiliar, uncomfortable, and difficult after years of restricted service as referee, mediator, and facilitator. The state finds itself now unable to meet the new demands of its citizenry because of choices it has made in the past.

Neoliberal analysts will have little that is critical to say of this passive and limited role of the state as the wave of globalization retreats. Firm in their belief that governments can do little or nothing directly to encourage economic recovery, they will consider the government's policy appropriate. Neoliberals will applaud the state for seeking to get the fundamentals right and then leaving the field to markets to do what they do best: generate economic activity, profits, and employment.

Those who argue that government has an obligation to intervene when markets fail will consider the inactivity of the state of unrequited dreams frustrating and shortsighted. The critics of the handmaiden state during the era of globalization triumphant will take cold comfort from the accuracy of their forecast of a state shorn of its capacity to meet social needs, even if it were to have the vision to try to do so.

THE GUARDIAN STATE

◆ ◆ ◆

The guardian state metamorphoses naturally from the social investment state as economic conditions change. The public-sector capacity, which the social investment state maintained during the period of expanding globalization, serves it well in the period of retrenchment. Habituated to adapting global pressures to domestic needs, and to using society's resources to support its weakest members, the guardian state has both the capacity and the predisposition to assume the role of society's protector in a time of crisis. Its public sector is larger than that preserved by the handmaiden state, and its core capacities to make social policy are more or less in place. The guardian state has the capacity to accommodate itself to a more activist role in times of economic difficulty and threats to security, and an interest in doing so. Since its priorities have been not only an efficient adjustment to the global marketplace but also the social well-being of its citizenry, it is well able to respond to citizens' renewed support of national sovereignty and national responsibilities, which are likely outcomes of globalization in retreat. The guardian state has meaningful choices to make, whereas the state of unrequited dreams has few if any at all.

CONCLUSION

◆ ◆ ◆

We have sketched four stylized models of the state, each pair embedded in two very different narratives of globalization—the first of triumph, the second of retreat and even reversal. The two narratives of globalization present different plausible futures, each difficult to dismiss with confidence. Globalization at either parametric value, we argue, offers more degrees of freedom than is conventionally thought.[21] We do not enter into the debate about whether one or the other future of globalization is the more likely. Nor do we maintain that these are the only plausible scenarios of the future. We do argue that both scenarios are plausible—and possible. We develop these two scenarios to help discipline the arguments, vary the conditions, and reflect upon state and society in a contingent future.

We develop at least two models under each condition of globalization to dramatize our argument that Canada and Canadians do have choices in their response to globalization. Globalization triumphant creates one set of constraints, principally through international institutions, international law, and global markets, all of which limit the fiscal and economic autonomy of the state. Even then, the Canadian state can respond in different ways. It can significantly reduce the size of government and choose to concentrate on mediating and assisting the adjustment of its citizens to global processes so that they are better positioned to compete. If the state makes this choice, it sheds much of its capacity to make social policy, but it continues to play an important, even essential, role in building all the relevant infrastructures and platforms for participation in the global economy. Or, the Canadian state can choose to invest socially, to enhance and broaden the basis of participation in global markets, but also to strengthen society by compensating and sustaining those excluded by the current phase of globalization. We argue that Canadian values, political culture, and institutions, as well as the history of most of the last hundred years, predispose the government as well as the citizens to favour a social investment state.[22]

Yet the challenge will be real. As national identity declines in salience, and as the state loses control of some of the important levers of growth, public trust and social solidarity will decline. In the face of a growing "democratic deficit," the social investment state must be able to persuade its most globally active citizens to invest at home in order to support and enhance the capacity of those who are marginalized by the latest phase of globalization. Skilled political leadership, reinforced by continuing reference to the values that Canadians share, will be needed to persuade Canadians to continue to invest, in order to bridge the gaps that exist.

> *In the face of a growing "democratic deficit," the social investment state must be able to persuade its most globally active citizens to invest at home in order to support and enhance the capacity of those who are marginalized by the latest phase of globalization.*

Despite all the challenges, the social investment state is the prudent and conservative choice. How the Canadian state responds when globalization is in its triumphant phase will have a significant impact on its capacity to respond should globalization stumble. The capacity that is eroded in the handmaiden state cannot easily be rebuilt when the parametric value of globalization changes. The handmaiden state, we suggest, creates a path dependency that seems to preclude the subsequent emergence of the guardian state. Should globalization reverse or slow significantly, it is very likely that the handmaiden state will be followed by the state of unrequited dreams. Ours is a cautionary tale of states that act purely as handmaidens to the processes of globalization.

Our stylized portraits of two pairs of states are heavily weighted toward an assessment of the capacity and inclination of the state, under varying conditions, to respond to social—and cultural—needs. We chose to examine the social dimensions of globalization in part because less attention has been paid to its social consequences than to its other dimensions, and in part because inattention to social justice in a period of rapid economic, cultural, and political change will be terribly costly in human misery. It will also jeopardize the promise that globalization brings to many who have been excluded from traditional structures of authority. ...

Contemporary globalization has come upon us so rapidly that collectively we hardly know what questions to ask, let alone how to answer them. Who, for example, should be included in—or excluded from—the international fora where crucial decisions affecting culture and society are made? States are understood to have a right of participation, based on the principle of sovereignty. But on what basis does a citizens' group acquire the legitimacy to participate? Does Greenpeace or the Business Council on National Issues get a seat at the bargaining table, but not the Grandmothers Against Free Trade or the Vancouver East Side Anarchist League? If so, why? On what basis? And who is to judge?

Currently, citizens and networks are not subjected to anything like the standards of accountability, transparency, and representativeness imposed on democratic governments, despite all the legitimate criticisms that can be made of these state-based processes. More formal involvement would require that this issue be addressed. How is this to be done?

Furthermore, how are non-state actors to be included in these global decision-making processes? The Internet and the World Wide Web seem to offer part of the answer, as they allow for substantial circulation of information between and among state and non-state actors, but it is hard to see how they could ever become the central media for political deliberation. Face-to-face meetings and direct negotiating fora will remain as central to international decision making as they are to domestic political life. How is a potentially vast array of organized interests and voices

introduced into a governing process without crippling its effectiveness? Countries have not been very successful at sorting out this dilemma at the national level; the problem multiplies exponentially at the global level.

Finally, what are the appropriate political institutions of a global governance system, and how can one best frame the appropriate global policy issues that need to be addressed? Most of the institutions have grown up in a "pre-global" world; is there any particular reason to believe that they are the most appropriate organizations, simply because they are there? And as for the appropriate policy issues, defining or framing the problem to be addressed can often be the most crucial step; who frames problems and through what process? ...

While one can point to several international institutions and practices that may represent the first green shoots of an emergent global civil and political order, these are not subject to even rudimentary, much less systematic, democratic control. As Mark Zacher observes, an explosion of international agreements, treaties, and tribunals has occurred in recent years, yet most remain executive-led and heavily bureaucratic, thickly insulated from popular pressures.[23]

Democratic states, constitutionally governed by the rule of law, will continue for some time to be the venue where the exercise of power is best held accountable and where legitimate and representative governance is best assured.

Canadians already have plenty of experience with the democratic deficiencies of executive federalism in the Canadian context.[24] "Executive federalism," disconnected from the publics it is allegedly serving, is as problematic at the global level as it is in the Canadian federation, or in the European Union. David Held has sought to develop a model of cosmopolitan governance that creates an overarching set of rights, obligations, and standards to govern the behaviour of all institutions, local, national, and international.[25] In this model, international institutions would become open, responsive, and accountable. Although groups of citizens are mobilizing to hold institutions accountable and to increase transparency, at present the accountability of international institutions is at best embryonic. International institutions remain a poor alternative to democratic, legitimate, and accountable states.

Democratic states, constitutionally governed by the rule of law, will continue for some time to be the venue where the exercise of power is best held accountable and where legitimate and representative governance is best assured. Indeed, it is likely that demands for representation and accountability will grow if globalization deepens, as citizens seek to assert control over important areas of public policy that directly affect their lives. The most promising arena for rule-governed popular contestation remains the democratic state. Certainly, international organizations, global private-sector corporations, military alliances, and even coalitions of non-governmental organizations do not provide the same opportunity. Nor, domestically, do cities, self-regulating industrial sectors, churches, or cooperative associations—at least, not yet. The modern, rule-governed democratic state is still unmatched in its capacity to provide accountability and representation. Whether connections among societies thicken as globalization advances, or borders re-emerge as globalization falters, our analysis suggests that it will be more important than ever to hold national governments accountable for their stewardship of society and to give voice to those who are excluded, as well as to those who are included, by current processes of globalization.

Notes

1. Yale Ferguson and Richard Mansbach, *Politics: Authority, Identities, and Change* (Columbia, SC: University of South Carolina Press, 1996).
2. … Kenichi Ohmae, *The End of the Nation State* (New York: Free Press, 1995), argues that "traditional nation-states have become unnatural, even impossible business units in a global economy." Susan Strange's similar argument is noteworthy: "The impersonal forces of world markets … are now more powerful than the states to whom ultimate political authority over society and economy is supposed to belong … the declining authority of states is reflected in a growing diffusion of authority to other institutions and associations, and to local and regional bodies." *The Retreat of the State: The Diffusion of Power in the World Economy* (Cambridge: Cambridge University Press, 1996), p. 4.
3. Janice Gross Stein, "The Privatization of Security," *International Studies Review*, 2002, [pp. 21–24].
4. See Manuel Castells, *The Rise of the Network Society*, 2nd ed. (Maiden, MA: Blackwell, 2000); and John Ruggie, *Winning the Peace: American and World Order in the New Era* (New York: Columbia University Press, 1996).
5. David Held, Anthony McGrew, David Goldblatt, and Jonathan Perraton, *Global Transformations: Politics, Economics, and Culture* (Stanford, CA: Stanford University Press, 1999), p. 437.
6. See Linda Weiss, *The Myth of the Powerless State* (Ithaca, NY: Cornell University Press, 1998).
7. Richard J. Barnet and John Cavanagh, *Global Dreams: Imperial Corporations and the New World Order* (New York: Simon and Schuster, 1994).
8. Thomas L. Friedman dubs this phenomenon "the electronic herd" in *The Lexus and the Olive Tree* (New York: [Farrar, Strauss and Giroux, 1999]).
9. Weiss makes these arguments in *The Myth of the Powerless State*. Indeed she argues that current neoliberal orthodoxy that glorifies markets is an Anglo-American construction.
10. In *Degrees of Freedom: Canada and the United States in a Changing World* (Montreal: McGill–Queen's University Press, 1997), editors Keith Banting and Richard Simeon conclude that both countries retain a significant degree of autonomy in shaping domestic policy, despite being confronted with similar external and internal pressures. Guiliano Bonoli, Victor George, and Peter Taylor-Gobby explore the reasons for the failure to converge in Europe, in *European Welfare Futures: Towards a Theory of Retrenchment* (Cambridge: Cambridge University Press, 2000). Francis Castles and Christopher Pierson explore similar issues with respect to the United Kingdom, Australia, and New Zealand, in "A New Convergence: Recent Policy Developments in the United Kingdom, Australia and New Zealand," *Policy and Politics* 24 (July 1996): 233–45.
11. Paul Pierson explores the impact of politics and policy legacies in the resistance to welfare state retrenchment in *Dismantling the Welfare State? Reagan, Thatcher, and the Politics of Retrenchment* (Cambridge: Cambridge University Press, 1994). See also his article "The New Politics of the Welfare State," *World Politics* 48 (1996): 2, 143–79.
12. A Gini index measure of family income inequality after taxes and transfers shows a score of 0.294 in 1980 and 0.298 in 1995. See Statistics Canada, *Income after Tax, Distribution by Size in Canada: 1995* (Ottawa: Supply and Services Canada, 1997), Table VI. These data do not reflect the cuts to social programs that came on stream in 1997.
13. Organisation for Economic Cooperation and Development (OECD), "Social Expenditures Statistics of OECD Member Countries: Provisional Version," *Labour Market and Social Policy Occasional Papers* 17 (Paris: OECD, 1996).
14. See the discussion of global and country inequalities in David R. Cameron and Janice Gross Stein, "Street Protests and Fantasy Parks," in David R. Cameron and Janice Gross Stein, eds., *Street Protests and Fantasy Parks: Globalization, Culture, and the State* (Vancouver: UBC Press, 2002), pp. 1–19.

15. Our four models differ from the matrix developed by the Government of Canada in its "Governing in an Information Society" project. See Steven A. Rosell, ed., *Changing Maps: Governing in a World of Rapid Change,* 2nd report of the project on governing in an information society (Ottawa: Carleton University Press, 1995). Our models of the state—namely, the handmaiden state, the social investment state, the state of unrequited dreams, and the guardian state—are nested within two scenarios that vary the pace, scope, and intensity of globalization. The analytic purchase comes from identification of path dependence and obstacles of movement across the two scenarios.

16. Mark Neufeld, "Globalization: Five Theses," paper presented at the Transatlantic Masters of Arts in Public Policy workshop, "Globalization and Public Policy," Toronto, May 10–21, 1999), available <www.chass.utoronto.ca/tamapp/papers.html>, accessed August 17, 2003.

17. The Standing Senate Committee on Social Affairs, Science and Technology, *Final Report on Social Cohesion*, June 1999, available <www.parl.gc.ca>, accessed August 17, 2003, ch. 4, p. 4. Banting makes precisely this argument in "The Internationalization of the Social Contract."

18. Standing Senate Committee, *Final Report on Social Cohesion*, ch. 2, p. 10.

19. Ibid., ch. 4, p. 2.

20. Paul Pierson dissents and argues that despite austerity and retrenchment, the welfare state has demonstrated surprising endurance. See *Dismantling the Welfare State?*, pp. 179ff.

21. Keith Banting, George Hoberg, and Richard Simeon, eds., *Degrees of Freedom: Canada and the United States in a Changing World* (Montreal: McGill–Queen's University Press, 1997). See also George Hoberg, Keith Banting, and Richard Simeon, "North American Integration and the Scope for Domestic Choice: Canada and Policy Sovereignty in a Globalized World," paper presented at the Annual Meeting of the Canadian Political Science Association, Sherbrooke, Quebec, June 6–8, 1999).

22. Very loosely, one might suggest that the social democracies of northern Europe represent empirical examples of the social investment state, and the United States and the United Kingdom empirical examples of the handmaiden state. Canada, typically, lies somewhere between these two poles.

23. Mark Zacher, "The Global Economy and the International Political Order: Some Diverse and Paradoxical Relationships," in Thomas Courchene, ed., *The Nation State in a Global/Information Era: Policy Challenges* (Kingston, Ontario: John Deutsch Institute for the Study of Economic Policy, Queen's University, 1997). See also Michael Th. Greven and Louis W. Pauly, eds. *Democracy Beyond the State? The European Dilemma and the Emerging Global Order* (Lanham, MD: Rowman and Littlefield, 2000).

24. See David Cameron and Richard Simeon, "Intergovernmental Relations and Democratic Citizenship," in *Governance in the Twenty-First Century: Revitalizing Public Service*, B. Guy Peters and Donald J. Savoie, eds. (Montreal: McGill–Queen's University Press, 2000), pp. 58–118. Parts of the final paragraph of this chapter are drawn from this article, pp. 102–3.

25. David Held, *Democracy and the Global Order: From the Modern State to Cosmopolitan Governance* (Stanford, CA: Stanford University Press, 1995).

Terms and Concepts

nation-state
globalization
global cities
economic globalization

path dependence
handmaiden state
social investment state
state of unrequited dreams

guardian state
global governance
non-state actors

Questions

1. What are the tasks of the state in the age of globalization?
2. Which of Cameron and Stein's two globalization scenarios is the more plausible in your view? Why?
3. What are things the state is no longer able to do?
4. Does globalization make it more important to have a strong state or a weak state?

Can Democracy Survive Globalization in an Age of Terrorism?

Benjamin R. Barber

Editors' Note

In his best-selling 1995 book, *Jihad vs. McWorld*, Benjamin Barber described global politics as a clash of the universalizing, homogenizing imperative of economic activity and the more particular attachments to home, land, and tribe that arise partly in reaction to it. A McDonald's in every city in the world may be a comfort to a travelling North American, but it is a provocation to many others who resist the imposition of alien images, moralities, and economic cultures on themselves and what is important to them. In this article, Barber continues his quest for some sort of rapprochement between the local and the global as they shape contemporary life.

While global communications and economic activity have brought undoubted benefits,

Barber insists that market capitalism, left to its own devices, is a ruinous, self-defeating, contradictory juggernaut. The market works best when it is brought under democratic political control. When economic life was largely confined to national states—when, in other words, foreign trade accounted for a relatively small portion of a nation's GDP—democratically elected governments could rein in market actors, attend to capitalism's more harmful side-effects, and increase the general welfare.

In a globalizing economic age, national states are less able to perform this necessary function. Yet there is no global counterpart to the nation-state to regulate global capitalism. Barber calls for an expansion of our sense of community to encompass the wider

world beyond traditional communities. He calls his readers to recognize and affirm a fundamental fact of life: global interdependence. With this recognition in place, he thinks that conceptions of community will change and that the political apparatus to tame global capitalism will eventually follow.

This essay is based on an address Barber gave to a Canadian audience at a conference in Calgary sponsored by the Sheldon Chumir Foundation for Ethics in Leadership. Yet it is unmistakably addressed to Americans. It is worth noting in this context that the United States is the strongest national economy in the world and also one with a relatively small portion of its GDP derived from international trade.

◆ ◆ ◆

Let me try to sketch out a picture of the two worlds in which people around the globe live—and the tensions between those two worlds. I think you will find that most questions of community values, how they can exist, how they can be nourished in a globalizing world refer to these two increasingly distinct spheres in which we lead our lives. One world is old,

familiar and traditional: the world of community. We know it well, and the Sheldon Chumir Foundation, I believe, was founded to nurture and explore the values that have traditionally animated this world of communities. Most human beings, if you ask them about the environment they live in, will first of all refer to the community: the familial and kinship associations, the wider

This article is an edited transcription of a keynote address delivered by Benjamin Barber at a Symposium of the Sheldon Chumir Foundation for Ethics in Leadership on April 26, 2002, in Calgary, Canada. The article was first published in 2002, paperback ISBN 0-9730197-1-9, title *Community Values in an Age of Globalization*.

civic, religious and work communities, the recreational and cultural groups to which they belong. That is the environment in which we pray, we work, we play, we create, we educate, we learn, we raise families. That's our immediate world. And for most of human history that has largely described for most people the compass of their lives.

But over the last fifty or perhaps a hundred years there has been a second, less invisible but sincerely felt environment, an environment of globalization. It has been a world of forces which we don't experience directly but which shape and condition almost everything we do experience. This is a global world that is increasingly interdependent, tied together by technology, by ecology, by the economy and now increasingly also by criminality, by disease, by violence and by terror. And that global environment, though we don't experience it directly, does shape the things that we do experience directly—our worlds of work, of religion, of prayer, of play, of art, of learning and indeed of our families. We can see today in the Middle East the way families are being literally torn apart by global forces of confrontation that lead young people to strap explosives on themselves and try to blow up other innocent people and martyr themselves. They march into the face of gunfire to be killed in the name of martyrdom. They are not reacting to the community when they do that but reacting to these anonymous but powerful conditioning global forces in which we are all increasingly engaged. The question that defines the set of issues that we want to look at ... is the relationship between those two environments: that immediate experience of community that we have in which relatives and friends and co-workers and colleagues and local politicians and pastors and rabbis and mullahs constitute our everyday experience; and these forces that increasingly (though we don't see them directly) shape everything that we do and increasingly interfere with, interdict, get in the way of the community experiences that go back to the beginning of time.

Now historically, the protector of community, the entity that has allowed communities to prosper over the last three hundred years, has been the nation-state: the independent, sovereign, autonomous, nation-state. Like globalization, the nation-state is not immediately visible—most of us experience our capitals, our national governments, only indirectly and occasionally. National government doesn't really encroach on our immediate lives but it stands in the background. It protects communities, providing their legal architecture; it oversees

economics, defining with its laws the nature of the corporation, the nature of economic contracts. It sets limits on the role that religion can play in public or private life, it supports the arts directly or indirectly. For three or four hundred years it has been the backdrop for the growth of local community. For better or worse, our community lives have unfolded within the nation-state. Moreover, over the last one hundred years, both our communities and the nation-states in which they have evolved have been increasingly democratic. Particularly in the West but around the world as well. Democracy, the nation-state and community life have gone hand in hand, evolving together, sharing similar problems and solving them through civic interactions among them. We have learned to think about the state as a sovereign and autonomous and independent entity and we have come to believe that our communities are safest, best preserved, most democratic when they are conditioned by the laws and regulations and oversight of the democratic nation-states to which we also belong. That's been the formula for success over a couple of hundred years.

> *Democracy, the nation-state and community life have gone hand in hand, evolving together, sharing similar problems and solving them through civic interactions among them.*

Around the turn of the last century with trade already globalizing, 12 to 14% of GNP of the nations engaged in trade were devoted to exports. Interdependence was already an emerging reality. With the two great world wars of the last century, it was apparent that individual nations no longer controlled their own destinies—hence "world" wars. Not the Franco-Prussian War or the Russo-Japanese wars, but global wars where states were no longer able to dictate their fates. Their territories were vulnerable. Their populations were vulnerable and the forces that conditioned their hopes were beyond their sovereignty. These wars, the Holocaust, the new totalitarian ideologies of Nazism and Communism, the Cold War, the coming of the atomic bomb, space exploration—all of them represented experiences of the limits of the nation-state, of sovereignty, of autonomy. All of them represented the limits of independence and the rise of an ineluctable interdependence. We Americans to the South, with our Declaration of Independence, proclaimed the possibility of an insular national life. Canada knew better but we Americans in the U.S. founded our destiny on the notion of an independent nation-state. Independent not just of mother Britain, but independent, period. We would control our own destiny our way. If we participated in wars we did it as an export product, fighting wars on foreign soil, bringing the boys (and girls) home again when it was over to a virgin territory untouched by the horrors of war and holocaust.

Before September 11, the last time foreign troops, enemies of America, assaulted it from within was when Britain burned down Washington in 1812. From that year until September 11, 2001, no foreign enemies had set foot on United States continental soil. No wonder the United States believed Americans could forge their own destiny inside of an envelope of two great oceans separated from the world, oblivious to it. This was the great American myth—that we could be separate from the world, sovereign in our own sphere. In the United States, this myth has coursed down through the centuries, more often vindicated than questioned.

Long after the idea had vanished in Canada and in Mexico and Latin America, we in the United States still believed that when there was trouble abroad, it was someone else's trouble, not ours; and if it touched us, then we strapped on the six guns, climbed on our horses, went out, found the bad guys, finished them off, and came home again to continue our lives. Even after September 11, that was the impulse of our president from Texas, to play the Lone Ranger and seek out the "evil ones," dispatch them and come home again. Yet September 11 demonstrated even to the most powerful nation in the world that no nation, however powerful, can in an age of globalization control its own destiny, take on its adversaries and enemies alone, deal with new forces that themselves are shaped by interdependence in an entirely independent way. Globalization and interdependence have become realities so persuasive and compelling that not even the United States is in a position to defy them. The new reality is interdependence: the terrorists of September 11 were, in a sense, our brutal tutors in teaching us this lesson. The terrorists were in many ways opaque, resistant to modernity: but they grasped and exploited (perhaps better than the United States) the interdependent character of the world in which they lived. They leveraged interdependence and the connectivity between nations; they understood the global financial system, whether it was a system of

world banks or whether it was the honey shops—that older system of international finance. They knew how to move their money, to communicate secretly, to use the Internet and all of those new technologies that, like it or not, link us together.

The new reality is interdependence: the terrorists of September 11 were, in a sense, our brutal tutors in teaching us this lesson.

There is indeed rather sad evidence that the terrorists had a better understanding of the interdependent character of the new world than the U.S. government did, because the government's response was to strike out at sovereign states, to try to find a nation-state address. We acted as if it was still the 19th century and somebody had crossed the Rhine and now we had to find who they were and push them back, and so we went looking immediately after September 11 for nation-states, those, as the President said, that harboured terrorists. In fact, the only states I could immediately identify that harboured terrorists around September 11 were Florida and New Jersey. Those were not the states that the President had in mind; but it teaches a sad lesson—that the terrorists were everywhere and nowhere; they didn't have a national address. They were not about nation-states and while the Taliban certainly had helped nurture some of the cells of al Qaeda as has been demonstrated with the destruction of the Taliban regime, al Qaeda survived. It moved on to Pakistan, another one of our "allies," and from there it can continue on to Indonesia or Yemen or Sudan or indeed to Berlin and Hamburg and Brussels and Miami, because the cells move in the interstices of the new global regime, inhabiting no region in particular. If we want to understand and deal with terrorism then we have to begin to confront the character of the new interdependence, the new globalization that is that background reality and that we sense only indirectly when, for example, the air is a little polluted in a wonderful fresh place like Calgary and you realize you can't really deal with it municipally and you can't deal with it by going to the legislature of Alberta and you can't really deal with it by going to the government of Canada either because, in fact, pollution has become a cross-frontier, a global problem. And if somebody gets

AIDS in Montreal you can't go to the Quebec government and say "let's put an end to this pestilence" and you can't go to Washington either, because, of course, AIDS is now a global plague and epidemiology requires a planetary perspective. The West Nile virus doesn't carry a passport and the Internet doesn't stop for customs inspections.

... the only states I could immediately identify that harboured terrorists around September 11 were Florida and New Jersey.

Interdependence means that the world's state borders are porous; traditional nation-states are no longer actors primarily responsible for the global condition because it is not within their power one by one to deal with global problems. Of course in many areas nation-states are still powerful, the primary presence in our lives, but in many others they are not. They are simply too large to deal with the things that touch us most immediately and too small to deal with global problems. The United States, the French like to say, are the hyper-power (*hyper-pouvoir*), but can the United States do anything about a little firm of, say, fifty or a hundred jobs that decides it wants to export those jobs to Nigeria or Indonesia? Can it control or even know what crosses its frontiers into the continental United States in container ships? Or on the Internet? Our sovereignty no longer is viable because we belong to an international system defined by new economies and new technologies that put our destiny beyond our control. Sovereign power simply isn't what it once was.

The West Nile virus doesn't carry a passport and the Internet doesn't stop for customs inspections.

This brings me to the central feature of the new globalization which gets to the role of community in a globalized world. Globalization has in fact evolved in a peculiarly asymmetrical form. We have globalized our market institutions—markets in capital, markets in goods, markets in commodities, markets in labour, markets in currency—but we have hardly begun even to think about globalizing our politics: that civic and democratic envelope of free institutions in which, for the last four hundred years, capitalism has grown up and been founded, and in which markets and their contradictions have been tempered and moderated. We have, as it were, ripped capitalism and capitalist markets out of that civic envelope of institutions that make it relatively productive, relatively efficient, less unjust than it would otherwise be, less Darwinian than it is in its naked form, and we have set it loose in an anarchic global environment where there is no analogous envelope of democratic and civic and political and legal institutions to be found. We have surrendered to anarchy, conspired in creating not a new world order but a new world disorder.

... we have, in effect, globalized most of our vices and almost none of our virtues.

Why do so many peoples who aren't part of the Western world find globalization so dangerous, so pernicious? Because to them it looks predatory, because to them it's a Darwinist jungle, because their experience of it suggests not order but anarchy, not growth but exploitation. They don't have the experience of living under a capitalist system that's closed in on all sides and limited by the law and by regulation and by the moderating influence not just of a capital state but of civil society and its myriad communities. More perhaps than the democratic state, democratic civil society in its local community manifestations has been crucial in tempering capitalism's impact on equality and justice. The church or the synagogue, the family, the philanthropic associations, the civic associations of local communities, have been the crucial arena in which capitalism has played out its entrepreneurial, competitive, rather Darwinian but nonetheless productive and efficient form of social organization. And it is the synergy between the two that saves us from capitalism's contradictions and at the same time allows us to enjoy its many benefits. This evolving synergy took three hundred years to develop, but we have almost overnight, in effect, abolished it in the global realm. Put bluntly, we have in effect globalized most of our vices and almost none of our virtues. Think about it: what's really global today? Crime. The syndicates that control drugs and prostitution and crime are global. Disease, plagues,

HIV, they are surely globalized. The problems we have with our environment, with the oceans, with the atmosphere are all global in nature. The exploitation and misuse of women and particularly of children have been globalized. Who are better seen as the true victims of globalization than children? They are always first in line in paying the costs of globalization. Look at the children on the streets of Brazilian cities, homeless, sometimes murdered so their organs can be farmed and sold in North American and European cities for medical operations. That's not hyperbole: it happens. Or look at the sex trade in Asia where eleven- and twelve- and thirteen-year-old boys and girls are offered up as virgins on the Internet to organized sex tours that help define the new international tourism. Look at the role of children as proxy warriors. Why do the old guys like Arafat and Sharon carry on and on and on and the children keep dying? Why do so many thirteen and fourteen year olds do the killing for the forty and fifty year olds? And the ones who get killed, whom you see at their feet, are also thirteen and fourteen and fifteen. We have watched the age of so-called suicide bombers get younger and younger, we have watched girls join the boys, and preteens beg to join the teenagers.

... globalization often means the wrecking of communities, their growing irrelevance in a world of forces beyond their control.

What is to be made of this? Does this reflect an anarchic global system of weak states and evolved chaos in which the most defenseless segment of our population is left unprotected because the civic and political and legal institutions that protect them within nation-states simply do not exist? The kids are without protectors. Certainly the market cannot protect them. That is not its job, which is to secure profits. That's what it's supposed to do. But that's exactly why we require other global institutions. Within nations, communities are children's best protectors because communities are the venues for family and church and civil association. But globalization often means the wrecking of communities, their growing irrelevance in a world of forces beyond their control. As Manuel Castels has shown in his remarkable trilogy *The Network Society*, increasingly the communities, the traditional communities, even those patriarchal communities that we don't approve

of anymore—at least they protected the children. They are being annihilated as a function of the new globalization—not incidentally but as a result of that globalization—and in the place of those communities we have found nothing to do their job.

In a word then, market capitalism stripped of the civic envelope is another term for anarchy. Anarchy, quite literally, means the absence of government, the absence of *archons*, the Greek word for governors. And the global regime right now is not a world order as we so often call it but a world disorder. To frame the questions that need to be asked properly, one must say "What's happening nowadays with big banks in the world disorder?" "How are investors faring in the world disorder?" For the world system is disorderly, anarchic, without legitimate governance mechanisms. There is power but it is undemocratic; there are those who would master it but they lack all legitimacy. The asymmetry this creates goes to the heart of the dangers we face. Because it's not just that in the global sector there's no democracy, there's no civic oversight, there are no political and community institutions. It's that those global and anarchic forces are themselves making war on community and making it harder and harder for us to preserve our communities whether it's in Calgary, or Detroit, or Bogotá, or Damascus.

In a word then, market capitalism stripped of the civic envelope is another term for anarchy.

Community is under assault because we are undone by these global forces which we cannot control. How do we normally control the communities in which we live, the villages and townships and municipalities, the provinces and states? Democracy has been the answer. We organize ourselves to oversee our institutions through choice and elections. We make the decisions about what we want, how we want our communities governed, how open, how closed. We don't always make wise decisions but in the democratic nations we make the decisions. But the decisions about the global environment are not being made by anybody in particular because there is anarchy. There certainly are people who are powerful and in an anarchic jungle, just the way there are certain animals that are more powerful than others in the real animal jungle. In the global market jungle, banks and investors and multinational corporations play the role of the most powerful animals but they don't really "govern" even as despots because they are at war with one another as well. The consequence is a world that isn't even very good for corporations and businesses. It attracts people out of what to capitalists appear to be the confines of democratic states. They believe they will find more working room, more profit, freer situations in the global environment. But it turns out that capitalism doesn't do very well there because in the absence of democratic oversight it once again falls prey to its own contradictions.

The great guarantor of competition has not been markets but the democratic state which, through its regulations, has assured a relatively fair playing field.

Capitalism is an ideology rooted in entrepreneurial competition. That's one of its great strengths. Yet left to its own devices it tends toward monopoly and the destruction of the competition it requires. The great guarantor of competition has been not markets but the democratic state which, through its regulations, has assured a relatively fair playing field. In the United States towards the end of the 19th century, after the Civil War, the great capitalist behemoths that grew up produced robber barons who exploited the American people and diminished competition and expropriated resources. They created huge monopolies in oil and coal and steel and railroads and, in time, rubber and then automobiles. And only with that great Republican Teddy Roosevelt, who recognized that the vaunted capitalist system was not working very well—not even for capitalism let alone for democracy—did the state develop countervailing institutions of oversight and regulation that saved capitalism from its own contradictions. We needed a more aggressive and interventionist state and in time, with President Wilson and the second Roosevelt, we caught up to what the Canadians and the Germans under Bismarck had understood much earlier: that for capitalism to be productive and fair, it must be contained within a democratic envelope. Capitalism produces goods more effectively and efficiently than it produces jobs, even though Henry Ford understood that without jobs there's no income for the consumers to buy all the things that capitalism produces. But again it's been the democratic state that helps assure that jobs are also produced so that there will be consumers to buy the goods of capitalism.

Now in the international marketplace, we are back to 1880 and an anarchy of outlaws both in the suites and in the streets. It's John D. Rockefeller in the oil fields. It's global robber barons, not because they're bad men but just because there's nobody to watch over and regulate them, because there's no effective international rule of law, because we haven't begun to re[-]create around them that civic and legal envelope for which Roosevelt reached at the end of the [19th] century. What do we do about it? I have some suggestions.

How do we create a global order [that preserves] our local communities that still give life and pleasure and creativity to all of us[,] … and [that] at the same time … permits us to produce something like a global community because only at such a global level can we address the challenges of globalization? Is community itself a stretchable and elastic enough entity that we can talk meaningfully about a global community? It's an interesting question because that is right now precisely Europe's problem. Can there really be a European community? It's called the EC, it's called the European Community, but to many residents of the continent it feels more like a technocracy—an economic market, to be sure, a financial and currency association, a defense alliance: but a community? Not yet. It's easier to talk about the Euro than the European, though Jean Monnet began with a dream of the European. Perhaps that is why countries like Denmark [(already part of the EC)] have had difficulties with Europe, and why countries like England [(still on the outside)] are so ambivalent about membership. Perhaps that is why Jean-Marie Le Pen is getting more rather than fewer votes because even on the left, many populists feel that whatever else Europe is, it's not yet a community, a civic community in which they feel an active participatory citizenship. Unfortunately, nobody has worked very hard to make it feel very participatory. They worked hard to create a technocracy of appropriate rules, to create a common market, to create a common currency. Yet at least among the younger generation of Europe there was an appetite for common citizenship and common identity as well: where was *their* Europe? So instead they have identified with the pop culture of North America, [w]ith MTV and Hollywood and the NBA[,] because those felt more cosmopolitan to them than the idea of Europe. Before then we even think about a global community we may have to think about what it might mean to forge a real European community.

This raises the central question about community itself: the question of whether communities are closed or open, democratic or hierarchical. The term community is itself ambivalent and ambiguous with respect to these characteristics. Community can mean "us versus them," and be closely associated with terms that suggest exclusivity such as solidarity, fraternity, sorority—us defined *in* by defining others *out*. Some of the most vicious wars today are being fought in the name of one community asserting itself against another community. What kinds of local communities can we nurture that will allow us also to be part of a national community and a global community? Multiculturalism, we know, is part of the answer, but of course multiculturalism comes in two parts: there is the "multi" suggesting variety and pluralism. But there is also the "culturalism" part, suggesting solidarity and singularity. As members of the multiculture African-Americans seem to resonate with variety and difference, but measured against Polish and Italian Americans, they are an exclusive and unique group whose differences pit them against other hyphenated Americans. The "multi" in multiculturalism looks outwards, the "culturalism" looks inwards. Each of the multicultural components of a multicultural country may see themselves as distinctive parts of a fragmented nation at war with their fellow citizens. The Québécois, no, they are not Canadians but fragmentary Canadians with their own identity; the Cree say, no they are not Québécois but fragmentary Québécois with their own identity … and so forth all the way on down. The parochialism of the idea of community in a globalizing world is then a problem for those who talk about "global community." Can the idea really be extended globally?

We are going to have to create some new global civic entity, whether it is captured by the idea of community or not. There has to be a new global civic envelope for global capitalism. For there is no going back. The anti-globalization movement—it isn't that. "Anti" was the name the cynical media used to create an oppositional image for the movement, not the name chosen by those who created the movement. The aim of the movement was not to reverse or take back globalization but to redirect and reform it. Globalization is the reality, whether we are talking about jobs or diseases or weapons or crime or investment or terrorism. We have to find a way not to bring markets back inside the nation-state but to extend democratic and civic and community organizations out into the world to re-envelope the forces—whether of the market or of criminal syndicates—so that we can bring order to the anarchy that currently defines their relations. We have to domesticate global anarchism the way we once domesticated American anarchism in the post–Civil War Wild West. We have to extend our civic ideals outwards. We have to find the way to use the NGO's that right now represent one form of civic organization inside of nations to create genuinely transnational entities that become a home for global citizenship.

There has to be a new civic envelope for global capitalism.

A global order is not just about law and legislation, a world federalism. It is also about global civil society and global citizens. We have *médicins sans frontières* and terrorists *sans* frontiers and capitalists *sans* frontiers: but where are the *citoyens sans frontiers*? The strongest and safest container for anarchism, for the disorders of the human soul, is not the law but community. For it is within the institutions of the community that citizenship is forged and it is citizenship that is the key to forging a democracy. Without global citizens, no global democracy.

Alexis de Tocqueville noticed when he traveled around the United States in the 1830s that it was not the federal government that endowed young America with a new and fresh sense of liberty, but the towns and municipalities. Freedom in America is local, he wrote: municipal. Near where people live and work. Speaker Tip O'Neill said the same thing a hundred years later when he insisted all politics is local. No one is born a citizen of the United States or of Canada or of Russia or of China. People are born in Calgary or Trenton or Montpelier and they begin to think about Alberta or New Jersey or Provence only later, and come to recognize their connection to Canada or the United States or France only later.

We begin life locally and our experience with democracy and citizenship starts locally too and only later does it extend out as we come to understand that, in order to control our localities and our municipalities, we have to control forces that move beyond them. In time we move out to the province and from there to the nation; and now, because of the proximity of global forces, we begin to recognize we must think globally as well.

We begin life locally and our experience with democracy and citizenship starts locally too and only later does it extend out ...

In fact, democracy in the modern world is beset by a powerful contradiction which globalization has exacerbated: participation is local, but power is central. We participate most easily in our townships and localities, but the power that shapes our lives is located in distant capitals and beyond. Once upon a time power and participation overlapped in municipalities and provinces. In ancient Athens power was local and community was local and citizenship was local and participation was local. Autarky and the lesser scale of politics meant citizens could control their world from their villages. But in today's world while we can participate here in a forum like this over the weekend—many of you are from Calgary and most of the rest are from elsewhere in Canada—the levers of power that affect the issues we want to talk about are where? In the Indonesian rain forest, being cut down to make matches for Japanese smokers? Up there in that hole in the ozone layer (the consequence of pollution), where dangerous radiation is seeping through to *our* towns? In the African hot zone rain forests where some new disease may be crossing over from animals to humans and where no local doctors we go to when we get infected have ever been? In distant war-zones whose outcomes affect us but whose causes are beyond us? The forces that impact our communities are simply way beyond the control of those communities—even our national communities. Farewell sovereignty.

This brings us back to where I began: the United States is no longer in a position to govern the forces that govern it. Unless it finds ways to collaborate and cooperate with other nations to create forms of local as well as global law. Local as well as global law. One of the great ironies of the United States today is, at the moment that we're out to catch and prosecute and bring to justice international terrorists, we have refused to ratify and become a member of the new international criminal tribunal which would be the perfect instrument to do it with. How crazy is that?

Caught up, as we are, in the myths of the 19th century, the great and good but increasingly obsolete myth of independence proclaimed in the Declaration of Independence, it is hard to recognize the new reality. The reality of interdependence. We still want to do it our own way, do it all with our own soldiers, impose our own unilateral solutions—as if our sovereignty were still unlimited and invulnerable. As if September 11 had never happened.

The challenge today is then to find ways to move beyond the 19th-century concepts of sovereignty, of nation-states, of Declarations of Independence—concepts too many nations still believe in. America, Russia, China, Egypt still play with the idea of independence, still cling to the belief that they can be powerful. But the era of independence is over, even for the most powerful nations. We need new ideas as "smart" as the bombs we drop in place of policy. We need a new Declaration of Interdependence to displace and replace that Declaration of Independence that has not just been America's founding document but the envy and a model for people all over the world who want to create their own democracies. Even today new states and transitional states proclaim their independence as if it were 1776 or 1789—most recently in East Timor. What a charming, what a disastrous mistake. For the reality we face is the reality of an ineluctable interdependence. What is required is a resonating new Declaration of Interdependence to symbolize our entry into a period when democratizing globalization is not a dream of idealists but a necessity for realists.

Let me conclude with a kind of provocation—a Declaration of Interdependence to which communities, individuals and states might actually subscribe. Would this be the beginning of the fashioning of a global community? Try this out:

A Declaration of Interdependence

recognizing that technological innovation, pandemic disease, crime syndication, ecology, new telecommunications systems, evolving weaponry, market economics and an expanding pop culture of pervasive consumer brands have rendered traditional territorial frontiers increasingly porous if not irrelevant; and

recognizing that the self-determination and sovereignty that once defined nation-states are no longer feasible in a world where networked transnational systems dominate the affairs of nations and where nation-states are no longer the primary actors in many international affairs; and

recognizing that governmental institutions and policies founded on national autonomy and sovereign independence are not only likely to fail in achieving their ends but may also compromise or even undermine those ends while endangering other peoples and states and the public goods and rights of human kinds as a whole; and

recognizing, finally, that as individuals living in the 21st Century, we have both rights with respect to and responsibilities in connection with a global entity, even if it does not yet have a structure or a constitution and even when the interests and goods of other communities to which we belong may sometimes be in tension with these global interests and goods …

We the people of this smalling world do hereby declare our interdependence both as individuals and legal persons and as members of distinct communities and nations and do pledge ourselves citizens of one world. Acknowledging herewith our responsibilities to the common interests and public goods of humankind as a whole and pledging to work both directly and through the nations and communities to which we also belong, to secure the rights of every person on the planet and to foster democratic policies and institutions expressing and protecting our human commonality while at the same time guaranteeing free spaces in which our distinctive religious, ethnic and cultural identities are protected from political, economic and cultural hegemony of every kind.

Might such a pledge, such a declaration, offer a starting place for those who, though still touched two hundred years after a glorious document was signed that pledged 18th-century men to the idea of freedom being protected by independent sovereign states, are ready to embrace interdependence? Might not this be an opportunity to recognize a new global reality in which liberty can no longer be protected, social justice can no longer be protected state by state by state by state, but can prosper only when we fashion a common community as broad as our common humanity? Only when we acknowledge that we all dwell on a common planet where the fate of the least prosperous will become the fate of those who are most prosperous. For in this new era, no nation, however powerful, is likely to survive in the long term unless the weakest are also permitted to survive, when no child, however well educated and promising her environment is, is likely to grow to old age unless children in the poorest communities around the world are also given the opportunity to do so. These are not byproducts of some new moral injunction but are mandates of necessity in a world that has become one, whether we like it or not.

Terms and Concepts

community
the great American myth
globalization

interdependence
connectivity

nation-states
civic envelope

Questions

1. Describe how globalization has affected the nation-state.
2. Barber argues that the events of September 11, 2001, taught Americans a lesson in interdependence. Do you agree?
3. Barber argues that we need a global civic envelope to tame global capitalism. What form do you think such a civic envelope should take?
4. How do you define community? How does your definition compare with Barber's? Can the idea of community be expanded to include myriad, diverse others whom we have not met and will never meet?
5. Barber describes the United States as a lone cowboy in an interdependent world of multilateral institutions. Do you agree with his assessment?

Governing Globalization—A World State, a Great-Power Concert, or a Renewed United Nations?

Joseph Masciulli

Editors' Note

Globalization is without question one of the most significant phenomena of the current age. Indeed, it is difficult to imagine any important aspect of life that has not been deeply affected by the various ways in which new technologies have managed to "shrink" our world; culture, business, education, health, leisure, and the environment have all been dramatically influenced by the increasing interconnectedness of the peoples of this planet.

While globalization has created many exciting possibilities, it also poses a number of significant challenges. In some cases (notably international trade) these challenges are sufficiently grave to have spawned a powerful political backlash—the so-called antiglobalization movement. The specific concerns of the antiglobalization movement are, of course, very interesting; yet underneath all of the particular problems lies another issue that is more interesting still: what political arrangements does the world require in order to be able deal effectively with each of those problems?

In this essay, Joseph Masciulli analyzes the political challenge of globalization—the gap between the global problems we face and the global institutions we have to deal with them. He then examines three different directions in which the world might move as we search for a form of global governance that will allow us to respond to the forces of globalization more effectively.

❖ ❖ ❖

And increasingly, there is a hopeless mismatch between the global challenges we face and the global institutions to confront them. After the Second World War, people realized there needed to be a new international institutional architecture. In this new era, in the early 21st century, we need to renew it.

Tony Blair[1]

INTRODUCTION
❖ ❖ ❖

Globalization includes technological, economic, cultural, and political processes of integration and interdependence that are occurring transcontinentally—involving both material forces and values.[2] Today we live in a world of *scientifically* and *technologically globalized* states, organizations, and individuals. Globalization is the current phase of what social scientists call "modernization"—processes of global trade, industrialization, urbanization, and the spread of empirically based science and technology extending back to the 16th century. Today, all global actors are actually or potentially globalized, because of the information and communication technologies (and other advanced technologies) that connect everyone and make us all more interdependent and integrated into one world, though still divided into a number of subworlds. Advanced technologies situate us all in a plurality of integrating worlds, in which significant exclusivities and inequalities persist.

The Communist government of authoritarian and nationalist China, for example, is doing its best to isolate the Chinese high-technology world from accessing political ideas found in the broader world of globalization; the government of North Korea, under dictator Kim Jong Il, adheres to an extreme policy of almost total isolation of that country from the rest of the world. Moreover, there is a vast "digital divide" between the richest countries and individuals and the poorest countries and individuals. Still, the infrastructure of information technology is spreading everywhere, including China and developing countries, to make all people potentially members of one world. In the last 200 years, our planet has shrunk. Global organizations situated in different geographical locations far apart simultaneously function in the real time frame of 24/7/365 mode.[3]

Ours is a dramatically new world in terms of the scope and intensity of interdependent relations, especially in the realm of worldviews and primary values. Think back to 1962, in the middle of the Cold War. Back then there was the Communist value system in the East, the capitalist and liberal democratic value system in the West, and the prosovereignty and anticolonial value system in developing countries of the South. But today most inhabitants of our integrating worlds can no longer protect their ideologies, lifestyles, cultures, religions, and civilizations—the particular values, beliefs, and forms of life that give the lives of both individuals and groups meaning—by remaining separated in local or regional majorities, and avoiding the perspectives of others with different beliefs, customs, and values living on the same planet. If you doubt these last statements, simply watch a world news program for a few days from the BBC or CNN or a global variant, and you will experience how interdependent "we" are with "others,"

no matter how geographically distant from each other people are. Isolationism is not an option.

Tony Blair—a controversial world leader and prime minister of the United Kingdom—recently stressed that "you can't have a coherent view of national interest today without a coherent view of international community." Blair said that our common problems, such as mass migration, the shortage of energy for development purposes, and global warming and other threats to our environment, require common action if they are to be effectively solved. Indeed, Blair paradoxically contended that "Globalization begets interdependence. Interdependence begets the necessity of a common value system to make it work. In other words, ... idealism [the belief in the ideals of constitutional democracy and human rights] becomes ... *Realpolitik* [power politics; emphasis added]." Blair went on to stress that he thinks there is increasingly "a hopeless mismatch between the global challenges we face and the global institutions to confront them" and, accordingly, recommended that we renew the "international institutional architecture" that was established after World War II. But the key to renewal is that "our common action" can and should be founded "on common values—of liberty, democracy, tolerance, and justice. These are the values that are universally accepted across all nations, faiths, and races, though not by all people within them. These are values that can inspire and unify. We need an international community that both embodies and acts in pursuit of these global values."[4]

Blair is right that we need to renew our global institutions, especially the United Nations (UN), and that we need to agree on common and universal values while allowing for cultural variations and particular civilizational emphases. The challenges of globalization require us to examine various options for global governance. Defined broadly, global governance means the way in which power is exercised over the world as a whole. The most complete form of global governance would be the establishment of a global government—a centralized world state with legislative, executive, and judicial authority and the power to enforce that authority. But global governance can also take other, "softer" forms: for instance, international treaties, covenants and conventions, international law, international organizations, and so on.

What, then, are the options for reforming global governance in the coming decades? Three main alternatives are possible. The first is some type of world state. The second is a great power concert, that is, an arrangement among the most powerful states to resolve key questions among themselves informally. The third alternative would be a stronger United Nations. I will argue that, on balance, the best of these options is the third: a renewed UN, strengthened by the acceptance of a common, consensual global ethic and by a common commitment to responsible and decent political dialogue.[5]

Global Problems

In globalized conditions, individuals, organizations, and states make more demands on the global order than in the past and have greater expectations of it. As we would expect, diplomacy in the classical sense—concerns about war and peace, territories, and international law—has been transformed and increasingly overlaps with cultural and foreign trade policies.[6] In the past, international concerns and interests were limited mostly to ensuring that no direct security or economic threats emerged from the international system. But today we have more extensive concerns and interests in global order, for this order is a source of more social goods and evils than in the past, given the high level of interdependence and integration that is developing.[7]

These social goods include 24-hour-a-day news information; diverse economic resources; human rights consciousness, rhetoric, and monitoring; humanitarian intervention; access to global social movements and international nongovernmental organizations (NGOs); and the sharing in an abundance of a variety of foods, cultural artifacts, lifestyles, and religious and civilizational perspectives. Potentially, there is a universal civilization in the making, incorporating the constructive elements of historical civilizations.

Social ills, however, seem to have overwhelmed our imaginations:

- Genocides, ethnic cleansings, massive human rights violations, brutal terrorist acts, cyber warfare, civil wars, and indiscriminate violence in failing states;
- An estimated 17 million refugees, a large number of internally displaced persons, and masses of illegal or forced migrants;
- The threats of global environmental degradation and imbalance, including global warming, acid rain, ozone holes, the depletion of nonrenewable resources, and the extinction of countless species of plant and animal life—all severely testing the planet's genetic diversity and holistic biosphere;
- The health challenges of global pandemics caused by the freer flow of pathogens because of air travel, tourism, and trade; AIDS and more traditional killer diseases; the threats to "human nature" posed by biotechnological experiments whose effects can now

more easily spread globally, including the biospheric ramifications of the "creation" of new human-non-human species anywhere in the world;
- The lack of global coordination of currency transactions and fiscal policies; the developing world's debt crisis; the resentment among these observers of the widespread celebration of global consumerism who are denied participation in it, even though this consumerism is creating a new class of indentured servants of credit card companies and the banks; the extreme poverty of one-fifth of humans who have not benefited from globalization;
- The inundation of traditional cultures, religions, and civilizations by vulgar, cheap, and commercial subcultures; and the potential clash of the major civilizations and religions, already realized to an extent in the global conflict between Americanization and extremist political Islam, and secularization and extremist political religious movements arising out of Judaism, Christianity, and Hinduism.

Globalization has directly caused, or exacerbated a significant number of these and other social ills.

To be sure, "deglobalization," remains possible in a number of imaginable future scenarios—repeated episodes of global terrorism or uncontrollable massive pandemics, financial meltdowns involving currencies or a global economic depression, a World War III fought with conventional weapons or both conventional and nuclear weapons. A future deglobalization, if it occurs, will necessitate a new type of statism and regionalism. This would involve economic protectionism and national or regional economic self-sufficiency by means of systematic censorship of the Internet and other aspects of global media and popular culture, a delegitimation of the World Trade Organization (WTO) and the UN, and other organizations seeking to integrate countries and peoples. The kind of mentality underlying calls for Fortress U.S.A., Fortress North America or Fortress Europe are extreme viewpoints today, but they could become more popular—in North America, Europe, and elsewhere—as national and regional responses to massive disruptions of the kind described above.[8]

If massive deglobalization is improbable (though possible), so too is complete globalization. Complete globalization would require the effective elimination of all current national, sovereign borders in favour of the free, global flow of scientific knowledge and technologies, goods and services, people, and ideas, and the use of English as the working language. Complete globalization would also require the replacement of the 192 current independent national governments (the current members of the UN, plus Taiwan) with some type of global government. A good indicator of complete globalization would be a future World Cup of Football/Soccer—the only global mass sport—in which the teams would no longer represent countries, but perhaps cities or corporate sponsors.

Today, then, the *status quo* is one of incomplete globalization with mitigated political "anarchy"—weak global governance and no global government. There is no centralized world government with effective legislative, judicial, executive, and enforcement power over the whole planet and its peoples. But there is some global governance—norms, laws, and organizations that are usually obeyed—provided by international treaties, covenants, conventions, and regimes (loose mixtures of norms, laws, and organizations in particular issue areas).

Today, then, the status quo *is one of incomplete globalization with mitigated political "anarchy"—weak global governance and no global government.*

Of crucial significance, however, is the growing consensus among state and corporate leaders and global activists that the *status quo* is not working, and that "we" (members of the human species) need globally coordinated and cooperative policy solutions to effectively solve global problems. This consensus is spreading, in large part, from the realization that environmental and health problems clearly cannot be solved by "bordered agents." The logic of environmental-health problems and solutions is being applied to other issue areas. Jürgen Habermas has expressed it well: "those who do not completely despair of the learning capacity of the international system have to rest their hopes on the fact that the globalization of ... dangers has in fact long since united the world into an involuntary community of shared risks."[9]

It is a common and alienating experience for many individuals and local, national, and international communities and organizations to experience themselves as objects of globalization, not its subjects, caught in "the whirlpool of an accelerating process of modernization that has been left to its own devices."[10] Developing countries have had little say in this new world order,

though China, India, Brazil, Nigeria, Indonesia, and other major developing states are trying to assert their influence at the UN, the WTO, and the G8 plus 5 meetings. As the post–World War II and post–Cold War hegemonic global leader, the United States has succeeded in liberalizing the world's economic and popular cultural markets. But the United States's role as the primary global coordinator has grown more difficult as developing countries have increasingly demonstrated their resentment toward that country's success and asserted their hard economic and demographic power, and soft-power influence, in not only the economic and cultural spheres, but also the political sphere.

States, corporations, and other global actors have failed to make economic globalization work better, or at least less badly, for the worst-off individuals and groups. The global free market today is distinguished "by the absence of any global authority to set minimal standards on issues like child labor, worker safety, the right to form a union, and environmental and animal welfare."[11] If globalization is not soon given more of "a human face"—a greater sense of compassion and fairness—the rich as well as the poor will be losers from the ensuing instability.[12] The current neoliberal solution to the problems of the global market assumes markets will regulate themselves; however, "markets are designed to facilitate the free exchange of goods and services among willing participants, but are not capable, on their own, of taking care of collective needs. Nor are they competent to ensure social justice. These 'public goods' can only be provided by a political process."[13]

If globalization is not soon given more of "a human face"—a greater sense of compassion and fairness—the rich as well as the poor will be losers from the ensuing stability.

Political intervention is needed to establish stability, protect the social sphere, and reduce inequality. Markets cannot take care of social needs. Moreover, the current regulatory financial institutions are being pressured by the growth of economic and financial power in Asia. To stay with the *status quo*—a global free trade regime with the absence of any authority to regulate pollution, global warming, or massive economic inequalities—and not move to a more robust system of international governance would not be good for human healthy survival and prosperity (leaving ethics and morality aside). For "objective" natural and demographic forces, if not altered by human planning and action, will continue to follow their own time line—to desertification, ozone layer depletion, and global warming; pathogenic pandemics and biotechnologically induced struggles for survival of the fittest between newer and older life forms; and human migration crises.

On the cultural level, the global situation is as dangerous. As more than one analyst has noted,[14] globalization tends to encourage a response in the form of a reaffirmation of local and traditional identities, whether nationalist, cultural, or religious, or all three combined. Samuel Huntington's thesis on the "clash of civilizations" is convincing in its basic version—in brief, that with globalization there will be more contacts between "civilizations" (super-cultures that unify nations, diverse smaller cultures, and their religious expressions), and as a result global value conflict is likely to increase because of non-Westerners' opposition to Westernization and Americanization. The U.S. War on Terror, (including the "coalition" occupation in Iraq, and NATO presence in Afghanistan) is above all a war against extremist political Islam. In this war, civilizational clashes are painfully evident and potentially explosive.[15]

In brief, prudent thinking and behaviour require that our global involuntary community of shared risks plan ahead to prevent and mitigate global social and natural evils. Clearly, the learning capacity of our involuntary global community will be severely tested by the challenges we face at this time.

Is a Global Government the Solution to Our Global Problems?

Hypothetically, a global government with centralized control over the whole planet and the whole human population could make, adjudicate, and enforce cosmopolitan law about economic and environmental regulations, ecology and biotechnology, and the just distribution of income and wealth. Global taxation and budgets would pay for all of this. All "wars" would be abolished and all types of violence would be dealt with by the world's criminal legal system and police as mere crimes and civil conflict.[16]

Global government does not exist today, nor is it likely to in the near future. Absent some actual global catastrophe, as we discussed above, such as a cosmic catastrophe, an ecological or biotechnological or pathogenic crisis of overwhelming proportion, or a World War III fought with nuclear weapons and other weapons of mass destruction (WMDs)—complete globalization with a centralized world government is neither likely in the foreseeable future, nor somehow inevitable in the longer term.[17] On the other hand, such a systemic crisis might result in sheer chaos or a move to massive deglobalization, if regions, states, and peoples turned inward in isolationist fashion, even though such isolationism would not be an effective response to the challenge to species survival. In the absence of such massive threats accompanied by enlightened nonisolationist responses, tight global coordination seems highly unlikely. Peoples in almost 200 states are not likely, short of massive emergencies, to act on "the domestic analogy" and integrate globally in the same way as national states integrated territories and jurisdictions on a more limited plane.[18]

Why not? Because there is not a sufficient sense of global political identity and mutual trust, because of the cultural diversity of our global community of shared risks, and because states are radically unequal in power. This general mistrust of "the others," for example, would make majoritarian voting and world referenda suspect and illegitimate in contrast to their well-established legitimacy within modern democracies. To be sure, reciprocal trust *could* develop globally over time through the growth of a global civil society united by human rights and the universal democratization of existing states, but that process might require centuries to be completed and could be reversed at any time. Optimists such as Benjamin Barber do not agree with this pessimistic timetable and general skepticism about a global democratic government. Barber views the growth of a global democratic community as imminent, because he is hopeful that enough people will progressively become committed to human rights and democratization, and reject the alternatives of commercialism, religious fanaticism, and authoritarianism. Barber's engaged optimism, however, borders on the utopian (imagining ideal political communities that do not exist and are not likely to exist, given human limitations).[19]

Nonetheless, given a massive enough global crisis and assuming that chaos or regional isolationism would not result, we can at least imagine a world government being imposed from above on world subjects. Currently the United States is the only "hyperpower," or global hegemonic power—a new Rome, but more powerful still—that could attempt an imperial feat. But short of some unlikely technological revolution in its military favour, even the United States could not succeed in imposing global imperial rule in an emergency situation because it lacks the necessary military and organizational resources that would be required to conquer the whole world. A transformation of a great power concert (see below) in a more centralized direction could more plausibly impose a weak global government from above, each great power policing its particular region and collaborating with other great powers globally.

... it is highly probable that a global government imposed from above would turn into the tyranny of regional majorities or authoritarian elites led by charismatic dictators ...

On the other hand, if accepted for more than a short period of time, even a weak global government would not be desirable. For it is highly probable that a global government imposed from above would turn into the tyranny of regional majorities or authoritarian elites led by charismatic dictators (indeed, these two forms of potential tyranny are not mutually exclusive). All things considered, we will continue to be better off with a plurality of states (even if regional federations should become states and the latter's number were to be reduced to a handful), accompanied by international organizations, as far as "offering people the largest number of opportunities for political action on behalf of peace, justice, cultural difference, and individual rights; and posing, at the same time, the smallest risk of global tyranny. ... Of course, opportunities for action are no more than that; they bring no guarantees; and conflicts are sure to arise among men and women pursuing these different values. .. [Still, this pluralism provides] a context for politics in its fullest sense and for the widest engagement of ordinary citizens."[20]

Philosopher Michael Walzer, the author of this quotation, is eloquent on the limitations of human nature in global politics, saying that the view that "reason [could be] in power in a global state—[is] as great a mistake (and a mistake of the same kind) as to imagine the future world order as a millennial kingdom where God is the king." For "the rulers required by regimes of this kind do not exist or, at least, do not manifest themselves

politically. By contrast, ... pluralism suits people like us, all-too-real and no more than intermittently reasonable, for whom politics is a 'natural' activity."[21] Walzer's skepticism about the goodness of a permanent world state leaves us with considerable latitude for reform and experimentation with forms of government and governance for our era of globalization, as long as we do not attempt to abolish all degrees of institutional and cultural pluralism in global politics.

Is a Concert of the Great Powers the Best Global Governance Solution?

Any extended series of terrorist attacks with WMDs or an unprecedented ecological, pathogenic, or biotechnological biospheric breakdown would result in fundamental changes in our current situation of weak global governance and no global government. If a global government of whatever kind were not established in response to such threats, it is likely that for reasons of survival and security the great powers—the states that rank highest in the possession of demographic, geographical, technological, economic, military, and strategic "hard power," as well as the possession of appealing cultural "soft" power—would act quickly, either through the U.N. Security Council or by way of an informal or formal great power concert or condominium. In a functioning concert system, however, the great powers would grant mutual, equal recognition only to one another, and seek recognition of a superior and more prestigious type for themselves from medium-sized, small, and micro states and the individuals who inhabit them all.

Today the great powers include one undisputed superpower (the United States). In addition, there are a number of major powers with global reach: the United Kingdom, France, Germany, China, Japan, Russia, and India. All have characteristically global ambitions, military and economic power, and influence. Finally, Brazil, Nigeria, and Indonesia are primarily regional powers, though in some issue areas have considerable global influence.[22] A great power concert united to respond to the threat of global chaos would be indistinguishable from a decentralized or confederal type of nondemocratic global government (the great powers would have an effective monopoly on a declared "legitimate" use of violence over planetary territory, even if only self-authorized).

The great powers have already learned that *ad hoc* concerts are the solution to the risks of WMDs and possible terrorist acts and regional chaos in their cooperation over unspecified threats posed by North Korea and Iran, for example. Dealing with these threats, they have demonstrated a great power style and mentality centred on resoluteness and vigorous action undeterred by external pressure. However, when great powers disagree—as, for example, about how to respond to particular crises when their national interests diverge—they cannot effectively pursue global governance goals.

A new concert would be a sustained cooperative agreement among the great powers to manage jointly the international system to prevent international disputes from escalating into war or global economic or other types of chaos. Such a limited multilateral approach would be based on the judgment that the UN, NATO, and the G8 all have essential limitations. Indeed, it is probable that any concert-based collective security architecture that would emerge in the post–Cold War era would consist of an *ad hoc* combination of regional bodies tied together by the interlocking membership of great powers. The concert would likely be regional in character, though not necessarily so. In a "fragile and disorderly multipolar world," this concert-based system with only *ad hoc* ties to the UN and other intergovernmental organizations could be expected to bring a modicum of order in the 21st century.[23]

[A great power concert] would lack global legitimacy and be a mere hard-power imposition on the other states.

However, this kind of "vigilante" UN Security Council would lack global legitimacy and be a mere hard-power imposition on the other states. Moreover, the great danger of a concert of great powers is for it to become transformed into an association of national security states—combining extreme nationalism (religiously defined or not), militarism, and extreme national security restrictions on civil society. The triumph of national security, neofascist states in the guise of antiterrorist, pro-order states, is a fearful possibility, given the prevalent rhetoric of some factions of the political leadership in the United States, Russia, China, Japan, and India, and in right-wing circles in the European Union.

Is the UN the Global Governance Solution?

The UN is not a world government or an exclusive great power concert, and does not pose the same dangers as a world government or concert would. The UN was founded as an idealist collective security organization devoted to peace, human rights, and the solution of global problems peacefully and cooperatively, but it also supported great power *realpolitik*. The latter is seen in the UN's reaffirmation of national sovereignty, independence, and nonintervention but, most dramatically, in the special permanent role (with the power of a veto) in the Security Council given to the victorious great powers of World War II—the United States, the Soviet Union, Britain, France, and China. By casting a veto (a negative vote) any of the permanent members can prevent a Security Council resolution from passing, even if the other 14 members of the Council vote affirmatively. (An abstention by a permanent member is *not* considered to be an application of the veto.)

The UN, as an intergovernmental organization, was not given a general monopoly on the legitimate use of organized violence to enforce its resolutions and decisions over the world's territory. But the Security Council does have that monopoly occasionally—whenever the five great powers, with the support of at least 4 of the 10 temporary members, can agree on a resolution to respond to a global threat and authorize a military operation. The Security Council stands out as the only organ of the UN that can issue binding, obligatory resolutions, and in effect can say what is or is not an act of "aggression" without fear of being contradicted by any higher body.[24] The central idea of the founders of the UN was that the great powers would guarantee collective security, and thus international peace and security, with their hard military and economic power and their soft power based on a commitment to human rights and the global rule of law.[25]

If we remember the tension always present in its dual foundation of realism and idealism, we can see that at most, the UN will remain limited to the goals of preventing wars or responding to aggressive wars, and preventing or responding to humanitarian catastrophes and "worldwide risks," including especially pathogenic and environmental risks (all goals tied to peace and human rights observance).[26]

There is a general understanding, though not a consensus, developing at the UN that there is a global duty to intervene, overriding national sovereignty, to protect victims of genocide, ethnic cleansing, massive human rights violations, and the chaos of failed states. However, to intervene effectively the UN should have sufficient revenue and its own standing military force to defend innocent civilians anywhere in the world immediately when so threatened—powers unlikely to be institutionalized in the UN in the near future, beyond the current *ad hoc* arrangements for money and military personnel.[27] Indeed, the central issue of UN reform is political—a matter of power and the prioritization of values—and touches most significantly on Security Council reform. Simplifying, one could suggest that for increased Security Council legitimacy, some transitional arrangement for including more current major powers—developing and developed—as permanent members would be wise. The most likely plan to be accepted by at least two-thirds of the members of the General Assembly and all five current permanent members would be a variant of a proposal being supported by India, Brazil, and Germany. This proposal requires that permanent membership (*without a veto initially*) be given to India, Brazil, and Germany, as well as to Japan and two African countries to be determined by the African Union.[28] The India-Brazil-Germany proposal's major strength is that the new arrangement they support would conform to the original logic of the Security Council, give the Council more legitimacy in the developing world, and make it a bulwark against a possible "clash of civilizations," since it would introduce greater religious and cultural-civilizational pluralism in the Council (four of the five current permanent members with a veto have Christian and European roots).[29]

Despite ongoing obstacles to Security Council reform, the UN's soft power is manifest in general in the almost universal acceptance of the *Charter,* the *Universal Declaration of Human Rights,* and many of the treaties derived from these documents. Moreover, the UN's soft power is manifest in experimental programs meant to respond to global problems and global risks—for example, in a highly innovative experiment in global governance, using networks to pursue the Millennium Development Goals (MDGs) through the UN's Social Compact Program. This program pursues the following goals: halving world poverty by 2015 and reducing infant mortality by two-thirds; halving the spread of HIV/AIDS and combating malaria and other diseases; achieving universal primary education; halving the number of people without access to safe drinking water; and promoting gender equality and environmental sustainability.

The Social Compact Program involves willing participants from international organizations, national governments, corporations, and civil society, while university-based research centres provide resources for learning and dialogue. Because networks operate horizontally, not vertically, all of the actors from the different sectors interact on an equal basis and have a shared conception of a normative framework.[30]

The global compact is a manifestation of soft power, and so is the *Millennium Declaration* ethical consensus. In the *Millennium Declaration* the leaders of over 150 countries declared that they are committed to common attitudes and values that would allow them to solve global problems together for our global community of shared risks, including making globalization positive for all the world's peoples. These common values and attitudes include solidarity (community); a sense of shared responsibility; and respect for nature, freedom, equality, and tolerance.[31]

To actualize these common global values, more reforms are needed. As a response to the evils caused or exacerbated by globalization, there is massive support for reform of the WTO to include human rights, labour, and environmental standards as an integral and necessary part of its agreements. The WTO should at least coordinate closely with the International Labor Organization (ILO) and the UN Environment Programme (UNEP) to effectively include these standards in trade pacts. Critics of the current negative dimensions of globalization also strongly support strengthening the International Monetary Fund and the World Bank to control capital flows to ensure that these institutions are more independently governed and loosely regulated by the central UN system, with more representation from developing countries. In general, reformers want UNEP and other UN agencies and NGOs that deal with human security issues to be strengthened and to coordinate their activities more effectively, so that they can implement human rights policies more effectively.

Two current (2006) reforms establishing a new smaller, more responsible, and more transparent Human Rights Council (replacing the old and discredited Commission on Human Rights), and a new Peacebuilding Commission to coordinate post-conflict restructuring challenges, show that UN reform can succeed and make globalization more positive for all the world's peoples.[32] In short, the UN's role in promoting human rights and human security in the face of armed conflicts and human rights violations—despite its tragic failures in Srebrenica, Rwanda, Sudan, and elsewhere—has had substantially positive results in lessening violent conflict and terrorism, and engaging in post-conflict resolution and reconstruction. We need to keep going in the direction of further UN reform, for with greater understanding of, and media attention to, global and regional problems, and "additional resources, more appropriate mandates, a greater commitment to conflict prevention and peacebuilding" far more can be achieved through the leadership of the UN, its allied agencies, member states, and NGOs.[33]

Lastly, in the current political tensions between the Bush Administration and (most of the members of) the UN, it is helpful to remember that "soft power does not depend [solely] on hard power."[34] The United States has insisted on a consistent unilateralist response, less so in Afghanistan, but more so in the Iraq War of 2003, which clearly violated the UN Charter and "just-war" criteria, *at least in its inception*. The Iraq War was a preventive war with little preemptive or reactive justification to fight imminent or actual aggression.[35] The Bush Administration has not been successful in making its case for the justice and prudence of the Iraq War in the global public sphere. There is an important lesson here for the global community of shared risks. The greatest economic and military power in the history of the planet could not use its hard power to win arguments in the UN's global public sphere. Nonetheless, the democratization efforts in Iraq do have UN support. So the United States–UN relationship is many-sided, but its negative dimensions are not open to easy resolution.

Thus, because of the UN's inclusiveness and because of the veto power of the current permanent members, the UN is easily paralyzed by great power action or inaction, embarrassed by the hypocrisy of many states as regards human rights implementation, and often ridiculed for its lack of resources in the areas of taxation and military capability to carry out its lofty ideals. Clearly, the UN is an imperfect intergovernmental organization, a universal and multipurpose IGO that continues to try to embody great power realism, human rights, and democratic idealism.[36]

Nonetheless, let us not forget the unprecedented historical achievement that the UN represents as the only global institution devoted to unceasing political dialogue, debate, and argument that includes everyone: "the primary condition of ideal speech, freedom from coercion, is thus partially present [today]. ... These venues such as the UN General Assembly, though they embody global inequalities of wealth and military power, are at least formally equal and organized to facilitate speech among the representatives of all states."[37]

... let us not forget the unprecedented historical achievement that the UN represents as the only global institution devoted to unceasing political dialogue, debate, and argument that includes everyone ...

The UN, as currently constituted, may not be the ideal solution to the governance challenges of our increasingly globalized word. On the other hand, it is clearly superior to the alternatives of a world state or a great power concert and has the potential to become better still with a small number of key reforms.

Notes

1. Tony Blair, "Our Values Are Our Guide," *The Globe and Mail*, May 27, 2006, p. A15. See Robert O. Keohane and Joseph S. Nye, *Power and Interdependence*, 3rd ed. (New York: Longman, 2001), pp. 228–63; and Thomas L. Friedman, *The Lexus and the Olive Tree*, updated ed. (New York: Anchor Books, 2000), pp. 3–16.

2. See Robert O. Keohane and Joseph S. Nye, *Power and Interdependence*, 3rd ed. (New York: Longman, 2001), pp. 228–63; and Thomas L. Friedman, *The Lexus and the Olive Tree*, pp. 3–16.

3. Thomas L. Friedman, *The World Is Flat*, updated ed. (New York: Farrar, Straus and Geroux, 2006), pp. 8–12.

4. *The Globe and Mail*, May 27, 2006, p. A15.

5. For an in-depth theoretical analysis of these governance issues, see Joseph Masciulli and Richard B. Day, "Governing a Global Community of Shared Risks," *Perspectives on Global Development and Technology*, 4 (2005): 681–706.

6. Jürgen Habermas, *The Postnational Constellation* (Cambridge, MA: The MIT Press, 2001), p. 71.

7. Ian Clark, "Globalization and the Post-Cold War Order," in John Baylis and Steve Smith, eds., *The Globalization of World Politics*, 3rd ed. (New York: Oxford, 2005), p. 729.

8. See Robert O. Keohane and Joseph S. Nye, *Power and Interdependence*, 3rd ed. (New York: Longman, 2001), Chapter 10; and David R. Cameron and Janice Gross Stein, "The State as Place amid Shifting Spaces," in David R. Cameron and Janice Gross Stein, eds., *Street Protests and Fantasy Parks: Globalization, Culture, and the State* (Vancouver: UBC Press, 2002), pp. 141–59.

9. Jürgen Habermas, *The Inclusion of the Other* (Cambridge, MA: The MIT Press, 1998), p. 186. See also Michael Walzer, who challenges us with the insight that "the combination of (many) weak states with weak global organizations brings disadvantages from both directions: the protection of ethnic and religious difference is inadequate and so is the protection of individual rights and the promotion of equality," in "Governing the Globe," in *Arguing about War* (New Haven and London: Yale University Press, 2004), p. 179.

10. Jürgen Habermas, *The Postnational Constellation*, p. 112.

11. Peter Singer, *One World: The Ethics of Globalization* (New Haven: Yale University Press, 2002), p. 92.

12. Richard Falk, *Human Rights Horizons: The Pursuit of Justice in a Globalizing World* (New York: Routledge, 2000), p. 1.

13. George Soros, *The Bubble of American Supremacy* (New York: Public Affairs, 2004), p. 91.

14. See Benjamin R. Barber, *Jihad versus McWorld: Terrorism's Challenge to Democracy, with a New Introduction* (New York: Ballantine Books, 2001); Samuel Huntington, *The Clash of Civilizations and the Remaking of World Order* (New York: Simon & Schuster, 1996).

15. Samuel Huntington, *The Clash of Civilizations and the Remaking of World Order*. Huntington's more particular hypotheses and prescriptions are more questionable—especially the prescription advocating Western technological and military superiority, and the predictive hypothesis regarding a possible, though not probable, major war between the United States and the West against Islam or China or both (*The Clash of Civilizations and the Remaking of World Order*, Chapter 12).

16. See Michael Walzer, *Arguing about War* (New Haven: Yale University Press, 2004), pp. xiii, 175.

17. See Alexander Wendt, "Why a World State is Inevitable," *European Journal of International Relations* 9 (2003): 491–542, who argues for inevitability, but in the far-off future.

18. Joseph S. Nye, Jr., "Transnational Relations, Independence, and Globalization," in Michael Brecher and Frank P. Harvey, eds., *Realism and Institutionalism in International Studies* (Ann Arbor: The University of Michigan Press, 2002), pp. 160–73.

19. See the preceding selection in this collection, Benjamin Barber's "Can Democracy Survive Globalization in an Age of Terrorism?" pp. 16–24.

20. Michael Walzer, "Governing the Globe," in *Arguing About War*, pp. 186, 190.

21. Ibid.

22. See Henry A. Kissinger, *Does American Need a Foreign Policy*, Rev. Ed. (New York: Simon & Schuster, 2002).

23. See W. Andy Knight and Joseph Masciulli, "Conclusion: Rethinking Instead of Tinkering—An Ethical Consensus and General Lessons," in W. Andy Knight, ed., *Adapting the United Nations to a Postmodern Era* (New York: Palgrave Macmillan, 2005), p. 244; and Charles W. Kegley Jr. and Gregory Raymond, "Great Power Politics in the 21st Century," in Charles W. Kegley, Jr. and Eugene Wittkopf, eds., *The Global Agenda* (New York: McGraw-Hill, 1998), pp. 182–83; see also Ian Clark, "Globalization and the Post-Cold War Order," in John Baylis and Steve Smith, eds., *The Globalization of World Politics*, 3rd ed. (New York: Oxford, 2005).

24. Only the new International Criminal Court—indirectly related to the Security Council but also independent of the latter—has the same enforcement power typical of national governments.

25. See Nigel Calder, *Introduction to Global Citizenship* (Edinburgh: Edinburgh University Press, 2003); Karen Mingst and Margaret Karns, *The United Nations in a Post–Cold War Era* (Boulder, CO: Westview Press, 2004); and www.un.org.

26. Jürgen Habermas, *The Postnational Constellation*, p. 106.

27. Peter Singer, *One World: the Ethics of Globalization*, p. 144.

28. The India-Brazil-Germany proposal also includes the addition of four new nonpermanent members; it is quite similar to the African Union's proposal, except that the African Union wants the power of the veto to be granted immediately to the new permanent members, and five new nonpermanent members instead of the four proposed by India-Brazil-Germany.

29. See www.un.org and www.reformtheun.org for documents; and *A More Secure World: Our Shared Responsibility—Report of the Secretary-General's High-level Panel on Threats, Challenges and Change* (New York: United Nations Department of Public Information, 2004); and *In Larger Freedom: Towards Security, Development and Human Rights for All—Report of the Secretary General* (New York: United Nations Department of Public Information, 2005) for a discussion of details about reforms.

30. John Gerard Ruggie, "The United Nations and Globalization: Patterns and Limits of Institutional Adaptation," *Global Governance* 9 (2003): 315.

31. See Mary Robinson, "Ethics, Human Rights, and Globalization." Lecture by Mary Robinson, former UN High Commissioner of Human Rights, given in 2002. Retrieved September 13, 2005, from www.weltethos.org/st_9_xx/9_144.htm.

32. The mechanics of institutional reform are not the crucial issue, unless they are perceived to be central because of power considerations. See Peter Singer, *One World: The Ethics of Globalization*, p. 145; and Edward Luck, "The UN Security Council: Reform or Enlarge," in Paul Heinbecker and Patricia Goff, eds., *Irrelevant or Indispensable: The United Nations in the 21st Century* (Waterloo, ON: Wilfrid

Laurier University Press, 2005), p. 144. It is difficult seeing any substantial reform of the Security Council occurring in the next few years, since the United States and the UN are in an overall tense relationship, though there is some cooperation between them. But the United States was not able to prevent the creation of the new Human Rights Council, even though it voted against the proposal.

33. See *Human Security Report 2005: War and Peace in the 21st Century*, (New York: Oxford University Press, 2005).
34. Joseph S. Nye, Jr., *Soft Power* (New York: Public Affairs, 2004), pp. 9–11.
35. See Michael Walzer, *Arguing about War*.
36. A good consequence of the UN's mix of idealism and realism is that it protects the UN from extreme moralism and legalism, which seek to evade political deliberation, if not abolish (national and global) politics altogether. For a critique of excessive legalism and moralism, see Peter Singer, *One World: the Ethics of Globalization*, p. 116.
37. Neta Crawford, *Argument and Change in World Politics: Ethics, Decolonization, and Humanitarian Intervention* (Cambridge, UK: Cambridge University Press, 2002), pp. 420–21.

Terms and Concepts

modernization
isolationism
realpolitik
global community of shared risks

great power concert
deglobalization
complete globalization
utopianism

hegemonic power
veto
Security Council reform
Millennium Development Goals

Questions

1. In what sense is there a gap between the global challenges we face and the global institutions that are supposed to handle them?
2. What are the obstacles to the emergence of a global government? Is global government a good idea?
3. What are the shortcomings of a great power concert as a mechanism of global governance?
4. What are the strengths and weaknesses of the UN as a mechanism of global governance?
5. What sorts of reforms are necessary to make the UN a more effective mechanism of global governance?

(4)

Political Ethics in an Age of Terror

Michael Ignatieff

Editors' Note

In 1939 a Gallop poll asked Americans whether they approved of deliberate bombing of civilian targets in wartime. Over 90 percent of respondents said no. Three days after the Japanese bombing of Pearl Harbor, 67 percent of American respondents favoured "unqualified and indiscriminate bombing of enemy cities."[1]

Such is the intemperance of peoples under attack. It is as understandable as it is volatile and dangerous. Immediate reactions to the events of September 11, 2001, were equally provocative, raising in a more contemporary context a longstanding problem liberal democracies face: to what lengths can free societies go in protecting themselves without betraying their very principles? In many ways the problem is even more difficult now: The United States was at war with a sovereign country in World War II; now it is engaged in a "War on Terror," a military engagement with a method whose practitioners are shadowy organizations, networks, and cells, but whose weapons can be every bit as threatening as those at the command of nation-states.

So, can liberal democracies sacrifice people's civil liberties in order to safeguard the constitutional order on which such freedoms are based? More simply, can the governments of Canada and the United States do bad things for good purposes? Are there occasions when they *must* do bad things for those ends? How do governments know for sure that the risk of harm to populations, institutions, or civil order is sufficiently great to justify pre-emptive action? Is it justifiable for police to hold in custody without decisive proof a suspect who may have information about a terrorist attack? Can that detainee be forced to give up information? Can he or she be tortured? If torture is unthinkable, is it proper, then, to wait until a terrorist attack has actually transpired in order to know for sure that particular agents committed particular harmful acts? How many innocent lives are we then prepared to sacrifice for our commitment to terrorists' civil liberties?

Ignatieff argues that in the real world, governments sometimes have no choice but to breach people's civil liberties. Such breaches are morally defensible, he suggests, only if they meet two conditions. First, the governments must recognize breaches as breaches. Second, those breaches must be justified in a properly open, democratic forum as necessary, effective, and limited to countering specific threats.

Ignatieff's bold but nuanced position has earned him the criticism of many, including many of his fellow liberals. Is his case for a robust, yet morally restrained antiterrorism policy persuasive?

◆ ◆ ◆

What lesser evils may a society commit when it believes it faces the greater evil of its own destruction? This is one of the oldest questions in politics and one of the hardest to answer. The old Roman adage—the safety of the people is the first law— set few limits to the claims of security over liberty. In the name of the people's safety, the Roman republic was prepared to sacrifice all other laws. For what laws would survive if Rome itself perished? The suspension of civil liberties, the detention of aliens, the secret assassination

---

1. Wretchard, "Hoist with One's Own Petard" The Belmont Club blog. Retrieved May 17, 2005, from http://fallbackbelmont.blogspot.com/2006/07/hoist-with-ones-own-petard.html.

of enemies: all this might be allowed, as a last resort, if the life of the state were in danger. But if law must sometimes compromise with necessity, must ethics surrender too? Is there no moral limit to what a republic can do when its existence is threatened? As Edward Gibbon retold the story of how the Romans slaughtered defenseless aliens in their eastern cities in 395 C.E. as a preemptive warning to the barbarians massing at the gates of their empire, he declined to consider whether actions that political necessity might require could still remain anathema to moral principle. But the question must not only be asked. It must be answered.

If the society attacked on September 11, 2001, had been a tyranny, these ancient questions might not be relevant. For a tyranny will allow itself anything. But the nation attacked on that bright morning was a liberal democracy, a constitutional order that sets limits to any government's use of force. Democratic constitutions do allow some suspension of rights in states of emergency. Thus rights are not always trumps. But neither is necessity. Even in times of real danger, political authorities have to prove the case that abridgments of rights are justified. Justifying them requires a government to submit them to the test of adversarial review by the legislature, the courts, and a free media. A government seeking to respond to an attack or an expected danger is required to present the case for extraordinary measures to a legislature, to argue for them with reasons that might convince a reasonable person, and to alter the measures in the face of criticism. Even after extraordinary measures receive legislative approval, they will still come under review by the courts.

Even in times of real danger, political authorities have to prove the case that abridgments of rights are justified.

The first challenge that a terrorist emergency poses to democracy is to this system of adversarial justification. The machinery of legislative deliberation and judicial review grinds slowly. Emergencies demand rapid action. Hence they require the exercise of prerogative. Presidents and prime ministers have to take action first and submit to questions later. But too much prerogative can be bad for democracy itself.

In emergencies, we have no alternative but to trust our leaders to act quickly, when our lives may be in danger, but it would be wrong to trust them to decide the larger questions of how to balance liberty and security over the long term. For these larger questions, we ought to trust to democratic deliberation through our institutions. Adversarial justification is an institutional response, developed over centuries, to the inherent difficulty of making appropriate public judgments about just these types of conflicts of values.[1] Citizens are bound to disagree about how far the government is entitled to go in any given emergency. Because we disagree deeply about these matters, democracy's institutions provide a resolution, through a system of checks and balances, to ensure that no government's answer has the power to lead us either straight to anarchy or to tyranny.

In a terrorist emergency, we disagree, first of all, about the facts: chiefly, what type and degree of risk the threat of terrorism actually presents. It would make life easy if these facts were clear, but they rarely are. Public safety requires extrapolations about future threats on the basis of disputable facts about present ones. Worse, the facts are never presented to the public simply as neutral propositions available for dispassionate review. They come to us packaged with evaluation. They are usually stretched to justify whatever case for action is being made. Those who want coercive measures construe the risk to be great; those who oppose them usually minimize the threat. The disagreements don't end there. Even when we agree about the facts, we may still disagree whether the risks justify abridgments of liberty.

These disagreements extend to the very meaning of democracy itself. For most Americans, democracy simply means what Abraham Lincoln said it was: government of the people, by the people, for the people. In this account, democracy is a synonym for majority rule. Popular sovereignty, through elected representatives, has to be the final arbiter of what the government can be allowed to get away with when it is trying to defend our freedoms and our lives. Democracies do have bills of rights but these exist to serve vital majority interests. When the executive branch of government suspends rights, for example, it does so in the interest of the majority of citizens. The public interests that these rights defend are defined by the elected representatives of the people, and courts must interpret what these rights mean in obedience to what legislatures and the people say the rights mean.[2] Defending a right of an individual, for example, to freedom of association in times of safety protects the liberty of all. But protecting that same individual in a time of emergency may do harm to all. A terrorist emergency is precisely a case where allowing individual liberty—to plan, to plot, to evade detection—may threaten a vital majority interest. A democracy has no more important purpose than the protection of its members, and rights exist to safeguard that purpose. Civil liberty, the chief justice of the U.S. Supreme Court has written, means the liberty of a citizen, not the abstract liberty of an individual in a state of nature.[3] Such freedom, therefore, must depend on the survival of government and must be subordinate to its preservation.

A democracy has no more important purpose than the protection of its members, and rights exist to safeguard that purpose.

What prevents such a system from falling prey to the tyranny of the majority is the system of checks and balances and, more broadly, the democratic process of adversarial justification itself. While injustice can always be justified if you have to justify it only to yourself, it is less easy when you have to justify it to other democratic institutions, like courts and legislatures or a free press. Thus presidents or prime ministers may not see anything wrong in a stringent measure, but if they know that this measure will have to get by the courts and the legislature, they may think twice.

Besides these constitutional checks and balances, there would also be the democratic check of competing social, religious, and political interests in the nation at large. One of the most lucid versions of this argument is to be found in *Federalist* No. 51, where in discussing the federal system's balance of federal and state power, the authors go on to say that while all authority in the United States will be derived from the power of the majority,

> the society itself will be broken into so many parts, interests, and classes of citizens, that the rights of individuals, or of the minority, will be in little danger from interested combinations of the majority. In a free government, the security for civil rights must be the same as that for religious rights. It consists in the one case in the multiplicity of interests and sects; and this may be presumed to depend on the extent of country and the number comprehended under the same government.[4]

Against this *pragmatic* view there is a *moral* view of democracy, which maintains that it is something more than majority rule disciplined by checks and balances. It is also an order of rights that puts limits to the power of the community over individuals. These limits are not there just for prudential reasons, to prevent governments from riding roughshod over individuals. The rights are also there to express the idea that individuals matter intrinsically. Democracies don't just serve majority interests, they accord individuals intrinsic respect. This respect is expressed in the form of rights that guarantee certain freedoms. Freedom matters, in turn, because it is a precondition for living in dignity. Dignity here means simply the right to shape your life as best you can, within the limits of the law, and to have a voice, however small, in the shaping of public affairs. Government for the people, in other words, is something more than government for the happiness and security of the greatest number. The essential constraint of democratic government is that it must serve majority interests without sacrificing the freedom and dignity of the individuals who comprise the political community to begin with and who on occasion may oppose how it is governed. Rights certainly owe their origin to the sovereignty of the people, but the people—and their representatives—must steer majority interests through the constraints of rights.

Democracies don't just serve majority interests, they accord individuals intrinsic respect.

Aharon Barak, president of Israel's Supreme Court, describes these two conceptions of democracy as "formal" and "substantive."[5] Other scholars have contrasted a "pragmatic" reading of the U.S. constitution with a "moral" reading.[6] In normal times, these two meanings of democracy—one stressing popular sovereignty, the other stressing rights; one privileging collective interests, the other privileging individual dignity—are interdependent. You can't have a democracy without rights, and rights cannot be secure unless you have democracy. But in terrorist emergencies, their relation breaks apart. What makes security appear to trump liberty in terrorist emergencies is the idea—certainly true—that the liberty of the majority is utterly dependent upon their security. A people living in fear [is] not free. Hence the safety of the majority makes an imperative claim. On this view, rights are political conveniences a majority institutes for its defense and is therefore at liberty to abridge when necessity demands it. Those who defend a rights-based definition of democracy will then argue that rights lose all effect, not just for the individuals at risk, but for the majority as well if they are revocable in situations of necessity.

Both sides then appeal to history and seek vindication of their claims. Those who think of democracy primarily in terms of majority interest point to the frequent abridgments of liberty in national emergencies past—from Lincoln's suspension of habeas corpus during the Civil War to the detention of illegal aliens after 9/11—and argue that democracies survive in part because they do not let rights stand in the way of robust measures. Moreover, robust measures do not prevent rights' returning in times of safety. Temporary measures are just that and they need not do permanent damage to a democracy's constitutional fabric. Those who put rights first will reply that yes, democracy survives, but rights infringements needlessly compromise the democracy's commitment to dignity and freedom. The detention of Japanese Americans during World War II would qualify as an example of majoritarian tyranny and misuse of executive prerogative, driven by fear and racial bias.[7] One side in the debate worries that caring overmuch about rights will tie the hands of a democracy, while the other insists that if rights are abridged, even for a few individuals, then democracy betrays its own identity.

Civil libertarians think civil liberties define what a democracy is. But the recurrently weak and shallow public support for civil liberties positions suggests that many Americans disagree. They believe that the majority interest should trump the civil liberties of terrorist suspects.[8] For these democrats, rights are prudential limits on government action, revocable in times of danger; for civil libertarians, they are foundational commitments to individual dignity that ought to limit governmental action in times of safety and danger alike. For one side, what matters fundamentally is that democracies prevail. For the other, what matters more is that democracies prevail without betraying what they stand for.

For one side, what matters fundamentally is that democracies prevail. For the other, what matters more is that democracies prevail without betraying what they stand for.

A further disagreement arises over the question of whether a country facing a terrorist emergency should base its public policy exclusively on its own constitution and its own laws, or whether it has any duty to pay attention to what other states have to say and what international agreements and conventions require. Some maintain that a democracy's commitments to dig-

nity are confined to its own citizens, not its enemies. Others point out that a democracy is not a moral island, sufficient unto itself. Thus, as many scholars have pointed out, the U.S. Constitution extends its protections to "persons" and not just to citizens.[9] Hence aliens have rights under U.S. law—as well as, of course, under international conventions to which the United States is a signatory. Enemy combatants have rights under the Geneva Conventions, and even terrorists retain their *human* rights, since these are inherent in being human and hence irrevocable. Others think this approach values consistency more than justice. Justice—to the victims of terrorist outrages—requires that terrorists be treated as "enemies of the human race" and hunted down without any regard for their human rights.[10]

When citizens of a democracy insist that what matters most in a terrorist emergency is the safety of the majority, they are usually saying that rights are at best a side constraint, at worst a pesky impediment to robust and decisive action. Those who think this are also likely to believe that international agreements, like the Geneva Conventions or the Torture Convention, should not limit what the United States can do in a war on terror. Since the threat is primarily directed at the United States, it must respond according to its own system of law, not according to anyone else's standards. To take this position, however, is also to assume that the lives of your own citizens matter more than the lives of people in other countries. It is, as Ronald Dworkin has pointed out, to base policy on the premise that Americans come first.[11] Those who disagree will usually be committed to the idea that a democracy's ethical commitments are universal and apply both to its own citizens and to its enemies.

These debates are also about whether some measures are just plain wrong. Consequentialists argue that measures which aim to save lives and preserve the security of the citizens cannot be wrong if they actually succeed in doing so. They are wrong only if they don't work—that is, if they produce a chain of further harms, like more terrorist attacks. Most civil libertarians take the view that some actions remain wrong even if they work. So torturing someone to divulge terrorist actions is wrong, no matter what useful information is extracted, and hence no democracy should ever have anything to do with torture. A third position lies between the two. It maintains that consequences can matter so much, for example, saving thousands of people from terrorist attack, that it might be worth subjecting an individual to relentless—though nonphysical—interrogation to elicit critical information. But this style of interrogation, which would push suspects to the limits of their psychological endurance, would remain a violation of their dignity. It would be a lesser evil than allowing thousands of people to die, but its necessity would not prevent it from remaining wrong.

This third position ... maintains that necessity may require us to take actions in defense of democracy which will stray from democracy's own foundational commitments to dignity. While we cannot avoid this, the best way to minimize harms is to maintain a clear distinction in our minds between what necessity can justify and what the morality of dignity can justify, and never to allow the justifications of necessity—risk, threat, imminent danger—to dissolve the morally problematic character of necessary measures. Because the measures are morally problematic, they must be strictly targeted, applied to the smallest possible number of people, used as a last resort, and kept under the adversarial scrutiny of an open democratic system.

> *... necessity may require us to take actions in defence of democracy which will stray from democracy's own foundational commitments to dignity.*

A lesser evil position holds that in a terrorist emergency, neither rights nor necessity should trump. A democracy is committed to both the security of the majority and the rights of the individual. Neither a morality of consequences nor a morality of dignity can be allowed exclusive domain in public policy decisions. If each of these ethical principles has legitimate claims, the resulting framework is going to be complex, to say the least. In it, there are no trump cards, no table-clearing justifications or claims. What works is not always right. What is right doesn't always work. Rights may have to bow to security in some instances, but there had better be good reasons, and there had better be clear limitations to rights abridgments; otherwise, rights will soon lose all their value. At the same time, a constitution is not a suicide pact: rights cannot so limit the exercise of authority as to make decisive action impossible. Finally, international standards matter. Nations are not moral islands: they should conform to international standards, both to comply with the treaties and conventions that nations have signed and to pay what Thomas Jefferson called "decent respect for the opinions of mankind."

> *... in a terrorist emergency, neither rights nor necessity should trump.*

A lesser evil morality is designed for skeptics, for people who accept that leaders will have to take decisive action on the basis of less than accurate information; who think that some sacrifice of liberty in times of danger may be necessary; who want a policy that works but are not prepared to make what works the sole criterion for deciding what to do. Such an ethics is a balancing act: seeking to adjudicate among the claims of risk, dignity, and security in a way that actually addresses particular cases of threat. An ethics of balance cannot privilege rights above all, or dignity above all, or public safety above all. This is the move—privileging one to the exclusion of the other—that produces moral error. They are all important principles—all must be weighed in the balance equally—and nothing trumps.

This is an ethics of prudence rather than first principle, one that assesses what to do in an emergency with a conservative bias against infringements of established standards of due process, equal protection, and basic dignity. A conservative bias assumes that in terrorist emergencies, the first response is usually wrong. Tried and tested standards of due process should not be hastily discarded. These standards are more than procedures, anchored in legal tradition. They reflect important commitments to individual dignity. Protection of the law means, concretely, that no one should be held indefinitely, without charge, without access to counsel or judicial review. Moreover, persons can be detained only for what they have done, not for who they are or for what they think, profess, or believe. A key conservative principle would be that blanket detentions and broad roundups of suspects are always a mistake, because they violate the law's principle of the individuality of guilt. It is invariably wrong to arrest or detain on the principle of guilt by association, based on race, ethnicity, or religious affiliation. Any detention policy must be targeted to individuals against whom probable cause can eventually be demonstrated. By these standards, the United States failed the test in its detention of nearly five thousand aliens, mostly single males of Muslim or Arab origin, after September 11. None have been found to merit charging with terrorist offenses. In retrospect, the whole exercise seems to have been as unnecessary as it was unjust.[12]

Any detention policy must be targeted to individuals against whom probable cause can eventually be demonstrated.

While a conservative bias will enable us to see through most of the overhasty reactions to terrorist emergencies, it may not be adequate when we have to face terrorists who control weapons of mass destruction. If the threat is sufficiently great, preemptive detention of suspects, together with military or police action to disarm, disable, or neutralize the threat, may be necessary. It is unrealistic to think that commitments to dignity, coupled with a conservative bias against departing from tried legal standards, will be sufficient to cope with any eventuality in the future. In the wake of another mass casualty terrorist attack, on or above the scale of September 11, most bets—and gloves—would be off. Even extreme necessity, however, cannot override democratic processes and the obligation to balance strong measures with basic commitments to full public justification.

If a war on terror may require lesser evils, what will keep them from slowly becoming the greater evil? The only answer is democracy itself. Liberal democracy has endured because its institutions are designed for handling morally hazardous forms of coercive power. It puts the question of how far government should go to the cross fire of adversarial review. Adversarial review procedures do not just pit one branch of government against another. Within each branch, there are, or should be, checks and balances, fire walls that guarantee the independence of institutions that perform intra-agency review. The General Accounting Office, for example, keeps the spending propensities of other federal agencies of the U.S. government in check. One branch of the Justice Department has recently criticized another branch's handling of administrative detainees after September 11, and that branch has changed its practices.[13]

In this process of adversarial review the test of reason is not the test of perfection. Citizens usually accept the decisions that result, and because democratic review affords a genuinely adversarial and open contest of opinions. Of course, even the most open process may produce perverse results. Senator Joseph McCarthy harassed and defamed individuals suspected of Communist sympathies in the full glare of publicity, and with the support, for a time, of majority opinion. While open proceedings are fallible, they at least create the possibility for correcting error. If McCarthy persecuted innocent people in open

proceedings, he was also brought down by open proceedings.[14] Ultimately, if open proceedings fail to produce answers that command the assent of citizens, it is up to citizens themselves to force the institutions—through public criticism and the electoral process—to come up with better answers. What is striking about democracy is the role of distrust in keeping the system honest. The system of checks and balances and the division of powers assume the possibility of venality or incapacity in one institution or the other. The ultimate safety in a democracy is that decisions filtered down through this long process stand less of a chance of being wrong than ones decided, once and for all, at the top.

The war waged against terror since September 11 puts a strain on democracy itself, because it is mostly waged in secret, using means that are at the edge of both law and morality. Yet democracies have shown themselves capable of keeping the secret exercise of power under control. So long as "a decision for secrecy should not itself be secret," secrecy can be controlled.[15] Legislatures can take hearings on sensitive intelligence matters in camera; judges can demand that state prosecutors justify secret hearings or the withholding of information from the defense. The redlines should be clear: it is never justified to confine or deport an alien or citizen in secret proceedings. Openness in any process where human liberty is at stake is simply definitional of what a democracy is. The problem is not defining where the redline lies, but enforcing it. A democracy in which most people don't vote, in which many judges accord undue deference to executive decisions, and in which government refuses open adversarial review of its measures is not likely to keep the right balance between security and liberty. A war on terror is not just a challenge to democracy; it is an interrogation of the vitality of its capacity for adversarial review.

A democracy in which most people don't vote, in which many judges accord undue deference to executive decisions, and in which government refuses open adversarial review of its measures is not likely to keep the right balance between security and liberty.

In a war on terror, I would argue, the issue is not whether we can avoid evil acts altogether, but whether we can succeed in choosing lesser evils and keep them from becoming greater ones. We should do so, I would argue, by making some starting commitments—to the conservative principle (maintaining the free institutions we have), to the dignity principle (preserving individuals from gross harms)—and then reasoning out the consequences of various courses of action, anticipating harms and coming to a rational judgment of which course of action is likely to inflict the least damage on the two principles. When we are satisfied that a coercive measure is a genuine last resort, justified by the facts as we can understand them, we have chosen the lesser evil, and we are entitled to stick to it even if the price proves higher than we anticipated. But not indefinitely so. At some point—when we "have to destroy the village in order to save it"—we may conclude that we have slipped from the lesser to the greater. Then we have no choice but to admit our error and reverse course. In the situation of factual uncertainty in which most decisions about terrorism have to be taken, error is probably unavoidable.

It is tempting to suppose that moral life can avoid this slope simply by avoiding evil means altogether. But no such angelic option may exist. Either we fight evil with evil or we succumb. So if we resort to the lesser evil, we should do so, first, in full awareness that evil is involved. Second, we should act under a demonstrable state of necessity. Third, we should choose evil means only as a last resort, having tried everything else. Finally, we must satisfy a fourth obligation: we must justify our actions publicly to our fellow citizens and submit to their judgment as to their correctness.

The challenge in assessing which measures might be permissible is to find a viable position between cynicism and perfectionism. Cynicism would maintain that ethical reflection is irrelevant: the agents of the state will do what they will do, and the terrorists will do what they will do, and force and power alone will decide the outcome. The only question to ask about these means is whether they work. The cynics are wrong. All battles between terrorists and the state are battles for opinion, and in this struggle ethical justifications are critical, to maintain the morale of one's own side, to hold the loyalty of populations who might otherwise align with the terrorists, and to maintain political support among allies. A counterterror campaign probably can be run only by cynics, by professionals schooled in the management of moral appearances, but even cynics know that some moral promises have to be kept if they are to be believed at all. Preventive detention to withdraw suspicious aliens from the general population

might disrupt terrorist networks, but it might so enrage innocent groups that they would cease to cooperate with the police. Torture might break apart a network of terrorist cells, but it would also engender hatred and resentment among the survivors of the torture and further increase their support among disaffected populations. There is simply no way to disentangle the technical question of what works from the political question of what impact such methods will have on the struggle for opinion that is the essence of any campaign against terror. Extreme measures, like torture, preventive detention, and arbitrary arrest, typically win the battle but lose the larger war. Even cynics know that Pyrrhic victories are worse than useless.

As for moral perfectionism, this would be the doctrine that a liberal state should never have truck with dubious moral means and should spare its officials the hazard of having to decide between lesser and greater evils. A moral perfectionist position also holds that states can spare their officials this hazard simply by adhering to the universal moral standards set out in human rights conventions and the laws of war.

There are two problems with a perfectionist stance, leaving aside the question of whether it is realistic. The first is that articulating nonrevocable, nonderogable moral standards is relatively easy. The problem is deciding how to apply them in specific cases. What is the line between interrogation and torture, between targeted killing and unlawful assassination, between preemption and aggression? Even when legal and moral distinctions between these are clear in the abstract, abstractions are less than helpful when political leaders have to choose between them in practice. Furthermore, the problem with perfectionist standards is that they contradict each other. The same person who shudders, rightly, at the prospect of torturing a suspect might be prepared to kill the same suspect in a preemptive attack on a terrorist base. Equally, the perfectionist commitment to the right to life might preclude such attacks altogether and restrict our response to judicial pursuit of offenders through process of law. Judicial responses to the problem of terror have their place, but they are no substitute for military operations when terrorists possess bases, training camps, and heavy weapons. To stick to a perfectionist commitment to the right to life when under terrorist attack might achieve moral consistency at the price of leaving us defenseless in the face of evildoers. Security, moreover, is a human right, and thus respect for one right might lead us to betray another.

> *To stick to a perfectionist commitment to the right to life when under terrorist attack might achieve moral consistency at the price of leaving us defenseless in the face of evildoers.*

A lesser evil morality is antiperfectionist in its assumptions. It accepts the inevitable that it is not always possible to save human beings from harm without killing other human beings; not always possible to preserve full democratic disclosure and transparency in counterterrorist operations; not always desirable for democratic leaders to avoid deception and perfidy; not always possible to preserve the liberty of the majority without suspending the liberties of a minority; not always possible to anticipate terrible consequences of well-meant acts, and so on. Far from making ethical reflection irrelevant, these dilemmas make ethical realism all the more essential to democratic reflection and good public policy. The fact that liberal democratic leaders may order the surreptitious killing of terrorists, may withhold information from their voters, may order the suspension of civil liberties need not mean that "anything goes." Even if liberties must be suspended, their suspension can be made temporary; if executives must withhold information from a legislature in public, they can be obliged to disclose it in private session or at a later date. Public disinformation whose sole purpose is to deceive the enemy might be justified, but deliberately misleading a democratic electorate with a view to exaggerating risk or minimizing hazard can never be. The same balancing act needs to be observed in other cases. If the targeted killing of terrorists proves necessary, it can be constrained by strict rules of engagement and subjected to legislative oversight and review. The interrogation of terrorist suspects can be kept free of torture. Drawing these lines means keeping in clear sight the question of whether these means reinforce or betray the democratic identify they are supposed to defend.

Keeping lesser evils from becoming greater ones is more than a matter of democratic accountability. It is also a matter of individual conscience. Hannah Arendt once argued that being able to think for yourself is a precondition for avoiding evil, especially in large bureaucracies where there is a premium against independent thought. She said that the one common denominator uniting opponents of Nazi rule in Germany was a capacity to ask, at all times, what kind of person one

was or wished to be. Those who refused to kill others, she said, "refused to murder, not so much because they still held fast to the command 'Thou Shalt Not Kill', but because they were unwilling to live together with a murderer—themselves."[16]

> *Public disinformation whose sole purpose is to deceive the enemy might be justified, but deliberately misleading a democratic electorate with a view to exaggerating risk or minimizing hazard can never be.*

No society can avoid official crimes and brutality unless this sense of responsibility is widely shared among public officials. Rules and procedures are not enough. Character is decisive, and there is some reason to think that democracies encourage the right kind of character. People who grow up in societies with constitutional rights are taught to believe that their opinions matter, that they are entitled to a certain fairness and due process in official dealings, and that they have a responsibility to the rights of others. But we cannot be sure that democracy teaches us all to do the right thing.

Moreover, no matter how good our moral learning we all stand in need of the scrutiny of good institutions. A war on terror puts these institutions under strain. It is not always possible to subject intelligence agents and Special Forces to full democratic scrutiny and control. Yet the agents themselves remain citizens, and their responsibility to the constitutional order they defend remains the tribunal of last resort to save them and us from a descent into barbarism. We depend for much of what we know about abuses of power on whistle-blowers, honest people who could not stand what they were being asked to do.[17] Any democracy that wants to fight a clean war on terror needs to safeguard the rights of whistle-blowers, in the most secret agencies of government, to tell the truth to elected officials and the media. The only way to prevent zones of impunity from opening up in our government is for legislatures to insist on their rights of oversight, for the media to continue to demand access, and for the law to sustain the rights of whistle-blowers to tell the truth.

But these are not the only moral checks on a war on terror. Internationally ratified human rights instruments, together with the UN Charter and the Geneva

Conventions, widen the audience of justification beyond the electorates of democratic states under direct attack, to a broader network of states and international bodies, whose views must be taken into account. Their views matter as well as a community of interests, and successful joint action against terrorism will soon become impossible if states disregard their allies, ignore their objections to national policies, and seek unilateral advantage or exemption from international commitments.[18]

International standards matter but we must not assume that nations always agree about what they mean. European countries disagree with the United States about the legitimacy of the death penalty, and they have refused to extradite terrorist suspects to the United States, where capital punishment may be the penalty. International conventions prohibit torture, but the exact point at which intensive interrogation passes over the redline into torture is a matter of dispute. The Geneva Conventions protect the idea of civilian immunity, but who counts as a civilian remains controversial. International conventions set standards, but each country may interpret them differently. How political leaders do so depends on what their domestic electorates appear to allow. But a political standard is not necessarily an ethically normless or relativist one. Public opinion will not accept simply anything. The norms that govern a war on terror are not the monopoly of government. They are susceptible to influence by moral entrepreneurship. Human rights activists and members of civil liberties NGOs will seek to raise the barrier of the morally permissible, while groups representing the military and the police may want to lower it. In any liberal democracy, standards for a war on terror will be set by adversarial moral competition.

As a contribution to this process of standard setting, I would propose the following tests for policy makers. First, a democratic war on terror needs to subject all coercive measures to *the dignity test*—do they violate individual dignity? Foundational commitments to human rights should always preclude cruel and unusual punishment, torture, penal servitude, and extrajudicial execution, as well as rendition of suspects to rights-abusing countries. Second, coercive measures need to pass *the conservative test*—are departures from existing due process standards really necessary? Do they damage our institutional inheritance? Such a standard would bar indefinite suspension of habeas corpus and require all detention, whether by civil or military authorities, to be subject to judicial review. Those deprived of rights—citizens and noncitizens—must never lose access to counsel. A third assessment of counterterror measures should be consequentialist. Will they make citizens more or less secure in the long run? This *effectiveness* test needs to focus not just on the short term, but on the long-term political implications of measures. Will they strengthen or weaken political support for the state undertaking such measures? A further consideration is *the last resort test:* have less coercive measures been tried and failed? Another important issue is whether measures have passed the test of *open adversarial review* by legislative and judicial bodies, either at the time, or as soon as necessity allows. Finally, "decent respect for the opinions of mankind," together with the more pragmatic necessity of securing the support of other nations in a global war on terror, requires any state fighting terrorism to respect its international obligations as well as the considered opinions of its allies and friends. If all of this adds up to a series of constraints that tie the hands of our governments, so be it. It is the very nature of a democracy that it not only does, but should, fight with one hand tied behind its back. It is also the nature of democracy that it prevails against its enemies precisely because it does.

Notes

1. Cass R. Sunstein, *Designing Democracy: What Constitutions Do* (New York: Oxford University Press 2001), 6–8, 13–47. Dennis Thompson and Amy Gutmann, *Democracy and Disagreement* (Cambridge: Harvard University Press, Belknap Press, 1996), 41–49.

2. John Hart Ely, *Democracy and Distrust: A Theory of Judicial Review* (Cambridge: Harvard University Press, 1980), 4: "thus the central function, and it is at the same the central problem, of judicial review: a body that is not elected or otherwise politically responsible in any significant way is telling the people's

elected representatives that they cannot govern as they'd like. ... This in America is a change that matters."

3. William H. Rehnquist, *All the Laws but One: Civil Liberties in Wartime* (New York: Knopf, 1998), 222.

4. *The Federalist* No. 51, http://memory.loc.gov/const/fed/fedpapers.html (accessed December 4, 2003).

5. For an account of how a Supreme Court seeks to balance the two meanings in times of terrorism, see A. Barak, "A Judge on Judging: The Role of a Supreme Court in a Democracy," *Harvard Law Review* 116, no. 1 (November 2002): 16–162, and especially 36–46 and 148–60.

6. Ronald Dworkin, "Philosophy and Monica Lewinsky," *New York Review of Books,* March 9, 2000; Ronald Dworkin, "Posner's Charges: What I Actually Said" (2000), http://www.nyu.edu/gsas/dept/philo/faculty/dworkin/ (accessed December 4, 2003). Ronald Dworkin, *Freedom's Law: The Moral Reading of the American Constitution* (Cambridge: Harvard University Press, 1996), vs. Richard Posner, *The Problematics of Moral and Legal Theory* (Cambridge: Harvard University Press, Belknap Press, 1999).

7. Peter Irons, *Justice at War* (New York: Oxford University Press, 1983), 9–13, 57–64. David Cole, "An Ounce of Detention," *American Prospect,* September 9, 2003.

8. *USA Today/*CNN Gallup Poll Results (August 2003), http://www.lifeandliberty.gov/subs/s_people.htm (accessed December 4, 2003). To the question "Do you think the Bush Administration has gone too far, has been about right or has not gone far enough in restricting civil liberties in order to fight terrorism?" between 55 and 60 percent of respondents say "about right," the numbers remaining stable since June 2002. Forty-eight percent of the sample believe that the Patriot Act gets the balance between liberty and security "about right."

9. David Cole, *Enemy Aliens* (New York: New Press, 2003).

10. For the idea of an enemy of the human race, see the discussion in Hannah Arendt, *Eichmann in Jerusalem: A Report on the Banality of Evil* (New York: Viking, 1963).

11. Ronald Dworkin, "Terror and the Attack on Civil Liberties," *New York Review of Books,* November 6, 2003.

12. Cole, *Enemy Aliens.*

13. *U.S. Justice Department Inspector General Report on Administrative Detention* (June 2003), http://www.usdoj.gov/oig/special/03-06/index.htm (accessed December 4, 2003).

14. Robert D. Marcus and Anthony Marcus, eds., "The Army-McCarthy Hearings, 1954," in *American History through Court Proceedings and Hearings,* vol. 2 (St. James, N.Y.: Brandywine Press, 1998), 136–51.

15. Dennis F. Thompson, *Political Ethics and Public Office* (Cambridge: Harvard University Press, 1987), 118; also Dennis Thompson, "Democratic Secrecy," *Political Science Quarterly* 114, no. 2 (Summer 1999): 181–93. See also *U.S. Senate Final Report of the Select Committee to Study Governmental Operations with Respect to Intelligence Activities* (Washington, D.C.: U.S. Government Printing Office, 1976), 11–14.

16. Hannah Arendt, "Personal Responsibility under Dictatorship," in *Responsibility and Judgment,* ed. Jerome Kohn (New York: Schocken Books, 2003), 44.

17. Daniel Ellsberg, *Secrets: A Memoir of Vietnam and the Pentagon Papers* (New York: Viking, 2002). For a whistle-blower's career in the CIA, see Robert Baser, *See No Evil: A True Story of a Ground Soldier in the CIA's War on Terrorism* (New York: Crown Publishers, 2002).

18. See Michael Ignatieff, ed., *American Exceptionalism and Human Rights* (Princeton: Princeton University Press, 2004).

Terms and Concepts

lesser evil	necessity	cynicism
adversarial justification	prudence	moral perfectionism
popular sovereignty	conservative principle	antiperfectionism
consequentialism	dignity principle	whistleblowers

Questions

1. According to Ignatieff, what are civil liberties for?

2. Ignatieff defends an ethics of the lesser evil in framing responses to terrorism. What is his case?

3. What roles does justification play in antiterrorism policy?

4. In deciding upon the means of combating terrorist threat, Ignatieff argues that rules are not enough. "Character is decisive." What does he mean?

5. What tests should be employed to determine the use of antiterrorism techniques?

6. What is Ignatieff's opinion of the guidance international treaties and protocols can give to the management of terrorist threats?

Making Canada Matter

John Ibbitson

Editors' Note

Canadian foreign policy rhetoric is familiar: Canada is the honest broker, a middle power, the archetypal peacekeeper, effective in its use of "soft power" to resolve international tensions, quick to deploy aid and humanitarian help to relieve distress around the globe, an enthusiastic supporter of the UN and myriad other international organizations and treaties. The image created by this rhetoric is that Canadian foreign policy is guided by values, not interests, and that these values are consonant with all that will make the world a better place in which to live. How much more responsible we are than the reckless Americans!

In this excerpt from his 2004 book, *The Polite Revolution*, *Globe and Mail* columnist John Ibbitson takes issue with almost every shibboleth undergirding Canadians' self-congratulatory opinions about their country's role in the world. Most of these home truths, he argues, are either plainly wrong or wild exaggeration. We say we are generous in our foreign aid, but the numbers tell a different story. We declare our participation in humanitarian efforts around the globe, but we are capable of little more than token contributions.

Canada does have a tradition of enthusiastic participation in UN peacekeeping and the brokering of international conflicts. But it also has a tradition of deadly effective participation in two world wars and in the NATO alliance.

Perhaps the greatest self-deception in the foreign policy story we tell ourselves is that our national independence is advanced by our shifting of national resources away from military defence to other domestic social policy purposes. Ibbitson suggests that this has merely produced a demeaning dependence on other countries, especially the United States, for our defence. We now have to hitch rides on other countries' aircraft to move our demoralized troops and meager resources from global hot spot to hot spot. This is no way to run an independent country.

As you read this essay, consider Ibbitson's most basic assumption: that active participation in the new global political order requires a muscular national defence force to protect national territory and to back up soft-power diplomacy.

◆ ◆ ◆

The framers of the original Canadian Constitution [awarded] the provincial governments all the powers that, in the nineteenth century, didn't seem so important but that, in the twentieth century, became the biggest game in town. Ottawa found itself in danger of being relegated to the sidelines as the great reforms in education, health, pensions, and welfare got underway. Fans of a strong, centralized federation feared that the national government might cease to mean anything in the eyes of its citizens.

To prevent that from happening, Ottawa used its spending power to intervene in spheres of provincial jurisdiction. We can now see that the federal intrusion did at least as much harm as good, by stifling provincial innovation, by creating an excessive transfer of wealth from successful jurisdictions to failing ones, and by creating fiscal crises at the provincial level whenever the federal power decided to reduce its financial commitment in an area of shared financing.

Even so, apologists for the status quo continue to defend the federal role in this sphere as essential to national unity. Without a direct—or, at the very least, a strong indirect—say in social-policy development, the federal power would have nothing to do, it would mean

Excerpts from Chapter 5 ("Making Canada Matter") of *The Polite Revolution: Perfecting the Canadian Dream* by John Ibbitson. Used by permission of McClelland & Stewart Ltd.

nothing to the lives of Canadians, and the very notion of Canada itself would begin to dissolve.

This reasoning, though it permeates both the federal bureaucracy and the ranks of the Liberal and New Democratic parties, is flawed. First, it has been proven demonstrably untrue in Quebec, which has jealously protected its exclusive jurisdiction in the domestic sphere, and which remains part of Canada despite the separatist forces that seek a divorce. Second, federal interference in domestic policy creates more alienation than it assuages. The warfare between the Ontario Conservative government of Mike Harris and the federal Liberal government of Jean Chrétien over health-care spending was often fiercer than that between Chrétien and Parti Québécois leader Lucien Bouchard. Federal policies from the Crow Rate to the National Energy Program to the Kyoto Accord have angered and alienated Albertans, who, along with British Columbians, mostly want to be left alone.

At the root of this federalist fallacy lies a chronic lack of appreciation for the latent power of the national government. The tragedy is that its obsession with social programs had led Ottawa to waste years of effort and countless billions of dollars meddling in other governments' business, while ignoring its own, more important, responsibilities. The first duty of a national government, superseding all others, is to protect its people from external or internal threat. Its second duty is to represent its people to the world. Successive federal governments have wilfully neglected to carry out this fundamental task. In consequence, this nation's defence and foreign policies lie in a shambles, with Canada discredited in the eyes of its citizens and the world. Nothing that Ottawa has achieved or attempted in the realm of its internal relations can excuse the disrepair into which external relations have fallen. This is our national disgrace.

> ... this nation's defence and foreign policies lie in a shambles, with Canada discredited in the eyes of its citizens and the world.

By the 1960s, it had become pretty clear that the Americans, with their military colossus, had assumed sole responsibility for the defence of the North American continent. That outcome had not been preordained. At the end of the Second World War, Canada was a major military power, with the world's third-largest navy and an army that had successfully taken one of the five beaches at Normandy on D-Day. Canada had played a significant role in helping to develop the technology that led to the creation of atomic weapons during the Second World War; this country could certainly have created its own nuclear deterrent, had it so chosen. Instead, Canada decided to concentrate on developing nuclear energy as a source of domestic power, a symbolically significant, as well as practical, decision. Similarly, Canada played an important role in the early days of the North Atlantic Treat Organization, with major responsibilities in the North Atlantic, a fleet that boasted two aircraft carriers, and a permanent expeditionary force of ten thousand on the continent. The NATO alliance also led to a sharp increase in the export of Canadian military technology. The development of the AVRO Arrow proved, if nothing else, that Canadian engineers could compete with the best in the world. Finally, through NORAD (the North American Aerospace Defense Command), the United States and Canada assumed joint responsibility for patrolling North American skies, principally to deter Soviet attack.

All of this was frittered away in the 1960s and 70s, as the federal government turned its energies to domestic issues, halved its commitment to NATO, and ceded effective responsibility for continental air and coastal defence to the United States. The Americans believed that a modern industrial nation could develop a robust social safety net while simultaneously protecting allies and neutral powers from the ongoing threat of Communist expansion. Canada, especially once Pierre Trudeau became prime minister, believed the Soviet menace was exaggerated, and that the national government should focus on improving the lives of its citizens. Since the Americans would look after us anyway, there was no need for Canada to take any meaningful role in its own defence.

> In the 1960s and 70s ... the federal government ... ceded effective responsibility for continental air and coastal defence to the United States.

This rationale is, frankly, baffling, because it came—and still comes—from the very citizens who are most concerned with protecting Canadian culture and sovereignty. What is sovereignty, if not a state's ability to deter and repel foreign encroachments? Granted, Canada could never have resisted an American invasion, but such an invasion was inconceivable. Canada was, however, under threat from Soviet attack throughout the duration of that empire. Some of those missiles in Russian silos were pointed at Canadian cities and Canadian defence centres. By any reasonable definition of sovereignty, the Canadian government had an obligation to provide a robust defence of its coastline, to field a strong contingent on the European front line of the Cold War, and to assert Canadian control over and under the ice of the Far North. Instead, the very nationalists who were determined to resist foreign domination of the Canadian economy, and who trumpeted a distinct, if amorphous, Canadian identity, happily surrendered Canadian sovereignty over its airspace and coastlines to the United States, by eroding the Canadian military to the point of irrelevance.

The diversion of public resources from defence to social services accelerated when the cost of those services escalated and the tax base weakened during the 1970s and 80s. The deterioration accelerated even further in the 1990s, when all resources were diverted to eliminating the federal deficit. With the return of surpluses in 1997, the first priority was to restore funding to health care and reduce taxes. The steady decline of the Canadian military became so serious that a Senate committee recommended in 2002 that Canada withdraw its forces from all overseas commitments, warning that our military had reached the point of effective collapse.[1]

The generation-long degradation of Canada's defence capacity simply reflected national values: a casual disregard for something that other countries are obsessively concerned with—namely, the physical ability to protect the nation's borders from incursion; an acceptance that American continental security interests are identical with Canadian interests, accompanied by trust that the Americans will protect our interests along with their own, without abusing that trust; and most important, a strong emphasis on the necessity of protecting social programs at whatever cost, including the cost of national defence. There are few, if any, countries in the world where butter so thoroughly trumps guns.

But there are other Canadian values, values that are increasingly being compromised as a result of Canada's relentlessly deteriorating military. As citizens become aware of those compromises, we may expect to see increasing impatience with the current state of the nation's defences, and increasing pressure to accelerate improvements.

Simply put, Canadians care about what happens in the world. We always have; that is why it was important that the Canadian government independently sign the Treaty of Versailles; why Canada assumed responsibility for its own foreign policy between the wars; why Canadian diplomats were heavily involved in designing the United Nations charter; why we were among the original participants in crafting NATO; why we have invested heavily in time and effort both within the Commonwealth and the Francophonie. Canadians are internationalists. Canadians are joiners.

Canadians are internationalists. Canadians are joiners.

The Canadian response to the Asian tsunami that devastated the nations bordering the Indian Ocean in December 2004 will probably be seen as a watershed moment in Canadian foreign policy. Canadians had responded admirably to previous humanitarian crises, both natural and man-made. This country's extraordinary response to the Vietnamese refugees (the "boat people") who fled their repressive regime in the wake of the collapse of South Vietnam contributed to our being awarded the Nansen medal in 1986, the only time the United Nations High Commission for Refugees has bestowed that prestigious prize on an entire country. Canadians also opened this country's doors to immigrants and refugees from Somalia and Ethiopia, when war and famine rendered the Horn of Africa virtually uninhabitable.

The tsunami, however, was different. Not only was the scale of the calamity virtually unprecedented—in the end, the tidal waves cost more than 260,000 lives—but these were no longer foreigners caught in a vortex of poverty and natural disaster. These people were family—kith and kin to the Indians, Sri Lankans, Indonesians, and Thais living in this country. The immediacy that the crises represented for millions of Canadians—including the five members of Parliament of Indian descent who accompanied Paul Martin on his trip to the region—doubtless contributed to the exceptional outpouring of $200 million that Canadians donated to the relief effort, matched by the $425 million contributed by the Canadian government. And yet, despite this effort, we came up short.

The Canadian military had created an emergency response unit known as DART (Disaster Assistance Response Team), specifically created for such emergencies. DART comes equipped with a field hospital, desalination equipment, and trained personnel—exactly what the situation called for. That is why the Italian government deployed its version of DART immediately. Forty-eight hours after the waves struck, the Italians had a field hospital in place in Sri Lanka, and were sending Canadian-made water bombers to the region to deliver emergency supplies to cut-off areas.[2] But DART took two weeks to get to Sri Lanka. The military was not to blame; they had mobilized DART within hours of the first reports, and had even secured Russian-made transport airplanes to ferry the team to the disaster area. But senior figures in the Department of Foreign Affairs questioned the need to send DART. It would be expensive, went the argument, and no formal request had actually been received from any of the stricken nations. Better to start out by sending some field observers into the region to see where the need might be. This, at a time when it was clear to everyone everywhere that the fatalities numbered in the tens of thousands at the very least. When citizens and reporters began asking "Where is DART?" Defence Minister Bill Graham, who had actually favoured immediate deployment, was reduced to stuttering explanations that the cost of sending the unit was so high that the money could be better spent on immediate relief. In that case, came the question, what's the use of the thing in the first place? Caught off-guard, politicians scrambled to redress the mistake, but by now the Russian transport planes were no longer available. It took a week before the government was able to announce the deployment of the team, and another week before it landed in Sri Lanka. Once in place, the experienced troops and workers of DART did their typically fine job. But for many Canadians who had not paid much attention to the state of Canada's military in recent years, the DART incident was revelatory.

They didn't know that, despite federal surpluses that had averaged $11.5 billion over the previous five years, the Canadian military had become so rundown that huge gaps existed in its ability to carry out its assigned missions. Canada deployed five hundred troops to Haiti in 2004, as part of a multinational effort to bring stability to the Western hemisphere's most wretched country. A Defence Department report revealed that the troops lacked, and were forced to scrounge for, such basic equipment as flak jackets, proper boots, and latex gloves.[3] When Canadian soldiers arrived in 2003 to lead the multinational force bringing stability to post-Taliban Afghanistan, their poorly armoured Iltis jeeps were unable to protect troops from land mines, one of which killed two soldiers. The expeditionary force initially lacked a field hospital and other vital support services, which it had to scrounge from allies.[4] And in all these so-called rapid foreign deployments, Canadian troops had to bum a lift, because this country lacks "heavy-lift capacity," the large airplanes needed to quickly transport troops and supplies to foreign destinations.

... the Canadian military had become so rundown that huge gaps existed in its ability to carry out its assigned missions.

There are also notorious deficiencies at home. The Canadian Coast Guard lacks the equipment and mandate to intercept foreign vessels entering Canadian waters that are suspected of smuggling illegal goods or illegal immigrants. And yet the Canadian navy, with its three, three-decade-old destroyers (a fourth has been mothballed to provide parts for the others), twelve frigates, and the newly acquired second-hand British submarines—one of which, the HMCS *Chicoutimi*, caught fire in 2004, killing one seaman—is hardly up to the task either. The ancient Sea King helicopters, only now being replaced, are unfit for any military. (One airman told the author that friends of his spend their days working on a Sea King that sits in a hangar and is never expected to fly again.) And as Denmark contests Canadian sovereignty in the Far North,[5] and other nations contemplate the possibility of sending commercial traffic through the Northwest Passage whether Canada grants permission or not, it is abundantly clear that this country lacks the military capacity to protect national interests in the Arctic archipelago. It comes down to this: No matter what task the Canadian military might be assigned, it is not up to it.

... it is abundantly clear that this country lacks the military capacity to protect national interests in the Arctic archipelago.

The decline of the national defence capacity, which is only now being tentatively slowed, is bad enough on its own, but what the Afghan, Haitian, and Indian

Ocean deployments reveal most clearly is that the deterioration of Canada's military has also led to the deterioration of this country's ability to project a coherent and respected foreign policy.

... the deterioration of Canada's military has also led to the deterioration of this country's ability to project a coherent and respected foreign policy.

For a young nation, Canada has a distinguished record in foreign affairs. Apart from the examples cited above, the efforts of then foreign minister Lester Pearson in 1956 to defuse the Suez crisis by introducing peacekeeping troops won our future prime minister the Nobel Prize. More recently, Canada led the fight among the developed nations within the British Commonwealth to impose sanctions that helped end apartheid in South Africa. We spearheaded the campaign to develop a treaty banning the use of land mines, and we were an important supporter of the new International Criminal Court. Our ratification of the Kyoto Protocol on global warming was central to its final passage, while Paul Martin helped fashion the G20 meeting of finance ministers from developed and developing nations. These foreign initiatives are part of what has been dubbed "soft power." According to the theory, Canada influences the world, not by virtue of its military powers or economic clout, but by promoting Canadian values of diversity, tolerance, and human right in international forums.

Perhaps the most important manifestation of Canadian soft power was "Responsibility to Protect," a United Nations report sponsored by the Canadian government and submitted to the world's governments in 2001. The document sets out a framework through which the UN and its member states could intervene in countries where governments were unable or unwilling to protect their own people from natural calamity or internal violence.

Response to "R2P" has been wary from many Third World countries, who suspect it may be used to legitimize neo-colonial interventions. Nonetheless, the philosophy behind the Canadian initiative will become increasingly dominant in the coming decades. In the twentieth century, nations emerging from colonial pasts jealously guarded the prerogatives of sovereign states, including rigid non-interference in internal affairs. The United Nations, whose General Assembly is dominated by these governments, has traditionally respected this principle, even when it has led to mass slaughter in Rwanda, or the more petty persecutions that African governments so often enjoy visiting on their own citizens. As more countries enter the privileged club of functioning liberal democracies, the atrocities committed by the holdouts against their own people will become less and less tolerable in the eyes of the international community. After all, if we could safely liberate the people of North Korea from that murderous dictatorship, which literally starves its own population while it develops nuclear weapons, wouldn't that be a blessing? Don't the people of Myanmar and Zimbabwe deserve every bit as much as you or I to live in free societies governed by the rule of law? God willing, the day will come in this century when citizens of all nations feel a responsibility to protect the most persecuted on the planet.

That day might come sooner rather than later, if Canada is able to persuade the General Assembly and Security Council to accept, at least in principle, the precepts of R2P. Unfortunately, this country is ill-positioned to press the case, for when it comes to contemporary foreign policy, Canada is something of a failed state of its own. Canadian foreign policy today is marked by so much contradiction and hypocrisy that it's hard to take anything that Ottawa says to the rest of the world seriously, which is why no one does.

Canadian foreign policy today is marked by so much contradiction and hypocrisy that it's hard to take anything that Ottawa says to the rest of the world seriously, which is why no one does.

First and foremost, Canadians have only belatedly begun to realize that a country's foreign policy is primarily its defence policy. Unless a nation is able to protect itself and to project force abroad, it will not be listened to, which is why Canada is not listened to. The reader might well ask: how can this be? Surely a nation is not respected or ignored based on its ability to wage war. Surely Canada won't be given a more respectful hearing if it demonstrates its capacity to invade Norway. Of course not. But projecting force in the 21st century is an evolving concept, one with which Canada is failing to keep pace.

Canadian officials point to the atrocities being committed against the people in the Darfur region of Sudan as a textbook case of how the R2P doctrine can be applied. The rape and murder of innocents by government-backed militias in 2004 appeared to be careening toward genocide, and continues to be—or at least should be—one of the more important areas of international concern. The global community has supported troop interventions by the African Union to protect the citizens of Darfur, and an international peacekeeping force is to be deployed to monitor a peace settlement between the Sudanese government and southern rebels. If that peace holds, it could also lead to a reduction in violence in Darfur.

But although Paul Martin personally visited Sudan in 2004, and although Canada has pushed hard for international action on Darfur, Canada's own contribution, in terms of financial support and of peacekeepers, has been largely symbolic: A token force of one hundred troops to assist the African Union in training and logistics, and $170 million in aid over two years. Most Canadians may not be fully aware that Canada, the country that invented peacekeeping, is no longer a significant contributor to peacekeeping activities around the globe. Canada ranks thirty-fifth among nations contributing peacekeeping forces, behind Nepal and Bangladesh. In fairness, the statistic is questionable, since it doesn't include Canadian forces stationed in the former Yugoslavia, who are there under the auspices of NATO. Nonetheless, the fact remains that Canada, which once committed peacekeeping forces whenever asked, from Cyprus to Cambodia, is often no longer able to respond to UN requests—or, more accurately, has to ask the UN not to ask us—simply because our military has deteriorated to the point where we have neither the troops nor equipment. Former journalist Andrew Cohen observed in *While Canada Slept* that "while Canada once supplied 10 per cent of the world's peacekeepers, it now contributes less than 1 per cent."[6]

Canada ... is often no longer able to respond to UN requests ...

The truth is that soft power only works when it is backed by hard power. The people of Darfur can be protected from the janjaweed militia only if the African Union is willing and able to carry out its mission to protect them. In this or other conflicts, First World military intervention may be needed to protect civilian populations, as happened in Haiti in 2004 and East Timor in 1999, or to provide financial or material support for regional coalition forces, as in Sudan. Anti-neocolonialists may decry what they see as naked imperialism disguised in humanitarian robes, but these imperialists may often be the only ones able to prevent mass starvation or slaughter. Responsibility to Protect means protecting with a strong arm.

The truth is that soft power only works when it is backed by hard power.

In fact, although many critics would deny it, a principle similar to that enshrined in Responsibility to Protect has already emerged over the past fifteen years. It has done so tentatively, inconsistently, and highly imperfectly. It has often originated in American determination to protect its own interest. But it has emerged nonetheless.

Kuwait, Somalia, Bosnia, Kosovo, Afghanistan, Haiti, Iraq. In all of these conflicts, an American-led international force—sometimes with United Nations approval, sometimes without—has intervened to deter aggressions by rogue governments, or to protect civilian populations from their own government. The interventions have sometimes failed. They have sometimes been prompted more by American perceived self-interest than collective altruism. They have always been attended by complications and unforeseen setbacks. Yet the principle is slowly emerging: coalitions of willing states, in the presence of an international emergency, have intervened to correct situations deemed intolerable. With the exception of the invasion of Iraq, Canada has participated in all of these coalitions. But that participation has probably done little to burnish Canada's image abroad. In every instance, our contribution was limited, not by our commitment to the cause, but by the forces we were able to contribute. Too often, the paucity of our resources rendered that contribution negligible.

If Canada truly does believe in a Responsibility to Protect, then it must develop the *capacity* to protect. At a minimum, this country must develop the ability to dispatch at least one brigade of troops, fully equipped for action in hostile territory, and able to deploy at very short notice without having to bum a lift or beg for supplies from allied forces. Even this would be a small fraction of what the British and Australian defence establishments—to name two of our English allies—are capable, but it would be a start.

It's about more than military might, though, or the lack of it. Canada's global profile in recent years has diminished in any number of ways, through our own inconstant and ill-chosen actions. Consider foreign aid. The developed nations committed, back in the 1960s, to devoting 0.7 per cent of their gross domestic product to foreign assistance. What most Canadians probably don't know is that Lester Pearson headed the commission that came up with the figure, and all prime ministers since Pearson have committed to meeting that target. In 2002, the world's richest countries renewed their pledge, promising to greatly reduce global poverty and its side effects by 2015. Canada was one of the nations that ratified this pledge. How dare we? This country has never come even remotely close to meeting the original target set by Pearson forty years ago. Instead, foreign aid has been steadily cut—Jean Chrétien's government slashed it by half from the level it was at during Brian Mulroney's tenure—until today it sits at around .28 per cent of GDP. Other nations have met the Canadian standard, including Norway, Sweden, Denmark, the Netherlands, and Luxembourg. Still others, including Britain, France, Spain, Finland, Ireland and Belgium, have set firm targets and are on their way to reaching the goal.

It's about more than military might, though, or the lack of it ... Consider foreign aid.

Critics of Canada's foreign-aid policy also rightly bemoan its lack of coherence or focus. As Andrew Cohen observes, our paltry contribution to overseas development should be concentrated on a few key countries where Canadian dollars could substantively help. But just as Canada can't resist joining every international forum that will have us, so too we can't resist being part of every relief effort, no matter how small our contribution might be. The Canadian International Development Agency delivers aid to more than one hundred countries, including China, which at last look was hardly a struggling, backward state. Canadian foreign aid must not only be increased, but it must be targeted to reach those countries where help is most needed and

can do the most good. For example, Canada can be proud of the passionate advocacy of Stephen Lewis in bringing home to the developed world the magnitude of the HIV/AIDS holocaust in Africa. Jean Chrétien's far-sighted plan to deliver anti-retroviral drugs to the region at low cost will be remembered as one of his most positive legacies. Canada might well conclude that combating HIV/AIDS in Africa is its principal goal in foreign aid. If so, then other programs, such as those in Latin America and Southeast Asia, might have to be wound down, so that all available resources can be focused on this particular fight.

To its credit, the federal government has finally moved to exploit one special area of potential that will involve little cost and could make a significant contribution. In Ukraine, in 2004, an exasperated population rose up against rigged elections, demanding a free and fair vote, open and democratic government, and closer ties to the democracies of Europe. That Orange Revolution overshadowed equally promising elections in Romania, leaving Belarus the last totalitarian holdout in Eastern Europe (Russia partially excepted). It is not being naive to predict that, with each passing year, more and more countries will progress steadily closer to democracy and the rule of law. In fact, this is the trendline.

Canada has an important and unique role to play in encouraging the spread of democracy around the globe. This country has considerable experience in election monitoring—our observers were at elections both in Ukraine in December 2004 and Iraq in January 2005—and a solid record in training police forces and judges in emerging democracies. More important still, our Constitution, with all its faults, has proven well adapted to managing the needs of a bilingual and multi-ethnic nation. We have lessons to teach and help to give in the development and coordination of local, regional, and national governance.

Canada has an important and unique role to play in encouraging the spread of democracy around the globe.

Foreign policy is also an instrument of economic development. Between 1993, the year NAFTA was signed, and 2004, Canada signed three free-trade agreements: with Chile, Costa Rica, and Israel. The United

States, on the other hand, despite George W. Bush's reputation for unilateralism and protectionism, signed twelve, and was hard at work on ten more. Canada should be able to negotiate free-trade agreements with anyone and everyone who is interested, from Australia to Brazil.

Supporting an expansion of Canadian trade in other markets need not and should not entail reducing Canadian political, cultural, and economic relations with the United States. Instead, the time has come to strengthen and deepen those ties.

Supporting an expansion of Canadian trade in other markets need not and should not entail reducing Canadian political, cultural, and economic relations with the United States.

There is a dark side to the celebration of Canada's growing ethnic diversity and cultural tolerance. Some observers, not content to celebrate this country's strengths, feel compelled to contrast the ongoing evolution of Canadian society with its American counterpart. They use it to rebut conventional wisdom that Canadians are, in most respects, pretty much like Americans. Canadians and Americans are *not* alike, these critics maintain. In fact, the two peoples are quite different in fundamental respects, and are growing further apart with every passing year, polarizing into opposing and incompatible camps. Implicit in this argument is the assumption that Canadians are not just different from Americans, but Canadians are *superior* to Americans, that American culture and society have embarked on a downward spiral even as Canada ascends toward Utopia.

Of course there are cultural differences between Canada and the United States. How could there not be? Our nation has not been scarred by the curse of slavery and the entrenched racial tensions it engendered. Nor can Canadians fully comprehend the mindset of a people who collectively preside over the most powerful and wealthy nation in all of human history. (And how differently would we manage things if *we* had such power?) Americans place a greater emphasis on individual liberty than Canadians, who are more attracted to the collective security of government intervention and communal rights. Although the American political

system in theory separates church more emphatically from state than does ours, the political influence of evangelical Christianity has always been strong in that society and appears to be growing, leading to a more socially conservative country, while Canada is steadily dismantling the former institutional ties between church and state, especially in Quebec, and there is no evidence, as yet, that religious fundamentalism is on the rise, at least as a political manifestation. (The fruitless efforts of the religious right to galvanize the opposition to federal same-sex marriage legislation in 2005 only served to reveal the weakness of the movement.) It is perfectly true than even Canadian conservatives would mostly vote Democrat in the United States. It also doesn't mean a thing.

For the truth is Americans and Canadians are so inextricably intertwined as to be inseparable. Now this has to be parsed, for there are several Americas, just as there are several Canadas. Atlantic Canadians share strong cultural and historical links with New Englanders. Quebeckers historically moved back and forth between the home province and Maine, New Hampshire, and Vermont. Ontario has been described by the political economist Thomas Courchene as an integral part of a de facto Great Lakes region-state, with closer economic ties to Michigan, New York, and Pennsylvania than to Quebec or Manitoba. Winnipeggers travel to St. Paul-Minneapolis for big-city shopping, while Prairie farmers know their compatriots south of the border understand better than anyone the challenges of farming in the North American Midwest. Alberta is closer than any other part of Canada to emulating the social conservatism, raw entrepreneurship, and petro-wealth of Texas, while Vancouver and Seattle are so closely intertwined that the local PBS station has hosted fundraisers in Canada. Canadian political elites like to point out that the dominant Canadian political ethos is most closely mirrored in the Democratic states of the Northeast, the Great Lakes, and the Pacific Coast, but that doesn't exactly hold, for there is equal resonance between Alberta, plus parts of Saskatchewan and Manitoba (all hotbeds of the original Reform movement), and the Red Republican states of the South and the Midwest. It would be more accurate to say that Canadians resemble, politically and culturally, the Americans they live closest to. And remember, just about everyone lies close to the Americans. Eighty per cent of the Canadian population lives within two hundred kilometres of the American border.

... Americans and Canadians are so inextricably intertwined as to be inseparable.

As for economic linkages, they are so intimate as to hardly require repeating. Forty per cent of Canadian GDP is tied to trade with the United States, which accounts for 85 per cent of Canadian exports. Since the signing of the 1988 Free Trade Agreement, Canadian exports to the United States have grown from $99 billion to $279 billion in value (counted in 2005 U.S. dollars) Canada is the United States' biggest supplier of imported energy. Our automotive industries are fully integrated. The Americans have $239 billion of capital invested in Canada, while Canadian investments in the United States total $191 billion. Canadians and Americans are business partners, friends, and family, all rolled into one.

This inescapable fact undermines the core argument made by those who favour keeping a healthy distance in American and Canadian relations. That argument is predicated on the assumption of different and diverging social values, displeasure with American foreign policy, and fear that Canada will lose its sovereignty—cultural, economic, and ultimately political—and its soul if it draws any closer to the American behemoth. The danger, however, is not that Canada will grow too close to the United States, but that we are growing too far apart. Trade irritants such as those that have emerged over softwood lumber, wheat, and the aftermath of the BSE cattle crisis threaten to rile the mostly calm waters of Canada–US trade. More important, both Mexico and China could surpass Canada as America's largest trading partner in coming decades, diminishing Canadian influence in Washington. And as America signs more and more trade agreements with other countries, Canada becomes simply one of a number of states with most-favoured trading status. We recede, rather than progress, in America's consciousness. One way to compensate, as mentioned above, is for Canada to seek trade agreements with other countries, and this is a policy worth pursuing aggressively. But it would be naive to imagine that Canadian trade will ever shift substantively from its American focus. Trade between Canada and the European Union, for example, is already mostly tariff-free. Yet trade with the EU represents no more than

1.8 per cent of Canadian GDP. The truth is, there isn't a lot that we have to sell them that they want to buy. They're just not into Ontario wines.

The danger ... is not that Canada will grow too close to the United States, but that we are growing too far apart.

A revived, consistent, and dynamic reshaping of Canada's role in the world would be reflected in a substantial upgrading of the Canadian military; an expanded and refocused program in foreign aid; improved efforts to export the Canadian experience in democratic governance; new trade agreements with other countries; and broader and deeper economic, security, and environmental co-operation with our friend—yes, our *friend*—and ally, the United States.

Such an aggressive expansion of Canada's role in the world would not come without a price. Federal subsidies in the domestic sphere would certainly diminish as a result of increased expenditures in defence and foreign aid. Any broad expansion of federally directed national social policy would have to be curtailed.

But fears that the federal government's importance in the lives of its citizens would diminish are misplaced. Canada is an outward-looking nation; its heritage as a settler country has made it so. As Canada bolsters and amplifies its role in the family of nation states, as its foreign policy, foreign-aid programs, and foreign presence become more credible, as its role matures within the United Nations, NATO, NORAD, the Commonwealth, the Francophonie, the G8, and new international forums yet to emerge, Canadians will look to Ottawa with pride and confidence, as the voice of Canada in the world, in a century when Canada can and should mean more to the world. This country has a unique role to play as liaison; a first-world, European culture increasingly dominated by polyglot races from around the globe; a bridge between English and French, European and Asian, American and everyone else. Canada, as the country that embodies the world, is the country that can make the world finally understand itself. And in that mission, the very thing that so many fear is being lost— the national identity, the national soul—will finally have been found.

Notes

1. Daniel Leblanc, "Keep troops at home, senators say," *Globe and Mail*, 13 November 2002, p. A4.
2. Hugh Winsor, "'Can do' general right choice for forces," *Globe and Mail*, 17 January 2005, p. A7.
3. Kevin Bissett, "Canadian troops left to beg for basic equipment," Canadian Press, 17 October 2004.
4. Stephen Thorne, "Canada seeks NATO help to run Kabul peacekeeping operation," Canadian Press, 21 February 2003.
5. Hans Island, a barren bit of rock between Ellesmere Island and Greenland, is claimed by both Denmark and Canada. War is unlikely, but both countries consider the island important. Ownership could affect control over future shipping routes, especially in the event of global warming, and there is always the possibility that oil or gas lies offshore.
6. Andrew Cohen, *While Canada Slept: How We Lost Our Place in the World*. Toronto: McClelland & Stewart, 2003, p. 29.

Terms and Concepts

sovereignty
Cold War

Canadian values
national defence capacity

soft power
hard power

Questions

1. Why is Canada irrelevant on the world stage, according to Ibbitson?
2. Ibbitson argues that "a country's foreign policy is primarily its defence policy." What are his reasons for saying so? Are they persuasive?
3. What national interests guide Canadian foreign policy? What values guide it?
4. How does the presence of the United States on Canada's southern border affect Canadian foreign policy?
5. Assuming Ibbitson is correct in his analysis of what needs to change in Canadian foreign policy, what should Canadians be willing to give up in order to finance a more muscular Canadian foreign policy? Are they willing to make the tradeoffs to update Canadian foreign policy?
6. Ibbitson argues that Canada has a unique contribution to make to democratization around the world. Explain.

Canadian Foreign Policy After September 11, 2001: Following the Wrong Path

Shaun Narine

Editors' Note

In the previous article in this collection, John Ibbitson argues that Canada needs a more muscular defence policy to secure a more independent foreign policy. In a world of sovereign states, countries are listened to and respected ultimately because they have the hard power to make their commitments stick. He also argues that the Liberal government's criticisms of American foreign policy were ill considered but also lightweight: for years the Liberals let Canada's armed forces languish, forcing us to depend more on others, including American forces, for security and the discharge of our international commitments. Since Ibbitson's words were published, Stephen Harper's Conservatives were elected to office and embarked on changes to both defence and foreign policies that largely reflect the approach he favours.

Canadians have always struggled with their relationship to the United States. Not a few have remarked that Canadian identity is essentially woven from the cloth of anti-Americanism. What is it about the United States that distinguishes that country from ours? Given the depth of the Canada–United States trade relationship, the amount of American TV Canadians watch, the number of American brands we wear and drive, the language we speak, and the American magazines we read, it is easy to conclude by saying: not much. The very similarities between the two societies perhaps are the source of our insistence that we are different.

On the other hand, some people maintain that despite these similarities, Canadians and Americans have distinct political values. Our social values are more "progressive" or "liberal." Our society is more secular in character. We are not as resistant to state action as are Americans. In foreign policy, Canadians see themselves as natural peacekeepers, more inclined to use the "soft power" of diplomacy, trading on an international reputation as an "honest broker." If this is true, then Canadians are different

from Americans and cannot be assumed to parrot the United States in international affairs. In Canadian politics, the question of foreign policy independence is often intimately tied to another, namely, Are Canadian interests similar to or different from those of the United States?

In this article on the perils and prospects of Canadian foreign policy independence, Shaun Narine argues that the Conservative government of Stephen Harper has violated a Canadian tradition of foreign policy independence by supporting the Bush Administration on so many aspects of the War on Terror. Bush's foreign policy has harmed the United States, the countries in which it has taken an especial political and military interest, and the international community. It will also, Narine suggests, harm those countries aligning their policies with Bush's. Under Stephen Harper, Narine maintains, Canada seeks a deck chair aboard a sinking ship.

◆ ◆ ◆

Canada and the United States have always shared a highly ambivalent relationship. This ambivalence has been most pronounced on the Canadian side. On the one hand, Canada has long presented itself as the United States's most important trading partner, its closest international ally, and a good neighbour, sharing an undefended border. On the other hand, Canada's history has been shaped by various military and political efforts designed to avoid being overrun by the United States, politically, economically, and militarily. The need to keep a healthy distance from the United States has long been understood by Canadian leaders as an important part of Canada's national identity and survival.

Canada's complex relationship with the United Stated became considerably more strained with the election in 2000 of George W. Bush as president. Bush came to power with a foreign policy agenda that was, in many of its basic elements, at odds with some long-held Canadian policies and interests. Bush's primary focus during his first months in office, however, was on domestic affairs. He paid little attention to international issues.

This changed with the terrorist attacks against the United States on September 11, 2001. These attacks had a transformative effect on some members of the Bush administration. Others in positions of power used the attacks as the pretence on which to pursue policies of American hegemony that they had long advocated. The overall effect was a singular American attack on the basic structures of the international order. These attacks culminated in the American (supported by a fictive "coalition of the willing") invasion of Iraq. At the time of this writing, that invasion has proven to be an unmitigated—albeit extremely predictable—foreign policy disaster for the United States. But it is a disaster that has had and continues to have profound implications for international order and stability.

... the U.S. War on Terror is a dismal failure and ... Canada ... has tied itself to this rapidly sinking ship.

This article explores the American "War on Terror" and the Canadian response to this highly questionable initiative. The basic argument is that the U.S. War on Terror is a dismal failure and that Canada—mostly for political reasons—has tied itself to this rapidly sinking ship. The article argues that the Conservative government of Stephen Harper entered office with an approach to foreign policy that was defined by an ideological commitment to the United States which is, on early evidence, digging Canada only more deeply into an intractable foreign policy morass. By contrast, the foreign policy that Canada should follow recognizes the growing value of internationalism and the need to remain an independent actor in a rapidly changing world.

THE UNITED STATES AND THE WAR ON TERROR
◆ ◆ ◆

George W. Bush began his tenure as president with a general lack of personal interest in foreign affairs. Bush was famous for being remarkably ignorant of the world outside the United States. He had expressed an aversion to "state building" and his foreign policy advisers seemed to be mostly hardcore realists who put a narrow, short-term understanding of American advantage at the forefront of policy making. Not surprisingly, this approach was not conducive to good foreign relations. From the outset, the Bush team made it clear that it was prepared to use international institutions when they served American national interests and ignore them otherwise. The Bush Administration quickly alienated much of the international community by adopting policies that harmed international order without any regard for the long-term consequences of such strategies.[1]

The terrorist attacks of 9-11 had the long-term effect of exacerbating the unilateral tendencies of the Bush Administration. The United States's immediate reaction was to declare a War on Terror and proceed to attack the terrorist organization al-Qaeda, which was operating out of Afghanistan. The subsequent invasion of Afghanistan took place with the overall approval of the international community and led to the overthrow of that country's Taliban regime. The next step in the U.S. War on Terror, however, proved to be far more controversial. Relying on rhetoric and innuendo, the Bush Administration led an ignorant American public into a war against Iraq.

The debates around the U.S. invasion of Iraq will continue for some time to come. The overall damage that American actions have done to the international system remains to be seen, but it is apparent that the damage is substantial. What is clear is that the war was illegal, it was a war of choice, and it was based upon a gross—and apparently deliberate—distortion of evidence.[2] Some debates centre on how deliberately the American government misled its people. There are equally interesting questions about the extent to which the ideologues within the Bush Administration misled themselves. Many Bush officials had been almost desperate to attack Iraq for many years. They used 9-11 as a pretext to do what they had long wanted to do. The ideological defence of this action tied it to the War on Terror. The basic argument—putting aside the innuendo that suggested that there were connections between al-Qaeda and the Iraqi regime of Saddam Hussein—was that terrorism originating in the Middle East was the product of a lack of "democracy" in the region. The overthrow of the Iraqi regime using American military power would lead to the establishment of a democratic Iraq that would then serve as an example to the rest of the Arab world. This blossoming of democracy would greatly reduce the terrorist threat to the United States. Not coincidentally, the positioning of American military bases in Iraq would enhance the United States's ability to control Iran and exert influence in the region.

The logical, historical, and moral problems with this argument are overwhelming. Iraq was deeply divided by religious and ethnic tensions; any democracy that resulted would surely reflect those tensions. In addition, after decades of Western and Russian intervention in the region, Islamic fundamentalist movements had become among the most politically popular in the Arab world and would surely gain considerable ground in true democratic elections in most Arab states. The notion that terrorism could be cured by democracy also failed to account for the many ways in which terrorism was a response to oppressive social and political forces.[3] Moreover, not all terrorism is the same. The ideologically driven, transnational terrorism of al-Qaeda, for example, was clearly distinct from the nationalist, politically driven terrorism of various Palestinian movements or Hezbollah in Lebanon. Lumping all of these groups together failed to appreciate the real complexity of the terrorist problem and the fact that Western powers were often complicit in causing it. Beyond all of this, there was the simple difficulty that terrorism was never an enemy that could be fought through military means. Any apparent military victory could be only temporary. Terrorism can be fought effectively only through international police work accompanied by deeper political strategies.

The events of 9-11 were spectacular, but they were only spectacular criminal acts, not acts of war. The U.S. attacks on al-Qaeda demonstrated this problem very effectively. On the one hand, the United States succeeded in killing many al-Qaeda operatives and crippling its organizational structure. On the other hand, al-Qaeda is not simply a terrorist organization but is much more influential and dangerous as an ideology.[4] As such, it does not have a head; it cannot be stopped. Anyone who adopts the ideology can consider themselves to be al-Qaeda.[5] This situation has been worsened by American bungling in Iraq. The invasion and occupation of Iraq, and all of the subsequent violence and abuse that followed, has done wonders for recruiting anti-Western terrorists, radicalizing many Muslims within Western states, and deepening the divisions between the Islamic and Western worlds.

Beyond the immediate problems inherent in the War on Terror, the U.S. actions did terrible damage to the entire post–World War II international order. Arguing that the realities of the post–Cold War era required that the rules of the system be changed, the Bush Administration came up with the "Bush Doctrine," a policy that allows the United States to use pre-emptive force against any state that it deems to be a real or potential threat. The invasion of Iraq was an expression of this doctrine. The real danger in this approach is that it attacks the very foundations of international order. While other major powers have decried the U.S. policy, these same states have quietly decided that what works for the United States can be made to work for them too. In the future, when any state decides to invade and occupy another, it will need to appeal only to its own self-declared sense of threat to justify its actions. This behaviour will be an obvious violation of international law, but if the United States can do it then any other state can too.

... U.S. actions did terrible damage to the entire post–World War II international order.

These actions have severely undermined the American standing in the larger world. Other world governments may have to deal with the United States, and many are forced to deal with it on its own terms for fear of being punished. While the United States can try to lead by force, however, it cannot lead through moral suasion. Joseph Nye used the term "soft power" to describe the ideological and moral appeals of American values to the rest of the international community.[6] Most analysts now agree that much of that soft power has been squandered under the Bush Administration. The international dislike and distrust of the United States, already very high, has hit unprecedented levels across almost the entire world. The fact that the United States is convinced of its own good intentions is hardly reassuring to the rest of world, which sees a "hyperpower" that is out of control. While in the short term this has not led to effective countercoalitions to United States power, it has meant that states that follow the U.S. lead run the risk of political costs at home. Moreover, many states are suspicious of the U.S. use of its power, believing, quite sensibly, that the Bush Administration has little sense of responsibility to the larger international community.

The international dislike and distrust of the United States, already very high, has hit unprecedented levels across almost the entire world.

Given this analysis, how has Canada responded to the changing American foreign policy, and how should it respond? Initially, Canada tried to walk a careful line between American preoccupations with security and Canada's need to pursue its own distinct interests. More recently, however, the new Conservative government of Canada, under Stephen Harper, has adopted a hard right-wing foreign policy that seems made in George Bush's Washington. The Conservatives have virtually abandoned a distinctive Canadian international identity and have, in some cases, overturned decades of established Canadian policy. Harper's pronouncements on the Middle East and terrorism are, doubtless, a reflection of his own ideological commitments. The overall effect has been to tie Canada, all too willingly, to a rapidly sinking ship and to run the risk of besmirching Canada's valuable image in the larger global community.

CANADA–UNITED STATES FOREIGN POLICY RELATIONS AFTER 9-11

◆ ◆ ◆

Historically, Canada has followed an extremely conservative foreign policy. After World War II, Canada's major preoccupation was maintaining good relations with its major allies, the United States and Great Britain. It is telling that Canada's primary concern during the 1956 Suez Crisis—the crisis in which Lester Pearson suggested the creation of the first UN peacekeeping force, and for which he subsequently won a Nobel Peace Prize—was to smooth relations between the United States and Britain, which had ended up on opposite sides of the conflict. During the Cold War era, Canada considered itself to be a "middle power"—a country that was influential in the corridors of the powerful, but which was not a major power itself. During the Cold War, the intermediary role of such actors was both clear and necessary. As a middle power, Canada promoted multilateralism and international law, while remaining clear that its national interest lay in an international order that worked to the benefit of the dominant Western powers.[7]

As a middle power, Canada promoted multilateralism and international law ...

In the post–Cold War era, the role of middle powers—particularly in a world ostensibly dominated by a single superpower—was not clear. Moreover, the problem was compounded by the fact that Canada lacked the resources or the political will to allocate the resources necessary to make it a major player on the world stage. Thus, during the 1990s the Canadian military was allowed to deteriorate. Canada, which had long prided itself on its participation in UN peacekeeping missions, quickly found itself incapable of supporting the UN in this way any longer. Canada declined from near the top of the list of UN contributors to peacekeeping missions to number 34. Canada's foreign aid contributions dropped precipitously as the country struggled with its internal financial crises.[8]

In the mid-1990s, Foreign Minister Lloyd Axworthy introduced the concepts of "human security" and "soft power" into the Canadian foreign policy lexicon. Human security was the idea that international security was ultimately dependent upon the security of individuals. The policy promoted "freedom from fear" and tried to argue that the focus on the state as the relevant international actor no longer made sense in a globalized world where security issues were far broader in scope and effect. Axworthy argued that Canada presented the world with an appealing set of values and that this "soft power" could translate into real influence in the emerging international system. The primary example of human security policy at work was Canada's leading role in promoting an international treaty banning land mines.[9] Many others criticized the human security approach, however, claiming that

Canada was trying to do foreign policy on "on the cheap." Canada had deliberately reduced its spending on both its military and foreign aid, and so lecturing other countries on how they should behave was the least expensive way in which to have an active foreign policy.[10]

Axworthy argued that Canada presented the world with an appealing set of values and that this "soft power" could translate into real influence in the emerging international system.

The human security approach was, arguably, an extension of Canada's traditional support for multilateralism and international law. Canada had long made the argument that an international system based upon common rules, norms, and values, and supported by international law, was in the best interest of Canada as well as the whole world. Robert Cox has described this approach as the "middle power *realpolitik*.[11] Canada followed this philosophy by actively promoting multilateral institutions and organizations such as the UN, NATO, and the International Criminal Court. In these bodies, Canada's status as a middle power was particularly effective.

The multilateral system created after World War II was, to varying degrees, created and supported by the United States, which saw its own interest in maintaining international institutions that it could dominate.[12] In the post–Cold War era, the United States began to backtrack on its general commitment to multilateralism. Without the competition of the Soviet Union to restrain and modify the American pursuit of self-interest, the United States reshaped the international financial, economic, and political systems to its even greater advantage. While the Clinton Administration pursued these policies with a certain degree of subtlety, the incoming Bush Administration was far more overt and crude in its intentions to use American power as a blunt instrument to pursue national interests, with little regard for the interests of other global actors. Canada found itself in a world where most states agreed on the continuing necessity of multilateral institutions, but where the United States was, apparently, in the process of abandoning

these established structures, except when they could serve immediate American interests.[13]

In the immediate aftermath of the 9-11 attacks, Canada was faced with the question of how to relate to the United States in a new era of fear and anger. Many Canadian commentators used the opportunity to argue that, for economic and geographical reasons, Canada's most important relationship was with the United States and securing that relationship was essential to Canada's survival. Canadian national interests, defined solely in terms of economic interests, required that Canada do whatever was necessary to reassure the United States of the Canadian commitment to American security. This included, essentially, creating a common North American security perimeter in order to preserve Canadian access to the all-important American market. The alternative, the argument went, was to leave Canada economically vulnerable to American security concerns. None of the 9-11 hijackers had any connections to Canada, but the nightmare scenario was a terrorist attack on the United States that, in some way, involved Canada as a staging ground.

The Canadian government accepted elements of this logic, and spent billions of dollars to enhance Canadian border security. Canada also adopted draconian antiterrorist laws that are currently under review. Canadian agencies may also have cooperated in at least some American operations that snared innocent Canadian civilians in the American security net.[14] Canada signed agreements allowing American military action in Canada under emergency circumstances. Nonetheless, there was little appetite among the Canadian public to simply turn Canadian sovereignty over to the United States.

On the foreign policy front, Canada was faced with a significant problem. Initially, after 9-11, the United States presented itself almost as a model international citizen. On the surface, the U.S government moved away from its unilateral ways and sought the assistance and the sanction of the international community in pursuing al-Qaeda, which it blamed for the attacks, into Afghanistan. The U.S. invasion of Afghanistan was carried out with the support of the UN and the larger international community.

Canada accepted the arguments in favour of the attack on Afghanistan and, while it did not participate in the invasion, Canada took on a considerable role in Afghanistan as part of NATO. The Canadian government also adopted an explicit policy position on Afghanistan. Making the credible argument that failed states are a breeding and staging ground for terrorism, the Canadian government made a serious commitment of resources toward helping Afghanistan rebuild. Canada thus defined its role in the War on Terror as fighting that war in military, social, and economic terms within Afghanistan.

Unfortunately for the international community, hot on the heels of successfully invading Afghanistan, the United States turned its attention to its real objective: Iraq. Largely losing interest in Afghanistan, the U.S. administration set about manufacturing a case for the invasion of Iraq. Most of the its attention focused on the claim that the regime of Saddam Hussein was very close to developing nuclear weapons and that a nuclear Iraq posed an intolerable danger to the international order. Among the less credible claims was that Saddam might give nuclear weapons to terrorists. Most of the international community remained unconvinced that war was necessary to disarm the Iraqi regime. In the end, the United States was unable to secure a specific UN Security Council resolution authorizing it to attack Iraq. It did so anyway, supported by Britain and a so-called "coalition of the willing." As already noted, the outcome of this adventure has proven disastrous. Weapons of mass destruction of any kind were never found in Iraq, and new information now suggests that American intelligence agencies, in particular the CIA, knew that the Iraqi regime was WMD free but were ignored or bullied by a White House that was determined to have its war.[15]

Canada thus defined its role in the War on Terror as fighting that war in military, social and economic terms within Afghanistan.

Canada was faced with a difficult decision during the run-up to the Iraq war. As after 9-11, many Canadian commentators argued that Canadian national interests dictated that Canada must support the United States. The suggestion that the United States would find ways to punish Canada both economically and politically if it were not given such support was a critical component of this argument. Others argued that Canada's traditional interests have been in creating and

maintaining an international system of law and rules, an important part of which is the UN. To ignore the fact that the American war was illegal because it did not have the sanction of the UN would be to undermine that institution. Moreover, it would be to ignore the many other ways in which the Bush Administration had acted to tear the fabric of international law and society. In the end, the government of Jean Chrétien decided not to participate in the war. The Canadian excuse largely centred around the argument that Canada was doing its part in the War on Terror by devoting resources to Afghanistan. Indeed, Canada's Afghan contribution freed up American troops to go to Iraq. In addition, Canada had committed so many of its relatively meagre military resources to Afghanistan that it had little left to contribute to any invasion of Iraq.

Ultimately, the Canadian decision to stay out of Iraq proved to be enormously popular with the Canadian public. Significantly, Stephen Harper, the leader of the Conservative Party, condemned this decision, even going so far as to publish an apology to the United States in the *Wall Street Journal*.[16] However, Canada did not simply oppose the war on principle; rather, it tried to maintain goodwill with the United States by arguing that it was still on board with general American policy, it was just fulfilling a different role in the execution of that policy. Nonetheless, in the larger international community, Canada gained enormous credibility and respect for its decision to resist American pressure to participate in the invasion of Iraq. Even before the fighting began, the Iraq War was one of the most unpopular conflicts-to-be in the history of the global community. Many people believed that the United States was acting out of a desire to seize Iraqi oil and exercise hegemonic power, not out of any desire to protect itself. The general international distrust of the Bush Administration contributed significantly to this negative impression of the United States.

Under the Liberal governments of Jean Chrétien and his successor, Paul Martin, Canada tried to walk a relatively fine line between appeasing the United States and maintaining an independent outlook and a sense that Canadian national interests may not accord with the unilateralism of the United States under George W. Bush.[17] However, the new Conservative government of Stephen Harper appears to have reversed this position. This is deeply problematic, not only because it does enormous damage to established

Canadian foreign policy traditions, but also because the policymakers in Washington have proven themselves to be both inept and corrupt. Their War on Terror is not only doomed to fail, but also already making the situation of terrorism and ideological/cultural polarization in the international system much worse. This was an entirely predictable effect. What is not clear is why Canada should tie itself to a policy that is both self-destructive and potentially very damaging to Canada's national cohesion at home and its positive image abroad.

DISCUSSION AND ANALYSIS

◆ ◆ ◆

Many commentators on Canadian foreign policy argue that the U.S. decision to abandon and undermine international institutions has left Canada with little choice but to adapt to the changing international order. Some observers have argued that with the failure of internationalism, Canada must adopt a regional approach to the world, which means accepting that Canada is part of a North American region and coming to terms with the domination of the United States. There are many problems with these arguments, however.[18]

First, the death of internationalism is neither assured nor even likely. The logic with which Canada approached the world during the Cold War era is as compelling today as it has ever been. It is in the interest of the entire world community to have a rule-governed international system. It is true that the international system has changed and that the emergence of a single superpower has had dramatic effects on the nature of world power. However, if Iraq has demonstrated anything, it is the real limits of American power and, indeed, the limited efficacy of military force in general. In Iraq, a relatively small (albeit diverse) insurgency, based in urban centres and situated within various ethnic/religious communities, has proven to be far too much for the American military to handle. This is true even though the U.S. military is no longer the primary target of the insurgency, and the single most important group in the country—the Shi'ite majority—has yet to turn against the Western coalition in any sustained way (though there are signs that this may happen soon). If American military power cannot pacify Iraq, then its utility in other parts of the world is highly limited. The United States has the most powerful and sophisticated military machine

ever constructed on the planet; its ability to smash things is unprecedented and unrivalled. But this is simply not enough. More tragically, the Bush Administration does not seem to have realized this point. Its continued willingness to use and encourage the use of force will create only "blowback" over time— the unintended, though quite predictable, consequences of intrusive policies.[19]

... the death of internationalism is neither assured nor even likely.

If there is to be any international progress, if international justice is to mean anything, it will happen only within a framework of international laws and rules. That is, multilateral institutions are even more important today than at any time in the past. The fact that the most powerful state in the system is acting to dismantle that system is not an argument for the weaknesses of the existing order. Rather, it is a demonstration of the dangers of unchecked power. For Canada, it makes little sense to abandon the international order. Even if the structures of power underpinning the system have changed, the logic of a rule-governed international society is as compelling as ever. Gwynne Dyer has argued that the achievement of the post–World War II era was a system that maintained international order and created a sense of shared values and goals. That slow, halting progress toward a genuine, rule-governed international order has been threatened by American unilateralism, but the threat is not yet irreversible.[20] As the United States experiences failure in the Middle East and elsewhere with its policies, it is possible to hope that it will begin to reform its approach to the international order. A more likely outcome, however, is that the United States will be forced to modify its approaches as its own limitations become apparent.

To many critics, economic arguments trump all other concerns. Canada is dependent on the United States for its economic prosperity. Therefore, in effect, it has no choice but to do whatever is necessary to keep the United States happy. This argument has innumerable difficulties. First, it assumes that the only things that matter to Canadians are economic in nature. This is certainly not true. Many recent studies have indicated that Canadians and Americans are growing further apart in many social values.[21] It seems unlikely that, in the long term, Canadians could be happy being associated with American policies that might be dramatically at odds with deeply held Canadian beliefs. Many Canadians are willing to accept an economic cost in order to be true to their values.

... multilateral institutions are even more important today than at any time in the past.

Second, the assumption that deeper integration with the United States will prevent political factors from affecting the economic relationship requires careful examination. The United States cannot harm or punish Canada economically without harming itself. Moreover, trade treaties such as NAFTA are supposed to separate economic relations from political considerations. If NAFTA has failed to protect Canada from the whims of American politics, the situation will not be improved by selling Canada's foreign policy independence in the name of economic access.[22]

As the world economy evolves and other major players—notably China—emerge, Canada's interest in being part of a regional bloc should decline. As connected as Canada is to the United States economically, and as much as that relationship has grown since the institution of NAFTA, this still does not mean that Canada must abandon its economic opportunities elsewhere. For more than a century the United States has been, by far, the biggest single economy in the world. That will change in the next few decades. For the first time in the modern era, there will be other economic powers in the world that can rival or surpass the American economic presence. It is impossible to gauge the full effects of this kind of unprecedented development. However, this reality probably means that the need for vibrant multilateral institutions is stronger than ever. It also means that Canada needs to be prepared to form powerful economic and political ties with other states outside the region. As world economic power shifts to Asia, Canada must be able to capitalize on the shift, rather than lock itself into a one-sided economic relationship with the United States. The fastest growing demographic in Canada today are people of Asian background. This means that the potential for greatly improved Canada–Asia economic relations is enormous and growing.

Canada's involvement in the War on Terror is already backfiring. The Canadian engagement in Afghanistan, however well intentioned, is already doomed to failure. Because the Western world turned its collective attention away from Afghanistan in order to launch another war in Iraq, the Afghan situation was all but forgotten and allowed to deteriorate. It is not clear that any amount of foreign intervention could have turned Afghanistan around. What is clear is that Canada lacked the resources to do this on its own, and now finds itself in a quagmire of its own. The Taliban is re-emerging as the dominant force outside the capital, Kabul, and local people are rapidly becoming tired of foreign occupiers who have a tendency to kill large numbers of civilians with aerial strikes. This is a sure-fire recipe for the locals to kill occupiers without distinguishing between Canadians, Americans, or British. In short, it is likely just a matter of time before Canadian forces in Afghanistan face a popular uprising. When that happens, the Western occupiers of the country will meet the same fate as so many other foreign occupiers of Afghanistan in the past.

Canada's involvement in the War on Terror is already backfiring.

The War on Terror also has detrimental effects at home. Every Canadian government has a legitimate stake in ensuring that Canada is not a staging ground for terrorism, be that directed at the United States or Canada itself. Securing the borders and ensuring internal security, however, are actions that can be taken without signing on to an American worldview that is deeply destructive both of international stability and Canadian domestic order. Inevitably, any effort to monitor and control terrorism in Canada will target the Islamic community. Given the growing number of Muslims in the country and Canada's avowed multiculturalism, this is an approach that must be handled with some delicacy and sensitivity. This is not helped when Canadian foreign policy can be interpreted as being deeply biased against the Muslim world.

At the time of this writing, the conflict between the West and the Arab/Islamic world has taken yet another turn for the worse. Israel has recently finished (July–August 2006) fighting a war against the Lebanese militia, Hezbollah. The conflict started when Hezbollah kidnapped two Israeli soldiers and killed three others in a cross-border raid, in an effort to acquire hostages who could be used to force Israel to return Lebanese prisoners.[23] Israel responded by launching a massive bombing campaign against targets all over Lebanon. Hezbollah replied by launching thousands of missiles against Israeli cities. By the time the present cease-fire was implemented, at least 1183 Lebanese were dead (the vast majority of these were civilians and about one-third children), and Lebanon's infrastructure was destroyed. About 118 Israeli soldiers were killed and 43 civilians.[24] Current evidence suggests that the United States and Israel had been planning an invasion of Lebanon for some time as an effort to smash Hezbollah and better position the United States for an offensive against Iran which, it fears, is pursuing the development of nuclear weapons. Thus, it appears that the United States is preparing to open up yet another front in its War on Terror against another Muslim state.[25]

... it is likely just a matter of time before Canadian forces in Afghanistan face a popular uprising.

When the conflict began, the new Conservative government and Prime Minister Stephen Harper came out unequivocally in favour of Israel—even though it was quickly evident that Israel was using force far in excess of anything that could reasonably constitute "self-defence." This radically pro-Israel position was a dramatic shift in Canadian foreign policy and, once again, parroted that of the United States. However, the position was fundamentally unbalanced and deeply insensitive to the grievances and perceptions of the Arab and Islamic worlds. At a time when the Western world, particularly the United States and Britain, was claiming that it was on a moral crusade against terrorists who target innocent people, the image of these same Western states refusing to condemn Israel's excessive use of force—indeed, in the case of the United States, actively encouraging and running interference for Israel in the UN and elsewhere—was not just contradictory, but also deeply hypocritical. The Arab–Israeli conflict stands as one of the major sources of tension between the West and the Arab/Islamic world. More generally, Israel is seen by much of the international community as being the beneficiary of a double standard that allows it to exercise force against

Arabs (notably the Palestinians) and defy international law and the international community with impunity. This particular issue was complicated by the fact that the United States and Britain were defending their tolerance of Israel's actions in Lebanon on the grounds that Israel was engaged in another part of the War against Terror. Thus, the complex, controversial, and highly polarizing politics of the Arab–Israeli dispute was tied up into the War on Terror, further undermining the legitimacy of that "war" to much of the world.[26]

There is no doubt that the radically pro-Israel shift in Canadian foreign policy will have detrimental effects for Canada's position in Afghanistan and in every other part of the Islamic world. It will also undermine the perception of Canada as a fair and just state across the entire international community. But it also reflects a worrying ideological commitment on the part of the Conservative government. Stephen Harper, unapologetically, believes that Canada is part of an "Anglosphere," a compact between English-speaking countries (i.e., the United States, Britain, Australia, and sometimes New Zealand), Canada's "traditional" allies, that overrides all other considerations.[27] Whether or not the "Anglosphere" is a fundamentally racist concept is open to debate; certainly, it seems to imply a commonality based as much—or more—on shared ethnicity as on shared values.[28] The word "traditional" sounds a great deal like shorthand for ethnocultural factors. Still, preaching solidarity with the United States and Britain simply because they are Canada's "traditional" allies is hardly an argument. If our traditional allies are pursuing destructive policies, it seems obvious that Canada should not feel any obligation to participate in such policies. A failure to follow the United States and Britain into misguided wars has nothing to do with Canada's commitment to its national security and the need to share information and resources with allies to protect security at home. The two issues are entirely separate.[29]

... preaching solidarity with the United States and Britain simply because they are Canada's "traditional" allies is hardly an argument.

What is particularly interesting about Harper's stand, however, is that it is entirely inappropriate in a multicultural and religiously diverse country such as Canada. Committing Canada to the "Anglosphere" ignores all of those Canadian citizens who are not "Anglo" (including, significantly, the Francophones of Quebec) and whose views of the merits of British imperialism—and imperialism in general—are more critical than those expressed by Prime Minister Harper. If the Conservative government does pursue a foreign policy based on perceived shared ethnicity, then it is excluding a huge and growing number of Canadians from participation not just in the foreign-policymaking process but from the Canadian polity itself.

CONCLUSION

◆ ◆ ◆

Canada's major concern in its relations with the United States should be ensuring that the country is not a staging ground for terrorism and maintaining economic ties with the American giant. These necessities, however, do not require that Canada accept an American world-view when it comes to terrorism or the relevance of multilateralism. Canada does not need to follow the American lead.

Canada's largest mistake has been in participating in the U.S. War on Terror. The Americans have, not surprisingly, completely bungled their prosecution of this war and are dragging the entire Western world into an intractable conflict. Canada did not need to be part of this, and should not have made the initial commitments. Terrorism does need to be countered, but it also needs to be understood and placed in perspective. By failing to do either, the United States has created an international mess that cannot be repaired without radical shifts in policy. Unfortunately, the new Conservative government of Canada seems poised to exacerbate all of these earlier mistakes.

Notes

1. Various international initiatives that the Bush White House has worked to undermine include the *Kyoto Treaty on Global Warming*, the International Criminal Court, the *Landmines Treaty*, and protections for the rights of children. The United States also abrogated the *Anti-Ballistic Missile Treaty*, opening the door to the development of missile defences and, many observers suspect, the weaponization of space. As part of the War on Terror the Bush regime has also undermined the Geneva Accords and various human rights protections. See Margaret Tutwiler, "The Lone Ranger," *Canada and the World Backgrounder*, (September 1, 2004): 24–29.

2. The war was "illegal" in that it was not approved by the UN Security Council, the only body that can authorize the use of force between states. States are allowed to use force in self-defence, but the United States could not present any credible argument that it was threatened by Iraq.

3. Ironically, while the United States refused to deal with the possibility that the al-Qaeda attack was the result of specific political grievances, the ideological justification for the Iraq war, with its focus on promoting democracy, is a tacit admission of American culpability in creating the circumstances that led to the September 11 attacks.

4. Jason Burke, "Think Again: Al Qaeda," *Foreign Policy* (May/June 2004): 18–26.

5. Yassin Musharbash, "The Terrorists Next Door," Salon.com, August 10, 2006. Retrieved March 21, 2007, from www.salon.com/news/feature/2006/08/10/london_plot/index.html.

6. Joseph Nye, *The Paradox of American Power* (Oxford: Oxford University Press, 2002).

7. Adam Chapnick, "Peace, Order and Good Government: The 'Conservative' Tradition in Canadian Foreign Policy," *International Journal*, vol. 60, no. 3 (Summer 2005): 635–50.

8. For an interesting discussion of Canada's foreign policy history and an argument about how Canada's international policy should be evolving, see Jennifer Welsh, *At Home in the World: Canada's Global Vision for the 21st Century* (Toronto: HarperCollins, 2004).

9. Interestingly, Canada's involvement in the *Land Mines Treaty* started as an accident. Canada was mistakenly included in a list of countries supporting such a ban and it was too embarrassed to correct the mistake. In the end, Canada decided to try to lead the process.

10. See Kim Richard Nossal, "Pinchpenny Diplomacy," *International Journal* (Winter 1998–1999): 88–105.

11. Robert Cox, "A Canadian Dilemma: The United States or the World," *International Journal*, vol. 60, no. 3 (Summer 2005): 678. Cox's discussion of Canada's foreign policy history and its relationship with the United States is excellent.

12. The UN became unpopular among American politicians only after the process of decolonization introduced many new states whose perceptions and interests were often at odds

with those of the United States. To Americans, the UN lost relevance as it could no longer be controlled.

13. For an excellent discussion of the Bush White House's approach to power and its failure to appreciate the intersubjective nature of political legitimacy, see Christian Reus-Smit, *American Power and World Order* (Cambridge, UK: Polity Press, 2004).

14. The case of Maher Arar, a Canadian citizen of Syrian birth, who was detained in New York by American authorities, then deported to Syria where he was imprisoned and tortured for almost a year, is the standout example of this. Mr. Arar was innocent of any wrongdoing and may have simply been recorded meeting someone else under police surveillance. The participation of Canadian authorities in Mr. Arar's situation remains unclear.

15. Ron Suskind, *The One Percent Doctrine* (New York: Simon and Schuster, 2006).

16. Stephen Harper and Stockwell Day, "Conservative Canadians Speak Out!," *The Wall Street Journal* (March 29, 2003). The letter emphasizes Canada's "historic" ties to Britain and the United States, and liberally adopts the rhetoric of George Bush in implying that the American invasion of Iraq is a battle against "evil" and for "civilization." Harper later channelled George Bush again when responding to the arrest of 17 Canadians on suspicions of planning a terrorist attack in Canada. At that time, he claimed that these individuals were attacking Canada because of their hatred of Canadian society, "democracy," and "freedom." He did not address the fact that the would-be terrorists were opposed to Canada's involvement in Afghanistan. See Peter Scowen, "A Bush League Response?" *Toronto Star* (June 11, 2006), p. D12.

17. See Stephen Clarkson and Erick Lachappelle, "Jean Chretien's Legacy in Managing Canadian-American Relations," *Canadian Foreign Policy*, vol. 12, no. 2 (Fall 2005): 65–82.

18. See, for example, Allan Gotlieb, "The Chrétien Doctrine" *Maclean's*, vol. 116, no. 13 (March 31, 2003): 42–44.

19. Chalmers Johnson, *Blowback: The Costs and Consequences of American Empire* (New York: Henry Holt Publishers, 2000).

20. Gywnne Dyer, *Future Tense: The Coming World Order* (Toronto: McClelland and Stewart, 2004).

21. Michael Adams, *Fire and Ice* Toronto: Penguin Books, 2003.

22. For further elaboration of these arguments, see Marie Bernard-Meunier, "The 'Inevitability' of North American Integration?" *International Journal*, vol. 60, no. 3, (Summer 2005): 703–12, and Jennifer Welsh, "Canada in the 21st Century: Beyond Dominion and Middle Power" *The Round Table*, vol. 93, no. 376 (September 2004): 583–93.

23. Five more Israeli soldiers died that day when their tank hit a mine inside Lebanon.

24. Figures are from Neil MacDonald, "Amnesty Urges UN to Probe Israeli Strategy," *The Financial Times* (August 23, 2006). Retrieved March 21, 2007, from www.ft.com/cms/s/65bf7dfa-3203-11db-ab06-0000779e2340.html.

25. Whether or not the United States goes ahead with this purported attack on Iran remains to be seen. The inconclusive outcome of the Israel–Hezbollah conflict may have delayed or indefinitely suspended U.S. military action against Iran. For a discussion of the United States–Israel plan, see Seymour Hersh, "Watching Lebanon," *The New Yorker* (August 21, 2006), pp. 28–33.

26. British support for the Israeli action was much more controversial inside Britain and within the governing Labour Party. Many Labour MPs and supporters were deeply angry at Prime Minister Tony Blair's continuing defence of Israel and his apparent willingness to toe the Bush Administration's party line.

27. John Ibbitson has discussed Harper's "Anglosphere" inclinations in a number of *Globe and Mail* columns, including "Empire Strikes Back in Harper's Rhetoric" (July 27, 2006) p. A10; "The Good Guys Will Win this War, Too" (August 11, 2006) p. A4; and "Tories File Foreign Policy Statement in Blue Box" (August 18, 2006), p. A4.

28. Precisely what "shared values" implies is open to discussion. A person can be a Canadian Muslim who believes in the "Western" values of liberty, democracy, and human rights and still arrive at the conclusion that the U.S. War on Terror violates all of those values.

29. For a further commentary on Stephen Harper's "continentalism" and his possible antipathy to Canada, see Michael Byers, "One Nation, Hold the Lament" *The Globe and Mail* (July 8, 2006), p. F7.

Terms and Concepts

national interest
unilateralism
multilateralism

War on Terror
Bush Doctrine
soft power

middle power
Anglosphere

Questions

1. What is Canada's foreign policy tradition?

2. How does American foreign policy under the Bush Administration violate that tradition?

3. According to Narine, why has Canada recently aligned its foreign policy with that of the United States?

4. Foreign policy determinants can be divided into external and internal or domestic determinants. What domestic determinants favour and discourage Canada–United States foreign policy alignment?

5. What alternatives does Canada have to political and economic alignment with the United States?

6. What is Narine's greater concern—that Canadian foreign policy be independent of that of the United States, or that Canadian foreign policy in substance not be similar to that of the Bush Administration?

Unit 1 Annotated Bibliography

Barber, Benjamin R. *Jihad vs. McWorld: How Globalism and Tribalism are Reshaping the World*. New York: Ballantine, 1996. This book, based on a famous 1992 essay in the monthly magazine *Atlantic*, describes world politics in terms of the potentially volatile interaction of homogenizing, universalizing forces of economics and technology on the one hand and particularizing forces of culture, religion, and territorial belonging on the other.

Berger, Peter L., and Samuel P. Huntington. *Many Globalizations: Cultural Diversity in the Contemporary World*. New York: Oxford University Press, 2002. This is a collection of essays on the particular effects of globalization in a variety of countries around the world. The essays suggest that globalization takes very different forms in different cultural contexts.

Booth, Ken, and Tim Dunne, eds. *Worlds in Collision: Terror and the Future of Global Order*. Basingstoke, UK: Palgrave Macmillan, 2002. This collection includes reflections on the post–September 11 world by leading scholars in the study of world politics. Topics covered include the nature of terrorism, U.S. power, political violence, international law, religion, culture, and morality.

Cameron, David R., and Janice Gross Stein. *Street Protests and Theme Parks: Globalization, Culture, and the State*. Vancouver; UBC Press, 2002. This collection of essays places culture at the centre of discussion of globalization.

Clarkson, Stephen. *Uncle Sam and Us: Globalization, Neoconservatism, and the Canadian State*. Toronto: University of Toronto Press, 2002. Clarkson, a professor of political economy at the University of Toronto, considers how the Canadian state has been changed in the past two decades as a result of the North American and global trade treaties that have constrained the political power of elected federal and provincial governments, and deepened integration into the United States.

Cohen, Andrew. *While Canada Slept: How We Lost Our Place in the World*. Toronto: McClelland and Stewart, 2003. Cohen laments Canada's withdrawal from its once vigorous financial and military commitments to world order and security.

Dyer, Gwynne. *Future Tense: The Coming World Order*. Toronto, McClelland and Stewart: 2004. Dyer presents a compelling and readable examination of the aftermath and possible consequences of the American invasion of Iraq. He examines the different ideological approaches, Islamic and neoconservative, that have fuelled conflict in the international system and assesses the likely outcomes.

Friedman, Thomas. *The World is Flat: A Brief History of the Twenty-First Century*. New York: Farrar, Strauss and Giroux, 2005. In this book *New York Times* columnist Friedman offers a lively account of economic globalization and its far-reaching effects on both the developed and developing world.

Fukuyama, Francis. *Nation-Building: Beyond Afghanistan and Iraq*. Baltimore: Johns Hopkins University Press, 2006. This collection of essays examines nation-building efforts in post-conflict situations. Essays draw upon recent American experience.

Fukuyama, Francis. *State-Building: Governance and World Order in the 21st Century*. Ithaca: Cornell University Press, 2004. Beginning from the premise that a major threat to international security is the weak state, Fukuyama examines the factors that turn weak, low-capacity states into functioning, high-capacity states that can expand their scope of operations to serve their citizens.

Fukuyama, Francis. *The End of History and the Last Man*. New York: Free Press, 1992. In this philosophical elaboration of his famous 1989 article entitled "The End of History?" Fukuyama describes the end of the Cold War as the final closing of fundamental ideological conflict in the world. Liberal political ideas have won, he argues.

Helliwell, John F. *Globalization and Well-Being*. Vancouver: UBC Press, 2003. This Canadian economist examines trade patterns between Canada and the United States, and how Canadian identity and other "border effects" condition them.

Hobsbawm, Eric. *The Age of Extremes: A History of the World, 1914–1991*. New York: Pantheon Books, 1994. Hobsbawm is an eminent British historian. This ambitious, sweeping work focuses on the economic and social forces that have shaped the 20th century, particularly capitalism and socialism. He does not find much to look forward to!

Homer-Dixon, Thomas. *The Upside of Down: Catastrophe, Creativity, and the Renewal of Civilization*. Toronto: Vintage, 2007. Canadian political scientist Homer-Dixon made his reputation by examining the causal relationship between environmental breakdown and political conflict. Here he examines the conditions under which complex societies like ours can adjust to new threats and challenges and renew themselves in the process.

Huntington, Samuel P. *The Clash of Civilizations and the Remaking of World Order*. New York: Touchstone, 1996. In this famous and controversial work, Huntington describes post–Cold War politics as a clash of seven cultures or civilizations. Culture and religion, he suggests, not economics, are the major political fault lines for the foreseeable future.

Hutton, Will, and Anthony Giddens, eds. *On the Edge: Living with Global Capitalism*. London: Vintage, 2001. This collection includes essays by such prominent intellectuals and journalists as Ulrich Beck, Robert Kuttner, Vandana

Shiva, Polly Toynbee, and Richard Sennett on political, economic, and cultural aspects of globalization.

Ignatieff, Michael. *The Warrior's Honour: Ethnic War and the Modern Conscience*. Toronto: Viking, 1998. This is a thought-provoking collection of essays reflecting on moral intervention in conditions of modern brutality.

Ignatieff, Michael. *The Lesser Evil: Political Ethics in an Age of Terror*. Princeton: Princeton University Press, 2004. Ignatieff, an academic and Canadian Member of Parliament, explores the vulnerability of open liberal societies to terrorism and suggests ways to reconcile antiterrorist policies with the protection of civil liberties.

Johnson, Chalmers. *The Sorrows of Empire*. Metropolitan Books, New York: 2004. In this book, Johnson offers a critical historical analysis of the "American Empire" that has developed since the end of the Cold War, discusses the military foundations on which it is built, and underlines the difficulties of maintaining an empire in the modern era.

Kagan, Robert. *Paradise and Power: America and Europe in the New World Order*. London: Atlantic Books, 2003. In this long essay, Kagan argues that deep political and economic fissures divide the United States and Europe, and that increasingly the United States assumes responsibility for world order while European countries concentrate on the social welfare of their own populations. Once partners, America and Europe are going their separate ways.

Kaldor, Mary. *New and Old Wars: Organized Violence in a Global Era*. Cambridge: Polity Press, 1999. Kaldor charts the rise of a new kind of brutal war, waged often for non-territorial purposes by nonstate forces, enriched by the global criminal trade in diamonds, guns, and drugs. She proposes a system of cosmopolitan law enforcement to confront it and prevent the human rights abuses associated with it in places like central Africa and the former Yugoslavia.

Kennedy, Paul. *The Parliament of Man*. New York: Random House, 2006. This book discusses the history of the United Nations and gives a balanced critical analysis of what we can expect from the United Nations in the future.

Klare, Michael. *Resource Wars: The New Landscape of Global Conflict*. New York: Henry Holt, 2000; rev. ed. 2001. This book describes the ways in which the Cold War has given way to a global scramble for oil, minerals, and water that will define a new generation of military conflict in places like Central Asia, the Middle East, and the South China Sea.

Knight, W. Andy, ed. *Adapting the United Nations to a Postmodern Era: Lessons Learned* (2nd ed.) Basinstoke, Hampshire: Houndsmills, 2005. This is a book of essays on United Nations operations in the recent past, and

provides an overview of the lessons learned from the successes and failures of these operations.

Rosenau, James. *Distant Proximities*. Princeton: Princeton University Press, 2003. This book provides an examination of the clash of integrating and fragmenting forces in contemporary globalization by a senior scholar in the field.

Stiglitz, Joseph E. *Globalization and Its Discontents*. New York: W.W. Norton and Company, 2002. Stiglitz critically examines the "Washington Consensus" and its effects on the international economy. The book provides an excellent overview of the workings of financial power and institutions in the world system.

Suskind, Ron. *The One Percent Doctrine: Deep Inside America's Pursuit of its Enemies Since 9/11*. This prize-winning journalist examines the public and private battles within the Bush Administration's war on global terror.

Walt, Stephen M. *Taming American Power*. New York: W.W. Norton and Company, 2005. Walt provides an accessible analysis of American foreign policy in the post–Cold War era and a description and analysis of the international response. This is a good examination from an American point of view of the problem of American power.

Walzer, Michael. *Arguing About War*. New Haven and London: Yale University Press, 2004. This is a collection of essays in which the author uses a just-war approach to discuss war and terrorism, and to argue against the project of creating a world state.

Waters, Malcolm. *Globalization*. London: Routledge, 1995. Waters gives a comprehensive introduction to the subject.

Watson, William. *Globalization and the Meaning of Canadian Life*. Toronto: University of Toronto Press, 1998. Watson argues that globalization is wrongly thought to constrain states. Canada has been subjected to globalizing forces for 400 years and, he argues, has considerable room to manoeuvre.

Weiss, Linda. *The Myth of the Powerless State*. Ithaca, NY: Cornell University Press, 1998. Weiss delivers a sustained critique of the view that globalization has disabled the modern state.

Welsh, Jennifer. *At Home in the World*. Toronto, HarperCollins, 2004. Jennifer Welsh examines the history and development of Canadian foreign policy and tries to present a blueprint by which Canada can play independent regional and global roles in the 21st century.

Wright, Lawrence. *The Looming Tower: Al-Qaeda and the Road to 9/11*. New York: Knopf, 2006. This is a comprehensive history of the al-Qaeda organization and its spectacular entrance onto the world stage in 2001. The book also traces the American response to the 9/11 attacks.

Unit Two

Introduction: Ideas and Ideologies

◆ ◆ ◆

Much ink has been spilt to define the concept of ideology. While there is no need to rehearse the long and tortured history of the idea, it is helpful to set out a few of its major themes. The Marxian account suggests that ideology is a complex of ideas and principles explaining and justifying an economic and political system whose oppressive, exploitive character would otherwise ruin it. Ideologies, therefore, prop up an illegitimate system and dupe its victims into thinking that their fate is necessary or somehow worth enduring. More recent versions of this notion suggest that ideology is tantamount to all those opinions and suppositions we consider to be common sense and not worth thinking about, questioning, or contesting. Ideology, in this view, governs ideas of the age and converts uncertain, contestable, and changeable states of affairs into conditions that are taken for granted.

Another view of ideologies associates them with the grand, revolutionary systems of thought that have directed their champions to transform society and human nature according to the dictates of some political blueprint. This view is often held by those who criticize the radical pretensions of leftists and fascists. In other words, those who see the status quo as inevitable, good, or both slap the label "ideological" on those who see the status quo as corrupt, evil, and open to concerted improvement. One observer defines ideology this way: "What persuades men and women to mistake each other from time to time for gods or vermin is ideology."[1] Ideologies allow two people to look at the same thing and see different objects. For example, consider two friends who are walking along a downtown street and who pass a prostitute. One remarks that the prostitute is an unfortunate victim of an oppressive cultural and political order in which women are reduced to sexual objects

CP (Vincent Thian)

Contrasting ideas of freedom and the good life are on display at a European beach.

for men's enjoyment, as commodities in the market for women's bodies. "If women had real political influence and if dominant patriarchal assumptions could be rooted out of society," she might say, "women would not feel the need to prostitute themselves." The other replies that in a liberal society people are in control of their lives and can decide what to do with themselves and their bodies. "Your moral judgments regarding their choices are quite irrelevant," he retorts. "You may disapprove of the prostitute's choices, but you should still respect them. What we should do is legalize prostitution, regulate it for the safety and health of prostitutes, and tax it for the benefit of society." A passerby of more conservative bent overhears the conversation. She deprecates both of these interpretations, suggesting that prostitution, whether legalized or criminalized, is a sign of the decay of moral order in any self-governing society. Of necessity, she avers, law enforces moral norms: "Decency is the province of the law."

Ideology helps to explain these different perceptions of the otherwise uncontroversial fact of prostitution. Ideologies provide us with answers to some important questions: Who are we? What is human nature? What is the good life? What are we fitted for? Are we fundamentally equal and, if so, on what basis? What is wrong with our society and our polity? What do we fear? What needs to be fixed in the world, how, and by whom? What is wrong with us? Why are we not happy, content, perfect, or self-directing? What are the causes of the evil surrounding us? How can we make things better? Political ideologies emphasize, in particular, the answer to this last question. Ideologies direct people to political action and give them a general guide to what must be done. It is one thing to have some general ideas about human nature, women's oppression, or the subversion of the "common sense of the common people," as populists like to say. It is quite another to have a developed theory of political

change based on an analysis of society and the causes of its various ills. Political ideologies provide the theoretical fuel for concerted political action.

In one way or another, each article in this unit gives its own answer to these questions. The authors discuss their views of the correct ordering of political society and the obstacles that stand in the way of that correct ordering. They also give a sense, explicitly or not, of what they consider human nature to be and what dimensions of the human condition are most politically consequential.

There is no standard list of political ideologies. Students years ago were given a thin gruel of conservatism, liberalism, socialism, and maybe nationalism and fascism. In an important sense, it can be argued that we are all now liberals, that liberal ideas are as familiar as the air we breathe, so that it is impossible to think entirely outside them. Nonetheless, the chapters in this section show us that the ideological scope of contemporary political debate remains wide and that there are plenty of differences within as well as between ideological traditions such as conservatism and feminism. At the dawn of the 21st century, the ideological landscape is harder to negotiate, or perhaps we are more sensitive to nuances that were always there. Feminism in its many varieties exerts a major influence on political discourse, as do liberal political and economic ideas. Multiculturalism increasingly receives critical attention. Different shades of conservative ideas compete for space on the right, while nationalist thinking, thought to be in decline owing to economic globalization, has proved reports of its demise to be premature.

This unit invites you to consider the following questions: Where do political ideologies come from? What causes ideologies to move in and out of fashion? Do political ideas and ideologies exert independent influence on political life and public policy? What influence do ideologies exert on one another?

---

1. Terry Eagleton, *Ideology: An Introduction* (London: Verso, 1991), p. xiii.

Classical Liberalism
and Civil Society

Loren E. Lomasky

Editors' Note

When a beginning university student is asked whether the state should regulate prostitution, criminalize drug consumption, or define marriage to exclude same-sex couples, he or she will likely respond: "As long as someone's actions do not harm others, those actions are his or her own business; the state and the morality of others should not interfere."

This is a quintessentially liberal answer to a range of public policy problems. So pervasive are liberal ideas that they act as the moral filter through which we pass any proposed law. At the root of liberal ideas is the principle that individual persons have a right not be interfered with in their decisions about the kind of life they wish to lead. It is important

that I chose my life, not someone else for me. And it is important that I be able to associate freely with whomsoever I choose.

But do people know what is good for them? Are not most lives the record of decisions badly made? Perhaps, say astute liberals, but the historical record speaks more strongly to the disasters incurred when self-appointed guardians of the good of others have made decisions for them.

Doesn't liberalism favour ways of life that maximize individualistic orientations to family, religious community, and nation, privileging the right of exit to the value of belonging? Liberals respond by noting that

there is nothing inherently individualistic about liberalism. Liberalism is as much about the ability to associate as disassociate.

Is not freedom for some in a liberal order bondage for others? Do not free markets—the concomitant of the classical liberal idea of noninterference—consign many to poverty while a few amass astounding wealth? What freedom is there in poverty? But, the liberal will retort, describe a realistic alternative that is as productive as the market without reducing whole populations to the whims of a central planning politburo.

This essay by Loren Lomasky is a lively and trenchant account of classical liberalism.

◆ ◆ ◆

I

Classical liberalism is the theory of the minimal state, the primary function of which is to vindicate individual rights by protecting against aggressors internal and external. But it also is a minimal philosophy. Liberalism offers an account of political justice.[1] It holds out no comprehensive catalog of the virtues, refrains from endorsing any specific conception of the good life, supplies no depiction of the delights of intimate association or communal solidarity. Its range of prescriptions can be

summarized as: Respect the rights of others. Beyond that, liberalism does not tell people what to do. These silences do not bespeak lack of interest in broader moral concerns, but rather are a strict consequence of liberalism's commitment to decentralizing questions of choice and value to individuals acting in their private capacity.

II

That individual human beings are the fundamental bearers of moral status is a postulate of liberalism. Their natural condition is one of liberty and equality.[2] More precisely, it is with respect to their liberty that they are equal. It is evident, says liberal forerunner John Locke, "that Creatures of the same species and rank promiscuously born to all the same advantages of Nature, and the use of the same faculties, should also be equal one amongst another without Subordination or Subjection."[3]

What one owes everyone in virtue of their status as rights holders is noninterference. Crucially, that is all that is owed.

Although that natural condition is stateless, it is not lawless. Human beings live under a natural law which, although ultimately authorized by God, is accessible independently of special revelation to all unimpaired adults via their rational faculties. What reason prescribes to them is peace and the preservation of all mankind. Respect for persons, natural rights to life, liberty, and property is the primary instrumentality through which this is achieved. These basic rights are understood by Locke and the ensuing liberal tradition as negative: that is, as rights not to suffer interference in one's peaceful pursuits rather than as entitlements to assistance.[4] Whatever one's ends or attachments may be, one must not pursue them in a manner that transgresses the rights of others. What one owes everyone in virtue of their status as rights holders is noninterference. Crucially, that is *all* that is owed.

A quick reading of this position supports the characterization of atomistic individualism. Lockean persons are minisovereigns, normatively separated one from another, free to go about their private businesses provided only that they refrain from bumping against others. The quick reading, though, is too quick. It confuses liberalism's strictures of minimal moral acceptability with an account of recommended forms of human sociality. For Locke and his liberal successors, if individuals are atoms, then—the occasional specimen of helium or xenon aside—they are atoms regularly prone to bind themselves to others in molecular formations of greater or lesser stability. No less for liberals than for Aristotelians and communitarians, human beings are social animals. If these theories diverge, it is with regard to the liberal postulate that communities are constituted by individuals and not vice versa. A life apart from a nexus of associations may be stultifyingly miserable, but it is up to individuals to decide with which societies they will affiliate. This holds true even for relationships originally unchosen, such as the primal unit of the family, as well as ethnos and nationality. Although these affiliations are not established *ab initio* through acts of choice, their centrality or lack of same in one's ongoing projects is a determination that devolves on individuals, not the discretion of collectives in which they find themselves. Most people will find their lives enriched through family or communal ties, but some will not; the latter are at liberty to detach themselves from these associations and seek others that are more fulfilling.

The one association, if it can be called that, from which one is not free to divorce oneself is the universal association with all other human beings. That is the proper domain for construing the rationale of the Lockean law of nature. One is obliged to respect the rights of everyone, no matter how little regard in which one holds them and the ends that move them. Because the demands consequent on rights are both universal and mandatory, it follows that a rationally sustainable order of rights will be sharply restricted in the scope of its demands so as to be minimally intrusive on individuals' prerogatives in deciding how they will construct their lives. A general requirement of noninterference, as opposed to precepts of beneficence and mutual support, is the least implicative standard of social coexistence. That is why it is especially suitable as the moral basis for the universal association— and why it is unsuitable for expressing the range of moral ties that bind people to each other in voluntary affiliations characterized by shared affections and commitments. If liberals did maintain that for the latter as well as the former the only moral considerations that apply are people's rights, then their theory would indeed be obtusely atomistic. But it does not and so it is not.

The one association ... from which one is not free to divorce oneself is the universal association with all other human beings.

Although we do not live in the natural condition, neither do we live entirely beyond its parameters. Hobbes takes the establishment of political order to be the nullification of the rights of the state of nature,[5] but Locke and the liberal tradition instead take it to be their vindication. The state of nature may be law-governed, but its interpretation and enforcement are precarious. Because of partiality toward oneself and loved ones and antipathy toward those of opposed interests, the task of upholding rights in anarchy is burdened by manifold "inconveniences."[6] From these the social contract is the recommended means of egress. The transition from anarchy to political society brings a legislature that can specify in a clear and determinate form persons' rights and duties under the law of nature, an executive to give effect to legislated ordinances, and a judiciary to rule on alleged violations. Through these institutional structures justice is more expeditiously served, but in all essentials it is the same justice that governs relationships among individuals in the state of nature. Most relevant for present purposes is that the political order is to be impersonal, neither privileging some rights-respecting personal project above others nor enshrining any preferred conception of so-called social justice or civically virtuous fraternity as the object of official state policy.[7] The state is to leave people at liberty to associate or dissociate as they choose, to transact among themselves either on a pecuniary or cash-free basis, and to pursue whichever forms of civility they see fit to follow—just so long, of course, as they refrain from violating rights in the process.

III

Where into the sort of liberal order described above does civil society fit? In one sense, nowhere. Beyond insisting on a regime of rights, liberalism simply does not prescribe concerning intermediaries between individuals and the state. That is liberal neutrality under one of its guises. But in another sense, though, implicit in liberalism is a profound appreciation of civil society, although not of any particular version in which it may present itself. By paring down the realm of the strictly obligatory to a minimum, a liberal order affords maximum latitude to voluntary association. One is not obliged to assume the station and associated duties of caste, community, socioeconomic class, religion, nationality, or kinship group. It is undeniably the case that such unchosen affiliations confer on most individuals handholds to satisfying and worthwhile lives, and liberal principles preclude interfering with people's choices to remain content within their confines. (There is no "forcing to be free" within classical liberalism; welfare liberalism allows much more scope for prodding people into what the illuminati take to be more authentically autonomous modes of life.) But it is also undeniably the

case that for many individuals the status to which they are born is unsatisfying and inimical to their good as they see it. Therefore, liberal principles similarly preclude interfering with people's capacity to exercise the exit option.

This is part of what is meant by liberalism's friendliness to civil society. A liberal society differentially privileges voluntary association over involuntary association. Indeed, all associations (other than the universal association of rights holders) are at least passively voluntary insofar as one's continued (though not initial) allegiance is discretionary. Severing deeply rooted ties may be imprudent and psychologically onerous, but it is permissible. Noninterference is mandatory; remembering to send Mother's Day cards is optional. Indeed, some critics maintain that this very partiality for voluntary forms of association evinces a deep inconsistency in liberal theory. Insofar as liberal principles refuse to afford protection to collectives against defection by their members, they do not display neutrality between voluntary and nonvoluntary modes of association.[8] This may be what Marx has in mind when he claims that bourgeois society dissolves what is solid, profanes all that is holy. In any event, the critique is misplaced. Liberal neutrality is not neutrality concerning *everything*[;] that would not be neutrality, but rather vapid mindlessness. Rather, it is specifically a refusal to take sides between rights-respecting types of activity. A liberal is not committed to neutrality between rapists and rape victims, neither is liberalism committed to neutrality between organizations that conscript their members and those that secure allegiance voluntarily. And of course it is individuals, not collectives, that are the primary moral unit within liberal theory. Associations do not possess a right to life that defection by members impermissibly jeopardizes.

Noninterference is mandatory; remembering to send Mother's Day cards is optional.

So much can be read off the surface of liberal theory. More speculatively, there is a deep rationale underlying a regime of rights that can be understood in terms of the value of voluntary associations from the perspective of those who have enrolled themselves. Liberals take rights very seriously; they are the heavy artillery of the moral arsenal. Rights engender maximally weighty claims with which transactors *must* comply. For one viewing from outside the liberal church, this insistence on respect for rights will seem somewhat mysterious, if not bordering on fanaticism. Rights block the realization of otherwise alluring social ends—for example, those of a redistributive nature intended to advance overall welfare or equality. They also impede paternalistic interventions designed to prevent individuals from doing harm to themselves.[9] The occasional misanthrope or ayatollah aside, no one would be comfortable with a regime in which state officials are entirely unchecked in their benevolent designs by individual rights. However, only classical liberals rule out as a matter of principle all intrusions into the protected moral space of competent individuals. One can, to be sure, embrace the inviolability of persons as a dogma, neither requiring nor admitting of justification. But a dogmatic liberalism is an unpersuasive liberalism. Assuming, then, that there is some basis to the liberal credo, on what can the near-absolute bindingness of rights be grounded?[10]

Liberals take rights very seriously; they are the heavy artillery of the moral arsenal.

It is no secret that liberal theorists differ among themselves with regard to the foundations of basic rights. Locke sees them as stemming from God's ownership of all creation, Kant as implied by the universal prescriptivism of the Categorical Imperative, Mill as validated by considerations of utility. And there are more. But one plausible route to the underpinnings of rights is to focus on the way they function in the lives of individuals who bear them. Each person stands in a unique relationship to those particular ends that are distinctively her own. Without gainsaying the relevance or morality of an impartial point of view from which one recognizes oneself to be merely one person among others, practical reason also allows—I would go further and say "requires"—partiality on the part of the agent toward those projects which she had made her own. I have discussed the logic of individuated practical reason at length elsewhere and will not attempt to reprise the argument here.[11] Skipping directly to the conclusion: rights are to be understood as establishing for individuals zones of limited sovereignty within which they

enjoy an immunity from demands on their moral attention and thus are free to direct themselves by their *own* moral lights rather than hitch their wagon to whatever happens to be in fashion or subscribed to by majorities. So important is the permission to be partial that it is allowed to override even very strong claims lodged from an impartialistic perspective. That is, there are many things that people *ought to do* that they may not be *compelled to do*. To phrase this in a way that will seem paradoxical to nonliberals, individuals have a robust right to do what is wrong.

… individuals have a robust right to do what is wrong.

Why should the personal, partialistic perspective be allowed to take precedence over the impersonal, impartialistic perspective? The most plausible strategy for framing an answer will be to underscore the necessity of self-directedness for lives that will be perceived from the inside to be worthwhile and meaningful. It is, then, a short step from the predominance of the voluntary to the importance of voluntary associations—that is, to a rich civil society. It is theoretically possible for a liberal to have a taste for a collection of Garbos who want above all else to be alone, but that would be most uncommon. Among the fundamental liberal rights is freedom of association, and there is every expectation that in the normal course of events it will regularly be invoked. That is why a characterization of liberal atomism is so thoroughly misleading. Privacy too will be prized by liberals, but this should not be understood as being in tension with liberal sociality. These are two sides of the coin of the overridingness of the voluntary.

I fear that the preceding discussion may seem unduly saccharine: just leave people alone and thereby allow them to live happily ever after. Would that that were so. Unfortunately, leaving people alone does not guarantee either in individual cases nor for aggregates results approaching the well-being optimum. That is why I believe it to be ill advised for liberal advocates to place all their bets with consequentialistic chips. Sometimes redistributionist measures of the welfare state really *do* eliminate more misery than they engender; sometimes paternalistic interventions really *do* keep individuals from damaging their own interests.[12] Few classical liberals would disagree with the proposition that on balance the welfare state's interventions do far more harm than good, including serious harms to intended beneficiaries;[13] nonetheless, an instrumental justification of liberal rights is both superficial and subject to forays by "reforms" that advertise themselves as *this time* having gotten the hang of actually helping. Liberals who make aggregate measures the primary criteria for acceptance of social rules are playing the other camp's game. As noted above, rights enter the moral arsenal as the device uniquely responsive to personal value. They legitimize and safeguard the judgments that issue from an individual's attachments to his own particular projects. Rights are to be respected not because they always/usually procure the greatest happiness for the greatest number, but because they afford individuals the moral space within which they can direct themselves according to their own conceptions of the good.

But not all self-direction is accurate direction. Economists may suppose within the confines of their models that agents are all perfect maximizers of their own well-being, but outside of those models that is distinctly not so. Due to excessive passions, inattentiveness, lethargy, illogicality, and intermittent bouts of stupidity we wander off the true path or, indeed, never quite manage to put ourselves on it. People make miseries of their lives through addicting themselves to harmful chemicals, betting on sure things that somehow finish seventh, marrying too impetuously, divorcing too impetuously, swallowing arterial plaque in the form of cheeseburgers, following their messiah to an out-of-the-way homestead in Waco. Had they chosen otherwise, their lives would have gone better. More arguably, had they not been afforded the prerogative to direct their choices along these detrimental lines, their lives would have gone better. A regime of maximum feasible liberty is friendlier than any other to life-enhancing choice making, but it is similarly hospitable to cul-de-sacs and poison pills. A liberal order can be viewed as the standing wager that people who guide their own projects rather than consign these to the putative wisdom of technocrats, benevolent despots, and philosopher-kings will do better than their more coddled cousins. And like any genuine wager, it is one that can be lost.

Classical liberalism historically has shown itself willing to assume that risk. In the seventeenth century it would have seemed to most people a rash leap into folly to suppose that a society could hold itself together

without a common religion to bind them into one ecclesiastical polity. In the eighteenth century there existed widespread skepticism concerning the desirability of an economic order in which entry and exit were not controlled by the crown and in which goods would be allowed to cross borders with minimal constraint. Nineteenth-century liberals offended against the received wisdom when they argued that the emancipation of women from their domestic role would not imperil the stability of the household and drown society in vice. And in the twentieth century, and now in the twenty-first, the majority hoots at the suggestion that we might wind down a war against drugs that has proven itself to be both unwinnable and extraordinarily profligate in the direct and collateral damages it causes; that employment contracts might be entered into on whatever terms to which the parties consent; that people might employ their own criteria concerning which foods and pharmaceuticals they will ingest; that an official state school system is no more necessary or desirable than an official state religion; and so on. In contrast, competing political philosophies such as welfare liberalism, conservatism, and social democracy show themselves to be considerably more risk-averse in their insistence on qualitatively and quantitatively more substantial direction from above.

Some may suspect that the preceding paragraph stacks the deck by listing only those wagers that have already shown themselves to be winners for liberalism (not including contemporary ones on which the moral bookmakers are still giving odds). By way of defense I note that the preceding four centuries have been a conspicuous winning streak for liberalism. The point is not that liberalism has been on a roll but that it (logically) could have been otherwise, and that many intelligent, well-informed observers at the time did indeed expect things to proceed otherwise. Marx, for example, announced the implosion of capitalistic economies to be imminent, and academics in the 1960s took seriously Khrushchev's boast that his society would bury ours. Many contemporary conservatives argue that feminist liberalization, removal of prayer from the schools, and tolerance of homosexual relationships are, even as we speak, leading us down paths to social disintegration. We may believe them to be mistaken, but they are not jousting against truisms. Liberalism's risks have shown and will, I believe, continue to show themselves to be well judged, but that is not because they are contrived.

... the preceding four centuries have been a conspicuous winning streak for liberalism.

Civil society is no less chancy. Across a wide swath of the political spectrum there exists consensus that a variety of structures intermediate between individuals and the state is necessary for the health of the polity. There exists no such consensus concerning the means through which those intermediate structures are most successfully nurtured. Might it not be the case that absent the deliberate application of political means to their sustenance, individuals will find themselves progressively more dissociated one from another, will secure entertainment while sitting alone in front of their wide-screen TVs and pursue companionship in chatrooms on the Internet? Is there cause for concern as attendance at PTA, Rotary, and chess club meetings plummets? What does it say about the health of the body politic that even on those occasions when individuals can be induced to leave the wired-in comforts of their homes for a few hours at the Bowlarama, they will increasingly eschew leagues and instead bowl alone?[14] One line of interpretation has it that these are the predictable fruits of a liberal non-interventionism that, in its apotheosis as unfettered individualism, takes it to be a matter of principle to refrain from opposing the centrifugal forces that fracture social bonds. Even if atomism is not implicit in the very foundations of liberalism, a desiccated collection of atoms is its long-term progeny.

Those espousing this viewpoint tend to issue calls of one sort or another for civic renewal.[15] Typically these entail the creation of new public programs, typically those programs that are to be funded from tax revenues, and typically those employed to design and manage these programs will be drawn from the same class of intellectuals who had proclaimed the urgency of these measures. This is not the place to hold such proposed remedies up to critical inspection; the primary intent of this essay is explication of liberalism's conception of civil society, not its defense. (To be sure, these tend to converge when explication involves exposing misconceptions and inaccurate stereotypes.) Instead, two brief observations: First, the existence of the civil society debate itself constitutes evidence that a laissez-faire attitude toward voluntary associations is by no means vacuously uncontroversial. Rather, it is to take a disputable—and disputed—stance on the question of whether voluntary associations when left to their own devices can adequately generate and regenerate themselves or whether guidance from above is required. Second, the diagnosis of an atrophied civil society cuts in both directions. Perhaps it is not the prevalence of liberal ideology that best explains developments inimical to a vibrant civil society, but rather the overriding of liberal strictures by an omnivorous public realm. Functions that formerly were mostly the domain of communal and charitable institutions have increasingly been taken over by the state. Ethnic and neighbourhood groups used to self-insure against unemployment and the death of a breadwinner, provide subventions for support of the indigent aged, float small loans to respond to emergencies, and provide both pecuniary and spiritual support to the "worthy poor." Now these mutual aid societies have gone the way of the dodo, and charity is increasingly supplanted by welfare state programs. One need not be an unrequited nostalgist for "[the] good old days," which in various respects were not so good at all, to observe that whatever benefits the expansion of the welfare state has conveyed, those benefits have not come free of associated costs. Among these are supplanting of the voluntary by the nonvoluntary. Those costs may or, as I am inclined to believe, may not have been worth incurring, but the point beyond dispute is that in at least this one regard it is welfare liberalism rather than classical liberalism that has done more damage to the infrastructure of civil society.

IV

Critics of classical liberalism may accept the charge that an expanding state realm narrows the space within which civil society can flourish. They are apt to respond, however, that this restriction is more benign, more manageable, and more limited in magnitude than constrictions originating from the other direction: the hegemony of corporate capitalism and its associated cash nexus. If in our private lives we are to be precariously situated between two gargantuas in the shadows of which we are dwarfed, then at least let them be opposed gargantuas. Insofar as the ministrations of the protective state neutralize in some measure the cold discipline of capitalism, then its interventions may on balance be more enabling than constraining: when flower power ruled the streets of San Francisco, this was known as capitalism with a human face.

Recall Marx's imprecations against the solvents unleashed by the ascendancy of the bourgeoisie. This is an early version of the call to arms against dehumanizing market forces, the most recent incarnation of which are warnings about the specter of globalization. To be sure, Marx and his epigones did not demonstrate themselves to be friends of civil society—their comradeship took a rather different form—but perhaps charity demands that the benefit of the doubt be accorded to those who alleged a parity between the oppressiveness of big corporations and the oppressiveness of big government when both were young. Enough time has passed to render that excuse stale. But whether in its early or late incarnations, the parity-of-oppression analysis is flawed for at least three fundamental reasons.

First, the comparison is immediately undercut by the simple observation that the putative oppression exercised by corporations cannot belong to the same genus as that exercised by states. Both are "powerful," but their powers takes radically different forms. States and their component parts exercise authority through coercive means. Possession of a monopoly on legitimate exercise of coercion is, indeed, the Weberian definition of the state. Corporations do not enjoy a prerogative of unleashing force against those who decline to purchase their wares or labor in their employ. Rather, whatever power they possess is a power of persuasion. They induce consumers to purchase by offering goods and services that in the subjective valuation of those consumers are more valuable than the money spent to secure those items. Similarly, employee services are procured by offering a wage that is more highly valued than alternative uses of the hours forgone. Nor is this sham persuasion, the sort that godfathers employ when they dangle offers that can't be refused. The business of business takes place in a highly competitive environment in which someone who is not persuaded to shop from/work for GM can take her dollars/labor to Ford or Chrysler or—thanks to the benefits of globalization—Volkswagen, Honda, Toyota, and a handful of other purveyors. Or she can choose to ride a bicycle. That corporations neither enjoy a monopoly nor have instruments of coercion at their disposal distinguishes them in the most obvious way from governmental instrumentalities.[16] Grammar to the side, *state* is a doggedly singular noun while *corporation* is capaciously plural.

> *Shopping is not the passive transformation of income into means of subsistence by cogs of the capitalist order, but rather a calculated manifestation of self-direction along avenues that one judges to be personally enhancing.*

A second and related point is that market structures and the transactions that take place within their ambit are not something *other* than civil society; they *are* voluntary association in one of its many forms. Corporate stockholders, whether individuals or institutions, have chosen to join their savings alongside those of willing others to undertake activities they believe will make their lives go better. Shopping is not the passive transformation of income into means of subsistence by cogs of the capitalist order, but rather a calculated manifestation of self-direction along avenues that one judges to be personally enhancing. Purchasing manifests individuality. It also typically is undertaken as an expression of sociability; as the father of two teenage daughters, I can speak with some authority on this matter. Nor is labor the alienation of one's species-being in the fetishistic practice of transforming one kind of commodity into others. The profession one selects, the trade-offs one makes between its pursuit and other employments of one's energies, the ends one serves through one's work: these too are manifestations of individuality through voluntary arrangements with willing others. If one chooses to "buy American" or not to work for companies that employ child labor in Southeastern Asian countries—or if one declines to limit one's consumption or labor in these ways—that is to take a moral stance. These are the free actions of free men and women in a way that "contributing" to Social Security or giving up cigarette smoking because the government has imposed punitive taxes are not. To be sure, there are important differences between market transactions and other forms of civil association, but that does not make the former any less a component of civil society than is singing in the Salvation Army choir or signing up for league bowling.

Third, I turn now to a consideration of those important differences. To spend an evening bowling with one's friends because one cherishes their company and wishes to join with them in a team activity is more edifying than charging them an hourly rate for one's kegler services. It does not follow that cash transactions are less creditable than those fraternally motivated. Rather, each is perfectly appropriate in its proper domain.

It was argued in section II that rights are to be understood not as the be-all and end-all of liberal morality, but rather as standards of peaceful interaction for members of the universal association. They are equipped to serve this function because they abstract away from particular affections and attachments so as to provide articles of justice claimed from everyone and owed to everyone. For less inclusive, more intimate groups, supplementation by other moral standards is requisite. Similarly, the cash nexus is the standard for economic interaction among the diverse participants in a vast (now global) market order. A market order is not, however, *only* a market order. Rather, it peacefully coexists with a diverse number and variety of less inclusive, more intimate groups. These include friends, families, neighborhoods, clubs, educational and philanthropic organizations, and the whole myriad of associations that constitute civil society. For these, the operative rule is not simply cash on the barrelhead. That is why it is odious for one friend to charge another for her time and companionship; it is culpably to misidentify something as what it is not. The precisely opposite mistake, however, is to apply patterns of intimacy and concern to transactions in which one is properly indifferent to the identity of the parties to whom one is thereby related. "Treat persons always as ends in themselves rather than as mere means."[17] Yes, but simply to acknowledge and respect the rights to life, liberty, and property of one's transactors is sufficient to certify their status as ends in themselves.

In revivals of Thornton Wilder's *Our Town* as well as in the currently fashionable philosophy of communitarianism there is a tendency to wax nostalgic over an era of tightly knit communities in which everyone knew everyone else, and all relationships were tinged with the personal. Perhaps in the eclipse of such modes of life we have lost something valuable. Or perhaps we have been released from stifling incursions on privacy and autonomy. Or perhaps both. In any event, for nearly all of us, the community of engagement and intimacy is no longer our home, certainly not our only home. We are plugged into international information systems, depend for our livelihoods and entertainments on people who are thoroughly anonymous to us, benefit from enormous welfare gains brought about through increasing economies of scale consequent on an unfathomably intricate division of labor. That is the condition of modernity. Whether one celebrates or bemoans its ascendancy, the question important for practice is: What are to be the terms of interaction within the national and international megalopolis? Marx answered this question with the bright idea of a centrally controlling dictatorship of the proletariat. Even then better proposals were on offer. Today we know with as high a degree of certainty as the human sciences afford that the singularly adequate regulative standard for large-scale economic systems is the price mechanism.[18] Money prices serve two crucial functions without which economies will founder. First, they convey information. Offers to buy and sell at a particular price inform transactors of effective demand for the good or service in question. Second, and equally important, prices conceal information. When buyer pays seller one hundred dollars for a carton of widgets, the only information conveyed is the willingness of the other party to transact at that price. Seller need not know whether buyer is an upstanding pillar of the community or something of a rogue; whether buyer is Christian, Jew, Druid, or none of the above; what buyer intends to do with the widgets once they are obtained; whether widget possession will truly enhance the life of buyer or instead lead him down the winding road to abject widget dependency. Nor need buyer trouble his mind concerning seller's personality and motivations. They simply come to terms at the striking price.

Some will object that economic activity so understood depersonalizes individuals. That claim is true. Exchange abstracts away all features of the transactors other than their liberty to transform one set of property holdings into another. There are two things to be said about such depersonalization. First, it is a necessary thing. Persons are endlessly rich and complex entities. If a precondition for exchange were "getting to really know" the opposite party, then economic relations would bog down in an epistemic morass. Prices abstract away from the personal good. But second, such depersonalization is a good thing. It is protective of privacy. If one had to bare one's soul to buy a newspaper or rent a video, then modern economies would indeed be ghastly panopticons. Moreover, depersonalization undercuts invidious grounds of discrimination. If people regularly buy from the vendor who offers the best goods at the best price, then whether that vendor is of the same religion or race or sexual preferences as oneself becomes immaterial. This is not to maintain, of course, that a capitalistic economy is immune from the perversities of prejudice, but it is to note that these all-too-common failings are meliorated by an impersonal price system. Compared with allocation via ties of consanguinity or political clout, capitalism is very much an equal-opportunity supplier.

... the components of civil society that operate via a cash nexus are thoroughly compatible with the existence of other modes of voluntary association not pecuniarily based.

This may seem efficient but also dreary, lifeless. If capitalistic means of production achieve their enormous efficiencies only by driving intimacy out of human relations, then perhaps the price of a market order is itself too steep. But if this is the mordant reflection that prompts critics of capitalism, they can release their apprehensions; the components of civil society that operate via a cash nexus are thoroughly compatible with the existence of other modes of voluntary association not pecuniarily based. Specifically, those that presuppose shared ideals or strands of affection cannot operate via monetary bids and offers. That is because the information abstracted away by prices is crucial for the sustenance of these more personal relationships. Just as basic rights do not exhaust for liberals the domain of morality but only provide the most inclusive standards of interaction, so too does the cash nexus not dominate liberal civil society, but rather is the basis for transaction where more committ[ed] and revealing relationship patterns are either not feasible or undesirable. By countenancing whichever voluntary associative choices individuals make, a liberal order is equally hospitable to both market and nonmarket arrangements.

... a liberal order is equally hospitable to both market and nonmarket arrangements.

As Adam Smith well knew, commercial society may be dynamically expansive, but it is not ubiquitous.[19]

Rather, it is interlaced with a myriad of noncommercial formations and affiliations. The succeeding two centuries of capitalistic development have not altered that fact. Nor is knowledge of it confined to a coterie of academic specialists. Ordinary men and women are able to preserve the separation in their common practice. Hiring labor is not like giving one's daughter her allowance; those who occupy both roles rarely confuse them. Americans are workers and consumers, but they are also joiners, volunteers, even league bowlers. For the most part, institutional structures spontaneously evolve to mark off the relevant distinctions. Sometimes governments employ legal sanctions to do likewise. For example, statutory prohibitions of prostitution and the sale of transplantable bodily organs express the conviction that the cash nexus is an inappropriate basis for relations of sexual intimacy or conveyances of the gift of life. That sentiment is not in itself discreditable. Unfortunately, when instantiated in law, it counterproductively tends to obliterate the sorts of distinction it intends to preserve. Sex for love and sex for cash are quite different activities that for some five thousand years have shown themselves quite able comfortably to coexist. Transplantation boasts a considerably shorter history, but there is no reason to suppose that donations from love and sales in pursuit of economic interest cannot coexist equally successfully.[20] By attempting to force all sexual activity and all organ transfers into the same Procrustean bed,[21] prohibitionists themselves undermine the distinction between pecuniary and nonpecuniary bases of civil association.

To conclude briefly: Liberal theory traditionally has paid scant attention to civil society. Nor has it much attended to love, beauty, athletic prowess, the wonderful palate-caressing properties of a classic Burgundy, poetry or, for that matter, metaphysics. Silence concerning the latter group should not be interpreted as hostility; neither should it be so interpreted with regard to civil society. Liberalism commends none of these, but it affords a place to all. If individuals acting in their private capacity should decide that the presence of any of these ingredients makes life go better than does its absence, then they are at liberty to act accordingly. With regard to items of potential value, liberalism is disinterested, not uninterested.

But although liberal theory does not speak explicitly of civil society, congeniality to it is implied at the most foundational level. That level is the inviolability of individuals' moral space within which they enjoy an extensive liberty to direct their affairs as they themselves see fit. By minimizing the scope of the mandatory, liberalism maximizes the domain of the voluntary. That, of course, includes voluntary association. Liberalism takes no sides concerning which forms of voluntary association are to be preferred over others; all such questions are devolved down to the level of the concerned individuals. Unless demonstrated otherwise, there is a presumption that there is no fixed upper bound to the number of flowers that can simultaneously bloom.

There exists no presumption, however, that once one has bloomed, it must be preserved forever in some sort of museum of species of sociality. Groups will wax and wane in response to the desires of the individuals who enter into them or defect. There exists no guarantee that the result either in the individual case or for aggregates will be auspicious. That is why a liberal order is the continuing wager that men and women left alone to direct their own affairs is the fitting and proper basis for human society.

Notes

1. Semantic shifts have rendered the term *liberal* slippery. The minimally interventionistic state of classical liberal theory has over the years taken on functions undreamed of by its philosophical forebears. The closest equivalent to the original meaning now in common usage is *libertarian,* but the proper scope of libertarian doctrine is a matter of intense debate among its votaries. *Classical liberalism* is accurate but ponderous. In what follows I shall employ *liberal* and its cognates with primary reference to the tradition that reigned from Locke though Mill. Where clarity requires a more finely honed distinction between the earlier and later stages of the semantic divide I shall employ, respectively, *classical liberalism* and *welfare liberalism.*

2. Traditionally this condition has been described as the *state of nature.* Although liberal theorists differ importantly in their understandings of the state of nature, for all of them its primary significance is as a normative baseline rather than as some bygone historical epoch.

3. John Locke, *Second Treatise of Government,* ed. Peter Laslett (Cambridge: Cambridge University Press, 1960), sec. 4.

4. Secondarily, Locke endorses a title to charitable provision for those who nonculpably fall below a level of resources necessary to sustain life and self-directed activity. Most of the liberal tradition follows Locke to justifying the existence of a background social safety net. In welfare liberal theories both the scope and prominence of this apparatus is markedly expanded. For elaboration of this point see Loren Lomasky, "Justice to Charity," *Social Philosophy and Policy* 12 (Summer 1995): 32–53.

5. With the significant exception of the right to do whatever one must to defend oneself from attack on one's life.

6. Locke, *Second Treatise,* sec. 13.

7. It is with regard to this restriction that welfare liberalism diverges most prominently from classical liberalism.

8. See, for example, Joseph Raz's critique of liberal neutrality in *The Morality of Freedom* (Oxford: Clarendon Press, 1986).

9. It goes without saying that this is not true of liberal welfare states that routinely effect transfers from the rich to the poor, the poor to the rich, and from one middle-class special interest group to another, and that are comparably busy with putting helmets on reluctant motorcyclists, deciding which pharmaceuticals patients will be allowed to ingest, and "helping" individuals give up smoking cigarettes by imposing punitive taxes on the noxious weed.

10. I discuss the near absoluteness of rights in "Rights Without Stilts," *Harvard Journal of Law and Public Policy* 12 (Summer 1989): 775–812.

11. See Loren E. Lomasky, *Persons, Rights, and the Moral Community* (New York: Oxford University Press, 1987), esp. chap. 2.

12. For example, although it is very likely that Food and Drug Administration edicts cost more lives than they save, it is also likely that laws requiring motorists to wear seatbelts on balance decrease death and serious injury.

13. E.g., rent control laws generate shortages of rental units; minimum wage laws turn the working poor into the unemployed poor; and so on.

14. See Robert Putnam, "Bowling Alone: America's Declining Social Capital," *Journal of Democracy* 6 (January 1995): 64–78. Although at first blush the demographics of bowling may seem to have only the most tenuous connection to concerns of social stability, in fact this essay has prompted a burgeoning literature discussing whether the alleged phenomenon is real and, if so, what implications ought to be drawn. See also David Brooks, "Civil Society and Its Discontents," *Weekly Standard,* February 5, 1996, 18–21; and Michael Sandel, "America's Search for a New Public Philosophy," *Atlantic Monthly,* March 1996, 57–74, for complementary reports from distant points of the political spectrum on the liberalism-induced pathologies of American civil society.

15. If I may be allowed an autobiographical excursion, for reasons still not entirely clear to me I was appointed four years

ago to the Scholars Panel of the National Commission on Civic Renewal, cochaired by William Bennett and Sam Nunn. Among panel members, the liberal etiology of civil decay was a popular theme.

16. "Obvious" is, admittedly, my personal gloss on the contrast. For many critics of markets it is far from obvious. They characterize as "coercive offers" consumption or employment proposals that induce individuals to transact because they represent the most highly valued opportunities open to them. Presumably this is taken to constitute coercion, because not to accept the offer is to acquiesce to a lower level of well-being than can be achieved by its acceptance. I confess that I am unable to find any plausibility in this position—as, I am sure, those who advance such views are unable to find any

plausibility in mine. Perhaps we are confronted here with the moral equivalent of color blindness. But whose?

17. Paraphrase of the third form of the Kantian Categorical Imperative.

18. The post-1989 collapse of the Soviet empire is but the latest piece of evidence confirming the proposition.

19. That is why the so-called Adam Smith problem of scholars endeavoring to render consistent the views expressed in *The Theory of Moral Sentiments* with those of *The Wealth of Nations* is mostly a phantom.

20. I have explored these cases in Loren E. Lomasky, "Gift Relations, Sexual Relations and Liberty," *Philosophical Quarterly* 33 (July 1983): 250–58.

21. No double entendre intended.

Terms and Concepts

humanity's natural condition
freedom of association
social contract
civil society

rights
zones of limited sovereignty
classical liberalism

welfare liberalism
capitalism
cash nexus

Questions

1. What is the role of the state in classical liberal thinking?
2. What are the differences between classical and welfare liberalism?
3. Lomasky argues that the right of noninterference is an essential feature of classical liberal thought. What are the limits to this right? What constitutes an attempt to interfere with another person's self-chosen conduct?
4. Lomasky argues that liberalism is a "genuine wager" that can be lost. Explain this remark.
5. Does the capitalist economy, dominated by large corporations, pose a problem for Lomasky's defence of individual autonomy?
6. Does classical liberal thinking privilege some ways of life over others?

The Universal Child-Care Benefit:
A Turning Point for Social
Conservatives?

Richard Myers

Editors' Note

Political parties attempt to represent polit-ical ideologies while they compete for political office, but they embody political ideas imper-fectly. Electoral imperatives cause parties to adjust their ideas in order to curry electoral support. Free-market ideas by themselves, for example, do not win elections in Canada. And political parties become homes for people who aspire to office at least as much as they seek fidelity to a political program. Competitive parties in Canada become "big tents" giving shelter to persons of diverse political views, united mainly by their desire to see the party do well in elections. Big-tent parties as a result are hard to identify on the political spectrum. They seem to want to be all things to all people. This has been the historical dilemma for the big parties in Canada, including the Conservatives.

Conservative parties have been dogged also by disagreement about what conservatism means. Conservatism once meant more than free-market economics. It also referred to the idea that a decent regime needs citizens of a certain moral character and that it must help cultivate that character. The emphasis on virtue is what is now called social conser-vatism. Liberal ideology, by contrast, holds that character formation is entirely a private matter and that individual choice is the key principle of liberal politics. Individual choice is now an almost unchallengeable political principle in Canada. For this reason, philoso-pher George Grant wrote in the 1960s that conservatism as a political ideology based on virtue, rather than choice, is now an impos-sible political platform.[1]

In the following essay, Richard Myers explores what conservatism means in contemporary Canada. Somewhat surprisingly, he argues that conservatives' success in Canada is tied to their skill in exploiting a principle at the heart of liberalism: individual choice.

◆ ◆ ◆

Whispered to conservatives: A reversion, a return in any sense or degree is simply not possible ... All priests and moralists have wanted to take mankind backward, to screw it back, to a former measure of virtue .... Even the politicians have aped the preachers of virtue at this point: today there are still parties whose dream it is that all things might walk backwards like crabs. But no one is free to be a crab. Nothing avails: one must go forward—step by step further into decadence (that is my definition of modern "progress.")

Friedrich Nietzsche,
The Twilight of the Idols, IX 43[1]

For some observers, the most significant aspect of the 2006 general election was the victory it represented for "social conservatives." Certainly much atten-tion was paid to the fact that many of the Conservative

---

1. George Grant, *Lament for a Nation: The Defeat of Canadian Nationalism.* [1965, 1978] (Montreal and Kingston: McGill-Queen's University Press, 2000), p. 81.

Article prepared for this publication. © Nelson, 2008.

Party's new candidates had close ties to evangelical churches and that 10 of those candidates managed to get elected. In addition, several prominent members of the new cabinet—Justice Ministers Vic Toews and Public Security Minister Stockwell Day, for instance—are staunch supporters of social conservative causes and organizations. On the policy front, social conservatives could also point to an important victory. One of the five top priorities in the Conservative platform was a policy plank dear to the hearts of social conservatives: a child-care allowance that could be used by families to subsidize stay-at-home caregivers. Opponents of social conservatism warn that the new government's policy on child care is merely the thin edge of a wedge that may force a kind of counterrevolution in Canadian social policy, including a rollback of rights to abortion and same-sex marriage. More generally, they fear that the Conservative approach to child care is indicative of a broader agenda to reduce government's role in addressing social problems by redefining social issues as family issues.[2]

While the introduction of what the government is now calling the Universal Child Care Benefit (UCCB) is certainly a breakthrough for social conservatives, predictions that this measure is the harbinger of a return to the social policy of the 1950s are almost certainly wrong. If anything, this social conservative victory is striking primarily because it comes in the context of a 30-year social conservative losing streak; and as we shall see, there is no reason to think that there has been any change in the underlying causes of that losing streak. The thesis of this essay is that the introduction of the UCCB points not to the imminent triumph of social conservatism, but to the way in which social conservatives will have to reinvent themselves if they hope to have any success in the future.

... this social conservative victory is striking primarily because it comes in the context of a 30-year social conservative losing streak ...

THE IDEOLOGICAL POSITION OF SOCIAL CONSERVATIVES

◆ ◆ ◆

One of the greatest challenges for the new student of politics is to decipher the meaning of the terms we commonly use to describe political ideologies. "Left," "right," "liberal," or "socialist" all appear to mean different things to different people, and even different things to the same people when used in different contexts. This challenge is as difficult with the term "conservative" as it is with any of the others. An astonishing range of political figures have been called conservatives; even though their fundamental beliefs would be completely antithetical, Stephen Harper and Kim Jong-Il, the dictator of North Korea, are both said to be "conservatives." As confusing as this may seem, it is important to resist the temptation to conclude that terms like "conservative" have no meaning at all, or that they mean whatever people say they mean. In reality, most of the confusion arises primarily because these terms are used in both a substantive and in a relative sense. Used relatively, the term "conservative" simply describes an attitude toward change. A conservative wishes to conserve whatever exists and opposes changing to something new. Kim Jong-Il and Stephen Harper both wish to maintain their countries as they are. To the extent that the political regimes of Canada and North Korea are dramatically different, the substance of what each wishes to maintain will differ dramatically: Communist dictatorship on the one hand and liberal democracy on the other.

What is it that Canadian conservatives wish to conserve?[3] Canadian conservatives themselves commonly draw a basic distinction between "fiscal conservatism" and "social conservatism." The first of these terms refers primarily to a set of beliefs in relation to such matters as tax policy, government spending and government regulation of commercial activity. Fiscal conservatives believe that government intervention in the economy often encumbers the sort of private enterprise that they deem essential to the creation of general prosperity. To begin with, they worry that government regulation of private economic activity will necessarily hamper the efforts of private entrepreneurs to create wealth. More generally, fiscal conservatives fear that welfare-state subsidies—whether to individuals, regions, or even corporations—necessarily distort the workings of the market and thereby create and entrench inefficiencies that cost everyone in the long run. They also claim that such subsidies undermine the enterprising spirit that is necessary to a successful market economy. One might say that what fiscal conservatives seek to conserve is a political economy based on the principle of "equality of opportunity." Their fear is that "big government" is undermining the classical liberal ideal of equality of opportunity as it pursues a more socialistic emphasis on "equality of result." Michael Alexander, a leading Canadian exponent of this view, puts it this way: "Canada's standard of living is declining because the group prevails over the individual in ways that undermine the equal opportunity ideal, and its natural companion, national prosperity."[4]

Social conservatives seek to conserve not a political economy grounded in the principle of equality of opportunity but what they call "traditional values." For many social conservatives, strong penalties for criminal behaviour (including capital punishment) or perhaps a more restrictive immigration policy might be part of the package of traditional values they espouse. At its core, however, social conservatism is a defense of the beliefs and practices related to the life of the traditional family, which they regard as the fundamental building block of a healthy society. For instance, social conservatives believe that marriage should exist only for heterosexual couples. Moreover, they worry that liberal (that is, permissive) attitudes toward abortion, sexual liberation, pornography, new reproductive technologies, and euthanasia endanger the status of the traditional family. In many cases, if not most, the social conservative's attachment to the traditional family either originates in, and/or is buttressed by, religious belief—usually (but not exclusively) some sect of Christianity.

The two main branches of contemporary Canadian conservatism are thus not only distinct in their focus, but stand in an uneasy relationship to each other. Though social conservatives as a group tend to support the economic objectives of fiscal conservatives, fiscal conservatives are often quite uncomfortable with the agenda of social conservatives. The source of the difficulty is reasonably evident. One might easily imagine a person who believes that the economic system should be based on equality of opportunity and who, at the same time, supports same-sex marriage and unrestricted access to abortion. Indeed, at the level of principle, there would seem to be a logical connection between these two positions. Fiscal conservatives believe in small government and leaving individuals as free as possible to shape their own economic fate. Their opposition to government regulation of what they regard as private economic matters carries over very naturally into an opposition to government regulation of private matters in general. In short, it is not only common, but perfectly understandable, that fiscal conservatives would in social matters be sympathetic to libertarianism—the view that government has no business telling us how to organize our private lives. This libertarian tendency can put fiscal conservatives in stark opposition to social conservatives, whose focus on "family values"

means that they actually favour an activist government, at least to the extent that they want governments to intervene in the social realm to prohibit activities of which they disapprove, such as abortion or pornography.

Though social conservatives as a group tend to support the economic objectives of fiscal conservatives, fiscal conservatives are often quite uncomfortable with the agenda of social conservatives.

In ideological terms, then, social conservatives hold a relatively isolated position. Their desire to use state power to enforce traditional values puts them in opposition not only to ideological liberals (for obvious reasons) and ideological socialists and feminists (who see "traditional family values" as a source of sexual inequality) but also to a large number of those who call themselves ideological conservatives.

THE POLITICAL POSITION OF SOCIAL CONSERVATIVES

◆ ◆ ◆

Their position of ideological isolation has led some social conservatives to conclude that their best political strategy is to try to advance their agenda through a political party of their own. In recent years, the chief example of such a party has been the Christian Heritage Party. The Christian Heritage Party has been fielding candidates in federal elections since 1988 in order to provide voters with a clear and uncompromising social conservative option.[5] The problem with this strategy, of course, is that the Canadian electoral system makes it virtually impossible for a new ideologically based party to succeed. Because we hold separate elections in each of our 308 electoral districts (as opposed to a single national vote based on party affiliation) only broadly based brokerage parties and narrowly based regional parties can succeed in the Canadian electoral system. The reality is that even if the Christian Heritage Party could pick up 20 percent of the vote in every riding in Canada, it would probably never win a single seat.

The alternative political strategy for social conservatives is to work within one of the major parties in the hope of influencing the national political agenda through their influence within that party. Many social conservatives have opted for this strategy, working within the old Progressive Conservative Party, the Reform Party, then the Canadian Alliance, and now the Conservative Party of Canada. This strategy has certainly been more fruitful insofar as the opportunity to run under the banner of a major national party has facilitated the election of individual social conservatives to Parliament. On the other hand, it is clear that social conservatives are merely junior partners in the Conservative Party and have relatively limited influence on policy. The causes of this are twofold. First, the Conservative Party includes many fiscal conservatives, moderate conservatives, and even just conservatives of convenience who are uncomfortable with (or even hostile to) social conservative ideology. Secondly, the Conservative Party understands that its aspirations for office depend on its capacity to attract support beyond its own core, that is, to reach out and attract voters from the broad middle ground of the Canadian political spectrum. This is especially true today as the minority Conservative government pins its hopes of a majority in the next elections on a large increase in seats from Quebec—the Canadian province that is least receptive to social conservative ideology. The majority of the Conservative Party's members are only too aware that even the slightest expression of certain social conservative views by any member of the caucus will trigger a torrent of allegations about "scary hidden agendas" from both the party's political rivals and the national media; and the experience of recent elections has demonstrated that such allegations, whatever their validity, can be very damaging.[6] Consequently, the strategy of the party leadership is to provide social conservatives with a sympathetic and respectful ear, pay lip service to certain social conservative ideals, provide enough minor concessions to maintain their interest in staying on board, but resist the adoption of any core social conservative policies.

The majority of the Conservative Party's members are only too aware that even the slightest expression of certain social conservative views by any member of the caucus will trigger a torrent of allegations about "scary hidden agendas" from both the party's political rivals and the national media; and the experience of recent elections has demonstrated that such allegations, whatever their validity, can be very damaging.

In essence, the political dynamic facing Canadian social conservatives is similar to that faced by their counterparts in the United States. The Republican Party, like the Conservative Party of Canada, is directed by moderate conservatives and fiscal conservatives. In order to collect the votes of social conservatives, the Republican leadership is happy to pay lip service to some of their causes and to throw them the odd policy bone, but it is careful not to give ground on anything fundamental.

The Conservative Party of Canada has taken a similar approach to Canadian social conservatives. For instance, while expressing some sympathy for the concerns of pro-life activists, the party was careful to adopt a resolution at its 2005 policy conference in Montreal stipulating that it would not legislate any kind of restriction on the right to abortion.[7] Even more illuminating is the Conservative approach to the same-sex marriage issue. Prior to the 2006 elections, the greatest concession made to social conservatives by the Conservative Party came in the context of the debate on same-sex marriage. Social conservatives are opposed to granting gays and lesbians the right to marry. In 2005, when the governing Liberals moved to legalize same-sex marriage through Bill C-38, the Conservative Party (along with some Liberals) voted against the bill. The Conservative position was not to prohibit same-sex unions altogether, as social conservatives wanted; instead, they called for legislation that would allow same-sex couples to be joined in "civil unions," with all the rights and privileges of marriage, while reserving the term "marriage" for traditional heterosexual unions. The Conservative position could hardly be described as radical; according to most polls, roughly half of Canadians agreed with it. Moreover, the governing Liberals had taken exactly the same position until just a couple of years earlier. On the other hand, most constitutional experts agreed that the compromise proposed by the Conservatives would not withstand a *Charter* challenge and could therefore be enacted only through the use of section 33, the notwithstanding clause. Because Mr. Harper has stated categorically that he would not use section 33 in this matter, the Conservative Party's support for this "compromise position" on same-sex marriage was really nothing more than a hollow display of "moral support" for the social conservatives in his party. Indeed, now that the Conservatives are in office, their strategy on same-sex marriage has become even more transparent. In another gesture of support for social conservatives, Mr. Harper agreed to hold a vote in Parliament on the same-sex issue sometime in the fall of

2006. In June of that year, however, he announced that the motion to be debated would not ask whether the Liberal legislation should be repealed, but merely whether the House wishes to re-open the debate on the question. Predictably, that motion failed, not only because the opposition members used their majority to defeat it, but also because Conservatives themselves "reluctantly conceded" that "the issue has already been settled," or "people are tired of fighting over this" or "it's time to move on."[8] Mr. Harper has thus cleverly managed to shore up his support with the party's social conservative wing (what other leader would have done this much for them?) without actually implementing any policies that might offend more moderate voters.

THE CHILD-CARE ISSUE

◆ ◆ ◆

Only on the issue of child care have social conservatives made a meaningful breakthrough. Here Mr. Harper has delivered exactly what his social conservative supporters were hoping for.

Only on the issue of child care have social conservatives made a meaningful breakthrough.

Child care has been on the national political agenda since the early 1990s. There are currently about two million children in Canada under the age of six. The mothers of two out of every three of these children work outside the home but only about 15 percent of children in this age group are in a regulated child-care centre. In most parts of the country, accessing a child-care centre that is both of good quality and affordable is difficult. Ever since the 1993 elections, the Liberal Party of Canada has made the establishment of a national child-care initiative a major element in its election platforms. The Liberals finally delivered on this promise in 2005.

Under section 92 of the *Constitution Act, 1867*, child care is a provincial jurisdiction. Led by Social Development Minister Ken Dryden, the federal government in 2005 negotiated a series of agreements with the provinces to introduce a national child-care initiative roughly resembling our medicare arrangements. Under these agreements, Ottawa would transfer $1 billion each year to the provinces in support of provincial child-care programs provided those programs were consistent with general guidelines established by Ottawa. In the 2006 elections, the Liberals committed to making these agreements permanent and they claimed that their policy would eventually lead to the creation of 625 000 new child-care spaces.[9] In other words, the Liberal position was to introduce a robust program of state-funded and state-regulated child-care centres.

While the Liberal policy was well received in many quarters, it did not please social conservatives, who saw it as just another example of "government's attempt to interfere in family life." Social conservatives believe that the traditional family is "the best health, educational and welfare unit ever devised" and that government initiatives to "assist" with these functions inevitably subvert the traditional family. State-run child care would be a perfect illustration of their position:

> There are differences in children who are raised at home during the early years and those raised in a child care system for over 20 hours a week. Children learn values and the importance of relationships from their parents, as they develop emotionally, spiritually and physically. Children raised in day care, however, do not spend the same amount of time to learn from the family and therefore do not have the same opportunity to acquire these values.[10]

Using data from a recent study by the Vanier Institute of the Family, the author of the document cited above goes on to argue that most Canadians agree with her position. The Vanier Institute study asked Canadians to rank various child-care options. The top choice was to have children cared for by one of the parents. Having them cared for by a grandparent was the second preference, while having them cared for by some other relative was third. Institutional day care was the lowest ranked of the five options.[11] According to social conservatives, the real political pressure for initiatives like the Liberals' comes from not from ordinary Canadians, but from government-sponsored lobbies and from unions hoping to expand their declining membership rolls through the creation of a large new class of public-sector jobs in state-sponsored child-care centres.[12] What the government should actually provide, according to social conservatives, is financial support for the kind of child care most Canadian parents actually want—care given in the home by a parent or a close relative.[13]

The Conservative Party's child-care platform in the 2006 elections was exactly what social conservatives were looking for. Mr. Harper promised that his party would terminate, after a one-year grace period, the agreements that Mr. Dryden had negotiated with the provinces. The Liberal child-care initiative would then be replaced with a two-part Conservative plan. One branch of the plan was the Community Child Care Investment Program, which established tax credits to encourage employers to create on-site child-care facilities. Conservatives claimed that this program would create up to 125 000 new spaces for child care over the course of five years. The other branch of the Conservative Platform was the Choice in Child Care Allowance, a taxable benefit of $100 per month paid to the parents of every Canadian child under the age of six.[14]

Child-care advocacy groups were highly critical of this Conservative platform. Some claimed that the idea of using tax incentives to encourage the creation of workplace child care had flopped in every other jurisdiction where it had been tried.[15] Others pointed out that the major financial challenge in child care is not the creation of spaces but the cost of operating them. Since the proposed new allowance of $100 per month would cover only about 10 percent of the average operating costs, it was argued that the Liberal plan would be far more beneficial for parents using institutional child care.[16] On the other hand, the large number of parents who do not use institutional child care, and would therefore receive absolutely no benefit under the Liberal plan, would, under the Conservative plan, be getting a cheque for $100 each month. Even if a substantial percentage of that allowance were taxed back, those who looked after their own children, or had them cared for by friends or family members, would still be much further ahead with the Conservative policy. No wonder social conservatives were pleased. Here was a policy that not only provided the kind of financial arrangements they had advocated, but also, and perhaps more importantly, implicitly conferred official legitimacy on their vision of child care. No longer would the federal government be privileging state-regulated child-care centres as the only approach deserving public support; the "traditional" approach to child care was now deemed equally valid.

POLITICAL ANALYSIS

◆ ◆ ◆

Policy analysts might have an interesting debate about the relative merits of the Conservative and Liberal approaches to child care in the 2006 elections. To the political analyst, however, the most interesting question

is the cause of the social conservative success with this issue. Does it signal the rising influence of social conservatism? Will it turn out to be the first in a series of social conservative victories? Or is the case of child-care policy basically anomalous, a political fluke that points to nothing beyond itself?

In order to come to terms with these questions, it is important to begin by noting two important ways in which the case of child care is politically distinct from other social conservative issues. First, unlike issues such as abortion or same-sex marriage, child care has a financial dimension that makes it as important to fiscal conservatives as it is to social conservatives. In *Securing Canada's Success*, its 2006 campaign platform, the Liberal Party described its child-care policy as "a great national endeavour on the same scale as the creation of Canada's public health care system."[17] Fiscal conservatives, with their instinctive dislike of big government, find such language alarming. To their ears, the comparison of child care with health care suggests the creation of a significant new entitlement, the cost of which will almost certainly balloon over time. Consequently, fiscal conservatives are as keen to prevent the emergence of an expensive new social entitlement as social conservatives would be to support traditional parenting. In the case of child-care policy, then, social conservatives have had important allies in the fiscal-conservative wing of their party, allies who are normally reluctant to support the social conservative agenda.

... fiscal conservatives are as keen to prevent the emergence of an expensive new social entitlement as social conservatives would be to support traditional parenting.

Of course, fiscal conservatives who have libertarian tendencies are normally scared away from social conservative policies because libertarians recoil from the notion that governments should tell people how to lead their lives. Here we see the second important distinction between the kind of policy that social conservatives normally support and their position on the issue of child care. Whereas social conservatives seek to prohibit women from having abortions or homosexuals from marrying, in the case of child care their objective has been *to win an entitlement for themselves rather than to deny one to others*. Indeed, instead of offending the libertarian ideal of freedom, the Conservative Party's approach to child care appeals to it. The genius in the Conservative strategy has been to frame the issue as a matter of choice and to then claim the moral high ground as the champions of choice. The Conservatives allege that the Liberal policy, by providing money only for state-regulated child-care centres, privileges that alternative at the expense of all others. According to Mr. Harper, this amounts to having "the federal government ... tell us how to raise our children."[18] By contrast, the Conservative policy of providing money directly to parents gives parents the power to choose the child-care option they prefer. Indeed, during the election campaign, the Conservatives went out of their way to emphasize the choice aspect of the issue by labelling their policy the "Choice in Child Care Allowance." Their 2006 election platform, *Stand up for Canada,* frames the difference between their position and those of the Liberals and NDP this way:

> The Liberals and the NDP believe that the only answer to expanding childcare in Canada is their one-size-fits-all plan to build a massive childcare bureaucracy which will benefit only a small percentage of Canadians. Only the Conservatives believe in freedom of choice in child care. The best role for government is to let parents choose what's best for their children, and provide parents with the resources to balance work and family life as they see fit—whether that means formal child care, informal care through neighbours or relatives, or a parent staying at home.[19]

The genius in the Conservative strategy has been to frame [child-care policy] as a matter of choice and to then claim the moral high ground as the champions of choice.

While it may have been a stretch to paint the Liberal policy as "telling Canadians how to raise their children," the Conservatives hit the political jackpot when Liberal Communications Director Tim Murphy foolishly took their bait, countering that the proposed Conservative policy would allow parents to use the child-care allowance to buy themselves "beer and popcorn." Conservatives pounced on Murphy's remarks, easily painting them as evidence of the Liberals' arrogance. Mr. Harper's team could now gleefully pin on the

Liberals all of the epithets normally hurled at social conservatives: rigid, narrow-minded, ideological, intolerant, and claiming to know better than you do what's good for you. The Conservatives, by contrast, came off as the party of flexibility and diversity, the party most willing to live and let live.

WHISPERED TO SOCIAL CONSERVATIVES: PLAY THE CHOICE CARD!

◆ ◆ ◆

The analysis above suggests that the social conservative victory on child care is better seen as a political anomaly than as a sign of the growing power of social conservatism. That victory depended in part on the unusual way in which this issue harmonized the interests of fiscal and social conservatives; more importantly, it depended on the Conservative Party's success at effecting a complete *inversion* of normal political categories, painting the Liberals into the corner of arrogant intolerance while portraying the social conservatives as the champions of choice. Fears or hopes that a social conservative victory on child care is just the prequel to social conservative victories on abortion or same-sex marriage thus seem highly implausible.

... social conservatives won this battle for the very same reason they have lost all the others: Canadians don't like it when their governments try to tell them how to lead their lives.

Indeed, to the extent that the social conservative victory on child care depended on an inversion of normal political roles, it actually serves to confirm the operative rule in today's game of politics: the choice card always wins. In other words, social conservatives won this battle for the very same reason they have lost all the others: Canadians don't like it when their governments try to tell them how to lead their lives.

The basic political truth for social conservatives is wonderfully expressed in the words of Nietzsche with which this essay begins. Social conservatives essentially seek to compel people to lead a life of "virtue"; that is, they seek to impose restraints on people's freedom of action in order to promote a traditional view of the right way to live. Such restraint is flatly inconsistent with the core principle of the modern liberal democratic world: that individuals must be free to live as they wish (provided only that they do others no harm). Nietzsche's use of the crab analogy is meant to suggest that attempts by social conservatives to limit freedom and choice in the name of virtue are simply doomed to fail because human beings are not crabs: they do not and cannot "walk backwards" in time; they cannot and will not resist the flow of history.

The child-care issue will mark a turning point for social conservatives only to the extent that they reinvent themselves in light of the lessons it offers. The first of these is that it is not merely futile, but also self-defeating to push political agendas that attack freedom in the name of virtue. Canadians will fiercely resist any attempt to legislate morality and will banish to political oblivion the "scary" people who seek to do so. On the other hand, the child-care case shows that social conservatives can win important victories if they give up their dreams of suppressing the choice of others and instead play the choice card themselves.

... the child-care case shows that social conservatives can win important victories if they give up their dreams of suppressing the choice of others and instead play the choice card themselves.

Playing the choice card means first of all coming to terms with the realization that social conservatives themselves constitute a cultural minority. Social conservatives sometimes have a tendency to think of themselves as "the moral majority," And their mode of argumentation certainly reflects a majoritarian mindset. The *reductio ad absurdum* ("next thing you know, homosexuals will want to adopt children!") and the appeal to authority (usually the Bible) are effective ways of rallying a majority to its flag. On the other hand, these methods are completely useless in terms of appealing to those outside one's own group. From the point of view of the political analyst, it is puzzling that what is clearly a minority group relies so heavily on the political tools of a majority, tools which are so poorly adapted to their situation. One might compare the social conservatives to a football team that is three touchdowns behind with five minutes to play and decides to go to its running game in order to eat up more of the clock.

In our modern world (and especially as it becomes increasingly a "postmodern" world that prizes "diversity" above all else), social conservatives would likely find it to their political advantage to acknowledge that theirs is a minority view and then to embrace that minority status and make it work for them. Instead of attempting to control the behaviour of all Canadians, they might pursue the more limited objective of creating conditions that will allow those who choose a more traditional lifestyle to do so more effectively. State support for choice in child care is a perfect example of what can be achieved in this respect.

To be sure, it would not be possible to recast as matters of choice all of the issues that are important to social conservatives. Yet there are at least some opportunities to replicate the success they have had with the child-care issue. A bigger, and potentially much more important, issue would be education. To the extent that social conservatives are primarily concerned with the transmission of values, it's difficult to imagine a realm of activity that would be more important to them than education. Social conservatives might well seek to use their status as a religious/cultural minority to push for more effective choice in schools and universities.

Notes

1. Friedrich Nieztsche (Walter Kaufmann, ed.) "Twilight of the Idols" in *The Portable Nietzsche* (New York, Viking Press, 1954) pp. 546–647.
2. Ann Porter, "The Harper Government: Towards a New Social Order? *The Bullet*, Socialist Project e-bulletin No. 21 (May 22, 2006). Retrieved April 23, 2007, from www.socialistproject.ca
3. I refer here to "small-c" conservatives, rather than members of the Conservative Party. It is a truism of Canadian politics that many members of the Conservative Party of Canada do not have any distinctively "conservative" views and could just as easily be members of the Liberal Party. The analysis in this paragraph and the next two refers to the subset of Conservative Party members who hold ideological views that could be described as distinctly conservative.
4. Michael Alexander, *Competing Against America: Why Canada Has Fallen Behind in the Race for Talent and*

Wealth (And What To Do about It) (Mississauga: John Wiley and Sons, 2005), p. 244.

5. See www.chp.ca. The Christian Heritage Party ran 45 candidates in the 2006 general elections.

6. Adam Daifallah and Tasha Kheiriddin, *Rescuing Canada's Right: Blueprint for a Conservative Revolution* (Mississauga, John Wiley and Sons, 2005), pp. 202–03.

7. *Rescuing Canada's Right*, p. 204.

8. Jennifer Ditchburn, "Tories Shy Away from Same-Sex Quagmire" *Canadian Press* (May 31, 2006). Retrieved June 7, 2006, from www.equal-marriage.ca/resource.php?id=507.

9. Liberal Party of Canada, *Securing Canada's Success*, pp. 27–28.

10. C. Gwendolyn Landolt, "Who Is In Charge of the Family." Retrieved March 2, 2007, from www.realwomenca.com/analyses/analyses_07.htm.

11. Horrified that one of their studies was being used to oppose funding for child-care centres, the Vanier Institute issued a press release suggesting that the results of its study were being taken out of context. Vanier Institute President Allan MacKay argued that the survey was merely indicating what Canadians would prefer "in an ideal world." See www.vifamily.ca/newsroom/media_06.html.

12. C. Gwendolyn Landolt, "Who Is In Charge of the Family?" Retrieved May 8, 2006.

13. "Statement on Child Care," REAL Women of Canada. Retrieved March 28, 2007, from www.realwomenca.com/papers/child_care.htm.

14. Conservative Party of Canada, *Stand up for Canada*, pp. 31–32. Retrieved March 28, 2007, from www.conservative.ca/media/20060113-Platform.pdf.

15. "The Community Child Care Investment Program: Does the Evidence Support the Claims?" Child Care Advocacy Association of Canada. Retrieved May 8, 2006, from www.childcareadvocacy.ca/action/codeBlue/pdf/Conservative_employer_tax_incentivefinal.pdf; and Rianne Mahon, "A Real Alternative: The Canadian Election and Child Care Policy" *The Bullet: Socialist Project*, e-Bulletin No. 12 (January 19, 2006).

16. "Children and Families Deserve More Than Empty Conservative Promises," Child Care Advocacy Association of Canada. Retrieved May 8, 2006, from www.childcareadvocacy.ca/action/election2006/pdf/children deservebetter.pdf.

17. Liberal Party of Canada, "Securing Canada's Success" p. 28 (2006 Election Platform).

18. John Gray, "Who Cares About Child Care?" Retrieved January 15, 2006, from www.cbc.ca/canadavotes/realitycheck/whocares.html.

19. Conservative Party of Canada, "Stand up for Canada," p. 31. One might argue that the Conservative platform on child care was not entirely "pro-choice" in that it did include, through the Community Child Care Investment Program (CCCIP), some money for the creation of child-care centres. One might regard that aspect of the Conservative platform as a compromise with the political mainstream. On the other hand, even the CCCIP reflects more of a "choice" orientation than the Liberal policy in that the resources for the creation of new centres are made available as an option to private employers and community groups rather than as a transfer to provincial governments.

Terms and Concepts

left
right

traditional values
social conservatism

fiscal conservatism
libertarianism

Questions

1. What are the differences between fiscal and social conservatism?
2. What explains the importance of the family to social conservatives?
3. Why has social conservatism had such a conspicuous losing streak in Canadian politics, according to Myers?
4. How do Liberals and Conservatives differ on child-care policy?
5. What explains the success of the Conservatives' Universal Child Care Benefit?
6. Myers suggests that only a "pro-choice" conservatism has a future. Do you agree? Why or why not?

The Politics of Feminism: An Introduction

Linda Trimble

Editors' Note

In the following article, written for this volume, Linda Trimble argues that women's advances in recent decades have stimulated a mostly misinformed backlash against feminism and those who identify themselves as feminists. She responds to this backlash, showing that feminism cannot be reduced to any simple formula or to stereotypes of "man-hating, anti-family, unfeminine, and usually lesbian, radicals." She presents feminism as being, at once, a social movement, a way of knowing the world, and an ideology—or, more precisely, a cluster of strikingly different ideological positions.

While "women's liberation" became a rallying cry in Western countries in the 1960s, feminism has a much longer history. Like other modern ideological positions, it can be traced back at least as far as the French revolution (when Mary Wollstonecraft published *A Vindication of the Rights of Woman*), and the industrial revolution. The 19th century saw the first political concessions in Britain to mass democracy in the gradual extension of the vote to men—not women. Philosopher and member of Parliament J.S. Mill sponsored a bill in the late 1860s to extend the vote to women—why, he asked, should a society deny itself the talents of half its members?—only to have it defeated. Women's political response to the incomplete democratic reforms of the times was a vigorous suffragette movement on both sides of the Atlantic. Its first success in Canada came when women won the right to vote in the three prairie provinces over a short span of time in 1916.

On the other hand, a women's movement of sorts emerged in response to the toll exacted by the factory system. Organizations were formed to push for things like improved sanitation, and, above all, to tackle the problem of alcoholism that was a working-class side-effect of industrialization. The Woman's Christian Temperance Union emerged out of this era as a force to be reckoned with; Louise McKinney, the first woman elected to the Alberta legislature in 1917, had cut her political teeth as a WCTU organizer. This kind of "social feminism," as it is sometimes called, defined for women a separate, maternal, and conservative role; their job was to protect families. Nellie McClung, who, with McKinney and three other Alberta women, successfully challenged the constitutional exclusion of women from appointment to the Senate, once declared: "Women have cleaned up things since time began; and if women ever get into politics there will be a cleaning-out of pigeon-holes and forgotten corners, on which the dust of years has fallen, and the sound of the political carpet-beater will be heard in the land."

Trimble's argument suggests that the vocabulary and targets have changed. Her survey of the diverse strands of contemporary feminism suggests at least three shared themes: (1) a rejection of the claim that biology determines gender roles; (2) a recognition of patriarchy in societal structures and ideas; and (3) a redefinition of politics to include both "public" and "private" spheres.

◆ ◆ ◆

Article prepared for this publication. © Nelson, 2008.

INTRODUCTION

◆ ◆ ◆

When I meet with the students in my women and politics class for the first time, I ask whether they identify themselves as feminists. Typically about half of the students are comfortable with the label because they see feminism as a positive, proactive and vital social movement. But the others are reluctant to embrace the "f-word," in part because feminism has been much maligned in popular discourses. Feminists are increasingly portrayed as man-hating, anti-family, unfeminine, and usually lesbian, radicals.[1] Feminism is cast as a socially and politically destructive doctrine that conveniently blames all of women's troubles on men. Moreover, my male students are not sure whether they are "allowed" to claim a feminist identity. While students sense that these representations of feminism tend to be homophobic, unfounded and misleading, they don't want to call themselves feminists and run the risk of being regarded as anti-male (or, in the case of the male students, "sissies"). Like many young Canadian women,[2] my students adopt an "I'm not a feminist, but ..." stance; they avoid the label while identifying with the goals of the women's movement, goals such as equal rights, recognition of women's unpaid work, a fairer division of household labour, and an end to discrimination based on sex, ethnicity, physical or mental ability and sexual orientation.

... male and female students alike are confused and ambivalent about feminism ...

My students reflect the backlash against feminism in contemporary Canadian society, a backlash prompted by stirrings of animus against the welfare state in the 1980s and propelled by neoliberal and neoconservative ideas in the 1990s.[3] In the new millennium, feminist thinking is increasingly marginalized by dominant discourses about the social order and the role of governments. Neoliberals want the state to do less, and feminism is associated with the era of big government and state intervention. Neoconservatives seek the reinstatement of patriarchal social relations and are rabidly anti-feminist. Women's groups are cast as a "special interest" seeking to impose their selfish, particularistic interests on so-called ordinary Canadians. It is, therefore, hardly surprising that male and female students alike are confused and ambivalent about feminism and the political salience of the women's movement.

This chapter is designed to challenge popular misconceptions about feminism by offering a clear overview of the subject. Keeping in mind the complexity and diversity of feminist thought and practice, the first section of the chapter defines the concepts essential to understanding feminism and provides a brief description of the major currents in feminist theory. Anti-feminist arguments, such as the myth of feminist orthodoxy (the idea that all feminists share a unified doctrine) and the notion that the women's movement has won the so-called battle of the sexes, are described and refuted in the second section. The third part of the chapter looks at the ways in which feminism has influenced Canadian political life and public policy, and shows that the feminist project is as yet incomplete. I conclude with some thoughts about the future of feminism in an era of neoliberal globalism, characterized by globalization, the shrinking state, and new information technologies.

WHAT IS FEMINISM?

◆ ◆ ◆

Feminism is complex because it is, at one and the same time, three interrelated forces. It is an *ideology* (a coherent system of ideas that helps people understand social and political forces and formulate a vision of the good life), an *epistemological framework* (a way of understanding what constitutes genuine knowledge, how humans know things, and who the knowers are), and a *social movement* (a constellation of diverse groups whose activities are designed to promote social, economic, cultural and political change).[4] The ideology, the epistemology and the socio-political action sponsored by the feminist movement reinforce, challenge and change one another because of the inevitable interaction between ideas and their translation into practice. In other words, feminism provides ideas for transforming human societies, these ideas fuel the women's movement, and the social and political consequences of feminist activities spawn changes to feminist theories. And the cycle begins anew; fresh ideas are born, inspiring new practices, and old ideas are called into question.

But what ideas underpin feminist thought and action, and why are these ideas such important agents of political change? Feminism in all three of its manifestations is informed by three important concepts, namely gender, patriarchy and oppression. *Gender* is the social construction of sex characteristics into ways of thinking about being male and female. Biology determines whether a person is labelled girl or boy, but much of what it means to be male or female is socially determined. For instance, there is no biological imperative behind North American parents' predilection for dressing baby girls in pink, boys in blue. That women menstruate until menopause is a function of their sex; that societies have treated menstruation as a taboo, to the extent of segregating menstruating women, is a function of gender codes. *Gender codes* are the roles, characteristics, resources, norms and expectations assigned to people based on their sex. They are often taken for granted and uninterrogated. We expect women and girls to look and act "feminine," while "macho" behaviour and rugged masculinity are the hallmark of the man's man. Fortunately, gender codes are not one-dimensional or permanent; they vary by place and culture, change over time, and are informed by social constructions of ethnicity, sexual orientation, age, social class, and physical or mental disability. For example, women of certain nationalities are chosen to serve as nannies under the live-in caregiver program on the grounds that they are more nurturing, caring and tolerant.[5] Disabled women are assumed to be asexual.[6] Certainly gender codes for women change as we age; an elderly woman decked out like Britney Spears would draw stares.

Gender codes, including the continued expectation that women will perform the majority of unpaid domestic and nurturing tasks, are developed and reinforced in two ways; *discursively* (though language, mass media, propaganda, and other methods of spoken and unspoken communication) and *materially* (through economic and physical realities such as threats of physical harm, individual and state coercion, economic necessity or lack of mobility). Contemporary North American mass media construct the family idyll, complete with the bumbling, gormless dad (epitomized by Homer Simpson), the hyper-competent, all-knowing "supermom" (see virtually any American situation comedy), and the witty, rebellious but obedient children (*Eight Simple Rules for Dating My Teenage Daughter*). Take a moment to consider the gender codes evident in any television or print advertisement and think about how they might shape the behaviour and goals of girls and boys, men and women. Material circumstances continue to condition norms of femininity and masculinity. Because women often have less wealth and fewer resources at their disposal, their life choices are constrained. While popular culture reifies the white, privileged, attractive working mother, material realities literally cast many women into the impossible role of homemaker/employee, struggling to manage a double

shift of full-time work in the paid labour force plus full-time unpaid work in the home. As these examples of coding indicate, the social construction of gender roles is by no means neutral or egalitarian. Gender codes continue to reinforce patriarchy.

... consider the gender codes evident in any television or print advertisement ...

Patriarchy is a concept that, very simply put, means male privilege and female subordination. Patriarchal ideas and practices have changed over time, and patriarchy is expressed differently in various cultures, but at a minimum patriarchy refers to rule by men in both the *private sphere* of home and family and in the *public sphere* of the economy, formal politics, organized religion, and other non-domestic pursuits. Patriarchy embodies various forms of male power: sexual, social, cultural, economic or political. That men denied women the right to vote is a key example of patriarchal attitudes and behaviour, and it illustrates a vital element of patriarchy: men have more power than women and greater access to what is valued by the social group.[7] In patriarchal societies, male dominance is institutionalized (that is, embedded in social, political, economic and cultural institutions) and normalized (assumed to be natural and functional). For instance, we tend not to question the fact that most politicians are male, that the vast majority of highly-paid sports figures are men, that there are few female CEOs, and that female ordination remains unheard of in many faiths.

Patriarchy embodies various forms of male power: sexual, social, cultural, economic or political.

Male dominance of economic and political power relations is accompanied in patriarchal societies by control of knowledge. This is why feminist thought and practice is concerned with epistemology. The production of knowledge includes the framing of what can possibly be true, who can know it, and how truth is to be represented. As feminist philosopher Simone de Beauvoir said, "Representation of the world, like the world itself, is the work of men; they describe it from their own point of view, which they confuse with absolute truth."[8] The exclusion of women from the public sphere and their virtual confinement to the household were common features of patriarchal societies until and including parts of the 20th century. This treatment of women was based in large part on knowledge claims, namely the assumption of male intellectual superiority and female inferiority. Political, scientific and intellectual elites accepted as a universal truth that women were the weaker sex, by nature designed to perform domestic and nurturing tasks. According to this patriarchal epistemological framework, women were incapable of being objective "knowers" and were thereby denied a role in knowledge production. Contemporary mainstream epistemology claims to be gender-neutral and universally applicable, when in fact it remains masculinist (constructed from the standpoint of men, more specifically privileged white men). For instance, political scientist and [conservative] activist Tom Flanagan maintains that the dearth of female political party leaders, coupled with women leaders' lack of success in bring their parties into political office, is explained by the "fact" that women are genetically programmed to be less competitive and less interested in power than are men.[9] Feminist theories show how masculinist epistemology upholds patriarchal ideas, institutions and practices; feminist organizing attempts to empower women to challenge patriarchal assumptions and assert their own knowledge of human relationships, economic forces and possible political solutions to perennial social problems.

Oppression is the final concept central to feminism, as the oppression of women maintains patriarchal power relations. Feminist philosopher Marilyn Frye defines oppression as "a system of interrelated barriers and forces which reduce, immobilize and mould people who belong to a certain group, and effect their subordination to another group."[10] The idea that women as a group are oppressed by men as a group, however, is too simplistic to accurately characterize feminist thinking. For one thing, feminist scholars and practitioners are increasingly sensitive to the fact that women's oppression often transcends the category "women" to include subordination based on ethnicity, sexual orientation, disability, class, and other social groupings. In other words, many women face multiple forms of oppression. Aboriginal women, for example, may experience the devastating impact of gender, class, race and cultural discrimination.[11] Secondly, in some circumstances, certain women may be in a position to oppress men or other women. Economically privileged women may use their wealth to exploit the labour of lower-class men or women, for instance by employing migrant workers, contracting the services of poor women as surrogate mothers, or hiring ethnic minority women as live-in domestic servants.

The third problem with the conceptualization of men as a group oppressing women as a group is that it implies unrelenting power on the part of men, and perpetual victimhood for women. To conceptualize women as passive subjects of male authority is disempowering and demobilizing. Many feminists argue that it is important to acknowledge women's continued oppression while celebrating women's tenacity, courage, persistence and potential to make change.[12] So, is oppression still useful as a concept? Yes; even though relations of domination and subordination are complex, variable and constantly shifting, on the whole women continue to have less power, liberty and social status than do men. That women continue to be victims of poverty, spousal abuse, spousal homicide, sexual assault, [and] sexual harassment is evidence of their subordination.

How does feminism take these ideas about gender, patriarchy and oppression and formulate them as an ideology? The rather unsatisfying answer to this question is that there is no single answer. Feminist thought is diverse, and although critics of feminism tend to portray feminists as walking in ideological lockstep, no feminist orthodoxy exists. This is not surprising given the multifaceted nature of feminism. Feminism offers "explanations for the pervasiveness of relationships of domination and subordination between men and women, for different perceptions of the relevance of class, racial and ethnic differences among women, and for a range of understandings about the changes required to redress exploitative and oppressive relationships."[13] Variants of feminist theory offer different, and sometimes competing, explanations for these phenomena. How can there possibly be only one explanation for the status of women and one vision of the changes required to promote women's equality when women are so diverse in their experiences, goals, needs and ideas? There are many ideas about the origins of inequality, solutions for problems of oppression and conceptions of new, more just social relationships to replace the patriarchal order.[14] Contemporary scholarship describes a panoply of feminisms, including liberal, socialist, radical, Marxist, maternal, left-wing, psychoanalytic, Black, anti-racist, Aboriginal, lesbian, separatist, cultural, French/postmodern, equal rights, poststructuralist, ecological, and cyber feminism. The next section provides overviews of the most commonly employed feminist theories, as well as examples showing how theory informs practical politics. Most discussions of feminism include liberal, radical, socialist and postmodern variants of feminist thought. To summarize these approaches to feminism parsimoniously strips them of their complexity, so what follows is an oversimplified account of these important feminist theories.[15]

Liberal feminism is arguably the most familiar of the feminist theories because its ideas are congruent with the dominant ideology of North American society, liberalism. Accordingly, most people associate feminism with claims for equal rights, and rights-based discourse is rooted in liberal thought. Liberal feminists see women's oppression as fostered by unequal treatment, namely denial of access to equal opportunities in employment, education, politics and the arts—in sum, an absence of the basic equality rights associated with citizenship.[16] It was not until the 20th century that women in Canada were granted the right to vote, stand for political office, sign contracts, remain in certain paid jobs after marriage, join the medical and legal professions, obtain loans from financial institutions in their own names, and so on. Liberal feminists argue that when women are denied the opportunity to become free, self-actualizing individuals, and are required to perform household duties without pay or recognition, they form dependency relationships with men. The solution lies in achieving equal civil and political rights, judicial fairness, and economic equality for women so they can make free choices. Liberal feminists lobby for an end to bias and discrimination in the paid labour force, and the promotion of bodily autonomy for women. While liberal feminists do look to the state for policies promoting women's equality, they also press for women's empowerment through egalitarian gender-role socialization and education.

The appeal of liberal feminism is that it focuses on women's liberty, arguing that a woman is truly equal when she can freely choose to be a homemaker, a plumber or a prime minister. As well, liberal feminism speaks the familiar language of rights, rules and fairness. Liberal feminism reveals the social, legal and political practices that prevent women from competing on an equal footing with men, and seeks to reform these practices. It is this reformist approach that inspires criticism of liberal feminism by those feminists seeking more radical change, namely proponents of feminist theories critical of liberalism itself.

Radical feminists regard liberal feminism as an inadequate challenge to patriarchal power relations because it seeks to tinker with these relations rather than to transform them. Radical feminists want to confront patriarchal power relations at their root, the sex/gender system, which refers to the ways in which biological imperatives like women's reproductive roles, combined with gender codes and compulsory heterosexuality, have been employed to uphold women's subordination to men. Veiling, foot binding, arranged marriage, genital mutilation, witch burning, wife killing, chastity belts, sexual assault, wife battering and sexual harassment are examples of male control of women's bodies and sexuality. Explanations for these practices and solutions to the problem of male domination of the female body differ according to the branch of radical feminist theory. Some early writers advocated androgyny, with each individual equally valuing her feminine and masculine characteristics, while others suggested opting out of patriarchal heterosexual relationships by practicing celibacy, lesbianism or separatism (women living in separate societies). Contemporary radical feminists writers are more inclined to accept bisexual, same-sex and heterosexual relationships on the grounds that a women's sexuality is hers to determine. The radical feminist's focus on the body illustrates concern with the ways in which biological determinism (the belief that "a woman's nature and all of her possibilities are determined by her biology"[17]) and sexual control lie at the root of male dominance and female subordination.

Radical feminism is important because it unearths patriarchal power relations in the private sphere, thus answering questions unexplored by liberal feminists. For instance, a radical feminist might point out that, despite the entrenchment of equality rights in the Charter of Rights and Freedoms, considerable political and economic progress, and laws protecting women from sexual harassment, stalking, rape and physical abuse, women continue to face physical and sexual violence. On the other hand, radical feminism suffers from being less well understood than its liberal counterpart, thus misrepresented. It is radical feminists who are cast as anti-male, and whose ideas are dismissed as "too radical."

Socialist feminism points out another source of gender-based oppression, the capitalist mode of economic production. Socialist feminists build on the insights of radical feminist thinkers by showing how patriarchy and capitalism act, often with the assistance of the state, as intersecting and mutually reinforcing systems. This theoretical approach brings material realities into the analysis, arguing that a woman's status is shaped by her role in economic production as well as in biological (and social) reproduction. The sexual division of labour in the family consigns domestic and nurturing responsibilities to women, thereby reinforcing the sexual division of labour in the paid workforce, funnelling the majority of women into part-time or casual, low-paying "pink collar" jobs. Moreover, capitalist economies are fuelled by the unpaid work performed by women in the household as well as the underpaid labour of women who make up a readily exploitable and disposable reserve army of labour upon which employers can draw in times of need. Socialist feminists point out that government laws and policies often uphold the relationship between patriarchy and capitalism, when, for example, they limit support for child care, restrict employment insurance to full-time or steady employees, support stay-at-home parents with tax credits, and generally reinforce women's economic dependency on men and/or the state. For instance, "spouse-in-the-house" rules for social welfare cut single mothers off social assistance when they have sexual relationships with men, on the assumption that any man enjoying sexual intimacy with a woman should support her economically. Socialist feminists believe that patriarchy cannot be dismantled as long as state-supported capitalism goes unchallenged.

Socialist feminism fills key gaps in liberal and radical feminist thought by explaining how the intersection of domestic, economic and state practices in capitalist societies maintains the oppression of women. Yet this branch of feminist theory has suffered in recent years with the decline of socialism and the fall of Communist regimes, and finds little public support in an era of neoliberal restructuring. That being said, resistance to globalization and neoliberal policies is increasingly evidenced in protest politics, with feminist and socialist social movements at the forefront of the anti-globalization critique.

Postmodern variants of feminism are most difficult to grasp but have inspired new and important directions for feminist inquiry. Postmodern feminism questions the existence of universal truths, arguing that since the symbolic order (our "taken for granted" world) is socially constructed, there can be no single version of any event or communication. Similarly, reality is not set, but is continually being structured, deconstructed and reconstituted by discourses (ideas, words, texts, images). The

discussion, above, of the ever-changing, and culturally variable nature of gender codes, nicely illustrates this key element of postmodern feminist theory. Postmodern feminists challenge any attempt to integrate feminist thought or practice into a unified whole on just these grounds. Indeed, postmodern feminist writers challenge the very concept of "woman" itself, arguing that women's diversity makes it impossible to conceive of an integrated women's identity or political project.

Seeing language as the main instrument of patriarchy, postmodern feminists employ counter-discourses to disturb and even displace the masculinist symbolic order. This is difficult because of male domination of language and knowledge. Postmodern feminists must somehow challenge the symbolic order when the instruments available are products of this order. One method adopted by some postmodern feminists is to disrupt the male view of reality by offering an alternative female/feminine view. In other words, women can "write themselves out of the world men have constructed for them by putting into words the unthinkable/unthought," including subversive and transformative ideas.[18]

While it is difficult to get a fix on much postmodern thought, as it is often deliberately obscure and even self-contradictory, postmodern feminism has been crucial to the evolution of feminist thinking and mobilizing because of its emphasis on women's diversity. Early feminism was often inattentive to multiple sources of oppression and tended to speak from a white, middle-class, able-bodied, and heterosexist standpoint. Many women pointed out that this mythical "universal woman" did not capture their particular experiences or social positions. Postmodern fracturing of the category "woman" has reinforced the need to recognize and celebrate women's differences from one another, especially when attempts to build coalitions and solidarity falter.

How do these diverse theoretical positions translate into political practice? Sometimes different variants of feminism lead to different positions on policy issues, while in other instances feminists take divergent stances. To see how different feminist theories examine a practical policy issue, let us look at prostitution as an example. Socialist and radical feminists tend to regard prostitution as a practice that degrades, abuses and exploits women. For radical feminists, prostitution epitomizes the victimization and objectification of women, with the male customer or pimp in the role of the oppressor, and the female sex-trade worker the vulnerable, dependent victim. For many radical feminists, prostitution represents an extreme form of exploitation of women's bodies. State regulation of the buying and selling of sexual services is supported by some radical feminists on the grounds that women need protection from sexual subordination and from the violence endemic to the sex trade. For instance, a radical feminist might applaud the B.C. government's decision to provide Vancouver-area prostitutes, while under threat from a serial killer ... with cell phones programmed to make 911 calls.

Similarly, socialist feminists see prostitution as gender-based exploitation characteristic of patriarchal societies, but also as illustrative of capitalist exploitation of women's labour. A woman's sexuality is commodified by prostitution, a result that at one and the same time is beneficial and harmful. On the one hand, by selling their sexual services, prostitutes defiantly assign economic value to physical labour that is otherwise unpaid, thereby challenging the sex/gender order. On the other hand, sex trade workers normally don't control their livelihood because their work is regulated by pimps, escort agencies[,] and the state. Socialist feminists would also point out that it is typically economic inequality based on gender, class, and ethnicity that leads women into the sex trade. State action, including criminalization of "communication for the purposes of prostitution,"[19] only masks the true problem, namely inequalities of wealth. There is no easy solution in a capitalist society. Socialist feminists might support the creation of collectives or cooperatives for prostitutes; while still commodified, their labour would be controlled by the sex-trade workers themselves.

A liberal would be inclined to argue that women freely choose to work in the sex trade. A liberal feminist would quibble with this interpretation, pointing out the paucity of employment options, especially for women without much formal education, and argue that prostitution is not usually the result of a truly autonomous choice. Women are constrained in the workplace by unequal pay, lack of access to permanent, full-time, well-paying jobs, and by sexual harassment and inadequate child care. Moreover, without a post-secondary education, most women have little to choose from besides low-wage jobs, so prostitution is often a rational option, one ensuring economic survival. The long-term solution for liberal feminists lies in greater access to education and job training coupled with workplace reform. While a liberal feminist is likely to support government attempts to ban child prostitution, as

children have not yet reached the age of consent or autonomy and need the protection of the state, most would be opposed to criminal sanctions against adult sex-trade workers. The liberal feminist focus on individual autonomy supports economic independence for prostitutes, coupled with the right of women to make decisions about their own bodies.

A postmodern feminist may challenge any totalizing characterization of the prostitute by pointing out that women who do this work for pay have different family histories, ethnicities, class positions and life goals. They cannot be homogenized, and their interests cannot be reduced to a single policy solution. As well, the project of the postmodern feminist is to show how the discursive construction of prostitutes and prostitution is as important as the physical and material realities associated with the act of prostitution itself. The postmodern feminist would ask how the sex trade worker is characterized in different texts, such as news reports, movies and books. Is she seen voyeuristically through a male gaze, or is she allowed to speak and act for herself? Is she stereotyped as the drug-addicted, pimp-dependent victim (imagery conveyed by many news reports) or is she portrayed as the good-hearted young woman temporarily down on her luck, in need of rescue by the "right man" (for example, the Julia Roberts/Richard Gere movie *Pretty Woman*). Postmodern feminists are likely to recommend the creation of new images of the sex-trade worker through texts imagined and communicated by the prostitute herself.

As this brief discussion has revealed, feminism in theory and practice features some core assumptions, but is marked by diversity of ideas and strategies. This diversity is a source of both weakness and strength. Because feminism defies easy characterization, its critics can stereotype feminist theory or practice by highlighting the most radical or provocative ideas (this problem is illustrated in the next section, on antifeminism). Conversely, by pointing out apparent contradictions in feminist thought, critics can maintain that feminism is too inconsistent to generate coherent ideas or facilitate practical political strategies for change. Diversity in thought and practice can also be positive, not least as inspiration for renewal. Feminism's flexibility means that when new ideas appear or old ideas are challenged, theories and projects may be demobilized, but they are rarely destroyed. Because a multiplicity of voices and ideas exist within feminist praxis, feminism is permeable and adaptable. Feminism is constantly reinventing itself.

> *... critics can stereotype feminist theory or practice by highlighting the most radical or provocative ideas ...*

Feminism is of necessity woman-centred, so can men be feminists? The feminist historian Gerda Lerner would answer no to this question, because she defines feminist consciousness as the awareness *of women* that because they belong to a subordinate and oppressed group they must *join with other women* to remedy discrimination and to create a society in which women will enjoy autonomy and self-determination.[20] But can't men be aware that women tend to be subordinated while men are privileged by patriarchal practices? Can't men join with women to remedy injustice and dismantle restrictive gender codes? In my view, of course they can. There are plenty of Canadian examples of men's involvement in feminist movements for social change. Men were active participants in the suffrage movement, which sought the vote for women. Toronto academic, writer and activist Michael Kauffman helped create the White Ribbon Campaign to end male violence toward women. However, while men can critique the status quo and work for change, women must claim power on their own behalf. There is an important difference between representation *for* women's interests (which can be carried out by both men and women), and representation *by* women (which can only be conducted by women).[21] Women themselves must identify the restrictions imposed by gender codes and develop appropriate strategies for empowerment.

ANTI-FEMINISM

◆ ◆ ◆

Anti-feminists dispute the very core of feminist thought, the idea that gender codes are socially constructed. As the following quotation illustrates, opponents of feminism see sex roles as natural, that is, as biologically determined.

> Moms are moms and dads are dads. So far no pill or twisted thinking can change the fact that women produce babies and, as nature intended, feed them from their breasts. Let us honour the father as the breadwinner, the hero who brings home the bacon. This is his position in the animal kingdom. Let the

mother be the nurturer, the caregiver, the producer of the next generation, the homemaker.[22]

Now feminists would not disagree with the assertion that gender roles are shaped by women's reproductive role. They would, however, take issue with the cornerstone of anti-feminism, the idea that the hetero-patriarchal family is best for men, women and children, and that any deviation from this norm is dangerous. Anti-feminist writer William Gairdner says society as we know it will crumble if the traditional family is disrupted. Gairdner calls radical feminists "the new barbarians of modern society" because they challenge the strict assignment of nurturing roles to women.[23]

Few Canadians believe that biology is destiny. The vast majority support equal rights for women, including reproductive choice, equality in the workplace, and equal benefit of the law.[24] Still, anti-feminism enjoys a certain currency because its proponents exploit two myths about feminism. The first is the myth of feminist orthodoxy—the notion of a unified and homogenous feminist position that is rigidly anti-male and anti-family. The second myth holds that feminism has triumphed and gender equality is now a reality. As one Canadian journalist put it, "the war's over," and women won.[25]

> *Few Canadians believe that biology is destiny.*

These two myths are often linked, with anti-feminist argumentation going something like this: The feminist movement has emerged victorious from the gender wars but because feminist activists do not wish to relinquish their power and notoriety, they continue to insist women are oppressed. Since women are in fact no longer subjugated by men, feminists justify their activism by promoting extremist, intolerant, anti-male ideas backed up by dodgy statistics and even outright lies. Journalist Donna Laframboise argues this case, insisting that since the "big battles have been won," a few radical feminist "nut cases" have taken over the women's movement.[26] These "extreme elements" insist "the entire male population is a menace," rail against heterosexual marriage, and attack the family. The credibility of these feminists is now in question, asserts Laframboise, because they use "sloppy arithmetic and skewed data" to mislead the public about issues like male violence against women. Similarly, *Edmonton Journal* columnist Lorne Gunter maintains feminists have perpetuated the "lie" that men are largely responsible for domestic violence, denying or covering up the fact that "women are as likely, perhaps even a little more so, to abuse their partners severely."[27] Feminists do this, claims Gunter, so they can preserve their "grip over politics, the media and, particularly, the courts."

Feminism challenges the patriarchal family, not the family *per se*; it is woman-centred, not anti-male; and while it features radical and transformative ideas, these ideas neither dominate feminist thought and practice, nor do they preclude competing ideas. For example, popular wisdom, and anti-feminist rhetoric, maintains that feminism single-mindedly lobbies for women's rights in the paid workforce and ignores the plight of stay-at-home moms. Yet, in 1997, Canada's largest umbrella feminist organization, the National Action Committee on the Status of Women (NAC), organized a conference to seek greater support and recognition for women's unpaid work in the home and to articulate the policy needs of homemakers.[28] But what about the argument that the women's movement has achieved most, if not all, of its goals, rendering feminism irrelevant and unnecessary? And are feminists really suppressing the truth about their success in order to maintain their grip on political power? Feminism has helped reshape Canadian politics and society, but as the data cited in the next section show, substantive equality is far from the reality for most women.

---

*Feminism challenges the patriarchal family,
not the family per se.*

FEMINISM AND POLITICAL ACTION IN CANADA

◆ ◆ ◆

Feminism, as expressed through the women's movement, has had a profound and measurable effect on Canadian society. The women's movement has "touched the lives of many Canadian women, radically transforming the nature of their everyday experiences."[29] My mother, who came with her family to Canada from Czechoslovakia in 1937, had her name changed by immigration authorities and school teachers, ran away from home at age 16 to escape an arranged marriage, and was pressured by social norms to quit her job after marrying my father, even though they needed both incomes. My life choices have been much freer thanks to the hard work of feminist activists. I have been able to make choices about reproduction, marriage, child care and work that simply were not available to women of my mother's generation. Until the 1940s and even later, laws and policies promoted the traditional family, assuming that women would marry, become financially dependent on their husbands, bear and rear children. For instance, the sale, distribution and use of birth control devices were all illegal acts until 1969. Abortion was also banned by the Criminal Code until 1969, and allowed under only very strict conditions until the law was struck down by the Supreme Court in 1988. Maternity leave and child-care centres were virtually unknown until the 1970s, and women could be fired from their jobs if they became pregnant.

At Confederation women were denied many basic citizenship rights because they were seen as incompatible with women's roles and the proper functioning of the patriarchal family. "Woman's first and only place is in the home," asserted political, religious and medical elites in turn-of-the century Canada. The early women's movement lobbied for several decades to win political and civil rights for women such as the right to vote, stand for office, own and control wages and property, enter the professions, stay in the workplace after marriage, and claim Canadian citizenship status in their own right.[30] These rights have been extended gradually to women, but not all at the same time. For example, the right to vote in federal elections was granted to white women in 1918, Asian and Indo-Canadians in 1948, status Indians in 1960, and persons with mental disabilities in 1991. Basic citizenship rights continue to elude some women despite the entrenchment of equality rights in the constitution. Rights in law don't necessarily translate into access to and enjoyment of formal entitlements. Immigration laws and regulations still work to keep women out of Canada on the basis of their race, class and gender.[31] Gays and lesbians … fought a long battle for the formal right to marry, a claim now [recognized] by Canadian courts [and Parliament].

A central goal of the women's movement has been to engender rights, that is, to interpret basic citizenship rights in ways that recognize women's experiences and needs. Engendering rights has transformed the defini- tion of what is political, as captured by the feminist slogan "the personal is political." For example, the right to bodily autonomy has only recently been con- ceptualized to include women's sexual autonomy within marriage. Until 1983 men could not be charged with raping their wives because it was assumed that a woman was in a constant state of sexual consent to her husband; as his sexual property, she had no right to say no. Similarly, the right to security of the person, which of necessity obliges the state to protect people from bodily harm, was not extended to women facing harm from spousal abuse until the mid-1980s. Before then it was argued that the state had no business intruding in or interfering with domestic relationships. Women's groups have brought to the political fore a range of issues previously considered private, or non-political, such as child care, the sexual division of labour in the home and workplace, unequal pay, reproduction, sex- role stereotyping in education and discrimination based on sex, ethnicity, sexual orientation and mental or phys- ical ability. The Canadian women's movement has pur- sued a variety of goals, including but certainly not limited to legal rights. Some groups eschew formal leg- islative politics, choosing instead to help women directly by providing services such as job counselling, rape crisis intervention, shelters for those forced to flee domestic violence, and language training for new immigrants.

The creation of the Canadian welfare state, which evolved between the 1930s and 1970s, provided some measure of social citizenship for women. Social citizen- ship, the right to basic economic welfare and security, is often referred to as the social safety net. The term *wel- fare state* means an approach to governance based on the belief that social citizenship can and should be fos- tered by governments, partly through the provision of universal social programs, including public education, health care, income security, and wage replacement. As a result of welfare state policies, some women have received help with domestic responsibilities, such as caring for children, elderly relatives, and people with special needs. As well, women have filled public sector jobs, working as nurses, teacher, social workers and clerical staff for municipal, First Nations, federal and provincial governments. Yet progress for women under the welfare state was limited, as programs often assumed the existence of stable, self-sufficient nuclear families with men as breadwinners, women as domestic labourers. The policies of the welfare state did little to

change the limited choices for women, namely eco- nomic dependency on men (marriage) or reliance on the state (social assistance). Woman-centred demands for national child care programs, recognition and funding of midwifery, language and job training for immigrant women, and culturally sensitive social welfare services have largely been ignored.

While the welfare state never fully incorporated women's realities and needs, it is now being eroded by Canadian governments in their quest to tackle stag- gering debt loads and balance budgets. Federal funding to the provinces has been reduced, sparking spending cuts to education, health care and social programs as well as restructuring measures such as privatization of government services, deregulation, and decentralization of programs and services. These shifts in fiscal and social policy are driven by changes to the global order. Neoliberalism, the ideological handmaiden of globaliza- tion, seeks the freest possible market for transnational capital, and thus espouses a larger role for the market and a smaller role for the state. Neoliberals want to replace government services with private-sector con- tracts, insist on individual self-reliance, and label as "special interests" those groups who make demands on the state. For most women, who rely more heavily than do most men on the welfare state, and who are far from achieving economic self-reliance, the shrinking welfare state is cause for alarm.[32]

If we accept the anti-feminist claim that most patri- archal practices have been erased and women can now compete on a level playing field with men, the neolib- eral edict of self-sufficiency is of little concern. If femi- nism has triumphed, women should be able to survive in an increasingly competitive marketplace. This view hinges on the assumption that women now have as much political and economic power as men and share equal access to the goods and resources valued by our society. Feminists would challenge this assumption on the grounds that many women do not yet enjoy eco- nomic autonomy and personal liberty, and political equality remains elusive. The majority of Canadian women are underemployed and underpaid. Women comprise the majority of part-time, casual and min- imum wage workers, holding 68 percent of Canada's lowest-paying jobs. Even those in full-time employment are disadvantaged by unequal pay, taking home an average of 73 percent of a man's paycheque.[33] Immigrant women, ethnic minority women, Aboriginal women, and women with disabilities are significantly more likely to be unemployed than other workers, male or female.[34] Women run greater risks than men of living in poverty, especially if they are single mothers, elderly, or have disabilities. Sadly, women who cannot rely on the financial support of men are likely to be poor.

... many women do not yet enjoy economic autonomy and personal liberty, and political equality remains elusive.

Women also remain markedly under-represented in political office. As of June 15, 2003, after a spate of provincial elections, women's share of the seats in federal, provincial and territorial legislatures is just over 20 percent.[35] The most recent elections across jurisdictions confirm the existence of an electoral glass ceiling for women, as the number of elected women has stalled and is unlikely to surpass 25 percent of the legislators in the near future. The one exception is Quebec, where women won 30 percent of the seats in the April 2003 election. Particular groups of women—ethnic minority, lesbian, Aboriginal, disabled—remain grossly under-represented in formal political institutions.[36] Government agencies designed to represent women's policy interests, such as the Canadian Advisory Council on the Status of Women and the Alberta Advisory Council on Women's Issues, have been dismantled, and NAC is struggling to stay afloat. At present, the political currency of the women's movement is at an all-time low because "it is being recast as just another special interest group whose claims for state intervention are both self-interested and oppositional to the collective interest."[37]

... women's share of the seats in federal, provincial and territorial legislatures is just over 20 percent.

Women continue to shoulder most of the responsibility for child-rearing and domestic duties, layering paid work on top of their household work and volunteer efforts. According to Statistics Canada, even those women with paid employment perform more than their share of domestic work, a situation that restricts their job mobility, chances of promotion and personal autonomy.[38] Women's liberty is further constrained by

violence inside and outside the home, as well as by women's fears of sexual and physical violence. While attitudes about a woman's place have changed dramatically, patriarchal notions persist. In 2001, female employees of a British Columbia telecommunications company finally won the right to wear slacks to work.[39] A 1997 survey of women elected to federal and provincial legislatures discovered that almost two-thirds of them had endured inappropriate, sexist or gender-based demeaning remarks.[40] Indeed, media coverage of B.C. New Democrat leader Joy MacPhail's [2003] decision to leave political life included a photo of her crying, made reference to her "changing hairstyles" and described her as "the sexiest woman in politics."[41] As these examples and the Statistics Canada data cited above show, feminists do not need to tell lies or fudge data when arguing that while progress for some Canadian women has been considerable, there is much ground yet to gain.

CONCLUSION

The political realm is changing rapidly. The state is shrinking, national boundaries are being eroded by forces of globalization, knowledge-based economies are redefining work, and Canada is among the most wired nations in the world, with the majority of its citizens travelling the information superhighway. What does all of this mean for feminism? Critics, including anti-feminists, might say feminism is doomed because it is mired in old paradigms. The evidence suggests otherwise, as feminism continues to change and progress. The women's movement has been shaped by globalization, with new information and communication technologies facilitating international organizing by feminists and coalition-building with other social movements. Women's groups from countries around the world are analyzing the impact of globalization on women, examining everything from the control of plant genetics by transnational agribusiness to the international sex trade in girls and women. Women's groups are inventing new ways to manoeuvre in a world that features increasing economic polarization, global terrorism, and permeable national boundaries.

The reaction of feminist thinkers and women's groups to new information and communication technologies (ICTs) illustrates the continued evolutionary potential of feminism. Some feminist theorists and activists are joining the wired world at the same time as they are challenging its underlying power dynamics. By analyzing the relationship between global capitalism and digital technology, measuring the impact of ICTs on women's work, and challenging male dominance of digital resources and discourses, feminists are deconstructing digital culture. Women's groups increasingly use the World Wide Web to create virtual communities, strategize and organize. A new breed of activists called cyberfeminists believes the Internet presents women with new possibilities for engineering social change.[42] This being said, there is no doubt feminism is under siege in an era of neoliberal globalism. Radical and socialist feminism in particular seem anachronistic in contrast to the neoliberal mantra of less government, individual economic autonomy, and global competitiveness. Long-standing feminist policy demands, such as a universal day care program, are seen as antithetical to the goals of the neoliberal order because they require government funding and state intervention in

the "private" market. Liberal feminism arguably stands the best chance of penetrating neoliberal roadblocks to change. "Freedom, personal autonomy, and economic independence remain key goals for Canadian women, and neoliberals are hard-pressed to argue against these values...."[43]

Because feminism challenges the status quo and envisions significant social, economic and political transformations, it disturbs those who resist change. Feminist action is met with anti-feminist reaction. Yet despite rumours of its demise and, in some quarters, insistence on its irrelevance, feminism remains alive and well because it lies at the heart of women's struggles for justice, equality and independence. As the economic, social and political context for these struggles changes, so does feminist thought and activism. Internal debates and external challenges alike will help feminism hold its course as the new millennium unfolds.

Notes

1. William Gairdner espouses this view in *The War Against the Family* (Toronto: Stoddart, 1992), p. 116.
2. See Brenda O'Neill, "On the Same Wavelength? Feminist Attitudes Across Generations of Canadian Women," in *Women and Electoral Politics in Canada*, ed. Manon Tremblay and Linda Trimble (Don Mills: Oxford University Press, 2003), pp. 178–91.
3. Linda Trimble, "Women and the Politics of Citizenship," in *Reinventing Canada: Politics of the 21st Century*, ed. Janine Brodie and Linda Trimble (Scarborough: Prentice-Hall, 2003), pp. 131–50.
4. This is adapted from Karen Offen, "Defining Feminism: A Comparative Historical Approach," *Signs* 114, 1 (1988): p. 119–57.
5. Tanya Schecter, *Race, Class, Women and The State: The Case of Domestic Labour* (Montreal: Black Rose Books, 1998), p. 122.
6. Judith Zelman, a disabled woman who uses a wheelchair, described the shock and consternation of colleagues and friends when she announced her pregnancy. Zelman felt the reaction was due in part to the assumption that disabled people are asexual and/or childlike. Judith Zelman, "Pregnant with Disability: Expecting but Unexpected," *Globe and Mail*, October 8, 1997, p. A28.
7. Lorraine Code, "Feminist Theory," in Sandra Burt et al., *Changing Patterns: Women in Canada*, 2nd ed. (Toronto: McClelland & Stewart, 1993), p. 19.
8. Quoted in Lorraine Code, *What Can She Know? Feminist Theory and Construction of Knowledge* (Ithaca and London: Cornell University Press, 1991), p. ix.
9. Linda Trimble and Jane Arscott, *Still Counting: Women in Politics Across Canada* (Peterborough: Broadview Press, 2003), p. 76. Trimble and Arscott show that women's lack of success in the leadership role is a function not of biology but of the fact that they typically take over wounded or ailing parties, parties without much chance of winning office.
10. Marilyn Frye, *The Politics of Reality: Essays in Feminist Theory* (Freedom, Calif.: The Crossing Press, 1983), p. 33.
11. Sally Weaver, "First Nations Women and Government Policy, 1970–92: Discrimination and Conflict," in Burt et al., *Changing Patterns*, 2nd ed., p. 128.
12. See Naomi Wolf, *Fire with Fire* (Toronto: Random House, 1993), pp. 135–42.
13. Roberta Hamilton, *Gendering the Vertical Mosaic: Feminist Perspectives on Canadian Society* (Toronto: Copp Clark, 1996), p. 4.
14. Jill Vickers, *Reinventing Political Science: A Feminist Approach* (Halifax: Fernwood, 1997), p. 196.
15. For a more thorough account of these theories, see Rosemarie Tong, *Feminist Thought: A Comprehensive Introduction* (Boulder and San Francisco: Westview Press, 1980).
16. For an elaboration of this argument see Trimble, "Women and the Politics of Citizenship."
17. Code, "Feminist Theory," pp. 22–23.

18. Tong, *Feminist Thought,* pp. 224–25.

19. Under the Canadian criminal code, selling sex is not illegal, but communication for the purpose of selling sex is against the law, as is operating a "bawdy house" and living off the avails of prostitution.

20. Gerda Lerner, *The Creation of Feminist Consciousness* (New York: Oxford University Press, 1993), p. 14.

21. Jane Arscott and Linda Trimble, "Introduction," in *In the Presence of Women: Representation in Canadian Governments,* ed. Jane Arscott and Linda Trimble (Toronto: Harcourt, 1997), p. 4.

22. Letter to the editor of the *Toronto Star,* quoted in Pat Armstrong and Hugh Armstrong, *The Double Ghetto,* 3rd ed. (Toronto: McClelland & Stewart, 1994), p. 144.

23. Gairdner, *The War Against the Family,* p. 302.

24. See O'Neill, "On the Same Wavelength?" p. 185.

25. Danielle Crittenden, "Let's Junk the Feminist Slogans: The War's Over," *Chatelaine,* August 1990, p. 38.

26. Donna Laframboise, "You've Come a Long Way, Baby … and for What?" *Globe and Mail,* July 26, 1997, pp. D1, D3.

27. Lorne Gunter, "Women Must Share Spousal Abuse Blame," *Edmonton Journal,* September 28, 1997, p. G8.

28. Paula Brook, "Every Mother Is a Working Mother," *Globe and Mail,* October 25, 1997, pp. D1, D3.

29. Burt et al., "Introduction," in *Changing Patterns,* 2nd ed., p. 9.

30. See Sandra Burt, "The Changing Patterns of Public Policy," in Burt et al., *Changing Patterns,* 2nd ed., pp. 213–15.

31. Yasmeen Abu-Laban, "Keeping, 'Em Out: Gender, Race and Class Biases in Canadian Immigration Policy," in Joan Anderson et al., ed., *Painting the Maple: Essays on Race,* *Gender and the Construction of Canada* (Vancouver: UBC Press, 1999), pp. 69–82.

32. Janine Brodie, *Politics on the Margins: Restructuring and the Canadian Women's Movement* (Halifax: Fernwood Press, 1995).

33. Canada, *Women in Canada, 2000* (Ottawa: Statistics Canada), available Statistics Canada site www.statcan.ca

34. Canada, *Women in Canada, 2000.*

35. See Trimble and Arscott, *Still Counting,* p. 50, and their Web site stillcounting.athabascau.ca, for updated information on women's status in electoral politics.

36. Regarding the representation of ethnic minority women, see Jerome Black, "Differences That Matter: Minority Women MPs, 1993–2000," in Tremblay and Trimble, *Women and Electoral Politics in Canada,* pp. 59–74.

37. Janine Brodie, "Restructuring and the Politics of Marginalization," in *Women and Political Representation in Canada,* eds. Manon Tremblay and Caroline Andrew (Ottawa: University of Ottawa Press, 1998), p. 34.

38. Canada, *Women in Canada, 2000.*

39. Jim Beatty, "Female Operators Okayed to Wear Pants," *National Post,* February 5, 2001, p. A8.

40. Trimble and Arscott, *Still Counting,* p. 112.

41. Canadian Press, "B.C. New Democrat Leader Joy MacPhail Quitting, Says Party Needs New Blood," Canada.com news, June 13, 2003.

42. See Melanie Stewart Millar, *Cracking the Gender Code* (Toronto: Second Storey Press, 1998), p. 60.

43. Trimble, "Women and the Politics of Citizenship," p. 147.

Terms and Concepts

patriarchy
gender codes
liberal feminism
radical feminism
socialist feminism

postmodern feminism
biological determinism
private and public spheres
neoliberalism
welfare state

engendered rights
equality
anti-feminism

Questions

1. Why does the word "feminism" elicit such strong reactions? Aren't we all now liberal feminists?

2. Have the battles of feminism been largely won? If not, what is left to be done?

3. Is there a common core of beliefs among the varieties of feminism?

4. How does feminism redefine the scope of politics? How does it challenge the family in particular as a social organization?

5. How does Trimble suggest that the growth of the welfare state, and its more recent scaling back, affect women in particular?

In Defense of Nationalism

John O'Sullivan

Editors' Note

"Nationalism" is not merely one of the most important political phenomena in today's world; it is also one of the most puzzling.

Since the era of Pierre Trudeau, English Canadians have been taught to think of nationalism as a bad thing—especially when practised by Quebecers. Trudeau made his career preaching that nationalism—which he understood as the idea that every "nation" should have its own state—is at its core intolerant and perhaps even racist.

Trudeau's response to Quebec nationalism was to try to build a Canada that would transcend nationalism in the directions of bilingualism and multiculturalism.

It would seem that Trudeau's plan was largely successful, for contemporary Canadians typically take great pride in our bilingual and multicultural identity. Indeed, we often point to these two principles as the crucial characteristics that separate us from the United States and its "melting pot." And yet, isn't

our pride in these distinctions ultimately a form of, well—*nationalism*?

In this provocative essay, John O'Sullivan explores the various meanings and forms of nationalism in the early 21st century. O'Sullivan is highly critical of some of the more popular opinions about nationalism. On the basis of his analysis, one might well wonder about the long-term viability of the particular form of nationalism that is ascendant in Canada today.

◆ ◆ ◆

To say that we live in an age of nationalism is both a platitude and a provocation. It is a platitude because there are more nation-states in the world of today than at any other time in history. Decolonization gave birth to several score new nation-states in Africa and Asia from the 1940s to the 1970s. The collapse of the Soviet Union and the breakup of the Yugoslav Federation released a number of "new" old nation-states from communist imprisonment across Central Europe to Central Asia. And unsatisfied nationalist movements today seek statehood from the Basque country to Palestine.

Yet nationalism also runs counter to other trends: namely, that the internet and globalization are shaping a borderless world in which multinational corporations are more powerful than governments; that transnational bodies from the European Union to the International Criminal Court are usurping powers

that once belonged to sovereign states; and that new non-governmental organizations claim to represent public opinion on international questions more faithfully than democratic governments. So nationalism looks increasingly constrained functionally even as its geographical sway extends.

To complicate matters further, there are influential intellectual trends in the advanced world that deny the legitimacy of nationalism altogether as an atavistic concept. Their adherents regard nationalism as an obstacle to human rights, international harmony and economic rationality. They accordingly seek to reduce the scope of national sovereignty in international affairs, transferring power upwards to global bodies and downwards to ethnic and other subgroups. Both President Bill Clinton and Prime Minister Tony Blair justified their Kosovo intervention in terms not simply of halting ethnic cleansing, but of defending the positive principle of multi-ethnic

"In Defense of Nationalism" by John O'Sullivan from *The National Interest*, Winter 2004/2005. Reprinted with permission.

statehood. And General Wesley Clark stated flatly: "There is no place in modern Europe for *ethnically pure* states. That's a 19th century idea and we are trying to transition into the 21st century, and we are going to do it with multiethnic states" (emphasis added).

To those who think of nationalism as a natural loyalty to one's nation and who therefore regard the Westphalian system of nation-states as an equally natural world order, this hostility to nationalism must be something of an intellectual mystery. Is railing against nationalism not as foolish as cursing the weather or complaining that water will not run uphill? Have not nations existed since time immemorial? Is it not reasonable as well as right that a people who lack their own state, such as the Kurds, should strive to acquire one or that a people who have their own state, such as the British, should seek to protect its sovereignty against legal erosion or military attack?

These questions probably strike most people in Western countries as common sense even today. But since the Second World War—not coincidentally—there has been an immense scholarly dispute over the naturalness of nationalism. Writing in *The National Interest* (Fall 1997), Anatol Lieven, the historian and journalist, summed up this debate:

> One side of the scholarly debate on the origins of nationalism stems ultimately from the belief that ... the roots of modern national allegiances lie in old and deeply felt ethnic, linguistic, religious and cultural differences ... In Western academia in recent decades, however, this approach has not been so much dissected as slashed to pieces by a range of scholars who have ... sought to expose the numerous ways in which nationalisms and, indeed, national traditions were artificially created in modern times.

Natural or artificial? These are the two points of view from which we are generally asked to choose. Good authorities can be cited to justify each of them. Suppose, however, that both viewpoints mix quite different things under the name of nationalism? Might they then not both be wrong—or at least oversimplified? Let me suggest that this is the case and that three quite different sorts of political commitment have been confused under one misleadingly similar heading.

These three concepts are, first, the political doctrine that the nation is the only legitimate basis for statehood; second, the political emotion of collective loyalty that might be attached to a nation, a race, a class, a religion or even a political ideology; and, third, the sense of national identity, sometimes called patriotism, that arises from living together under the same institutions and sharing a common language and culture over time.

... that three quite different sorts of political commitment have been confused under one misleadingly similar heading.

The concepts may seem indistinguishable at first hearing. And they are all linked, as we shall see. But they also differ fundamentally. To see exactly how, let us examine each one in detail, beginning with nationalism as a doctrine of statehood.

Elie Kedourie's classic book *Nationalism* opens with this simple but dramatic definition:

> Nationalism is a doctrine invented in Europe at the beginning of the 19th century. It pretends to supply a criterion for the determination of the unit of population proper to enjoy a government exclusively its own for the legitimate exercise of power in the state and for the right organization of a society of states. Briefly, the doctrine holds that humanity is naturally divided into nations; that nations are known by certain characteristics which can be ascertained; and that the only legitimate type of government is national self-government.

Those sentences are quite literally mind-altering. At least they altered my own mind when I first read them, persuading me that my own unexamined sense of nationalism as a natural emotion like love of family was simply a misconception. Once we grant Professor Kedourie's definition, moreover, we are drawn eventually to the conclusion that nationalism is not just an intellectual error, but also a destructive one.

To begin with, the doctrinal nationalism he condemns is rooted in a false and ideological conception of statehood. Its underlying error is to suppose that legitimate statehood must rest upon some universally valid principle. In fact, states are the product of history and accordingly rest upon many different foundations—dynasty, ethnicity, culture, religion, ideology, conquest and revolution.

No sensible statesman asks of a state: "Is it based upon a recognizable nation?" (Or, as Clinton and Blair might prefer, "is it multi-ethnic?") He asks rather: "Is it stable? Does it have generally accepted boundaries? Does its government really control its territory? Does it enjoy the loyalty of its citizens?" And so on. If these questions can be answered more or less positively, then it scarcely matters whether population of the state is ethnically pure, as for instance Norway, or composed of several ethnic groups, as for instance the United Kingdom. It is likely to be a reasonably successful state and an orderly presence on the international scene.

Doctrinal nationalism is also rooted in a false account of history. As a matter of historical fact, very few states can trace their origins to ethnically distinct peoples that have remained uncontaminated by their neighbors over the centuries. That is why historians and teachers were conscripted in the 19th century—and more recently in the Balkans—to trace their present nation back to ancient times with the help of maps, poems and ancient scripts. The objection to this is not that it is patriotic in effect—so is much good history— but that it is false and invented for a political purpose.

As a matter of historical fact, very few states can trace their origins to ethnically distinct peoples that have remained uncontaminated by their neighbors over the centuries.

As it happens, in Europe, where doctrinal nationalism was itself invented, very few existing states fitted the nationalist theory. In Hugh Seton-Watson's words: "Every England has its Ireland, and every Ireland had its Ulster." Nationalism was therefore divisive—not in the modern sense of stimulating debate, but because it encouraged national minorities to seek the breakup of the state in which they were allegedly imprisoned, and because it gave neighboring states a pretext to intervene on their behalf. Conflict was perhaps inherent in the circumstances of Mitteleuropa. At the very least, however, doctrinal nationalism aggravated it.

If doctrinal nationalism is easy to dismiss or condemn, does that demolish nationalism of other kinds? After all, how many people who think of themselves as nationalists because they love their country hold the opinions of the 19th century German intellectuals who largely dreamt up this theory of nationalism? Most of them would never think of asserting that nationality is the only legitimate basis for statehood. Yet they experience strong emotions of loyalty and allegiance to their country.

Recognition of this truth is the beginning of the second theory. This theory sees nationalism as a form of collective political loyalty that is usually attached to the nation but that is capable of being separated from it and re-attached to some other unit of humanity. The most

famous theorist of this form of nationalism is also its most famous critic, namely George Orwell in the essay "Notes on Nationalism."

Orwell begins by specifying that nationalism is not to be confused with patriotism. In his formulation, the former is aggressive and power hungry, the latter defensive and devoted to celebrating a particular way of life. In order to justify this distinction he has to define nationalism in a singular and arguably eccentric way: namely, as "The habit of identifying oneself with a single nation or other unit, placing it beyond good and evil, and recognizing no other duty than that of advancing its interests." He then extends this definition to cover almost every political unit of humanity. Nationalism in this extended sense, he argues, covers a variety of movements, including communism, Zionism, pacifism, political Catholicism and anti-Semitism, and he observes, finally, that the devotee of some transferred nationalism, such as a Stalinist or a pan-Europeanist, is able to be much "more nationalistic, more vulgar, more silly, more malignant, more dishonest than he could ever be of his native country or any unit of which he had a real knowledge."

In other words, Orwell's essay is not really about nationalism as other people understand the word at all; it is an essay on power-worship. That becomes clear in Orwell's crucial concession that nationalism is probably least dangerous when it is attached to one's own country—when it is no more than a harsh variant of patriotism—and most virulent when it is attached to some other unit of humanity. If proof were needed for this proposition, it would come in the support that the political intellectuals on the Left have given to such foreign utopias as Stalinist Russia, Maoist China, Cuba and North Vietnam over the years, transforming themselves into ideological chauvinists and justifying torture and mass murder in the process.

... Orwell's essay is not really about nationalism as other people understand the word at all; it is an essay on power-worship.

Let me now turn to the third concept of nationalism. This is the argument that people come to share a national identity, mutual loyalty and sense of common destiny as the result of sharing the same language and culture and of living under the same institutions over a long period of time.

This group to which people feel loyal may be a tribe, an *ethnos*, a people in an ethnic sense. Or it may be a group that was originally diverse ethnically but that has become a single people, through time and intermarriage, rather like an extended family. Or it may consist of the subjects of a dynasty who originally felt no attachment to the state but who developed one over time. Or it may consist of immigrants to a settler society, such as Australia or the United States, who assimilate to a common culture and identity established before their arrival. What matters is that over time they come to feel that they are part of the same collective body and feel a loyalty to it and to its symbols, whether the monarchy in the UK or the flag in the United States.

Because shared language and culture are at the root of this political loyalty, a wider national identity naturally replaces more local identities in periods when we see the spread of communications. In the early 19th century, nationalism spread because it was transmitted by new organs of mass circulation, in particular, newspapers, pamphlets, novels, popular histories and so on. These enabled many more people to feel a sympathy for—and to forge an identity with—others beyond the boundaries of their village or province. Nationalism of this kind is, as we shall see, inseparable from improved communications.

Now, the constructivist historians object that this sense of common sympathy is an artificial construct planned by governments and built with the help of intellectuals and artists from Sir Walter Scott to Rudyard Kipling. A new sense of national identity was manufactured in Britain, for instance, by persuading the English, the Welsh, the Scots and (some of) the Irish that they were a people gifted with Protestant liberty in peril from continental Catholic absolutism. As the historian Noel Malcolm has pointed out, however, while the process of building may have been artificial, it drew upon real materials. The Catholic powers in 18th century Europe were largely absolutist and Britain was a free society by contemporary standards. Louis XIV and Napoleon were threats to British independence. If artifice too played a part, the short answer to the constructivist historians is Burke's observation that "Art is man's nature."

Once we grant that conventional patriotism is real, even if artifice went into its construction, however, is it also virtuous? Orwell comes near to conceding that it is. Describing the nationalism of power-worship that he despises, Orwell remarks in passing that "its worst follies have been made possible by the breakdown of patriotism and religious belief." He hesitates almost immediately, warning that "if one follows this train of thought, one is in danger of being led into a species of conservatism." But the damage has been done. He has conceded what conservatives have long contended. When patriotic sentiments have been expelled from polite discourse, all manner of brutish ideologies rush in to occupy the vacant space—whether that space is the public square or the human heart.

When patriotic sentiments have been expelled from polite discourse, all manner of brutish ideologies rush in to occupy the vacant space—whether that space is the public square or the human heart.

Indeed, we might consider the three types of nationalism we have been discussing not as three distinctive concepts but as three states in a process of collective ideological conversion. First, an existing national identity ceases to satisfy its former adherents for a variety of possible reasons—defeat in war, internal religious oppression, political boredom, the influence of bad companions, and so on. We might concede (with a bow to the constructivists) that such national identities, once abandoned, seem invented and imposed to those no longer under their sway. In the second stage these ex-patriots, now vulnerable to the attractions of the power-worshipping ideologies listed by Orwell, adopt one of them as a new, more authentic and more rational identity. And when they do so, the scales fall from their eyes. The possessors of this new self-conscious identity are soon seized by a missionary impulse to spread the good news. That leads them to the third stage of doctrinal nationalism. To convert others, they must first demystify the false identities still extant and demonstrate the rationality of their chosen identity. Hence they develop a doctrine to establish that their new identity is the only real and legitimate kind. And that doctrinal nationalism now sets out to replace the national identity whose weakness started the entire process.

There is an inevitable rivalry between ideological nationalism of this kind and taken-for-granted national identities rooted in a shared culture. Pre-existing loyalties are an obstacle to any new political identity that is striving to assert itself. These rivalries can sometimes be murderous—real men and real women perished in

Stalin's campaign to kill nations to create a new Soviet man. With the demise of Soviet communism and the corresponding decline in some power-worshipping ideologies cited by Orwell, however, it might seem that there are no more power-worshipping ideologies and doctrinal identities to disturb us—and that more traditional identities can therefore rest secure. In fact, however, there are two important new examples of doctrinal nationalism entering the lists: multiculturalism in the United States and the European Idea across the Atlantic.

The word multiculturalism means many things, but in its largest sense it is an alternative national identity for the United States. It seeks to replace the present political system of liberal democracy based upon rights-bearing individual citizens with one of multicultural democracy in which the fundamental unit is the ethnic or cultural group with its own worldviews, values, history, heritage and language. It holds that people should express their political aspirations through membership in such groups. And it predicts that in the future, national sovereignty will devolve upwards towards transnational bodies and downwards towards these now semi-autonomous groups.

It is hard to take those ideas seriously, because they clash sharply with the liberal U.S. Constitution, in part because, if implemented, they would transform the United States into a larger version of Lebanon or Northern Ireland, and in part because there has been a unifying upsurge of American nationalism since September 11. But the fact that something cannot work does not mean it will not be tried. Multiculturalism remains the orthodoxy in law schools, corporate America and elite institutions. If nothing else, it is likely to sharpen the sense of ethnic grievance, to chip away at national cohesion, and to obstruct improvements in homeland security. Insofar as multiculturalism is a rising nationalism, then, it is one that threatens not foreign countries but internal security and stability in the United States.

The "European Idea" rests somewhat more openly upon hostility to existing European nations and their national identities. Its justifying claim is that the European Union has overcome the shameful legacy of the European nations that were responsible for two world wars and threaten the peace of the Balkans today. Since its foundation in the 1950s the EU has been a bulwark against the recrudescence of such dangerous nationalism, ensuring that nations like France and Germany will never go to war again. The United States

should be grateful, since GIs will never again die in European civil wars.

Every single argument in this list is either highly questionable or plainly false. Half the states involved in the First World War were multinational empires such as Austria, Hungary and czarist Russia. The Second World War was caused by the colliding ambitions of the two great transnational ideologies hostile to nationalism: Nazism, with its belief in the racial hierarchy transcending nations, and communism, with its belief in a class hierarchy transcending nations. It was local nationalisms in Britain and occupied Europe that provided most of the morale to resist fascist ideologies. Indeed, nationalism is being used as a synonym for interstate rivalry. But the European Union is not proposing to abolish the system of states, merely to create a larger state in a world of larger states—in other words, to replicate 1914 on a larger scale.

Nor is the EU the cause of the post-war peace in western Europe. Rather, it is the consequence of that peace. As the dates plainly show—NATO was established in 1949 and the EU's forerunner in 1957—what has ensured a European peace since 1945 is the military and diplomatic presence of the United States. And this security has enabled countries to trust their neighbors and form cooperative arrangements in the economic, political and military affairs from which they would have shrunk.

It is, finally, hard to characterize as anti-nationalist a political idea that asserts Europeans are a single people, united by a culture, whose manifest destiny is to form a single state with its own flag, anthem, currency, citizenship, foreign policy, armed forces, parliament and government. In every other context people who believe this kind of thing are called nationalists. If therefore the EU is the latest incarnation of European nationalism rather than an antidote to it—as its supporters claim—it should surely receive more skeptical scrutiny than it has done until now.

If therefore the EU is the latest incarnation of European nationalism rather than an antidote to it ... it should surely receive more skeptical scrutiny than it has done until now.

Particular skepticism should be directed towards the democratic credentials of this new Euro-nationalism. The traditional nation-state rooted in a shared language and culture has proved to be the most—indeed the only—reliable incubator of democratic government accountable to the people. Multiculturalism is hostile to majority rule in principle and yet has produced no plausible substitute for it except for power-sharing arrangements like those of Northern Ireland, which require an external umpire to enforce them. And as the Europeans admit with their phrase the "democratic deficit," the EU has still not developed an acceptable democratic structure. Its proposed constitution, for instance, retains the extraordinarily authoritarian arrangement whereby an unelected and largely unaccountable commission has a monopoly on initiating legislation.

Some defenders of the EU claim that this admittedly undemocratic provision is offset by the increased powers of the European parliament. But this greatly exaggerates the representative nature of the Euro-parliament. Though formally democratic by virtue of being elected, it has no continent-wide European public opinion to which it might be accountable. It debates in several languages—some of its key terms, such as "federalism" and "subsidiarity" mean quite different things in the different languages. It consists not of European political parties but of *alliances* of national political parties that represent quite different political attitudes in their respective countries. It is divided not by continent-wide political philosophies—there are none—but either by national concerns or by the interests of the EU political elite, including itself. And it is elected by a very small percentage of the eligible voters in elections that turn not on European issues but on the fortunes of national governments and opposition parties. The fundamental problem underlying all these difficulties is that there is no single European *demos*—no European people united by a shared language, culture and history—which the parliament can represent and to which it is accountable. Living under the same European institutions is not enough. And no *demos*, no democracy.

Many proponents of the "European Idea" resist the notion that a shared language and culture are necessary components of nationality and democracy. When faced with the question of what holds the state together, they offer two answers: liberal institutions and social-democratic transfer payments. Under liberal institutionalism (Michael Ignatieff's "civic nationalism" seen from another angle), citizens are held together by a strong state which protects citizens and their rights and enables them to go about their business peacefully. They therefore owe the state their loyalty. Unless it brutally oppresses constituent groups, they have no right to secede and found their own state.

Yet this position presents almost as many problems as doctrinal nationalism. As Noel Malcolm points out: How strong is a state going to be if people are taught to think of it merely as a geographic area containing a certain number of human beings endowed with rights? If such a state holds in small nations against their will, it is likely to be further weakened by the reality that not all of its citizens will in fact be loyal. And as the recent fates of Yugoslavia and Czechoslovakia illustrate, a velvet divorce will sometimes have happier consequences than a loveless marriage maintained by force. It is probably no accident, as some people used to say, that the United States, founded as it is on the principle of popular consent, has until recently taken great care to inculcate the national language and a common culture in both immigrant and native-born citizens.

According to the second answer—financial flows—governments promote national solidarity first by transferring resources from favored to disadvantaged groups and, second, by encouraging all citizens to participate in entitlement programs, like Social Security, that subtly promote an ethic of equal citizenship. As long as the state retains the fiscal ability to keep the checks flowing, it can maintain national cohesion even without a shared national identity rooted in culture and language.

But what happens when the treasury runs out? The costs of financial flows are rising rapidly in the advanced world because of aging populations. Research shows that those paying the costs of financial flows are more willing to fund government transfers if they are linked to the recipients by the ties of sympathy and fellowship that exist in a shared national culture. The more diverse a society is, the less willing it is to spend money on welfare. In the new globalized economy, the fiscal costs of transfer payments will be easier to avoid by emigration, capital movements and competition between governments to attract scarce capital investments. So the time is approaching when financial flows, far from being a method of sustaining national harmony, will become a positive threat to it.

Social democratic states are already responding to these pressures by seeking to ensure that neither individual nor corporate citizens can escape their controls. They seek to close tax havens, transform trade agreements into vehicles for extending regulations, impose taxes on international financial flows, establish international regulatory bodies, "harmonize" regulations upward in bodies such as the EU, and so on. As a result, transnational bodies gain new powers, NGOs gain influence over more decisions, and international civil servants gain more profitable careers. It would be a rash man who bet against such a constellation of forces—and against the global social democracy that they imply. In effect governments are forming cartels—the EU is one such—to maintain near-monopoly prices for their services.

But these large cartel structures suffer even more fiercely from the same defects as "economic" states. They are remote, undemocratic and unsupported by a shared culture and language—indeed, they are bitterly divided by such factors. So they are likely to exhibit even more fissiparous tendencies than afflict the states forming them. What they will mainly transfer upwards is crises.

Both transnational political structures divorced from democratic consent and national political structures that are not rooted in a shared culture and language are likely to prove fragile and, while they last, disruptive. Why governments and public intellectuals should have decided that they are morally obliged to erect both states and international agencies on exactly the opposite assumptions is a mystery. If they stick to this course, however, one day it will become a tragedy.

Both transnational political structures divorced from democratic consent and national political structures that are not rooted in a shared culture and language are likely to prove fragile and while they last, disruptive.

Breathes there a man with soul so dead,
Who never to himself hath said,
'This is my own, my native land!'
Whose heart hath ne'er within him burn'd
As home his footsteps he hath turn'd
From wandering on a foreign strand?
If such there breathe, go, mark him well;
For him no minstrel raptures swell;
High though his titles, proud his name,
Boundless his wealth as wish can claim;
Despite those titles, power and pelf,
The wretch, concentrated all in self,
Living, shall forfeit fair renown,
And, doubly dying, shall go down,
To the vile dust from whence he sprung,
Unwept, unhonour'd, and unsung.

—Sir Walter Scott

Terms and Concepts

atavistic
ethnos
nationality

Westphalian system
doctrinal nationalism

European Idea
multiculturalism

Questions

1. How is it "both a platitude and a provocation" to say that we live in an age of nationalism?
2. O'Sullivan argues that when people talk about "nationalism" they are often confusing three quite distinct political commitments. What are they?
3. How does Orwell define nationalism and how does he criticize it? What is O'Sullivan's objection to Orwell's position?
4. O'Sullivan claims that multiculturalism is actually a new form of doctrinal nationalism. How so?
5. What is the "European Idea" and why is O'Sullivan so skeptical of it?
6. In what sense is O'Sullivan's piece a "defense" of nationalism?

Social Democracy in Theory and Practice—The Way Ahead

Edward Broadbent

Editors' Note

The last two decades have not been easy for social democrats in Canada. At the national level, the New Democratic Party has in recent times been hard pressed to maintain official status in the Commons. Even in provinces where it has managed to get elected, its performance in office has alienated traditional supporters who claim that NDP governments are virtually indistinguishable from their predecessors.

At the same, the NDP has been attacked from the other direction. In a generation shaped by the neoconservative argument that government is the problem, by the imperatives of spending and tax cuts, and by the striking of international trade deals in which states willingly surrender some of their policy options, social democrats are accused of swimming against the tide. Their conviction that governments have a strong role to play in providing services and balancing against the inequalities of a market economy has been dismissed as quaint and impractical.

Ed Broadbent was national leader of the NDP at its political high-water mark. In this essay, part of a collection by various thinkers struggling with the question What's Left?,[1] he reiterates a social-democratic position that he distinguishes from liberal individualism in its understanding of human beings, rights, and the role of government. The social-democratic tradition stretches back to late-19th-century Europe, where the first mass workers' parties grew out of factory industry. It includes, in Canada, the formation of the Co-operative Commonwealth Federation, which issued its Regina Manifesto in the early years of the Great Depression, and the introduction of universal public health care in Saskatchewan in the 1960s.

Early on, social democrats set themselves apart from Marxism in rejecting the course of revolution and in making peace, more or less, with capitalism. Their goals were more modest, and arguably even conservative: to ameliorate inequality and redistribute wealth.

To that end, social democrats proposed to "harness" and limit the scope of the market through planning, progressive taxation, public services, and support for cooperatives as a form of social ownership of the economy. Many of these themes can still be found in Broadbent's essay. There is, he writes, no meaningful citizenship without the substantive equality that gives people the opportunity to participate in public affairs.

Broadbent's essay has two primary targets. On one hand are those tempted to follow the so-called "third way" pioneered in Britain by Tony Blair's Labour Party, which is widely criticized even by some of his own MPs as being far too cozy with global capitalism. Note Broadbent's references to "continental European social democrats," who not only form governments, but also have "managed to retain the benefits of market economies without becoming market societies." On the other hand are those tempted to remake the NDP into a broad oppositional coalition of activist groups that does not aspire to govern.

❖ ❖ ❖

Canada does not need another Liberal Party. Nor does it require, in this era of right-of-centre politics, a party comprised of good-to-be-in-permanent-opposition self-described "radicals." It needs a re-invigorated New Democratic Party that is confident about the relevance of social democracy to the well-being of the majority of Canadians. Today, most of the governments in western continental Europe are social democratic: a distinct type of politics and society responsible for transforming the lives of millions of ordinary people. These countries have tough-minded governments who preside over market economies and understand that there must be an emphasis on substantive equality if liberty is to be an equitably experienced aspect of democratic citizenship. What Canada's Liberals and the "radicals" have in common is rejection of social democracy. The former have no commitment to substantive equality. And the latter have nothing but disdain for markets.[1]

Looking at the past decade, we can see that when it comes to social justice, ideology matters and governments count. While Canada, Britain and the United States went one way during this period, social democrats went another. Changes in the economies of all OECD countries, resulting from technical innovation and globalization, widened the market-income and wealth gap between classes and regions. Continental European governments responded by looking for ways to extend the social charter and by becoming economically more efficient. In contrast, Canadian, British and American governments slashed social programs and deepened inequality. The Danes and the Dutch introduced globally competitive labour market flexibility without cutting back on social benefits or rights of their workers. And while market-produced levels of child poverty in Sweden and Canada were virtually identical during this period (around 24%), after government intervention only 2.6% of Swedish kids remained in poverty whereas in Canada, the percentage was six times greater—and in Britain and United States the situation was even worse. (Five continental European countries almost eliminated child poverty as the numbers in Canada continued to grow.) And while Britain, Canada and the United States stood back and watched profitable companies lay off workers, the French government responded to such action with measures to strengthen the rights of workers and tax changes which will penalize profitable companies if they seek greater profitability by even more layoffs. While the rich in Germany, Sweden and the Netherlands continue to send their children to the well-funded public schools attended by everyone else, our wealthiest province has embarked upon a two-class system of education already firmly entrenched in the United States and Britain. And in the same three European countries, productivity increases, averaged over the period, equaled that of the United States. In sum, continental European social democracies see social justice and economic efficiency not in competition, but as complementary components of national policy. They also understand that liberty and equality should be seen, not in conflict, but as mutually reinforcing.

How did this come about? Social democracy took off during the post–World War II years, a by-product of strong unions and social solidarity fostered by the war. Democratic citizens were determined to build a new social order, one that would combine social and economic justice with our liberal political institutions. The goal was to ensure that all citizens were equally entitled to a range of universal social rights. These would not be allowed on the basis of the market but provided as rights of citizenship. It was understood that market economies were required to generate the necessary wealth for these new egalitarian social rights.

However, it was also understood that for this to happen, a market economy required an intervening government. This combination—social rights, market economy, and activist government—laid a strong foundation in Europe for what was neither Marxist, nor liberal, but rather a novel, expanded notion of democratic citizenship. Social democrats there and in Canada contended that such societies could achieve a much higher level of personal freedom and distributive justice than had ever been thought possible. This notion of the need for deeply embedded social rights, alongside the operations of the market economy, is unique to social democracy.

Modern liberals have a deeply embedded and unresolved conflict. On the one hand, they would agree that the goal of a tolerant, open society should be to ensure that all human beings have the equal right to the development of their talents and interests. At the same time, they remain wedded to the ethic of the market place: economic rewards should be allocated on the principle of greater amounts going to those with greater innate ability *or* to those who make a more energetic effort *or* who perform a task that the market values. Assuming the existence of laws to stop the formation of cartels and government guarantees to ensure that no person or family remains in abject poverty, according to this ethic, any resulting inequalities are exactly as they should be.

Although any such market system entails serious material inequalities at birth, for the modern liberal, equal access to education or post-industrial skills training should make it possible for all individuals to compete more or less equally. In terms of rights, what citizens need are only equal civil and political rights. It's using these rights politically and in the economy that will lead to the justified material inequalities produced by the market. Seen by a modern liberal who accepts the ethic of the market place, a "just society" that also includes social and economic rights would be an oxymoron. This is because such rights, by definition, alter significantly the distribution results of the market.

Instead of egalitarian social and economic rights of citizenship, liberals prefer "safety-net" welfare. While preserving other serious inequalities, this is intended (in principle) to ensure that no one is destitute. [As prime minister,] Jean Chrétien [did] not proclaim the need for a range of social rights for all. Instead, he justifie[d] Liberal social policy by asserting, "governments must help those who cannot help themselves." Canada's other conservative[s] who remain equally wedded to the market-ethic strongly agree.

... we see equality and freedom to be inextricably connected.

Social democrats differ from other Canadians on precisely this issue. Like the modern liberal, we see the goal as each citizen having the equal right to develop his or her talents and to participate equally in shaping political decisions. However, when we talk about equality, we do not take this to mean simply equality before the law, or the equal right to participate in politics, or the equal formal entitlement to have access to employment, or gender and sexual equality, or the freedom to purchase goods and services in the marketplace. Social democrats believe in all these rights, but more as well.

For us the degree of substantive equality in society matters a great deal if the equal right to development is to exist. And it is in this context that we see equality and freedom to be inextricably connected. To act freely is to make choices. In any society that lacks a significant degree of material equality, we see it as self-evident that the capacity to act freely is also unequal. In a market economy, most goods and services are bought and sold. Whether for baseball games, food on the table, music lessons, kids' clothing, or a holiday—to exercise free choice requires cash. The less cash, the less choice; the less choice, the less freedom. Rich families not only have more money, they have more freedom. Citizenship is unequal.

... democracy's goal of equal and participatory citizenship can only be achieved by government measures designed to provide more real equality.

We social democrats therefore reject the market mechanism as the means for ensuring an equitable distribution of the wealth of a nation. It is inherently unfair. Nor do we accept as adequate, measures intended to achieve only equality of opportunity. We strongly assert that democracy's goal of equal and participatory citizenship can only be achieved by government measures designed to provide more real equality. Only combining progressive taxation with social rights that remove many goods and services entirely from market criteria can do this. Only by becoming social democratic in shaping market outcomes can the liberal goal of the equal right of all to full human development take place.

MARKETS: HARNESSED AND SUBVERTED
◆ ◆ ◆

To social democrats, the prospect of ever-increasing social equality necessarily involves a complex set of relationships that serve to both harness and subvert the power of the market. They see the process of democracy as the most effective means of ensuring that men and women do not become enslaved to the severe inequality and commercialization of life that results from unfettered markets. While they see the innovative efficiency of markets as the best means of ensuring the production, distribution and sale of most goods and services, social democrats believe that certain goods, services and activities are so important that they should be ensured as a matter of right to all citizens. And, to achieve democracy's objective of participatory citizenship, social democrats seek means to make both the corporate and public sectors responsive and accountable to workers and citizens.

By ensuring that the negative results of market forces are effectively countered by non-market social rights and other government action in selective parts of the economy, in the arts and the environment, continental European social democrats have managed to *retain [the] benefits of market economies without becoming market societies*. Progressive taxation *and* the strong presence of social and economic rights that ensure major elements of equality for all citizens in the essentials of personal and family life can considerably reduce the negative effects of market-based inequalities. Put in terms appropriate to our age, as long as ordinary citizens can send their children to good public schools, have free comprehensive health services, benefit from income and retraining programs when they are unemployed, buy a computer, have an annual paid vacation with access to healthy air and clean beaches, and retire with dignity, most will regard with neither envy nor contempt the existence of an affluent few. They will simply want to get on with their own lives.

... continental European social democrats have managed to retain the benefits of market economies without becoming market societies.

It is the presence of strong, universal social rights—whose specific content varies over time—that has made possible the sense of freedom and social equality experienced by millions of ordinary people. Free from the time demands and anxiety otherwise needed to make personal market decisions about health, pensions, child care, and university education, citizens in established social democracies are literally freer to choose how to spend their time: listening to Bach, playing soccer, or drinking beer and talking with friends on a sunny afternoon.

By drawing upon our own history, Canadian social democrats can find a rich source of ideas that can inspire us in the building of such a society. It was a Canadian social democrat who first drew together the amalgam of secular and religious values which subsequently emerged in 1948 as the Universal Declaration of Human Rights. John Humphrey, a professor of law at McGill University, became the world's first public servant with a human rights mandate. Invited to go to the United Nations to serve a committee chaired by Eleanor Roosevelt, he produced the first draft of the Universal Declaration. Taken along with its companions, the Covenant on Economic, Social and Cultural Rights and the Covenant on Civil and Political Rights, the result constitutes a deeply social democratic global objective.

Instead of seeing liberty and equality in conflict, these values are correctly understood to be mutually reinforcing. Instead of seeing individuals as permanently in competition with each other, they are portrayed as members of communities with obligations as well as rights. At the outset of all three documents there is the important recognition of the importance of equality. All men and women are seen to have an equal claim to a life of dignity *and* an equal claim to the resources needed to achieve it. To have such a life, a wide range of human rights are spelled out, among which are included the freedoms of speech, association and assembly; the right to health care and education; and the right to equal pay for equal work. The right to form and join a trade union is the only right found in all three documents. Governments are obligated to foster and promote these rights within a framework of the rule of law. Citizens must in turn have "duties to the community in which alone the free and full development" of the human personality is said to be possible. All bodies within society, including implicitly corporations, are obligated to act [in a manner] consistent with the principles of the Universal Declaration. As a unifying foundation for both domestic and foreign policy, there is no better guide for Canadian social democracy in the twenty-first century.

When I went to South Africa a few years ago, it was no surprise for me to find that Nelson Mandela saw in these rights and obligations the foundation for his country's new constitution. Nor with its narrow definition restricted to only political and civil rights and free market capitalism, is it surprising that the United States has not ratified the Covenant on Economic, Social and Cultural Rights.

POLITICS MATTERS
◆ ◆ ◆

There is an important difference between the rights covenants when it comes to obligations for governments. Once ratified, a national government is obligated to implement without qualification the provisions of the Covenant on Civil and Political Rights. In general, this is what we did in Canada in 1982 with our Charter of Rights and Freedoms. On the other hand the Covenant on Economic, Social and Cultural Rights takes into account the different level of economic development among nations. This means that on-going political debate about priorities within any given country plays a crucial role. Ideology counts. Political leadership and political power matter. Decisions to spend or not to spend on a social right must be made. Will it be tax cuts or health care? [Selection] of priorities *within* the family of social rights must also be done. How much for health care and how much for education?

We do not allocate political and civil rights on the basis of a means test. Nor should we do so with the right to health, post-secondary education or child care.

Successful, functioning social democracies are the product of a positive and complex mix of ideology, political leadership, and institutional practice. Should a social democratic state modify or eliminate a significant number of universal social programs it would, of course, at some point cease to be social democratic. Just as the United States today can be seen as a liberal society that never aspired to social democratic status, so too could the Scandinavian and other European countries revert to a pre-social-democratic character. We Canadians, who first came to describe ourselves as "sharing and caring" people only after years of strong universal social programs (health, pension, unemployment insurance), could soon lose both the practice and the self-description. Recent policies of the federal and most provincial governments have undermined strong universal programs in health and education. The more these foundational institutions are changed, the less we will see ourselves as sharing and caring. We do not allocate political and civil rights on the basis of a means test. Nor should we do so with the right to health, post-secondary education or child care.

In seeking redress for the violation of either a political or a civil right, we naturally turn to the courts. In the case of social rights, redress requires a political act. Apart from the failure to implement a regulation, which may permit judicial review, disputes about the level of benefit of a social right, like its establishment in the first place, are political issues. Values, leaders, and ideology count. Citizens acting as equals in the political process first established social rights. As we Canadians have seen, they can also be taken away in the same process.

INDIVIDUALISM: DIFFERENT VISIONS, DIFFERENT REALITIES

◆ ◆ ◆

A social democracy should be seen for what it is: a principled, functioning, real alternative to the American-style liberal democracy favoured by Canada's flag-waving Liberals who prefer tax cuts to rebuilding and extending our social rights. The liberal sees an individual's life as unfolding in a society that stands in an antagonistic relationship to the state and in which citizens are essentially in competition with one another. The liberal then designs all institutions to make sure that they mesh with such a divisive goal.

We social democrats make different assumptions, beginning with the rejection of the competitive individualist model. Our rejection is *not* based on a utopian counter-vision, which naively sees humans as unalienated, altruistic beings. Instead it rests on a view of humanity that is much closer to reality than the caricature promoted by liberal individualism. Social democratic individualism incorporates cooperation. It is an individualism derived from an understanding of reality: human beings are inescapably social creatures and they have both personal and shared goals.

For the social democrat, there are two important universally observable qualities of human beings that should receive equal weight in assessments of potential economic and political structures—our disposition to pursue personal gain and our disposition to act cooperatively in implementing shared objectives with others. Most of us want personal and family satisfaction but we have also created in Canada 175,000 volunteer organizations to do things with and for our neighbours. We want to do such things within civil society *and* by means of government programs. Any polity that does not take into account these two basic human characteristics at best does a disservice to its citizens. Any proposed political agenda that puts its emphasis exclusively on either of these dispositions is seriously flawed.

The social democrat sees in his or her version of society, which matches a market driven economy with a regime of social rights, the answer to this century's most famous political question: what is to be done? Unlike the liberal, classical or neo, the social democrat sees the human capacity to cooperate as a practical and moral foundation for a global agenda for social rights and a healthy environment, objectives radically dissociated from market criteria. Unlike Marxists, old or new, the social democrat does acknowledge as productively

useful our permanent disposition to seek our own benefit. A form of market economy matched with social
rights is not, therefore, either a compromise of liberal-
democratic principles or some half-way step to a
Marxist utopia. It is instead the best kind of society that
can be constructed, given these two differing aspects of
our nature. It provides for a broad range of individual
and collective rights and for the opportunity for personal and community good. However, since the social
democrat's deep commitment to political democracy
entails the acceptance of pluralism, there will always be
the option to broaden or narrow the degree of equality
within society: to eliminate or maintain poverty, to recognize or withhold collective cultural identity rights for
minorities, to respect, or not, divergence in sexual orientation, or to make bureaucracies more or less responsive to citizens.

*... the social democrat sees the human
capacity to cooperate as a practical and
moral foundation ...*

Within the complex matrix of the democratic state,
social democrats will normally be located among those
supporting the first option in these pairs of choices at
any given time—all of which expand human liberty for
more people beyond the parameters set either by market
forces or by tradition. However, competing political priorities can result in different decisions. Bad or mistaken
leadership can also do so—as can the presence or
absence of a vigorous civil society and the winning or
losing of elections. Social democracy is a democracy and
that means there can be no predetermined outcomes.
There is no golden calculator available as a guide to perfect solutions. Nor should there be in a free society.

CIVIL SOCIETY AND THE PARTY

◆ ◆ ◆

The movement towards greater levels of equality has
always been a product of the interrelation between civil
society and elected members of parliament. Many social
democratic parties themselves emerged from the
activism of unions and a variety of other groups within
civil society, who had the goal of achieving political
power in order to make changes in governmental
policies. In Europe, through coalitions and majority

governments, there has been remarkable political success
at the national level in translating good policies into legislation that has benefited millions. Here in Canada,
with New Democratic Party (NDP) governments at the
provincial level and an effective presence of the NDP in
Ottawa, rights and benefits for workers, pensioners, the
sick, women, Aboriginal Peoples, visible minorities and
gays and lesbians are much higher than in the United
States, which lacks a social democratic party. Like any
human institution, our party has experienced failures,
setbacks and bad decisions. But any serious assessment
based on egalitarian concerns would reach the same conclusion as Pierre Trudeau when he acknowledged that
our presence has been a key element in bringing about
progressive change in Canada. At the federal level in the
1980s and in the minority government a decade earlier,
the NDP was significant in its impact. Canada has strong
provisions in the Constitution Act of 1982 ensuring the
equality rights of women and the historic rights of
Aboriginal Peoples because of work done in civil society
by the women's movement and Aboriginal leadership—
and because the NDP was in Parliament, writing, persuading and moving adoption of key causes.

The relationship between the Party and active
groups within civil society is important and complex.
When out of power, the Party is part of civil society,
i.e., it is not a part of the governing structure and joins
with other bodies in helping to shape public debate.
However, unlike any other institution within civil
society, it actually aspires to govern. It periodically goes
to the people and asserts [that], if elected as a government, it would put in place such-and-such policies and
laws, or if elected in opposition it would apply pressure
to the elected government to adopt the same laws and
policies.

In developing its political agenda the Party must
listen to civil society. It must in particular take into
account and learn from those groups who are closest to
its philosophical orientation. But as a rule, it should
neither seek nor accept affiliation with them. (The one
exception is the trade union movement—to which I will
return shortly.) Women's groups, environmentalists,
anti-poverty activists, and human rights organizations,
student bodies, and the diverse groups critical of many
aspects of corporate power and globalization: all of
these provide needed critiques of the status quo and
many provide thoughtful answers.

These advocacy groups are of great importance to
democratic life. They bring serious matters to public
attention and are often the major source of ideas for

significant innovation by governments. To remain cred-ible as organizations, they should remain completely independent of all political parties, promoting with integrity the particular agendas for what they believe needs to be done. They should attempt to influence all democratic parties although it is clear that some will be more open to their proposals than others. A social dem-ocratic party, for its part, must remain independent of them. This is not simply because within every category, e.g., environment, anti-poverty, human rights, there are groups whose agendas differ from one another, as well as groups that are knowledgeable and some that are not. More fundamentally, it is the Party's unique responsi-bility to translate a political critique into governmental action. In this sense, a political party is like no other group in civil society.

... it is the Party's unique responsibility to translate a political critique into governmental action. ... If it promised without thinking and cannot deliver when elected, it shatters its own credibility.

The Party must consider the evidence presented by a civil society organization. It must also take into account counter priorities and claims made by other groups and citizens. It must recommend so much spending for housing, education, and health—and do so in an accountable, responsible way to the community. An organization campaigning to eliminate child poverty can in good faith recommend the spending of so many millions of dollars to achieve this goal. A social demo-cratic party cannot adopt the same agenda without first critically considering the amount of money needed to act on other social priorities. Only the Party as a civil society organization, whether in government or in opposition, has such serious and broad-ranging respon-sibility. If it promised without thinking and cannot deliver when elected, it shatters its own credibility. It must be prepared to say "no" before elections to many demands made by conscientious citizens because of its obligations to give equal consideration to the proposals of other conscientious citizens.

The trade union movement is the notable exception to the general rule that civil society groups and the party should remain structurally independent and unaffili-ated. There are a number of reasons for this. Many social democratic parties came into being because either wholly or in part they were created by trade unions. The NDP's birth in 1961 was the product of the Cooperative Commonwealth Federation (CCF), organized labour and individual progressive Canadians. Deeper than the mere fact of creation is the reason for it. In virtually all developed democracies, the trade union movement has as its *raison d'être* the task of redistributing power and income for the benefit of workers. This is within the workplace the equivalent of the broader struggle for equality in society as a whole which is the hallmark of a social democratic party. It's no accident that in many communities across Canada, many of the executives of the first branches of the CCF and of the first trade union locals consisted of the same individuals. Organized labour, with leaders elected by its members, sees as its mission a struggle for justice for all men and women as workers (whether or not they are members of unions) and has seen in the party its preferred instrument for political change in society. This has provided a natural and unique fit between the Party and trade unions. No other group within civil society is in a similar position.

These strong ideological and institutional goals pro-vide solid grounds for affiliation of trade union bodies within the party. (The question of providing funds for the party is an important but separate matter. See point (6) in my suggestions for a new political agenda at the end of this essay.) The Party and the trade union move-ment in Canada have been in strong agreement on most of the issues of the day—each providing input and sup-port to the other. As autonomous organizations, how-ever, they have differed, and on occasions these differences have been serious. This is inevitable and should not take away from the profound common agenda that they uniquely share: the building of a more egalitarian workplace and society.

THE FUTURE

◆ ◆ ◆

As I indicated at the outset of this essay, in continental Europe where social democracy is most deeply embedded in the minds and institutions of its citizens, the egalitarian essence of social citizenship continues to underpin the legislative agenda. In Canada, Britain and the United States, we have been moving backwards. Instead of encouraging market growth *within* a political framework of social justice, market and corporate pri-orities have been encouraged to dominate. Instead of countering the effects of market-produced inequality, the governments of Chrétien, Blair and Clinton have fostered it. The rich in all three countries have an increasing share of the after-tax income. (President Bush, with the support of Democrats, has exacerbated the problem with his recent tax measures.) Chrétien's recent election victory moved Canada even closer to a "low-tax" nation—i.e., one with poor social services like Britain and the United States. As a percentage of GDP, Blair's government is spending at about the same low level on social services as was Margaret Thatcher in 1984. It is actually allocating less to education.[2] In all three countries, the level of poverty, in general, and for children in particular, is impossible to find in any continental social democracy. We also find these Anglo-American governments' records on the environment lamentable. Once again, it was the Europeans who pushed for global reform at the Bonn meeting on the Kyoto environmental agreement in the summer of 2001.

We must not allow the avaricious aspects of current capitalism at home and abroad to wipe out the great postwar social reforms ...

The world recently celebrated the fiftieth anniversary of the Universal Declaration of Human Rights. That remarkable postwar document includes the much older political and civil rights as well as the new social and economic rights. Despite their birth dating back three hundred years, political and civil rights are still under attack, as seen in the continuing persecution and discrimination related to religious, ethnic, racial and sexual-orientation differences. Though vigilance on these rights is obviously essential, it is more than fortunate that the principle of political and civil rights has become deeply embedded in Canada and most other developed democracies. Citizens' rights involving the freedoms of religion, speech, assembly, association, voting and due process are defended quite vigorously by the establishment media as well as by academics and an active human rights community. However, this has not been the case with threats, abuses, or even clear violations of the social and economic rights which have been the major addition to the human rights agenda in this century. These rights require direct government intervention in the economy to alter its distributive effects on the side of equality. Editorial writers and virtually all political parties in Canada except the NDP are now the

leading enemies of social and economic rights, in most cases ignorant of the fact that Canada committed itself to the Covenant on Economic, Social and Cultural Rights in 1976. While they readily denounce the emergence of ethnic cleansing or censorship, they either endorse or openly foster the dismantling of Canada's social rights. They appropriately insist that the democratic state, through our courts and parliaments must protect the right of an author to publish or a child with AIDS to go to a public school. But they readily acquiesce or even celebrate when a government dismantles a pension scheme, eliminates a housing benefit, or ignores the claim of workers to a union at home or abroad—all of which are internationally recognized human rights and favour those with less power and income. These rights are as central to human dignity as political and civil rights. While neo-liberals may revert to pre–Second World War standards of citizenship and remain ideologically consistent, social democrats cannot. Social democrats stand for more equality, or they stand for nothing.

We must not allow the avaricious aspects of current capitalism at home and abroad to wipe out the great postwar social reforms of this century. Policies that promote the removal of all "shackles" to the global movement of capital, now as in the nineteenth century, reveal the self-serving ideology of the dominant classes. Trade policies that protect the mobility and property rights of corporations but ignore the human rights of millions of workers are not neutral. They tip the balance in favour of the few over the many and foster the growing global inequality. The elites that advocate such policies need reminding that earlier in [the last] century laissez-faire capitalism denied real freedoms to millions, exacerbated class conflict, and helped destroy some democracies while seriously destabilizing them all. Those young and old who today are demanding an end to unaccountable corporate power are involved in a struggle crucial to the future of democracy.

Trade policies that protect the mobility and property rights of corporations but ignore the human rights of millions of workers are not neutral. They tip the balance in favour of the few ...

In addition to the fundamental need to keep and extend our social rights as citizens, other serious concerns about the unregulated market have also emerged in our time. If we are to preserve the environment on a sustainable basis, complete the struggle for gender equality, take into account the legitimate claims to identity of certain minorities, and foster the development of non-commercial cultural options, we require an activist government.

Only the mendacious or those ignorant of recent history can continue to argue that the Anglo-American neo-liberal version of capitalism on a global scale could possibly avoid either the serious social instability or the commercialized inequality that were its legacy for the nation state in the first half of the twentieth century.

The answers to the problems produced by economic globalization, whether in the North or the South, are not to be found in either the economic status quo, or the rejection of markets as a key element in economic development. Rather, as two distinguished individuals have recently argued, the answer is to be found in combining markets with more and deeper democracy. Harvard economist Dani Rodrik has said national governments should be able to de-link from international trade obligations when they conflict with deeply held national norms and values. Amartya Sen, the Nobel Prize winner in Economics, has made a similar but broader-ranging democratic argument. In effect, the kind of social democratic development that has already produced economic growth in the context of equality and freedom within a handful of the world's democracies must be deepened at home and extended on a global basis.

We must reject outright the economic neo-liberal[ism] and institutional conservatism of the Liberal government in Ottawa. To achieve true citizens' equality in Canada we need significant improvements in fleshing out both our political and social rights. Parliamentary and electoral reform is badly needed. Our cities need new powers. To help build a better world, we must be efficient and support trade but insist that globalization include rules that will ensure that when in conflict, the human rights and environmental needs of democratic peoples will trump the trading-based property rights of corporations. In Parliament in 1982 we rejected proposals to include property rights in the Constitution. We did so because of the fear that such entrenchment would lead to legal disputes which could jeopardize the more fundamental social and environmental priorities decided upon by elected legislators. What we sensibly decided in 1982 should be rejected in domestic law is now embodied in international trade

agreements. This is absurd and anti-democratic—and must be changed.

During the coming years, the only way the important domestic and international proposals for reform made by social democrats, human rights, environment, poverty, and women's groups earlier this year at Quebec City will be implemented is by change in domestic and international law. This will happen in Canada neither by remaining in the streets nor as a consequence of good arguments. Protest and reason are never sufficient in a democracy. Change has occurred in Canada at the national level when the Liberals saw demonstrations and arguments directly reinforced by the possibility of electoral defeat in Parliament. This has happened when federal governments were confronted by a principled party on the left which is committed to winning elections. In 1945, Mackenzie King took significant steps towards the creation of the Canadian welfare state. It was not a coincidence that he did so only after the Cooperative Commonwealth Federation had almost won Ontario in 1943, formed a government in Saskatchewan in 1944, and led national public opinion polls for the first time in 1945. Medicare became a national reality only after the NDP won power and showed it could be done at the provincial level. Political power matters, but so does the [fear] of losing it.

Canada's social democratic party, the NDP, is now going through a serious and positive process of renewal. Its members can be proud of its contributions to Canada. It now needs a revised structure, an updated agenda, and a new name. The Party should be finally called "social democrat" because that is what it has been for forty years. What will not change is its profound commitment to equality which is what makes it unique in our history.

As mentioned earlier, the Universal Declaration of Human Rights embodies the fundamental values of social democracy. This political and economic philosophy is spelled out in greater detail in the International Bill of Rights which includes the Universal Declaration on Human Rights as well as the Covenant on Economic, Social and Cultural Rights, and the Covenant on Civil and Political Rights. By 1976, Canada had committed itself to all three. These obligations to extend liberty and broaden equality by enlarging the scope of civil, economic, political and social rights provide benchmarks against which we can measure human progress at home and abroad. For Canadians, they could serve as a major source of inspiration. For the Party, they should serve as guideposts for charting the direction of future national and international policies. What follows are some suggestions for future development in these areas:

1. A critique of the federal Liberals' failure to live up to their domestic and international obligations contained in the Covenant on Economic, Social and Cultural Rights, complemented by related concrete policy proposals, particularly on low-income housing and child poverty.

2. Detailed policy suggestions aimed at overcoming the lack of democratic transparency and accountability in international trade discussions and institutions, particularly those associated with the WTO, regional trade agreements, and global financial institutions. As one component of needed reforms, Canada should be insisting that when there is a conflict between an international human right and any provision in a trade agreement, the right should trump. This is what our Charter of Rights and Freedoms means at home. The same principle should hold internationally.

3. Proposals aimed at bringing civil society organizations and government officials into forums of regular engagement on policy matters. These forums would have to respect the ultimate independence of each but would encourage ongoing exchange on contemporary concerns.

4. A comprehensive and specific strategy to translate the Kyoto agreement on climate change into action. A Party policy committee could be mandated to show specifically how we can have sustainable development *and* concentrate on new industries that can take advantage of a growing global demand for equipment and machinery related to sources of energy other than petroleum.

5. A carefully-thought-out agenda for making corporations more accountable for their employees and their national and international communities, as well as their shareholders. Trade unions have already made significant progress in redistributing the benefits of a market economy by negotiating higher wages, improved health and safety standards, better pensions, and extended vacations for their members, thereby raising standards for working men and women generally. But much more is required, notably in the international context involving human rights (which include workers' rights) and the environment. Specific reform ideas for domestic and international institutional change are available. They need to be translated into concrete policies to be brought before the people of Canada and the international community.

6. Finally, major reforms to broaden the political rights of citizenship. For example:

   a. The Party should lead the way in proposing and promoting a thought-out, revised, democratic electoral system, one which would combine elements of the existing single member constituency with proportional representation.

   b. Corporations and unions and all other collective entities should be banned from financially contributing to federal political parties and candidates. The governments of Quebec and Manitoba made such democratic reform by insisting that apart from the government itself, only individual Canadians should be allowed to provide money for either parties or individuals seeking political office. This moves to much more equality in a citizen's capacity to influence policy debates and electoral results.

Notes

1. In reading a document released on July 26, 2001, by a group who want either a significantly changed New Democratic Party or a new party, a person from Mars could be excused for thinking that the second half of the twentieth century had somehow disappeared. This statement, "The New Politics Initiative: open, sustainable, democratic," contains four references to social democracy, all of which are pejorative. The movement and its leaders are portrayed as "condescending," acting "from on high," or as a "paternalistic elite." Its accomplishments in Canada and elsewhere in the world are ignored. The positive legacy of thousands of party activists and leaders alike in Canada and throughout the world is simply passed over. It's a virtual certainty that none of the drafters of this document would describe themselves as supporters of a social democratic philosophy. The level of discussion about markets is best indicated by MP Svend Robinson, a member of the coordinating committee of the New Politics Initiative. At a conference at McGill University in May, 2001, Mr. Robinson did not agree with the serious arguments being made by social democratic economists that markets should be tamed or made subservient to broader social goals, including equality. "Markets," he said, "like mad dogs, should be put down."

2. See Tony Judt, "'Twas a Famous Victory," *New York Review of Books,* July 19, 2001.

Terms and Concepts

social democracy	liberal	cooperation
citizenship	civil, political, and social rights	civil society
equality	freedom	political parties
market economy	progressive taxation	

Questions

1. How does the author distinguish between social democrats and liberals in terms of their understanding of human beings, rights, and the role of government vis-à-vis society?

2. Why is a social-democratic party still important? Why not just a federation of civil-society organizations and activists?

3. If market economies, as Broadbent observes, generate inequality, why has he made his peace with capitalism? Why does he think it can be "harnessed"?

4. Can individuals be "free" without the means to exercise their freedom?

Unit 2 Annotated Bibliography

Beiner, Ronald. *Liberalism, Nationalism, and Citizenship*. Vancouver, UBC Press, 2003. Beiner defends the ancient idea that citizenship is a human calling and considers citizenship in light of globalization, multiculturalism, and human migration.

Berlin, David Z., and Howard Aster, eds. *What's Left? The New Democratic Party in Renewal*. Oakville: Mosaic Press, 2001. Scholars and activists in this collection of essays debate the future of social democracy in Canadian politics.

Betz, Hans-Georg. *Radical Right-Wing Populism in Western Europe*. New York: St. Martin's Press, 1994. Betz provides an analysis of the rise of populism in France, Italy, and Germany.

Calhoune, Lawrence E. *Civil Society: The Conservative Meaning of Liberal Politics*. Malden, MA: Blackwell, 2002. The author makes a subtle argument for the public place of tradition and community to give contemporary liberal politics a sustainable, conservative cast.

Epstein, Richard A. *Skepticism and Freedom: A Modern Case for Classical Liberalism*. Chicago: University of Chicago Press, 2003. This is a vigorous defence of classical liberal ideas—primacy of individual choice, the laissez-faire economic organization—without recourse to older generalizations about human nature or natural law.

Freyfogle, Eric T., ed. *The New Agrarianism: Land, Culture, and the Community of Life*. Washington: Island Press, 2001. This book collects a series of contemporary essays that demonstrate a reinvigoration of agrarian ideas and practices concerned with land, food, and community.

Frum, David. *Dead Right*. New York: New Republic Books; Basic Books, 1994. A sweeping, polemical attack on the welfare state by a leading neoconservative.

Galston, William A. *Liberal Pluralism: The Implications of Value Pluralism for Political Theory and Practice*. New York: Cambridge University Press, 2002. Galston argues that liberal societies should tolerate as much cultural, religious, and moral diversity as is consistent with civil coexistence.

Giddens, Anthony. *Beyond Left and Right: The Future of Radical Politics*. Stanford: Stanford University Press, 1994. Giddens argues that a new "middle" or "third way" must be fashioned as an alternative to obsolete distinctions between left and right in democratic politics. Giddens has influenced such political leaders as Tony Blair and Bill Clinton.

Giddens, Anthony, ed. *The Progressive Manifesto: New Ideas for the Centre-Left*. Cambridge, UK: Polity Press, 2003. The articles in this collection explore different dimensions of what a progressive vision of politics should look like in the 21st century. The contributors seek a middle course between market capitalism and socialist centralism.

Gidengil, Elisabeth, and Brenda O'Neill (eds.). *Gender and Social Capital*. Oxford: Taylor and Francis, 2006. This collection of essays takes up Robert Putnam's concept of social capital as the foundation of healthy democratic life and examines it from the perspective of gender distinctions.

Gilligan, Carol. *In a Different Voice*. Cambridge, MA: Harvard University Press, 1982. Gilligan's book is an important and frequently cited contribution to the debate surrounding gender difference.

Gray, John. *Two Faces of Liberalism*. New York: New Press, 2000. Gray examines the effect of cultural and moral diversity on liberal understandings of toleration and pluralism.

Grosby, Steven. *Nationalism: A Very Short Introduction*. Oxford: Oxford University Press, 2005. This is a brief and current overview of nationalism as a political, social, philosophical, and anthropological phenomenon.

Holmes, Stephen. *Passions & Constraint: On the Theory of Liberal Democracy*. Chicago: University of Chicago Press, 1995. Holmes offers a thorough defence of the liberal constitutional regime.

Hubbard, Ruth. *The Politics of Women's Biology*. New Brunswick: Rutgers, 1990. Hubbard, who decided to write about science after becoming a respected biologist, describes what she sees as the patriarchal nature of science. Scientific inquiry, she claims, has been part of the power structure that has subjugated women.

Ignatieff, Michael. *Blood and Belonging: Journeys into the New Nationalism*. Toronto: Viking, 1993. Ignatieff delivers a study of nationalism in several contemporary locations, including Yugoslavia, Germany, and Quebec.

Ignatieff, Michael. *Human Rights as Politics and Idolatry*. Princeton: Princeton University Press, 2001. "The most essential message of human rights is that there are no excuses for the inhuman use of human beings," argues Ignatieff. He offers the universal liberal case for the enforcement of human rights across the world.

Ignatieff, Michael. *The Rights Revolution*. Toronto: Anansi, 2000. This Canadian human rights scholar explores the moral and liberal philosophical foundations of the *Canadian Charter of Rights and Freedoms*.

Kheiriddin, Tasha, and Adam Daifallah. *Rescuing Canada's Right: Blueprint for A Conservative Revolution*. Toronto: Wiley, 2005. This is a trenchant defence of a new, more libertarian conservatism that marries individual choice and minimal government.

Kymlicka, Will. *Politics in the Vernacular: Nationalism, Multiculturalism, and Citizenship*. Toronto: Oxford University Press, 2001. Kymlicka examines the relationships among liberalism, multiculturalism, and nationalism in the contemporary North American setting.

Laycock, David. *The New Right and Democracy in Canada: Understanding Reform and the Canadian Alliance.* Toronto: Oxford University Press, 2002. Laycock analyzes the ideology of right-wing populism and its expression in recent Canadian party politics.

Loney, Martin. *The Pursuit of Division: Race, Gender, and Preferential Hiring in Canada.* Montreal and Kingston. McGill–Queen's University Press, 1998. Loney furnishes a trenchant critique of feminist and multiculturalist claims of systemic discrimination and the need for preferential hiring policies.

Miliband, Ralph. *Socialism for a Sceptical Age.* London: Verso, 1994. This book, written after the collapse of Communist regimes in Eastern Europe, restates the case for the possibility of a socialism that can win popular support and create an economy under democratic control.

Newman, Jacquetta, and Linda White. *Women, Politics and Public Policy: The Political Struggles of Canadian Women.* Oxford: Oxford University Press, 2006. This is an examination of feminist initiatives in political action and public policy.

Pateman, Carole. "Feminism and Democracy." In *Democratic Theory and Practice,* ed. Graeme Duncan. New York: Cambridge University Press, 1983. A classic essay by one of the foremost feminist critics of liberal democracy. Pateman believes that liberal democratic politics purposefully and wrongly limit the political participation of women and citizens of lower socioeconomic status.

Plamondon, Bob. *Full Circle: Death and Resurrection in Canadian Conservative Politics.* Toronto: Key Porter, 2006. This is a detailed but accessible account of recent battles of ideas and factions within Canadian conservatism.

Radcliffe Richards, Janet. *The Sceptical Feminist: A Philosophical Inquiry.* London: Penguin, 1980. The author traces the nature of gender inequality, identifies its causes, and critically assesses the arguments justifying it.

Richards, John, Robert D. Cairns, and Larry Pratt, eds. *Social Democracy Without Illusions.* Toronto: McClelland & Stewart, 1991. The editors have collected useful essays on some of the key questions facing Canadian social democrats.

Rosenblum, Nancy, ed. *Liberalism and the Moral Life.* Cambridge, MA: Harvard University Press, 1989. Rosenblum provides a collection of essays laying out the key debates in which liberalism is currently embroiled.

Sandel, Michael J. *Democracy's Discontent: America in Search of a Public Philosophy.* Cambridge, MA: Belknap Press, 1996. Sandel supplies a communitarian critique of modern, "procedural," individualistic liberalism.

Sandel, Michael, ed. *Liberalism and Its Critics.* New York: New York University Press, 1984. Sandel's collection of articles examines critiques of American liberalism.

Smith, Anthony. *National Identity.* London: Penguin, 1991. This is a concise and balanced review of ethnic and other forms of nationalism.

Tamir, Yael. *Liberal Nationalism.* Princeton: Princeton University Press, 1993. Tamir argues that liberal values and national feeling can be quite compatible and mutually reinforcing.

Young, Iris Marion. *Justice and the Politics of Difference.* Princeton: Princeton University Press, 1990. Young critically examines the relationship between universal citizenship and group differences based on gender, ethnicity, and race.

Unit Three

Introduction: Citizenship and Democracy

❖ ❖ ❖

A popular e-mail circulating through cyberspace asks readers to consider what it would be like working for a "company" whose 300 employees have the following characteristics: 30 have been accused of spousal abuse; 9 have been arrested for fraud; 14 have been accused of writing bad cheques; 95 have directly or indirectly bankrupted at least two businesses; 16 are currently defendants in lawsuits; 12 have been arrested on drug-related charges; and so on. The "company" in question is the Canadian House of Commons.

E-mails like this are intended not only to get a laugh but also to confirm us in our contempt for our so-called elected representatives in the halls of political power. For those who think MPs are upstanding citizens, e-mails like this are intended to set them straight. Leave aside for the moment whether the allegations noted are true. Leave aside the fact that most of the characteristics involve allegations and accusations, which are easy to make and over which the recipient has little control—indeed, being a politician means being subject to allegations of all sorts, as well as the odd pie in the face. Leave aside the absence of statistics indicating the level of immorality and profligacy in the general Canadian population. Leave aside also that such contempt for politicians is not new. Mark Twain once said, "Suppose you were an idiot. And suppose you were a member of Congress. But I repeat myself." Politicians themselves sometimes find it useful to take up the antipolitician rant. Ronald Reagan once said, "The government is like a baby's alimentary canal, with a happy appetite at one end and no responsibility at the other."

What gives e-mails like this their power is the assumption that elected representatives are worse people than the rest of us, that they are unrepresentative in a moral sense. Either they are corrupt by nature—corrupt people will seek avenues to practise corrupt conduct—or the system makes them corrupt.

Why do we have such contempt for politicians? Why are our expectations so high? What of the maxim that democratic peoples get the governments they deserve? Is the problem political representation itself? Perhaps citizens in democracies should participate more deeply in their governance so that if things go wrong, they will have only

© Micah Walter/Reuters/Corbis

For many, democratic citizenship entails standing up for one's view, not just voting for them.

themselves to blame. In other words, the principle of representation itself creates a distinction between government and the governed, and citizens are placed at one remove from political power.

An important strand in the history of political thought holds that the general population should not directly wield power, since most people are unwilling and unfit to assume the responsibilities of self-government. Representation in this sense is a constitutional safety valve, protecting people from themselves.[1] Contemporary writers also find that the demands made of government are so numerous and complex that citizens as a collective body cannot be expected to spend the time necessary to manage political affairs.

Other strands see representation as a relic in mature democracies with ever more highly educated populations. In addition, electronic information technologies afford us the opportunity to bring large populations into circles of governance. If a democracy is to be true to its name, power must be returned to the people.[2]

Citizenship is a legal as well as a sociological matter: citizens of a state are entitled to exercise the full measure of rights, ranging from political and legal rights to social welfare entitlements. How one gains citizenship varies from state to state. Generally, one becomes a citizen of a country by being born there. However, there have been conspicuous exceptions to this rule. Until 1999, the Federal Republic of Germany operated under a 1913 citizenship code that defined citizenship on the basis of ethnicity. This code effectively deprived over 7 million residents of non-German ethnic background (either guest workers or their descendants) of the rights of citizenship.

In most cases, those not born in a country can be naturalized as citizens by making an application and satisfying certain conditions; for example, living in the country for a minimum period, demonstrating a knowledge of the country's history and politics, and pledging allegiance to the country and its constitution. Such conditions are always a matter of political debate. Some argue that conditions should be stringent, especially when the host country boasts a generous welfare state. Others maintain that rigorous conditions are unacceptably exclusive in an age in which all persons are held to be possessors of universal rights.

When the discussion of citizenship shifts from rights to obligations, the sociological dimension of citizenship comes to the fore. Citizenship is a matter of membership, belonging, and identification, a fact clearly evident in the pomp and ritual associated with citizenship ceremonies. What can be expected of a citizen? What sacrifices of time and energy must citizens make? How exactly are the rights and duties of citizenship expressed in 21st-century democracies?

Several articles in this unit consider the issues of participation and belonging, as well as the rights of citizenship. They explore how people participate and in what ways democratic citizenship is hampered.

---

1. An excellent example of this suspicion of democracy is *The Federalist Papers,* a compilation of late-18th-century newspaper articles written by James Madison, Alexander Hamilton, and John Jay, all of whom influenced the ratification of the American Constitution of 1791. The most prominent fathers of Canadian Confederation in 1867 were no less suspicious of popular government.
2. Robert Dahl, *How Democratic Is the American Constitution?* (New Haven: Yale University Press, 2002).

Civic Disengagement in Contemporary America

Robert D. Putnam

Editors' Note

"Capital" refers to any asset that can be used to increase the efficiency of a production process. More efficient processes lead to more profits. Capitalism is that economic system in which profits are reinvested in capital to increase efficiencies and profits further. A screwdriver is a form of physical capital a cabinetmaker can use to make cabinets quickly, efficiently, and with the prospect of making more money on their sale. Likewise, someone can go to school and use that education to be more productive as a computer analyst than he or she would be without that training. Education is a way to develop human capital.

Harvard political scientist Robert Putnam is concerned with a new dimension of capital altogether: social capital. Social capital refers to patterns of human interaction and norms of reciprocity that make people individually as well as collectively healthier, safer, and more prosperous. If we "only connect," we will get along in ways that produce wealth, health, and happiness. There is something obvious in this. If I slip in the bathtub before an appointment with friends, someone will soon miss me and find out what happened. If I know no one, it could be days

before help arrives, if at all. But there is more to it than this. Social capital refers to norms of generalized trust among strangers, allowing them to interact, trade, and engage in mutual help without fear of being cheated or harmed.

What of the political effects of social capital? Putnam argues that civic engagement is the seed of political citizenship, the basis for people's participation in the common life of the community and polity. He notes that the decline of the stock of social capital is associated with increases in incivility—rude behaviour and cheating on taxes, for example. The more people see their fate as distinct from that of others and that of the community as a whole, the less they contribute to the welfare of others. Market economies and democratic politics depend on social capital and will wither without it.

Putnam is famous for arguing, as he does here, that social capital in the United States is in a period of decline. Americans love to bowl, he notes, and the number of bowlers is increasing, but the number of people who bowl in leagues is declining. People eat

together less than they used to. People gamble a lot, but they play less bridge—a quintessentially social game—and visit casinos more. He argues that entertainment television consumption accounts for one-third of the social capital declines in recent years. Entertainment TV substitutes simulated social capital for the real thing: we watch actors building and enjoying social capital instead of doing it ourselves.

How does Putnam know what he knows? Many a pundit bemoans contemporary individualism, but such jeremiads seem to be based on impressions rather than systematic inquiry. Putnam supports his argument by reference to extensive survey data and statistical correlations. The major problem with this method of inquiry is that one needs things to count. Formal membership in permanent organizations is easy to count, but informal patterns of connectedness may be more difficult to examine. Putnam has been criticized for basing his decline thesis on formal memberships, not more comprehensive examinations of people's social activity. In this and in more recent work, Putnam responds to the critics and holds fast to his theory of social capital decline.

❖ ❖ ❖

Robert Putnam, "Civic Disengagement in Contemporary America," *Government and Opposition* 36(2) (Spring, 2000): 135–56. Reprinted with permission of Blackwell Publishing Inc. This is the text of the Government and Opposition/Leonard Schapiro lecture delivered at the London School of Economics on May 6, 1999.

Over the past two generations the United States has undergone a series of remarkable transformations. It has helped to defeat global communism, led a revolution in information technology that is fuelling unprecedented prosperity, invented life-saving treatments for diseases from AIDS to cancer, and made great strides in reversing discriminatory practices and promoting equal rights for all citizens. But during these same decades the United States also has undergone a less sanguine transformation: its citizens have become remarkably less civic, less politically engaged, less socially connected, less trusting, and less committed to the common good. At the dawn of the millennium Americans are fast becoming a loose aggregation of disengaged observers, rather than a community of connected participants.[1]

In social science terms, Americans have dramatically less "social capital" than they had even 30 years ago. Social capital simply refers to the social norms and networks that enhance people's ability to collaborate on common endeavours. These social norms and networks have important consequences, both for the people who share and participate in them and for those who do not. All things being equal, social capital makes individuals—and communities—healthier, wealthier, wiser, happier, more productive and better able to govern themselves peaceably and effectively.

At the dawn of the millennium Americans are fast becoming a loose aggregation of disengaged observers, rather than a community of connected participants.

Social capital is a term originating in an analogy with two other forms of capital. The first, physical capital, is simply some tangible object that makes a person more productive than he or she would otherwise be. A screwdriver is a bit of physical capital. So, if an individual saves his money and buys a screwdriver, he can repair more bicycles more quickly. That physical capital improves his productivity.

The second form of capital, human capital, is a term coined by economists about a quarter-century ago. The term draws an analogy between buying a screwdriver and going to school. An individual can save up her money to pay for education or training, and she will be more productive than she would have been if she lacked that human capital. Moreover, there are external effects. People around her benefit from the fact that she is more educated and more productive: they learn from her knowledge, and enjoy the fruits of her labour.

Like physical and human capital, social capital may have individual and collective effects. A person who is involved in networks, particularly networks with certain features, will be more productive than a demographically identical individual who is not so involved. Networks and organizations with high levels of trust and reciprocity are especially conducive to efficient collective action. One need only imagine trying to function in a low-reciprocity environment, where each person had to look over her shoulder and worry about being undercut by somebody else. So distracted, each individual would be less productive than if she could count on the others. That example demonstrates the meaning of social capital—and the fact that social networks have consequences. They tend to produce norms of reciprocity, and that tends to enable people to be more efficient.

What has happened to America's stock of social capital—its civic norms, networks and organizations? My best estimate is that by many different measures the stock has been depleted by roughly one-third since the early 1970s. Of course, that broad conclusion masks a lot of variation. Some measures of social capital have declined more; others have declined less. But, broadly speaking, the trends are pronounced and consistent.

... by many different measures the stock [of social capital] has been depleted by roughly one-third since the early 1970s.

Take trust, for example. The degree to which Americans have faith in their government and politics, their social institutions and their fellow citizens has dropped dramatically over the past two generations. In the 1960s, when the American National Election Studies asked Americans whether they trusted the government to do what is right "just about all" or "most" of the time, seven out of ten respondents said Yes. In 1999, fewer than two out of ten respondents agreed. That is a 75 per cent drop, reflecting a 30-year erosion of faith in democratic institutions. People have similarly jaded evaluations of the performance of religious institutions and unions and business and universities and so on.

Americans are also far less likely to trust one another—which is logically quite different from trusting public authorities. A variety of different kinds of evidence makes this clear. In round numbers, nearly two-thirds of Americans a generation or two ago said they trusted other people: today, the fraction is closer to one-third. And there is some reason to believe, though the evidence on this is much spottier, that Americans are actually less honest than they used to be, meaning the decline in trust may be an understandable response to an actual decline in trustworthiness.

"BOWLING ALONE"

◆ ◆ ◆

Other indicators of declining connectedness are equally surprising and should be of deep concern to Americans as citizens. Five years ago, in a short article called "Bowling Alone,"[2] I reported familiar trends, such as that Americans are a lot less likely to vote than they were 25 or 30 years ago. There's been about a 25 per cent decline in the fraction of Americans who vote, and that's true at all levels—national, state and local. The article used metaphors like "bowling" and "choral societies" to indicate that political participation is embedded in social activity more generally. It is important not to mistake what might be a broad social trend for merely a political trend. And, indeed, the decline in voting is only one of many indicators of civic and social disengagement.

The "Bowling Alone" article reported, for example, a massive decline in participation in local parent-teacher associations, an especially ominous development given that PTA participation is one of the most common forms of civic engagement in America. The fraction of American parents who belong to a PTA has fallen by roughly half since the 1950s. Note that this is not a 50 per cent decline in absolute numbers, but rather a 50 per cent drop in the fraction of relevant population that is participating. Obviously, during the baby boom, there were more parents, and so, not surprisingly, there were more parent-teacher association members. It is necessary, therefore, to statistically adjust for the declining numbers of school-aged kids since that time to get at the interesting indicator, which is the propensity of parents to participate in PTAs. Simply put, parents have only about half the propensity today that they did in the 1960s.

This is also true for what we might colloquially call the "animal clubs"—that is, fraternal organizations. In the United States, most men's organizations are named for animals: The Lions, Moose, Elks, Eagles and so on. "Bowling Alone" showed how all of those organizations have experienced declining membership since the mid-1960s or mid-1970s. Again, these declines reflected a population-adjusted drop in the propensity to join these organizations. The story is the same for women's clubs and also for the group that inspired the article's title, bowling clubs.

Bowling is big in America. The sport consists of throwing a ball down a lane and knocking pins down. The player who knocks the most pins down wins. You can bowl by yourself, as many people do, or you can bowl in teams. Bowling is very popular, the most popular participant sport in America. It is also one of the most egalitarian sports, in the sense that participation is not especially correlated with social class. This is a middle-class and working-class sport. It is a sport that is far more diverse than are many other sports by gender, marital status, race and educational attainment. Because bowling attracts all types, it is an interesting social barometer.

The nature of the game affords important opportunities for face-to-face interaction. Normally, two teams, with five players apiece, square off in a game. But at any given point, there are only two people up at the lane, rolling the ball or getting ready to do so. That leaves eight people who are not doing anything except sitting on a semicircular bench and waiting their turn. Most of the time, they chat about the previous night's game or the latest gossip. But occasionally and inevitably, they will also discuss whether the local bond issue should pass, or whether the trash is picked up promptly, or how the local schools are performing. So, in a profound sense, those eight people sitting in the back are involved in civic deliberation, even if it is not recognized as such at the time. They are having a conversation with other folks that they see regularly, and in a context of mutual understanding. They know Joe always says crazy things, so they know how to interpret what Joe's position is; they know that Barbara is always on top of matters, so they pay attention to her point of view.

Bowling is increasingly popular in America. The fraction of people who bowl has risen by roughly ten per cent over the last decade or so. But bowling in leagues, bowling in teams, is down by forty per cent. That is of importance to the bowling industry because it turns out that people who bowl in teams drink four times as much beer and eat four times as many pretzels. The money in that industry is in the beer and pretzels, not in the ball and shoe rentals. So, the bowling industry actually worries a lot about the decline of league bowling. Everyday citizens should be concerned as well, but for a different reason: less team bowling means less civic deliberation.

The fraction of people who bowl has risen roughly ten per cent over the last decade or so. But bowling in leagues, bowling in teams, is down by forty per cent.

That short article touched off a debate in America about the so-called "bowling alone" issues, because claims made on the basis of a couple of gripping examples may not be broadly generalizable. Both ordinary people and other scholars responded with thoughtful questions, insights and critiques that have helped to enhance understanding of the changing scope and nature of social capital in America.

Here, I update "Bowling Alone" by presenting new evidence on trends in American civil life. Parenthetically, it would be fascinating to determine whether comparable trends exist in other countries. But for the time being, I address four questions:

First, what's been happening to civic life in America?
Second, why?
Third, so what—why should we be concerned?
And fourth, what do we do about it?

WHAT HAS HAPPENED TO CIVIC LIFE IN AMERICA?

◆ ◆ ◆

It turns out that answering this question is more methodologically complicated than it might appear. There are many approaches, but each one has serious drawbacks. For example, examining the membership in fixed-named organizations, such as the Lions or Elks Clubs, provides some sense of the vitality of those particular organizations, and it allows roughly comparable measures of organizational activity over long periods of time. However, that approach does not capture the possible displacement of members from old organizations to new ones. Thus, examining membership in a set of long-established organizations does not necessarily

provide a valid picture of social connectedness trends in general. Instead, it is necessary to use myriad approaches to answering the question, on the theory that each approach can make up for the shortcomings in some other approach.

As an initial cut, I have gathered membership data on a large number of voluntary associations over the course of the twentieth century. These were all organizations with local chapters where people met face-to-face, rather than advocacy organizations whose members do not do anything more than send a cheque to national headquarters. For example, I have collected data over time on the percentage of Catholic men who belong to the Knights of Columbus; the percentage of Jewish women who belong to Hadassah; the percentage of rural kids who belong to 4-H; the percentage of middle-aged men who belong to one of the animal clubs, and so on. These percentages reflect what corporate executives call "market share."

Astonishingly, the market share of all of these organizations followed virtually the same trajectory over time. Over the course of this century, all of these organizations showed rising market share, year after year, for the first half of the twentieth century. More doctors belonged to the American Medical Association, more women belonged to women's clubs, more Catholic men belonged to the Knights of Columbus, and so on. A graph would show a long rise from 1900 to roughly 1960. There is only one notch in that graph, which comes in a dramatic, catastrophic decline in membership in the Depression years, as one might expect. Many organizations lost half of their members in four or five years.

But then, astonishingly, beginning around 1945, America experienced what may well have been the greatest organizational boom in its history. Membership in most groups (as a fraction of the relevant of the population group) basically doubled between 1945 and 1960. And that is true in virtually all of these organizations after the Second World War. It is perhaps no surprise that there were more members of the American Legion, a veterans' group, right after the Second World War. But it is quite surprising that the Grange, a nineteenth-century organization of farmers, showed a similar boom in membership. The Girl Scouts and Boy Scouts and 4-H, which are all organizations for kids, showed a boom, as did the League of Women Voters, and so on.

Then, in the 1960s, suddenly, surprisingly, and mysteriously, all of these groups almost simultaneously began to experience stagnation in their market share.

Soon after, their market share began to fall. Most of these groups did not notice because the number of people—the pool of potential members—was growing, and that partially offset the declining propensity for potential members actually to join. In other words, club secretaries kept track of actual members, not what fraction of potential members had actually signed up. So it took some time before voluntary association leaders realized that there was something happening to their membership. And, of course, their first thought was they had done something wrong—a bad programme chair that year, dues that were too high, or whatever. For a good while, many organizations engaged in tough self-analysis. There are scores of consultants' reports commissioned by these organizations analyzing the question, "Why are we in trouble?"

… in the 1960s, suddenly, surprisingly, and mysteriously, all of these groups almost simultaneously began to experience stagnation in their market share.

Of course, what was happening to one organization was happening to all of them, though the declines did not all happen at exactly the same time. The first of the organizations to maximize their market share was the National Federation of Women's Clubs, which peaked in 1957. The last organization to hit the wall, appropriately enough, was a civic organization in Middle America called the Optimists. Their peak year was 1980, but they have not plunged so far that they are at the level of the other organizations that started declining earlier.

Interestingly, these trends also hold for professional organizations, even though it looks on the surface that they could be an exception to the general organizational downturn. With rising rates of professional education in America, membership in these organizations has soared since mid-century. The American Bar Association (lawyers) had more than ten times as many members in 1991 as it had in 1945; the American Medical Association (doctors) more than doubled its membership in that time-frame. Professional associations of engineers, dentists and architects also posted huge increases. But, in terms of the market share—the fraction of professionals who actually belong to their respective professional association—the trend looks exactly like the trend in other voluntary groups. That is, professional association posted rising membership rates until about 1960 or 1965, and then began a steady decline. The American Medical Association hit the wall in 1961, for instance. Again, the Association's leaders did not notice it right away because the number of doctors was growing so rapidly that the expanding pool made up for the fact that the Association was capturing a smaller and smaller share of that pool.

But that evidence in itself does not prove anything. Although suggestive, it is not conclusive insofar as membership data from specific organizations do not necessarily reflect an underlying propensity to join groups in general. A critic might ask—and many did—whether this analysis is limited to old-fashioned organizations on their way out. Indeed, there is an inherent problem with this kind of analysis in that organizations that have long-term membership data are by definition organizations that have been around for a long time. So, critics asked, what if there is a whole new set of organizations that people are joining instead: New Age encounter groups, Alcoholics Anonymous and Drugs Anonymous, book clubs and so on? What if people are dropping out of older, better-known organizations but not dropping out of organizations entirely? That is the first critique. The second critique goes as follows: maybe Americans are no longer formally joining groups or going to organizational meetings (that feels kind of square and "1950s-ish" anyhow) but people *are* still hanging out together, maybe even more than they used to. Perhaps they are going to bars, like the one on the popular American television programme *Cheers,* where (according to the programme's slogan) "everybody knows your name." Hanging out with friends at the bar fosters social capital just as much as hanging out at the bowling alley does.

I had been aware of these problems, but it was not immediately obvious how to get around them. For example, it would be nice to know the number of picnics that people went on every year since 1975, but I know of no "national picnic registry." Likewise, it was not obvious how to find good data on how many club meetings people attended, not just meetings of well-known clubs for which no organizational records existed. Astonishingly, just as the methodological situation was looking very dire, two rich new sources of data became available, and between them, they not only confirmed the "Bowling Alone" story, but also made it much more compelling. My critics had suggested that if we took a more comprehensive look at social capital in America—not just membership in old-fashioned organizations—things might not look so bleak. With the new data we could take a much wider view of various forms of social connectedness, and with that new evidence things actually looked bleaker than I had originally suggested.

The first of these datasets was actually known to exist, but the data were not previously available for analysis. This dataset consists of surveys conducted by a reputable polling firm called the Roper Organization. Roughly every month for 25 years, Roper asked 1,000 Americans—a good nationally representative sample every month—a set of questions that had the following form:

Now here is a list of things some people do about government or politics. Have you happened to have done any of those things in the past year?

- Attended a public meeting on town or school affairs. [Note that this asked about any public meeting, and that the meeting could have been about any number of specific issues.]

- Served in a committee for some local organization. [Again, note that the question asks about membership in *any* organization, not just in one of a handful of well-established organizations.]

- Become or served as an officer of some club or organization.

- Written your congressman or senator.

- Held or run for political office.

Now, few people run for office, of course. But when 1,000 people a month are surveyed for 25 years, the cumulative number of respondents adds up pretty fast—there are 415,000 people in the Roper dataset. In that large a survey, with that large a sample, you can get statistically reliable estimates of the number of people who run for office, or who have written letters to the editor of the newspaper, or who belong to local good government organizations, or who have signed petitions. In all, the surveys asked about twelve different ways in which one can be politically or civically involved. Unbelievably, according to these surveys, participation in every single one of those activities massively declined over the period. For example, between the early 1970s and the early 1990s, there was a decline of about 40 per cent in the fraction of Americans who served as a club officer, and a decline of 35 per cent in the fraction who attended a public meeting. All told, there was a decline of about 25 per cent in the fraction of Americans who had done any of the twelve activities in the previous year.

> *With the new data we could take a much wider view of various forms of social connectedness, and with that new evidence things actually looked bleaker than I had originally suggested.*

The declines were not of equal magnitude across all types of activity. That, in itself, is intriguing, and helps to illuminate how the character of American civil society is changing. The sorts of activities that a citizen can do alone without coordinating with anyone else—activities such as signing a petition or writing a letter to an elected official—are down just 10 to 15 per cent over this period. On the other hand, activities that involve coordinating with somebody else—activities such as public meetings—are down far more sharply, about 40 to 50 per cent. Obviously, if you go to a meeting and there is nobody else there, it is not a meeting. Likewise, it is hard to be a secretary of an organization if the organization has no other members to elect you. This evidence is consistent with the following explanation: everybody has cut back a little bit. Each individual decision has ripple effects, and these individual ripples together have a multiplicative, rather than an additive, effect that makes group coordination especially challenging.

Because the Roper dataset is so large, it lends itself to many interesting analyses. But the major conclusion emerging from them is that all kinds of organizations (not just traditional organizations) have experienced this same kind of decline in membership. That implies that although there are obviously some new groups now that did not exist 30 years ago, they do not begin to make up for the catastrophic declines in membership of the traditional mainline organizations.

> *... all kinds of organizations (not just traditional organizations) have experienced this same kind of decline in membership.*

The second newly available dataset is, in many ways, even more useful.[3] Every year since 1975, the market research firm DDB has commissioned a survey that asks 3–4,000 Americans a whole range of "lifestyle" questions. Most of these questions center on what brand of car or laundry detergent or some other product they prefer. But 25 years ago, one of the marketers realized that companies could more easily sell products if they knew about the background and tastes of potential customers. Therefore, the surveys contain a lot of questions about people's attitudes toward family, race differences, economic policies, politics and so forth. But the surveys also ask an even more interesting set of questions: how many times, in the course of the last year, did you take part in various specific social activities?

For example, the survey asks, "How many times in the last year did you go to church?" (That's useful information for the marketers because church-goers turn out to buy and send more Christmas cards.) But, unbeknownst to the survey designers, they created what is probably the best data series in America on the frequency of church attendance. The DDB data, among other things, can be examined together with other surveys that ask about church attendance to see if all the data sources are telling the same general story.

Besides inquiring about church attendance, the DDB survey asked:

- How many times last year did you go to a club meeting?
- How many times last year did you have friends over to your house?
- How many times last year did you go to a dinner party?
- How many times last year did you work on a community project?
- How many times last year did you volunteer?
- How many times last year did you play cards?
- And certainly not least, how many times last year did you go on a picnic?

So, it turns out, there is after all a record of picnicking in America. Consistent with other trends, the frequency with which Americans go on picnics has been cut in half over the past quarter-century. Americas went picnicking, on average, four times a year in 1975, but only twice in 1999.

Consistent with other trends, the frequency with which Americans go on picnics has been cut in half over the past quarter-century.

Another social activity that is popular in America is card-playing. Even today, card-playing is actually much more common than is going to movies. The average American plays cards about twice as often as he or she goes to the cinema. However, the new data make clear how rapidly that form of social entertainment is disappearing.

In the late 1950s, 40 per cent of American adults played bridge regularly. That number is now about 8–9 per cent, and bridge is mostly confined to retirement communities. Bridge is essentially dying out. If you say "bridge" to an audience of young people, it sounds as "whist" does to Americans of my generation. That is, it is a game that you have vaguely heard of, but you cannot imagine any real person playing it. Indeed, card-playing is dropping at such a fast rate that a straight line projection has card-playing disappearing from America in little more than a decade. If card-playing continues its 20-year downhill slide, the activity will disappear.

Now perhaps that is not the end of the world—unless you are a card manufacturer. But, actually, card-playing is important because card games are intrinsically social. In bridge, for example, the players are not allowed to talk about the game, but they have to talk about something. At its height, bridge was probably the most important site for extra-familial, cross-gender discussions in America. That was an age in which leisure activities were very gendered. But mixed bridge was common. Now it has just about disappeared.

Americans are doing other things instead. For example, going to casinos is up. However, casino gambling is anything but a social activity. Casinos consist of hundreds of people in enormous rooms who are sitting and pulling levers by themselves. Some people are choosing to play bridge on the Internet. These are games involving real people, but there is almost never any side-talk. There is not talk about how the players feel about the local schools. Of course, such talk would be misplaced, because two players' local schools are almost certainly in different localities or even different countries.

In short, the collapse of actual card-playing is much larger than the rise in Internet card-playing; but even if the Internet version had perfectly replaced the face-to-face version, the Internet version would not generate the kind of social capital that matters. Traditional card-playing will face extinction once the number of card-players sinks below a certain threshold. Once that threshold is passed, it does not make sense for any given individual to learn the rules. It is a coordination problem, in game theory terms. Just as bird populations collapse at the end for lack of adequate partners, so card-games are on the road to collapse for the same reason.

Club activity is also in dramatic decline. In 1975, the average American attended twelve club meetings annually, or one a month. That figure is now at five a year, and it is declining at such a rate that clubs, like card-playing, will disappear in the 2010s unless something changes.

The DDB surveys also asked, "How many times last year did you go to a bar?" It turns out that activity is down a lot, as well. Several independent survey archives confirm that going out in the evening (to a bar, night club, disco, etc.) has declined by about 30 per cent. That finding is especially surprising because going out tends to be a "singles' activity" and there are more singles in America now compared to a generation ago. I do not know where these singles are hanging out, but it is not in any of the social settings that the surveys could pick up.

Virtually all of the informal social activities—going to club meetings, going to church, having dinner parties, having friends over, going out to bars, going on picnics, etc.—show a substantial decline. The decline is also monotonic, meaning that the prevalence of the activity does not fluctuate from year to year, but rather it just keeps going down in survey after survey.

The DDB surveys not only measure Americans' retreat from civil society, but they also record the nation's much-noticed move toward incivility. The survey asked, "How many times in the course of the last year did you give the finger (make a rude gesture) to another driver?" The latest answer is 2.2 times nationwide, running as high as 4.8 times among Americans under 30. Even more intriguingly, the dataset contains information on respondents' self-reported cheating on their income tax. It turns out that cheating on one's income tax is strongly correlated with the number of times one issued a rude gesture to another driver. This find, of course, could provide a powerful clue to the Internal Revenue Service about whose income tax returns to audit.

> The DDB surveys not only measure Americans' retreat from civil society, but they also record the nation's much-noticed move toward incivility.

But the most astonishing single finding in this entire dataset concerns how often people have dinner with members of their family. It turns out that the frequency with which people have dinner with their family has declined by nearly one-third since the mid-1970s. This is not simply because fewer people are married. This figure refers only to married people, who are increasingly eating alone.

> ... the fact that Americans are disengaging from their families may be the more troubling trend.

Somehow, "eating alone" does not have the same rhetorical cachet as "bowling alone," but the fact that Americans are disengaging from their families may be the more troubling trend. We have been going to clubs for five or six hundred years, but people have been breaking bread with their life partner much longer. It is hard to think of any society in which families do not dine together. So, to have that activity on the road to disappearing in one or two generations is an alarming trend—almost like watching a major species go into extinction.

WHY IS SOCIAL CAPITAL ERODING?
◆ ◆ ◆

Charting the changes in American civil society is easier than explaining their causes. To find the source of social trends, social scientists often act like an epidemiologist looking for the source of a disease: they scout around for "hot spots," or pockets of the population where the trend might be concentrated. In the present context, one might ask, "Who used to have lots of picnics but stopped doing so?"

Looking for social trend hot spots is complicated, however, by the fact that declines in civic and social activity are remarkably equal across all segments of American society. The trends are down among men and down among women. They are down among the rich, and among the poor and the middle class. They are down among people with graduate education, and they are down among high school drop-outs, and among people at all levels in between. The trends are down in central cities, and they are down in suburbs, and they are down in small towns. Even though club meetings and other forms of social capital are more common in small towns than in central cities, the trends are the same in both places. The decline in social capital has also hit all areas of the country: the East Coast, and West Coast, the South, and even the comparatively social-capital-rich upper-Midwest.

However, there is one bright spot in an otherwise bleak picture. Today's older generation appears to have been somewhat immune from the virus that is depressing social and civic participation. People who are in their 60s and 70s today are nearly as participatory as were people who were in their 60s and 70s several decades ago—and in the case of volunteering in the community, today's seniors are actually much more participatory than were seniors in earlier generations.

In general, participation often declines with age, but if we examine the evidence contained in the newly available longitudinal survey archives, we can hold age more or less constant and examine generational differences. Suppose that all Americans were lined up, left to right, from those born in the 1900s to those born in the 1970s. Then suppose that these people are asked a series of questions: how often do you read the newspaper, how many picnics did you go on last year, how often do you go to clubs, how often do you go to church, how often did you go to a public meeting last year? Among those on the left side of the line, those born from 1910 to 1930, the fraction who do all those activities would be very high, as it always has been. These people constitute what I call the "long civic generation."

That generation was born in the years leading up to the mid-1930s. People who were born in the late 1930s and early 1940s are still quite active, but they are a little less active than are the people born in the 1920s and early 1930s. That generational decline would continue for the next four decades. Compare people born in the 1920s with their grandchildren, born in the 1970s. The grandparents are three times as likely to read a newspaper, twice as likely to vote, and twice as likely to trust other people; and the older folks go to clubs three times as often.

The obvious objection is, "So what? Maybe when the grandchildren get to [be] their grandparents' age, the younger cohort will be joining clubs and doing all those activities just like their grandparents." Unfortunately, there is no evidence for that optimistic supposition. In technical terms, there is little evidence that the different participation rates across age groups represent a life-cycle phenomenon. Virtually all the evidence suggests instead that this is a cohort, or generational, phenomenon.

The generational finding is the only strong clue as to what might have caused the decline in civic partici-

pation and social capital over the past 25 or 30 years. But it is a striking clue. It also has serious implications for the future because this long civic generation, the people who came of age during the Great Depression or the Second World War, are now in their seventies and eighties and nineties and do not have many years left to contribute. The cohorts coming up behind them, those who came of age after the Second World War, seem to have been exposed to some anti-civic X-ray that made them wary of participation in social and public life. As a result, voluntary organizations are graying because middle-aged people and new retirees are not replacing the long civic generation as members and officers. The average age in church pews and club meetings is rising.

> ... those who came of age after the Second World War ... seem to have been exposed to some anti-civic X-ray that made them wary of participation in social and public life.

On a positive note, there is some evidence of a slight upturn in civic participation among people now in their twenties. They do not quite match people in their forties and fifties, but the twenty-somethings are more civic than are people in their thirties. So at the very front end of this long-run trend, civic help might be arriving. In the meantime, however, old age continues to take away the most civic people in America, and this process will keep driving down the average rate of civic engagement and voting for at least the next 20–30 years.

In sum, the process of "generational replacement" is the single most important reason for the erosion of social capital and civic participation. It accounts for about half of the overall decline. What about the other half?

One obvious possibility is that more Americans are working, and working longer hours, and so they simply do not have time for voluntary activity. That explanation has intuitive appeal. Surprisingly, though, an increase in work hours is but a tiny part of the problem. This is because, although women are working more hours outside the home than they used to, men are actually working fewer hours outside the home than they used to, on average. In addition, among women, work has two effects that go in opposite directions. Because work takes time, it cuts down on some forms of involvement; but because it exposes women to wider networks, it also increases the likelihood that they will be an officer of a club, for example. Changes in work patterns, notably the proliferation of two-career families, account for only about 10 per cent of the decline in civic participation.

One might expect that economic hard times and economic discontent are part of the explanation. Others, by contrast, speculate that affluence has caused rampant individualism. But these factors cannot explain very much because over the last 25–30 years the economy has gone up and down and up and down. During the 1970s Americans faced tough times economically, whereas throughout most of the 1990s, the American economy experienced a huge boom. But through good times and bad, social capital kept going down and down. So it seems unlikely that this is simply an economic phenomenon.

Urban sprawl is probably an accomplice. For every ten minutes of time one spends commuting, there is a 10 per cent cut in almost all forms of social engagement— 10 per cent fewer dinner parties, 10 per cent fewer club meetings, and 10 per cent fewer church services attended. The church attendance figure is especially revealing because most church services are not held on working days. In other words, that pattern implies that there is something about urban sprawl, other than simply the time people are stuck in a car, that keeps them from attending social and civic events. Most likely, urban sprawl has created a geographical separation between the places where people work, the places where they live and the places where they shop. That dispersion has fragmented citizens' sense of community. The best estimate is that urban sprawl and subordination are responsible for about 10 per cent of the decline in civic engagement.

Finally, and significantly, there is the advent of television. TV comes onto the stage at just the right moment to help explain the decline in civic life, and TV has come to occupy a sizeable fraction of Americans' free time. The new dataset makes clear how powerful the correlation is between watching TV and being a civic slug. The most powerful predictor of an individual's level of civic engagement is the answer to the following question: "Television is my primary form of entertainment—agree or disagree." Half of Americans agree, and half disagree. Which way they answer turns out to be a better predictor of their involvement than is their level of education, which is normally the strongest demographic correlate of civic activity.

The best estimate from the data is that the proliferation of entertainment television is responsible for about one-third of the decline in civic participation.

An important caveat is in order. Television per se is not the problem. For example, watching television news is done by people who are older and more civically engaged. But most of Americans' time in front of the tube is spent not watching the news, but rather watching entertainment, and that is strongly negatively correlated with civic activity. It is not clear from the data whether television causes people to be less engaged, or whether people who do not want to be engaged watch television instead. Probably, the causal arrow points in both directions. The best estimate from the data is that the proliferation of entertainment television is responsible for about one-third of the decline in civic participation. Television works in two ways. It contributes to the generational-replacement explanation (because the older civic generation is not as hooked as the younger cohorts are), and television keeps people of all ages in their living rooms.

SO WHAT?
◆ ◆ ◆

The erosion of social capital in America matters in many important ways. This is not merely about an ageing generation's nostalgia for the tranquil 1950s. Rather, the stark reality is that, in many measurable ways, the health of our communities and even our own health depends importantly on our stock of social capital.

This investigation of the state of social capital in America is an outgrowth of an earlier study of Italy.[4] That study set out to investigate a rather obscure topic: why some regions of Italy were better governed than other regions were. There were clearly parts of Italy that were poorly governed, and there were other parts of Italy that were well-governed. The research question was, "What could explain those differences?"

Many hypotheses presented themselves: differences in economic wealth, differences in the education level of the residents, differences in political party systems, and so forth. Some of these factors, such as the level of modernization and economic development, did matter. But it took years of research before it became clear that there was a secret ingredient, a trace element in the soil, that made some regional governments function better than others did. That secret ingredient turned out to be choral societies and football clubs—that is, various forms of community involvement.

Some communities had higher levels of involvement in political life but also in social life. Civic engagement is not purely a matter of politics, which is why "choral societies" is an effective metaphor and an efficient predictor of good government. Dense networks of civic engagement had given rise to a norm of reciprocity— "I'll do this for you now, without expecting anything back immediately from you, because down the road, somebody else will do something for me, and anyhow, we'll all see each other on Thursday night at the choral society." Based on that research, if you tell me how many choral societies there are in a community of Italy, I will be able to tell you, plus or minus three days, how long it will take the average citizen to get his health bills reimbursed. The correlation is strong.

Now communities that have lots of choral societies also turn out to be wealthier, and for some time we thought that this was because wealth produces choral societies. That is, in economically underdeveloped regions, the poor residents do not have the time, energy, or inclination to join choral societies. But, actually, that story is exactly backward. It was not that wealth had produced the choral societies, but rather that the choral societies had produced the wealth. That is, the patterns of connectedness predated the differences in wealth. If a region, for whatever reason, happened to have lots of choral societies, it did not begin wealthier, but it gradually became wealthier. Those more connected regions also had healthier citizens, and happier citizens. At the risk of overstatement and simplification, choral societies explain economic development, good government, happiness.

It was not that wealth had produced the choral societies, but rather that the choral societies had produced the wealth.

It turns out that there is a large body of research on the positive effects of community connectedness. This research shows, among other findings, that educational systems do not perform well in places where people are not engaged in their communities or schools. And where social capital is weak, people are much more likely to cheat on their taxes.

… where social capital is weak, people are much more likely to cheat on their taxes.

The crime rate is closely related, too. Suppose a mayor wanted to reduce crime in the city, and she had a choice between two strategies: increase by 10 per cent the number of cops on the beat, or increase by 10 per cent the number of neighbours who know one another's first name. The latter approach—building social capital—is likely to be the more effective crime-fighting strategy. The fact that Americans do not know their neighbours' first names as well as they once did is an important part of the reason for the crime rates that have been much higher than they were in the 1950s and 1960s, notwithstanding recent favourable developments.

If you smoke and belong to no groups, it is a close call as to which behaviour is worse for you.

Finally, social capital has profound consequences for people's health. There are many excellent prospective studies that can disentangle the causes from the effects. Controlling for an individual's blood chemistry, gender, age, status as a smoker and level of exercise, the chances of dying over the next year are cut in half by joining one group. This is about the same order of magnitude as quitting smoking. If you smoke and belong to no groups, it is a close call as to which behaviour is worse for you. There are several reasons why social capital is conducive to health. Partly, it is social support— if you slip in the bath-tub and do not show up at church, someone will notice and come to check on you. But social capital appears to operate mainly through physiology, or biochemical effects. Going to meetings actually lowers individuals' stress level, hard as that is to believe.

WHAT CAN WE DO ABOUT IT?
◆ ◆ ◆

Over the course of the last generation, a variety of technical, economic and social changes have rendered obsolete a stock of American social capital.

Because of two-career families, sprawl, television and other factors, Americans are no longer as eager to find time for the PTA, or the Elks Club, or the Optimists. There are measurable bad effects for the United States that flow from this social capital deficit.

Now, return to a hundred years ago. At the end of the nineteenth century in the United States, the stock of social capital in America was in a similarly depleted state. America had just been through 30–40 years of dramatic technological, economic and social change that had rendered obsolete institutions and informal patterns of social engagement. Urbanization, industrialization and immigration meant that people no longer had the tight communities of friends that were present back on the farm, and they no longer had the institutions they had enjoyed back in the village in Poland or in Iowa.

At the end of the nineteenth century, America suffered from all of the same symptoms of the social capital deficit that the nation has experienced over the past couple of decades. These include high crime rates, decay in the cities, concern about political corruption, poorly functioning schools, and a widening gap between the rich and everyone else. Then as now, the erosion of social capital happened for the same reason: technological change rendered obsolete the ways Americans had previously connected.

Then, amazingly, Americans fixed the problem. In a very short period of time, at the end of the nineteenth century, most of today's more important civic institutions were invented: the Boy Scouts, the American Red Cross, the League of Women Voters, the National Association for the Advancement of Colored People (NAACP), the Knights of Columbus, the Sons of Norway, the Sons of Italy, the Urban League, the Kiwanis Club, the YWCA, the 4-H Club, the Rotary Club, the Community Chest and most trade unions. It is actually hard to name a major civic institution in American life today that was not invented at the end of the nineteenth century or the beginning of the twentieth century.

In that period, as now, it was very tempting to say, "Life was much better back in the old days." At the end of the nineteenth century, "the old days" meant "on the farm," when everyone knew each other. Similarly, it might be tempting today to say, "Life was much nicer back in the 1950s. Would all women please report to the kitchen? And turn off the television on the way." Of course, America should no more return to the days of

gender segregation than it should return to a pre-industrial agricultural economy. Instead, Americans today must do what their forebears did a century ago: create new institutions to fit new times. Americans need to reinvent the Boy Scouts or the League of Women Voters or the Sons of Italy.

Here, there is a close connection between British history and American history. Many of the organizations that were "invented" in the United States at the end of the nineteenth century actually were imported from England, where they had been invented in the mid-Victorian era, probably in response to very similar social problems. Such organizations include the Boy Scouts and the Salvation Army. These patterns suggest that there may be periods in many countries, not just the United States, in which there are bursts of civic reconstruction. Now, the challenge to Americans as a people is to put in a hard ten or twenty years figuring how to reconnect in an era of new demographic, economic and cultural realities. It is not an option to say "It doesn't matter if we connect with other people." There are measurable reasons why connecting does matter.

It remains to be seen what those new ideas and strategies will be. Some might seem a little crazy. One can only imagine the response in some quarters when civic leaders said creating an organization called the Boy Scouts would be a solution to the street-urchin problem—that if urchins get shorts, beanies and badges, this would be a substitute for friends on the farm. In hindsight, we can see which inventions of that period were successful; but it is harder to see the ones that were unsuccessful. Today as then, there will be a lot of false starts.

Quite interestingly, the late nineteenth century was a period almost unique in American intellectual history in the sense that there was a very close connection, and a lot of direct exchanges, between academics and practitioners. Some American academics are now trying to create a similar situation in which scholars no longer spend all their time writing for obscure journals read only by other scholars, but rather spend more time learning from practitioners who are addressing vital public issues. In short, addressing the social capital deficit in contemporary society is far from a hopeless task, but it will require that social scientists descend from our ivory tower. That is, of course, a challenge to which the London School of Economics has long been dedicated, and it is the task that lies before American social science today.

Notes

1. Because this essay was originally delivered as a lecture, I forgo extensive citation. However, the lecture drew heavily on the material subsequently published in my *Bowling Alone: The Collapse and Revival of American Community* (London: Simon & Schuster, 2001), and I there provide much fuller documentation of the arguments presented in synthetic form here. I want to thank Kristin Goss for her skilled help in editing my extemporaneous oral remarks into written form. I am also grateful to Sir Nicholas Bayne and Rosalind Jones for their forbearance during the unavoidable delay between my original lecture and the appearance of this written essay, as well as for their exceptional hospitality during my visit to LSE.

2. Robert D. Putman, "Bowling Alone: America's Declining Social Capital," *Journal of Democracy,* January 1995, 65–78.

3. This is a dataset of which social scientists were previously unaware. I learned about it by accident when a graduate student at the University of Minnesota wrote a term paper critical of "Bowling Alone" that included a footnote saying that there was a dataset that he had learned about from his marketing professor that might be relevant to this. So, I followed up that lead, and the firm that owned the dataset—DDB—allowed us to use it for this project.

4. Robert D. Putnam, with Robert Leonardi and Raffaella Nanetti, *Making Democracy Work: Civic Traditions in Modern Italy* (Princeton: Princeton University Press, 1993).

Terms and Concepts

civic participation
social capital
trust

social connectedness
informal and formal civic
    participation

bowling alone
reciprocity

Questions

1. Putnam argues that social capital has both individual and collective effects. Explain.

2. Putnam distinguishes life cycle from generational patterns of change in social capital. What does he mean? Which pattern of value changes is linked with the decline in social capital?

3. What explains the decline in social capital in the United States?

4. After cataloguing the elements of social capital decline, Putnam offers his readers hope for the future. On what is this hope based?

5. Putnam argues that trust is a good thing. Is it possible to have too much trust in others, such as politicians?

6. Do you talk about politics and public affairs with others? If so, how often and in what context? How important are such discussions to your political education and your citizenship?

Republic.com

Cass Sunstein

Editors' Note

A long-running debate among political scientists concerns the relation between economics and political life—more specifically, what economic system most conduces to democracy. Marxists and liberal capitalists disagree on many things, but they are as one on the point that economics and politics are tied closely together.

Cass Sunstein generally believes that economic freedom, as embodied in free markets in goods and services, supports political democracy. He has a lot of evidence on his side. Socialist regimes have been poor examples of democratic vitality.

But there are tensions in the relationship between democracy and the market, as Sunstein argues in the following essay.

Democracy is premised on collective self-government, the notion that citizens as a whole unite in common concern for the welfare of the political community. Democratic life is properly concerned with deliberation among citizens about what is best for the community. For Sunstein, democracy is not merely about voting once every four years. It is about committing oneself to a process of intellectual and political engagement with others to arrive at common positions on public affairs. For such a commitment, people need opportunities to encounter ideas with which they are unfamiliar and with which they would not normally choose to acquaint themselves. Accordingly, a democracy, properly constituted, provides many opportunities for people to confront—willingly or not—

new ideas, new people, and new conceptions of the common good.

The logic of the economic marketplace, on the other hand, is to cater to people's settled preferences. The market is about the maximization of choice. The market is where I satisfy my desires, not where I am confronted with different, sometimes unwelcome and disturbing, views of what is right, good, and just.

Democratic life for Sunstein is a careful negotiation between the logic of the market and the demands of republican citizenship.

As you read his argument, consider whether electronic technologies like the Internet fit better with the logic of political sovereignty or with the marketplace.

◆ ◆ ◆

For countless people, the Internet is producing a substantial decrease in unanticipated, unchosen interactions with others. Many of us telecommute rather than travel to work; this is a rapidly growing trend. Rather than visiting the local bookstore, where we are likely to see a number of diverse people, many of us shop for books on Amazon.com. Others avoid the video store or the grocery because Kosmo.com is entirely delighted to deliver *Citizen Kane* and a pizza. Because of MP3 technology, a visit to the local music store may well seem a hopeless waste of time. Thus communications specialist Ken Auletta enthuses, "I can

sample music on my computer, then click and order. I don't have to go to a store. I don't have to get in a car. I don't have to move. God, that's heaven."[1]

If you are interested in anything at all—from computers to linens to diamonds to cars—Buy.com or MySimon.com, or Bloomingdales.com, or Productopia.com, or Pricecan.com, or any one of hundreds of others, will be happy to assist you. Indeed, if you would like to attend college, or even to get a graduate degree, you may be able to avoid the campus. College education is already being offered on line.[2] A recent advertisement for New York University invites people to attend "the Virtual College at NYU" and emphasizes that with virtual education, you can take a seat "anywhere" in the class—and even sit alone.

It would be foolish to claim that this is bad, or a loss, in general or on balance. On the contrary, the dramatic increase in convenience is a wonderful blessing for consumers. Driving around in search of gifts, for example, can be a real bother. (Can you remember what this used to be like? Is it still like that for you?) For many of us, the chance to point-and-click is an extraordinary improvement. And many people, both rich and poor, take advantage of new technologies to "go" to places that they could not in any sense have visited before—South Africa, Germany, Iran, stores and more stores everywhere, an immense variety of specialized doctors' offices (with some entertaining surprises as you search; for example, Lungcancer.com is a law firm's Website, helping you to sue, rather than a doctor's site, helping you to get better). But it is far from foolish to worry that for millions of people, the consequence of this increased convenience is to decrease the set of chance encounters with diverse others—and also to be concerned about the consequence of the decrease for democracy and citizenship.

Or consider the concept of *collaborative filtering*—an intriguing feature on a number of sites, and one that is rapidly becoming routine. Once you order a book from Amazon.com, for example, Amazon.com is in a position to tell you the choices of other people who like that particular book. Once you have ordered a number of books, Amazon.com knows, and will tell you, what other books—and compact discs and movies—you are likely to like based on what people like you have liked. Other Websites, such as Qrate.com and Movielens, are prepared to tell you which new movies you'll enjoy and which you won't—simply by asking you to rate certain movies, then matching your ratings to those of other people, and then finding out what people like you think about movies that you haven't seen. Collaborative filtering is used by CDNOW, Moviefinder.com, Firefly, and increasingly many others. We have seen that TiVo, the television recording system, is prepared to tell you what other shows you'll like, based on what shows you now like.

Collaborative filtering is only the beginning. "Personalized shopping" is becoming easily available, and it is intended, in the words of a typical account, to "match the interests and buying habits of its customers, from fabric preferences to room designs to wish lists."[3]

Or consider the suggestion that before long we will "have virtual celebrities.... They'll look terrific. In fact, they'll look so terrific that their faces will be exactly what *you* think is beautiful and not necessarily what your neighbor thinks, because they'll be customized for each home."[4] (Is it surprising to hear that at least one Website provides personalized romance stories? That it asks you for information about "your fantasy lover," and then it designs a story to suit your tastes?)

In many ways what is happening is quite wonderful, and some of the recommendations from Amazon.com and analogous services are miraculously good, even uncanny. (Thousands of people have discovered new favorite authors through this route.) But it might well be disturbing if the consequence is to encourage people to narrow their horizons, or to cater to their existing tastes rather than to form new ones. Suppose, for example, that people with a certain political conviction find themselves learning about more and more authors with the same view, and thus strengthening their existing judgments, only because most of what they are encouraged to read says the same thing. In a democratic society, might this not be troubling?

... a free society creates a set of public forums, providing speakers access to a diverse people and ensuring in the process that each of hears a wide range of speakers, spanning many topics and opinions.

The underlying issues here are best approached through two different routes. The first involves an unusual and somewhat exotic constitutional doctrine, based on the idea of the "public forum." The second involves a general constitutional ideal, indeed the most general constitutional ideal of all: that of deliberative democracy. As we will see, a decline in common experiences and a system of individualized filtering might compromise that ideal. As a corrective, we might build on the understandings that lie behind the notion that a free society creates a set of public forums, providing speakers access to a diverse people and ensuring in the process that each of us hears a wide range of speakers, spanning many topics and opinions.

THE IDEA OF THE PUBLIC FORUM

◆ ◆ ◆

In the common understanding, the free speech principle is taken to forbid government from "censoring" speech of which it disapproves. In the standard cases, the government attempts to impose penalties, whether civil or criminal, on political dissent, libelous speech, commercial advertising, or sexually explicit speech. The question is whether the government has a legitimate, and sufficiently weighty, reason for restricting the speech that it seeks to control.

This is indeed what most of the law of free speech is about. But in many free nations, an important part of free speech law takes a quite different form. In the United States, for example, the Supreme Court has ruled that streets and parks must be kept open to the public for expressive activity. In the leading case, from the early part of the twentieth century, the Court said, "Wherever the title of streets and parks may rest, they have immemorially been held in trust for the use of the public and time out of mind, have been used for the purposes of assembly, communicating thought between citizens, and discussing public questions. Such use of the streets and public places has, from ancient times, been a part of the privileges, immunities, rights, and liberties of citizens."[5] Hence governments are obliged to allow speech to occur freely on public streets and in public parks—even if many citizens would prefer to have peace and quiet, and even if it seems irritating to come across protesters and dissidents when you are simply walking home or to the local grocery store.

> A distinctive feature of the public forum doctrine is that it creates a right of speakers' access, both to places and to people.

To be sure, the government is allowed to impose restrictions on the "time, place, and manner" of speech in public places. No one has a right to set off fireworks or to use loud-speakers on the public streets at 3:00 a.m. to complain about global warming or the size of the defense budget. But time, place, and manner restrictions must be both reasonable and limited. Government is essentially obliged to allow speakers, whatever their views, to use public property to convey messages of their choosing.

A distinctive feature of the public forum doctrine is that it creates a *right of speakers' access, both to places and to people*. Another distinctive feature is that the public forum doctrine creates a right, not to avoid governmentally imposed *penalties* on speech, but to ensure government *subsidies* of speech. There is no question that taxpayers are required to support the expressive activity that, under the public forum doctrine, must be permitted on the streets and parks. Indeed, the costs that taxpayers devote to maintaining open streets and parks, from cleaning to maintenance, can be quite high. Thus the public forum represents one area of law in which the right to free speech demands a public subsidy to speakers.

JUST STREETS AND PARKS? OF AIRPORTS AND THE INTERNET

◆ ◆ ◆

As a matter of principle, there seems to be good reason to expand the public forum well beyond streets and parks. In the modern era, other places have increasingly come to occupy the role of traditional public forums. The mass media, including the Internet, have become far more important than streets and parks as arenas in which expressive activity occurs.

> … a free society requires a right to access to areas where many people meet.

Nonetheless, the Supreme Court has been wary of expanding the public forum doctrine beyond streets and parks. Perhaps the Court's wariness stems from a belief that once the historical touchstone is abandoned, lines will be extremely hard to draw, and judges will be besieged with requests for rights of access to private and public property. Thus the Court has rejected the seemingly convincing argument that many other places should be seen as public forums. In particular, it has been urged that airports, more than streets and parks, are crucial to reaching a heterogeneous public; airports are places where diverse people congregate and where it is important to have access if you want to speak to large numbers of people. The Court was not convinced, responding that the public forum idea should be understood by reference to historical practices. Airports certainly have not been treated as public forums from "ancient times."[6]

But at the same time, members of the Court have shown considerable uneasiness with a purely historical test. In the most vivid passage on the point, Supreme Court Justice Anthony Kennedy wrote: "Minds are not changed in the streets and parks as they once were. To an increasing degree, the more significant interchanges of ideas and shaping of public consciousness occur in mass and electronic media. The extent of public entitlement to participate in those means of communication may be changed as technologies change."[7] What Justice Kennedy is recognizing here is the serious problem of how to "translate" the public forum idea into the modern technological environment. And if the Supreme Court is unwilling to do any such translating, it remains open for Congress and state governments to do exactly that. In other words, the Court may not be prepared to say, as a matter of constitutional law, that the public forum idea extends beyond streets and parks. But even if the Court is unprepared to act, Congress and state governments are permitted to conclude that a free society requires a right to access to areas where many people meet. Indeed, Websites, private rather than public, might reach such conclusions on their own, and take steps to ensure that people are exposed to a diversity of views.

WHY PUBLIC FORUMS? OF ACCESS, UNPLANNED ENCOUNTERS, AND IRRITATIONS

◆ ◆ ◆

The Supreme Court has given little sense of why, exactly, it is important to ensure that the streets and parks remain open to speakers. This is the question that must be answered if we are to know whether, and how, to understand the relationship of the public forum doctrine to contemporary problems.

We can make some progress here by noticing that the public forum doctrine promotes three important goals.[8] First, it ensures that speakers can have access to a wide array of people. If you want to claim that taxes are too high or that police brutality against African-Americans is widespread, you are able to press this argument on many people who might otherwise fail to hear the message. The diverse people who walk the streets and use the parks are likely to hear speakers' arguments about taxes or the police; they might also learn about the nature and intensity of views held by their fellow citizens. Perhaps some people's views will change because of what they learn: perhaps they will become curious, enough so to investigate the question on their own. It does not much matter if this happens a little or a lot. What is important is that speakers are allowed to press concerns that might otherwise be ignored by their fellow citizens.

On the speakers' side, the public forum doctrine thus *creates a right of general access to heterogeneous citizens*. It is important to emphasize that the exposure is shared. Many people will be simultaneously exposed to the same views and complaints, and they will encounter views and complaints that some of them might have refused to seek out in the first instance. Indeed, the exposure might well be considered, much of the time, irritating or worse.

Second, the public forum doctrine allows speakers not only to have general access to heterogeneous people, but also to specific people and specific institutions with whom they have a complaint. Suppose, for example, that you believe that the state legislature has behaved irresponsibly with respect to crime or health care for children. The public forum ensures that you can make your view heard by legislators, simply by protesting in front of the state legislature itself.

The point applies to private as well as public institutions. If a clothing store is believed to have cheated customers or to have acted in a racist manner, protestors are allowed a form of access to the store itself. This is not because they have a right to trespass on private property—no one has such a right—but because a public street is highly likely to be close by, and a strategically located protest will undoubtedly catch the attention of the store and its customers. Under the public forum doctrine, speakers are thus permitted to have access to particular audiences, and particular listeners cannot easily avoid hearing complaints that are directed against them. In other words, listeners have a sharply limited power of self-insulation.

Third, the public forum doctrine increases the likelihood that people generally will be exposed to a wide variety of people and views. When you go to work or visit a park, it is possible that you will have a range of unexpected encounters, however fleeting or seemingly inconsequential. On your way to the office or when eating lunch in the park, you cannot easily wall yourself off from contentions or conditions that you would not have sought out in advance, or that you would have avoided if you could have. Here too the public forum doctrine tends to ensure a range of experiences that are widely shared—streets and parks are public property—and also a set of exposures to diverse views and conditions. What I mean to suggest is that these exposures help promote understanding and perhaps in a sense freedom. As we will soon see, all of these points can be closely connected to democratic ideals.

We should also distinguish here between exposures that are *unplanned* and exposures that are *unwanted*. In a park, for example, you might encounter a baseball game or a group of people protesting the conduct of the police. These might be unplanned experiences: you did not choose them and you did not foresee them. But once you encounter the game or the protest, you are hardly irritated; you may even be glad to have stumbled across them. By contrast, you might also encounter homeless people or beggars, asking you for money and perhaps trying to sell you something that you really don't want. If you could have "filtered out" these experiences, you would have chosen to do so. For many people, the category of unwanted—as opposed to unplanned—exposures includes a great deal of political activities. You might be bored by those activities, and wish that they were not disturbing your stroll through the street. You might be irritated or angered by such activities, perhaps because they are disturbing your stroll, perhaps because of the content of what is being said, perhaps because of who is saying it.

The most ambitious uses of public forums are designed to alert people to arguments as well as experiences ...

It is also important to distinguish between exposures to *experiences* and exposures to *arguments*. Public forums make it more likely that people will not be able to wall themselves off from their fellow citizens. People will get a glimpse, at least, of the lives of others, as for example through encountering people from different social classes. Some of the time, however, the public forum doctrine makes it more likely that people will have a sense, however brief, not simply of the experiences but also of the arguments being made by people with a particular point of view. You might encounter written materials, for example, that draw attention to the problem of domestic violence. The most ambitious uses of public forums are designed to alert people to arguments as well as experiences—though the latter sometimes serve as a kind of shorthand reference for the former, as when a picture or a brief encounter has the effect of thousands of words.

In referring to the goals of the public forum doctrine, I aim to approve of encounters that are unwanted as well as unplanned, and also of exposure to experiences as well as arguments. But those who disapprove of unwanted encounters might also agree that unplanned ones are desirable, and those who believe that exposure to arguments is too demanding, or too intrusive, might also appreciate the value, in a heterogeneous society, of exposure to new experiences.

GENERAL INTEREST INTERMEDIARIES AS UNACKNOWLEDGED PUBLIC FORUMS (OF THE WORLD)

◆ ◆ ◆

Of course there is a limit to how much can be done on streets and in parks. Even in the largest cities, streets and parks are insistently *local*. But many of the social functions of streets and parks, as public forums, are performed by other institutions too. In fact society's general interest intermediaries—newspapers, magazines, television broadcasters—can be understood as public forums of an especially important sort.

The reasons are straightforward. When you read a city newspaper or a national magazine, your eyes will come across a number of articles that you would not have selected in advance. If you are like most people, you will read some of those articles. Perhaps you did not know that you might have an interest in minimum wage legislation, or Somalia, or the latest developments in the Middle East; but a story might catch your attention. What is true for topics is also true for points of view. You might think that you have nothing to learn from someone whose view you abhor. But once you come across the editorial pages, you might well read what they have to say, and you might well benefit from the experience. Perhaps you will be persuaded on one point or another, or informed whether or not you are persuaded. At the same time, the front page headline, or the cover story in *Newsweek,* is likely to have a high degree of salience for a wide range of people.

Unplanned and unchosen encounters often turn out to do a great deal of good, both for individuals and for society at large. In some cases, they even change people's lives. The same is true, though in a different way, for unwanted encounters. In some cases, you might be irritated by seeing an editorial from your least favorite writer. You might wish that the editorial weren't there.

But despite yourself, your curiosity might be piqued, and you might read it. Perhaps this isn't a lot of fun. But it might prompt you to reassess your own view and even to revise it. At the very least, you will have learned what many of your fellow citizens think and why they think it. What is true for arguments is also true for topics, as when you encounter, with some displeasure, a series of stories on crime or global warming or same-sex marriage or alcohol abuse, but find yourself learning a bit, or more, from what those stories have to say.

Unplanned and unchosen encounters often turn out to do a great deal of good, both for individuals and for society at large.

Television broadcasters have similar functions. Maybe the best example is what has become an institution in many nations: the evening news. If you tune into the evening news, you will learn about a number of topics that you would not have chosen in advance. Because of the speed and immediacy of television, broadcasters perform these public forum-type functions even more than general interest intermediaries in the print media. The lead story on the networks is likely to have a great deal of public saliency, helping to define central issues and creating a kind of shared focus of attention for many millions of people. And what happens after the lead story—dealing with a menu of topics both domestic and international—creates something like a speakers' corner beyond anything ever imagined in Hyde Park.

None of these claims depends on a judgment that general interest intermediaries always do an excellent job, or even a good job. Sometimes such intermediaries fail to provide an adequate understanding of topics or opinions. Sometimes they offer a watered-down version of what most people already think. Sometimes they suffer from prejudices of their own. Sometimes they deal little with substance and veer toward sound bites and sensationalism, properly deplored trends in the last two decades. What matters for present purposes is that in their best forms, general interest intermediaries expose people to a range of topics and views at the same time that they provide shared experiences for a heterogeneous public. Indeed, general interest intermediaries of this sort have large advantages over streets and parks precisely because most of them tend to be so much less local and so much more national, even international. Typically they expose people to questions and problems in other areas, even other nations. They even provide a form of modest, back-door cosmopolitanism, ensuring that many people will learn something about diverse areas of the world, regardless of whether they are much interested, initially or ever, in doing so.

... in their best forms, general interest intermediaries expose people to a range of topics and views at the same time that they provide shared experiences for a heterogeneous public.

Of course general interest intermediaries are not public forums in the technical sense that the law recognizes. These are private rather than public institutions. Most important, members of the public do not have a legal right of access to them. Individual citizens are not allowed to override the editorial and economic judgments and choices of private owners. In the 1970s, a sharp constitutional debate on precisely this issue resulted in a resounding defeat for those who claimed a constitutionally guaranteed access right.[9] But the question of legal compulsion is really incidental. Society's general interest intermediaries, even without legal compulsion, serve many of the functions of public forums. They promote shared experiences; they expose people to information and views that would not have been selected in advance.

REPUBLICANISM, DELIBERATIVE DEMOCRACY, AND TWO KINDS OF FILTERING
◆ ◆ ◆

The public forum doctrine is an odd and unusual one, especially insofar as it creates a kind of speakers' access right, subsidized by taxpayers, to people and places. But the doctrine is closely associated with a longstanding constitutional ideal, one that is very far from odd: that of republican self-government.

From the beginning, the U.S. constitutional order was designed to be a republic, as distinguished from a monarchy or a direct democracy. We cannot understand the system of freedom of expression, and the effects of new communications technologies and filtering, without reference to this ideal. It will therefore be worthwhile to spend some space on the concept of a republic, and on the way the American constitution understands this concept, in terms of a deliberative approach to democracy. The general ideal is hardly limited to America; it plays a role in many nations committed to self-government.

In a republic, government is not managed by any king or queen; there is no sovereign operating independently of the people.[10] The American Constitution represents a firm rejection of the monarchical heritage, and the framers self-consciously transferred sovereignty from any monarchy (with the explicit constitutional ban on "titles of nobility") to "We the People." This represents, in Gordon Wood's illuminating phrase, the "radicalism of the American revolution."[11] At the same time, the founders were extremely fearful of popular passions and prejudices, and they did not want government to translate popular desires directly into law. Indeed, they were sympathetic to a form of filtering, though one very different from that emphasized thus far. Rather than seeking to allow people to filter what they would see and hear, they attempted to create institutions that would "filter" popular desires so as to ensure policies that would promote the public good. Thus the structure of political representation, and the system of checks and balances, were designed to create a kind of filter between people and law, so as to ensure that what would emerge would be both reflective and well-informed. At the same time, the founders placed a high premium on the idea of "civic virtue," which required participants in politics to act as citizens dedicated to something other than their self-interest, narrowly conceived.

This form of republicanism involved an attempt to create a "deliberative democracy." In this system, representatives would be accountable to the public at large. But there was also supposed to be a large degree of reflection and debate, both within the citizenry and within government itself.[12] The aspiration to deliberative democracy can be seen in many places in the constitutional design. The system of bicameralism, for example, was intended as a check on insufficiently deliberative action from one or another legislative chamber; the Senate, in particular, was supposed to have a "cooling" effect on popular passions. The long length of service for senators was designed to make deliberation more likely; so too for large election districts. The Electoral College was originally a deliberative body, ensuring that the president would result from some combination of popular will and reflection and exchange on the part of representatives. Most generally, the system of checks and balances had, as its central purpose, the creation of a mechanism for promoting deliberation within the government as a whole.

From these points it should be clear that the Constitution was not rooted in the assumption that direct democracy was the ideal, to be replaced by republican institutions only because direct democracy was impractical in light of what were, by modern standards, extremely primitive technologies for communication. Many recent observers have suggested that, for the first time in the history of the world, something like direct democracy has become feasible. It is now possible for citizens to tell their government, every week if not every day, what they would like it to do.[13] Indeed, Websites have been designed to enable citizens to do precisely that (Vote.com is an example). We should expect many more experiments in this direction. But from the standpoint of constitutional ideals, this is nothing to celebrate[;] indeed it is a grotesque distortion of founding aspirations. It would undermine the deliberative goals of the original design. Ours has never been a direct democracy, and a good democratic system attempts to ensure informed and reflective decisions, not simply snapshots of individual opinions, suitably aggregated.[14]

HOMOGENEITY, HETEROGENEITY, AND A TALE OF THE FIRST CONGRESS

♦ ♦ ♦

There were articulate opponents of the original constitutional plan, whose voices have echoed throughout American history; and they spoke in terms that bear directly on the communications revolution. The antifederalists believed that the Constitution was doomed to failure, on the ground that deliberation would not be possible in a large, heterogeneous republic. Following the great political theorist Montesquieu, they urged that public deliberation would be possible only where there was fundamental agreement. Thus Brutus, an eloquent antifederalist critic of the Constitution, insisted, "In a republic, the manners, sentiments, and interests of the people should be similar. If this be not the case, there will be a constant clashing of opinions; and the representatives of one part will be continually striving against those of the other."[15]

It was here that the Constitution's framers made a substantial break with conventional republican thought, focusing on the potential uses of diversity for democratic debate. For them, heterogeneity, far from being an obstacle, would be a creative force, improving deliberation and producing better outcomes. If everyone agreed, what would people need to talk about? Why would they want to talk at all? Alexander Hamilton invoked this point to defend discussion among diverse people within a bicameral legislature, urging, in what could be taken as a direct response to Brutus, that "the jarring of parties … will promote deliberation."[16] And in an often forgotten episode in the very first Congress, the nation rejected a proposed part of the original Bill of Rights, a "right" on the part of citizens to "instruct" their representative on how to vote. The proposed right was justified on republican (what we would call democratic) grounds. To many people, it seemed a good way of ensuring accountability on the part of public officials. But the early Congress decided that such a right would be a betrayal of republican principles. Senator Roger Sherman's voice was the clearest and most firm:

The words are calculated to mislead the people, by conveying an idea that they have a right to control the debates of the Legislature. This cannot be admitted to be just, because it would destroy the object of their meeting. I think, when the people have chosen a representative, it is his duty to meet others from the different parts of the Union, and consult, and agree with them on such acts as are for the general benefit of the whole community. If they were to be guided by instructions, there would be no use in deliberation.[17]

Sherman's words reflect the founders' general receptivity to deliberation among people who are quite diverse and who disagree on issues both large and small. Indeed, it was through deliberation among such persons that "such acts as are for the general benefit of the whole community" would emerge. Of course the framers were not naive. Sometimes some regions, and some groups, would gain while others would lose. What was and remains important is that the resulting pattern of gains and losses would themselves have to be defended by reference to reasons. Indeed, the Constitution might well be seen as intended to create a "republic of reasons" in which the use of governmental power would have to be justified, not simply supported, by those who asked for it.

We can even take Sherman's conception of the task of the representative as having a corresponding conception of the task of the idealized citizen in a well-functioning republic. Citizens are not supposed to press their self-interest, narrowly conceived, nor are they to insulate themselves from the judgments of others. Even if they are concerned with the public good, they might make errors of fact or of value, errors that can be reduced or corrected through the exchange of ideas. Insofar as people are acting in their capacity as citizens, their duty is to "meet others" and "consult," sometimes through face-to-face discussions or if not through other routes as, for example, by making sure to consider the views of those who think differently.

> *… to the extent that both citizens and representatives are acting on the basis of diverse encounters and experiences, and benefiting from heterogeneity, they are behaving in accordance with the highest ideals of the constitutional design.*

This is not to say that most people should be devoting most of their time to politics. In a free society, people have a range of things to do. But to the extent that both citizens and representatives are acting on the basis of diverse encounters and experiences, and benefiting from heterogeneity, they are behaving in accordance with the highest ideals of the constitutional design.

E PLURIBUS UNUM, AND JEFFERSON VS. MADISON
◆ ◆ ◆

Any heterogeneous society faces a risk of fragmentation. This risk has been serious in many periods in American history, most notably during the Civil War, but often in the twentieth century as well. The institutions of the Constitution were intended to diminish the danger, partly by producing a good mix of local and national rule, partly through the system of checks and balances, and partly through the symbol of the Constitution itself. Thus the idea of *e pluribus unum* (from many, one) can be found on ordinary currency, in a brief, frequent reminder of a central constitutional goal.

Consider in this regard the instructive debate between Thomas Jefferson and James Madison about the value of a bill of rights. In the founding era, Madison, the most important force behind the Constitution itself, sharply opposed such a bill, on the ground that it was unnecessary and was likely to sow confusion. Jefferson thought otherwise, and insisted that a bill of rights, enforced by courts, could be a bulwark of liberty. Madison was eventually convinced of this point, but he emphasized a very different consideration: the unifying and educative functions of a bill of rights.

In a letter to Jefferson on October 17, 1788, Madison asked, "What use, then, it may be asked, can a bill of rights serve in popular Government?" His basic answer was that the "political truths declared in that solemn manner acquire by degrees the character of fundamental maxims of free Government, and as they become incorporated with the National sentiment, counteract the impulses of interest and passion."[18] In Madison's view, the bill of rights, along with the Constitution itself, would eventually become a source of shared understandings and commitments among extremely diverse people. The example illustrates the founders' belief that for a diverse people to be self-governing, it was essential to provide a range of common experiences.

TWO CONCEPTIONS OF SOVEREIGNTY, AND *HOLMES VS. BRANDEIS*

◆ ◆ ◆

We are now in a position to distinguish between two conceptions of sovereignty. The first involves consumer sovereignty, the idea behind free markets. The second involves political sovereignty, the idea behind free nations. The notion of consumer sovereignty underlies enthusiasm for the "Daily Me"; it is the underpinning of any utopian vision of the unlimited power to filter. Writing in 1995, Bill Gates cheerfully predicted, "Customized information is a natural extension.... For your own daily dose of news, you might subscribe to several review services and let a software agent or a human one pick and choose from them to compile your completely customized 'newspaper.' These subscription services, whether human or electronic, will gather information that conforms to a particular philosophy and set of interests."[19] Or recall ... [Bill] Gates' celebratory words in 1999: "When you turn on Direct TV and you step through every channel—well, there's three minutes

of your life. When you walk into your living room six years from now, you'll be able to just say what you're interested in, and have the screen help you pick out a video that you care about. It's not going to be 'Let's look at channels 4, 5, and 7.'" This is the principle of consumer sovereignty in action.

The notion of political sovereignty underlies the democratic alternative, which poses a challenge to Gates' vision on the ground that it may well undermine both self-government and freedom, properly conceived. Recall here John Dewey's words: "Majority rule, just as majority rule, is as foolish as its critics charge it with being. But it never is *merely* majority rule.... The important consideration is that opportunity be given ideas to speak and to become the possession of the multitude. The essential need is the improvement of the methods and constitution of debate, discussion and persuasion. That is *the* problem of the public."

Consumer sovereignty means that individual consumers are permitted to choose as they wish, subject to the constraints provided by the price system, and also by their current holdings and requirements. This idea plays a significant role in thinking not only about economic markets, but also about both politics and communications. When we talk as if politicians are "selling" a message, and even themselves, we are treating the political domain as a kind of market, subject to the forces of supply and demand. And when we act as if the purpose of a system of communications is to ensure that people can see exactly what they "want," the notion of consumer sovereignty is very much at work.

Of course the two conceptions of sovereignty are in potential tension. A commitment to consumer sovereignty may well compromise political sovereignty if, for example, free consumer choices result in insufficient understanding of public problems, or if they make it difficult to have anything like a shared or deliberative culture. We will create serious problems if we confound consumer sovereignty with political sovereignty. If the latter is our governing ideal, for example, we will evaluate the system of free expression partly by seeing whether it promotes democratic goals. If we care only about consumer sovereignty, the only question is whether consumers are getting what they want. The distinction matters for policy as well. If the government takes steps to increase the level of substantive debate on television or in public culture, it might well be undermining consumer sovereignty at the same time that it is promoting democratic self-government.

We will create serious problems if we confound consumer sovereignty with political sovereignty.

With respect to the system of freedom of speech, the conflict between consumer sovereignty and political sovereignty can be found in an unexpected place: the great constitutional dissents of Supreme Court Justices Oliver Wendell Holmes and Louis Brandeis. In the early part of the twentieth century, Holmes and Brandeis were the twin heroes of freedom of speech, dissenting, usually together, from Supreme Court decisions allowing the government to regulate political dissent. Sometimes Holmes wrote for the two dissenters; sometimes the author was Brandeis. But the two spoke in quite different terms. Holmes wrote of "free trade in ideas," and treated speech as part of a great political market, with which government could not legitimately interfere. Consider a passage from Holmes' greatest free speech opinion.

> When men have realized that time has upset many fighting faiths, they may come to believe even more than they believe the very foundations of their own conduct that the ultimate good desired is better reached by free trade in ideas—that the best test of truth is the power of the thought to get itself accepted in the competition of the market, and that truth is the only ground upon which their wishes safely can be carried out. That at any rate is the theory of our Constitution.[20]

Brandeis' language, in his greatest free speech opinion, was quite different.

> Those who won our independence believed that the final end of the state was to make men free to develop their faculties; and that in its government the deliberative forces should prevail over the arbitrary.... They believed that ... without free speech and assembly discussion would be futile; ... that the greatest menace to freedom is an inert people; that public discussion is a political duty; and that this should be a fundamental principle of the American government.[21]

Note Brandeis' suggestion that the greatest threat to freedom is an "inert people," and his insistence, altogether foreign to Holmes, that public discussion is not only a right but "a political duty." Brandeis sees self-government as something dramatically different from an exercise in consumer sovereignty. On Brandeis' self-consciously republican conception of free speech, unrestricted consumer choice is not an appropriate foundation for policy in a context where the very formation of preferences, and the organizing processes of the democratic order, are at stake.

... it is indispensable to ensure that the system of communications promotes democratic goals. Those goals emphatically require both unchosen exposures and shared experiences.

In fact Brandeis can be taken to have offered a conception of the social role of the idealized citizen. For such a citizen, active engagement in politics, at least some of the time, is an obligation, not just an entitlement. If citizens are "inert," freedom itself is at risk. This does not mean that people have to be thinking about public affairs all or most of the time. But it does mean that each of us has rights and duties as citizens, not simply as consumers. As we will see, active citizen engagement is necessary to promote not only democracy but social well-being too. And in the modern era, one of the most pressing obligations of a citizenry that is not inert is to ensure that "deliberative forces should prevail over the arbitrary." For this to happen, it is indispensable to ensure that the system of communications promotes democratic goals. Those goals emphatically require both unchosen exposures and shared experiences.

REPUBLICANISM WITHOUT NOSTALGIA
◆ ◆ ◆

These are abstractions; it is time to be more concrete. I will identify three problems in the hypothesized world of perfect filtering. These difficulties would beset any system in which individuals had complete control over their communications universe and exercised that control so as to decrease *shared communications experiences and exposure to materials that would not have been chosen in advance but that nonetheless are beneficial,* both to the person who is exposed to them and to society at large.

The first difficulty involves fragmentation. The problem here comes from the creation of diverse speech communities, whose members make significantly different communications choices. A possible consequence is considerable difficulty in mutual understanding. When society is fragmented in this way, diverse groups will tend to polarize, in a way that can breed extremism and even hatred and violence. New technologies, emphatically including the Internet, are dramatically increasing people's ability to hear echoes of their own voices and to wall themselves off from others. An important result is the existence of *cybercascades*—processes of information exchange in which a certain fact or point of view becomes widespread, simply because so many people seem to believe it.

The second difficulty involves a distinctive characteristic of information. Information is a public good in the technical sense that once some person knows something, other people are likely to benefit as well. If you learn about crime in the neighborhood or about the problem of global warming, you will probably tell other people, and they will benefit from what you have learned. In a system in which each person can "customize" his own communications universe, there is a risk that people will make choices that generate too little information, as least to the extent that individual choices are not made with reference to their social benefits. An advantage of a system with general interest intermediaries and with public forums—with broad access by speakers to diverse publics—is that it ensures a kind of social spreading of information. At the same time, an individually filtered speech universe is likely to underproduce what I will call *solidarity goods*—goods whose value increases with the number of people who are consuming them.[22] A presidential debate is a classic example of a solidarity good.

The third and final difficulty has to do with the proper understanding of freedom and the relationship between consumers and citizens. If we believe in consumer sovereignty, and if we celebrate the power to filter, we are likely to think that freedom consists in the satisfaction of private preferences—in an absence of restrictions on individual choices. This is a widely held view about freedom. Indeed, it is a view that underlies much current thinking about free speech. But it is badly misconceived. Freedom consists not simply in preferences satisfaction but also in the chance to have preferences and beliefs formed under decent conditions—in the ability to have preferences formed after exposure to a sufficient amount of information, and also to an appropriately wide and diverse range of options. There can be no assurance of freedom in a system committed to the "Daily Me."

Notes

1. Alfred C. Sikes and Ellen Pearlman, *Fast Forward: America's Leading Experts Reveal How the Internet Is Changing Your Life* (New York: Morrow & Company, 2000), p. 210 (quoting Ken Auletta).

2. In some ways these developments are entirely continuous with other important social changes. The automobile, for example, has been criticized for "its extreme unsociability," especially compared with railway, "which tended to gather together … all activity that was in any way related to movements of freight or passengers into or out of the city." George Kennan, *Around the Cragged Hill: A Personal and Political Philosophy* (New York: W. W. Norton & Company, 1993), pp. 161, 160. Far more important in this regard has been what may well be the dominant technology of the twentieth century: television. In the words of political scientist Robert Putnam, the "single most important consequence of the television revolution has been to bring us home"—Robert D. Putnam, *Bowling Alone: The Collapse and Revival of American Community* (New York: Simon & Schuster, 2000), p. 221. And the result of the shift in the direction of home has been a dramatic reduction—perhaps as much as 40 percent—in activity spent on "collective activities, like attending public meetings or taking a leadership role in local organizations" (p. 229).

3. See "Art Technology Group Powers Living.com," Headline News from Around the Industry, Sun Microsystems site, available industry.java.sun.com/javanews/stories/story2/0,1072,17512,00.html, accessed August 16, 2003.

4. Sikes, *Fast Forward*, p. 208 (quoting Alvin Toffler).

5. *Hague v. CIO*, 307 US 496 (1939). For present purposes, it is not necessary to discuss the public forum doctrine in detail. Interested readers might consult Geoffrey Stone et al., *The First Amendment* (New York: Aspen Publishers, Inc., 1999), pp. 286–330.

6. See *International Society for Krishna Consciousness v. Lee*, 506 US 672 (1992).

7. See *Denver Area Educational Telecommunications Consortium, Inc. v. FCC*, 518 US 727, 802–3 (1996) (Kennedy, J., dissenting).

8. See the excellent discussion in Noah D. Zatz, "Sidewalks in Cyberspace: Making Space for Public Forums in the Electronic Environment," *Harvard Journal of Law & Technology* 12, 1 (Fall 1998), 149.

9. See *Columbia Broadcasting System v. Democratic National Committee*, 412 US 94 (1973).

10. An especially illuminating elaboration of republican ideals is Philip Pettit, *Republicanism: A Theory of Freedom and Government* (Oxford: Oxford University Press, 1999).

11. See Gordon Wood, *The Radicalism of the American Revolution* (New York: Vintage Books, 1993).

12. From the standpoint of American history, the best discussion of deliberative democracy is Joseph M. Bessette, *The Mild Voice of Reason: Deliberative Democracy and American National Government* (Chicago: University of Chicago Press, 1984). There are many treatments of deliberative democracy as a political ideal. For varying perspectives, see Amy Gutmann and Dennis Thompson, *Democracy and Disagreement* (Harvard: Belknap Pr, Harvard University Press, 1998); Jürgen Habermas, *Between Facts and Norms: Contributions to a Discourse Theory of Law and Democracy* (Cambridge: Polity Press, 1997); and Jon Elster, ed., *Deliberative Democracy* (Cambridge: Cambridge University Press, 1998).

13. A popular treatment is Dick Morris, *Vote.com* (Los Angeles: Renaissance Books, 2000).

14. To be sure, one of the central trends of the last century has been a decrease in the deliberative features of the constitutional design, in favor of an increase in popular control. As central examples, consider direct primary elections, initiatives and referenda, interest group strategies designed to mobilize constituents, and public opinion polling. To a greater or lesser extent, each of these has diminished the deliberative functions of representatives, and increased accountability to public opinion at particular moments in time. Of course any evaluation of these changes would require a detailed discussion. But from the standpoint of the original constitutional settlement, as well as from the standpoint of democratic principles, reforms that make democracy less deliberative are at best a mixed blessing. Government by initiatives and referenda are especially troubling insofar as they threaten to create ill-considered law, produced by sound-bites rather than reflective judgments by representatives, citizens, or anyone at all. For valuable discussion, see James Fishkin, *The Voice of the People* (New Haven: Yale University Press, 1995).

15. Herbert J. Storing, ed., *The Complete Anti-Federalist* (Chicago: University of Chicago Press, 1981), p. 31.

16. *The Federalist*, No. 70, 426–27.

17. Joseph Gales, ed., I *Annals of Congress* 733–45 (1789).

18. Marvin Meyers, ed., *The Mind of the Founder: Sources of the Political Thought of James Madison* (Lebanon, NH: Brandeis University Press/University Press of New England, 1981), pp. 156–60.

19. Bill Gates, *The Road Ahead* (New York: Penguin USA, 1995), pp. 167–68.

20. *Abrams v. United States*, 250 US 616, 635 (Holmes, J., dissenting).

21. *Whitney v. California*, 274 US 357, 372 (1927) (Brandeis, J., concurring).

22. For more detailed discussion, see Cass R. Sunstein and Edna Ullmann-Margalit, *Solidarity in Consumption*, University of Chicago Law School, John M. Olin Law & Economics Working Paper No. 98, April 28, 2000, available papers. ssrn.com/sol3/papers.cfm?abstract_id=224618, accessed August 17, 2003.

Terms and Concepts

collaborative filtering
public forum
deliberative democracy
general interest intermediaries

republican self-government
direct democracy
antifederalists
the republic of reasons

consumer sovereignty
political sovereignty
the "Daily Me"
solidarity goods

Questions

1. What is a public forum?

2. Does the Internet expand or narrow people's views of politics, economics, and society?

3. Is deliberative democracy in conflict with liberalism, as Lorne Lomasky defines it in his selection in this collection, "Classical Liberalism and Civil Society, pp. 72–82.

4. How can consumer and political sovereignty come into mutual tension?

5. Identify the public spaces most familiar to you. Do they conform to Sunstein's conception of the public forum?

Value Change and the Rise
of New Politics

Neil Nevitte

Editors' Note

Everyone knows the old truisms about parents and children. "The apple," according to one, "does not fall far from the tree." "Like father, like son," goes another. These home truths suggest continuity and the power of families to determine the attitudes and conduct of future generations.

Neil Nevitte finds these truisms wanting. He argues in this essay that there are profound and deepening intergenerational changes occurring in developed "advanced industrial" democracies like Canada. Younger people do not harbour the same values as their elders. They think about political issues differently and engage the political process differently than their elders. And it is not just because young people are young. Nevitte builds on the pioneering work of political scientist Ronald Inglehart to suggest a theory to explain intergenerational value change and

the rise of "postmaterialist" political culture. He also cites survey evidence from around the world to support his claim that this is no idiosyncrasy, but rather a global movement sweeping the prosperous postindustrial countries.

What causes intergenerational value change? Nevitte points to changes in the way our economies are organized. A common job in the 20th century was a life-long position in a "smokestack" manufacturing company. The position was probably unionized. The job required low skills and low educational attainment. Such manufacturing jobs once contributed most of the wealth of the country. Today, high-skill, high-knowledge jobs in the service sector are the economic drivers. Now we make machines to do the work people used to do, and to make the machines requires workers with high education, who command

high salaries. Our societies are advanced industrial, and increasingly postindustrial.

Advanced industrial citizens have the time, income, and inclination to aspire to more than just a new car or refrigerator. They now pursue "higher order" goals of an aesthetic, expressive sort. Political life, according to Nevitte, is no longer simply about setting the conditions for increased wealth and employment. It is about the pursuit of more ethereal goals like "quality of life," the recognition of identities, and the advancement of expressive capacities of individuals. So people in advanced industrial democracies pursue new political objectives. They also do politics differently, increasingly preferring "direct action" to deference to elites who make the decisions for them. These are the "new politics" of advanced industrial democracies.

◆ ◆ ◆

INTRODUCTION

◆ ◆ ◆

Significant changes have taken place in the value landscape of most advanced industrial states over the course of the last half century, and these value shifts have had a profound impact on our social, economic, and political lives. The rates of value change vary from

one country to the next but there is clear evidence that the direction of those changes is the same in each and every advanced industrial state. These transformations are the result of a combination of factors including both the structural changes that are usually associated with the transition from industrialism to advanced industrialism, and the fact that citizens in advanced states have experienced a historically unprecedented period of sustained

Article prepared for this publication. © Nelson, 2008.

prosperity. Together, those dynamics help to explain why Canadians, like citizens in other advanced industrial states, are increasingly moving away from old politics toward new politics.

This chapter begins by highlighting the key elements of this value transformation. It then turns to consider some of the prevailing explanations for why these value changes have taken place. The final section presents some survey research evidence gathered over the course of the last 20 years. As we will see, those data provide fairly convincing evidence supporting these theories of value change. Moreover, they help to explain why politics in advanced industrial states have become more boisterous over the last two decades and why Canadians, like citizens elsewhere, have become harder to govern than they once were.

VALUE FORMATION

◆ ◆ ◆

Values lie at the core of human decision making. These values not only form the basis of personal judgments, but also shape decisively what people expect from their friends, their neighbours, their communities, and their environment (Rokeach 1968). When it comes to the political world, values help us to determine which issues are important during election campaigns, why voters are attracted to some candidates but not others, and indeed, whether some people decide to vote at all. Significantly, values also provide the foundation for what citizens expect from their governments (Feldman 1988; Nevitte 2002; Gidengil et al. 2005).

The common starting point for most accounts of the rise of new politics is the observation that individual values are neither inherent nor randomly distributed within populations. Rather, these deep-seated dispositions are acquired through the process of socialization. Individuals internalize their core values during their formative years—usually by the end of their teenage years. And once people have reached young adulthood their value sets are relatively stable; they tend to persist throughout the rest of their lifecycle (Dalton 1977, 1996; Inglehart 1971). If values change they do so slowly. If we have experienced a period of gradual value change then the question becomes, Which values do people acquire during their formative years?

The answer to that question is central to most interpretations of the shift from old politics to new politics. One of the most influential explanations for the rise of

new politics is supplied by Ronald Inglehart (1971, 1988) who draws on the insights of Abraham Maslow, an influential psychologist. According to Maslow (1954), the kinds of values that people acquire through processes of socialization depend a great deal on the environment individuals are exposed to during their formative years. Maslow's pioneering insight was his theory that identified a "needs hierarchy." People have both lower-order and higher-order needs. Lower-order needs refer to those things that are basic to human survival: the need for security and sustenance. Once lower-order needs are ensured, according to Maslow, people's priorities tend to turn to higher-order needs. Thus people who face economic and physical insecurity during their formative years, according to Maslow, tend to become preoccupied with such lower-order needs as safety and sustenance. Inglehart labels these outlooks "materialist orientations." By contrast, individuals who are socialized under conditions of material security and affluence can take their security and material needs for granted. These individuals tend to become preoccupied with higher-order needs; they place a much higher priority on aesthetic and intellectual ideas, or the needs for belonging and for esteem. Inglehart labels these core higher-order needs "postmaterialist values."

The common starting point for most accounts of the rise of new politics is the observation that individual values are neither inherent nor randomly distributed within populations.

Economists were among the first to consider how Maslow's theory might apply to other types of social behaviour. They observed that those people who had first-hand experience with the Great Depression developed completely different savings habits from those who were born later. People socialized during hard times tend to save more because their primary concern during their formative years was with their material insecurity. Greater savings provide a material safety net. Using the same kind of logic, Inglehart applies a combination of socialization theory and the hierarchy of needs to explain how and why political values have changed in the advanced industrial world. Inglehart speculates that people who were born after the Great Depression and World War II have no first-hand experience with those great physical and economic traumas of the 20th century. Consequently, they will be more likely than those of preceding generations to internalize postmaterialist outlooks. By contrast, those who experienced material and physical insecurity during their formative years would be far more likely to have absorbed materialist outlooks. Materialist outlooks form the foundation of old politics, which focuses on the creation and maintenance of welfare states and on the politics of wealth distribution. Postmaterial politics, by contrast, tend to be more preoccupied with such quality-of-life issues as the environment, diversity, and the freedom to pursue nontraditional lifestyles.

Postmaterial politics ... tend to be more preoccupied with such quality-of-life issues as the environment, diversity, and the freedom to pursue nontraditional lifestyles.

STRUCTURAL CHANGE AND VALUE CHANGE

◆ ◆ ◆

Publics in most advanced industrial states have enjoyed not only sustained prosperity over the past few decades, but also other structural changes that have had an important impact both on how postmaterialist values have spread and on the dynamics of new politics. One such structural change concerns the rapid expansion of the middle class. A significant characteristic of the shift from deep industrialism to advanced industrialism is the decline in the proportion of the workforce that is devoted to traditional "smokestack" manufacturing and the corresponding growth of the workforce employed in

service sectors and the knowledge economy (Huntington 1974).

A second related and important structural change concerns the truly striking explosion in access to postsecondary education. Knowledge-based economies cannot grow and be competitive without knowledge workers. Consider the following data: In 1960 about 16 percent of Canadians between the ages of 20 to 24 were in postsecondary educational institutions. By 1990, the proportion of that group involved in postsecondary education more than quadrupled to 66 percent. The expansion of postsecondary education opportunities is a pattern common to all advanced industrial states.

The explosion of educational opportunities has consequences that reach far beyond the workforce. Rising levels of formal education are clearly associated with the increasing occupational, social, and geographic mobility of populations. But exposure to higher levels of education by larger segments of the population has a significant impact on the political world: educated publics tend to be more interested in, and knowledgeable about, politics. Exposure to formal education also equips people with the kinds of skills, and confidence, that encourage people to be more outspoken and to be politically engaged (Dalton 1996). More importantly, educated publics are more engaged and active. Those leading the shift away from materialist values and toward postmaterialist outlooks not only come from the postwar generation, but also come disproportionately from those with higher levels of formal education.

One feature of the transition from old politics to new politics concerns how the shift in values has shaped the changing *content* of public debate. Figure 14.1 summarizes

Figure 14.1   Value Change

Old Politics		New Politics
Economic growth: concerned with the accumulation of wealth (affluence)	⇒	Quality of life and social consciousness
Class conflict	⇒	Individual freedom
Public order and national security	⇒	Social equality
Traditional lifestyles	⇒	Issue driven: minorities, gender roles, homosexuality, environment, animal rights
Representative and hierarchical institutions: deference toward authority	⇒	Decentralization of traditional governmental institutions: self-actualization
Political participation largely electoral	⇒	Participatory in direct action politics and social movements

Source: World Values Surveys (Canada) 1981, 1990, 2000.

some of these key dimensions of change. Another feature of the shift from old politics to new politics concerns the changing *style* of politics: In the new politics world, citizens are less passive, less satisfied with traditional hierarchies, more outspoken, and more knowledgeable (Nevitte 1996).

In the new politics world, citizens are less passive, less satisfied with traditional hierarchies, more outspoken, and more knowledgeable.

THE COMPARATIVE EVIDENCE

◆ ◆ ◆

Our focus so far has been on sketching out what drives the shifts from old to new values, and what consequences this transformation has for the political dynamics of advanced industrial states. But what about the evidence? Are there any data that shed direct light on the extent to which these value changes are taking place?

The best available source of evidence for exploring value change comes from the World Values/European Values Surveys (W/EVS) (see Halman 2001; Inglehart et al 2004). Since the early 1980s, researchers with the World and European Values research group have conducted surveys of random samples of citizens in multiple countries throughout the world, including Canada. These surveys are useful not only because they focus primarily on measuring values, but also because the surveys are reliable; they repeatedly asked the same values questions in each participating country for more than two decades. Values tend to change slowly and so it is difficult to detect value change over a short period of time. Fortunately, these values data now cover two decades. The W/EVS are particularly useful for exploring the evolution of new politics because all of the surveys contain the now standard set of questions used to measure materialist and postmaterialist outlooks.

The place to begin is with the basic data. Is there evidence of growing postmaterialist outlooks among the Canadian population? The data summarized in Figure 14.2 indicate a clear value shift; the levels of postmaterialist values in Canada have almost doubled. Just over 16 percent of Canadians qualified as postmaterialist in 1981; that increased to almost 30 percent by 2000. It turns out that these levels of postmaterialism are consistent with changes that have occurred in other

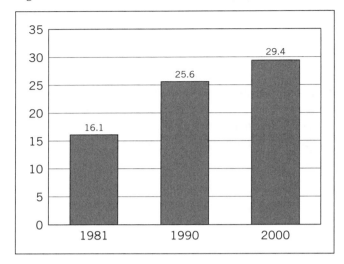

Figure 14.2   Postmaterialists in Canada (%)

advanced industrial states. The proportion of the Canadian population that qualifies as postmaterialist is marginally lower than those found in some Scandinavian countries (Halman 2001) but somewhat higher than those found in southern Europe (Inglehart et al 2004). The important point is that the trajectories of value change are the same, from one country to the next: postmaterialist outlooks are steadily spreading. That finding is consistent with what the theory predicts.

A second implication of the theory is that postmaterial attitudes ought to be more common among younger generations because older generations are more likely to have been socialized under conditions of material and physical insecurity. In effect, the expectation is that there will be generational differences in materialist and postmaterialist values distributed within the population. Canadian population data provide a simple example. In 1981, when the Canadian World Values data were collected, about 40 percent of the Canadian population was born before 1945. By 2000, the year when the latest Canadian values data were collected, only 20.9 percent of the Canadian population was born before 1945. According to the theory, we should expect to find higher levels of postmaterialism among the younger generations. And that is exactly what we do find. As data in Figure 14.3 show, that same pattern of generational difference is consistently found in a variety of other countries. In this case, the vertical axis on the graph is a percentage difference index, which simply measures the percentage of materialists minus the percentage of the postmaterialists in each country. Notice that the data from each country slope in the same direction. To be sure, there is evidence of some variation in the levels of

Figure 14.3   Age Difference in Value Priorities

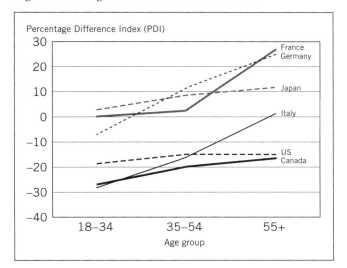

postmaterialism from one country to the next. But those in the older generations (over 55 years of age) are consistently more materialist than their younger counterparts.

A second set of predictions coming from the new politics view of value change concerns issue priorities. If the transformation from old politics to new politics is linked to the increased importance postmaterialists attach to quality of life considerations, then we would expect to find empirical evidence indicating that materialists and postmaterialists consistently take different issue positions on a variety of issues. Moreover, if the theory generally applies to publics in all advanced industrial states, then we would expect to find evidence of issue differences between materialists and postmaterialists in quite different national settings. We can examine the World Values Surveys data to explore that expectation.

Figure 14.4 compares where materialists and postmaterialists stand on three issue areas: homosexuality,

Figure 14.4   Support for Issues by Value Priority and Country

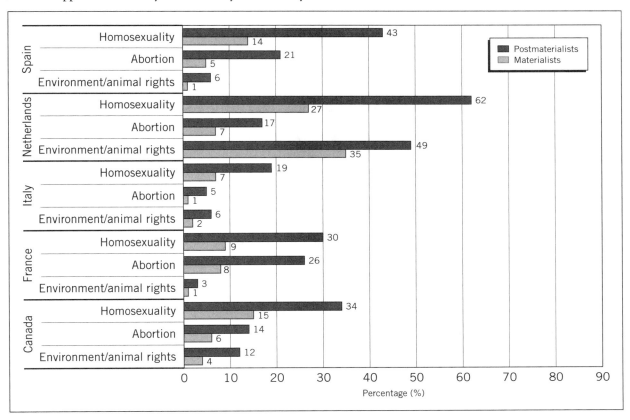

Questions:

Abortion: Abortion is always justifiable.

Homosexuality: Homosexuality is always justifiable.

Environment/animal rights: Member of a conservation, environment or animal rights group.

Source: European & World Values Surveys, 2000.

abortion, and support for environmental and animal rights. In this case, we consider comparable data collected in 2000 in five countries—Spain, Netherlands, Italy, France, and Canada—all of which qualify as advanced industrial states. The most striking finding concerns the consistency of the differences between materialists and postmaterialists.

Regardless of which country is under consideration, postmaterialists are always significantly more likely than materialists to view "homosexuality" as justifiable and "abortion" as justifiable, and they are consistently more likely than materialists to report that they are members of groups supporting such new politics issues as environmental protection and animal rights. Once again there is some evidence of national variations. Dutch respondents, for example, seem to be more "liberal" in their views about homosexuality and abortion than are

their Italian counterparts. The more impressive point is that in every country for which we have data, postmaterialists are twice as likely as materialists to think that homosexuality is "justifiable."

On balance, these survey data clearly do provide support for the contention that postmaterialist value priorities underpin issue positions that are consistently different from those of their materialist counterparts. The fact that there seem to be significant differences between materialists and postmaterialists on the issues of the day would not matter much, perhaps, if the growing ranks of postmaterialists lacked any interest in politics—if they were politically passive and disengaged. The theory of new politics outlined at the beginning, however, predicted precisely the opposite. Recall that it was precisely because of the structural changes associated with the shift from deep industrialism to advanced industrialism that new politics theory

Figure 14.5   Political Interest and Protest Activity by Value Priority and Country

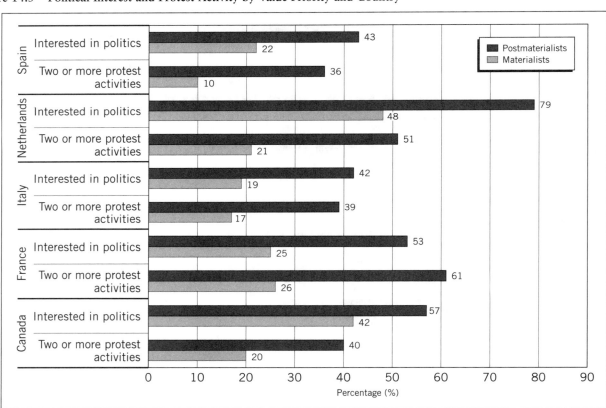

Questions:
Interested in politics: "How interested would you say you are in politics? Very interested, somewhat interested, not very interested, not at all interested." The responses include those who say they are "very interested" and "somewhat interested."
Two or more protest activities: Respondents who had participated in two or more of the following protest activities were included in the analysis: signed a petition, joined in a boycott, attended lawful demonstrations, joined unofficial strikes, occupied buildings.

Source: European & World Values Surveys, 2000

predicts that the politics of advanced industrial states will become more boisterous (Huntington 1974; Dalton 1996; Putnam and Pharr 2000). People with higher levels of formal education tend to be more interested in politics. Greater interest in politics, in turn, provides the motivation both to become better informed about the political world, and to be more active and engaged in that world (Nie et al 1996). Moreover, those higher levels of political activity do not just mean that supporters of the New Politics agenda are more likely to vote; it means that they may be more likely than their old politics counterparts to engage in such higher levels of "direct political action" as signing petitions or joining boycotts (Barnes et al 1979; Dalton and Keuchler 1990).

Once again, we can turn to the survey evidence to see if there is any support for both of these claims. Figure 14.5 compares the levels of political interest and protest activity of materialist and postmaterialists among publics from the same five countries as in Figure 14.4.

The basic findings are unequivocal. Postmaterialists are consistently more likely than materialists to say that they are interested in politics. Moreover, they are consistently more likely than materialists (about twice as likely) to say that they have participated in at least two types of political behaviour that qualify as "protest activities."

CONCLUDING DISCUSSION

◆ ◆ ◆

What do these findings collectively mean for Canada's political landscape? The consistency of the rise of post-materialist values among Canadians is one finding that warrants careful consideration. If the data presented in Figure 14.2 are projected forward it is tempting to conclude that in another few decades the vast majority of the Canadian public will be embracing postmaterialist outlooks. But there are several reasons for caution about that kind of projection.

First, it is certainly the case that many Canadians have enjoyed far more prosperity, over a far longer period, than their predecessors could have imagined. But that prosperity has not been equally shared; a significant proportion of the Canadian population lives in poverty.[1] As long as that remains the case, we would expect those who are socialized under conditions of poverty to continue to internalize materialist outlooks.

A second and related point concerns the dynamics of population replacement in this country. About one in

eight of Canada's citizens come from other parts of the world. Indeed, Canada is more dependent on immigrants for population replacement than all other advanced industrial states with the single exception of Australia. In the 1950s and early 1960s the bulk of Canada's immigrants came from Europe. That pattern has now completely reversed. Since the 1980s the vast majority of Canada's immigrant population has come from the poorer regions of the world. To the extent that these new Canadians were to have been socialized under conditions of material and often physical insecurity, then we would expect them to have internalized materialist outlooks. Poverty is stubborn and it is not likely that the significant pockets of poverty can be eradicated overnight. Nor is it likely that the patterns of immigration that have been in place for the last twenty 25 years will change in the short run. The combined effects of these two dynamics, according to the theory, will be to feed the ranks of those holding materialist values and to slow the pace of rising postmaterialism.

There are also the economic conditions within Canada to consider. We began this chapter with the observation that one of the main reasons postmaterialist outlooks have steadily grown is because of the period of economic growth and prosperity that Canadians have enjoyed since the 1950s. There is no guarantee, however, that citizens of advanced industrial states will escape economic reversals in the future. Even such short-lived economic shocks such as the oil crisis in the late 1970s and the spike in inflation rates in the early 1980s had a substantial impact on people's sense of security. Those economic shocks, as the theory predicts, produced a temporary reversal away from postmaterialism and an increase in materialist outlooks.

Political factors also matter. People's sense of material and physical security is driven not only by economic factors. Materialism and postmaterialist values do not simply rise and fall along with the stock market; political shocks—war or terrorism—also have the potential to undermine people's sense of security.

A second general interpretation needs to be elaborated and concerns the claims, first, that new politics is more boisterous than old politics and, second, that Canadians are harder to govern than they once were. Both of these claims are grounded in the linkages between value change *and* structural change. The data clearly show (Figure 14.4) that postmaterialists are significantly more likely than materialists not only to be more interested in politics but also to engage in direct action protest strategies. Part of the reason for those differences is attributable to the fact that postmaterialists also have significantly higher levels of formal education than their materialist counterparts.[2] Thus those with higher levels of formal education are more likely to be outspoken and active in the political arena, and the priorities they promote are also systematically different from those of the rest of the population. In effect, the postmaterialist message is more forcefully presented in public discourse and is more difficult to ignore. Canadians now are not more difficult to govern because postmaterialists are more vocal and active than materialists. They are more difficult to govern because of the co-existence of multiplying value differences within a single public. The materialist set of value outlooks anchors old politics and within that axis the old left and old right disagree, typically, about the size of the state, about what and how much the state should do, and about the distribution of wealth. The postmaterialist value outlooks, by contrast, divide this traditional axis, creating a new left and a new right that coexist along with the old left and the old right. Canadians are harder to govern because it is harder for representative institutions, such as political parties, to coherently represent an increasingly fragmented value landscape.

Notes

1. Some 11 percent, according to Statistics Canada's Low-income cut-off (LICO). LICOs identify "the income thresholds below which Canadians likely devote a larger share of income than average to the necessities of food, shelter and clothing" (Statistics Canada 2006).

2. The connection between higher levels of formal education and holding postmaterialist values holds in every advanced industrial state. See Abramson and Inglehart 1995.

Bibliography

Abramson, Paul and Ronald Inglehart. *Value Change in Global Perspective*. Ann Arbor: University of Michigan Press, 1995.

Barnes, Samuel, Max Kaase, Klaus Allerback, Barbara Farah, Felix Heunks, Ronald Inglehart, Kent Jennings, Hans Klingemann, Alan Marsh, and Leopold Rosenmay. *Political Participation: Mass Participation in Five Western Democracies*. Beverly Hills: Sage, 1979.

Dalton, Russell, and Manfred Kuechler. *Changing the Political Order: New Social and Political Movements in Western Democracies*. New York: Oxford University Press, 1990.

Dalton, Russell. "Was There a Revolution? A Note on Generational versus Life Cycle Explanations of Value Differences," *Comparative Political Studies* vol. 9, no. 4. 1977: 459–73.

———. *Citizen Politics*, 2nd ed. New Jersey: Chatham House Publishers, 1996.

European and World Values Surveys. Retrieved April 28, 2007, from www.europeanvalues.nl/index2.htm.

Feldman, Stanley. "Structure and Consistency in Public Opinion: The Role of Core Beliefs and Values," *American Journal of Political Science* vol. 32, 1988: 416–40.

Gidengil, Elizabeth, Andre Blais, Neil Nevitte, and Richard Nadeau. *Citizens*. University of British Columbia Press, 2005.

Halman, L. *The European Values Survey: A Third Wave*. Tilburg, Netherlands: European Values Survey and Work and Organization Research Centre, Tilburg University, 2001.

Huntington, Samuel P. "Post-industrial Politics: How Benign Will It Be?" *Comparative Politics*, vol. 6, 1974: 147–77.

Inglehart, Ronald. "The Silent Revolution in Europe: Intergenerational Change in Post-Industrial Societies," *The American Political Science Review* vol. 65, no. 4, 1971: 991–1071.

———. "The Renaissance of Political Culture," *The American Political Science Review* vol. 82, no. 4. 1988: 1203–30.

Inglehart, Ronald F., Miguel Basanez, Jaime Diez-Medrano, Loek Halman, and Ruud Luijkx. *Human Beliefs and Values: a Cross-cultural Sourcebook based on the 1999–2002 Value Surveys*. Mexico City: Siglo XXI, 2004.

Maslow, Abraham. *Motivation and Personality*. New York: Harper, 1954.

Nie, Norman H., Jane Junn, and Kenneth Stehlik-Barry. *Education and Democratic Citizenship in America.* Chicago: University of Chicago Press, 1996.

Nevitte, Neil. *The Decline of Deference: Canadian Value Change in Cross-National Perspective.* Toronto: Broadview Press, 1996.

———.(ed.) *Value Change and Governance in Canada.* Toronto: University of Toronto Press, 2002.

Putnam, Robert D., and Susan J. Pharr. *Disaffected Democracies.* Princeton: Princeton University Press, 2000.

Rokeach, M. *Beliefs, Attitudes, and Values: A Theory of Organization and Change.* San Francisco: Jossey-Bass, 1968.

Statistics Canada. "Income of Canadians," *The Daily.* March 30, 2006. Retrieved March 26, 2007, from www.statcan.ca/Daily/English/060330/d060330a.htm.

Terms and Concepts

generational value change
needs hierarchy
socialization

old politics
new politics
materialist values

postmaterialist values
direct political action

Questions

1. Compare your own political views with those of your grandparents. In what respects are they the same? In what ways do they differ?

2. Name five political issues that have recently dominated the national news. Which ones are "new politics" issues and which ones are not? Defend your answers.

3. Is voter turnout decline in Canada evidence for or against the new politics thesis?

4. The new politics thesis suggests that people feel a shrinking competence gap between themselves and politicians. If this were true, how would it manifest itself? Is this what you see in contemporary Canadian politics?

5. Nevitte argues that postmaterialist political orientations assume and depend upon the existence of strong economic growth. Do such orientations support such growth or undermine it?

6. How do new politics concerns fit with conventional distinction between "right" and "left" in Canada?

May the Weak Force Be with You: The Power of the Mass Media in Modern Politics

Kenneth Newton

Editors' Note

The news does not simply appear on TV, ready for our consumption. Nor is it simply generated by events "out there" in the world. The news is produced, "stories" are constructed, and decisions are made about what stories make the news and what will be passed over. This creates the suspicion that the stories told are those of the journalists, not those of the people in the stories. When one country is at war with another, does the TV news story indicate that country A is retaliating against an aggressive attack by country B, or does it emphasize civilian casualties caused by country A's bombing campaign? The media spin events in different ways, presumably to create different political interpretations.[1]

The inquiry into media bias—whether the news favours certain political actors, partisan positions, or political ideologies—has not yet produced a consensus. For every discovery of left-wing bias there is an equal but opposite insistence that the right-wingers have a stranglehold on news reporting.[2] This is perhaps to be expected. Partisans rarely consider others' criticisms seriously. If someone disagrees with his or her view of the role of the state in the economy, for example, the partisan can take comfort by saying that critics simply do not understand his or her position, or that the media have brainwashed the critics into thinking as they do.

Preoccupations with the political orientation of media bias may have distracted us from careful consideration of the extent of media influence and how it works. Kenneth Newton's recent article from the *European Journal of Political Research* offers a new analysis of these questions. According to him, many current assumptions about media bias are questionable. Among other things, he concludes that media power depends a great deal on characteristics of the news consumer. Paradoxically, news junkies may be more immune to media influence than most people.

◆ ◆ ◆

INTRODUCTION
◆ ◆ ◆

Many social scientists, journalists and social commentators share a worry about the increasingly powerful and malign effects of the mass media. These effects are powerful, they claim, because the mass media permeate almost every corner of society, and have a strong tendency to undermine, even destroy, many of the mass attitudes and behavioural patterns upon which democracy depends and because

---

1. Randal Marlin, *Propaganda and the Ethics of Persuasion* (Peterborough: Broadview, 2003).
2. For example, Lydia Miljan and Barry Cooper, *Hidden Agendas: How Journalists Influence the News* (Vancouver; UBC Press, 2003); Noam Chomsky, *Chronicles of Dissent* (Vancouver: New Star Books, 1992).

Kenneth Newton, "May the Weak Force Be with You: The Power of the Mass Media in Modern Politics" from the *European Journal of Political Research*, Volume 45:2 (March 2006), pages 209–34. Reprinted with permission of Blackwell Publishing.

of their tendency to undermine democratic leaders and institutions. Originally the term 'videomalaise' was coined to describe the effects of television news on political attitudes and opinion (Robinson 1976a, 1976b), but the claim has broadened in the past twenty-five years to cover all forms of television, newspapers, radio, films and, most recently, e-mail and the World Wide Web. Therefore the term 'media malaise' is used here as an umbrella term to cover the claim that the mass media have a substantial and malign impact on politics and social life.

Media malaise is not a school of thought, even less a coherent or well-articulated theory of media effects. It is a mood, or climate of opinion, but it is strongly and widely held among politicians, journalists and the general public, as well as academics in the social sciences. It covers far more than politics, extending to anti-social behaviour (violence in the media), poor school performance and illiteracy (watching television rather than reading), poor health and eating habits (the 'couch-potato'), passivity rather than activity (watching television rather than doing), an inability to develop social skills (the 'computer nerd'), the decline of community (television and social capital) and the growth of an aggressive possessive individualism (advertisements and entertainment media).

... neither theory nor evidence is strong enough to sustain the broad and general claims found in the media malaise literature.

It is not claimed here that all social scientists, even less all media experts, share a common concern with media malaise. On the contrary, some contest the idea, but they are a small group. As Norris (200: 11) puts it, the voices of those who are sceptical about the mass media have been 'drowned out by the Greek chorus of popular lament for the state of modern journalism.' Nor is it true that there is no good theory or empirical research to support the idea of media malaise. On the contrary, there is evidence to show that the media can be powerful and sometimes malign. The central argument here, however, is that neither theory nor evidence is strong enough to sustain the broad and general claims found in the media malaise literature.

This article is concerned primarily with the political impact of the mass media, arguing that they are generally a weak force in politics and government. They can

and do exercise some direct and independent influence over some aspects of political life, and can even exercise a strong or crucial one under certain circumstances, but normally their impact is mediated and conditioned by a variety of other and more powerful forces. The second part of the media malaise claim, that the media exercise a malign influence, will not be tackled here, in part because it is dealt with elsewhere (see Holtz-Bacha 1990; Bennett et al. 1999; Newton 1999; and especially Norris 2000).

To make its case this article presents an argument in three parts. The first part summarizes the large amount of literature on the powerful and pernicious political effects of the mass media in order to show that the media malaise theory is not a straw man set up to be knocked down with ease, but a widespread argument developed by a large number of social scientists. The second part reviews the various ways in which media messages are themselves mediated by forces that can dilute, deflect or even destroy them in some cases, or, alternatively, magnify their effects in other cases. The third part will present some evidence to illustrate aspects of the claim that the mass media are generally a weak force.

MEDIA MALAISE
◆ ◆ ◆

Table 15.1 presents an analysis of the various ways that the media are said to have an adverse effect on modern government and politics, together with references to some—certainly not all—of the English-language literature on the subject. It makes the point that a great many writers have made a great many claims of a great many kinds about the ways in which the mass media have an adverse impact on democratic government and politics. Some of the work is by journalists, but the great majority is by specialists in media research, many of them distinguished in the field.

Not all the authors appearing in Table 15.1 argue that the mass media are the only cause of concerns about modern democracy, or even the main cause. Nor do all of them argue that the media have only negative effects. Yet a great many dwell on the negative effects, and some concentrate almost exclusively on them. Nor is it contended that all the statements in Table 15.1 are wrong; many are partly right, as often as not because they make correct or partially correct observations about the nature or content of the mass media, but then

Table 15.1   The Mass Media as a Powerful and/or Malign Force: Summary of Claimed Effects

Mass Attitudes and Opinions

Ignorance and incomprehension. The constant flow of new news, combined with increasingly brief and superficial treatment of unconnected and unexplained events, contributes to public ignorance and incomprehension of politics (Ansolabehere et al. 1991; Hart 1994; Gabler 1998; Debord 1990; Blumler & Gurevitch 1995: 213; Ranney 1983: 80, 82; Baudrillard 1987; Schiller 1973: 24–29; Kalb 1998; Shawcross 1984; Adatto 1990).

Debased public discourse. The sensational, superficial and sound-bite content of the news media debase the quality of public debate and understanding of politics (Dautrich & Hartley 1999; Fallows 1997; Schudson 1995; Hachten 1998; Kalb 1998; Schulz 1998; Patterson 1980, 1994). The news media reduce complex, many-sided issues to two antagonistic camps (Epstein 1973: 227), turn politics into infotainment or show business (Gabler 1998; Hallin 1991; Dautrich & Hartley 1999; Fallows 1997; Schudson 1995; Hachten 1998; Patterson 1994; Dahlgren 1995). The news is impoverished by the conflict between politicians and journalists (Blumler 1997). Some claim that by its very nature, television (including news and current affairs programmes) is doomed to entertain and amuse (Postman 1985).

Political fatigue. Voters have sometimes become so bored and irritated by the huge amount of election news that they avoid television news and newspapers during the campaigns. For these people, there is not too little serious political news and comment in the mass media, but a great deal too much (Franklin 1994: 131, 151; Wober 1992: 2; MacArthur & Worcester 1992: 5).

Mainstreaming. Television is said to homogenize us (Sartori 1989: 43; Kubey & Csikzentmihalyi 1990: 100). The more we watch television, the more we conform to its beliefs, attitudes and values and the more we take up mainstream opinions (Kerbel 1995: 8; Gerbner et al. 1982).

The mean world effect. The mass media, especially television, create fear, alienation, distrust and cynicism because of its attack journalism and its focus on conflict and bad news (Lang & Lang 1966, 1968; Robinson & Sheehan 1983; Robinson 1976a, 1976b; Gerbner et al. 1984; Edelman 1987; Cappella & Hall-Jamieson 1996; Philo 1990; Patterson 1994: 93; Kerbel 1995: 6, 124; Blumler & Gurevitch 1995: 215; Ranney 1983: 79; Schulz 1998; Holtz-Bacha 1990).

Undermining social capital. Television drags people from their communities and its associations, and isolates and privatizes them in their living rooms (Putnam 1995).

Attitude instability. The rapidly changing flow of news and issues, coupled with fluctuating opinion polling figures, causes instability in public opinion (Smith 1981: 178).

Mass and Elite Behaviour

Falling election turnout. According to Ranney (1983: 80–86) and Maarek (1995: 225–226), the media contribute to falling election turnout because they bore electors with too much politics and make elections foregone conclusions by predicting election winners. Others emphasize the importance of negative campaigning and bad news as a cause of declining turnout (Ansolabehere et al. 1993, 1995: 24–26; Entman 1995: 153).

Falling party membership and identification. The shift from news and commentary about parties and policies to candidates and personalities has weakened party ties and partisanship (Wattenberg 1984; Fiorina 1980; Pfetsch 1996).

Packaging and presentation are favoured over political substance. The mass media encourage the concern of politicians with packaging and presentation rather than policy content (Maarek 1995; D.K. Davis 1995: 330; Franklin 1994; Hall-Jamieson 1984).

Policy instability and short-termism. Because of way the media covers the rapid flow of political events and fluctuating opinion poll figures about them, politicians are encouraged to become short-term pragmatists (Maarek 1995: 226).

Political Processes

Incumbency effect, shortening political lives. Some argue that the mass media strengthen the electoral position of incumbents (Graber 1993: 273–275), others that political lives are shortened by attack journalism and the pitiless glare of publicity (Ranney 1983: 147–150; Meyrowitz 1995: 133).

Table 15.1 (*Continued*)

Fast forward effect. As competing channels of news try to outdo each other with new news and scoops, the pace of political life accelerates (Ranney 1983).

Privatisation and the re-feudalisation of politics. The commercialization of the press, and its concentration of ownership and control, has re-feudalised the public sphere and turned it into a private matter between the state and media corporations (Habermas 1979: 198).

Democracy and Its Institutions

Decline of parties. The mass media undermine the need for party members and so undermine party membership (Ansolabehere et al. 1991; Maarek 1995: 204; Negrine & Papathanassopoulos 1996).

The presidentialisation of leadership. Focus on a few well-known political leaders creates or strengthens a presidential style of politics (Ranney 1983).

Diminished responsibility and accountability of leaders. The heavy concentration of episodic news stories of a human interest kind serves to draw attention from general policy issues and hence undermines the responsibility of leaders for the consequences of their policies (Iyengar 1991; Entman 1995: 155).

Political overload and ungovernability. The media fuel public demands and so overloads governments and creates ungovernability (Crozier et al. 1975; Ranney 1983: 154).

Loss of political trust and confidence in institutions. The mean world effect results in loss of trust in political leaders, loss of confidence in democratic institutions and loss of satisfaction with democracy itself (McKeod et al. 1997).

Undermining democracy. The mass media undermine democratic leaders and cause loss of confidence in democracy and its institutions (Crozier et al. 1975).

proceed to speculate, assume or assert that these will have adverse effects on government and politics. For example, it is claimed that 'attack journalism'—highly critical muck-raking, investigative journalism—shortens the political lives of democratic leaders, or can even destroy them (Ranney 1983: 147–150; Meyrowitz 1995: 133). One can think of examples to fit the theory, from Gary Hart, Richard Nixon, Michael Dukakis and Gerald Ford, to Edward Heath, John Major, Neal Kinnock and Lionel Jospin. All were attacked by the media and all soon faded from national political life. This, however, is to cherry-pick examples to suit the theory.

For all the destructive power claimed for attack journalism, it should not be forgotten that the modern world has some unusually long-lived political leaders, including Thatcher, Major, Blair, Kohl, Mitterand, Chirac, Gonzales, Fraser, Hawke, Keating, Howard, Trudeau, Chrétien and Mulroney. John Major served as prime minister for a long time in spite of a particularly bad press. Ken Livingston, villainised by the British media in the 1980s and 1990s as a 'loony-lefty,' bounced back without public relations or party support to become

Mayor of London and a popular political figure. More systematic evidence on government longevity shows that it did not decline in twenty Western states from 1950 to 1983 (Budge & Kenman 1990: 162), which were also the years in which the attack power of the mass media is reputed to have grown substantially.

Even if it were true that the mass media increasingly attack governments and political leaders by focusing on bad news, it is still necessary to show that it is the media and not political events that cause the damage. Did Nixon resign because the media attacked him, or because of the events of Watergate? Did the press do the damage or was it mainly the messenger that brought the news? Did Kinnock, Dukakis and Jospin fail to achieve the highest office, and did Heath, Ford, Spiro Agnew and (eventually) Thatcher fall from grace because journalists did not like them or because they failed to impress voters and/or their political colleagues? In these cases, as in so many others, it is difficult to understate the methodological problems of showing clear cause and effect relationships between the mass media and political outcomes.

Even if it were true that the mass media increasingly attack governments and political leaders by focusing on bad news, it is still necessary to show that it is the media and not political events that cause the damage.

This point about the methodological problems of demonstrating mass media causes and effects is important, and needs to be heavily stressed. It applies, of course, as much to media malaise writings as it does to the present argument that the media are a weak force. However, the point is methodological problems allow exaggerated or false claims to be made for media effects without fear of empirical rebuttal. Given the lack of hard evidence and the great difficulties of establishing clear cause and effects relations, assumption and speculation fill the gap, and since it is difficult to disprove these, then *prima facae* plausibility is often the toughest test of the assertions. What follows is an attempt to introduce a broader theoretical framework, with some evidence, into thinking about mass media effects on government and politics.

MEDIATING THE MEDIA

◆ ◆ ◆

Some of the forces mediating media effects are well understood, and widely known. These will be passed over quickly in order to concentrate on more recent or less commonly discussed considerations.

Minimal Effects: Psychological Mechanisms and the Media Market

The minimal effects tradition of media research stresses the great importance of individual and structural factors in restricting the mass media to a reinforcing role (Lazarsfeld 1968; Blumier & McQuail 1968; McQuail 1987: 233–237, 253–254; Miller 1991: 1–4). On the individual level, people use a variety of psychological mechanisms to minimise media effects, including self-selection, distortion, misinterpretation and suppression. At the structural level, a competitive media market provides consumers with what they want to see, hear and read, in much the same way that supermarkets deliver goods at the price

consumers are able and willing to pay. To the extent that the commercial media are bound by the golden chains of the market to satisfy consumer demand, it is as much a matter of audiences shaping the media as the other way round. Competition also means that the mass media are not a single entity delivering the same message to a single mass audience, but a varied and competing set of mediums delivering varied and competing messages to varied audiences.

Some media markets are more oligopolistic than competitive, and increasing concentration of ownership and control weakens media pluralism. Even so, Western societies have not produced media monopolies along the lines of totalitarian systems, and to the extent that there is pluralism and competition, different channels of communication must bow to consumer demand, political and otherwise. For example, in Britain, the *Observer* newspaper opposed the Suez War of 1956, promptly lost a large proportion of its readers and provided itself and other papers with a lesson about the commercial importance of swimming with the tide. It is also clear that voters in the West use a wide variety of sources of political information (Dautrich & Harley 1999: 45), and thereby expose themselves to competing views and messages. To this extent, the impact of any one channel or message may be off-set, counter-balanced or neutralised by others (Zeller 1992: 185–215; 1996: 20). It will not do to assume either that the Western media are a monolithic block, selling essentially the same political message, or that citizens are fools who believe whatever they read in the newspapers.

It will not do to assume either that the Western media are a monolithic block, selling essentially the same political message, or that citizens are fools who believe whatever they read in the newspapers.

The Mass Media Are Embedded in Society

Implicit in many statements about media effects on society is the idea that somehow the media are quite separate and distinct from society, firing their poison arrows into it from a distance. In fact, the mass media are an integral part of society, sharing many of its values, operating within many of its constraints (organisational, economic, cultural and legal), drawing its journalists from it, and reflecting its concerns to a greater or lesser extent. In other words, the media are deeply embedded in and part of society. They are subject to its influences much like other institutions: journalists and editors do not arrive on earth from Mars or Venus, they are social products like the rest of us, albeit, maybe, rather special ones, like many other occupations. This not only makes it difficult to sort out the great entanglement of cause and effect relationships running between the media and society, but suggests caution in making statements about how the media affect society without regard to how the media and its messages are themselves products of society and influenced or determined by it.

Trust in the Mass Media

The less a medium is trusted and the less it is believed, the less its influence (Schiller 1973: 79–80). One of the most notable features of the Western media is the generally rather low esteem it commands from the general public. Two waves of World Values Surveys in seventeen democracies in the early 1980s and early 1990s show that the press ranks with trade unions at the very bottom of a table covering ten sets of public and private institutions (Newton & Norris 2000: 55; see also Dautrich & Hartley 1992: 82–90; Kerbel 1995: 10–12). While confidence ratings for the press are 40 per cent or lower, those for the police and the education system are 60 per cent or higher. Another survey of trust in the media in the Member States of the European Union (*Eurobarometer 57*, Spring 2002) shows that an average of 44 per cent of adults trust the press, 61 per cent trust the radio and 55 per cent trust television. Tabloid newspapers are generally trusted far less than broadsheets, but tabloids comfortably outsell broadsheets. In general, the power and influence of the media are reduced to the extent that trust in them is not high, and trust in the mass media is still lower.

The less a medium is trusted and the less it is believed, the less its influence ...

Values, Attitudes and Opinions

Public opinion has three main layers: opinions are the most superficial and most changeable; attitudes are more deeply rooted and less changeable; values are the core foundations on which opinions and attitudes are built. Values are the least susceptible to outside influences, and have a general and pervasive influence over attitudes and opinions (Zaller 1992: 23; Van Deth & Scarbrough 1998). How are values formed and changed? The answer seems to be that they are shaped mainly by such things as social class, religion, ethnicity, age, gender, education and personal experience. These are the strong forces that mould public opinion— the classical variables of the behavioural sciences. Where values, attitudes and opinions are strongly held, where individuals have first hand experience and knowledge of an issue, and where the issue is seen as closely tied to class, race, religious, and gender interests, then the impacts of the mass media are likely to be secondary.

Zaller's (1996: 17–78) impressive attempt to demonstrate 'massive media effects' illustrates the point. He found that highly aware liberals in the United States reduced their support for the Vietnam War when anti-war communications in the American media increased in intensity between 1964 and 1966. In strong contrast, highly aware conservatives became *more* supportive of the Vietnam War in the same period, in spite of the increased intensity of anti-war communications. They strengthened their views because they tagged anti-war messages as liberal, and were therefore able to reject them. Zaller writes (1996: 57):

> In fact ... there was as much support for the Vietnam War in 1970 among highly aware conservatives as there had been in 1964. Such doggedness in the face of extremely frustrating real-world outcomes is explained by the fact that highly aware conservatives received a consistent set of pro-war messages and cues from people they respected.

In other words, in their battle with 'real-world outcomes' and the liberal press, conservative values triumphed among highly aware conservatives. Yet where liberal values coincided with the increasingly liberal and critical account of the progress of the Vietnam War in the mass media, the liberal point of view was strengthened. It seems that people do not so much believe what they read in the newspapers, but read what they believe in the newspapers. The import of Zaller's careful research seems to be that the liberal press did have the effect of changing attitudes towards the war, but only among liberals who were predisposed to believe the news about the real world.

*It seems that people do not so much
believe what they read in the newspapers,
but read what they believe in
the newspapers.*

A different body of literature on the importance and effect of political campaigns reaches exactly the same conclusions. If the mass media are a political weak force, then one would expect political campaigns, a form of political persuasion that operates primarily through the mass media, also to be a weak force. The conclusions of Schmitt-Beck and Farrell (2002) in a book on political campaigns suggests that this is the case. They found that campaigns do matter in some respects, but this depends on upon circumstances. As they put it:

> [I]f the voters are not buying then there is not much a campaign can do about it ... referendum campaigns have the best chance of converting opinion on new, unclear and complex issues that are unrelated to existing political cleavages, but on established issues with clear partisan connotations, the best they can hope is to mobilize their supporters ... the more aware voters are, and the more clear their political predispositions are, the less likely campaigns are to affect opinion, while the more likely they are to mobilise people. (Schmitt-Beck & Farrell 2002: 188–192)

This conclusion is consistent with Zaller's finding (1996: 57) that highly aware conservatives in the United States did not 'buy' the anti-Vietnam War messages of the liberal press between 1964 and 1970 because news about what was actually happening in the war was overridden and discounted by their conservative values.

Social Networks

Recent research has revived the Katz-Lazarsfeld research on the importance of social networks and discussions as an influence that filters media messages and helps individuals interpret them. Recent work of this kind tends to emphasise the impact of social networks, rather than the more top-down view of opinion leaders and the two-step flow of communication developed by Katz and Lazarsfeld. According to Schmitt-Beck's (2003: 258) study of public opinion in Britain, Spain, the United States and West Germany: 'If media messages are not in accord with the prevailing opinion of a

recipient's discussion network they will be rejected and not taken into account at the ballots.' According to an American study (Beck et al. 2002: 68–69), the primary sources of political cues in the 1992 presidential campaign are 'personal networks and groups, not the modern mass media, which has often been ceded greater electoral significance. Organizations and personal discussants serve as more consequential carriers of partisan messages than the media' (see also Robinson & Levy 1986; Roessler 1999; Wright et al. 1969; Huckfeldt & La Due Lake 1998; and on the importance of conversations as an influence on voting, see Pattie & Johnston 1999).

These studies show that while the mass media carry messages, it is personal networks and discussion that exercise a strong influence [on], even determine, how these messages are received and interpreted. The mass media do not so much influence opinion as provide the raw materials that social networks mould into different shapes. If this is the case, then a further important conclusion may follow. If social networks and discussions are important for the way in which social groups interpret media messages, then what appear to be media effects, even what appear to be massive media effects, may be the result of interaction between media content and social networks. In other words, uncovering a strong association between media messages and public opinion may tell us less about media effects than about how they are amplified by networks and discussions. What appears to be a media impact may, in fact, be a network effect.

*The mass media do not so much influence
opinion as provide the raw materials
that social networks mould into
different shapes.*

To summarise, this section of the article has argued that the media are mediated by an array of factors that can modify their impact on individuals and institutions. Where values and beliefs are strongly held, where individuals have firsthand knowledge and experience of an issue, or where the issue is tied to the interests of class, race, religion, age and gender, and the discussion networks associated with them, then the impact of the media is likely to be weaker. Where people know and care little about the issue, and where it is remote from their everyday experience of life and their values, then

Figure 15.1   Mediating the Media

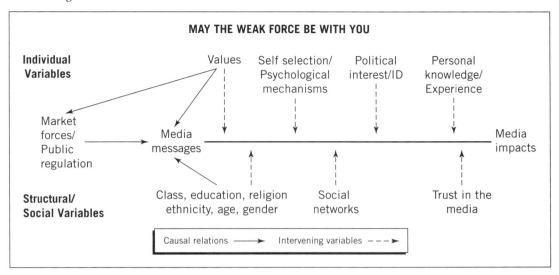

the impact of the media may be greater. This argument is sketched out in a simplified diagrammatic form in Figure 15.1.

THE MASS MEDIA AS A WEAK FORCE: SOME EVIDENCE

◆ ◆ ◆

This section of the article will present some evidence to illustrate the claim that the mass media are a weak force whose effects may be modified, diluted or even negated by mediating factors.

Telemythology: Clinton and Reagan

Probably the best single example of attack journalism in recent times is the feeding frenzy over the Clinton-Lewinsky scandal in the American mass media. According to media malaise theory, no president could possibly withstand such enormous and concerted pressure of media criticism. Unfortunately for the theory, not only did Clinton's ratings as a president remain comparatively high, but the Democrats actually gained Congressional seats a few months after the scandal broke, much to the surprise of political scientists who know about mid-term elections. Clinton's ratings as an individual plummeted, but his comparatively high ratings as a president barely wavered. Zaller's (1998, 2001) explanation is that his presidential ratings were

not affected so much by the media coverage of the scandal as by the mainsprings (i.e., the strong forces) of American politics—namely, peace, economic prosperity and ideological moderation. Zaller writes (1998: 186): 'No matter how poorly informed, psychologically driven, and 'mass mediated' public opinion may be, it is capable of recognizing and focusing on its own conception of what matters.' And this in the United States, which is reputed to have the worst informed, most psychologically driven and heavily mass-media-influenced public opinion in the world.

If the mass media have the power to shorten or destroy political careers then presumably they can use the same power to build up and support political leaders and prolong their lives. Ronald Reagan is a prime example: the camera loved him, his style was warm and re-assuring, and he was the 'kind of guy you couldn't stay mad at for long.' He was much admired by the Washington press corps who presented him as a very popular president whose appeal was based largely on his use of the media to establish rapport with the people. As Iyengar (1991: 1) writes: 'The unprecedented public popularity and significant policy success of President Reagan, for instance, have been widely attributed to his mastery of television.' A charisma, it must be said, that was backed up by a large, skilled and effective team of spin-doctors. The only fault with this account is that, in his own time, Reagan had the lowest ratings of any president since 1946. His popularity has, nonetheless, become part of modern telemythology created by the Washington press corps and academic media specialists (see Schudson 1995: 125–141), who were impressed by his communication skills. The press corps persuaded itself of two falsehoods. First, Reagan's outstanding ability to perform for the cameras must have made him a smash hit with the voters. And second, since the Washington press corps told the public that Reagan was immensely popular, the public would act accordingly and make him so.

Thatcher and the Failure of Political Marketing

Britain in the 1980s is an excellent place to test the strength of the mass media, especially of newspapers. The country had a highly centralised national newspaper system, and most regular newspaper readers see one of the eleven national dailies and/or one of the nine national Sunday papers. As a result, Britain had nine of Western Europe's eleven biggest selling newspapers, with sales of the dailies totalling 13.5 million and the Sundays, 13.7 million. The national press in Britain was also highly partisan, nailing their party political sympathies firmly to their mastheads. Moreover, Conservative newspapers accounted for between 65 and 75 per cent of national sales in the three election years, most being not just Conservative, but strongly Thatcherite in their politics.

For its part, the government was eager and able to provide the material that most Fleet Street editors were seeking. The government firmly believed in the power and importance of public relations and was prepared to spend ever-increasing amounts of time, effort and money on the packaging and presentation of its politics for public consumption. It built up a powerful, efficient and highly centralised public relations machine under the leadership of Thatcher's press secretary, Bernard Ingham. By the end of the 1980s Ingham's office, the Government Information Service (GIS) in Downing Street, controlled the entire government's propaganda efforts, serving as a clearing and coordinating centre for *all* central government departments (Cockerell et al. 1988; Franklin 1994: 82–95). In effect, Ingham had become the country's Minister of Information, or as one journalist said, 'the real Deputy Prime Minister' (quoted in Franklin 1994: 85). He certainly ran one of the largest government public relations operations anywhere in the democratic world. By 1989, it had increased its annual budget to very nearly £200 million and employed a staff of 1,200 press officers, journalists, radio producers, film makers, editors and support staff. From 1986 to 1989, government expenditure on

advertising was second only to the multinational conglomerate, Unilever (Scammell 1990). In 1987 and 1988 the Central Office of Information paid for over 30,000 television advertising spots, more than 9,000 newspaper advertisements, and in excess of 100 publicity campaigns, 1,800 publications, 140 films, videos and commercials, and 140 separate exhibitions (Franklin 1994: 100). It should be emphasised that a good proportion of this spending was mainly devoted to apolitical matters such as safety in the home, public health and safe driving, but increasingly large amounts were devoted to political matters of direct relevance to controversial aspects of government policy.

In short, Britain in the 1980s is an excellent limiting case in which to study media and government propaganda effects. There can be few other times or places in the Western world when circumstances were so favourable to 'massive media effects.' Among the issues of importance to the Thatcher government, four stand out as vital to its core interests: the poll tax, privatisation, taxing and spending, and Thatcher's personal image. The poll tax was a flagship of the Thatcher government. Staking her own and her government's reputation on its success, she put huge effort and budgetary resources behind its publicity campaign. A high-pressure media campaign was launched in which more than £10 million was spent on videos, tape recordings and press releases. Some 25 million leaflets for individuals, 1.5 million booklets for businesses and a special leaflet about tax rebates were produced. In 1989, 23 million leaflets were distributed at a cost of £1.8 million, followed by a £3.1 million campaign aimed at television and the local and national press (Deacon & Golding 1991).

Public approval of the tax was fairly constant at around 25 per cent between 1987 and 1990, but opposition rose steadily from 45 to 76 per cent. At the peak of one of the biggest publicity campaigns ever launched by a British government, and large by the standard of democratic governments and businesses anywhere, 71 per cent of the populace thought the poll tax was 'a bad idea.' In 1990, when the tax was introduced in England and Wales, 54 per cent were 'very strongly opposed' and another 22 per cent were 'fairly strongly opposed'; 22 per cent were in favour. When the tax was abolished a year after its introduction, two-thirds of the population thought it was a bad idea and wanted rid of it, while only 7 per cent thought it a good idea worth keeping (Butler et al. 1994: 260). The government even failed to get its own positive sounding name attached to the tax ('Community Charge'), which was always known as the anachronistic and 'bad' poll tax. The government also failed to lay the blame for the failure of the tax at the door of local government, though it tried hard to do this. Central government was clearly blamed for what came to be known as the worst idea in the world. The failure of the huge public relations campaign for the poll tax is easy to explain with weak force theory. It is not possible to convince the public of something it does not want to believe, especially if it has firsthand knowledge and experience of the matter. Everyone was required to pay the poll tax.

It is not possible to convince the public of something it does not want to believe, especially if it has firsthand knowledge and experience of the matter.

The campaign to persuade the British public of the merits of privatisation was equally expensive and time consuming, and met with no more success. Well over £240 million was spent on the attempt to sell privatisation to the British public, but the opinion polls (Table 15.2) show that it was never popular. At no point in any given privatisation campaign was it approved by much more than 40 per cent of the population. In fact at no time in the history of any privatisation campaign was the highest point of popularity higher than the lowest point

of unpopularity. The more the government campaigned, the more money it spent and the longer the programme lasted, the more unpopular the issue became. It might be claimed that privatisation would have been even more unpopular without the campaigns, but this is implausible given the abysmal levels of approval to start with. By the early 2000s, privatisation was more popular, but this may tell us more about how people get used to what they have, than about the persuasive powers of advertising.

A third policy area of critical importance to the government was the political battle for cutting taxes and public services. Once again Thatcher and her government fought long and hard, using the full weight of the government's large and expensive public relations machine, plus the huge support she had from the national press. The British public never bought the idea. Throughout the 1980s, tax spenders outnumbered cutters by a clear margin, and the balance shifted heavily towards the spenders year on year. In 1979, when Thatcher came to power, spenders and cutters were equal at 37 per cent each, but by 1987 tax cutters were 11 per cent and service extenders were 66 per cent (Crewe 1988: 38).[1]

Thatcher got a very favourable press for most of the 1980s from Fleet Street, which heavily supported her and her policies. She also put huge amounts of money, time and effort into constructing a favourable image of herself. Her clothes were chosen carefully, her voice

Table 15.2   Advertising Costs and Approval Ratings (in per cent) of Privatisation Campaigns

		Public Approval		Public Disapproval		
	Cost (£m)	*High*	*Low*	*High*	*Low*	*Dates*
British Telecom (BT)	25	42	26	59	43	10/83–12/94
British Aerospace						
British Gas	40	36	24	59	41	5/85–12/94
Water	40	22	10	83	62	8/88–12/94
Electricity	76	38	17	73	47	3/88–12/94
Coal Board	Not Known	36	31	56	51	8/88–3/91
Steel	Not Known	43	35	50	45	8/88–7/98
British Rail	Not Known	40	11	75	49	8/88–5/94
Post Office	Not Known	15	11	77	74	5/94–10/94

Sources: Costs: Franklin (1994: 103); approval/disapproval figures: *Gallup Political and Economic Index*. Figures for the last four privatisations are not available.

modulated, her speech-making coached, her body language schooled, her hairstyle softened, her interview technique honed and her television style trained by experts. Public appearances, photo-opportunities and sound bites were stage managed down to the last detail (Franklin 1994: 149–150; Bruce 1992: 55; Seymour-Ure 1991). What effect did all this have? Not a lot, it seems. Throughout her time as prime minister, the British public saw her realistically—there is ample polling data showing that she was seen as tough, determined, shrewd, decisive, able and a leader, but she was also seen as uncaring, unlistening, unlikeable, divisive, out of touch and destructive (see Tables 15.3 and 15.4). By comparison, the leader of the opposition, Neil Kinnock, was perceived as a far poorer politician, but a better human being (Table 15.3). In case it is thought misleading to compare a prime minister in the hot seat to a leader of the opposition who has an easier job and has served for a shorter time, Table 15.4 compares Thatcher and Major as prime ministers. The same picture emerges: Thatcher was highly rated as a politician, but poorly rated as an individual. Major's scores were the reverse.

In spite of ten years of concentrated public relations effort, Thatcher's image did not change much. She was always seen as being a bit out of touch, divisive and destructive (Table 15.5), although these views grew over time. Moreover, in spite of her electoral success and for all her media support from the press, she had, after Heath, the lowest satisfaction ratings of any postwar prime minister [Table 15.6]. Like Reagan's popularity as president, her popularity as a prime minister was more myth than reality. British citizens saw her daily on television and they were well able to make up their own minds about what they saw.

Table 15.4   Popular Perceptions of Thatcher and Major (September 1990) (in per cent)

	Thatcher	Major
Strong personality	79	9
Ability to deal with other world leaders	62	13
Ability to lead	53	20
Ability to talk straight	34	28
Knows what they are talking about	29	22
Able to unite the country	15	61
Sincere	10	52
Honesty	9	37
Friendliness and warmth	6	68
Understands problems of ordinary people	4	72
Willing to listen	3	84

Source: Gallup Political and Social Index, 1991.

Table 15.5   Thatcher's Image

	April 1979	April 1989
Tries hard in her job	93	83
Speaks her mind	81	90
Strong personality	79	93
Good speaker	75	80
Knows what she's talking about	75	63
Knows about the problems of the cost of living	73	38
Thinks a lot of herself	54	75
Not in touch with ordinary people	52	75
Doesn't come over well	46	36
Talks a lot but doesn't do much	39	43
A snob	37	54
Divides the country	37	72
Destructive ideas	25	41

Source: Gallup Political and Economic Index, 1979–1989.

Table 15.3   Popular Perceptions of Thatcher and Kinnock (May 1986) (in per cent)

	Thatcher	Kinnock
Tough	68	17
Determined	66	33
Sticks to principles	60	28
Shrewd	45	19
Decisive	42	17
Caring	8	42
Listens to reason	6	44
Likable as a person	5	50

Source: Gallup Political and Social Index, 1987.

Table 15.6   Satisfaction as a Prime Minister Compared to Other Postwar Leaders (in per cent)

		Average satisfaction score	Low	High
1945–1951	Atlee	47	37	66
1951–1955	Churchill	52	48	56
1955–1957	Eden	55	41	70
1957–1963	Macmillan	51	30	79
1963–1964	Douglas-Hume	45	41	78
1964–1966	Wilson	59	48	76
1966–1970	Wilson	41	27	69
1970–1974	Heath	37	31	45
1974–1976	Wilson	46	40	43
1976–1979	Callaghan	46	33	59
1979–1983	Thatcher	40	25	52
1983–1987	Thatcher	39	28	53
1987–1990	Thatcher	38	23	52
1990–1992	Major	51	46	59
1992–1997	Major	24	16	36
1997–1998	Blair	72	62	83

Note: The question asked was 'Are you satisfied or dissatisfied with ... as Prime Minister?'
Source: Gallup, Political and Economic Index 418, July 1995: 10 (1945–1997 figures) and Gallup monthly reports thereafter.

CONCLUSIONS
◆ ◆ ◆

Any attempt to establish media effects is riddled with tricky methodological problems, and any conclusions about them must be exceedingly cautious and accompanied by all sorts of caveats—including the weak force theory propounded here. Nevertheless, weak force theory seems to have more theoretical and empirical plausibility than strong force theory. The powers of the mass media are weak because they are often diluted, deflected or even destroyed by more powerful influences that mediate the media by intervening between them and their effects of wider society. The mediating strong forces are mainly those of social class, religion, age, education, gender, social networks and discussions, trust in the media, personal values, and personal knowledge and experience. Equally, these strong forces may also heighten media effects so that what appears to be a

media impact is, in fact, the result of an interaction between the media and their mediating forces.

The evidence presented here (about the Vietnam War, the Clinton and Lewinsky affair, Reagan, political campaign effects and Thatcher's public relations) suggests that media impacts are constrained by three paradoxes. First, those who are least interested, involved and knowledgeable about politics are the most susceptible to media influence, but the least likely to expose themselves to their influence. Second, the more people know about and have firsthand experience of something, the more likely they are to take an interest in media coverage of it, but the more likely they are to trust their own judgments rather than media's. Third, the more they try to persuade people of a political position, the less likely they are to be seen as impartial and neutral, and the less likely they are to be influential. The most partisan press is the least trusted and least influential.

> *... those who are least interested, involved and knowledgeable about politics are the most susceptible to media influence, but the least likely to expose themselves to their influence.*

This is not to say that the media cannot be a force or a strong force. To say that they are a weak force is to acknowledge that they are a force, and to say that they are normally or usually a weak force is to acknowledge that they can be a strong force under the right circumstances. Zaller's studies of the Vietnam War era and the Clinton-Lewinsky affair, as well as the evidence about the effect of political campaigns, show that media are weak where people already have entrenched values and opinions, but may be stronger on matters that are new, complex and unrelated to existing cleavages and values. Finally, the merit of arguing that the mass media are a weak force is that it avoids the false dilemma of whether the media have either minimal or massive effects. It suggests that one should focus instead on the sorts of circumstances in which the mass media have weaker or stronger effects, an approach that seems likely to be a more productive research agenda than arguing about whether they are not a powerful force.

Note

1. Crewe provides a good deal more evidence about the general failure of the Thatcher government to win support for many of its policies.

References

Adatto, K. (1990). *Sound bite democracy: Network evening news presidential campaign coverage, 1968 and 1988* (Research paper R-2). Cambridge, MA: Joan Shorestein Barone Center, Harvard University.

Altheide, D. L. (1976). *Creating reality: How TV news distorts events.* Beverly Hills, CA: Sage.

Ansolabehere, S., Behr, R. & Iyengar, S. (1991). Mass media and elections: An overview. *American Politics Quarterly* 19: 109–139.

Ansolabehere, S., Behr, R. & Iyengar, S. (1993). *The media game.* New York: Macmillan.

Ansolabehere, S., Behr, R. & Iyengar, S. (1995). *Going negative: How attack ads shrink and polarize the electorate.* New York: Free Press.

Ansolabehere, S., Behr, R. & Iyengar, S. (1995). Evolving perspectives on the effects of campaign communication. In P. C. Wasburn (ed), *Research in political sociology, Volume 7: Mass media and politics.* Greenwich, CT: JAI Press.

Baudrillard, J. (1987). *The evil demon of images.* London: Left Bank Books.

Beck, P. A. et al. (2002). The social calculus of voting: Interpersonal, media and organizational influences on presidential choice. *American Political Science Review* 96(1): 57–73.

Bennett, L. W. (1996a). *The governing crisis: Media, money and marketing in American elections.* New York: St. Martin's Press.

Bennett, L. W. et al. (1996b). *News: The politics of illusion.* New York: Longman.

Bennett, L. W. et al. (1999). 'Videomalaise revisited': Reconsidering the relations between the public's view of the media and trust in government. *Harvard International Journal of Press/Politics* 4(4): 8–23.

Blumler, J. G. (1997). Origins of the crisis of communication for citizenship. *Political Communication* 14(4): 395–404.

Blumler, J. G. & Mcquail, D. (1968). *Television in politics: Its uses and influence.* London: Faber & Faber.

Blumler, J. G. & Gurevitch, M. (1995). *The crisis of public communication.* London: Routledge.

Bourdieu, P. (1998). *On television and journalism.* London: Pluto Press.

Bruce, B. (1992). *Images of power.* London: Kogan Page.

Budge, I. & Keman, H. (1990). *Parties and democracy: Coalition formation and government functioning in twenty states.* Oxford: Oxford University Press.

Butler, D., Adonis, A & Travers, T. (1994). *The failure of government: The politics of the poll tax.* Oxford: Oxford University Press.

Calcutt, D. (1998). Democracy under threat. In H. Stephenson & M. Bromley (eds), *Sex, lies and democracy: The press and the public*. London: Longman.

Cappella, J. N. & Hall-Jamieson, K. (1996). News frames, political cynicism and media cynicism. *Annals of the American Academy* 546 (July): 71–84.

Capella, J. N. & Hall-Jamieson, K. (1997). *Spiral of cynicism: The press and the public good*. New York: Oxford University Press.

Carruthers, S. L. (2000). *The media at war*. Basingstoke: Macmillan.

Chomsky, N. & Herman, E. (1988). *Manufacturing consent*. London: Vintage.

Cockerell, M. et al. (1988). *Sources close to the prime minister*. London: Macmillan.

Corner, J. (1995). *Television form and public address*. London: Edward Arnold.

Corner, J. & Peis, D. (2003). *Media and the restyling of politics*. London: Sage.

Crewe, I. (1988). Has the electorate become 'Thatcherite'? In R. Skideldsky (ed), *Thatcherism*. Oxford: Blackwell.

Crozier, M., Huntington, S. P. & Watanuki, J. (1975). The crisis of democracy: Report on the governability of democracies to the trilateral commission. New York: New York University Press.

Curran, J. & Seaton, J. (1997). Power without responsibility. The press and broadcasting in Britain. London: Routledge.

Dahlgren, P. (1995). *Television and the public sphere*. London: Sage.

Davis, D. K. (1995). Mass and modernity: The future of journalism in a post Cold War and postmodern world. In P. C. Wasburn (ed), *Research in political sociology, Volume 7: Mass media and politics*. Greenwich, CT: JAI Press.

Davis, D. K. (1995). Media: Becoming an autonomous force. In P. J. Davies (ed), *An American quarter century*. Manchester: Manchester University Press.

Dautrich, K. & Hartley, T. H. (1999). *How the news media fail American voters: Causes, consequences and remedies*. New York: Columbia University Press.

Deacon, D. & Golding, P. (1991). When ideology fails: The flagship of Thatcherism and the British local and national media. *European Journal of Communication* 6(3): 291–315.

Debord, G. (1990). *Comments on 'The Society of the Spectacle.'* London: Verso.

Edelman, M. (1987). *Constructing the political spectacle*. Chicago, IL: University of Chicago Press.

Entman, R. M. (1989). *Democracy without citizens: Media and the decay of American politics*. New York: Oxford University Press.

Entman, R. M. (1995). Television, democratic theory and the visual construction of poverty. In P. C. Washburn (ed), *Research in political sociology, Volume 7: Mass media and politics*. Greenwich, CT: JAI Press.

Epstein, E. J. (1973). *News from nowhere*. New York: Random House Vintage Books.

Fallows, J. (1997). *Breaking the news: How the media undermine American democracy*. New York: Vintage Books.

Fiorina, M. (1980). The decline of collective responsibility. *Daedalus* 109: 25–74.

Franklin, B. (1994). *Packaging politics: Political communications in Britain's media democracy*. London: Edward Arnold.

Freedman, J. (2002). *Media violence and its effects on aggression: Assessing the scientific evidence*. Toronto: University of Toronto Press.

Gabler, N. (1998). *Life the movie: How entertainment conquered reality*. New York: Knopf.

Gerbner, G. et al. (1982). Charting the mainstream: Television's contribution to political orientations. *Journal of Communication* 32(2): 100–127.

Gerbner, G. et al. (1984). Political correlates of television viewing. *Public Opinion Quarterly* 48(1): 283–300.

Graber, D. (1993). *Mass media and American politics*. Washington: Congressional Quarterly Press.

Habermas, J. (1979). The public sphere. In A. Mattelart & S. Seigelaub (eds), *Communications and the class struggle, Volume 1*. New York: International General.

Hachten, W. A. (1996). *The troubles of journalism: A critical look at what's right and wrong with the press*. Hillsdale, NJ: Lawrence Erlbaum.

Hall-Jamieson, K. (1984). *Packaging the presidency: A history and criticism of presidential advertising*. New York: Oxford University Press.

Hall-Jamieson, K. H. (1992). *Dirty politics: Deception, distraction and democracy*. Oxford: Oxford University Press.

Hallin, D. (1991). *Sound bite news: Television coverage of elections. 1968–88*. Washington, DC: Woodrow Wilson Centre for International Scholars.

Hart, R. (1994). *Seducing America*. New York: Oxford University Press.

Holtz-Bacha, C. (1990). Videomalaise revisited: Media exposure and alienation in West Germany. *European Journal of Communication* 5: 78–85.

Huckfeldt, R. & La Due Lake, R. (1998). Social networks as social capital: Individual and collective incentives for political participation. *Political Psychology* 19: 567–584.

Iyengar, S. (1991). *Is anyone responsible: How television frames political issues*. Chicago, IL: University of Chicago Press.

Iyengar, S. (1997). Overview. In S. Iyengar & R. Reeves, *Do the Media Govern?* Thousand Oaks, CA: Sage.

Iyengar, S., Peters, M. B. & Kinder, D. R. (1982). Experimental demonstrations of the 'not so minimal' consequences of television news programs. *American Political Science Review* 76: 848–858.

Kalb, M. (1998). *The rise of the new news (Discussion paper D-34)*. Cambridge, MA: Joan Shorenstein Centre, Harvard University.

Kellner, D. (1990). *Television and the crisis of democracy.* Boulder, CO: Westview Press.

Keane, J. (1991). *The media and democracy.* Oxford: Polity Press.

Kerbel, M. R. (1995). *Remote and controlled: Media politics in a cynical age.* Boulder, CO: Westview Press.

Kurbey, R. & Csikszentmihalyl, M. (1990). *Television and the quality of life: How viewing shapes everyday experience.* Hillsdale, NJ: Lawrence Erlbaum.

Kurtz, H. (1998). *Spin cycle: How the White House and the media manipulate the news.* New York: Simon & Schuster.

Lang, K. & Lang, G. (1966). The mass media and voting. In B. Berelson & M. Janowitz (eds), *Reader in public communication.* New York: Free Press.

Lang, K. & Lang, G. (1988). *Politics and television.* Chicago, IL: Quadrangle.

Lazarsfeld, P. (1968). *The people's choice.* New York: Columbia University Press.

Maarek, P. J. (1995). *Political marketing and communication.* London: John Libby.

Manheim, J. B. (1976). Can democracy survive television? *Journal of Communication* 26: 84–90.

MacArthur, B. & Worcester, R. M. (1992). Preaching to the uninterested. *UK Press Gazette,* 6 April.

McChesney, R. W. (2000). *Rich media, poor democracy: Communication politics in dubious times.* New York: New Press.

McGuire, W. (1986). The myth of massive media impact. Savagings and salvagings. *Public Communication and Behavior* 1: 173–257.

McKeod, J. et al. (1977). Decline and fall at the White House: A longitudinal analysis of communication effects. *Communication Research* 4: 3–22.

McQuail, D. (1987). *Mass communication theory: An introduction.* London: Sage.

Meyrowitz, J. (1995). How television changes the political drama. In P. C. Wasburn (ed), *Research in political sociology: Volume 7: Mass media and politics.* Greenwich, CT: JAI Press.

Miller, W. (1991). *Media and voters.* Oxford: Oxford University Press.

Mughan, A. (2000). *Media and the presidentialization of parliamentary elections.* Basingstoke: Palgrave.

Negrine, R. & Papathanassopoulos, S. (1996). The 'Americanization' of political communication: A critique. *Harvard International Journal of Press/Politics* 1(2): 45–62.

Newton, K. (1999). Politics and the news media: Mobilization or media malaise? *British Journal of Political Science* 29: 577–599.

Newton, L. & Norris, P. (2000). Confidence in institutions: Faith, culture or performance. In S. J. Pharr & R. D. Putnam (eds), *Disaffected democracies: What's troubling the trilateral democracies?* Princeton, NJ: Princeton University Press.

Noelle-Neumann, E. (1983). Return to the concept of powerful mass media. *Studies in Broadcasting* 9: 66–112.

Norris, P. (2000). *A virtuous circle: Political communications in postindustrial societies.* Cambridge: Cambridge University Press.

Parenti, M. (1986). *Inventing reality: The politics of the mass media.* New York: St. Martin's Press.

Parenti, M. (1992). *Make-believe media: The politics of entertainment.* New York: St. Martin's Press.

Patterson, T. E. (1980). *The mass media election: How Americans chose their president.* New York: Praeger.

Patterson, T. E. (1994). *Out of order.* New York: Vintage Books.

Pattie, C. & Johnston, R. (1999). Context, conversation and conviction: Social networks and voting at the 1992 British General Election, *Political Studies* 47 (5): 877–889.

Pfetsch, B. (1996). Convergence through privatization? Changing media environments and televised politics in Germany. *European Journal of Communication* 8(3): 425–450.

Philo, G. (1990). *Seeing and believing.* London: Routledge.

Postman, N. (1985). *Amusing ourselves to death: Public discourse in the age of show business.* New York: Viking-Penguin Books.

Purvis, H. (2001). *Media, politics and government.* Fort Worth, TX: Harcourt.

Putnam, R. D. (1995). Tuning in, tuning out: The strange disappearance of social capital in America. *PS* 28(4): 664–683.

Raboy, M. & Dagenais, B. (1992). Introduction: Media and the politics of crisis. In M. Raboy & B. Dagenais (eds), *Media, crisis and democracy.* London: Sage.

Ranney, A. (1983). *Channel of power: the impact of television on American politics.* New York: Basic Books.

Robinson, J. P. & Levy, M. R. (1986). Interpersonal communication and news comprehension. *Public Opinion Quarterly* 50: 160–175.

Robinson, M. (1975). American political legitimacy in an era of electronic journalism: Reflections on the evening news. In D. Cater & R. Adler (eds), *Television as a social force.* New York: Prager.

Robinson, M. J. (1976a). American political legitimacy in an era of electronic journalism: Reflections on the evening news. In D. Cater & R. Adler (eds), *Television as a social force.* New York: Praeger.

Robinson, M. J. (1976b). Public affairs television and the growth of political malaise: The case of 'The selling of the Pentagon.' *American Political Science Review,* 70(2) 409–432.

Robinson, M. J. & Sheehan, M. (1983). *Over the wire and on TV.* New York: Russell Sage Foundation.

Roessler, P. (1999). The individual agenda-designing process: How inter-personal communication, egocentric networks and mass media shape the perception of political issues by individuals. *Communication Research* 26: 666–700.

Sabato, L. J. (1991). *Feeding frenzy: How attack journalism has transformed American politics.* New York: Free Press.

Sartori, G. (1989). Video power. *Government and Opposition* 24(1): 39–53.

Scammell, M. (1990). Political advertising and the broadcasting revolution. *Political Quarterly* 61(2): 200–213.

Schiller, H. (1973). *The mind managers.* Boston, MA: Beacon Press.

Schmitt-Beck, R. (2003). Mass communication, personal communication and vote choice: The filter hypothesis of media influence in comparative perspective. *British Journal of Political Science* 33 (Part 2): 233–259.

Schmitt-Beck, R. & Farrell, D. (2002). Do political campaigns matter? In D. Farrell & R. Schmitt-Neck (eds), *Do political campaigns matter? Campaign effects in elections and referendums.* London: Routledge.

Schudson, M. (1995). *The power of the news.* Cambridge, MA: Harvard University Press.

Schultz, W. (1998). Media changes and the political effects of television: Americanization of the political culture? *Communications* 23(4): 527–543.

Seymour-Ure, C. (1991). *The British press and broadcasting since 1945.* Oxford: Blackwell.

Shawcross, W. (1984). *The quality of mercy.* London: Andre Deutsch.

Smith, A. (1981). Mass communications. In D. Butler, H. Penniman & A. Ranney (eds), *Democracy at the polls.* Washington, DC: American Enterprise Institute.

Starker, S. (1991). *Evil empires: Crusading against the mass media.* London: Transaction.

Stephenson, H. & Bromley, M. (1998). *Sex, lies and democracy: The press and the public.* London: Longman.

Theobald, J. (2000). Radical mass media criticism: Elements of a history from Kraus to Bourdieu. In D. Berry (ed), *Ethics and media culture: Practices and representations.* Oxford: Focal Press.

Van Deth, J. & Scarborough, E. (1998). The concept of values. In J. van Deth & E. Scarborough (eds), *The impact of values.* Oxford: Oxford University Press.

Wattenberg, M. (1984). *The decline of American political parties, 1952–1980.* Cambridge, MA: Harvard University Press.

White, T. (1973). *The making of the president, 1972.* New York: Bantam.

Wober, M. (1992). *Televising the election.* London: ITC.

Wright, J. C. et al. (1989). How children reacted to televised coverage of the space shuttle disaster. *Journal of Communication* 39: 27–45.

Zaller, J. (1992). *The nature and origins of mass opinion.* Cambridge: Cambridge University Press.

Zaller, J. (1996). The myth of massive media impact revived: New support for a discredited idea. In D. C. Mutz, P. M. Sniderman & R. A. Brody (eds), *Political persuasion and attitude change.* Ann Arbor, MI: University of Michigan Press.

Zaller, J. (1998). Monica Lewinsky's contribution to political science. *PS* (June): 182–189.

Zaller, J. (2001). Monica Lewinsky and the mainsprings of American politics. In L. W. Bennet & R. M. Entman (eds), *Mediated politics: Communications in the future of democracy.* Cambridge: Cambridge University Press.

Terms and Concepts

media malaise	causality	social networks
attack journalism	correlation	weak force theory
trust		

Questions

1. Is everyone equally subject to media influence? What factors may make some more resistant to it than others?

2. Newton suggests that "social networks" stand between the media and consumers of political information. What is his argument?

3. Why is 1980s Britain such a good test case for the media power thesis?

4. Newton discusses the media as a group. Are all media alike in their capacity to inform and influence?

The Flight from Politics

Reg Whitaker

Editors' Note

Politics is a kind of human activity. Do people engage in politics because political life is somehow intrinsic to human life and flourishing—because politics is sewn into the fabric of our being? Or do they do so because politics is a necessary way to get other important things they want? In other words, is politics an end in itself or a means to other ends? Do we suffer politics to get other good things or do we find ourselves in politics?

Citizens in liberal democracies are exposed to both views but the liberal interpretation of politics—that it is a necessary evil in which we engage to get other desirable things— seems to prevail. When political activity is not strictly necessary or fruitful—in any event, the object of a voluntary decision about what is right for the individual— liberal people will avoid it. Liberals generally balk at compulsory service to the polity,

either by means of military duty or by compulsory voting.

What happens when great numbers of people flee from politics? Is this a sign that the polity is working well or in a state of crisis?

Reg Whitaker understands the flight from politics to be a dangerous development in which partisans of both the right and the left have been complicit. As his essay indicates, the flight from politics involves much more than declining voter turnout in general elections. It involves a preference for litigation of rights claims over the wrangling of parties in parliamentary squabbles. It involves a populist discourse that seeks to give political power to voters through referenda and initiatives. It involves the pursuit of treaties to lock into place, beyond easy political amendment or repeal, rules of the global economic game that favour some and adversely affect others.

Hoping to reverse the flight from politics, Whitaker offers a more traditional party-parliamentary politics founded on the arts of deliberation, compromise, negotiation, and the brokerage of disparate interests. One senses from his essay that he believes this will not only revivify the social-democratic left but also attend to the rejuvenation of the Canadian polity.

Partisans of all stripes will have to weigh the merits of his argument against the gains they have made by "non-political" means. Many will think the game of politics is not worth the candle. Others will wonder whether the flight from politics is just politics in a new form. Still others will never overcome the view that compromise and negotiation are dirty, discreditable arts.

◆ ◆ ◆

Since the Charter of Rights and Freedoms came into effect in 1982, there has been both praise and criticism of its effects on Canadian democracy. Enthusiasts claim the Charter has been inclusionary, helping make room for previously excluded or marginalized citizens, thus widening and deepening democratic participation. Critics have blasted the Charter and the "rights talk" that has come in its wake as inherently undemocratic. Puzzlingly, this criticism has come from critics on opposite sides of the ideological divide.

Marxist legal scholar Michael Mandel has excoriated the "legalization of politics." Yet from the right, Ted Morton and Rainer Knopff are equally hostile. They see the Charter facilitating the evasion of democratic political negotiation. It is worth quoting their words at length:

> Our primary objection to the Charter is that it is deeply and fundamentally undemocratic ... in the more serious sense of eroding the habits and temperament of representative democracy. The growth

Reg Whitaker, "The Flight from Politics," *Inroads* 11 (2002), 187–202. Reprinted with permission.

of court room rights talk undermines perhaps the most fundamental prerequisite of decent liberal democratic politics: the willingness to engage those with whom one disagrees in the ongoing attempt to combine diverse interests into temporarily viable governing majorities. Liberal democracy works only when majorities rather than minorities rule, and when it is obvious to all that ruling majorities are themselves coalitions of minorities in a pluralistic society. Partisan opponents, in short, must nevertheless be seen as fellow citizens who might be future allies. Representative institutions facilitate this fundamental democratic disposition; judicial power undermines it.

Peter Russell, writing from a more centrist position, issued an early warning of the effects of transferring policymaking from the legislative to the judicial branch. This would, he argued, represent "a further flight from politics, a deepening disillusionment with the procedures of representative government and government by discussion as means of resolving fundamental questions of political justice." I take Russell's words as my text, noting that he referred to a "further flight from politics" and a "deepening disillusionment with the procedures." The flight from politics is a deeper, wider, and more worrying phenomenon than scholars squabbling over the Charter of Rights have usually allowed.

Morton and Knopff see the emergence of a Court Party, a leftist amalgam of centralizers, "equality seekers," "social engineers, civil libertarians, and post-materialists," all intent on winning enforceable victories in court that they have failed to win through the electoral and legislative processes. This party is, they assert, fundamentally authoritarian, since it has failed to win consent in the democratic marketplace. This is a partial view. There is a flight from politics, but it is more widespread than Charter litigation alone. Nor is it simply a left-wing phenomenon. The right, too, has attempted to flee the political arena rather than fight democratically, and to impose its preferred policy solutions upon the country by fiat. This has largely taken the form of locking Canada into global economic regulatory regimes, international commercial agreements, and binding dispute resolution mechanisms which impose neo-liberal agendas and constrain governments, both federal and provincial, from using a variety of collective policy instruments. This too is a "legalization of politics" and generates many of the same anti-democratic effects, although for different purposes.

The specific origins of this general flight from politics can be situated in the late 1960s and early 1970s. It was in this period that emergent trends in Canada coincided and reinforced one another. The challenge to federalism of Quebec nationalism moved into a new phase with the sovereignty movement. At the same time, a long-term decline in deference to hierarchy and authority had begun in the rest of Canada, undermining the existing mechanisms of elite accommodation that had served to hold the country together in the past, and exacerbating the task of meeting the sovereigntist challenge. This was the specific Canadian variant of a legitimacy crisis, but there was another crisis, more widely based, in this period. Conservative thinkers and business-oriented think tanks (such as the Trilateral Commission) began developing an "ungovernability" argument, that democratic governments were being swamped by "demand overload," as previously quiescent sections of the democratic citizenry began raising their voices and the stakes of redistribution. Retroactively, conservatives waging the cultural wars of the 1980s and 1990s looked back at the 1960s and 1970s as the era when consensus broke down, anarchy broke out, and the delicate fabric of social and cultural order was seriously rent. Left-wing observers have been more sanguine, even romantic, about the last era when social justice seemed a leading priority, and new possibilities were opening up after the stifling conformity of the 1950s had begun to dissipate. Dispassionately, we can say, whatever spin one puts on it, that this period was one in which the political ante was being dramatically upped, at the same time as the rules of the game were being challenged. This was an explosive combination. We are still feeling the fallout.

THE LEFT'S CHALLENGE: EMBEDDING SOCIAL RIGHTS

◆ ◆ ◆

Morton and Knopff's picture of the Court Party is a bit of a caricature, but they do have one good point. The left in Canada never made the transition from the margin to the mainstream through building a mass socialist or social democratic party capable of seriously contesting national political office. The New Right did do this, with the rapid emergence of the Reform/Canadian Alliance, a party that not only showed remarkable growth capacity, starting from scratch, but also appropriated "democracy" from the left in the process. While the Alliance stalled outside the corridors of power, its past perform-ance in helping transform the dominant political dis-course in Canada should not be discounted. The left did change the discourse as well, but failed to follow up with the kind of political work that has made Reform/ Alliance so influential in policy terms. Having placed culture, identity, gender, ethnicity, race, and sexuality on the agenda, the left was largely diverted from political action in the traditional, parliamentary, sense, and instead focused on consciousness raising, protest, rights recognition, and the pursuit of litigation rather than leg-islation. The ironic result has been that the new identity politics has generated a reaction in the form of rightwing populism that has been relatively more successful in the electoral arena, and has impeded, although not defeated, the left's attempt at winning cultural hegemony for its ideas. However, the New Right has been more or less a sideshow in relation to the larger response of the neo-liberal right, described later.

The left in Canada never made the transition from the margin to the mainstream through building a mass socialist or social democratic party capable of seriously contesting national political office.

There is a huge literature on Charter litigation. I am more interested in the wider political implications and effects of the rise of rights talk as a dominant left-wing discourse. At any rate, rights talk preceded the Charter. One could even argue that the Charter was the result of the rise of rights talk, rather than the reverse.

Situating the Charter in its political and historical context, it is evident that its appearance on the agenda was as a political tool enabling the Trudeau govern-ment to partially divert attention away from a different kind of rights talk that had begun to dominate consti-tutional discourse in Canada: the right to national self-determination of Quebec and its potential for either breaking up federalism or forcing its radical decentral-ization. When eight premiers opposed Trudeau's patri-ation plan in 1981, the proposed addition of the Charter to the package focused popular support. A wide variety of groups testified about what ought to be in a Charter, subtly shifting attention away from what had been the primary question—certainly for Quebec—of the legitimacy of unilateral patriation itself. But the widening of the constitutional field

beyond the traditional question of the collective rights and jurisdictions of governments to encompass the rights of individual citizens and groups in civil society could not have been as successful a political tactic, had not the ground already been prepared by a prior and fundamental shift in the society.

... the widening of the constitutional field beyond the traditional question of the collective rights and jurisdictions of governments to encompass the rights of individual citizens and groups in civil society could not have been as successful a political tactic, had not the ground already been prepared by a prior and fundamental shift in the society.

It is not difficult to understand the motives that led the left of the post-1960s toward emphasis on rights over parliamentary politics. The old social democratic left had opted primarily for the parliamentary route, embodied in the organic relationship between the trade unions and the NDP. Its successors were generally marked by a pervasive sense of exclusion or at least marginalization from political institutions. In reality, trade union affiliation with a political party stalled indefinitely in third party status in national politics was a sign not of the influence of the union movement but of its ineffectuality.

The new groups seeking to place their concerns on the political agenda could not fail to note that business, by playing both of the two mainstream brokerage parties, and by bringing influence to bear directly on the policy process via pressure groups and business associations, had incomparably more success than labour. Feminists, Aboriginals, environmental-ists, racial minorities, gays and lesbians did not abandon the party political field altogether. There was, however, a tendency to concentrate on mobilizing pressure to bear on the institutions of policymaking, often directly on the bureaucracy, or indirectly on the parliamentary parties through organizing demonstra-tions of their supporters. This had the advantage that purity of ideals and fidelity to group interest could be maintained more easily. Activists who opted for party politics were condemned as sellouts by their former comrades.

There was another reason to bypass political par-ties, although in retrospect this appears as a warning sign of problems for the left. Parties, even self-styled "democratic" parties like the NDP, are inevitably, in pluralist societies, brokerage institutions, despite their ideological tag and their trade union affiliation. Getting minority group policy concerns onto the party platform usually involves the kind of policy brokering, the trade-offs and compromises, that previously marginalized groups have identified as structural barriers to their recognition. Faced with the gritty reality of making deals and playing old-fashioned coalition politics even in pursuit of movement ideals, many shrank back in revulsion. This only pointed toward a deeper problem, one that many on the left remain reluctant to acknowledge. There is no natural alliance of the excluded and marginalized. There are conflicts between groups and within groups. Party activity highlights and exacerbates these tensions. Operating as new social movements along identity lines avoids (or evades) some of the tensions and costs of coalition building.

There is no natural alliance of the excluded and marginalized.

As the political history of the past decade shows only too clearly, however, extra-parliamentary activity imposes a different set of costs. Groups operating from relatively narrowly defined bases can be perceived as "special interests" opposed to the public good. However infuriating this designation may be to movement people, and however much the application of the special interest category has been decried and denounced by writers in, or sympathetic to, the movements, this interpretation has in a sense defined the terms of political discourse on behalf of the New Right. Reform/Alliance formulates a concept of the general will of the people that is directly opposed to the selfish, albeit fragmented, minority wills of the special interests. Moreover, the right has largely succeeded in popularizing its own partial view. When neo-liberal governments intent on imposing their agendas face weak, fragmented opposition in parliaments, opposition spills into the streets and labour disruptions, as in Ontario during the initial wave of the Common Sense Revolution from 1995 to 1999, or in British Columbia in 2002 under the Liberal government of Gordon Campbell. The "special interest" focus of the street opposition tends to be utilized by the government in its own defence, emphasizing successfully that it alone speaks for the general or public good.

As for the tactic of acting directly on the bureaucracy, liberal bureaucrats quickly learned how to absorb and co-opt some of the energies of the social movements with special targeted programs and largely symbolic representational gains. Feminists were put in charge of programs targeting women's groups. Multicultural programs were, and are, a relatively cheap way of paying off party supporters in the ethnic communities with taxpayer dollars and minor positions on boards and panels, etc. Pay and employment equity programs are representational ghettoes for minority spokespersons. Representation becomes something of an end in itself, partially displacing more substantive policy goals, and is more easily satisfied by government, at a lower price tag.

... liberal bureaucrats quickly learned how to absorb and co-opt some of the energies of the social movements with special targeted programs and largely symbolic representational gains.

In this context, it is not surprising that the left has laid heavy focus on rights. For previously marginalized groups seeking favourable policy outcomes, but suspicious of using the route of party politics, rights are a kind of currency to be deployed for strategic advantage. Capital may hold the big properties on the Monopoly board, but rights are also properties on the same board. To see how these properties can be played successfully, there is the instructive example of the pay equity settlement in the federal public service.

A long-standing dispute dating back to 1983 concerning the dollar value to be placed on pay equity in the federal public service was sent to a special tribunal on appeal by the Public Service Alliance of Canada (which had just signed a collective agreement that included a negotiated settlement for the employees affected). The tribunal, using a highly technical, if not arcane, formula, ruled that some 200,000 federal employees, mainly but not entirely female, should receive retroactive compensation that might amount to between $4 and $5 billion. The PSAC, as well as feminist and equity advocacy groups, insisted that this award was the employees' right. The government did not dispute the right, but did dispute the dollar value put upon it. The only recourse was to appeal to the courts (which, it should be noted, are as insulated from political accountability as human rights tribunals). In 1999, the government lost in the Federal Court, and then capitulated totally. The point is not who was right or wrong, rather it is that instead of settling for a compromise amount negotiated in the process of collective bargaining, the PSAC elected for rights litigation on the gamble that if they won, they would win it all. And so they did.

Could a decision to allocate over $4 billion to these particular 200,000 people be justified as rational public policy? The question does not even arise in this case, because it was fought as rights litigation in the venue of politically unaccountable tribunals and courts where public policy rationales take a back seat to rights. Yet the outcome was sufficiently expensive to the federal government to have real effects on other potential beneficiaries of government expenditures. It also proved later to be divisive for rank-and-file PSAC members, some of whom have questioned the disproportionate gain for one group among the membership.

Following the government's capitulation, an op-ed piece appeared in the *Globe and Mail*, contributed by a feminist, singularly graceless in victory. The writer was apparently incensed that views critical of pay equity in this case had been widely expressed by parliamentarians, newspaper columnists, and others. This apparent hostility to democratic debate could perhaps only be understood in the optic of rights. If pay equity is a right, even the particular dollar value placed on it by the administrative and adjudicative machinery set up to interpret this right partakes of the same sacrosanct and unquestionable aura as fundamental human rights. The deliberative process, in this optic, is reconfigured as a field on which these fundamental rights are thrown into question and threatened. Rights become a refuge or protective haven for those fleeing the insecurities of politics.

Rights become a refuge or protective haven for those fleeing the insecurities of politics.

Nowhere has rights talk been more pronounced than in Aboriginal demands. To be sure, Aboriginal peoples were clearly the most marginalized and excluded among all the groups vying to influence the policy agenda. Moreover, Aboriginal claims are national in nature and scope, which distinguishes them from those of other rights claimants, save the Quebecois. Sovereigntists have for extended periods held political

office in Quebec, with all the jurisdictional power that implies, which distinguishes their position sharply from the relatively powerless First Nations. First Nations do have a past history of nation-to-nation treaty relations, and an armoury of land claims as a tool for expanding political influence. Because their claims are national, while their bases are so weak and marginalized, it was perhaps inevitable that Aboriginal groups would focus on rights rather than a political process that was stacked severely against them in numbers, and was culturally alien and forbidding terrain for would-be Aboriginal politicians.

This tendency was reinforced when Aboriginal bands turned mainly to lawyers for advice from outside their own communities. Alan Cairns has eloquently elucidated the impact that legal discourse has had on the political position of Aboriginal communities in relation to non-Aboriginal society. Rights talk fits the Aboriginal situation in so many ways, but at the same time, it generates political barriers. Rights as trumps can be very effective weapons in winning courtroom battles. Yet the adversarial mentality fostered in the courtroom may also polarize political opposition. It certainly does little to build the kind of mutual trust between Aboriginal and non-Aboriginal society that would favour the compromises and trade-offs necessary for livable and durable accommodations. The fact remains that whatever the outcome of rights adjudication, the Aboriginal and non-Aboriginal communities will remain living side by side and sharing the costs and the benefits of the condominium they both inhabit. Unfortunately, the arts of compromise have withered, on both sides, to the point where in 2002, the British Columbia government carried out a referendum in which the non-Aboriginal majority asked to voice their views on Aboriginal rights. To Aboriginals, such a process is inherently insulting and degrading. Yet it is simply a further step in the progressive shrinkage of the space for compromise and negotiation between the communities, a process to which Aboriginal reliance on rights adjudication has itself contributed. The potential for conflict is particularly heightened where Aboriginals and non-Aboriginals compete for resources, for example fishing on both west and east coasts. Here Aboriginal rights sometimes trump non-Aboriginal rights, within the common framework of a market that does not readily accommodate traditional rights that effectively exclude non-Aboriginal fishermen, and a common framework of government regulatory policy that Aboriginals may claim the right to disregard. The

Burnt Church fiasco in New Brunswick illustrates the worst implications of this inherent contradiction.

Unfortunately, the arts of compromise have withered ...

Rights-driven political discourse on the left has a number of victories to its credit, enough that activists continue to lean heavily on rights talk. The paradox is that it is precisely these victories that generate ever more concerted opposition from the right. Morton and Knopff are right that the "Court party," taking this characterization at face value for the moment, is a result of political failure, and rights talk a substitute for confronting the right in the electoral arena. But in any event, the right had a more powerful riposte in store than politics alone.

THE RIGHT'S ANSWER: "ECONOMIC CONSTITUTIONALIZATION"

◆ ◆ ◆

By the mid-1970s, the "ungovernability" of liberal democracies had fostered the monetarist revolution that swept through Western treasury departments more rapidly and completely than Keynesianism had in the 1940s. The coincidence of high inflation and high unemployment ("stagflation") discredited Keynesian fiscal management, but more importantly, monetarism, or supply-side economics, concealed a thinly veiled political response to the political forces that had grown to threaten business ascendancy in the earlier decade. Thatcherism and Reaganism represented the political counterattack to trade unions and social movements, first seizing the Conservative party from the "wets" and the Republican party from the "liberals," then taking command of the national policy agenda to strike at their opponents. They were not, however, content simply to win the immediate battles, and then settle in for the inevitable swing of the pendulum back in the other direction. Instead, faced with a new sense of "entitlement," a rights consciousness on the part of those groups previously marginalized, and stiff resistance to rollbacks and downsizing of the welfare state and the power of unions, they sought ways of placing their neoliberal agenda beyond the reach of politics and politicians. The right had come to believe that democracy itself could be a threat to capitalism if social rights and entitlements were permitted to become a permanent part of the structure of democratic decision-making. It was, however, now considered equally futile to combat this threat by the ordinary politics of compromise and negotiation (the post-Keynesian consensus politics of the 1950s as practised by the Churchill-Macmillan Tories and the Eisenhower Republicans), or to contest it on the left's own terrain, that of the embedding of social rights.

The right had come to believe that democracy itself could be a threat to capitalism if social rights and entitlements were permitted to become a permanent part of the structure of democratic decision-making.

Globalization is an important part of the right's riposte, which is why in the early 21st century, "anti-corporate" and "anti-globalization" movements are more or less synonymous. As is well understood on all sides, economic globalization takes policy tools out of the hands of democratically accountable governments and places them beyond the reach of political parties, activists, and the associations of civil society to lobby or influence. Even if the "wrong" people get in charge of national states, they can do less damage than they could in the past because they have fewer tools with which to do damage. The pressures of international competitiveness are insistent and, from the point of view of the left, insidious in sapping the capacity of political actors to even imagine credible collective solutions to social inequalities, let alone set in motion redistributionist forces that might undermine competitiveness.

Globalization need not be an abstract concept. It is embodied in specific international agreements binding on the signatory states. In Canada's case, we might start with the Canada-U.S. Free Trade Agreement, expanded into NAFTA and perhaps next into the proposed Free Trade Agreement of the Americas. When the original bilateral deal was being negotiated in the late 1980s, Ronald Reagan provided a prescient metaphor when he declared that the proposed agreement would form the "economic constitution of North America." Constitutions are the fundamental laws, the ground rules, structuring the roles of the governors and the governed, majorities and minorities, and the relations between individuals and groups. Neither party to the first agreement wanted anything to do with political superstructures, *à la* Europe. But they were quick to see the advantages of an "economic constitution" in structuring the roles of the public and private sectors and setting enforceable limits on public policy that would constrain future governments from acting irresponsibly and threatening free markets.

… Ronald Reagan provided a prescient metaphor when he declared that the proposed [free trade] agreement would form the "economic constitution of North America."

A further irony of the FTA lies in how this "constitution" was imposed upon Canada. The Mulroney Tories had breathed not a word about free trade in their victorious election of 1984, and had no intention of submitting the agreement to the citizenry for approval. It was the unelected Senate, which happened to be still dominated by Liberal appointees, that forced a national election prior to approval of the pact. The ensuing contest was dominated, as no other election campaign in Canada's history, by this single issue. The contest took on all the aspects of a national referendum on the FTA and on the direction of Canada's future. If it had been a formal referendum, the FTA would have lost, as parties opposed to the agreement took majorities in all provinces save Quebec and Alberta. But it was not a referendum, it was an election run on the usual first-past-the-post rules with two parties dividing the anti-free trade sentiment and one party, the governing party, supporting it. The electoral result was another Tory "majority," and a free trade future was undertaken on behalf of a minority of the voting citizenry.

Once in place, crucial clauses in these trade agreements closed certain doors forever to policy-makers in Canada. Most notable are the continental energy resource rules that clearly make another National Energy Program, like that of the Trudeau Liberals in the early 1980s, not merely politically impractical, but illegal ("unconstitutional," in effect). Of course, the Trudeau-era NEP was a policy disaster unlikely to be repeated. But the general point is significant: any future energy resource policy that is designed to serve primarily the Canadian national interest, as opposed to continental and global markets, is not permissible. In the

early 1980s, Alberta fought Ottawa bitterly over the NEP, and the Mulroney Tories pledged to scrap the entire program. Once in office, they were better than their word—with the FTA in their pocket, they ensured that no subsequent government could ever mount anything like the NEP again. Thus the ordinary politics of give and take have been trumped by the extraordinary politics of fundamental rule setting, by the constitutionalization of politics.

… the ordinary politics of give and take have been trumped by the extraordinary politics of fundamental rule setting, by the constitutionalization of politics.

In the immediate aftermath of the implementation of the FTA, there was another telling example of constraints imposed on Canadian policy-makers. Privatization of state enterprise and the ascendancy of the market over "politics" are high on the neo-liberal agenda. Although existing Crown corporations are protected, any future attempt to use this policy instrument runs afoul of clauses permitting American corporations operating in Canada to sue for compensation for future business lost when government enters the market to provide goods or services. The Ontario NDP had a longstanding promise to nationalize private automobile insurance if elected. The NDP had done just that in Manitoba, Saskatchewan, and British Columbia. (Parenthetically, it might be noted that even free market economists acknowledge that public automobile insurance can reduce costs by rationalizing administrative infrastructure, and consolidating insurance with licensing, government safety checks, etc.) Yet when the NDP won the Ontario election of 1990, they did not press ahead with their promise. Instead, they hired Canada's former free trade negotiator, Simon Reisman, to assess the potential liability to American private insurers under the FTA if Ontario proceeded with nationalization. On Reisman's advice, the NDP dropped the plan altogether. This has obvious implications in other potential areas for public enterprise. Thus an important element in the social democratic policy agenda has been permanently blocked, and the neo-liberal market-driven alternative has been enshrined in the "constitutional" fabric. Little attention has been paid to this development, since social democrats have pretty much dropped any commitment to public enterprise from their programs. Nor is this policy instrument apparently much on anyone's mind these days. Its absence from the policy agenda is itself a tribute to the success of the neo-liberal strategy of constitutionalizing their program, and rendering alternatives "unconstitutional." Alternatives are thus placed out of sight, out of mind. The triumph of neo-liberal discourse in the media, the compelling logic of competitiveness in the absence of alternative views, are thus powerfully reinforced by the quasi-constitutional effect of binding international agreements well beyond the reach of domestic politics to rectify or even modify.

The same is of course true for the nascent instruments of global governance: the WTO, the World Bank, the IMF, the G-8, and existing and proposed global regimes for countering terrorism, international crime, money laundering, illegal drug traffic, etc., or for regulating licit global finance and enterprise, such as the aborted (but by no means dead) Multilateral Agreement on Investment. All of these have in common the surrender of national sovereignty to multilateral regimes of regulation and control. In most cases, national sovereignty is limited to the formalities of compliance with the agreed-upon international rules. This does not mean that the national state has been marginalized. The coercive capacities of national states to enforce international agreements are crucial elements in the functioning of global governance. There would be no rules at all without national states to enforce them. And of course the state with the heaviest armoury of coercive power at its disposal, the United States, is the world's most influential power. Despite the current efforts of the Bush administration to impose its own unilateralist solutions on a wide range of global problems, it is obvious to all but the White House and Congress that not even the world's only superpower can run the world without the active cooperation of a host of other states. But this also means constraints and limits upon American behaviour. Far more is this the case for smaller, less influential, states like Canada. Increasingly, Canada finds itself exercising its coercive power to enforce rules that are not of its own making, in which its voice has been at best only one input, and which sometimes may even be at variance with specific Canadian interests.

The current coalition to prosecute the war on terrorism offers an instructive lesson in the paradox of the multilateral defence of national security. When Parliament passed C-36, the Anti-Terrorism Act, it was instructed that many of the controversial provisions (which drew heavy criticism from many quarters) were simply fulfillments of Canada's obligations to its allies in the coalition and to a series of international agreements on combating terrorism to which Canada was a signatory. Instead of legislating its own rules regarding the governance of cyberspace, now considered a potential battleground for cyber-terrorism, Canada simply adopted the recent (and highly controversial) European Convention on Cyber Crime.

The ironies of giving up sovereignty to save sovereignty are even more acute—one might even say, flagrant—in regard to Canada-U.S. border security issues, when multilateralism gives way to one-to-one relations with a neighbour of vastly disproportionate power. Pressure for harmonization of immigration security rules and practices comes from the U.S., but also from a very influential big business lobby in Canada. The latter obviously is concerned with the costs imposed on business by blockages at the border, which is perfectly understandable. However, if some kind of broader "perimeter security" accord is struck, or—extending the logic further as a number of lobbyists have done—if some deeper customs union arrangement is negotiated making Canada and the U.S. an inner core of NAFTA with free movement of goods, services and labour, as in the European Union, then the business lobby gains a double benefit. Not only will cross-border business flows be facilitated, but in innumerable ways, Canadian governments will be yet further constrained from undertaking policy initiatives or even administering rules of conduct that are at variance with American practices—which will mean, of course, less fear of departures from pro-business, free market approaches.

As globalization proceeds, complaints about the "democratic deficit" have grown. There is no question that the objective effect of international regulation and cooperation in governance is to make authoritative decision-making more and more remote from people, less and less accountable. This is, after all, the point. Europe represents an attempt to construct a political superstructure to govern economic integration, but despite direct election to the European Parliament, cries of "democratic deficit" and frustration at a largely unaccountable "Eurocracy" have been widespread. For Canada, ever closer economic integration with the U.S. is not accompanied by any development of a North American political superstructure. The Americans will not hear of anything that diminishes their sovereignty, and in any event, the gross disproportion of size and weight between the two countries means that any political superstructure would bury Canadian voices.

Nor are there any structures for giving voice to "global civil society," to use this somewhat overheated and under-examined phrase. The only sites where democratic accountability mechanisms exist are nation states. Ironically, these are also the sites for the absolutely necessary and irreplaceable enforcement function. This coincidence represents a potential weak point for the security of neo-liberal globalization processes.

The anxiety of capital to move rule-making out of the reach of meddling at the national state level is driven by ideology, of course, but also by the more straightforward concern for predictability. Investment is future-oriented and thus risky; it also leaves investors exposed to changes in the rules that may affect their returns. Thus binding international rules are like entrenched charters of rights for capital. The adjudication of these rights has taken an interesting turn that reinforces the argument I am making. Increasingly, disputes arising from international business activities are being resolved by binding resolution mechanisms. Some of these are institutionalized in agreements like NAFTA and the WTO. Decisions, however distasteful they may be to individual parties and at whatever cost to national practices, have to be accepted. Less widely noticed than these treaty arrangements is the equivalent growth of supra- (or extra-) national dispute resolution mechanisms for conflicts arising among transnational corporations, none of whom are willing to see their disputes submitted to the legal jurisdiction of any particular state. Out there, in the global space of flows, is a burgeoning case law for what amounts to transnational corporate jurisprudence. There is thus a double democratic displacement at work—not only are the "constitutional" rules being drawn up out of the reach of democratically accountable institutions, but the adjudication of this new body of global "rights" is also taking place out of reach of democratic oversight.

There is anti-democratic blowback onto the national states themselves. National electorates grow distrustful of political parties that fail to deliver on their promises, and cynical about political systems that seem powerless to protect them from the effects of globalization. The voting electorate shrinks, as disillusioned citizens turn away from electoral politics, leaving the field to parties targeting, through "narrowcasting" marketing strategies, influential and wealthier groups in the population with a stake in electing governments able and willing to protect them from redistributive policies.

Capitalizing on this curious combination of populism and fiscal conservatism, neo-liberal parties attempt to extend the quasi-constitutional entrenchment of the rights of capital into the domestic sphere through populist devices like referenda limiting taxation, and self-constraining laws forbidding governments from incurring deficits. More common in the U.S. than in Canada, there are growing examples here as well. Ontario, for instance, has provided that cabinet ministers in governments that run deficits will have their salaries slashed to help make up the shortfall. Ostensibly designed to protect citizens (i.e., taxpayers) from the depredations of politicians currying favour with "special interests" through redistributive programs, these devices attempt to embed barriers to redistribution in the political process itself, thus reinforcing in the domestic sphere the constitutionalization of corporate rights via globalization.

Another domestic spin-off of globalization is the enhancement of centralized executive power in the federal government. Observers have been pointing out for some time now that globalization has a decentralizing impact on regionally divided states. Would-be breakaway nationalisms, like Quebec in Canada, or Scotland in the U.K., have been emboldened and made more credible by the new economic frameworks of NAFTA or Europe that have diminished the salience of the national states in administering regional development. Tom Courchene has argued that Ontario is moving inexorably out of the federalist orbit and into a new status as a North American "region-state." Without quarrelling with the general thrust of these arguments, which are compelling enough and supported by a wealth of empirical evidence, a counter-tendency sparked by globalization has been less often noted. In the absence of effective supranational authority with teeth, national states are the sites for enforcement of global regulation and governance. This places increasing responsibility on national governments as the effective *interlocateurs valables* in dealing with other governments and with the emergent agencies of global governance. Precisely because they deal on a government-to-government basis outside direct day-to-day accountability to national legislatures, press and public, this has the effect of centralizing power in the executive branch, and, more precisely, in heads of government.

Another domestic spin-off of globalization is the enhancement of centralized executive power in the federal government.

Recently, much criticism has been directed at the centralization of power in the office of Prime Minister Jean Chrétien, and the associated one-party dominance of his Liberals. This has been identified as a source of the malaise of democracy in Canada, as in journalist Jeffrey Simpson's categorization of Ottawa as a "friendly dictatorship." The roots of this quasi-monolithic power are many. It is demonstrably the case that Mr. Chrétien's role as Canada's negotiator with the world and the lack of participation in these negotiations by the political opposition in Parliament, feeble oversight by the media of what goes on behind the closed doors of international meetings, and even the exclusion of the provinces until the deals are signed, are strong contributing factors to the concentration of largely unaccountable power in the PMO.

... the concentration of power at the top has continued, and, if anything, strengthened further, as the recent histories of Alberta, Ontario, and British Columbia indicate.

There were clues to this development in Canada's own political history. Executive federalism, with its emphasis on intergovernmental relations and even intergovernmental diplomacy, contributed to executive domination of both federal and provincial branches of government. Premiers became potentates able to wheel and deal largely out of the control or oversight of their legislatures, which in any event were often skewed to overwhelming government majorities and fragmented, ineffectual oppositions. As Meech Lake and Charlottetown demonstrated, there were limits to the tolerance of Canadians for the deals struck behind closed doors by their first ministers. But the concentration of power at the top has continued, and, if anything, strengthened further, as the recent histories of Alberta, Ontario, and British Columbia indicate. In each case, premiers Ralph Klein, Mike Harris, and Gordon Campbell have run quasi-dictatorships that opponents would be reluctant to describe as "friendly."

As the focus of economic decision-making shifts away from Canada and onto the wider global stage, and the crucial importance of the national state as the coercive enforcer of the global rules is emphasized, the power of the prime minister is enhanced vis-à-vis his provincial counterparts. This trend has been thrown into sharp relief in the aftermath of the events of Sept. 11, and the dedication of the Western alliance, including Canada, to a war on terrorism and to security as the leading priority on national policy agendas.

At a stroke, the legitimacy of the national government has been dramatically enhanced, and that of the provinces diminished. Efforts by premiers to get back on to the agenda—the Tory government in Ontario has detailed part of its provincial police force to track non-citizens and report results to Immigration Canada; the premier of B.C. has bizarrely pleaded for a "Zip-Loc bag around North America"—have been ineffectual, as have the efforts of the premier of Quebec to re-establish momentum for sovereignty post-Sept. 11.

When national security is an anxiety not merely of government elites but of civil society faced with terrorist threats to civilians, the national government becomes a renewed focus of popular support and allegiance. Moreover, coercion becomes legitimation. The role of the federal government as enforcer, manifest in relation to countering terrorism, and in policing the spreading movement to disrupt and protest globalization, doubtless raises its profile, both positive and negative, but it is a profile of the state as soldier, spy, and cop, not as economic or social policy-maker. The abrasive and violent conflicts between state and "civil society" (I use this latter term somewhat ironically, given that the state can count on majority backing in containing these protests) evident at APEC, Quebec City, and Kananaskis, are themselves indications of how far things have drifted from the negotiation, compromise, and trade-offs that were the stuff of ordinary politics in the past. Protestors may ask sarcastically "who elected the bankers?" but the uncommitted public can, and does, ask just as sarcastically, "who elected the protestors?"

Just as the extraordinary politics of rights (on both left and right) have usurped the old politics of negotiated agreement, so too the apocalyptic politics of "globalization" vs. "anti-globalization" have superseded the intricate and delicate task of reforming and rebalancing a complex system of interests and alliances. Protestors can retain their purity and remain "uncompromised," but the forces sustaining globalization proceed imperturbably, facing opposition that can be policed, rather than negotiated with. And the chief political beneficiary is a quasi-one-party government in Ottawa.

HALTING THE FLIGHT?

◆ ◆ ◆

There is some reason to believe that the flight from politics may finally be drawing to a close. Incessant rights talk on all sides has resulted in an impasse and a growing revulsion against a democratic deficit that is multifaceted and innocent of particular ideology. The very domination of national politics by one party, itself an indication of democratic malaise, bears within it the seeds of democratic regeneration. The political success of the Liberals has been defined against the background of the turn in party politics in 1993 toward new programmatic, ideological parties. The BQ and Reform were in a sense both products of the flight from the old brokerage politics of compromise and negotiation, and each arose on the ashes of the Mulroney Tories, the brokerage that failed. Reform has changed its name, twice changed its leader, splintered, and is now seeking to re-establish a sense of direction. The BQ's sole ideological *raison d'être,* sovereignty, is going nowhere, and the BQ is drifting with it. The Liberals have succeeded in this landscape not simply because their opponents are fragmented and hopeless, but because the Liberals have seized the potential ground from them. They have done this because they alone have kept alive the brokerage principle and the arts of political prudence and compromise. Unfashionable as these arts have appeared since the 1960s, and however fatal they proved to the Tories, they remain practical requirements for national governance in a pluralist society. In aid of one-party rule, they appear to bolster the democratic deficit. But they also offer the way forward for the return of party competition and a healthier democratic debate. For this to happen, the rhetoric of rights must be ratcheted down, and the constitutionalization of politics rolled back. The self-interest of party politicians may be the best reason to believe that such a development will take place.

The Liberals have succeeded in this landscape not simply because their opponents are fragmented and hopeless, but because the Liberals have seized the potential ground from them.

Another hopeful sign of change may be discerned in that old nemesis of ordinary politics, the Quebec question. The Supreme Court Secession Reference and the Clarity Act that followed remain highly controversial in Quebec. But what is striking in the high court's reasoning and in the logic of the federal legislation is their attempt to find a compromise between the recognition of Quebec's right to national self-determination and the recognition of the rights of the rest of Canada. Both parties are enjoined to find common ground for bargaining in good faith. Rights, even the collective rights of nations, cannot be trumps, but the compromises of politics must take these rights into account.

At this point, hopeful signs of realism in the contestation of globalization seem more remote. Yet the widespread and broadly based evidence of discontent with the direction of global governance has opened up some potential space for greater popular input into the process—if protestors will take up the challenge of becoming partial insiders, as well as outsiders. The institutions of global governance do depend crucially upon the participation of national states as enforcers. Since these same governments have to worry about their legitimacy and their standing with their own electorates, there is room for encouraging protestors to bring their concerns to the international bargaining table.

If there is any positive effect of the terrible events of September 11, it has been to refocus attention on the health of the community as a whole, and on the state as an instrument with a positive role to play in protecting and supporting the civil society—not privileged parts of it, but all of it. When everyone begins to realize that the entire enterprise of placing their own interests out of the reach of others, and thus out of the reach of political negotiation, is self-defeating, the sooner we can return to the prosaic terrain of ordinary politics: the compromises, trade-offs, and half-loaves that indicate mutual respect and the recognition of one's own limits.

Terms and Concepts

Court party	economic constitutionalization	WTO
politics	globalization	MAI
ungovernability	democratic deficit	APEC
rights talk	the brokerage principle	
"special interests"	NAFTA	

Questions

1. What is politics?
2. How have both the right and the left been implicated in the flight from politics?
3. How has globalization been implicated in the flight from politics?
4. Is rights talk a flight from politics or politics by other means?

5. What are the roles of citizens and political parties in Whitaker's vision of a properly functioning political order?
6. In a liberal society, do people have an obligation to engage in the political life of their community?

Unit 3 Annotated Bibliography

Adams, Michael. *Fire and Ice: The United States, Canada and the Myth of Converging Values*. Toronto: Penguin, 2003. Canadian pollster Adams argues that subtle but important differences in social and political values distinguish Canadians and Americans, and that these differences are becoming more pronounced. Contrary to received views, he finds that Canadians are the more "revolutionary" in their social attitudes than Americans.

Barney, Darin. *Prometheus Wired: The Hope for Democracy in the Age of Network Technology*. Vancouver: UBC Press, 2000. Barney discusses not only the democratic potential, but also the dangers associated with new technologies.

Cairns, Alan C. *Charter Versus Federalism: The Dilemmas of Constitutional Reform*. Montreal: McGill-Queen's University Press, 1992. In his vintage style, Cairns investigates the deep divisions and difficulties encountered over the past 25 years.

Cairns, Alan C. *Citizens Plus: Aboriginal Peoples and the Canadian State*. Vancouver: UBC Press, 2000. Cairns attempts to reconcile the diversity represented by Aboriginal peoples in the Canadian polity with the sense of belonging and shared fate provided by a common citizenship.

Coates, Ken. *The Marshall Decision and Native Rights*. Montreal and Kingston: McGill–Queen's University Press, 2000. Coates discusses a controversial recent Supreme Court of Canada decision on Aboriginal rights and examines alternative means of advancing historic resource rights of First Nations in Canada.

Dobrowolsky, Alexandra. *The Politics of Pragmatism: Women, Representation, and Constitutionalism in Canada*. Toronto: Oxford University Press, 2000. This book explores different explanations of feminist involvement in constitutional change in Canada.

Elshtain, Jean Bethke. *Democracy on Trial*. Concord, ON: Anansi, 1993. Elshtain has a fervent plea for the renewal of American civil society.

Everitt, Joanna, and Brenda O'Neill, eds. *Citizen Politics: Research and Theory in Canadian Political Behaviour*. Toronto: Oxford University Press, 2002. This collection of essays explores citizen attitudes and participation in Canada, including voting behaviour, public opinion, political activism, and social movements.

Flanagan, Thomas. *First Nations? Second Thoughts*. Montreal and Kingston: McGill–Queen's University Press, 2000. Flanagan disputes historical arguments buttressing Aboriginal claims for differential constitutional status in Canada and argues instead that common citizenship based on liberal principles is both fair and to the material advantage of Aboriginal people in this country.

Fukuyama, Francis. *Trust: The Social Virtues and the Creation of Prosperity*. New York: Free Press, 1996. Fukuyama examines the foundations of prosperous societies around the world. He argues that all such societies rest on a foundation of social trust, the ability of citizens to trust in the reliability and honesty of anonymous others in their societies. He explores the sources of social trust.

Gidengil, Elisabeth, André Blais, Neil Nevitte, and Richard Nadeau. *Citizens*. Vancouver: UBC Press, 2004. This is a brief, sobering study of Canadians' knowledge of politics and their patterns of participation in political life.

Harrison, Lawrence E., and Samuel P. Huntington, eds. *Culture Matters: How Values Shape Progress*. New York: Basic Books, 2000. This collection of essays explores the relationship between cultural beliefs and economic and political development, in North America and around the world.

Ignatieff, Michael. *The Rights Revolution*. Concord, ON: Anansi, 2000. Ignatieff discusses the effect of human rights and the *Canadian Charter of Rights and Freedoms* on Canadian identity, public discourse, and citizenship.

Inglehart, Ronald, and Christian Welzel. *Modernization, Cultural Change, and the Human Development Sequence*. New York: Cambridge University Press, 2005. The authors assemble a large body of international survey data to suggest that processes of economic and technological modernization are changing political values in the direction of gender equality, individual autonomy, and demands for democracy.

Mancuso, Maureen, Michael M. Atkinson, André Blais, Ian Greene, and Neil Nevitte. *A Question of Ethics: Canadians Speak Out* (2nd ed.). Toronto: Oxford University Press, 2006. This book examines survey evidence of what Canadians consider the bounds of acceptable political conduct, from conflicts of interest and patronage to lying and personal morality.

Milner, Henry. *Civic Literacy: How Informed Citizens Make Democracy Work*. Hanover: University Press of New England, 2002. Milner compares Canada to other countries to show that citizens' knowledge of public affairs is a crucial part of civic engagement and political participation. He examines proposals to increase levels of civic literacy.

Norris, Pippa, and Ronald Inglehart. *Sacred and Secular: Religion and Politics Worldwide*. New York: Cambridge University Press, 2004. The authors argue that modernization processes foster a decline of religious belief. While developed societies continue to secularize, religious belief will prevail among fast-growing population in parts of the world where modernizing forces have yet to achieve a full impact.

Putnam, Robert, ed. *Democracies in Flux: The Evolution of Social Capital in Contemporary Society*. New York: Oxford University Press, 2002. This collection of essays examines the state of social capital in democracies around the world. Putnam is famous for arguing that social capital is in decline in the United States. Essays in this volume suggest that the country is exceptional in this regard.

Rosenblum, Nancy L., and Robert C. Post, eds. *Civil Society and Government*. Princeton: Princeton University Press, 2002. This is an excellent collection of essays examining the idea of civil society in historical, theological, and philosophical perspective.

Sniderman, Paul, Joseph F. Fletcher, Peter H. Russell, and Philip E. Tetlock. *The Clash of Rights: Liberty, Equality, and Legitimacy in Pluralist Democracy*. New Haven: Yale University Press, 1996. The authors provide a comprehensive study of Canadians' opinions on the politics of rights in the Charter era.

Taras, David. *Power and Betrayal in the Canadian Media* (2nd ed.). Peterborough, ON: Broadview, 2000. This is a wide-ranging discussion of trends that weaken the political functions of the media.

Taylor, Charles. *The Malaise of Modernity*. Concord, ON: Anansi, 1991. Taylor, a Canadian philosopher, locates the crisis of contemporary political life in the character of modern individualism, the primacy of instrumental reason (technology, efficiency), and the threat of "soft despotism" in which people retreat from participation in citizen self-government in favour of material comforts.

Verney, Douglas. *Three Civilizations, Two Cultures, One State: Canada's Political Traditions*. Durham, NC: Duke University Press, 1986. A sweeping historical analysis of Canada's traditions and contradictions.

Unit Four

Introduction: Contemporary Politics at Home

◆ ◆ ◆

To many students, the branch of political science that deals with institutions might seem dull when compared with other fields of the discipline. While the study of ideologies is characterized by lively debates over principles of political philosophy, and the study of international relations focuses on questions of global war and peace, the study of institutions entails mastering the detail of what sometimes appear to be incomprehensibly complex webs of quaintly named rules and offices. But there is much more to the study of political institutions than meets the eye.

For a typical Canadian, the phrase "political institution" likely conjures up an image of our magnificent Parliament Buildings. This association between institutions and buildings is not surprising because buildings connote permanence and stability—key characteristics of political institutions. But people refer to the family as an institution as well and families are not normally associated with buildings. The example of the family points to the truth that any institution, at its core, is really a kind of relationship: a web of norms and understandings that bind people and dictate how they will interact with each other. The institution we call "parliament" is thus not primarily a group of buildings but a set of norms and rules governing what our elected representatives do and how they do it.

The fact that institutions are fundamentally sets of norms and rules suggests an important insight. Rules are not devised randomly; they typically aim at some purpose. One might say that they have an "inner logic." For instance, the new rule in NHL hockey that eliminates the centre line for purposes of two-line passes is designed to increase the available area of play and to speed up the game. The same observation may be made with respect to our political institutions. The rule that divides consideration of a bill into three distinct "readings" is designed to ensure an orderly and rational discussion: the first reading allows for a general introduction of the bill, the second reading addresses its main principles, and the third allows for a discussion of the bill's details once the main principles have been accepted. In the end, the study of political institutions is not about mastering detail for the sake of mastering detail; it is about figuring out the inner logic of how our institutions work.

This first insight leads to a second: political institutions are not neutral. To the extent that institutions have an inner logic, it is important to understand how the logic of our institutions will shape the political decisions we

Parliament and the Supreme Court buildings stand stolidly above the Ottawa River.

make. Our electoral institutions provide one of the more obvious illustrations of this point. Not only does our single-member plurality system help determine the kinds of parties we will have (by favouring brokerage parties over ideological parties); at times, it will even determine who wins the election. For instance, in New Brunswick's 2006 provincial elections, the structure of our electoral system produced an outcome in which the Liberals won a majority of the seats even though the Conservatives had a larger share of the popular vote.

To the extent that an institution is really a set of norms and rules, it is important to appreciate the interplay between specific rules and the broader norms that inform them. In 2006, the House of Commons adopted a resolution affirming that the Québécois constitute a "nation" within Canada. One of the great questions raised at the time was how the declaration of this new norm would affect other institutional arrangements. Specifically, does it entail the transfer of special powers to the Government of Quebec?

Is the Impossible Possible?
Electoral Reform and
Canada's Provinces

Harold J. Jansen

Editors' Note

Political scientists study political activity—what politicians say and do; what forces they create, exploit, or oppose; and what groups they assemble to support them in their various campaigns. But to do this well, political scientists must also understand the institutional context in which political life unfolds. An institution is not a building or physical structure; it is a settled arrangement, a set of generally accepted rules and understandings that structure, define, and give expression to human activities. Institutions can and do change but they usually do so slowly and with some difficulty. This is what is both frustrating and valuable about them.

Democratic electoral politics take place within the institutional context of an electoral system—those rules defining the manner in which citizens' votes are translated into parliamentary representation for elected candidates and political parties. As Harold Jansen makes clear in the following essay, electoral systems matter. Different systems produce different results and present political actors with different incentives. All institutions are biased, said one political scientist a long time ago. In other words, the rules of the game affect how it is played and who wins. The rules, then, should be well understood and carefully chosen.

Though Canada uses one of the most simple, easily understood electoral systems in the world, most Canadians cannot give an account of how it operates and what sorts of biases it produces. It is not that Canadians are dull; it is simply that they think little of the terms on which politics take place. But this is changing. There is more and more interest in all facets of electoral politics in Canada: the influence of money in party operations; the timing of elections and who gets to decide election dates; the apparent problem of declining voter turnout; the use of referenda instead of elected politicians to decide matters of public interest; and, finally, the problems associated with our electoral system.

Jansen suggests that many Canadian jurisdictions—but not all of them—may be on the cusp of significant electoral system change in Canada. Jansen explains why electoral reform is afoot in some parts of the country. He leaves to us to speculate why it is a dead letter elsewhere. Another important theme in his essay is that there are institutional incentives embedded in not only electoral systems but also processes selected to decide upon electoral reform.

❖ ❖ ❖

Electoral reform with respect to the House of Commons is not going to happen. Not now. Not soon. Not ever.[1]

—Roger Gibbins

For almost as long as we've been conducting elections in Canada, there has been debate about the way we elect Members of Parliament to Canada's House of Commons. Critics of Canada's electoral system point to its propensity to create artificial majorities, the marginalization of smaller parties, and the system's contribution to increased regionalism. In recent years, the debate has become even more intense, with increased academic attention, popular mobilization through groups such as Fair Vote Canada, and even some attention at the elite level—electoral reform came up in the English leaders' debate for the 2006 federal election. Despite decades of debate, there has been little action. It is no wonder that commentators increasingly see electoral reform as an impossibility.

The same is not true at the provincial level. Over the last five years, several Canadian provinces have shown a willingness to do more than engage in debate. Five provinces are going or have gone down the path of considering electoral reform, and many have held or will hold referendums on the issue. Although electoral reform at the federal level seems moribund, at the provincial level it is very much alive. In this essay, we will consider the debate over the single-member plurality system in Canada, the actions of provincial governments, and what we can learn from the provincial experience for considering electoral reform in Canada.

Although electoral reform at the federal level seems moribund, at the provincial level it is very much alive.

THE DEBATE OVER THE SINGLE MEMBER PLURALITY SYSTEM

◆ ◆ ◆

Although electoral systems may seem like an esoteric concern, of interest only to political scientists, they do matter. Electoral systems are not neutral things: they can have a profound impact on the nature of electoral competition. They affect the actions and strategies of political parties and voters, the major actors in elections. Different electoral systems translate votes into seats in different ways and the way this translation happens provides incentives for parties and voters to alter their behaviour accordingly.

When we describe electoral systems, we typically make a distinction between two elements: district magnitude (the number of representatives elected in each district) and the electoral formula (the formula by which we decide how the votes in a district are translated into seats). In Canadian federal politics, each of the 308 electoral districts elects one Member of Parliament; in other words, the district magnitude is equal to one. The formula used is the plurality formula: whichever candidate gets the most votes (note that this is not a majority) becomes the Member of Parliament. When we put these two elements together, we can describe Canada's electoral system as a single-member plurality (SMP) system, although it often commonly called the "first past the post" system. In Canada, the federal government and all of the provinces and territories use the SMP system for their elections.

Electoral systems are not neutral things: they can have a profound impact on the nature of electoral competition.

The SMP system has a number of effects. These are well documented, so we will review them only very briefly here.[2] The SMP system tends not to translate party votes into seats in a way that accurately reflects the shares of their popular votes. The party that wins the most seats wins more seats than it "deserves" according to its share of the popular vote. Particularly important is the ability of the SMP electoral system to create a majority government for a party when it receives less than a majority of the vote, a phenomenon known as a "manufactured majority." In federal politics, the Liberals earned three consecutive majority governments from 1993 to 2004, but in none of those elections did the party earn a majority of the vote. In fact, in 1997, the SMP system manufactured a majority Liberal government out of only 38.5 percent of the vote. Sometimes, the system can even produce "wrong winners," sometimes known as "spurious majorities." This is a situation where the party that gets a majority of the seats is not a party that received the most votes. In Canadian federal politics, this has happened only once (in 1896), but it is a relatively common occurrence at the provincial level.[3]

In the Canadian context, one of the major challenges has been that the SMP system exacerbates regionalism in Canada. In a seminal article on the electoral system, Alan Cairns pointed out that the electoral system distorts the parliamentary representation of larger parties. For example, in the last several elections, the Liberals have been overrepresented in Ontario and have earned fewer seats than they "deserve" in the West; the reverse is true of the Conservatives. Cairns also pointed out that small parties with support spread across the country tend to fare less well than those parties with geographically concentrated support. In the 2006 federal election, for example, the Bloc Québécois had the support of 10.5 percent of Canadian voters; the NDP 17.5 percent of the vote. The BQ, though, earned 51 seats and the NDP earned 29 seats.[4] Obviously, a big part of the problem is that parties are weaker in some regions than others, but the electoral system plays a role in magnifying these pockets of strength and weakness, making the Canadian political party system look more regionalized than it actually is. Given Canada's preoccupation with national integration and regionalism, this feature of the electoral system has been the primary impetus behind electoral reform initiatives.[5]

Although these features of the SMP system lead many people to advocate for changes to the system, some defend it or are at least skeptical about what electoral reform might accomplish. Defenders of the system point out that majority government allows government to act decisively and enables voters to hold their elected officials accountable for their actions. It is more difficult to hold a coalition government comprising a number of parties accountable for its actions, because governmental decisions are the product of compromise and negotiation between parties. Furthermore, the process of government formation in a system where there is no clear majority party involves negotiations between parties; voters may have little ability to vote a party out of office. If many voters desert a particular party to punish it for its actions, that party might be able to stay in government by negotiating successfully with other parties.

The major alternative to the SMP system is some form of proportional representation (PR), where party seat shares are generally proportional to party vote shares. Under a PR system, a party with 40 percent of the vote would get 40 percent of the seats. PR systems can be implemented in a variety of ways, from a simple vote for a party that gets translated into seats allocated from lists provided by political parties (list PR) to more complex implementations such as the mixed-member proportional (MMP) and single-transferable vote (STV) systems, which we will discuss later. Advocates of PR argue that this system would more accurately reflect the voters' wishes, largely put an end to manufactured majorities, and reduce the exaggeration of the regionalization of party system. Skeptics, though, suggest that well-intentioned institutional reforms may have unintended consequences,[6] or that PR may not improve regionalism much because it would undermine the other institutional arrangements that have grown around the SMP system to accommodate regional considerations.[7]

WHY ELECTORAL SYSTEMS ARE HARD TO CHANGE

◆ ◆ ◆

Debates like this over Canada's SMP system have been raging for years. Despite this, the electoral system has remained basically intact, seemingly impervious to attempts to alter it. Electoral systems provide incentives for certain kinds of behaviours and strategies. Those parties adept at these behaviours and strategies will tend to be successful. The party in power, then, is usually a beneficiary of the electoral system in place and, hence, has little reason to change it. Even parties in opposition are not always that supportive of changing the electoral system. Even if the system is not currently benefiting them, they reason that if they can marginally increase their vote shares, the system will begin to work in their favour. Furthermore, the members of their party caucuses hold seats that they won under the current system and individual members might oppose a reform that, even if it were to increase the overall number of seats for their party, might threaten their own seats.

The self-interest of elected politicians is thus a significant barrier to electoral reform. This dynamic leads analysts such as Roger Gibbins (quoted at the beginning of this article) to conclude that the prospects for electoral reform are very bleak. Without question, Canadian history is on Gibbins's side. Despite the decades of discussion of electoral reform, there has been no real progress. The comparative evidence also supports Gibbins's contention: electoral systems rarely change.

The self-interest of elected politicians is ... a significant barrier to electoral reform.

The fact is, though, that they do change. It happens rarely, but it does happen. In the late 19th and early-20th centuries, a rash of countries switched from plurality and majoritarian systems to proportional representation systems.[8] More recently, countries with long-established electoral systems switched. In the 1990s, New Zealand, Italy, and Japan all made significant changes to their electoral systems. Clearly, the problem of institutional self-interest is not insurmountable.

THE PROVINCES LEAD THE WAY

◆ ◆ ◆

Further evidence that electoral systems can change comes from Canada's provinces. Although there hasn't been much progress on electoral reform at the national level, at the provincial level we see a fair amount of activity. Five provinces—British Columbia, Ontario, Quebec, New Brunswick, and Prince Edward Island—have all undergone or are undergoing processes to examine their electoral systems. Although at time of writing there has been no actual reform, the provinces are considering reform in a way not seen at the national level. These initiatives remind us that, when it comes to electoral reform, Canada's provinces have always been the leaders. Over the decades, Canada's provinces have experimented with a variety of electoral mechanisms, including multi-member districts, drawing the electoral map to ensure the representation of particular minorities, and even the use of majority and proportional electoral systems for provincial elections.[9] This is a testament to one of the advantages of a federal system: it makes it possible for provinces to experiment with different public policy and institutional arrangements.

... when it comes to electoral reform, Canada's provinces have always been the leaders.

What accounts for this spate of electoral reform initiatives in the Canadian provinces? Part of this is driven by dissatisfaction with recent provincial election results.[10] The dissatisfaction seems to be greatest with two outcomes of the SMP system. The first is a tendency to produce overwhelming majorities, leaving little opposition in the provincial legislature. This was clearly a factor in two of the provinces considering electoral reform. Prince Edward Island has had chronic problems with small oppositions in the last couple of decades, often with only one or two MLAs sitting in the opposition benches. New Brunswick also had that problem in recent years; famously, the Liberals won every seat in the 1987 election, rendering the legislature devoid of opposition MLAs. Furthermore, although the B.C. Liberals' commitment to considering electoral reform

predated the 2001 election, only 2 of the 79 MLAs elected in that election were members of the opposition.

The second phenomenon is the "wrong winner" problem. Quebec experienced this in its 1998 provincial election when more Quebec voters supported the Liberals than the BQ, but the BQ won more seats and formed a majority government. The root of this problem is that Anglophone and allophone voters tend to be too concentrated in too few electoral districts; the Liberals win these districts by significant margins, while the Parti Québécois (PQ) wins more close races. This means that the PQ is far more efficient at converting its popular votes into seats. British Columbia experienced a wrong winner in 1996, when the Liberals outpolled the NDP, but the NDP won a majority government. Most recently, in the 2006 New Brunswick provincial election, the Liberals defeated the Conservative government despite having received fewer votes. Although there are many strange results associated with the SMP system, the spurious majority stands out because it so egregiously seems to violate the idea of translating voter support into a mandate to govern.

An explanation focusing on provincial dissatisfaction with election results faces two problems. The first is why Ontario is considering electoral reform. Although Ontario experienced decades without a change of government, in the last 20 years, Ontario's elections have been highly competitive: three different parties have formed governments, oppositions have been sizeable, and there have been no experiences with spurious majorities. The evidence from Ontario suggests that there is something else driving the process besides mere dissatisfaction with the way the system is running.

Besides the puzzle of the Ontario case is the question of timing. As Carty notes, these problems with the SMP system are hardly new. Lopsided electoral results have long been a feature of provincial elections; there have been "wrong winners" in past elections.[11] Why has electoral reform become an issue at this point? It is impossible to answer this question definitively, but part of the answer lies in the greater democratic expectations of citizens. Canadian citizens are less deferential than they once were; furthermore, they are better educated and more knowledgeable, and are less willing to accept inegalitarian social and political arrangements.[12] This decline in the culture of deference may make politicians eager to capitalize on public dissatisfaction with traditional democratic practices, by promising to reform elements of the political system. The electoral system has now entered the agenda at the provincial level. A similar rise in democratic sentiment played an important role in sparking the electoral reforms of the late 19th and early-20th centuries.[13]

This decline in the culture of deference may make politicians eager to capitalize on public dissatisfaction with traditional democratic practices, by promising to reform elements of the political system.

Provincial political elites have also displayed a willingness to entertain changing a system that has benefited them. One of the striking things about this round of provincial electoral reform is that it has been led and guided by provincial premiers, the very people we would expect to stymie the process.[14] Some of these premiers experienced deathbed conversions while they served in opposition. The remarkable thing is that these commitments have remained even as they moved into government. For example, B.C. Liberal leader Gordon Campbell first promised an electoral system review in 1999, while he was leader of the opposition. As premier, his commitment to the process remained.[15] Therefore, the assumption that electoral reform is impossible because of the self-interest of political leaders may not be entirely accurate. At the very least, the calculus of self-interest may be changing. If political elites perceive that championing electoral reform (or at least initiating a process of electoral reform) is electorally advantageous, then political self-interest can help the cause of electoral reform, not just hinder it.

GOING PUBLIC

◆ ◆ ◆

If growing public dissatisfaction with the political process is part of what is motivating electoral reform, we also see this in the way electoral reform is being considered in the various provinces. One of the central features of this wave of electoral reform initiatives has been broad public involvement. Although the provinces have used different processes to consider electoral reform, public involvement is playing a role everywhere.

Quebec's electoral reform process has been characterized as driven by the Liberal government of the day and, indeed, much of the reform debate and process

has been driven by political elites.[16] Even Quebec's government-dominated process, though, has seen significant public involvement. In 2003, an Estates General (a broadly based representative consultative assembly), with more than 1,000 delegates, endorsed electoral reform, kicking off the process.[17] After the provincial Liberal government developed a draft electoral reform bill, it turned it over to a committee comprising nine Members of the National Assembly and eight ordinary citizens. Six of the citizens drafted their own report, calling for a more proportional electoral system than that proposed by the government, among other reforms.[18] Although the Quebec process has to this date been more government-driven than elsewhere, it too has incorporated a significant degree of public involvement.

The most ambitious and dramatic use of citizen involvement has come in British Columbia and is being emulated in slightly modified form in Ontario. In B.C., Premier Gordon Campbell decided to turn over the entire process to citizens through the creation of a Citizens' Assembly. Campbell wanted to ensure that citizens had a role to play in drafting a new electoral system for the province so that it did not just reflect the concerns of parties and governments.[19] Along with a chairperson for the assembly, B.C. randomly selected one man and one woman from each of the 79 provincial electoral districts and chose two aboriginal members as well.[20] In early 2004, these 161 people gathered regularly in Vancouver and underwent a crash course in electoral systems. In the spring, they then returned to their districts (and travelled to other districts) for public consultations. Over the summer, the assembly members waded through the hundreds of public submissions to the assembly. Finally, in the fall of 2004, they gathered in Vancouver to debate various electoral systems for B.C. The members of the assembly chose a single-transferable vote (STV) system over a mixed-member proportional (MMP) system as their preferred alternative to the SMP system.

New Brunswick and P.E.I. have followed a tried and true model of institutional change: a government commission to study the problem and to recommend changes. Both of these provinces, though, have opted for citizen involvement in the form of referenda. The use of referenda to effect electoral system change has become a defining feature of the provincial electoral reform processes. All of the provinces but Quebec have used or have committed to using referenda to decide whether electoral reform should proceed. B.C. was the first to vote on electoral reform. In a May 2005 referendum, 58 percent of B.C. voters supported the Citizens' Assembly proposal to adopt STV. However, B.C.'s Liberal government had specified ahead of time that any change needed to receive the support of 60 percent of the voters and had to get support of the majority of voters in 60 percent of the province's 79 electoral districts. The referendum easily passed the second threshold, with a majority of voters in 77 of the 79 districts supporting the change, but fell just short of the first threshold. Despite the fact that the referendum did not meet the mandated threshold, the government felt it could not ignore the strong support expressed for STV. It instructed an Electoral Boundaries Commission to draw up a new electoral map with districts for both the existing SMP system and an electoral map for the proposed STV system. With concrete electoral systems in hand, voters will then be asked to vote on the proposal in a second referendum in May 2009, in conjunction with the provincial election then. The supermajorities of 60 percent approval and 60 percent of the electoral districts will be in place for that referendum as they were for the first. Besides B.C., the other province to have voted on electoral reform has been P.E.I. In the fall of 2005, P.E.I. held a referendum on a proposed switch to a Mixed-Member Proportional (MMP) system in which MMP was ultimately rejected by 64 percent of the Island's voters. As in B.C., the P.E.I. plebiscite had a dual 60 percent popular vote/majority in 60 percent of the districts threshold.

The stage is set for at least one other referendum on electoral reform as well. If the Ontario Citizens' Assembly decides to recommend a change to the system, that change will be put to the people on Ontario in a referendum. The legislation for the referendum proposes the same dual thresholds used in B.C. and P.E.I.[21] The defeat of Bernard Lord's Conservative government in New Brunswick in September 2006 (ironically, a "wrong winner" election) has thrown plans for an electoral reform referendum in that province into doubt. In June 2006, the Lord government had announced a May 2008 referendum on whether to accept the Commission on Legislative Democracy's proposed MMP system or keep the existing SMP system. Unlike their counterparts in other provinces, however, the government in New Brunswick announced that it would accept a simple majority (50 percent + 1), with the additional requirement that voter turnout for the referendum must be at least 50 percent.[22] As of May 2007, it is not clear whether the Liberal government of New Brunswick will carry through with the previous government's commitment.

Clearly, then, citizens have become central actors in electoral reform at the provincial level. This is indicative of a more participatory and egalitarian ethos that seems to be reshaping Canadian politics. This is not only leading to demands for electoral reform, but also transforming the very way these demands are implemented.

... citizens have become central actors in electoral reform at the provincial level.

DIFFERENT PROCESSES, DIFFERENT OUTCOMES
◆ ◆ ◆

Besides having chosen different processes, the provinces have also opted for different electoral systems. This reflects the fact that different regions have different needs and, hence, require different electoral systems.[23] Taking this logic further, this also illustrates that the answer as to the "best" electoral system cannot be answered in the abstract; a system that works well in one context may not be appropriate in another or may create more problems than it solves.

Although it is certainly the case that the provinces have opted for different electoral systems, reflecting local conditions, it would be hard to overlook the fact that three of the four provinces that are well on the way down the electoral reform path (that is, all provinces but Ontario) have opted for some form of a mixed-member proportional (MMP) system. The basic idea of a MMP system is that a certain proportion of seats (typically half, but it could be more or less) are elected using a single-member electoral system, such as the SMP system. The rest of the seats are allocated from party lists in such a way as to compensate the parties for the distortions in the translation of seats to votes in the SMP district seats. Consider, for example, a party that gets 30 percent of the vote, but only 20 percent of the seats in the single-member districts. If that province allocated half of its legislature seats to single-member seats and the other half to party lists, when the list seats were allocated, that party would be overcompensated to bring its overall share of the seats back up to 30 percent. The idea of a MMP system is to try to ensure proportional outcomes while retaining single-member districts, so that voters living in a district have a representative who is "theirs."

MMP systems can be altered in many ways and those details can change the way the system operates in response to local conditions. For example, altering the balance between single-member seats and compensatory list seats will affect how proportional the results are: the more list seats you have, the more proportional your results will be. The system can be further tweaked by applying the list seats either system-wide (that is, at the provincial/national level) or at a regional level. Furthermore, MMP systems typically impose a threshold: a party must earn a minimum share of the vote (typically 3 or 5 percent) or win a seat in a single-member district in order to qualify for compensatory list seats. The method of election in single-member districts can be altered to use a method other than the SMP system. The MMP model the B.C. Citizens' Assembly was considering, for example, would have used the alternative vote to elect members in single-member districts.[24] Finally, voters can have either one vote or two. If they have one vote, they vote for a particular party candidate and that vote is also considered a vote for the party for which that candidate runs. With a two-vote system, voters vote for a candidate and then for the party list they prefer; the candidate may or may not be from the same party.

The provincial MMP proposals demonstrate the flexibility of the MMP system in response to local conditions. The proposed reform in P.E.I. was an MMP system with 17 members elected in single-member districts using the plurality rule, and 10 members elected from province-wide districts. P.E.I. would also have imposed a threshold of 5 percent on the party vote in order to qualify for compensatory seats. Residents of New Brunswick, according to the 2003 Commission on Legislative Democracy, would also be voting on an MMP model; theirs has a balance of 36 single-member seats with 20 party-list seats elected in four multi-member districts. Voters would cast separate ballots for the candidate in their single member-district and for the party to determine their preferred party. The compensatory seats are allocated at a regional level, reflecting the importance of the regional distribution of the Francophone minority in that province. Quebec's plan would retain 77 Members of the National Assembly (MNAs) elected in "divisions" using the SMP system. There would be 24–27 districts, most of which would comprise three divisions. Most districts would elect 3 SMP MNAs and 2 list seats. Voters would cast only one vote, which would be used to elect a candidate in the single-member district and as a choice of party.

Although these reforms are all different in the sense that their specific details would likely affect the electoral outcomes, they are all variants of a MMP system. The predominance of these systems is not a surprise. There has been an increasing consensus among both students and practitioners of electoral system design that a mixed-member system provides "the best of both worlds."[25] These systems combine the relationship between constituents and elected representatives on the one hand (the ombudsman function) and the proportional outcomes of PR systems on the other. The electoral design phases in all three of these provinces was more elite dominated, relying on experts and academic support. Most recent electoral reforms in the world have been in this direction.[26]

> There has been an increasing consensus among both students and practitioners of electoral system design that a mixed-member system provides "the best of both worlds."

B.C. stands out as the exception in its decision to opt for the single transferable vote (STV). In the family of electoral systems, STV is a relatively more complex option. STV districts are multi-member districts. In Ireland, the districts elect anywhere between 3 and 5 members. In the B.C. case, the Citizens' Assembly proposed districts that would elect between 2 and 7 members. Each party would nominate as many candidates as it wanted to in the district. Voters would then rank the candidates in order of preference. These votes could be cast in any order that voters wish, either supporting candidates of one party, or crossing between parties and independent candidates. In the classic form of this, voters can mark as many or as few preferences as they wish.[27]

When sorting out who wins the seats, first all of the ballots are counted and an electoral quota is determined, based on the district magnitude of the district.[28] The quota is the vote threshold that a candidate has to reach in order to be declared elected. After a quota has been calculated, the ballots are sorted by candidate according to the first preferences indicated on them. If any candidate has more first-preference votes than the quota, he or she is declared elected. Election officials then remove votes in excess of the quota (the surplus) and distribute those among the other candidates according to the second preferences indicated on them. Once we are done distributing surplus votes, if we still have not declared enough candidates to be elected, we then eliminate the candidate with the lowest number of votes and distribute those ballots among the other candidates according to the subsequent preferences. We go through this process of distributing surpluses and eliminating candidates until we have either elected the required number of candidates or we are left with only the required number of candidates.

STV tends to produce relatively proportional results among parties, which means that it would likely address many of the shortcomings of the SMP system. STV, however, is unusual among PR systems for a number of reasons. First, voters cast their votes for candidates and not for political parties. Second, voters have almost unlimited freedom to cast their votes as they choose; they can opt to vote a strict party line and support only candidates from within a party, or they can mix and match between parties and independent candidates. Third, a party's candidates have to compete against not only the candidates of other parties, but also each other. Forcing a party's candidates to compete against one another for votes generally inhibits party unity and can encourage factionalism. All told, STV is not an electoral system conducive to strong, disciplined parties. Systems that use party lists (such as MMP) give greater control to parties and party elites and may encourage party unity; STV does not do that. It produces more proportional outcomes than SMP (although likely less so than most MMP systems), but it does so in a less party-centred way.

B.C.'s decision to opt for such an unusual electoral system cries out for explanation. After all, STV is not a particularly popular electoral system. Although STV has the distinction of being the only PR system to have been used for legislative elections in Canada, at the national level, only three countries currently use it: Ireland, Malta, and Australia (for elections to its Senate). Although STV has some vocal supporters, the recommendation of the B.C. Citizens' Assembly alienated a number of people who otherwise support electoral reform.[29]

Why would B.C. choose this? It seems likely that the process used for electoral reform (a citizens assembly) largely contributed to the outcome. Although the members of the assembly largely felt that STV best accomplished the goals they set for the electoral process, it is critical that the people making the choice were

approaching reform from the standpoint of citizens. Ken Carty, who also functioned as the B.C. Citizens' Assembly's Chief Research Officer, argues that in choosing STV, the assembly consciously chose a voter-centred electoral system rather than a party-centred system, such as MMP. The members of the assembly were concerned with more than issues of electoral fairness—they wanted their political system to be less adversarial and to have less party discipline.[30] In other words, they wanted weaker parties and thought STV would strengthen the hands of voters and individual MLAs, while weakening political parties. This anti-party sentiment runs through much of the work of the assembly, from the options used to flesh out the electoral system proposals they discussed[31] to the final report.[32] In an opinion piece published shortly after the assembly made its recommendation, Gordon Gibson, the architect of the process, pointed to the dislike of STV by politicians.[33] A process that explicitly excluded candidates and political parties undoubtedly contributed to the recommendation that emphasized voters rather than parties.

Besides the fact that STV may have best fit the assembly's understanding of what it wanted in an electoral system, there were certain constraints that militated against the choice of an MMP system. One of these was that the Citizens' Assembly interpreted its mandate as to address only the way MLAs are elected in B.C. The assembly did not feel it could increase (or decrease) the number of MLAs.[34] That can make it difficult to implement an MMP system. In order to be sure that you have enough MLAs on party lists to ensure a proportional outcome while still having enough single-member MLAs to ensure that districts are geographically small enough to be represented effectively, a larger legislature might be necessary. Furthermore, in any particular election, MMP may also require the temporary addition of a few seats to a legislature in order to represent the parties properly, a phenomenon known as "overhang" seats. This would be difficult to do in the context of a fixed assembly size.

Finally, although STV is arguably a more complex electoral system in its operation and potential effects, it is actually easier to design. Once you have made a decision to opt for an STV system, there are relatively few details to be worked out. Designing an MMP system is a considerably more complex undertaking. Decisions about one aspect of the design have implications for other elements. MMP systems are thus inherently more difficult to design in committee and in a compressed time frame such as was seen in the B.C. Citizens' Assembly.[35] This does not mean that citizens are incapable of understanding the tradeoffs; it is just that it is considerably more complicated to do so. Evidence for this comes from the Citizens' Assembly itself. The assembly chose to construct an STV system first, because it was a simpler task.[36] In fact, at the end of the process of designing a potential MMP system for B.C., there were several aspects of the system upon which the Assembly had not yet decided.[37]

The key observation here is that not only local conditions but also the electoral design process matters. It is possible that, had B.C. opted for a different process, another outcome (such as MMP) might have resulted. The experience of Ontario's Citizens' Assembly will be instructive in this regard. By adopting B.C.'s process and applying it to a different political context, Ontario will provide an interesting comparison to what happened in B.C.

> *... not only local conditions but also the electoral design process matters.*

WHAT WOULD IT TAKE TO HAPPEN FEDERALLY?

◆ ◆ ◆

The provincial experience does show that, at a minimum, a serious consideration of electoral reform is possible, even if electoral reform itself has still proven elusive. What lessons can we draw from the politics of electoral reform at the provincial level? What would it take for electoral reform to make it onto the national political agenda?

The first thing we would need to see is some anomalous electoral results at the national level. Although we have certainly seen these in the differential treatment of small parties nationally and the regional disparities in party representation, we have only rarely seen situations like those that have seemed to spur the reform agenda at the provincial level: overwhelming majorities with little opposition or the spurious majority (or "wrong winners") problem. Were a government to be elected that had a majority of the seats despite another party having won more votes, more attention would be paid to the electoral system's role in creating majority governments.

It is possible that we are seeing a different kind of anomaly at the level of federal politics.

One of the major arguments put forth against PR electoral systems is that they create a perpetual situation where there are no majority governments, making it difficult to get things done, leading to frequent elections, and making it hard to hold governments accountable for their actions. If we were to have a series of minority governments, Canada could experience all the supposed disadvantages of a proportional electoral system without its major advantage: a more accurate reflection of popular support for parties.[38] This frustration could help create a climate conducive to electoral reform.

One of the clear lessons from the provincial experience is that leadership matters. Electoral reform needs to be championed by political parties; it needs to leave the realm of academic discussion and activist debate to become part of partisan political discourse. As we have seen from the provinces, the actions of premiers and party leaders are critical in getting electoral reform on the agenda. There is some sign that is happening to a minor extent at the federal level, as the NDP has talked about electoral reform in the last couple of election campaigns. The NDP's record on this is somewhat suspect, however. Despite the fact that we have had provincial NDP governments in four Canadian provinces, not one has moved to reform the electoral system, seemingly content to benefit from it. Even the actions at the national level cast some doubt on the NDP's commitment to the cause. In the 2004 federal election campaign, NDP leader Jack Layton demanded a referendum on proportional representation as the price for NDP support of a minority government.[39] One year later, however, when a Liberal minority government required NDP support to stay in power, the NDP asked for short-term policy gains, not electoral reform.

> *One of the clear lessons from the provincial experience is that leadership matters.*

Although political leadership is clearly necessary, public opinion can help create conditions where championing a discussion of electoral reform can become politically advantageous for a party. There is some evidence of dissatisfaction with the way elections are conducted in Canada. There is strong support for better representation for smaller political parties, for a proportional allocation of party seats, and for coalition governments. At the same time, though, Canadians are also strongly supportive of strong majority governments, a key attribute of the SMP system and one seemingly at odds with these other values.[40] Furthermore, there is also evidence that Canadians do not fully understand their electoral system as about half of Canadians erroneously believe that candidates require the support of a majority of the voters to be declared elected and/or believe that a government must win a majority of the votes in order to govern.[41] It is not clear, then, that the preconditions of strong public support for change are in place at the national level.

One of the more likely scenarios is for one of Canada's provinces to reform its electoral system. If the reform were successful—that is, the provincial government functioned effectively and voters were satisfied with the system—we could expect that it might increase pressure on the federal government to change accordingly. As the provinces have moved to discuss electoral reform, there has been pressure on other provinces and the federal government to follow suit. There is no guarantee, however, that other provinces or the federal government would emulate the reformers; Alberta and Manitoba used STV for decades without anyone following their leads.

Electoral reform is often written off as impossible due to the well-honed instincts for self-preservation common among political leaders. The experiences of Canada's provinces, though, indicate that electoral reform can make it onto the political agenda and be considered in a serious way. With increasing public demands for greater democracy and accountability, and political elites increasingly willing to respond to those demands, the impossible is looking more and more possible.

Notes

1. Roger Gibbins, "Early Warning, No Response: Alan Cairns and Electoral Reform," in Gerald Kernerman and Philip Resnick, eds., *Insiders & Outsiders: Alan Cairns and the Reshaping of Canadian Citizenship* (Vancouver: UBC Press, 2005), p. 49

2. For a discussion of the effects of the single-member plurality system, see Law Commission of Canada, *Voting Counts: Electoral Reform for Canada* (Ottawa: Law Commission of Canada, 2004), pp. 8–12.

3. Alan Siaroff, "Spurious Majorities, Electoral Systems and Electoral System Change," *Commonwealth & Comparative Politics* 41 (2003): 146–47.

4. Alan C. Cairns, "The Electoral System and the Party System in Canada, 1921–1965," *Canadian Journal of Political Science* 1 (1968): 55–80.

5. Harold J. Jansen and Alan Siaroff, "Regionalism and Party Systems: Evaluating Proposals to Reform Canada's Electoral System," in Henry Milner, ed., *Steps Toward Making Every Vote Count: Electoral System Reform in Canada and its Provinces* (Peterborough: Broadview, 2004), pp. 43–44.

6. Richard S. Katz, "Problems in Electoral Reform: Why the Decision to Change Electoral Systems Is Not Simple," in Henry Milner, ed., *Steps Toward Making Every Vote Count: Electoral System Reform in Canada and its Provinces*, pp. 97–100.

7. John C. Courtney, "Electoral Reform and Canada's Parties," in Henry Milner, ed., *Steps Toward Making Every Vote Count: Reassessing Canada's Electoral System*, pp. 91–99.

8. André Blais, Agnieszka Dobrzynska, and Ingrid H. Indridason, "To Adopt or not to Adopt Proportional Representation: The Politics of Institutional Choice," *British Journal of Political Science* 35 (2005): 182–90.

9. Manitoba used the STV form of PR to elect MLAs from Winnipeg between 1920 and 1953; Alberta did the same for MLAs from Edmonton and Calgary between 1926 and 1955. Both provinces used the alternative vote in roughly the same periods to elect MLAs from rural areas; B.C. used AV in 1952 and 1953.

10. William Cross, "The Rush to Electoral Reform in the Canadian Provinces: Why Now?," *Representation* 41 (2005): 78–80.

11. R. Kenneth Carty, "Regional Responses to Electoral Reform," *Canadian Parliamentary Review* 29, no. 1 (2006), 22; elsewhere, R. Kenneth Carty, "Canadians and Electoral Reform: An Impulse to Doing Democracy Differently," *Representation* 40 (2004): 177, notes that lopsided election results are the "dirty secret" of provincial elections.

12. Neil Nevitte and Mebs Kanji, "Canadian Political Culture and Value Change," in Joanna Everitt and Brenda O'Neill, eds., *Citizen Politics: Research and Theory in Canadian Political Behaviour* (Toronto: Oxford University Press, 2002), 56–73.

13. Blais, Dobrzynska, and Indridason.

14. Carty, "Regional Responses," p. 23; Carty, "Canadians and Electoral Reform," p. 176.

15. Norman Ruff, "Electoral Reform and Deliberative Democracy: The British Columbia Citizens' Assembly," in Henry Milner, ed., *Steps Toward Making Every Vote Count: Electoral System Reform in Canada and Its Provinces*, pp. 236–39.

16. Carty, "Canadians and Electoral Reform," pp. 179–80.

17. Brian Doody and Henry Milner, "Twenty Years after René Lévesque Failed to Change the Electoral System, Québec May Be Ready to Act," in Henry Milner, ed., *Steps Toward Making Every Vote Count: Electoral System Reform in Canada and its Provinces*, pp. 273–74.

18. M. Mustapha Archarid et al., "Rapport remis á la Commission spéciale sur la Loi électorale," retrieved April 12, 2006, from www.assnat.qc.ca/fra/37legislature2/commissions/csle/rapport_comite_csle.pdf.

19. Ruff, 236.

20. Elections B.C. randomly selected 100 people for every riding. Those people were invited to meetings explaining the Assembly and the duties of members. Some people pulled out at that point. Names of the remaining people were divided by sex and pulled from a hat. One man and one woman were selected for each constituency. A supplementary selection was undertaken for two aboriginal members.

21. Government of Ontario, Democratic Renewal Secretariat, "McGuinty Government Introduces Referendum Legislation," retrieved October 24, 2006, from http://ogov.newswire. ca/ontario/GPOE/2006/10/24/c3947.html?lmatch=&lang=_e.html.

22. "Electoral Reform on Tap for N.B.?" *Halifax Daily News*, June 21, 2006, p. A13.

23. R. Kenneth Carty, "Regional Responses."

24. Alternative voting requires voters to rank-order the candidates; the ballots are transferred to ensure that the winning candidate has a majority of the vote in the district.

25. Matthew Soberg Shugart and Martin P. Wattenberg, eds., *Mixed-Member Electoral Systems: The Best of Both Worlds?* (Oxford: Oxford University Press, 2001); Patrick Dunleavy and Helen Margetts, "Understanding the Dynamics of Electoral Reform," *International Political Science Review* 16 (1995): 9–29.

26. Patrick Dunleavy and Helen Margetts, "Understanding the Dynamics of Electoral Reform," *International Political Science Review* 16 (1995): 9–29.

27. Australian Senate elections require that voters rank each and every candidate for a district's seats; the BC Citizens' Assembly explicitly rejected this option.

28. The most common quota used is the Droop quota, which divides the total number of votes cast by the number of representatives to be elected plus one, drops the remainder, and adds one to the total. For example, if a district were to elect five MLAs and there were 6,300 votes cast in the district, we would divide 6,300 by 6 (the number of MLAs plus one) to get 1,050. We would then add one to the total to get a quota of 1,051.

29. For example, Doris Anderson, a past president of Fair Vote Canada, a national interest group pushing for electoral reform, denounced STV. See Doris Anderson, "Is a Single Transferable Vote the Way to Go? NO: The Message Should Be Clear for Ontario, STV Is Just Plain Dumb," *The Globe and Mail*, May 6, 2005, p. A21.

30. R. Kenneth Carty, "Turning Voters into Citizens: The Citizens' Assembly and Reforming Democratic Politics," *Democracy and Federalism Series*, 3 (2005), Institute of Intergovernmental Relations, Queen's University, retrieved April 23, 2007, from www.iigr.ca/pdf/publications/384_Turning_Voters_into_Citi.pdf.

31. For example, the STV option decided by the assembly excluded Australian-style "above the line" voting that allows voters to endorse a party-determined ranking of candidates. It did so because limiting the power of parties was central to the decision. See "Record of Proceedings of the Citizens' Assembly on Electoral Reform, September 25–26, 2004," retrieved March 30, 2007, from www.citizensassembly.bc.ca/resources/Record_of_Proceedings_Sept25-26,2004.pdf, pp. 8–9. The MMP system was designed with open lists that allow voters to have maximum choice. See "Record of Proceedings of the Citizens' Assembly on Electoral Reform, October 16–17, 2004," retrieved March 30, 2007, from www.citizensassembly.bc.ca/resources/reports/dmaclachlan-3_0410231052-507.pdf, pp. 8–9.

32. Citizens' Assembly on Electoral Reform, *Making Every Vote Count: The Case for Electoral Reform in British Columbia*, Technical Report (2004), p. 16.

33. Gordon Gibson, "Why Party Politicians Don't Like STV," *Vancouver Sun*, December 14, 2004, p. A15.

34. Although the terms of reference for the assembly did not explicitly rule out an increase in the size of the legislature, the terms of reference stated that the recommendation had to be "limited to the manner by which voters' ballots are translated into seats in the Legislative Assembly." See "Citizens' Assembly on Electoral Reform Terms of Reference and Duties of the Chair," retrieved March 30, 2007, from www.citizensassembly.bc.ca/resources/terms_of_reference.pdf.

35. I am grateful to Lisa Young for this observation.

36. Citizens' Assembly on Electoral Reform, *Technical Report*, p. 91; in the Technical Report's list of critical decisions to be made about various electoral systems, there were four listed for STV, and 12 listed for MMP; see Appendix 10.

37. Citizens' Assembly on Electoral Reform, *Technical Report*, p. 92.

38. For an elaboration on this, see Matthew Soberg Shugart, "Canada 2006: A Dysfunctional FPTP System" retrieved January 24, 2006, from http://fruitsandvotes.com/?p=506.

39. Steven Chase, "A Vote on the Way Canada Votes," *The Globe and Mail*, June 24, 2004, p. A6.

40. Centre for Research and Information on Canada, *Portraits of Canada 2004*, retrieved March 9, 2007, from www.cric.ca/pdf/cahiers/cricpapers_jan2005.pdf.

41. Darrell Bricker and Martin Redfern, "Canadian Perspectives on the Voting System," *Policy Options* (July–August 2001): 22.

Terms and Concepts

electoral systems
proportional representation
mixed-member proportional
single-transferable vote
single-member plurality

manufactured majorities
spurious majorities
district magnitude
electoral formula
Citizen's Assembly

electoral quota
independent candidates
party candidates
majority government
minority government

Questions

1. Explain the principal differences between single-member plurality and proportional representation electoral systems.

2. To what problems in Canada is electoral system reform a solution?

3. What factors seem to determine or promote electoral reform? When do they become more important than those forces resisting change?

4. Should an electoral system ideally foster the voter's selection of an individual candidate or of a political party?

5. Proportional representation systems facilitate the parliamentary election of more parties and of small parties with narrow agendas. Is this desirable or is it something an electoral system should be designed to avoid?

6. According to Jansen, from where does the energy for electoral reform come—political elites, voters, interest groups, academics, or media?

What Is Asymmetrical Federalism and Why Should Canadians Care?

Gerald Baier and Katherine Boothe

Editors' Note

Canadians are strong believers in equality. But this conviction hides as much as it reveals; for, as Aristotle pointed out over 2000 years ago, the language of equality begs the question, Equal in what respect? If we believe in the equality of nations, then we face the claim that Québec is a nation and should be considered one of three founding peoples in Canada: the French, the English, and the First Nations. If we believe in equality of provinces, then Québec is one province among ten with no particular special status. Yet, Québec nationalists insist that Québec is not a province but the homeland of the French language in Canada and the territorial base of the Québec national identity. In one view, Québec is one of three equal units; in the other it is reduced to one in ten. Believing in equality solves nothing: we must address the tough question first posed by Aristotle.

Federalism has been the principal means by which the Constitution has dealt with the distinct cultural and linguistic character of Québec. The French-language majority of the province was given a provincial government it could control. The Constitution assigned government jurisdiction in policy fields of particular importance to the majority population. In most respects all provinces were given the same powers, and each could exercise that jurisdiction according to the priorities of its local population. The constitutional status of the provinces was equal, but with that equal allocation of powers each province could enact different policies. When provinces enjoy the same constitutional status relative to the federal government and one another, federal arrangements are symmetrical.

For some political actors, this is not enough. They argue that some provinces are very small, and others very large. There are some differences across provinces that are so significant that they require differential or special constitutional status or powers. One or more provinces should have constitutional powers, representation in the central institutions of Canadian government, or special influence in the amending formula in the Constitution, that others do not have. This is asymmetrical federalism. Asymmetrical arrangements are as necessary and obvious for some as they are controversial for others.

Understanding the politics of asymmetry is essential to understanding why Canada is a difficult country to govern. In this essay, Gerald Baier and Katherine Boothe examine the idea of asymmetrical federalism and how it operates in Canadian constitutional politics.

◆ ◆ ◆

INTRODUCTION

◆ ◆ ◆

Given the complexity of most federal systems of government, Canadians can be forgiven for not always appreciating all of the subtleties of power sharing and negotiations that go on between their two constitutionally recognized levels of government. To add to the confusion, politicians eager to suggest that they are doing things differently than their partisan opponents or predecessors will often coin new terms to describe their unique approach to federal–provincial relations.

Article prepared for this publication. © Nelson, 2008.

Canadians are thus faced with an abundance of "federalisms," the basic system modified by adjectives like "cooperative," "collaborative," "open," or "new." "Asymmetrical" federalism is yet another descriptor of Canada's federal system, and, like others, is full of subtleties and perhaps multiple meanings or even contradictions. Federal and provincial politicians in Canada have recently begun to celebrate the idea of asymmetry and at least claim to have enshrined it as a principle of Canadian federalism.

What exactly does asymmetrical federalism mean, and why should Canadians care? We take asymmetry to mean treating different parts of a federation differently from one another (i.e., not symmetrically). How that actually happens can often be complicated. There are a variety of ways that asymmetry can be put into practice but depending on the context, some kinds of asymmetrical federalism are more important than others. This essay looks at the different types of asymmetry and at the state of asymmetry in Canadian federalism and speculates on the kinds of asymmetries that Canada may need to remain a relatively smoothly running federation.

We recognize that to say that any given federation is asymmetrical seems a truism. Perfect uniformity of size, population, or characteristics such as language and culture is an impossibility. In their most readily identifiable characteristics the subunits of any federation are naturally unequal. But, there are kinds of natural diversities and inequalities that are more consequential than others. A federation in which a single province or state contains the overwhelming majority of the population will obviously operate differently than a federation where there are groups of big and small subunits, or where population is relatively equally distributed. A federation in which one or two states or provinces are the only among several with a majority of practitioners of one language or religion will work differently than a federation with a relatively homogenous linguistic or religious makeup. Asymmetrical federalism is the attempt to recognize those differences and take them into account in the setting of the decision-making rules and political institutions of the federation. A wildly diverse federation could operate with no asymmetrical features at all and treat its unit parts the same regardless of their differences. We argue that the extent to which a federation sincerely tries to accommodate its differences through asymmetrical features is worth caring about, as it is ultimately revealing of the values that underlie the

federation itself. Whether the Canadian federal system is making appropriate use of the potential of asymmetrical federalism is a question of concern.

> ... the extent to which a federation sincerely tries to accommodate its differences through asymmetrical features is worth caring about, as it is ultimately revealing of the values that underlie the federation itself.

THE IDEA OF ASYMMETRY
◆ ◆ ◆

Federations are always characterized by differences and inequalities. Asymmetry is about according those inequalities or differences some kind of standing in decision making. If economic or other practical conditions differ from state to state or province to province, the necessary preconditions for asymmetry exist. As Canadians are acutely aware, a look at the map of any federation usually reveals startling differences of geography, climate, and population patterns. There are invariably deviations among the subunits of a federation in physical size, population (size and demographic features), natural resources, economy, language, and culture. Although it would be theoretically possible to modify subunit boundaries to create more uniform units, in most federations this is such a remote possibility that we can safely think of these differences as "natural."[1] We should not go so far as to classify differences as asymmetries. Doing so misses a critical step. Asymmetry exists only if the relevant differences are recognized *politically*; otherwise they are just differences and more suitable as research subjects for geographers or demographers. It is not inevitable that underlying differences be accommodated by asymmetrical arrangements; in most federations many "natural" differences go unrecognized by political relationships.

Asymmetries matter because they are *relational*, that is, they are alterations in the otherwise natural relationship that subunits have with the central government or with each other. Most asymmetries are likely to be used positively, to grant special treatment or recognition to a subunit. This can be done out of a sense of justice, or can be a status secured in the negotiations that bring in new subunits, or entice them to stay. The possibility of negative asymmetry is not unheard of, but usually results in a claim for equal treatment from the province or state affected.

Federations are always characterized by differences and inequalities. Asymmetry is about according those inequalities or differences some kind of standing in decision making.

One of the earliest writers on asymmetrical federalism, Charles Tarlton, contrasts an asymmetrical system with a "model symmetrical federal system, [where] each state would maintain essentially the same relationship to the central authority."[2] This factor is important because it means that some political or policy differences between subunits, such as the choice of different provincial sales tax rates or provincial relations with municipalities in Canada, should not be characterized as asymmetries. Provinces have autonomy in their constitutionally assigned jurisdictions, and differences in their approaches to similar problems are to be expected. Therefore, it is more useful to conceptualize asymmetries *as differences in relationships within a federation* (for example, control over different policy areas for different governments) rather than simple differences in policy choices within an area that all subunits have the same constitutionally assigned jurisdiction.

Asymmetrical arrangements must be *political* as well as *relational*. Keeping in mind that asymmetries are primarily a means for accommodating difference, we can categorize types of asymmetries according to the *venue* for accommodating difference (constitutional and nonconstitutional) and the *type of difference* to be accommodated (where the most important division is between cultural/linguistic differences, what we call recognition differences, and other pragmatic, often economic, differences).

Authors often distinguish types of asymmetry as being *de facto* (in fact) or *de jure* (as a matter of law), but as noted above, *de facto* asymmetries often become conflated with differences and inequalities or what we called above the preconditions for asymmetry. It is actually difficult to draw a clear dividing line between *de facto* and *de jure* asymmetries. For example, constitutional opt-out/opt-in provisions, which allow a subunit to choose whether it wishes the central government to administer a particular policy area as part of a national program, or whether the subunit would rather receive its share of central government

funds and administer the policy area itself, are difficult to place. When these provisions are constitutionally entrenched, but used to create different programs only by some subunits, should they be characterized as *de facto* or *de jure* asymmetries?

Using the categories "constitutional" and "nonconstitutional" avoids this problem and focuses attention on the venue in which the asymmetrical relationship is expressed. Constitutional asymmetries appear in the constitutional texts or other constitutional forms such as organic statutes, conventions, or judicial interpretations. They might include the division of jurisdictional responsibilities, procedures for constitutional amendment, and legal processes (such as Québec's unique civil code in Canada).[3] Another important element of constitutional asymmetry is institutional: asymmetrical relationships may be expressed in the design of the upper and lower legislative houses of the national government, the judiciary, and other political institutions. Note that this is a fairly narrow definition of institutions: they are themselves defined by constitutions, statutes, or stable constitutional conventions. Nonconstitutional asymmetries are expressed in policy, political practice, or habit, and may also be contained in intergovernmental agreements, particularly in federations characterized by bargaining among federal and provincial executives, such as Canada. Note that the difficult-to-classify opt-out provisions may be constitutional or nonconstitutional, depending on whether the relationship being opted out of is formal or informal. For example, provisions for opting out of a constitutionally assigned jurisdiction are a constitutional asymmetry, whereas opting out of an intergovernmental agreement is nonconstitutional.

The second dimension we use to categorize asymmetries is the type of difference the asymmetrical relationship accommodates. Although it could be argued that all asymmetrical arrangements recognize or acknowledge difference in some way, dividing these differences into recognition-based differences (primarily culture and language) and pragmatic differences (often but not necessarily economic) reflects a central distinction of purpose. Recognition asymmetries do not necessarily accommodate practical interests. Many federations seek to minimize recognition-based asymmetries with singular national mythologies or cultures (i.e., a melting pot not a mosaic). More accommodative federations, Canada among them, may actually seek opportunities to recognize and even affirm the maintenance of a different status for different parts of the country. Recognition-based asymmetries are generally an effort to preserve differences that equal treatment by the national government might otherwise diminish. For example, by giving a culturally distinct subunit control over policy areas pertaining to a matter like language, the subunit is able to preserve its distinctiveness, perhaps even enhance it. Recognition asymmetry is not without controversy. Canada's constitutional struggles in the 1980s and 1990s turned in large part on efforts to grant recognition asymmetry, and several participants in those constitutional wars staked out positions quite hostile to that very idea.

Pragmatic asymmetries, on the other hand, are often meant to mitigate the effect of natural differences. For example, regional development programs may be designed to reduce economic disparities between subunits. This is not always the case, of course. Recent discussions in Canadian health policy demonstrate that some provinces may enter asymmetrical relationships with the national government to realize policy preferences unrelated to language or culture.

Canada's constitutional struggles in the 1980s and 1990s turned in large part on efforts to grant recognition asymmetry, and several participants in those constitutional wars staked out positions quite hostile to that very idea.

For example, Alberta's unavailing motions toward a "third way" for health care might have resulted in enough reductions in federal transfer payments to amount to an asymmetrical funding arrangement with the national government. The table below provides some more examples of the four types of asymmetries we have described here.[4]

Varieties of Asymmetry

---

1. Venue for Accommodating Difference
   a. Constitutional
      - Constitutional/statutory/institutional
      - Jurisdiction, amendment, legal processes, etc.
   b. Nonconstitutional
      - Policy, practice, habit
      - Nonbinding intergovernmental agreements
2. Type of Difference to be Accommodated
   a. Recognition
      - Recognize and preserve cultural/linguistic differences
      - "Distinct society" clause
      - Only New Brunswick and Québec in *la francophonie*
      - New Brunswick's constitutionally entrenched bilingualism
      - Only Québec choosing to opt in on immigration and parental leave benefits
      - Recognize and mitigate/accommodate more pragmatic differences (often but not necessarily economic)
   b. Pragmatic
      - Mobility rights [s. 6(4), *Charter*]
      - Asymmetrical representation of provinces in House and Senate
      - Regional development programs
      - "Side deals" in intergovernmental relations

WHAT ARE THE IMPLICATIONS OF ASYMMETRY?

Some asymmetries may be expected to preserve differences, and others to mitigate or even lessen differences. Different types of asymmetry will have different implications, and will be more or less important depending on the type of federation. For example, recognition-based asymmetries may have different implications for national unity and federal trust in a federation with multiple culturally or linguistically distinct subunits than in a federation that is basically culturally or linguistically homogenous, but with one distinctive subunit (such as Québec). We might also expect asymmetries to affect the equality of citizens and/or subunits, and in some cases, the levels of stability, legitimacy, and democratic participation in a federation.

When Canadians think about asymmetrical federalism, they are usually focused on the importance of constitutional, recognition-based asymmetries. Québec's cultural and linguistic distinctiveness within Canada, and its traditional demands for formal constitutional recognition, seem to demand no less.[5] Canadians outside Québec, including federal politicians committed to constitutional change, often want to demonstrate the capacity for the federation to protect group identities through formal powers and accept the government of Québec as a *de facto* representative for the French fact in Canada. Those opposed to recognition asymmetry usually wish to endorse a different political philosophy, either a liberal conception that puts the idea of individual rights ahead of group rights and characteristics, or one that challenges the idea that Québec alone needs recognition.

When Canadians think about asymmetrical federalism, they are usually focused on the importance of constitutional, recognition-based asymmetries. Québec's cultural and linguistic distinctiveness within Canada, and its traditional demands for formal constitutional recognition, seem to demand no less.

Canadians may have to pay greater attention to the role of nonconstitutional, recognition asymmetries, although it has been argued that these types of arrangements may be less satisfactory when it comes to easing tensions in multinational federations.[6] Recognition just seems more sincere (and judicially enforceable) when it is enshrined in the Constitution. Canadian authors though have begun to focus attention on more informal and pragmatic asymmetries.[7] We revisit this point in the conclusion.

HOW MUCH ASYMMETRY DOES CANADA REALLY HAVE?

◆ ◆ ◆

Given our stricter definitions for what truly qualify as elements of asymmetrical federalism, how does Canadian practice measure up? Canada's constitutional asymmetries, not surprisingly, start in the text itself. The initial division of powers in sections 91 and 92 of the *Constitution Act* did not contemplate much if any asymmetry in the basic assignment of legislative jurisdictions to the provinces. The division of powers leaves a lot of room for provincial variation in the formulation of basic institutional arrangements in the provinces. For example, the nature and structure of provincial court systems are decisions left to the provinces in section 92(14). That the provinces have used some of their assigned powers differently, however, is a sign of provincial autonomy, not asymmetry. The recognition that Québec will use civil law, while asymmetrical, is perhaps still more a matter of the province exercising autonomy in an area where it has constitutional jurisdiction. Given that the civil code was already in use for private law in that province, its preservation is probably more a matter of pragmatic than recognition asymmetry.[8]

Where special needs related to jurisdiction might have necessitated some asymmetry in the Constitution, the Fathers of Confederation preferred to universalize entitlements for the provinces with the unstated presumption that only some will take up the offer. That is probably the appropriate interpretation of the separate schools provisions in section 93 of the *Constitution Act, 1867*. That section limited provincial autonomy to alter existing arrangements for separate denominational school boards and extended the right to such boards to all provinces post-Confederation. The amendments to the Constitution that brought Manitoba, Alberta, Saskatchewan, and Newfoundland into Confederation altered the application of section 93 for those individual provinces in ways that may be considered asymmetrical. Even more explicitly, section 93A was added to the Constitution in 1997, exempting Québec from section 93's provisions altogether.

As the section 93 example illustrates, the terms of union for provinces that joined after Confederation do make some asymmetrical overtures. The guarantee of certain rights such as subsidized ferry service for Prince Edward Island were features of the settlements necessary to lure those provinces into Confederation. Few of those terms of union create asymmetrical differences for the provinces in terms of jurisdiction. One exception was the seeming preclusion of Alberta and Saskatchewan from complete jurisdiction over nonrenewable natural resources, their ownership, and raising of revenue from their extraction. That seemingly negative asymmetry was remedied by the addition of section 92A in the 1982 amendments to the Constitution.

In terms of representation, both houses of Canada's national legislature have asymmetrical features. While the lower house is nominally a house of representation by population, some effort has been made to preserve higher levels of representation for smaller or older provinces, a practice that may be considered asymmetrical. The guarantee (in Section 51A of the *Constitution Act*) that no province will have fewer Members of Parliament than Senators (the so-called "Senate floor") has resulted in the overrepresentation of PEI and New Brunswick in the lower house. Constitutional changes in the *Representation Act, 1985* required that no province have fewer representatives than it did as a result of the redistribution of house seats in 1976. This "grandfathering" provision again overrepresents some of the smaller provinces in the lower house.

In terms of representation, both houses of Canada's national legislature have asymmetrical features.

Likewise the upper house was always meant to be asymmetrical. The Senate of Canada, like the Senate of the United States, recognizes asymmetry by treating unequals equally. The unequals in this case are regions, a concept sometimes coterminous with provincial boundaries and sometimes not. Canada's Senate regions are Ontario, Québec. the Maritimes (Nova Scotia, New Brunswick, and PEI) and the Western provinces, each of which is entitled to 24 senators. By having equal representation for four separate regions (plus individual senatorial seats for the territories and a half dozen for Newfoundland and Labrador) the upper house not only represents sober second thought, but nominally the regions. Its ineffectiveness at being a voice for regional concerns is usually considered to be more a result of its general lack of electoral legitimacy and the appointment practices of past governments. Advocates of Senate reform have usually been hostile to the particular asymmetry of the present representational compromise and instead advocate the American-style equal representation of all provinces, big or small.[9]

The amending formulae for future changes to the Constitution are in some ways asymmetrical, though somewhat deceptively so. The challenge for their authors, dating back to early attempts at finding an amending procedure in the 1960s, was to recognize both the different stakes that some provinces would attach to constitutional change, and the informally held notion that Québec needed to have the ability to block constitutional changes that would inhibit its autonomy or uniqueness. Amending proposals such as the Fulton-Favereau formula, and the amending formulae eventually enshrined by the 1982 changes, acknowledge that some kinds of constitutional change required equal treatment of the provinces (in its way an asymmetry for the smaller provinces) and that other kinds of change should be possible with something closer to a simple popular majority, with some weighting of the process to ensure that population (and thus big provinces) would not always win the day.

The distinct-society clause proposed in the Meech Lake Accord, a package of constitutional amendments attempted in the mid-1980s, was perhaps the most asymmetrical constitutional recognition ever contemplated

for the Canadian federation. The distinct-society clause was meant to be an interpretive clause, that is, a signal to courts and governments to interpret the remainder of the Constitution (including the *Charter of Rights and Freedoms*) in a way consistent with the recognition of Québec as a distinct society within Canada. Just like section 1 of the *Charter*, which requires courts to allow reasonable limits on rights if other values of a free and democratic society are being pursued, distinct society could potentially limit rights. The individual rights enshrined nationally in the Charter would, in theory, be subject to limits that advance the prior guarantee that the National Assembly of Québec could make laws to promote and preserve the distinct society of that province.

The distinct-society clause proposed in the Meech Lake Accord, a package of constitutional amendments attempted in the mid-1980s, was perhaps the most asymmetrical constitutional recognition ever contemplated for the Canadian federation.

Opponents of the clause were probably more upset with its special treatment of one province than with its potential to limit individual rights. It is by no means clear that, armed with the distinct-society clause, Québec's National Assembly would have embarked on a program of laws to radically repress languages other than French, or to make laws that would somehow revive Duplessis-era notions of the traditional roles of family, religion, and society.[10] The *Charter* already provides justification for legislatures that want to pass laws that limit *Charter* rights in the pursuit of some other legislative objective. Section 1 of the *Charter*, another interpretive clause, acknowledges that the rights in the Constitution are subject to limits that can be demonstrably justified in a free and democratic society. Combined with the Supreme Court's endorsement of the value of federalism and the protection of minorities in the *Reference Re: Secession of Québec*, one could reasonably expect the Court to uphold laws aimed at the protection of Québec's distinct society regardless of the failure to include an explicit guarantee in the Constitution. The clause clearly recognized that Québec was different than other provinces and would have enshrined that recognition in the Constitution. In fact, that recognition was the whole point.

Asymmetries are much more common in the nonconstitutional elements of the Canadian federal system. Accommodative practices such as regional representation in the federal cabinet or the (unofficial) appointment of a Québec lieutenant to the prime minister are indications that all provinces are not created equal in the operation of the national government. The interactions of governments through intergovernmental relations, and the accords and agreements that are the product of those relationships, often result in asymmetrical outcomes. This is particularly true when one accepts that the definition of nonconstitutional includes arrangements that still have some expression in law. For example, following the 1995 Québec referendum, the Parliament of Canada passed legislation lending its veto over constitutional change to provinces and regions of the country. If this were a practice enshrined in the Constitution we would have to classify it differently. Because the law can be easily revoked by a future parliament, it seems more appropriate to classify it as nonconstitutional, but still a recognition-based asymmetry.

Some nonconstitutional asymmetries have significant consequences for the provinces that they affect. Offshore oil and gas is a growing industry in some of Canada's coastal provinces. Jurisdictionally those resources are assigned to the federal government by the Constitution. Through a series of accords with Newfoundland and Labrador and Nova Scotia, the two Atlantic provinces most engaged in the oil and gas business, the federal government has essentially created an asymmetrical arrangement that not only allows those provinces to be actively engaged in the regulation of the offshore resources, but exempts them from some substantial revenue clawbacks that would otherwise significantly affect their entitlements under the federal equalization program.[11] Other coastal provinces have not been given the same generous treatment; in fact, British Columbia is still under a federally imposed moratorium on offshore oil exploration.

Additionally, intergovernmental agreements and accords are not always one-size-fits-all products. Side deals for individual provinces, often involving federal revenues, might be seen as asymmetrical. The post-1995 era of intergovernmental relations, marked as it was by Québec's refusal to negotiate with the federal government and the provinces, featured a unique asymmetry summarized by some as "federalism with a footnote." Intergovernmental agreements in the period, the Social Union Framework Agreement among them, often acknowledged that they were agreed to by the federal government and nine of the provinces and that a separate agreement, signalled by an asterisk or in a footnote, would be reached bilaterally between the Québec and federal governments to provide similar services or programs. Many of the conditions and results were roughly the same, but a symbolic asymmetry was recognized.[12]

The post-1995 era of intergovernmental relations, marked as it was by Québec's refusal to negotiate with the federal government and the provinces, featured a unique asymmetry summarized by some as "federalism with a footnote."

Opt-in/opt-out asymmetries, as we noted above, can have constitutional and nonconstitutional expressions. When provinces choose to use constitutional powers available to all provinces, but selectively taken up, they must negotiate implementation agreements with the federal government. The agreements are generally malleable and subject to revision over time, with some exceptions. Québec's choice to have a public pension plan is a relatively permanent asymmetry. However, its choice to use its share of jurisdiction for immigration requires it to have considerable interaction with the federal government to create the programs that other provinces will not. That the option is available to all provinces makes the asymmetry less obvious perhaps, but it is a pragmatic recognition that some provinces will attach more importance to some issues than will others.

Likewise, the federal government can have asymmetrical effects in the delivery of its own programs. Many of those asymmetries are pragmatic ones, recognizing the challenges that provinces face in providing similar services when they have different geographic and economic circumstances. Federal programs for regional development are generally asymmetrical. While there are programs for most parts of the country, including those regions that nominally do not need development assistance, the bulk of funding is likely to go to those provinces where the perceived need is greatest.

HOW MUCH ASYMMETRY SHOULD CANADA HAVE?

◆ ◆ ◆

As we demonstrated above, asymmetrical arrangements are a response to the natural differences that exist in any federation. We have emphasized that not all asymmetries are created equal. Particularly important is the difference between asymmetry for pragmatic reasons and asymmetry for symbolic or recognition purposes. The latter kind of asymmetry, particularly when constitutionalized, tends to be much more controversial, as debate over the distinct-society clause clearly demonstrated. The institutionalization of "special" rights or status for one province or a category of provinces runs up against a general liberal, egalitarian attitude and pits notions of collective rights against the dominant North American individual rights paradigm.

The institutionalization of "special" rights or status for one province or a category of provinces runs up against a general liberal, egalitarian attitude and pits notions of collective rights against the dominant North American individual rights paradigm.

Canada, like all federations, is unique in the structure of its natural differences. The differences that come from geography, language, and culture are what made federalism appealing in the first place for a country whose political culture at its founding certainly could not have been more adoring of unitary, parliamentary government. To repeat a point we have made already, federalism alone is not asymmetry. The asymmetry that counts is political and relational. When thinking about the kinds of asymmetry that Canada needs or should have it is important to keep in mind that not all of the proposals or practices that elites currently identify as asymmetrical may truly be so. Asymmetry has taken on a kind of currency in intergovernmental relations and the mega politics of Québec and Canadian nationalism that is meant to signal a general attitude of compromise and accommodation and respect for provincial autonomy, but real asymmetry is measurable on simple indicators like those we have suggested here.

If Canada needs some asymmetrical arrangements they might not be of the kind that is most obvious or

that most commonly advocated by proponents of reform in the federal system. Canadians demonstrated sufficient frustration with attempts at constitutional reform in the 1990s; most governments and leaders have shied away from grand proposals for constitutional change and exercises in national self-definition. As a result, there has been less call for "distinct–society" kinds of asymmetry. Accompanying that trend has been a lingering feeling that there are still institutional deficiencies in practices like electoral systems, party discipline, and the deliberative capacity of our legislatures. Many of the provinces have undertaken efforts at democratic reform focusing on internal institutional reforms at the provincial level (largely electoral systems). Successive federal governments have also talked about making changes to the operation of Parliament. The Council of the Federation has tried to change the way that governments interact with each other. If all these changes occur, they may remedy some concerns about the quality of Canadian democracy, but they may also have the potential to alter and even undermine some of the informal practices that have helped to accommodate the natural asymmetries of the federation.[13]

Given the nature of the Canadian federation and the long-standing accommodative challenge of Québec (including continuing fears of separation), it is no surprise that asymmetry initiatives still focus on Québec. Recognition asymmetry is the tool most likely to be used to address the big questions of national unity. The old Levesque-era notion of sovereignty association is in some ways just an extreme form of federalism: one province having a singularly different relationship with the rest of the federation. Given the general support for the idea of treating provinces equally for most constitutional entitlements, excessive constitutional asymmetry seems an unlikely prospect, even if it would highlight the willingness of Canada outside Québec to be accommodating.

The kind of asymmetry that the Canadian federal system requires most might be the nonconstitutional forms that are focused less on recognition and more on mitigating pragmatic differences. In fact these practices might be the pressure release that makes constitutional recognition of differences less necessary. As long as the federal government wishes to use its spending power as a way of having influence on areas of provincial jurisdiction, these kinds of accommodations are necessary. If intergovernmental relations become more formalized as a result of the kinds of internal institutional changes on the democratization agenda, those kinds of informal accommodations may be less easy to achieve.

The kind of asymmetry that the Canadian federal system requires most might be the nonconstitutional forms that are focused less on recognition and more on mitigating pragmatic differences.

CONCLUSION

♦ ♦ ♦

Relations between Ottawa and the provinces in the early years of the new century have, like the late years of the last, been marked by a real dependence on nonconstitutional intergovernmental agreements. No federal government has been willing to genuinely open the constitutional file since the failure of the Charlottetown Accord referendum in 1992. Informal changes to the way that the federation works have been hammered out through pacts and accords—some general, others quite specific. This approach is more piecemeal than the comprehensive constitutional change of the past; governments appear to be responding to issues and crises as they arise rather than setting out longer-term goals or principles for the federation. The result has been some "flavour-of-the-month" approaches to intergovernmental relations. In the early period after the Charlottetown Accord, the flavour was to show Quebeckers that federalism worked. Other projects have included pledges toward a "social union" and the reduction of Canada's internal trade barriers. Asymmetry has taken on some of the characteristics of the latest flavour of the month without much of the substance that we have argued is a necessary part of recognizing differences.

In 2004, the federal government negotiated a comprehensive Health Accord with the provinces that offered the provinces more funding in exchange for provincial commitment to national goals on waiting times for basic services. The Accord included an appendix that recognized Québec's distinctiveness and its ability to impose its own unique standards and measures for wait-time goals. The appendix defines asymmetrical federalism as "flexible federalism that notably allows for the existence of specific agreements and arrangements adapted to Québec's specificity."[14] This doesn't appear to mean much beyond recognizing the ability of Québec to implement policy in its constitutionally prescribed field of health care in whatever manner it chooses. What is worrying is that talking the

language of asymmetry without actually following through with genuine power may be a dangerous practice. According seemingly preferential treatment may bother Canadians outside Québec, and that province gets genuinely little extra autonomy or capacity in return. Nods to asymmetry, even if it is little more than a rhetorical asymmetry, may give the public impression of special treatment for Québec in ways that older, less celebrated forms of conciliation might not have. In other words, the quiet accommodation of difference through flexible arrangements that has been a trademark of Canadian federalism's durability is now set aside for essentially shallow acknowledgments of difference that are trumpeted as genuine asymmetry.

One of the paradoxes of recognizing differences in a federation is that even though differences complicate relationships, there is often little incentive to reduce or eliminate them.

One of the paradoxes of recognizing differences in a federation is that even though differences complicate relationships, there is often little incentive to reduce or eliminate them. Reducing pragmatic differences of economic conditions or fortune is an obvious exception. Asymmetrical relationships that recognize cultural and linguistic diversity in federations intentionally perpetuate difference, or at the least protect diverse characteristics from being universalized. Granting such recognition can be tricky, particularly in constitutional arrangements, as it can have an alienating effect on parts of the country that do not see a need for differential treatment. Nonconstitutional recognition can help recognize important differences, but can fail to give the real power necessary to really protect differences, which is presumably the point of asymmetry. The choices facing governments in dealing with difference seem to give them few good options. If asymmetrical federalism has an appeal, it is in the goodwill that the federal system is extending to one of its parts by recognizing the need for a different arrangement for one or more of its parts. If new arrangements are advertised as asymmetrical, but offer little real difference in relationships, they get the worst of both worlds, and asymmetry becomes just another meaningless adjective to append to our current description of how intergovernmental relations are done. The idea will quickly be in danger of losing its appeal.

Notes

1. In Canada there have occasionally been calls for unification of the Maritime provinces or of the prairie provinces to give those regions a more equal footing with the larger provinces. As Alan Cairns notes, the Maritime provinces have tenaciously resisted amalgamation on more than one occasion (see "The Governments and Societies of Canadian Federalism," *Canadian Journal of Political Science* X, December 1977, 701.) For an example of such a proposal, see John J. Deutsch and Fred R. Drummie, *The Report on Maritime Union: Commissioned by the Governments of Nova Scotia, New Brunswick, and Prince Edward Island* (Fredericton: Maritime Union Study, 1970).

2. Charles D. Tarlton, "Symmetry and Asymmetry as Elements of Federalism," *Journal of Politics* 27 (September, 1965): 861–874.

3. Michael Burgess, "Asymmetrical Federalism and Federation," in Michael Burgess, *Comparative Federalism: Theory and Practice*, (New York: Routledge, 2006).

4. David Milne includes a table that informed our choice of examples; see "Equality or Asymmetry: Why Choose?" in Ronald L. Watts and Douglas M. Brown (eds.) *Options for a New Canada* (Toronto: University of Toronto Press, 1991).

5. See, for example, Peter M. Leslie, "Asymmetry: Rejected, Conceded, Imposed," in Leslie F. Seidle (ed.), *Seeking a New Canadian Partnership: Asymmetrical and Confederal Options* (Toronto: Institute for Research on Public Policy, 1994); and Reg Whitaker, "The Dog That Never Barked: Who Killed Asymmetrical Federalism?" in Kenneth McRoberts and Patrick Monohan (eds.), *The Charlottetown Accord, the Referendum, and the Future of Canada* (Toronto: University of Toronto Press, 1993).

6. See for example Alain-G. Gagnon, "The Moral Foundations of Asymmetrical Federalism" in Alain-G. Gagnon and James Tully (eds.). *Multinational Democracies* (Cambridge, UK: Cambridge University Press, 2001); and John McGarry, 2005, "Asymmetrical Federalism and the Plurinational State," paper presented at the 3rd International Conference on Federalism, Brussels, 3–5 March. Retrieved March 29, 2006, from http://federalism2005.be/en/home/conference_papers.

7. See the 2005 Institute of Intergovernmental Relations Working Paper series on asymmetry, which includes a number of papers concerned with asymmetry in the 2004 Health Accord.

8. Guy Laforest suggests that the retention of Lower Canada's uniqueness in the Constitution was seen as a pragmatic or political necessity by the founders. He cites as early evidence of constitutional asymmetry the securing of the Civil Code for Québec. See "The Historical and Legal Origins of Asymmetrical Federalism in Canada's Founding Debates: A Brief Interpretive Note," *IIGR Working Paper 2005* (8) (Institute of Intergovernmental Relations, Queen's University, 2005).

9. Senators Jack Austin and Lowell Murray introduced legislation in the Senate in the fall of 2006 intended to pursue a constitutional amendment to increase Senate representation for Alberta and British Columbia—the two most disadvantaged provinces under the terms of the present representational formula.

10. Opponents of the Québec government's sign laws would probably differ on this point. For an impassioned example see, Mordecai Richler, *Oh Canada! Oh Quebec!: Requiem for a Divided Country* (New York: Viking, 1992).

11. See in particular the 2005 accords that limit the effect of oil and gas revenues on equalization entitlements. *Agreement between the Government of Canada and the Government of Newfoundland and Labrador on Offshore Revenues, 2005* and *Agreement on Offshore Revenues between the Government of Canada and Nova Scotia, 2005*.

12. Alain Noël, "Without Quebec: Collaborative Federalism with a Footnote" *Policy Matters* Vol. 1 Issue 2 (March, 2000).

13. Gerald Baier, Herman Bakvis and Douglas M. Brown, "Executive Federalism, the Democratic Deficit and Parliamentary Reform" in G. Bruce Doern, ed., *How Ottawa Spends 2005–2006* (Montreal and Kingston: McGill-Queen's University Press, 2005).

14. "Asymmetrical Federalism that Respects Quebec's Jurisdiction," *Press release,* September 15, 2004; retrieved May 26, 2006, from www.hc-sc.gc.ca/hcs-sss/delivery-prestation/ fptcollab/2004-fmm-rpm/bg-fi_quebec_e.html.

Bibliography

Agreement between the Government of Canada and the Government of Newfoundland and Labrador on Offshore Revenues, 2005.

Agreement on Offshore Revenues between the Government of Canada and Nova Scotia, 2005.

"Asymmetrical Federalism that respects Quebec's jurisdiction," *Press release,* September 15, 2004; retrieved May 26, 2006, from www.hc-sc.gc.ca/hcs-sss/delivery-prestation/fptcollab/2004-fmm-rpm/bg-fi_quebec_e.html.

Baier, Gerald, Herman Bakvis, and Douglas M. Brown. "Executive Federalism, the Democratic Deficit and Parliamentary Reform." In G. Bruce Doern (ed). *How Ottawa Spends 2005–2006*. Montreal and Kingston: McGill-Queen's University Press, 2005.

Brock, Kathy L. "Accord and Discord: The Politics of Asymmetrical Federalism and Intergovernmental Relations." *IIGR Working Paper 2005*. Institute of Inter-governmental Relations, Queen's University, 2005.

Burgess, Michael. "Asymmetrical Federalism and Federation." In Michael Burgess. *Comparative Federalism: Theory and Practice*. New York: Routledge, 2006.

Cairns, Alan. 1977. "The Governments and Societies of Canadian Federalism," *Canadian Journal of Political Science* X, December.

Conservative Party of Canada. (nd). "Open Federalism." *Conservative Party of Canada webpage*. Retrieved March 14, 2007, from www.conservative.ca/EN/2692/41617.

Deutsch, John J. and Fred R. Drummie. *The Report on Maritime Union: Commissioned by the Governments of Nova Scotia, New Brunswick, and Prince Edward Island.* Fredericton: Maritime Union Study, 1970.

"First Minister's Meeting on the Future of Health Care 2004," *Press release,* September 16, 2004. Retrieved March 14, 2007, from www.hc-sc.gc.ca/hcs-sss/delivery-prestation/fptcollab/2004-fmm-rpm/index_e.html.

Gagnon, Alain-G. "The Moral Foundations of Asymmetrical Federalism." In Alain-G. Gagnon and James Tully (eds.). *Multinational Democracies*. Cambridge. UK: Cambridge University Press, 2001.

LaForest, Guy. "The Historical and Legal Origins of Asymmetrical Federalism in Canada's Founding Debates: A Brief Interpretive Note." *IIGR Working Paper 2005* (8). Institute of Intergovernmental Relations, Queen's University, 2005.

Leslie, Peter M. "Asymmetry: Rejected, Conceded, Imposed." In Leslie F. Seidle (ed.). *Seeking a New Canadian Partnership: Asymmetrical and Confederal Options.* Toronto: Institute for Research on Public Policy. 1994.

McGarry, John. "Asymmetrical Federalism and the Plurinational State." Paper presented at the 3rd International Conference on Federalism, Brussels, March 3–5, 2005. Retrieved March 19, 2006, from http://federalism2005.be/en/home/conference_papers.

Milne, David. "Equality or Asymmetry: Why Choose?" In Ronald L. Watts and Douglas M. Brown (eds.) *Options for a New Canada.* Toronto: University of Toronto Press, 1991.

Noël, Alain. "Without Quebec: Collaborative Federalism with a Footnote." *Policy Matters* Vol. 1 Issue 2 (March 2000).

Tarlton, Charles D. 1965. "Symmetry and Asymmetry as Elements of Federalism." *Journal of Politics* 27 (September): 861–74.

Whitaker, Reg. "The Dog That Never Barked: Who Killed Asymmetrical Federalism?" In Kenneth McRoberts and Patrick Monohan (eds.). *The Charlottetown Accord, the Referendum, and the Future of Canada*. Toronto: University of Toronto Press, 1993.

Terms and Concepts

federalism	constitutional asymmetry	pragmatic asymmetry
asymmetrical federalism	nonconstitutional asymmetries	"federalism with a footnote"
natural diversities	recognition asymmetry	

Questions

1. What is asymmetrical federalism? Why do some federations have it?

2. What is the difference between provincial autonomy and asymmetry?

3. In Canada, is constitutional asymmetry most evident more in the division of powers, the design of central institutions, or the rules for amending the Constitution?

4. Is asymmetry more evident in constitutional or nonconstitutional elements of the Canadian federation?

5. How might we determine when "natural" differences or inequalities among provinces ought to be recognized in asymmetrical constitutional forms?

6. Are there some natural diversities that are simply too great to be accommodated by asymmetrical devices in Canada? If so, what would be the evidence for this?

Just What the Doctor Ordered: Private Health Insurance and the *Charter*

Thomas M. J. Bateman

Editors' Note

Normally, courts try people for alleged breaches of a law. The question is whether the facts of the case meet the legal definition of the infraction. But when the *Charter* is involved, the courts are asked to measure a law against the constitutional standard contained in the *Charter*. In a sense it is the law that is on trial. In a trial, the accused can say, "I didn't do it." In the age of the *Charter*, the accused can say, "Whether I did it is irrelevant. The law violates a *Charter* right and is therefore null and void." When courts engage this latter argument, they exercise what is called judicial review.

It is a truism of this country's political life that Canadians love their *Charter of Rights*. After all, who wouldn't want constitutionally entrenched safeguards for our fundamental rights? Who wouldn't want to give judges the power to prevent bigoted majorities from engaging in blatant acts of racism, as our

country did in the notorious case of the Japanese-Canadians in World War II?

Yet scholars have pointed out that *Charter* decisions almost never deal with black-and-white cases of human rights abuses. Most *Charter* decisions actually involve questions in the grey zone, matters on which reasonable and fair-minded people will reasonably disagree. To the extent that *Charter* cases often have important consequences for public policy, then, political scientists are faced with some important but difficult questions about the *Charter*'s status as a political institution. Where and how should we draw the line between "rights" and "policy?" How far into the realm of "policy" should the courts go as they grapple with questions of "right?" What are the political implications of having courts deal with matters that are at least to some extent questions of policy?

In thinking about these questions, it is important to keep in mind the nature of judicial decision making. As legal institutions, courts arrive at decisions by applying principles. Where the necessary principles don't yet exist, the courts must develop them. Once developed and adopted, any new principle usually becomes a binding precedent for all future decisions. Not surprisingly, then, one typical problem in judicial decision making is the law of unintended consequences. A principle generated to solve one legal question may subsequently push courts to deal with other questions in surprising ways. In this article, Thomas Bateman explores a recent and controversial *Charter* decision in which a precedent from a case in the 1980s has driven the Supreme Court to strike a significant blow against Canada's single-tier public health care system.

◆ ◆ ◆

In June 2005, Canadians witnessed a clash of national icons. One icon is the country's health care system, premised on access to medically required services on the basis of need, not ability to pay. Roy

Romanow, Chair of the Commission on the Future of Health Care in Canada, intoned at the beginning of his final report that in their discussions with him, "Canadians have been clear that they still strongly support the core values on which our health care system is premised—equity, fairness, and solidarity. These values are tied to their understanding of citizenship. Canadians consider equal and timely access to medically necessary services on the basis of need as a right of citizenship, not a privilege of status or wealth."[1]

Such access is assured by what is called a single-payer model—government payment for the provision of medical services to patients who need them. It is contrasted with the American model, characterized by the dominance of profit-oriented private health insurance. Tens of millions of Americans go without health insurance, and while no one is denied care in extreme situations, ability to pay does go a long way to determine one's access to health care services. In Canadian iconography, this provides a stark and uplifting Canadian–American comparison. According to Romanow, "Canadians view medicare as a moral enterprise not as a business venture."

The other great icon is the *Canadian Charter of Rights and Freedoms,* a statement of not only technical rights and interpretive provisions but also fundamental Canadian values, those threads that bind an otherwise provincialized, fragmented, multicultural political community. So profound has been the *Charter*'s effect on the national consciousness that undergraduate students typically think that the *Charter is* the Constitution. The courts' interpretation of the *Charter* is also associated (in the public mind, if not always in the case law) with all things correct and proper: personal liberty, freedom of speech, equality and nondiscrimination, and the right to be treated decently by the criminal justice system.

Shocking it was, then, when four members of a seven-justice Supreme Court of Canada panel declared invalid a provision of Québec's health care legislation that prohibited the purchase of private health insurance. This was not supposed to happen. The *Charter* is about rights and equality and fundamental Canadian values. Canadian health care policy is egalitarian, efficient, and not American. The two should thrive in loving embrace. Alas, the *Charter* was taken up as the sword to pierce the heart of Canadian health care. Supporters of the *Charter* (who most often are supporters of the principle of universal access in Canadian health care) must have squirmed in discomfort at reading a *Charter* decision that opened the door to private health insurance. And the *Charter*'s long-time opponents (many of whom are pro-market conservatives) must have felt equally uncomfortable reading a welcome decision based on a constitutional document they disdain and rendered by an institution they distrust.

This essay will show that the Supreme Court's invalidation of Quebec's ban on private health insurance is rooted in an earlier judicial invalidation of Canada's criminal ban on abortion, which itself opened the legal door to private abortion clinics. Consideration of the connection between these two cases will shed light on both the prospects and perils of using courts to advance public policy objectives. The law of unintended consequences applies to judicial politics as well as to politics more generally.

THE CHARTER: AN ALTERNATIVE POLICY-MAKING TOOL

◆ ◆ ◆

The *Canadian Charter of Rights and Freedoms* is not normally considered a policy-making tool. Instead, it is commonly seen as a statement of fundamental rights and freedoms—and these things are basic to the whole polity, more fundamental than public policies. Laws and government policies come and go, the conventional wisdom has it, but rights are permanent, supreme, and beyond partisan and ideological dispute.[2] This is what is attractive about rights: if I have them, no one can take them away; and since rights are moral principles, they are resistant to compromise.

The Canadian Charter of Rights and Freedoms *is not normally considered a policy-making tool.*

If the conventional wisdom were true, there would, first, be a bright, clear line between rights and public policy. Second, judges would understand their role narrowly—to interpret constitutional law, not "make it up." Third, the meaning of the rights contained in the *Charter* would be clear and relatively uncontroversial. Fourth, the public would have relatively modest expectations of what the *Charter* would do to influence Canadian society. Fifth, only rarely would government violate fundamental rights; much room would be left for governments and legislatures to debate the merits of this or that public policy.

All of these propositions are debatable. Taking the last point first, very rarely indeed is a court required to consider a breach of a fundamental liberal democratic value. More frequently they are asked to decide between competing, plausible secondary applications of a core value of liberal democracy in Canada.[3] Here is one example. Canada, like all liberal democracies, upholds freedom of speech and press. We do not abide censorship and generally think that public discussion is improved and democratic governance guaranteed by free discussion of both comfortable and uncomfortable topics. Freedom of speech is a core Canadian value. But we do not think the right should be enjoyed or exercised absolutely. Naturally some limits on it should exist. We will agree on some limits; for example, rules that people should not joke about bombs and terrorism in airport security checkpoints. But on other limits, like the criminal prohibition of public communications that promote hatred against identifiable groups, reasonable people will disagree, and have done so.[4] Reasonable people will disagree about state-enforced limits on the activities of interest groups during general elections.[5] Canada would be no less a liberal democracy committed to freedom of speech were it to have different policies in these areas. These kinds of decisions dominate courts' attention. It is the secondary application of core values, not the core values themselves, that constitute the stuff of judicial review.[6]

The proposition that Canadians have modest expectations of the courts is also questionable. For many Canadians the courts are among the most trusted institutions, and judges are highly esteemed. They certainly rank much higher than politicians.[7] Even when politicians have attempted to open up the Supreme Court of Canada appointment process to parliamentary review, they have felt great pressure not to "politicize" the courts by subjecting candidates to unseemly partisan questioning. Canadians enthusiastically supported the *Charter*'s entrenchment in 1982.[8] They continue to express general or diffuse support for the Supreme Court of Canada and its role in enforcing *Charter* rights, even though they may quarrel with this or that particular decision.[9]

The meaning of *Charter* rights is anything but clear and uncontroversial. The *Charter*'s provisions are drafted in general, "open-textured" language intended to anticipate and apply to unforeseen factual circumstances. Citizens' right to vote, for example, in section 3, may seem simple enough, but does it say anything about the quality or actual power of a vote—whether one vote has as much weight in determining the election of a representative as another?[10] Does section 3 indicate whether persons imprisoned for criminal convictions can be denied the vote for the duration of their sentences?[11] *Charter* rights do not interpret themselves; they need judicial interpretation. And sometimes, judicial interpretation changes. Courts will reverse themselves on the

meaning of *Charter* rights. For example, in 1991 the Supreme Court ruled that the Canadian Minister of Justice could surrender fugitives to the United States to face justice there even if the fugitive faced the death penalty upon conviction. While Canadians may not countenance the death penalty, the majority of the Court reasoned, we should not impose our views on other countries.[12] Ten years, later, the Court ruled that, except in "exceptional circumstances" (left unexplained), the minister could not surrender such fugitives unless he or she obtained assurances from the receiving country that the death penalty would not be imposed.[13]

Sometimes the text of the Constitution does not even enter as the basis for judicial decision making. In the 1998 *Secession Reference*,[14] in which the Court had to decide if it was constitutional for Quebec unilaterally to declare independence from Canada, the Court relied on "principles of the Constitution" to dispose of the reference, not least because the Constitution was silent on the constitutionality of secession. More recently, in a speech on the judicial function, Chief Justice Beverly McLachlin argued that

> even inclusive, written constitutions leave much out, requiring us to look at convention and usage. In addition, the broad, open-textured language used in constitutional documents admits a variety of interpretations. In order to resolve the interpretational issues that may arise from this language, judges may need to resort to conventions and principles not articulated in the constitution itself.[15]

This brings us to the judges' view of their role in the *Charter* era. Supreme Court justices have been mindful that they are part of a constitutional system in which legislatures and governments (the executive, including elected members drawn from the ranks of legislatures, and permanent staff in the public service) are legitimate, democratically accountable policy makers. Judges acknowledge that when they exercise judicial review, they engage in a sort of "dialogue" with the other institutions of Canadian democracy over public policy and its relationship to constitutional rights. Such a dialogue in their view allows no interlocutor to have the final say.[16] On the other hand, justices have sometimes taken a very broad view of their role. Frequently they intone that the Constitution "is a living tree" and must be given a "large and liberal interpretation" consistent with the activist purposes set for it.[17] They have referred to "evolving standards of decency" that ought to cause courts to alter the definition of rights as time passes.[18]

When clear statements of the framers' intentions for the meaning of a *Charter* provisions have been put before the Court, judges have at times either ignored those intentions or accorded them little weight.[19]

Judges' interpretive creativity stems significantly from the difficulty in distinguishing a *Charter* right from a public policy claim. Secondary constitutional values—those concrete applications of core liberal democratic rights or values—take courts into public policy territory and potentially into conflict with the priorities of legislatures and public opinion. When confronted with difficult cases, judges often begin their reasons by noting that their job is not to decide the merits or wisdom of a policy, but the constitutionality of a policy. This is a distinction, as we will see, more easily made in principle than in practice.

> *... there is a minoritarian quality to courts as decision-making institutions. People who lose, or who will probably lose, in the majoritarian halls of Parliament, find courts attractive.*

It is precisely the blurriness of this line that invites activists, reformers, and interest groups to use the courts and the *Charter* to advance policy goals they failed to achieve in other institutional venues like Parliament or the bureaucratic policy process. Courts are different from executive and legislative institutions in a crucial respect: they are institutionally insulated from the pressure of public opinion and democratic vote getting. Judges enjoy security of tenure until 75 years of age and cannot be subject to political influence. Courtrooms are, in a famous formulation, forums of principle where the winning argument depends on its cogency and persuasiveness, not on the number of electors who like it. Accordingly, there is a minoritarian quality to courts as decision-making institutions. People who lose, or who will probably lose, in the majoritarian halls of Parliament, find courts attractive. There, they do not need to prove how many people support them. In addition, rights are valid regardless of the number of people who assert them. Liberal democracy is not merely about majority rule; it is about majority rule hemmed in by a catalogue of rights and freedoms democratic majorities must not abrogate. So while courts are important guardians of liberal democratic stability and decency, they are also attractive alternative venues for public policy making. It all comes down to the skill with which a *Charter* claimant can convert a policy claim into a rights claim a court can properly entertain.

THE CASE OF ABORTION AS PROLOGUE
◆ ◆ ◆

Canada's public policy regarding abortion until 1988 was an awkward settlement or compromise between extreme positions. One extreme position was that abortion to the moment of birth should be entirely a woman's personal prerogative. The other was that abortion in all circumstances is the murder of a human being and must be criminalized to protect the life of the unborn from conception to birth. Section 251 of the *Criminal Code* criminalized the procurement of abortions, but made exceptions for those abortions performed to save the life or health of the pregnant woman. "Life" and "health" were undefined. The *Code* required that such "therapeutic" abortions be performed in hospitals with surgical facilities and approved beforehand by a committee of a minimum number of doctors applying the *Code*'s criteria. Many hospitals were too small to have therapeutic abortions committees and were not required to have them and to perform abortions in any event. Committees operating in hospitals across the country applied the life or health criteria differently—strictly in some places, liberally in others. Some had easy access to abortion, others not.

Abortion rights proponent Dr. Henry Morgentaler wanted to change this. He lobbied Parliament for changes to the abortion law but failed. MPs were uninterested in disturbing an awkward and unprincipled, but stable, policy settlement. Morgentaler then opened a private clinic, flagrantly in violation of the *Code*, and performed abortions for a fee. For this he got standing in court to protest that the law under which he was charged was a violation of rights protected by the 1960 *Canadian Bill of Rights*. He lost the constitutional challenge but won acquittals from sympathetic juries. He received lots of attention. But then, Morgentaler was looking for a fight. He published articles stating that he had performed thousands of illegal abortions and in 1973 he allowed CTV cameras into his clinic to film a Mother's Day airing of a complete abortion procedure.[20]

The *Charter* provided Morgentaler with the legal pretext he needed to win through the courts what he could not in Parliament. Section 7 of the *Charter* reads:

> Everyone has the right to life, liberty and security of the person and the right not to be deprived thereof except in accordance with the principles of fundamental justice.

Several interpretive possibilities were open to him. He could have argued that his own economic liberty rights were infringed by the criminalization of abortion. This tack would not have gained him much public sympathy—moral crusaders do not wish to be considered in it for the money—and it would have required the courts to interpret section 7 to include economic or property rights. This the courts were reluctant then and since to acknowledge.[21]

Instead he based his case on *women's* section 7 rights, not his own, something courts do not normally allow. He made two other arguments that gained traction. First, he argued that abortion is an intensely personal decision that is properly within a zone of individual freedom beyond the legitimate reach of the state. To decide to abort a fetus, in other words, is an aspect of the section 7 right to liberty. Madam Justice Bertha Wilson was on the panel of seven justices and found this argument the most persuasive. She wrote

> The *Charter* is predicated on a particular conception of the place of the individual in society. An individual is not a totally independent entity disconnected from the society in which he or she lives. Neither, however, is the individual a mere cog in an impersonal machine in which his or her values, goals and aspirations are subordinated to those of the collectivity. The individual is a bit of both. The *Charter* reflects this reality by leaving a wide range of activities and decisions open to legitimate government control while at the same time placing limits on the proper scope of that control. Thus, the rights guaranteed in the *Charter* erect around each individual, metaphorically speaking, an invisible fence over which the state will not be allowed to trespass. The role of the courts is to map out, piece by piece, the parameters of the fence.[22]

For her, abortion fit inside the fence she erected.

Wilson was unable to attract the support of her colleagues on the panel for her reasons. Four other justices struck down the abortion law but did so by accepting Morgentaler's second main argument. The *Charter,* they argued, did not guarantee a right to abortion; it does, however, guarantee a right to security of the person, which is infringed by the operation of the rules Parliament created to provide for therapeutic abortions. State-imposed limits on access to abortion do infringe a woman's security of the person, because the delays increase anxiety and also increase the health risks associated with later-term abortion procedures. Against this

consideration is the state's legitimate interest in the life of the fetus. But because the abortion committees do not exist in all hospitals, and because the "life or health" standard is applied differently from place to place, many women do not in practice have access to therapeutic abortions. So the defence against a criminal charge the law provides—that a threat to life or health excuses a pregnant women from a conviction—is really illusory. It is a defence a woman in a real situation cannot make. A principle of fundamental justice is that defences to criminal charges cannot be illusory. Thus the infringement of the right was not in accordance with a principle of fundamental justice. The law was found unconstitutional by a vote of 5–2 justices.

> *One consequence of Morgentaler's litigation was that abortions became a legitimate private, for-profit medical business.*

Dr. Morgentaler successfully used the courts to pursue his pro-choice policy agenda. He was able to articulate a pro-choice position in terms of *Charter* rights and have the court frame abortion for public policy purposes not as a matter of criminal justice but as a matter of health. Since 1988 Morgentaler has lobbied and litigated for public provision and funding of abortions as a matter of health (outside criminal regulation). In the meantime, he has continued to operate his private fee-for-service clinics as a medical entrepreneur. One consequence of his litigation was that abortions became a legitimate private, for-profit medical business.

DR. CHAOULLI AND THE EXTENSION OF THE LOGIC OF *MORGENTALER*
◆ ◆ ◆

The battle over Canadian health care is largely a battle between two health care models. One model is that medical services are like other services available in the marketplace. Consumers should pay for what they get. Health care can be very expensive, so the market will provide insurance people can purchase to protect them against costly, unforeseen medical services. Health insurance would operate just like automobile or house insurance. Those who want a lot of insurance coverage will pay more. Those who are at greater risk of health problems will also pay more. Such premium differentials, according to this model, are good because they create the right incentives to reduce one's risks of disease. If I know that smoking increases the cost of my health insurance by 40 percent, I may decide not to smoke. If health care is free to me, I can smoke cigarettes and remain confident that I need not pay extra for the health care I will eventually need to remedy my heart and lung disease. In the market model, you can get the health care you want, but you had better be prepared to pay for it.

The other is the public health care model according to which health care is not a market commodity but an essential public service that ought to be available to everyone based on need, not ability to pay. While medical services may be delivered by doctors operating as private contractors, those doctors ought to be paid by the government, not patients or their private insurers. Doctors are paid according to schedules of fees for services that are negotiated by doctors' associations and governments. Everyone, regardless of income, is entitled to the same standard of care. Citizenship is not two tier; nor should health care be two tier. In this view, government is an unlimited liability insurance provider. If the government does not pour enough money into the system, and if demand for services exceeds supply, health services are rationed by the emergence of wait lists for treatment. In this model, you will get the same standard of health care as everyone else, but you had better be prepared to wait for it.

In the market model, you can get the health care you want, but you had better be prepared to pay for it.

Quebec medical doctor Jacques Chaoulli had worked for years without success to change health care policy in Quebec to be allowed to operate a private hospital. Meanwhile, Quebecker George Zeliotis had waited for what he considered too long a time to get a hip replacement. Faced with political obstruction, they took a page from Morgentaler's playbook and fashioned a constitutional argument to persuade the courts to break a deadlock the politicians were afraid to touch. They jointly applied to a Quebec court for a motion to have Quebec's legislated ban on private health insurance (PHI) struck down as contrary to section 7 of the Canadian *Charter* and a related provision of the *Quebec*

Charter of Human Rights and Freedoms.[23] They lost at trial and on appeal to the Quebec Court of Appeal. However, they scored a narrow but crucial 4–3 victory at the Supreme Court of Canada.

In the public model, you will get the same standard of health care as everyone else, but you had better be prepared to wait for it.

Dr. Chaoulli did not argue that he had an economic or property right to practise medicine for profit. Nor did he argue that Canadians had a constitutional liberty right to purchase PHI. He might have considered the claim that Canadians have a right to timely health care but this would have been a long shot. Classic formulations of rights in Western liberal democracies are negative in character—rights are asserted by individuals *against* state action, not to require state action. Law professors consider that the next stage in the evolution of rights will be the judicial recognition of positive social rights to state action to provide minimal standards of education, income, health care, and social security. Some Canadian jurists also find positive rights attractive, but a majority of the Supreme Court has not yet affirmed them.[24]

... Chaoulli articulated a patient's right to security of the person, not a patient's right to PHI, nor a doctor's right to practise in private clinics and hospitals.

Dr. Chaoulli took a more conservative route, relying on the Court's 1988 decision in *Morgentaler*. Chaoulli argued that once the state provides access to medically required services based on need, any state-induced delay in access could cause stress, anxiety, and risk of medical harm sufficient to constitute a breach of the right of security of the person contrary to section 7 of the *Charter*. The province of Quebec prohibited the purchase of PHI, ostensibly to protect the integrity of the public health care system whose fundamental principle was access to health care based on need, not ability to pay. Chaoulli argued that this ban on PHI was what caused such long and potentially harmful wait lists in that province. So Chaoulli articulated a patient's right to security of the person, not a patient's right to PHI, nor a doctor's right to practise in private clinics and hospitals.

In section 7 *Charter* cases, it is not enough for the *Charter* rights claimant to show that the right to security of the person is breached. Such a right is not and cannot be absolute. The government can limit such rights if it can show that the limit is in accordance with principles of fundamental justice. It is a principle of fundamental justice that state limitations on the right to security of the person not be arbitrary. A nonarbitrary limit would be one in which there is a logical and *demonstrable* connection between the ban on PHI and the state's legitimate desire to protect the public system. If the court could not be convinced by Quebec government counsel that the ban on PHI is necessary to protect the public health care system as we know it, then a section 7 infringement will be made out and the ban on PHI would be struck down.

Three justices hearing the appeal were unpersuaded by Dr. Chaoulli's argument. Chaoulli's real objective, in their opinion, was to seek the Court-mandated privatization of Quebec health care. But courts do not decide the merits of social policy, they insisted. They were not even happy with the application of section 7 to social policy issues like health. Section 7, they wrote, is preeminently concerned with criminal justice policy, not health care and other difficult matters resting outside the courts' traditional competence. Indeed for this reason, they claimed, the precedent in the 1988 *Morgentaler* case does not even apply here: *Morgentaler* involved the application of section 7 to a provision of the criminal law. Chaoulli's appeal was about social policy simply.

Reluctantly, the dissenters agreed that the right to personal security was infringed in this case due to delays in access to health care but found Quebec's measures not to be arbitrary at all. The PHI ban, they argued, flows logically from Quebec's interest in preserving the integrity of public health care. Further, there is plenty of evidence that PHI does nothing to reduce, and may even increase, wait lists, evidence the trial judge found persuasive and which it is not the proper role of an appeal court to question.

But four of seven justices on the Supreme Court panel delivered just what the doctor ordered: an invalidation of the ban on PHI. Chaoulli's use of the "*Morgentaler* doctrine" worked. The state, wrote three of four justices in the majority, created a

virtual monopoly for the public health scheme. The state has effectively limited access to private health care except for the very rich, who can afford private care without need of insurance. This virtual monopoly, on the evidence, results in delays in treatment that adversely affect the citizen's security of the person. Where a law adversely affects life, liberty, or security of the person, it must conform to the principles of fundamental justice. This law, in our view, fails to do so.[25]

It fails to do so because other provinces and other OECD countries allow PHI in various forms while preserving the integrity of the principle of access to health care based on need. The PHI ban, according to the Court majority, is an excessive and unsupported infringement of rights in the service of a broader, legitimate state objective. As a remedy, the majority held that Quebec will be able to sustain a ban on PHI only if it reduces wait times to acceptable levels.

DISCUSSION
◆ ◆ ◆

Chaoulli's stunning victory could have been otherwise. Seven justices heard the appeal in June 2004 and rendered their decision in June 2005. Two vacancies on the Court were filled in August 2004. The two new appointees, Justices Rosalie Silberman Abella and Louise Charron, did not participate in the appeal. What if they had? The result could have been different. Justice Abella boasts a long public record of speeches, articles, and judicial decision testifying to her left-leaning social progressivism. It is hard to imagine her voting for PHI. Judges are not eunuchs and the law, especially constitutional law, is not mechanically applied to produce the "right" result every time. Judges have different experiences, different views of the judicial function, and different political ideologies, and all these influence their view of the cases coming before them. Appeal courts have panels of at least three judges and the Supreme Court attempts to sit with the full panel of nine as often as possible to eliminate the distortions associated with panel composition. Nonetheless, panels of seven or fewer sit frequently and this adds extra unpredictability to the legal enterprise.[26]

Be that as it may, the Court was recruited to take sides in a broader policy debate of long standing. For years Parliamentarians and former politicians have struggled with ways to contain health care costs and provide Canadians with timely access to care. Former Saskatchewan Premier Roy Romanow chaired a Royal Commission that recommended that more resources be poured into the system. A Senate committee chaired by former Trudeau aide Michael Kirby toyed with private health insurance but in the end recommended experimentation with contracted private delivery of publicly funded services.[27] Kirby also recommended that governments provide a health care guarantee: if provinces cannot provide care within a certain period, they must pay to have that care provided in other jurisdictions. More ominously, the Kirby committee warned, if governments will not provide for more timely care, then "the failure to deliver timely health services in the publicly funded system, as evidenced by long waiting lists for services, is likely to lay the foundation for a successful *Charter* challenge to laws that prevent or impede Canadians from personally paying for medically necessary services in Canada, even if these services are included in the set of publicly insured health services."[28] In support of this position, the Kirby Committee relied heavily on a C. D. Howe Institute study written by Stanley Hartt and Patrick Monahan that laid out the constitutional argument.[29] The majority in *Chaoulli* accepted this argument *in toto,* which is not entirely surprising. Kirby and some of his Senate colleagues submitted an intervener factum to the Court in *Chaoulli* and had Monahan and Hartt draft it for them.

The Court's decision in *Chaoulli* makes it tempting to conclude that the judges are really running the public policy show in Canada, that we are turning into some sort of jurocracy. Things are not quite this simple. First, courts uphold laws and administrative conduct against *Charter* challenges much more often than they declare them unconstitutional.[30] Second, they cannot easily take the initiative in effecting a revolution. They can decide only matters that come before them—in most cases as applications for leave to appeal. The Supreme Court can decide only which leaves to appeal it will grant. Third, the courts have generally been careful not to question legislative objectives but instead examine the means by which legislatures attempt to realize those objectives. They are tinkerers more than revolutionaries.

Finally, courts lack the resources of the revolutionary. Courts do not have an army or police forces at their command. They cannot spend money. They depend on *voluntary* compliance with their decisions for their power. Accordingly, they are on a leash whose length is measured by the extent of public confidence. They may occasionally lead or follow, but cannot disregard settled views about the just and unjust.[31] They can afford criticism of this or that decision, as long as diffuse support for the judiciary as such is not endangered.

All this having been said, the Supreme Court of Canada in *Chaoulli* pushed section 7 jurisprudence further into fields of social policy where courts have traditionally

feared to tread. It added the imprimatur of *Charter* rights to a gathering movement to privatize aspects of Canadian health care. While the Court was careful not to claim Canadians had a right to PHI, subtleties get lost in media coverage. People generally do not read court decisions but they do read headlines like "Champions of Private Health Care Find Satisfaction in Supreme Court Ruling"[32] and "Ruling Has Canada Planting Seeds of Private Health Care."[33] Canadians would be forgiven for thinking private health care is now a constitutional right. While it is tempting to blame misperceptions on media, in fact the Supreme Court has for years taken many steps to explain its decisions to media and to make its decisions more accessible to the public. It does bear some responsibility for the dissemination of its decisions.[34]

> *… the Supreme Court of Canada in Chaoulli pushed section 7 jurisprudence further into fields of social policy where courts have traditionally feared to tread.*

In law as in politics, the law of unintended consequences applies. Years ago, Henry Morgentaler's policy goal was to widen women's access to abortion. He acted to secure constitutional and policy space for private, for-profit abortion clinics. He expressed no interest in privatizing Canadian health care and in fact has worked for the coverage of abortion in provincial medical insurance plans. But his winning legal arguments set a precedent for the constitutional protection of private medical services. Once accepted by the Supreme Court, this precedent was out of his hands and available to others for their purposes. A curious legacy of Morgentaler's legal adventure may be the further privatization of health care in Canada.

> *A curious legacy of Morgentaler's legal adventure may be the further privatization of health care in Canada.*

CONCLUSION

◆ ◆ ◆

The Supreme Court of Canada was not driven inexorably to do what Dr. Chaoulli ordered. There is great flexibility in the language of the *Charter,* and there are several alternative precedents from which the Court could choose in supporting its decision one way or the other. In addition, the personnel on the Court and on the panel hearing Chaoulli's appeal could have been different, and this could well have altered the outcome. Litigants like Chaoulli cannot be guaranteed the outcomes they seek. Why then did Chaoulli spend the tens of thousands of dollars on a gamble?

Part of the answer is that Chaoulli and other supporters of private health insurance were getting nowhere in the normal policy-making venues. Canadian politics has experienced a real gridlock on health care policy—lots of concern about its operation combined with lots of resistance to change. Such is the effect of our having elevated the health care system to the status of health care icon. In a sense, Chaoulli had nothing to lose by resorting to the courts. If Chaoulli had lost, he would nonetheless have gained a lot of free publicity since the courts are now a staple of media coverage. A loss would merely affirm the status quo. In any case, as was discussed above, the Court does occasionally reverse itself, so a loss would not necessarily be for all time. Depending on the wording of a negative decision, new circumstances in future—longer wait times, more evidence of patient suffering while in the queue for treatment—could lead to a different result.

As it happened, Chaoulli scored an important, though limited, victory. He got a high court to agree that long wait times were a constitutional problem and that a ban on PHI was equally constitutionally problematic. Now the case for a private, market model of health care could occupy some of that high moral ground reserved until now for the proponents of the public model. Chaoulli got the Supreme Court of Canada to join him in a campaign for change of Canadian health care policy.

Notes

1. Canada, Commission on the Future of Health Care in Canada, *Building on Values: The Future of Health Care in Canada—Final Report* (Ottawa, 2002), p. xvi.
2. Mary Ann Glendon, *Rights Talk: The Impoverishment of Political Discourse* (New York: Free Press, 1991).
3. Peter H. Russell, "The Political Purposes of the Canadian Charter of Rights and Freedoms" *Canadian Bar Review* 61:1 (1983), pp. 30–54.
4. *R. v. Keegstra*, [1990] 3 S.C.R. 697.
5. *Harper v. Canada (Attorney General)*, [2004] 1 S.C.R. 827.
6. Christopher Manfredi, *Judicial Power and the Charter: Canada and the Paradox of Liberal Constitutionalism,* 2nd ed. (Toronto: Oxford University Press, 2001), chapter 6.
7. Leger Marketing, "Profession Barometer, 2006" (March 20, 2006). Retrieved June 12, 2007, from www.legermarketing.com/eng/tencan.asp.
8. James B. Kelly, *Governing with the Charter: Legislative and Judicial Activism and Framers' Intent* (Vancouver: UBC Press, 2005), chapter 2.
9. Joseph E. Fletcher and Paul Howe, "Public Opinion and Canada's Courts" in Paul Howe and Peter H. Russell, eds., *Judicial Power and Canadian Democracy* (Montreal-Kingston: McGill-Queen's University Press, 2001), pp. 255–96. For signs of change to this view, see Lori Hausegger and Troy Riddell, "The Changing Nature of Public Support for the Supreme Court of Canada" *Canadian Journal of Political Science.* 37:1 (March 2004), pp. 23–50.
10. *Reference re Prov. Electoral Boundaries (Sask.)*, [1991] 2 S.C.R. 158.
11. *Sauvé v. Canada (Chief Electoral Officer)*, [2002] 3 S.C.R. 519.
12. *Kindler v. Canada (Minister of Justice)*, [1991] 2 S.C.R. 779.
13. *United States v. Burns,* [2001] 1 S.C.R. 283.
14. *Reference re Secession of Quebec*, [1998] 2 S.C.R. 217.
15. Chief Justice Beverly McLachlin, "Unwritten Constitutional Principles: What Is Going On?" 2005 Lord Cooke Lecture, Wellington New Zealand, December 1, 2005. Retrieved March 21, 2007, from www.scc-csc.gc.ca/aboutcourt/judges/speeches/UnwrittenPrinciples_e.asp.
16. See the discussion of the dialogue metaphor in *Vriend v. Alberta,* [1998] 1 S.C.R. 493. Also, Kent Roach, *The Supreme Court on Trial* (Toronto: Irwin Law, 2001); and Peter Hogg and Allison Bushell, "The Charter Dialogue between Courts and Legislatures (Or Perhaps the Charter Isn't Such a Bad Thing After All)" *Osgoode Hall Law Journal* 35 (1997), pp. 75–124.
17. *Law Society of Upper Canada v. Skapinker*, [1984] 1 S.C.R. 357; *Hunter v. Southam Inc.,* [1984] 2 S.C.R. 145; *R. v. Big M Drug Mart Ltd.*, [1985] 1 S.C.R. 295; *Reference re Same-Sex Marriage*, [2004] 3 S.C.R. 698.
18. *United States v. Burns.*
19. *Reference Re s. 94(2) of the British Columbia Motor Vehicles Act*, [1985] 2 S.C.R. 486; *R. v. Morgentaler*, [1988] 1 S.C.R. 30 per Justice Wilson at 163–72.
20. F. L. Morton, *Morgentaler v. Borowski: Abortion, the Charter, and the Courts.* (Toronto: McClelland & Stewart, 1992), p. 37.

21. To the extent that it mattered, the *Charter*'s framers were clear that property rights were expressly excluded from the *Charter*. Kelly, *Governing with the Charter*, p. 55.

22. *Morgentaler,* at para. 224.

23. For the purposes of this essay, the legal differences between the Quebec and Canadian Charters will be ignored. The constitutional arguments made with respect to the two documents were nearly identical.

24. See *Gosselin v. Québec (Attorney General),* [2002] 4 S.C.R. 429.

25. *Chaoulli,* para. 46.

26. Andrew Heard, "The Charter in the Supreme Court of Canada: The Importance of Which Judges Hear an Appeal" *Canadian Journal of Political Science.* 24:2 (June 1991), pp. 289–307.

27. Canada, Senate Committee on Social Affairs, Science and Technology, *The Health of Canadians—The Federal Role: Final Report of the Standing Senate Committee on Social Affairs, Science and Technology*, vol. 6 (Ottawa: The Senate, 2002), chapter 5. Retrieved March 16, 2007, from www.parl.gc.ca/37/2/parlbus/commbus/senate/com-e/soci-e/rep-e/repoct02vol6-e.pdf.

28. *Ibid.* at 103.

29. "The Charter and Health Care: Guaranteeing Timely Access to Health Care for Canadians" *C.D. Howe Institute Commentary: The Health Papers* 164 (May 2002). Retrieved March 16, 2007, from www.cdhowe.org/pdf/commentary_164.pdf.

30. See James B. Kelly, "The Charter of Rights and Freedoms and the Rebalancing of Liberal Constitutionalism in Canada, 1982–1997." *Osgoode Hall Law Journal* 37 (1999), pp. 625–95.

31. Gerald Rosenberg, *The Hollow Hope: Can Courts Bring About Social Change?* (Chicago: University of Chicago Press, 1991); Jeffrey Rosen "The Day After *Roe*" *The Atlantic* (June 2006), pp. 56–67.

32. Kazi Stastna and Irwin Block, *CanWest News,* June 10, 2005, p. 1.

33. Clifford Krauss, *New York Times*, February 20, 2006, pp. A1–A4.

34. See Florian Sauvageau et al, *The Last Word: Media Coverage of the Supreme Court of Canada* (Vancouver: UBC Press, 2006).

Terms and Concepts

single-payer model

secondary applications

two-tier health care

positive social rights

jurocracy

law of unintended consequences

Questions

1. Which institution is better situated to decide between competing secondary applications of a fundamental right, a legislature or a court?

2. When and why would people such as Morgentaler or Chaoulli use courts to advance their public policy objectives?

3. What was Morgentaler's legal strategy in his challenge of Canadian abortion law? Why was his choice of strategy significant?

4. In what sense was Chaoulli's legal strategy grounded in that of Morgentaler?

5. What is the significance of Chaoulli's case for our health care system? What is its significance for the *Charter* as a political institution?

Climate Change Policy: Why Hasn't Canada Walked Its Kyoto Talk?

Ian Urquhart

Editors' Note

Public policy refers to those actions, commitments, and statements governments make to achieve a certain objective. It is what governments choose or choose not to do.[1] It is, of course, a matter of great debate what governments ought to do. This question is the province of political ideology and political philosophy. But once this question is settled, it remains for political actors to decide how exactly they propose to achieve their objective. Can an objective be achieved by a new law? If so, then what kind of law? A criminal law providing for imprisonment, or a regulatory provision providing for fines as penalties? Perhaps a change to income tax legislation is desirable, entitling people to a tax advantage if they spend their money in ways that advance the government's objective. Or maybe the government should mandate that children be educated in certain ways so that they grow to act in a manner consistent with government goals. As often as not, governments declare themselves in favour of certain objectives, but do little actually to achieve them.

How should political actors decide on the public policy instrument of choice for a particular situation? One important factor is to decide how much government should intervene in people's lives for the sake of the government objective. Also, it is important to consider how effective a particular policy tool is likely to be. Finally, a policy tool must be considered in terms not only of what it will achieve, but also what other government objectives it may frustrate.

These questions are at the forefront of one of the most complex debates of our time: climate change. A minority of naysayers notwithstanding, a strong scientific consensus exists on the effects of greenhouse gas (GHG) emissions on climate change. How, then, to reduce GHG emissions in terms that both achieve the desired result without sacrificing other goods people consider important? Since GHG emissions are in large part a product of economic growth, and since most people and most governments consider economic growth a nonnegotiable social and economic objective, the real issue is how to reverse human-induced climate change without impairing economic prosperity.

As Ian Urquhart indicates in this essay, almost everyone is agreed on the need to do something about climate change. On the question of policy instrument, however, disagreement prevails.

❖ ❖ ❖

1.   Kenneth Kernaghan and David Siegel, *Public Administration in Canada: A Text,* 4th ed. (Toronto: ITP Nelson, 1999), p. 126.

The Government of Canada has a concrete plan to fight climate change. It's an ambitious plan ...

—*Liberal Foreign Affairs Minister Pierre Pettigrew, December 8, 2005*

The Government of Canada is working towards a "Made in Canada" approach to deliver real change and real results for all Canadians, in our common campaign to clean up our air and to reduce our greenhouse gas emissions."

—*Conservative Environment Minister Rona Ambrose, June 7, 2006*

It's a perfectly sensible strategy. Everyone wants to appear green without doing anything.

—*David Montgomery, consultant to the Canadian Association of Petroleum Producers, June 3, 2006*

CANADA'S INCONVENIENT TRUTH

◆ ◆ ◆

The *Oxford Dictionary* defines an urban myth as "an entertaining story or piece of information circulated as though true." Former United States Vice President Al Gore (or, as he likes to say, the man who used to be the next President of the United States) revises an urban myth about a frog and boiling water to good effect in *An Inconvenient Truth*, his widely acclaimed documentary on the dangers of climate change. The revised myth, as told in a cartoon segment in the movie, is that a frog that jumps into a container of boiling water, feeling the water's life-threatening temperature, will hop out immediately. But, if you put a frog in warm water and then heat the water toward the scalding point the frog will sit contentedly in the pot, unmindful of its imminent death. When the water gets hotter and hotter the frog will ... be rescued! This summarizes Gore's hope for the human frog. Before humanity pays the ultimate price we will find the political will needed first to stabilize and then reduce greenhouse gas (GHG) emissions to rescue ourselves from the ever-hotter climate pot we find ourselves in.[1]

The theatre audience around me loved Gore's story. I wonder if they think the urban myths spun by Liberal and Conservative governments alike in Canada about climate change are as entertaining. Both perpetuate the myth that they take the threat of global warming seriously. The Liberal version of the story, told by the Chrétien and Martin administrations, was a tale where Canada's public policy initiatives to reduce Canada's GHG emissions matched the strength of Liberal rhetoric about the severity of the climate change threat. The version told by Stephen Harper's Conservatives, like the Liberal one before it, dutifully swears allegiance to the need to act on climate change. It trumpets what any serious student of Canadian climate change already knows—a decade of Liberal climate change policies did nothing to move Canada closer to meeting Canada's GHG emissions reduction commitments established under the terms of the 1997 Kyoto Protocol. But, in the first few months of the Harper minority government, there were no signs that the Conservatives, unlike the Liberals, would adopt measures placing Canada firmly on the path of reducing this country's GHG emissions. The Conservatives, after all, had avoided any mention—let alone endorsement—of the Kyoto Protocol's GHG reduction targets in their 2006 election platform. By the early summer of 2006, the Harper government's actions consisted first of cancelling ineffective Liberal climate change policies, and second, only promising to develop and introduce a "made-in-Canada" approach to the climate change issue in the fall of 2006.

This chapter on the politics of climate change has several objectives. Its overriding concern is to try to explain the policies adopted by successive Liberal and Conservative governments. In that regard the reader is asked to pay particular attention to a handful of international and domestic factors: international agreements and pressures (including the American thirst for secure sources of oil), corporate interests, and the constitutional division of powers between Canada's national and provincial governments. It begins by discussing the science of climate change and the details of the Kyoto Protocol. It then outlines and explains the GHG emissions policies that our Liberal and Conservative governments have produced.

SKEPTICS, STICKS, AND SCIENCE

◆ ◆ ◆

The Oxford Research Group has warned that climate change represents a far more serious threat to global security than international terrorism.[2] The United States Pentagon's Office of Net Assessment is quoted in its report as claiming that climate change is a threat that "vastly eclipses" terrorism.[3] The likely effects of climate change—rising sea levels, shifting precipitation patterns, increased average temperatures—in turn are likely to increase human suffering and social unrest; social impacts such as these will have "long-term security implications for all countries which are far more serious and destructive than those of international terrorism."[4]

But how likely are these changes? Are we, through our accelerated use of fossil fuels, responsible for the average temperature increases recorded since the late 1800s? Have we created and are we exacerbating global warming? Judging by the messages coming from some policy makers and some media outlets—especially in the United States—we might be exaggerating global warming's significance and human responsibility for the phenomenon. One study of articles published by four leading American newspapers about the human contribution to climate change between 1988 and 2002 discovered that more than one-half of the articles sampled gave roughly equal treatment to the opposing sides of the issue. Fifty-three percent of the 636 articles paid roughly as much attention to the assertion that global warming is part of a natural cycle as to the contrary position that human activities are important contributors to global warming. Senator James Inhofe, the Republican Chair of the United States Senate Committee on Environment and Public Works, famously has called the idea that human activities are responsible for global warming today "the greatest hoax ever perpetrated on the American people." He has been especially critical of the so-called "hockey stick" graph of global temperature change. This graph, likened to a hockey stick lying on its shaft with its blade pointed skyward, suggested that average global temperatures recently have risen sharply after centuries of relative stability. According to Inhofe, this interpretation of the temperature record is alarmist. It ignores the significance of the Medieval warm period (approximately 1000 A.D.) and the Little Ice Age (approximately 1700 A.D.). That these prior periods of warming and cooling were unrelated to human behaviour is used by Inhofe and other climate change skeptics to try to cast doubt on the links currently made between fossil fuel–driven industrialization and today's changes.

Have we created and are we exacerbating global warming?

Unfortunately, such skepticism and journalistic balance badly misleads the public about the state of scientific

understanding about the relationship between human activities and global warming. Over the last generation a consensus first formed and then strengthened among the world's climate scientists. This consensus maintains that human behaviour is responsible for most of the recent global warming. This consensus animates the climate assessments prepared by the Intergovernmental Panel on Climate Change (IPCC), arguably the most authoritative collection of climate scientists on earth. Its 2001 climate change assessment, based primarily on peer-reviewed scientific studies, concluded: "There is new and stronger evidence that most of the warming observed over the last 50 years is attributable to human activities."[5] The IPCC's perspective on human culpability is shared widely in the scientific community. For example, all American scientific associations with expertise on climate change—the National Academy of Sciences, the American Meteorological Society, the American Geophysical Union, and the American Association for the Advancement of Science—have agreed with the IPCC's 2001 statement. In Canada, the Canadian Meteorological and Oceanographic Society, described as Canada's climate science "brains trust," has called on governments to make severe GHG emission cuts.[6] The credibility of these views is underlined emphatically by a statistical analysis of 928 abstracts of global climate change articles published in refereed journals between 1993 and 2003. None of the articles disputed the consensus view.[7] When it comes to the science of climate change there is no scientific dispute—human behaviour is warming our planet to an increasingly worrying degree. As the cartoon character Pogo famously said on a 1970 Earth Day poster: "We Have Met the Enemy and He Is Us."

When it comes to the science of climate change there is no scientific dispute— human behaviour is warming our planet to an increasingly worrying degree.

WHAT IS THE KYOTO PROTOCOL?
◆ ◆ ◆

Alberta's former Premier Ralph Klein, a vigorous opponent of the Kyoto Protocol, could have been speaking for many Canadians when he said nearly five years after the Kyoto Protocol was signed that "People still don't know what Kyoto means other than it's a city in Japan."[8] Legally, the Kyoto Protocol amends the United Nations Framework Convention on Climate Change (UNFCCC), an international agreement signed at the United Nations Earth Summit held in Rio de Janeiro in June 1992. The need for Kyoto arose out of the scientific consensus just noted. By the mid-1990s this consensus viewed the GHG emission reductions established by the UNFCCC—that developed countries should reduce their GHG levels to 1990 levels by the year 2000—as insufficient. The parties to the Convention subsequently agreed to negotiate a protocol to set stiffer GHG emission reductions for the Annex I parties (these parties are the developed countries—the OECD nations, Russia, and the former socialist countries of Eastern Europe). The Kyoto Protocol was the product of those negotiations. It called on the Annex I parties to reduce GHG emissions by an average of 5.2 percent from their 1990 levels by 2008–2012. It asked Canada to reduce its emissions to 6 percent below 1990 levels (to 571 megatonnes from 607 megatonnes).[9]

Two thresholds had to be crossed before this international agreement came into effect. First, 55 of the signatories to the UNFCCC needed to ratify the Protocol. This condition was satisfied in 2002. Second, the 55 (or more) ratifying states needed to contain enough of the 41 Annex I countries to account for 55 percent of that group's carbon dioxide emissions in 1990. This second threshold proved to be a potential "Protocol breaker." When the United States announced in 2001 that it did not intend to ratify Kyoto, this second threshold became more difficult to cross because of the significance of the U.S. share of total Annex I country GHG emissions—more than one-third (36.1 percent in 1990). Without American participation the vast majority of the remaining Annex I countries needed to ratify Kyoto in order for the Protocol to come into effect. Furthermore, the absence of the United States delivered a *de facto* Kyoto veto power to the Russian Federation since the latter country's share of Annex I GHG emissions in 1990 was 17.4 percent. Without Russian participation, the 55 percent threshold could not be crossed.[10] Russia used this leverage well in subsequent negotiations devoted to fleshing out the details of the Protocol. For example, its threat to pull out of Kyoto unless it received very generous credits for carbon sinks—sinks are growing forests and other vegetation that remove carbon from the atmosphere—succeeded.[11] Russia also used its pivotal position to secure European support for Russian entry into the World Trade Organization.[12] In

November 2004 Russia ratified the Protocol; on February 16, 2005, the Kyoto Protocol came into force.

Kyoto's significance never rested in the possibility that its very modest GHG emissions reductions target would save humanity from the dangers posed by dramatic climate change. Climate science then and now recognized that much more dramatic cuts in carbon dioxide emissions—cuts in the order of 60 percent or more—are needed just to stabilize carbon dioxide emissions at 450 to 550 parts per million (ppm).[13] The bottom end of this range, considered to be the most the earth can tolerate before dangerous and very damaging consequences become widespread, is only 18 percent higher than the record level of 381 ppm recorded by American climate scientists in early 2006.[14] How can the implementation of an agreement that will do little to slow the rate of global warming be described as "an audacious commitment"?[15] Given Kyoto's obvious shortcomings, why is there support for the Protocol, especially from within the industrialized nations that solely bear the duty of meeting Kyoto's GHG emission reduction targets? One reason may be found in the value of establishing an international institution and processes for addressing GHG emissions. Kyoto's provisions on issues such as definitions, procedures, and institutions for measuring carbon emissions, for registering carbon credits, for monitoring, and for compliance potentially offer a valuable framework for managing GHG emissions more effectively in the future. As William Nordhaus concluded

> the major merit of the new accord is that it is the first experiment with market instruments in a truly global environmental agreement. There is little appreciation of the importance of "institutional innovations" of this kind, and even less appreciation for the fact that there are no mechanisms for dealing with economic global public goods like global warming. For this reason, the Kyoto-Bonn Accord may be a useful if expensive guinea pig. Operating the Kyoto-Bonn mechanism will provide valuable insights on how complicated international environmental programs will work. It is hard to see why the United States should not join with other countries in paying for this knowledge.[16]

Paul Roberts offers another rationale for supporting Kyoto—one that may perhaps be especially appealing to environmentalists. He suggests climate change is "the *only* real driver" to a new, zero-carbon or far less carbon-intensive energy economy.[17]

Kyoto's significance never rested in the possibility that its very modest GHG emissions reductions target would save humanity from the dangers posed by dramatic climate change.

THE PHONY WAR

◆ ◆ ◆

For nearly seven months after Germany's invasion of Poland in September 1939 Europe was in the "phony war"—a lull in military operations that ended with Germany's invasion of Norway in April 1940. When it comes to climate change Canada has been "fighting" a phony war since it signed the Climate Change Convention at the Rio Earth Summit, and there are few signs this will change soon. In 1992 Canada emitted 606 megatonnes of GHGs. By the beginning of 2003 Canada had sent numerous signals over the preceding 10 years of its commitment to reduce GHG emissions. In 1995 the federal government introduced its National Action Program on Climate Change; in 1997 Canada signed the Kyoto Protocol—ostensibly strengthening the commitment made through the UNFCCC in 1992; in 2000 the federal government unveiled its *Action Plan 2000 on Climate Change*; in 2002 the national government introduced its *Climate Change Plan for Canada*. By 2003, notwithstanding these commitments and policy initiatives, Canada's GHG emissions had skyrocketed to 740 megatonnes—180 megatonnes or 32 percent higher than the country's Kyoto target of 560 megatonnes.

Why was the federal government so spectacularly unsuccessful in moving Canada toward keeping its Kyoto commitment? Policies that address climate change can be located along a continuum of coerciveness. Toward the noncoercive end would be public information campaigns, advertisements urging voluntary action, and cash or tax incentives and subsidies for increased energy-use efficiency. Toward the coercive end, policies include regulations forcing automakers to improve fuel-efficiency standards, strict limits on the amounts of GHGs a firm may emit, and increased taxes on gasoline. Throughout the 1990s Canadian climate-change policy took the noncoercive path, relying on information, exhortation, and voluntary participation to try to get people and

businesses to reduce GHG emissions. Clearly, as the federal inventory of GHGs underlines, these measures were an unmitigated failure.

Throughout the 1990s Canadian climate-change policy took the noncoercive path, relying on information, exhortation, and voluntary participation to try to get people and businesses to reduce GHG emissions.

The national policy package introduced in 2002 punctuated the national government's intent to stay on this path and avoid the more coercive one. The *Climate Change Plan for Canada* (2002) treated very leniently the large industrial emitters—oil and gas companies, coal, oil, and gas-fired electrical utilities, and mining/manufacturing firms. The emissions reduction ceiling established for these industries (55 megatonnes) amounted to just 23 percent of the reductions Canada would have to make from "business as usual" emissions levels in 2010. This share was less than half of the 53 percent contribution these industries actually made to Canada's GHG emissions total in 2002.[18] Government also promised not to ask industry to pay for "a large proportion" of its GHG emission permits.[19] In addition to free permits industry would be able to meet its remaining reduction requirements through whatever approach was most cost effective—reducing smokestack emissions and/or purchasing emission permits surplus to other firms' needs. In fact, the policies proposed in this document bore a striking resemblance to the climate-change policy preferences outlined by the Canadian Association of Petroleum Producers (CAPP). The CAPP wanted different plans for different sectors—Ottawa adopted this wish; the CAPP wanted reduction targets to be based on emissions intensity—Ottawa endorsed this approach for large industrial emitters.[20]

Further details about the distance the federal government would go to accommodate industry's concerns appeared after the *Climate Change Plan for Canada* was released. In December 2002 federal Natural Resources Minister Herb Dhaliwal made two significant commitments to Canadian industry. First, companies would not have to pay more than $15 per tonne for reducing their GHG emissions. Second, he offered additional specifics for how Ottawa would apply the emissions intensity approach to the oil and gas sector. "With respect to the volume of emissions," he wrote, "the Government will set the emissions intensity targets for the oil and gas sector at a level not more than 15 percent below projected business-as-usual levels for 2010."[21] Canada's two largest oil sands producers then announced that these commitments would have only a very marginal impact on production costs. Suncor put these costs at between 20 and 27 cents per barrel; Syncrude estimated a range of 22 to 30 cents per barrel.[22]

This conciliatory theme also animated the sections of the 2003 federal budget devoted to climate change. There the government continued to shy away from the taxation and regulatory options, preferring instead the policy options of exhortation, incentives, and domestic/international markets where GHG reduction credits would be traded as commodities. No taxes were aimed at heavy industry. Instead, the budget allocated $2 billion to be spent over five years on various climate change initiatives—funds for research and development, for tax incentives for renewable energy, and for unspecified targeted initiatives and partnerships.

This eagerness to avoid burdening Canada's largest industrial concerns with many of the costs of reducing GHG emissions was embraced even more tightly in Project Green, the last climate change initiative introduced during Paul Martin's tenure as prime minister. Project Green called for the Large Final Emitters (LFEs) to contribute even less to reducing Canadian GHG emissions than did the *Climate Change Plan for Canada*. Originally called upon to contribute just 23 percent of Canada's official reductions (55 megatonnes) Project Green reduced that contribution to 17 percent (45 megatonnes). Measures proposed in 2002 in order to soften the overall and financial impact on large industrial emitters—such as the $15 per tonne maximum cost, the emissions intensity approach and safeguard, and access to emissions trading—were retained in Project Green. In fact, according to a simulation conducted by Jaccard et al, these measures probably would have meant that LFEs would have reduced their own emissions by only 15 megatonnes during the first Kyoto commitment period. The simulation predicted that 9 megatonnes would come from the purchase of international permits since it was assumed that these permits would cost no more than $15 per tonne.[23]

FROM TWEEDLEDUM TO TWEEDLEDEE?

◆ ◆ ◆

In the January 2006 federal election the Conservative party, led by Stephen Harper, won the most seats and formed a minority government. As the Conservatives prepared to reconvene Parliament several signs pointed to the growing problems a warming climate posed for Canadians. Mountain pine beetles continued their assault on the lodgepole pine forests of the interior of British Columbia and swept across the Rocky Mountains into Alberta. Previously controlled by cold snaps or weeks of very cold winter weather, the beetle has thrived in the absence of those conditions. More temperate winters in British Columbia's interior for well over a decade now have produced what the Canadian Forest Service labelled "the largest known insect infestation in North American history." Claiming more trees than wildfires or logging, the mountain pine beetle plague is radically disrupting the ecological balance in the Canadian West. Its threat to Western timber communities is arguably far more serious and potentially devastating than those presented by trade disputes over softwood or environmentalist attacks on "industrial forestry."[24]

As the Conservatives prepared to reconvene Parliament several signs pointed to the growing problems a warming climate posed for Canadians.

In the far north the Inuit echoed the forest scientists' conclusion that Canada already is witnessing significant, damaging ecological changes courtesy of global warming. Some there described the winter of 2005/06 as the worst—meaning the warmest—they had ever seen. The Inuit are greatly concerned that exceptionally warm winters are no longer the exception; they fear they are becoming the new normal. The ecological disruptions occurring in Canada's Arctic are too long to list here. Suffice it to say that shrinking and thinning Arctic ice sheets (confirmed by NASA scientists) look to be changing the Arctic ecology and threatening Inuit ways of life in profound ways. As one Inuit elder in Pangnirtung noted about contemporary climatic conditions: "These are things that all of our old oral history has never mentioned. We cannot pass on our traditional knowledge, because it is no longer reliable."[25]

Judging by the Conservative government's actions stories such as these did not move Environment Minister Rona Ambrose and her cabinet colleagues. [As of] the summer of 2006 it appears the Harper government takes climate change no more seriously than did the Chrétien and Martin administrations. The Conservatives' dislike for Kyoto was hinted at in their 2006 campaign platform. There they chastised the Liberals for signing "ambitious international treaties," for sending "money to foreign governments for hot air credits," and for not helping Canadians in their own country. Once in power the Conservatives pulled the plug on more than a dozen of the spectacularly ineffective Liberal climate change programs—programs such as the "one tonne challenge" advertising campaign in which comedian Rick Mercer urges the audience to reduce their individual greenhouse emissions by one tonne per year.

... it appears the Harper government takes climate change no more seriously than did the Chrétien and Martin administrations.

Environment Minister Ambrose went so far as to say that it would be impossible for Canada to meet its Kyoto obligations in the first commitment period without crippling the economy. Canada required a longer, unspecified timeframe in order to address climate change. Further, the Conservatives needed more time to craft a "made-in-Canada" plan that would address climate change (the plan also would address clean air, water, land, and energy). This plan was scheduled to be unveiled in the fall of 2006. All public statements by the federal Environment Minister suggest that the Conservatives will follow very closely the approach outlined in the party's election platform. There the party promised to

Address the issue of greenhouse gas emissions, such as carbon dioxide (CO_2), with a made-in-Canada plan, emphasizing new technologies, developed in concert with the provinces and in coordination with other major industrial countries.[26]

In a June speech to the Canadian Club Ambrose reportedly indicated that technology "would be a key driver" of the Conservative approach to climate change.[27] In line with this emphasis on technology the Minister also expressed her government's interest in the newly minted Asia-Pacific Partnership for Clean Development and Climate, a six-nation partnership dedicated to establishing "a voluntary, non-legally binding framework" to facilitate the development and use of cost-effective, cleaner technologies and practices among its signatories. For environmentalists this interest in joining a voluntary network constituted a further retreat from Kyoto, a suspicion strengthened by the fact that only one of the six founding partners—Japan—has committed to reducing GHG emissions under Kyoto.[28] Ambrose claimed it was ludicrous to interpret these signals as meaning her government had abandoned Kyoto. But, to some of the federal scientists who worked intimately on climate change issues, the early Conservative record on climate change, at the very least, was discouraging. Reportedly, some federal climate change scientists were so disappointed with the Harper government's stance that they considered leaving their careers in the federal public service.[29]

It would be surprising and uncharacteristic of the business community not to try to socialize the risks and costs of these new technologies by asking Canadian taxpayers to bear most of the cost of their development and implementation.

Environmentalists were quick to attack the Harper government's early approach to climate change. The Sierra Club gave the Conservatives an F for their climate change performance.[30] Are such attacks justified? On the one hand, it seems abundantly clear that the Conservatives, like the Liberals before them, have no intention of unlocking the gate to the more coercive climate change policy path. But what about the idea that technological change (encouraged in a noncoercive manner) can rescue us from the global warming pot? The National Roundtable on the Environment and Economy offers considerable support for this technological hope (without commenting on how this change would be implemented). In fact, the Roundtable regards technology as something of a magic bullet when it comes to balancing increased fossil fuel production with reducing GHG emissions. Its report concluded that "existing and near-term technology" could deliver a 60 percent reduction in GHG emissions from today's levels by 2050. And these dramatic results would not demand any sacrifice in respect to population, economic, or energy export growth. But, before Canadians rush out to celebrate this attractive promise to reduce our GHG emissions, several caveats should be considered. First, the Roundtable's scenario relies heavily on carbon sequestration and storage (CCS) technology and assumes this technology will be perfected. Without such a perfected technology the dream of increasing oil and gas production while reducing GHG emissions will remain nothing more than that. The report also left to future analyses the all-important political issues of cost and who will pay for new technologies such as CCS. Here, the parameters established by the Martin government could prove very relevant. Large final emitters will surely remind the Harper government in future negotiations over issues such as CCS of the generous treatment they were scheduled to receive from the Martin government. It would be surprising and uncharacteristic of the business community not to try to socialize the risks and costs of these new technologies by asking Canadian taxpayers to bear most of the cost of their development and implementation.

EXPLAINING NATIONAL GHG EMISSIONS POLICY

◆ ◆ ◆

Tom Keating's comprehensive examination of post–World War II Canadian foreign policy stresses the importance of multilateralism to understanding government behaviour.[31] Multilateralism has enabled Canada to pursue national objectives as well as international norms. Canadians take considerable pride in this orientation to global affairs. Among other things multilateralism has been "important as a counterweight to an exclusively continentalist foreign policy."[32] Canada's Kyoto record, where the federal government clearly has not "walked the talk," effectively repudiates the multilateralism Canadians are so proud of. Where should we look to explain what Heather Smith described as our "terribly tarnished" image in respect to international environmental policy?[33]

Federalism may be one place to start in trying to understand Canada's failure to make any progress in implementing Kyoto. Constitutional provisions and interpretations regarding the environment, natural resources, and international treaty implementation undoubtedly complicate federal thinking about how to address climate change. The sections of the *Constitution*

Act, 1867 dealing with the division of powers are silent when it comes to the environment. The right to legislate on environmental issues essentially is shared between the national and provincial levels of government.[34] Each level of government enjoys constitutional powers enabling it to legislate in ways affecting the economic, social, and biophysical dimensions of environmental quality. Provincial authority over natural resources (sections 92A and 109) and property and civil rights (section 92.13) are important constitutional foundations for provincial environmental legislation. Federal powers in respect to the criminal law, fisheries, and peace, order, and good government (sections 91.27, 91.12, and the preamble to section 91) provide strong roots for federal legislative initiatives.

Federalism may be one place to start in trying to understand Canada's failure to make any progress in implementing Kyoto.

Judicial review of the treaty-making power in the Canadian Constitution has strengthened the shared character of implementing international environmental agreements such as the Kyoto Protocol. In the early days of the Great Depression the Judicial Committee of the Privy Council (JCPC), then Canada's highest court of appeal, ruled in the *Radio Reference* case (1932) that the federal government enjoyed exclusive powers to make and to implement international treaties, even when the subject matter of the treaties fell within areas of provincial jurisdiction. But, just five years later in the *Labour Conventions* case (1937) the same court stripped Ottawa of these unqualified treaty implementation powers. "(T)he Dominion cannot," wrote Lord Atkin, "merely by making promises to foreign countries, clothe itself with legislative authority inconsistent with the constitution [to] which gave it birth."[35] Provincial legislation would be required to implement treaties touching areas of provincial jurisdiction. Ottawa could continue to negotiate such treaties but they could be implemented only by provincial legislatures.

This interpretation of federalism's consequences for Kyoto seemingly coloured Prime Minister Chrétien's assessment of his policy options in 2002. "For the implementation of Kyoto," he said, "we need the collaboration of the provinces. We don't have all the jurisdiction to do it."[36] However, Chrétien's assessment of the federal government's limited powers was likely too pessimistic. Nothing in the federal–provincial division of powers, for example, prevents Ottawa from introducing taxation measures to discourage GHG emissions. And, the Supreme Court has appeared to open the door to reconsidering Lord Atkin's restrictive interpretation of the federal treaty power. As Peter Hogg noted, it may very well be the case that the federal treaty power could be enhanced if the Supreme Court reconsiders this issue.[37] Federalism may have complicated federal decision-making on climate change; but we overrate its significance if we conclude that federalism prevented Ottawa from taking more aggressive actions.

... Chrétien's assessment of the federal government's limited powers was likely too pessimistic. Nothing in the federal–provincial division of powers, for example, prevents Ottawa from introducing taxation measures to discourage GHG emissions.

Some insist that implementing Kyoto will cripple the competitiveness of Canadian industry. The essence of this argument, made by virtually every major Canadian industrial association, is that, since the United States and Mexico are not committed to reducing their GHG emissions, implementing Kyoto will drive jobs and investment dollars south. The persuasiveness of this argument rests more with who makes it—the leading representatives of the Canadian business community—than with its substantive merits. An impressive list of economists have argued that the essence of the competitiveness fears raised by business, namely, that environmental protection generally takes place at the expense of competitiveness, is a "false dichotomy."[38] There is "no evidence" that environmental standards, such as energy efficiency standards, harm the international competitiveness of manufacturers.[39] Strict environmental regulations, if they stimulate innovation and upgrading of a firm's capital stock, actually may increase competitiveness.[40] Furthermore, there is little evidence that environmental regulations are crucial factors when it comes to making corporate investment and relocation decisions.[41] Finally, as the president of the Pew Center on Global Climate Change noted, improving corporate competitiveness actually has proven to be an important motivation for companies to try to reduce their GHG emissions.[42] Notwithstanding these arguments to the contrary, the fear-mongering campaigns of organizations such as the Canadian Manufacturers and Exporters cannot be ignored when trying to understand the reluctance of the federal government to match its climate change rhetoric with meaningful actions.[43]

There is "no evidence" that environmental standards, such as energy efficiency standards, harm the international competitiveness of manufacturers.

Related to this point is the recognition that federal governments, Conservative and Liberal alike, have been very receptive to lobbying by the Canadian oil and gas industry since the mid-1980s. They collectively have eliminated the pall cast over the petroleum sector by the federal National Energy Program (NEP) of 1980. Beginning with the dismantling of the NEP by the Mulroney government, federal administrations have offered olive branch after olive branch to the petroleum producers. The Canada–United States Free Trade Agreement (FTA) of 1988 effectively closed the book on the more nationalist, multinational-hostile style of federal intervention that characterized Canadian energy policy from the 1970s through to the introduction of the NEP. Through the FTA and the North American Free Trade Agreement (NAFTA), the federal government agreed to impose important limits on its taxation and energy supply management powers—limits sought by the energy industry. Significant federal tax policy changes introduced in the 1996 Budget helped launch the current flood of oil sands investments sweeping across northern Alberta. The federal government, in other words, has proven to be a good friend to the energy industry for more than 20 years now. Signing and then ratifying Kyoto did nothing to change that attitude. Consequently, the federal government has preferred collaboration to confrontation with the energy sector when it comes to GHG emissions.

As the references to the free trade agreements will suggest to some, the FTA and NAFTA are important institutional contributors to Canada's spectacular failure to make any progress in reducing GHG emissions. With respect to energy, NAFTA was designed to increase Canadian energy production and exports to the United States and to limit the ability of Canadian governments to privilege Canadians when it came to using our own energy resources. In Larry Pratt's words,

"NAFTA is rooted in a producer's viewpoint because of the near-exclusive emphasis it gives to expanding production in a wider market. It also reflects conservative fears of the national government."[44] Domestic petroleum production and export statistics certainly illustrate a spectacular increase in oil and gas exports during the free trade era. Combined crude oil and natural gas production in Canada grew by an impressive 61 percent from 1990 to 2003; petroleum exports over this period grew by a staggering 144 percent; net oil and gas exports rose even more—by 180 percent.[45] Put more starkly, 94 percent of the domestic production increase over this period was exported and virtually all of these exports went to the United States. Virtually every drop of new petroleum produced in Canada since 1990 has been shipped to American markets.

The statistical record also suggests that surging oil and gas exports "contributed significantly to emission growth" since 1990.[46] The GHG emissions associated with oil and gas exports rose by 149 percent over this period. Emissions resulting from all export-related oil and gas production amounted to more than 29 percent of the total increase in GHG emissions growth between 1990 and 2003.[47]

Beginning with the dismantling of the NEP by the Mulroney government, federal administrations have offered olive branch after olive branch to the petroleum producers.

The policy history of Kyoto demonstrates clearly that the noncoercive path leads us nowhere. If Canadians want to honour their international commitments and reduce GHG emissions their governments need to intervene more coercively. NAFTA has made this route more difficult for several reasons. First, NAFTA's pro-production/ anti-state foundations have worked well. They generated impressive petroleum production increases and even more impressive increases in GHG emissions.[48] Second, NAFTA's Article Six, the energy chapter, handcuffs Canadian policy makers; it prevents them from developing GHG emissions reduction strategies that favour Canadian consumers and/or companies at the expense of Americans. Article 604's export tax provisions, for example, prevent the national government from funding GHG emissions reduction initiatives through an export tax on energy. Under NAFTA, export taxes may be levied only if they also are imposed "on any such good when destined for domestic consumption." The identical policy making principle, "do unto Americans only what you also proceed to do unto Canadians," applies to the possibility of reducing Canadian GHG emissions by export restrictions, reducing the volume of oil and natural gas sold in the American market. Article 605, with its "proportional access requirement," eliminates this option. Under the terms of Article 605 Canada can reduce its energy exports to the United States only if it reduces the energy available for Canadian consumption by the same percentage. The border is erased; two energy markets are now one.

Production cutbacks, in other words, must be shared equally between American and Canadian consumers of Canadian energy. If, for example, the United States continues to consume 63 percent of all oil produced in Canada (as it did over the 2001–03 period) then, if oil production was cut back in order to reduce GHG emissions, these cutbacks would have to be applied equally to American and Canadian consumers. The United States would be entitled to receive 63 percent of whatever reduced amount of petroleum was produced on Canadian soil. So, while NAFTA does not prevent reducing energy exports to the United States it does require any such reductions to be accompanied by cuts to the supplies of petroleum sold to Canadians. It is hard to imagine a rational politician favouring this policy option given the suicidal electoral logic flowing from the interaction between production cuts and the proportional access requirement. In the NAFTA setting this policy option likely would anger not only Alberta and the oil and gas industry but also consumers and voters throughout the rest of the land.

A GHG emissions or "carbon" tax is another option that seems to offend Canadian political rationality. This approach, as implemented in the United Kingdom, is one that does not necessarily call for an increase in the total tax burden and has been favoured by some economists and environmental nongovernmental organizations (ENGOs).[49] The British government has introduced a revenue-neutral carbon levy through which increases to corporate energy costs were balanced by reductions in the National Insurance taxes paid by employers.[50] Michael Ignatieff endorsed a version of this approach—higher taxes on nonethanol blends of gasoline, reduced taxes on ethanol blends— during the 2006 federal Liberal leadership campaign. Panned by fellow Liberal leadership contenders, business editors, and groups such as the Canadian Taxpayers Federation, it is anything but certain that Canadian voters would respond favourably to Ignatieff's proposal since it appears to call for shifting the taxation burden onto individuals. Pogo's sage observation may be proven right once again.

When it comes to climate change policies Canada's Liberal and Conservative governments faithfully have followed what David Montgomery described as "a perfectly sensible strategy"—wanting to appear green without doing anything. Those who regard global warming as the most important policy issue facing humanity in the 21st century must be troubled by this "made-in-Canada" inaction. Future generations will be the judges of just how inconvenient this particular Canadian truth will be.

> *When it comes to climate change policies Canada's Liberal and Conservative governments faithfully have followed what David Montgomery described as "a perfectly sensible strategy"—wanting to appear green without doing anything.*

Notes

1. GHGs trap heat in the earth's atmosphere. The three primary GHGs are carbon dioxide, methane, and nitrous oxide. Carbon dioxide is the most common of the three.
2. Richard Norton-Taylor, "Climate Change a Bigger Security Threat than Terrorism, Says Report," *Guardian Unlimited,* June 12, 2006. Retrieved March 17, 2007, from www. guardian.co.uk/climatechange/story/0,,1795486,00.html.
3. Chris Abbott, Paul Rogers, and John Sloboda, "Global Responses to Global Threats: Sustainable Security for the 21st Century," (Oxford: Oxford Research Group, 2006). Retrieved March 17, 2007, from www.oxfordresearchgroup. org.uk/publications/briefings/globalthreats.htm.
4. Ibid., 9.
5. Intergovernmental Panel on Climate Change, *Climate Change 2001: Synthesis Report,* 5. Retrieved March 17, 2007, from www.ipcc.ch/pub/un/syreng/spm.pdf.
6. Peter Calamai, "Experts Rebuke Tory Kyoto Stand; Scientists Decry Change in Policy, Call for Bigger Emission Cuts," *Toronto Star,* June 2, 2006, p. A3.
7. Naomi Oreskes, "Between the Ivory Tower: The Scientific Consensus on Climate Change," *Science,* vol. 306, no. 5702 (December 3, 2004), p. 1686.
8. CBC News, "Alberta to Fight Ratification of Kyoto," September 4, 2002. Retrieved March 17, 2007, from www.cbc.ca/stories/2002/09/03/kyoto_reac020903.
9. A megatonne equals 1 million tonnes. A subsequent revision to Canada's 1990 GHG emissions placed them at 596 megatonnes. This revision means that Canada must reduce its GHG emission levels to 560 megatonnes by 2008–12 from their 2003 level of 740 megatonnes—a 24 percent reduction. The revision is taken from Environment Canada, *Canada's Greenhouse Gas Inventory: 1990–2003* (October 2005), p. 4. Retrieved March 23, 2007, from www.ec.gc.ca/pdb/ ghg/inventory_report/2003_report/toc_e.cfm.
10. Together Russia and the United States accounted for 53.5 percent of Annex I country emissions in 1990.
11. Gilles Trequesser, "Haggling Over Fine Print of Climate-change Treaty," (Reuters), November 9, 2001.
12. "Kyoto Ratification," *The Washington Post,* November 6, 2004, p. A22.
13. Paul Roberts, *The End of Oil: On the Edge of a Perilous New World.* (Boston: Houghton Mifflin Company, 2004), pp. 124–27.
14. David Shukman, "Sharp Rise in CO_2 Levels Recorded," March 14, 2006. Retrieved March 17, 2007, from http://news.bbc.co.uk/2/hi/science/nature/4803460.stm.
15. Roberts, *The End of Oil,* p. 127.
16. William D. Nordhaus, "Global Warming Economics," *Science,* Vol. 294, no. 5545 (November 9, 2001), p. 1284.
17. Roberts, *The End of Oil,* p. 123.
18. These figures and percentages are taken from Canada, *Climate Change Plan for Canada,* (2002) and Environment Canada, *Canada's Greenhouse Gas Inventory: Overview 1990–2003,* (Ottawa: Environment Canada, 2005).
19. *Climate Change Policy for Canada,* p. 31.
20. Emissions intensity is a controversial idea in climate-change politics. It refers to the amount of GHG emissions produced relative to a unit of output or production. The controversy arises because it is possible for emissions intensity to fall while total emissions of GHGs rise. For example, if a firm reduces its emissions intensity by 10 percent but increases its output by 25 percent, its aggregate greenhouse emissions will increase.
21. See "Letter to Mr. John Dielwart, Chairman, Canadian Association of Petroleum Producers from the Honourable Herb Dhaliwal, P.C., M.P.," December 18, 2002. Retrieved August 5, 2006, from www.nrcan-rncan.gc.ca/media/ newsreleases/2002/2002147a_e.htm.

22. "Kyoto Impact Minimal, Suncor Says," *The Globe and Mail,* January 10, 2003, p. A1; "Kyoto Oil Sands 'Scare' Eases," *The Globe and Mail,* January 10, 2003, p. B1; "Trust Puts Kyoto Costs at up to 30 Cents a Barrel," *The Globe and Mail,* January 25, 2003, p. A13.

23. Marc Jaccard et al, *Burning Our Money to Warm the Planet: Canada's Ineffective Efforts to Reduce Greenhouse Gas Emissions* (Toronto: C.D. Howe Institute, 2006), pp. 12–13. The ineffectiveness of federal initiatives was pointed out in the first edition of this chapter. See Ian Urquhart, "The Devil is in the Details: Implementing the Kyoto Protocol," in Thomas Bateman and Roger Epp (eds.), *Braving the New World: Readings in Contemporary Politics* (3rd ed.), (Toronto: Nelson, 2004), pp. 199–208.

24. Doug Struck, "'Rapid Warming' Spreads Havoc in Canada's Forests," *The Washington Post,* March 1, 2006, p. A1.

25. Doug Struck, "Inuit See Signs in Arctic Thaw," *The Washington Post,* March 22, 2006, p. A1. Readers who regard the Inuit accounts as too impressionistic may instead be persuaded by the conclusions of the Arctic Climate Impact Assessment prepared under the auspices of the Arctic Council. Its scientific data largely confirmed the accuracy of the Inuit accounts. See Cambridge University Press, *Arctic Climate Impact Assessment,* (New York: Cambridge University Press, 2005).

26. Conservative Party of Canada, *Stand up for Canada,* p. 37.

27. Paul Vieira, "Critics of Kyoto Compromise 'Self-serving,' Minister Says: Not about Finger-Pointing," *The National Post,* June 8, 2006, p. A1.

28. The six founding members were Australia, China, India, Japan, the Republic of Korea, and the United States.

29. "Tory Kyoto Policy Spooks Federal Scientists," June 12, 2006. Retrieved July 12, 2006, from www.cbc.ca/Canada/ Ottawa/story/ot-scientists20060612.html.

30. Mike De Souza, "Tories Fail to Make Sierra's Grade: Alberta Given "F" over Oilsands," *Calgary Herald,* June 17, 2006, p. A11.

31. Keating defines multilateralism as both "the practice of multilateral diplomacy and … policies supporting the establishment and maintenance of institutions and associations that facilitate and support the practice of multilateral diplomacy." Tom Keating, *Canada and World Order: The Multilateralist Tradition in Canadian Foreign Policy* (2nd ed.) (Don Mills: Oxford University Press, 2002), p. 4.

32. Ibid., p. 12.

33. Smith made these comments during a public lecture at the University of Alberta on January 12, 2003. For details of her lecture see Geoff McMaster, "Kyoto's Half-Truths," retrieved March 17, 2007, from www.expressnews.ualberta. ca/article.cfm?id=3727.

34. For examinations of the constitutional background of environmental policy in Canada, see Marcia Valiante, "Legal Foundations of Canadian Environmental Policy: Underlining Our Values in a Shifting Landscape," in Debora L. VanNijnatten and Robert Boardman (eds.), *Canadian Environmental Policy: Context and Cases* (2nd ed.) (Don Mills: Oxford University Press, 2002); and Mark S. Winfield, "Environmental Policy and Federalism," in Herman Bakvis and Grace Skogstad (eds.), *Canadian Federalism: Performance, Effectiveness, and Legitimacy,* (Don Mills: Oxford University Press, 2002).

35. Peter H. Russell, Rainer Knopff, and Ted Morton, *Federalism and the Charter: Leading Constitutional Decisions* (Ottawa: Carleton University Press, 1989), p. 110.

36. Steven Chase, "Provinces Have Kyoto Role, PM says," *The Globe and Mail,* April 24, 2002, p. A4.

37. Peter W. Hogg, *Constitutional Law of Canada* (2nd ed.) (Toronto: Carswell, 1985), p. 252.

38. Michael E. Porter, "America's Green Strategy," *Scientific American,* Vol. 264, no. 4 (April 1991), p. 168.

39. Duncan Brack with Michael Grubb and Craig Windram, *International Trade and Climate Change Policies,* (London: Royal Institute for International Affairs/Earthscan Publications, 2000), p. 54.

40. Porter, "America's Green Strategy." This argument is made more elaborately in Michael E. Porter and Claas van der Linde, "Toward a New Conception of the Environment-Competitiveness Relationship," *Journal of Economic Perspectives,* Vol. 9, no. 4 (Fall 1995), pp. 97–118.

41. Brack et al., *International Trade and Climate Change Policies,* p. 9; Pierre Marc Johnson and André Beaulieu, *The Environment and NAFTA: Understanding and Implementing the New Continental Law* (Washington: Island Press, 1996), pp. 45–46; some of these corporate investment and relocation studies are cited in Porter and van der Linde, "Toward a New Conception," p. 109.

42. "Climate Change: Myths and Realities," remarks by Eileen Claussen, at the Swiss Re conference "Emissions Reductions: Main Street to Wall Street," July 17, 2002. Retrieved March 17, 2007, from www.pewclimate.org/press_room/speech_ transcripts/transcript_swiss_re.cfm.

43. The centrepiece of the Canadian Manufacturers and Exporters campaign is the report "Pain Without Gain: Canada and the Kyoto Protocol," (February 2002).

44. Larry Pratt, *Energy: Free Trade and the Price We Paid,* (Edmonton: Parkland Institute, 2001), p. 20.

45. Environment Canada, *Canada's Greenhouse Gas Inventory: 1990–2003,* (Ottawa: Environment Canada, 2005), p. 11.

46. Ibid., 10.

47. Canada, Environment Canada, *Canada's Greenhouse Gas Inventory: Overview 1990–2003,* (Ottawa: Environment Canada, 2005), p. 2. These emissions rose from 28 megatonnes in 1990 to 69 megatonnes in 2003.

48. It should be stressed that the energy chapter of NAFTA restricts only state intervention that limits energy production. State intervention that promotes production—"existing or future incentives for oil and gas"—receives a nod of approval in Article 608 of this chapter.

49. Versions of the carbon tax proposal may be found in Jaccard et al, *Burning Our Money to Warm the Planet* and Sylvie Boustie, Marlo Raynolds, and Matthew Bramley, *How Ratifying the Kyoto Protocol Will Benefit Canada's*

Competitiveness, (Pembina Institute for Appropriate Development, June 2002), pp. 22–23.
50. See United Kingdom, Department of Environment, Food and Rural Affairs, *Climate Change Agreements: The Climate*

Change Levy, retrieved March 17, 2007, from www.defra.gov.uk/environment/ccl/intro.htm. Significantly, road fuel gas—an item that would have targeted individual Britons—was exempted from this tax.

Terms and Concepts

climate change
greenhouse gas emissions
"hockey stick" graph
Kyoto protocol

carbon credits
North American Free Trade
  Agreement
exhortation

incentive
regulation
socialization of risk

Questions

1. Why is it relatively easy for citizens and policy makers to ignore global warming?

2. How did the federal Liberal governments of Jean Chrétien and Paul Martin attempt to tackle GHG emissions in Canada?

3. How does Urquhart explain the benefits of the Kyoto Protocol, given its modest potential effect on GHG reduction?

4. Who, in your opinion, is ultimately responsible for GHG emissions—corporations or consumers? How might your answer to this questions influence your choice of public policy tool?

5. How does the federal division of powers complicate Canadian environmental policy?

6. What constraints limit the federal government's options on GHG reduction policy?

The Canadian Prime Minister: Revisiting *Primus* in Canadian Politics

Donald J. Savoie

Editors' Note

When Canadians compare the power and prestige of the office of Canadian prime minister with that of the office of president of the United States of America, they generally conclude that the American president is a far more powerful figure in American government than is the prime minister in Canadian government. Such a conclusion is understandable. The President is the head of state and senior executive of the most powerful country on the planet. The American president is usually at the centre of international summits and routinely uses his influence to broker conflicts beyond the shores of the United States. By contrast, the Canadian prime minister is a diminutive presence on the world stage.

It is important to keep in mind that comparing offices is not the same as comparing countries. If we are interested in comparing the relative power of the prime minister and president, then we must see how each office relates to other institutions in its respective regime. Despite the president's enormous profile on the world stage and in American politics, it is likely true that the Canadian prime minister is a more powerful figure in Canadian politics than is the president in American politics.

Donald Savoie's essay is concerned not so much with this Canada–U.S. comparison as with establishing that the power of the prime minister has increased in Canadian politics and government over the last generation. Prime-ministerial power has increased to such an extent that it has affected the nature of parliamentary government in this country.

Savoie explores the manner in which prime ministers have become so dominant.

Recent political events attest to the strength and attractions of the institutions of prime ministerial power. During the 2005–06 federal election campaign, Conservative leader Stephen Harper urged more democratic accountability, by which many of his supporters understood more MP autonomy and less executive domination. Their hopes were dashed when Prime Minister Harper limited his cabinet ministers' remarks to scripted talking points, controlled media relations with meticulous care, punished Conservative MPs like Garth Turner for speaking independently, and allowed a vote on extending Canada's mission in Afghanistan after deciding to extend the mission anyway.

◆ ◆ ◆

Canadians have known for some time that their prime minister wields a great deal of power. But what they may not know is that developments since the late 1960s have been such that when it comes to the political power inherent in their office, Canadian prime ministers now have no equal in the West.

In the past three decades Canadians have witnessed major changes in the way they are governed, changes that have generally attracted little notice. Public debate in Canada since the late 1960s has focused on actual or proposed constitutional changes and not on the internal machinery of the federal government. In any event, changes to the machinery of government rarely,

Article prepared for this publication. © Nelson, 2008.

if ever, enjoy much media or public profile. Yet the evolution of the machinery of government, particularly within the federal government, has had far-reaching consequences for the public service, public policy, Canadian federalism, and ultimately for Canadians themselves.

I maintain ... that power no longer flows from ministers, but from the prime minister, and unevenly at that.

This paper challenges long-established conventions or understandings about how our government works. Gordon Robertson, former secretary to the Cabinet, explained nearly thirty years ago that in our system "ministers are responsible. It is their government."[1] The Privy Council Office in its 1993 publication on the machinery of government argued that "we operate under the theory of a confederal nature of decision making where power flows from ministers."[2] I maintain, to the contrary, that power no longer flows from ministers, but from the prime minister, and unevenly at that.

This chapter begins by looking at the forces which have, in more recent years, strengthened the hand of the prime minister in government. It then reviews the levers of power available to the prime minister and new developments that have made him or her *primus* in all things, rather than simply *primus inter pares*.

NATIONAL UNITY
◆ ◆ ◆

One's place in history matters a great deal to prime ministers. No Canadian prime minister wants the country to break up under his or her watch. Thus, one of the main tasks at hand is keeping the country united, and no other politician in Canada feels so directly responsible for Canadian unity as the prime minister. Indeed, should Canada break up, the prime minister will be the first to be held to account. The result is that many policy issues ranging from cuts in spending to trade negotiations are now routed to the Prime Minister's Office or the Privy Council Office to assess their impact on national unity. The impact is felt in all areas and in all sectors from the obvious (e.g., regional development) to the less obvious (e.g., trade issues). Andrew Cooper, for example, writes "the decisive impact of the constitutional issue in this

matter inevitably stymied the government's ability to perform effectively in the concluding phase of the Uruguay Round."[3]

... many policy issues ranging from cuts in spending to trade negotiations are routed to the Prime Minister's Office or the Privy Council Office to assess their impact on national unity.

THE MEDIA
◆ ◆ ◆

There is plenty of evidence to suggest that how the media go about their work has changed substantially in recent years. Today, the media, much like society itself, are less deferential to political leaders and political institutions. Nothing is off limits any more. In addition, the media have become important political actors in their own right.

The age of 24-hour television and the intense competition between the electronic and print media have put relentless pressure on journalists to produce something new or provocative. In addition, the electronic media can hardly follow a government decision-making process and, in any case, they have little interest in describing how it works. Their focus is on political actors and the one who matters most to their audiences, and is turned to for answers in any policy field, is the prime minister.

Today's media have a greater capacity than ever before to ferret out errors or miscues in government. Access-to-information legislation is one factor and a greatly expanded role of the Office of the Auditor-General is another. The media can now, on very short notice, turn an issue, however trivial, into an important file. What constitutes an important file is any issue that makes it to the front page of *The Globe and Mail*, *The National Post*, or *La Presse*. It then becomes highly political, and at that point the prime minister and his advisors will want to oversee its development. Senior officials from either the Prime Minister's Office or the Privy Council Office or both, will, on behalf of the prime minister, manage the issue to limit any political fallout.

The media will also concentrate on party leaders at election time rather than on selected party candidates, even those enjoying a high profile. Journalists buy seats on the chartered aircraft of party leaders and follow them everywhere. In Canada, at least, the media and, by extension, the public, focus on the clash of party leaders. For one thing, there are the leaders' debates on national television, in both English and French. How well a leader does in the debates can have an important impact, or at least be perceived to have an important impact, on the election campaign, if not the election itself.

Increasingly, Canadian political leaders appear to be the only substantial candidates in the election race. In the past, Canada had powerful Cabinet ministers with deep roots in the party or strong regional identification and support. One thinks of Jimmy Gardiner, Chubby Power, Jack Pickersgill, Ernest Lapointe, Louis St. Laurent, Don Jamieson, and Allan MacEachen. We no longer seem to have powerful regional or party figures who can carry candidates to victory on their coattails or speak to the prime minister from an independent power base in the party. Alain Cairns, for example, writes that "early Cabinets were collections of regional notables with independent bases of their own who powerfully asserted the needs of their provinces at the highest level in the land .... now, however, regional spokesmen of such power and authenticity are only memories, although the regional basis of Cabinet appointment continues."[4]

In Canada, winning candidates on the government side are aware that their party leader's performance in the election campaign explains in large measure why they themselves were successful. The objective of national political parties at election time is more to sell their leaders to the Canadian electorate than it is to sell their ideas or their policies. Canadian elections invariably turn on the question of which person—not which party—will form the government. It should come as no surprise, then, that if the leader is able to secure a majority mandate, the party is in his debt, and not the other way around.

The objective of national political parties at election time is more to sell their leaders to the Canadian electorate than it is to sell their ideas or their policies.

Canadian national political parties are not much more than election-day organizations, providing the fundraising and poll workers needed to fight an election campaign. They are hardly effective vehicles for generating public policy debates, for staking out policy positions, or for providing a capacity to ensure their own party's competence once in office. Regional cleavages in Canada, as is well known, dominate the national public policy agenda, and national political parties shy away from attacking regional issues head-on for fear they will split the party along regional lines and hurt its chances at election time. The thinking goes, again at least in the parties that have held power in Ottawa, that the issue is so sensitive and so politically explosive that it is better left in the hands of party leaders and a handful of advisors.

Since Trudeau, Canadian prime ministers have made themselves into television personalities. The same cannot be said of Cabinet ministers. A Gallup poll conducted in 1988 is very revealing on this point. It reported that only 31 percent of respondents could name a *single* Cabinet minister four years after the Mulroney government had come to power. In addition, only 5 percent of the respondents could identify Don Mazankowski, deputy prime minister and one of the most, if not the most, powerful member of Mulroney's Cabinet.[5]

Access to information legislation has also had an important impact on government operations. The legislation has generated a demand for good political firefighters and safe pairs of hands in Ottawa to manage political crises. The prime minister, for example, as head of the government, will want to have the best political firefighters by his side in his own office or in the Privy Council Office. It explains in part why, when a fire becomes difficult or when a potential problem emerges, information and power are drawn to the centre.[6] This too serves to strengthen the hand of the prime minister.

THE POLICY PROCESS
◆ ◆ ◆

There are now two policy process in Ottawa. One is best described as policy by announcement (e.g., Kyoto, the Millennium Scholarship Fund), the other is an elaborate interdepartmental, consultative, and porous process. One depends solely on the prime minister and his court of advisors while the other depends on a complicated interdepartmental and stakeholder consultative process. This suits the prime minister just fine. When he decides that something is important to him, he will take charge and get his way. For other things, he will be content to just see the process run its course under the watchful eye of his department, the Privy Council Office. One process enables the prime minister to have his way on things that matter to him and the other enables him to keep an eye on and control other issues. In any event, the prime minister is secure in the knowledge that, in Jean Chrétien's words, "in our system, a minister proposes but it has to be decided by the Prime Minister."[7]

There are now two policy processes in Ottawa.

THEY ARE NOW ALL THE PRIME MINISTER'S MEN AND WOMEN
◆ ◆ ◆

The centre of government has changed a great deal since Trudeau came to power in 1968. The Trudeau reforms had a profound impact on how policies and decisions are made in Ottawa and they are still being felt today. In the pre-Trudeau days, strong ministers would strike an alliance with their deputy ministers and together decide if, when, and how departmental policies or programs should be overhauled or adjusted. The minister would then bring the matter to Cabinet to get a green light to proceed.[8]

Cabinet, Trudeau and his key advisors concluded, did not have the capacity to challenge a strong minister, to identify and debate the various options. In order for ministers to make it their government, the argument went, they needed a capacity and support at the centre of government and in Cabinet to discuss the "lines of solutions" and make policy.

The Trudeau Reforms
- Established Cabinet committees with authority
- Considerably expanded and strengthened Privy Council Office and the Prime Minister's Office
- Appointed deputy ministers increasingly from outside departmental ranks
- Central agency experience made a prerequisite for advancement
- Mandate letters prepared at the centre of government when ministers and deputy ministers are appointed; these letters point up issues that should be attended to and identify priorities that should be pursued

A capacity was indeed created at the centre of government with both the Prime Minister's Office and the Privy Council Office growing substantially in size during the 1970s. Several spending reduction measures introduced during the past several years, including the ambitious program review exercise (1994–96), have had limited impact on these two offices. The Prime Minister's Office and the Privy Council Office today employ over 800 officials, in contrast with 250 in 1969. These figures are all the more remarkable given that the size of the federal government today, as Treasury Board Secretariat officials are often proud to report, is about what it was in the late 1960s.

The Prime Minster's Office now employs over 800 officials, in contrast with 250 in 1969.

The Trudeau reforms did attenuate the powers of strong ministers and strong line departments. But they did not strengthen Cabinet as a collective decision-making body. Rather, they strengthened considerably the hand of the prime minister and his advisors. One minister in the Chrétien government observed that "Cabinet is no longer a decision-making body; it is a focus group for the prime minister."[9] This analogy is not much of an overstatement. In fact, Chrétien himself wrote before he became prime minister that a minister "may have great authority within his department, but within Cabinet he is merely part of a collectivity, just another adviser to the prime minister. He can be told what to do and on important matters his only choice is to do or resign."[10]

"Cabinet is no longer a decision-making body; it is a focus group for the prime minister."

The Trudeau reforms have also enabled prime ministers since Trudeau to cope with the political overload problem confronting all modern governments. The term "political overload" speaks to a sense of urgency in government matters and of being overwhelmed by both events and things to do. Prime ministers, again since Trudeau, have decided that the best way to deal with the overload problem is to focus on a handful of policy issues and to rely on central agencies to manage the rest. All of the major policy initiatives in Trudeau's last mandate, including the national energy program, the Constitution, and the "six and five" wage restraint initiative, were organized outside the government's formal decision-making process. Similarly, Mulroney side-stepped Cabinet in pursuing constitutional reform, the Canada-U.S. free trade agreement, and the establishment of regional development agencies. Chrétien did the same for the Millennium Scholarship Fund and the Kyoto agreement.

Prime ministers, again since Trudeau, have decided that the best way to deal with the overload problem is to focus on a handful of problems and to rely on central agencies to manage the rest.

Pollsters can also help the prime minister decide what is important to Canadians and what is not, what is politically sensible and what is not. Prime ministers since Trudeau have had a pollster in their court of advisors. Trudeau had Martin Goldfarb, Mulroney had Allan Gregg, and Chrétien has Michael Marzolini. It is also important to recognize that the prime minister no longer needs to rely on regional ministers for an understanding of how government policies are being received. Public opinion surveys are more reliable, more objective, less regionally biased, more to the point, and easier to cope with than ministers. They can also be used to deal with any public policy issue. Surveys can enable prime ministers and their advisors to challenge the views of ministers. After all, how can even the most senior ministers dispute what the polls say?

... the prime minister no longer needs to rely on regional ministers for an understanding of how government policies are being received.

During the Trudeau years, a new breed of advisors arrived on the scene in Ottawa and they made their presence felt. Lobbyists happily took up special causes, mostly those tied to big business. Though it is not at all

clear precisely what kind of expertise lobbyists peddle around Ottawa, one would need to be extremely naive to assume that this development has not had a significant impact on the Ottawa decision-making process. Senior lobbyists, particularly the discreet ones, can be extremely useful to prime ministers. If a prime minister needs a second opinion on advice provided by ministers and senior public servants, he can turn to one of several senior lobbyists who are only too happy to oblige by reporting the views of clients or the results of public opinion surveys.

In the late 1970s, the Privy Council Office also began the practice of preparing mandate letters for delivery to ministers on the day of their appointments. It has since become an integral part of the Cabinet-making process. Mandate letters are also now handed to all ministers when they are assigned to a new portfolio. All ministers in the Chrétien government, for example, were given a mandate letter at the time he formed the government in 1993 and again in his second mandate in 1997 and once again in his third mandate in 2000.

What are the contents of these mandate letters? In most cases, they are brief, only about two to three pages in length. They are also tailored to the recipient. That is, a mandate letter to a newly appointed minister will be different from one to a veteran minister. In the first instance, it will outline basic information about becoming a Cabinet minister, including conflict-of-interest guidelines, and the need to respect the collective nature of Cabinet decisions. In all cases, the letters will delineate issues the minister should attend to and identify priority areas, if any, to be pursued. Here, again, there are two basic mandate letters. One states, in effect, "Don't call us, we'll call you." That is, the prime minister has decided that the department in question should not come up with a new policy agenda or legislative program. In these cases, the message is essentially: keep things going, do not cause any ripples, and keep out of trouble. In other instances, the letter will refer to particular policy objectives and major challenges. In these cases, they can be quite specific, singling out proposed legislation, a special concern that needs attending to, or a program that needs to be overhauled.

Mandate letters are now also prepared for newly appointed deputy ministers. Here again the purpose is to outline the main challenges the new deputy ministers will be confronting and the priorities they will be expected to follow. This development, combined with several others, has served to weaken further line departments in relation to the centre. Indeed, deputy ministers, in many ways, have become as much a part of the centre of government as they are the administrative heads of their departments.

Mandate letters ... have served to weaken further line departments in relation to the centre.

A detailed study, "Changing Profile of Federal Deputy Ministers, 1867 to 1988," is very revealing. It reports that the time deputy ministers spend in a particular department has declined to three years from the average of twelve in the early period of Confederation. Unlike their predecessors, therefore, deputy ministers no longer stay with and retire in their department. As the profile study points out, "They can no longer head the same department for many years."[11] Moreover, in Ottawa, recruitment of deputy ministers now easily crosses the boundaries between departments, while countries such as France and Germany have remained loyal to the tradition that the permanent head of the department is chosen from its senior ranks. Another study reveals that "experience in a central agency, most notably in the Privy Council Office, is now a virtual prerequisite for deputy minister appointment."[12] A still more recent study reveals that deputy ministers are increasingly drawn from central agencies and that the bulk of their work has to do with interdepartmental issues. Two deputy ministers interviewed for the study report that they now spend anywhere between 75 and 95 percent of their time on horizontal issues.[13]

It is important to note that deputy ministers are appointed by the prime minister, not the relevant minister. The prime minister is, of course, free to turn to several sources for advice on who would make a strong deputy minister. But no one has more influence in this area than the Clerk of the Privy Council Office. What about the role of ministers? It varies. A few of the more senior ministers have a kind of *droit de regard*. But precious few ministers enjoy or have enjoyed this privilege. In addition, the *droit de regard* is considered a privilege, not a right, even in the case of the most senior ministers, and it can be revoked at any moment if the prime minister so decides. Marc Lalonde and Allan MacEachen enjoyed a *droit de regard* under Trudeau, as did Don Mazankowski under Mulroney and Paul Martin under Chrétien. But the Clerk, better than most, knows which ministers have the *droit de regard* on the appointment of their deputy ministers and will have the good sense to

have a private chat with them on a possible appointment or even recommend the individual favoured by the minister. The minister, having in turn gained the confidence of the prime minister, will also be wise to the ways of government and will promote someone who is well known and respected by the Clerk. In other words, both a senior minister and the Clerk know that confrontation on the appointment of a deputy minister is not in their interest and they will usually do what is necessary to avoid it.

Other ministers will be informed of possible choices, and still others (the great majority) will simply be told a day or two in advance who will be appointed as their deputy minister. There have been occasions when even that courtesy was not observed. One former minister reveals that he first learned of the identity of his deputy minister on the radio in the morning while shaving.[14] Privy Council Office officials explain that deputy ministers are often appointed in a "DM shuffle," which can involve several appointments at a time, and that it would not be realistic to shop around names to see which minister is interested in whom.

LOOKING BACK
◆ ◆ ◆

The past thirty years or so reveal that important decisions are no longer made in Cabinet. They are now made in federal-provincial meetings of first ministers, on Team Canada flights, where first ministers can hold informal meetings, in the Prime Minister's Office, in the Privy Council Office, in the Department of Finance, in international organizations, and at international summits. In Canada, national unity concerns, the nature of federal-provincial relations, and the role of the media tend, in a perverse fashion, to favour the centre of government in Ottawa. The prime minister and his or her advisors dominate the policy agenda and permeate government decision-making to such an extent that they trust only themselves to oversee the management of important issues. In a sense, the centre of government has come to fear ministerial and line department independence more than it deplores line department paralysis.

Primus was challenged by his own caucus and party in the spring-summer of 2002. Jean Chrétien, perhaps sensing that he would lose a leadership review vote scheduled for February 2003, announced in the summer of 2002 his intention to leave office in February 2004. The party, because of its ability to hold a leadership review vote, can call in question the prime minister's stay in office. It is important to note, however, that the policy does not provide for the turfing-out of a prime minister, but only forces a leadership convention even if the prime minister is able to secure a majority of seats in the previous general election.

The past thirty years or so reveal that important decisions are no longer made in Cabinet.

We need to put the events of spring-summer 2002 in context. The opposition had posed no serious threat to the governing Liberal party from the day Jean Chrétien was sworn in as prime minister in 1993. The Progressive Conservative party, it will be recalled, collapsed in 1993 and two regional parties emerged—one in western Canada and one in Quebec—which served to give the Liberal party access to political power for the past ten years with no indication that things will change in the near future. But political power is not forever. In the current context, when Canadians become disenchanted with the prime minister, they must look to a change of leadership in what has been described as the natural governing party.[15] To be sure, there are many facets to Canada's democratic deficit, but the fact that there is no opposition party that is national in scope and that poses a serious threat to the party in power ranks at the top of the list.

The challenge for a long-serving prime minister, then, is to pay particular attention to leadership review votes following general elections. If the prime minister can successfully navigate such a vote, he or she will continue to hold most of the government's political power. It will be recalled that following Chrétien's announcement that he would be a slowly departing prime minister, former Prime Minister Joe Clark declared: "The problem facing Parliament is that the prime minister has virtually absolute control and that is not democracy. The solution is to break up that control."[16] Indeed, within a month of his announcing his decision to retire, Chrétien, we are informed, decided "to make an international commitment" (i.e., on Kyoto) without first informing all the members of his Cabinet, and this event was described as "just one example of the power he now wields."[17] It appears that a Canadian prime minister, even when he has to wear

the "lame duck" label, can still have his way on issues that matter to him, on the Budget and on appointments. This does not leave much room for others to exercise political power.

What are the prospects for change? There are signs that Canadians are starting to take note of the prime minister's power and that they would like to see change. Paul Martin, former Finance Minister and the leading candidate to replace Chrétien as Liberal leader, spoke about the democratic deficit in a major speech to students at Osgoode Law School on October 21, 2002. He declared that "everyone in Ottawa believes that the key to getting things done is … who do you know in the PMO?" His solutions? Loosen the hold of party discipline over members of Parliament by overhauling the role of standing committees, provide parliamentary committees an opportunity to review senior government appointments and give "greater scope and opportunity for private members' bills for MPs and to change substantially legislation."[18]

… prime ministers have not been known in the past to part willingly with their power once they have climbed all the way up to the Prime Minister's Office.

The fact that Martin would make the power of the prime minister an important issue in his bid to win the leadership of the Liberal party is revealing. The reforms he proposes are modest; but it is a start, and it may well spur other political leaders to advance other proposals to reform our national political institutions. The real test, however, is what a politician does when he or she is actually sitting in the prime minister's chair. Prime ministers have in their hands virtually all the levers of power, and so they decide if and when reforms should or can be initiated. Much like tigers do not like to part with their stripes, prime ministers have not been known in the past to part willingly with their power once they have climbed up all the way to the Prime Minister's Office. In brief, it is up to the prime minister to reduce the power of *Primus* and there is a very strong possibility that once in office he or she will be comfortable with the status quo and that "*Primus* in all things" will remain part of the Canadian political system for at least the foreseeable future.

Notes

1. Gordon Robertson, "The Changing Role of the Privy Council Office," *Canadian Public Administration,* 14, 4 (Winter 1971): 497.

2. Canada, *Responsibility in the Constitution* (Ottawa: Privy Council Office, 1993).

3. Andrew F. Cooper, *In Between Countries: Australia, Canada and the Search for Order in Agricultural Trade* (Montreal: McGill-Queen's University Press, 1997), p. 217.

4. Alain Cairns, *From Interstate to Intrastate Federalism in Canada* (Kingston: Institute of Intergovernmental Relations, 1979), p. 6.

5. See John Crosbie, *No Holds Barred: My Life in Politics* (Toronto: McClelland and Stewart, 1997), p. 301.

6. See, among others, Donald J. Savoie, *Governing from the Centre: The Concentration of Power in Canadian Politics* (Toronto: University of Toronto Press, 1999), chapter 7.

7. Prime Minister Jean Chrétien in year-end interview (2002) with CBC-Television, December 18, 2002.

8. Savoie, *Governing from the Centre,* p. 235.

9. Jean Chrétien, *Straight from the Heart* (Toronto: Key Porter Books, 1985), p. 85.

10. Jacques Bourgault and Stéphane Dion, "The Changing Profile of Federal Deputy Ministers, 1867 to 1988," Research Paper no. 2 (Ottawa: Canadian Centre for Management Development, March 1991), p. 28.

11. Frank Swift, "Strategic Management in the Public Service: The Changing Role of the Deputy Minister" (Ottawa: Canadian Centre for Management Development, November 1993), p. 63.

12. See Savoie, *Governing from the Centre,* p. 116.

13. Jacques Bourgault, *Le rôle et les défis contemporains des sous-ministres du gouvernement fédéral du Canada* (Ottawa: Centre canadien de gestion, 2002), pp. 15–40.

14. John Tait et al., "Discussion Paper on Values and Ethics in the Public Service" (Ottawa: Privy Council Office, December 1996), p. 45.

15. Reg Whitaker, *The Government Party: Organizing and Financing the Liberal Party of Canada, 1930–58* (Toronto: University of Toronto Press, 1977).

16. Quoted in "Democracy Rule by the People? Not in Canada," *National Post,* October 9, 2002, p. A1.

17. Quoted in "PM's Power Threatens to Even Make Cabinet Irrelevant," *National Post,* October 16, 2002, p. A1.

18. See, among others, Susan Delacourt, "Martin Vows to Empower the MP," *National Post,* October 22, 2002, p. A1.

Terms and Concepts

primus inter pares

mandate letters

Prime Minister's office

Privy Council Office

droit de regard

democratic deficit

ministerial responsibility

policy processes

line departments

the "DM shuffle"

political overload

Questions

1. How have changes in the senior public service appointment processes influenced prime ministerial power?

2. A maxim of parliamentary government is that the concentration of political power produces the concentration of political responsibility. A prime minister who is *"primus* in all things" can be held responsible for all things. Is this an effective reply to Savoie's concerns?

3. Canada has a history of populist political parties that support ways of returning power to the people by mechanisms of direct democracy. Would more power to the people limit prime ministerial power?

4. To what extent are criticisms of the institutions of parliament really criticisms of the people and parties occupying them at any given time?

5. Does Canada have a democratic deficit?

6. Assuming Savoie's analysis is correct, what do you recommend to reduce the power of the prime minister?

Are Canadian Political Parties Empty Vessels: Membership, Engagement and Policy Capacity

William Cross and Lisa Young

Editors' Note

Party was once synonymous with faction—a divisive, dangerous cabal of people united in opposition to the general welfare of the political order. These days parties are considered vital to the health of democratic societies. Democracies stand for civil freedom and an enfranchised educated citizenry. Diverse views about public policy and the common good are expected and encouraged. Out of the welter of conflicting views comes more thoughtful, refined, and widely supported law. Political parties are among the most important vehicles for the development and mobilization of diverse views of the common good. In contrast to other organizations like interest groups and think tanks, parties afford citizens a direct role in selecting candidates for elected office.

Modern political parties are complex organizations. They are groups of like-minded individuals dedicated to electing their representatives to public office. Members help to select party officers who run the party machine, finance the parties' activities, and vote for representatives at election time. Parliamentary members of the party, however, are subject to different responsibilities than non-parliamentary members. The elected members are responsible to party members for what they do but also to those who elected them (very few of whom are party members) and to all constituents, even those who voted for the losing candidates. Party members typically have a narrower view of the political landscape than the parliamentary party member. Tension is inevitable.

One measure of the health of a democracy is the vitality of political parties as membership organizations. By this measure, Canada suffers from a political sclerosis. Party membership is quite low and in apparent decline. William Cross and Lisa Young trace this decline to the dissatisfaction felt by party members with the relatively modest role they play within our political parties. Cross and Young propose that membership would increase and parties would be strengthened if people were given a more meaningful role in the development of party policy. One important question is whether Canadian traditions and party structures are flexible enough to accommodate the reforms the authors propose.

❖ ❖ ❖

INTRODUCTION
❖ ❖ ❖

In the period just after Confederation, the notion that membership or involvement in a Canadian political party was a form of public service would have been considered quite peculiar. More accurate would have been the idea that activism on behalf of a political party was a route into the public service, as civil service jobs

were awarded to loyal supporters of the governing party. In the contemporary era, with fewer opportunities for political parties to dispense patronage, it is more plausible to think about party membership as a form of public service, as most party members are volunteers motivated by a desire to play a role in political life.

In fact, drawing on the Study of Canadian Political Party members, our 2000 survey of members of what were then Canada's five major political parties,[1] we find that individuals are drawn to party membership not by a desire to further their personal interests but rather by support for their party's policy stance and as participants in intraparty personnel contests. This conforms to a notion of public service as volunteerism motivated by a desire to participate in or influence discussions of public policy and party affairs. Volunteers have traditionally played a significant role in Canadian political parties as campaign workers, supporters of candidates for party leadership or nomination, and local organizers. In the contemporary era of professionalized, media-oriented politics, however, the already circumscribed role of the Canadian party member has been limited even further. In our survey, we found that party members are not satisfied with their ability to shape party policy and are particularly resentful of the extent to which political professionals have usurped the role of the party member.

To the extent that party membership in Canada is a form of public service and thus contributes to the vibrancy of political life in the country, we should be concerned that the rates of party membership appear to be dropping, the average party member is nearing retirement age and is not being replaced, and rates of activism within parties are relatively low. All of these tendencies are products of complex social change, reinforced by institutional constraints that have historically limited the role of Canadian party members. As such, they defy easy solutions. We argue, however, that one approach that might encourage party membership and help political parties to fulfill their roles in public life would be to encourage parties to develop policy foundations.

... we should be concerned that the rates of party membership appear to be dropping, the average party member is nearing retirement age and is not being replaced, and rates of activism within parties are relatively low.

PARTIES WITHOUT MEMBERS—THE COMPARATIVE CONTEXT

◆ ◆ ◆

Studies of political party organization and membership in Western Europe and North America in recent years point to significant changes in party organization, driven by declining rates of membership in political parties. The

most notable of these studies is a book entitled *Parties Without Partisans* (Dalton and Wattenberg 2000), the title of which telegraphs a key concern about the development of party organization in these established democracies. The consensus among political scientists who study political parties in established democracies is that rates of party membership have declined over the past three or four decades (Scarrow 2000; Norris 2002; Heidar and Saglie 2003). The extent of the decline and the rate at which it has occurred vary by country, but the overall trend is in a downward direction. Moreover, rates of activism tend to be very low, and in many cases declining, among party members in these industrialized democracies (Scarrow 2000; Norris 2002; Heidar and Sagile 2003; Gallagher and Marsh 2002; Whiteley and Seyd 2002).

Although these findings have profound implications for the role of political parties in modern democracies, they must be placed in context. When measuring numbers of party members or the rate of party membership in the electorate, the initial basis for comparison is usually the 1950s or 1960s. Susan Scarrow (2000, 94–5) points out that "it was only in the 1950s and 1960s that many countries had parties of both the left and the right successfully pursuing mass enrolment strategies. Before and after this period, parties exhibited an uneven pattern of commitment to, and success in, enlisting supporters in permanent organizations." As Scarrow points out, the period from the Second World War until the 1970s was a historical anomaly, with unusually high rates of membership. Using this time as a basis for comparison overstates the magnitude of the decline.

... affluent countries generally have lower rates of party membership than other democracies.

Even if the decline in rates of membership is somewhat exaggerated by the basis for comparison, there remains the question of why membership rates began to fall after reaching these unprecedented highs in the postwar era. Norris's (2002) cross-national analysis makes it clear that this is a phenomenon of affluent established democracies; in fact, she finds that affluent countries generally have lower rates of party membership than other democracies. This finding lends general support to the modernization thesis, which holds that various aspects of the modern social and political order in advanced industrialized nations lead to a weakening of the bond between the public and political parties (Dalton and Wattenberg 2000, 10–11).

More specifically, the modernization thesis suggests that increases in education, changing values held by citizens, changing modes of social organization, the rise of the mass media, tendencies toward professionalization and changes in technology all combine to weaken citizens' attachment to political parties and to discourage membership in party organizations. At the level of the individual citizen, higher rates of education result in "cognitive mobilization" of citizens. With greater intellectual resources at their disposal, these individuals become self-sufficient political actors who are less deferential to political elites and less inclined to look to elites for political cues, opting instead to make their own choices (Dalton and Wattenberg 2000, 10–11). More complex patterns of social organization, when combined with this cognitive mobility, reduce the basis for group mobilization. Individuals in these postindustrial societies are less inclined to identify themselves as members of a social group—such as the working class—and are consequently less available to be mobilized as group members. Overall, these individual-level changes result in a smaller supply of individuals who can be mobilized to partisan activity.

Aspects of social organization in modern societies also contribute to declining membership in political parties. In particular, the rise of the electronic mass media supplants the role of party members in spreading the party's message, and the rise of public opinion polling reduces party leaders' need to gather information about the mood of the electorate from party members. Norris (2002) finds empirical evidence for this assertion. In her cross-national analysis, she finds that rates of party membership are lower in countries that have a high rate of ownership of television sets. From this, she concludes that the electronic broadcast media act as a substitute for party mobilization in established democracies. Parties communicate with voters not through volunteers who spread the word but via carefully crafted television advertisements.

Along with the rise of electronic media and opinion polling comes a professionalization of parties, in which fundraisers, pollsters and communication consultants come to fill the functions that were once the preserve of members of political parties. As a consequence, the conduct of politics goes from a labour-intensive undertaking in which volunteer labour was a necessity for an electorally competitive party, to a capital-intensive activity in which money, rather than volunteer labour, is essential to electoral success. In essence, technological changes have reduced parties' demand for active members in these affluent, established democracies.

Given these trends, it would be reasonable to predict that political parties may one day become organizations without members. If party leaders do not need members to run election campaigns, maintain party organization and serve as informational conduits between the electorate and the party leadership, then why should they continue to recruit party members? In considering this question, it becomes clear that party members serve functions other than those listed above. First, parties gain legitimacy from their membership; if they are not able to point to some membership base, they may lose credibility in the eyes of the electorate. The existence of a membership base lends an air of legitimacy to decisions made by the party, not the least of which are the selection of a leader and the choice of candidates for legislative office. Second, members can be important assets in intraparty battles (Scarrow 2002, 100). As long as party constitutions give party members a voice in selecting party leaders, there will be an incentive for aspirants to mobilize members into the party to support their quest for the leadership.

This raises the question of how parties can recruit new members from the cognitively mobile and atomized societies that we find in most established democracies. Comparative studies show that parties have responded to this challenge in large part by moving in the direction of "plebiscitary" party organization, in which members are accorded direct votes in the selection of party leaders and on selected matters of party policy and direction (Scarrow 1999; Seyd 1999; Whiteley and Seyd 2002, 213). In their research in Britain, Whiteley and Seyd (2002) conclude that such techniques may increase the size of a party's membership but do not increase the rate of activism within the party.

A strategy that parties facing such challenges often adopt is to turn to the state for financial support that allows them to purchase the services of professionals to maintain party organization (Kata and Mair 1995; van Biezen 2004). Increasingly, political parties are portrayed in both academic and political discourse as "public utilities" that perform services that are necessary to electoral democracy and that must be supported financially by the state. Certainly, with the advent of quarterly funding for Canadian political parties at the federal level, we can see that Canadian parties have, to varying degrees, adopted this strategy (Young et al 2005). If state funding reduces a party's need to maintain an active base of members and supporters, it may exacerbate tendencies toward party organization in which members play a minimal role.

PARTY MEMBERSHIP IN CANADA: AN OVERVIEW

◆ ◆ ◆

How does Canada fit into this picture of declining party memberships? On one hand, there is little evidence that rates of membership in Canadian parties have declined substantially. In her comparative analysis, Scarrow (2000, 88) observes that the United States and Canada "do not support the picture of 'decline,' though they do match the picture of contemporary parties as lacking strong membership bases." In essence, the golden era of the mass membership party never dawned in Canada.

... between 1 and 2 percent of Canadians belong to a political party on a year-to-year basis. This places Canada at the bottom of the list of Western democracies.

Few Canadians choose to belong to political parties on an ongoing basis. An Institute for Research on Public Policy study by Howe and Northrup (2000, 89) found that 16 percent of respondents claim to have belonged to a political party at some point in their lives. This figure probably includes a significant number of "partisans" of a party who have never formally held membership. Our best estimate, from an examination of membership patterns over time, is that between 1 and 2 percent of Canadians belong to a political party on a year-to-year basis. This places Canada at the bottom of the list of Western democracies.

Moreover, Canadian party members are much older than the general population. In our survey, we found half our respondents were senior citizens, and only one in 20 was under age 30. Some of this age distortion may be explained by respondent bias, as seniors are more likely to participate in mail surveys than are their younger counterparts. However, this factor alone cannot explain the degree to which Canadian political party membership appears to be "greying." Similar findings are reported in a study conducted by the IRPP in 2000, which found that only 5 percent of Canadians aged 18 to 30 have ever belonged to a political party (either federal or provincial),

compared with one-third of those over age 60 (Howe and Northrup 2000). The same question was asked in a survey conducted in 1990; at that time, 10 percent of respondents aged 18 to 30 reported having belonged to a party. This decline over time in the rate of party membership among youth lends some credence to the idea that Canadian political parties, as membership organizations, are in decline.

No Canadian political party has achieved the kind of mass membership enrolment that characterized mass parties of the mid-twentieth century. The co-operative Commonwealth Federation (CCF) and then the New Democratic Party (NDP) represented an effort to build a mass-type party in Canada, but neither party was able to achieve the kind of social encapsulation that leftist parties in Western Europe achieved. This may in part reflect the limited salience of class identities in the Canadian context, but it is also a product of the unique circumstances of Canadian political parties. R.K. Carty (2002, 729) notes that Canadian parties must accommodate differences among diverse and shifting coalitions of supporters, and have "little in the way of the material or ideational glue that traditionally holds political parties together." As a consequence, "the conventional model of a centralized, disciplined mass membership party, speaking with one voice, and committed to offering and delivering an integrated and coherent set of public policies has never been the way to do this successfully" in the Canadian experience (Carty 2002).

Although the Canadian party system did not experience the full effects of the rise of the mass party in the mid-twentieth century, the formation of the NDP and changing expectations about internal democracy did provide a stimulus for the two traditional brokerage parties to increase the influence of their members. During the 1960s and 1970s, the grassroots party memberships gained greater influence over the selection of the party leader, gained the power to oust a party leader and won some influence over setting party policy (see Carty, Cross, and Young 2000, 110–11). As a result of these developments, the traditional influence of Canadian party members at the local level, especially in controlling local party affairs and selecting candidates, was enhanced by a new influence over the selection of the leader at the national level.

Members' entitlements to vote in local nomination contests and in national leadership contests are the two significant entitlements that accompany membership in a Canadian political party. It is not surprising, then, that levels of membership in Canadian political parties follow a cyclical pattern. The number of members who belong

Table 22.1   Number of Members for the Liberal Party of Canada in the Four Largest Provinces, 2002 and 2003

	2002	2003	% increase
Ontario	38,000	126,000	232
Quebec	28,000	65,000	132
British Columbia	4,500	38,000	744
Alberta	4,000	22,000	450

Source: R. Kenneth Carty and William Cross, "Can Stratarchically Organized Parties Be Democratic: The Canadian Case," *Journal of Elections, Public Opinion and Parties* 2006, 16 (2): 93–114, 103.

to each party can double or even triple in election years and in years when the party is selecting a leader. Table 22.1 shows the dramatic increase in Liberal Party membership in each of the four largest provinces in the run-up to its 2003 leadership vote. Candidates seeking either the party's nomination or its leadership mobilize supporters into the party, bolstering the membership ranks. However, after the contest is over, many of these individuals drop out of the party, leaving the stalwarts who maintain the party organization between elections. The vast majority of these members take no further part in party activities. This cyclical pattern suggests that voters are willing to join a party when they see some value offered in exchange for their taking out membership: a vote in the party's leadership or nomination contest. When these contests are not imminent, however, these individuals let their membership lapse.

… voters are willing to join a party when they see some value offered in exchange for their taking out membership: a vote in the party's leadership or nomination contest.

This raises the important question of why voters who are open to the possibility of participating in party politics will not maintain ongoing memberships. We suggest that the answer to this question is, at least in part, that voters do not see membership in political parties as a way of influencing the country's politics (aside from personnel selection). The Howe and Northrup survey (2000) offers some evidence of this. They find that, by a three-to-one margin, Canadians believe that

belonging to an interest group is a more effective way of influencing public policy than is participation in a political party. This public perception is not erroneous, as even the parties' core group of consistent members are largely dissatisfied with the role they play in ongoing party decision-making. (We discuss this in some detail below.)

… members remain valuable to Canadian parties primarily as a source of public legitimacy, and as a resource in intraparty contests.

The cyclical pattern of membership numbers suggests that party members remain a valued resource for party leaders in intraparty contests. The same modernizing factors that have decreased party leaders' demand for party members in other industrialized democracies are also at work in Canada, however. Canadian political parties have availed themselves of the services of opinion pollsters for checking the public mood, and use television and other electronic media as their primary means of communicating with voters. Canadian parties have become professionalized organizations in which volunteer labour is simply less necessary than it once was. In short, members remain valuable to Canadian parties primarily as a source of public legitimacy, and as a resource in intraparty contests.

When we examine organizational changes in the major political parties over recent decades, we find clear signals that parties continue to seek members as a source of legitimacy. Led by the Reform Party/Canadian Alliance, Canadian parties have shifted their organizational modes in the direction of plebiscitary models of internal party democracy (Young and Cross 2002b). The clearest manifestations of this are the move to give every party member a direct vote in the selection of party leader, the moves of three of the major parties (the Canadian Alliance, the Progressive Conservatives and the Bloc Québécois) away from decentralized forms of party membership in favour of a national party list and the occasional use of referendums within parties on crucial policy issues (See Carty, Cross and Young 2000, chap. 6). The move toward plebiscitary democracy in Canadian parties had its greatest momentum in the 1990s, but the majority of reforms implemented during this period remain in place. While the merits and the success of these initiatives are subject to debate, their existence is a clear sign that the leaders of Canadian parties continue to see a value in trying to recruit and retain party members outside of leadership contests.

Not only do few Canadians belong to parties, but those who do are not particularly active. Our data, collected during a non-mobilization period when we suspect only the most stalwart of party supporters maintained their memberships, indicate that fewer than half of these party members engage in ongoing party activity. Our survey shows that 4 in 10 members report spending no time on party activity in a typical month, and an additional 2 in 10 commit less than one hour per month. As shown in figure 22.1, we found significant variance among the parties in this regard, with the Liberal and Progressive Conservative parties having fewer members who are disengaged from party activity than do the newer parties. This may be a governing party effect with activists more likely to participate in a party that has access to the levers of government and the accompanying patronage powers.

Not only do few Canadians belong to parties, but those who do are not particularly active.

Figure 22.1   Proportion of Members Participating in Party Activity in a Typical Month, Canada, 2000 (percent)

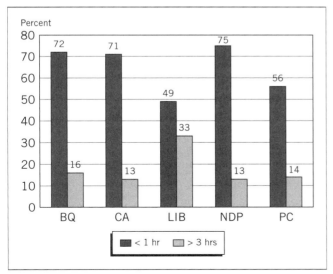

Source: "Study of Canadian Political Party Members," 2000.
Note: The figures for the Liberal Party exclude respondents from Quebec to correct for a sampling problem in that province.

Figure 22.2   Proportion of Members Who Have "Ever" Participated in Party Activities, Canada, 2000 (percent)

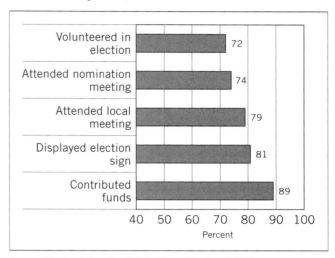

Source: "Study of Canadian Political Party Members," 2000.

Similarly, 4 members in 10 report not having attended a single party meeting during the past year, and fewer than 4 in 10 attended more than two meetings. And, as illustrated in figure 22.2, almost one-quarter of members report that they have never attended a meeting of their local party association or volunteered in an election campaign. While participation rates of 75 percent may seem high, it must be kept in mind that the question asked of members was whether they had "ever" done each of the activities, and also that the population being surveyed was the stalwart (interelection) party members. On the other hand, 9 in 10 members report having contributed funds to the party. Many then appear to be what we might call "chequebook" members, willing to contribute funds to the party but not active in party affairs in any way that may be thought of as akin to public service.

WHY DO CANADIANS JOIN POLITICAL PARTIES?
◆ ◆ ◆

Theoretical accounts suggest three categories of motivation for belonging to a political party (Young and Cross 2002a). The first category—material incentives—harkens back to the post-Confederation era of Canadian politics, when patronage provided ample incentive for membership. The broad category of material incentives includes patronage appointments and government contracts as well as more general inducements like career advancement. The second category—social incentives—offers potential participants the company of like-minded individuals and social or recreational opportunities. The third category—collective or purposive incentives—gives individuals an opportunity to assist in achieving the party's collective policy or ideological goals.

In most but by no means all industrialized democracies, material and social incentives have declined in importance over time. Civil service reforms and changing political values have reduced the practice of patronage, thereby reducing the parties' ability to offer material incentives to potential members. As recreational opportunities have expanded and the bases of social organization on which mass parties were formed have ended, parties have been less able to offer social incentives to membership (Ware 1996). This leaves the category of collective incentives as the primary set of motivators for partisan involvement.

If membership in a political party is a form of collective action, then it is subject to what Olson (1965) identified as the "free rider problem." Olson argues that people have no incentive to participate in political action if they can benefit from the outcome without joining in the mobilization. "Free riders" are individuals who enjoy the benefits of a mobilization without participating in the campaign. In the context of political party activism, the question is this: If party involvement provides only collective benefits, what incentive does an individual have to join a political party?

Although there have been no comprehensive studies of the motivations for Canadians to join political parties, much of the literature suggests that supporting a candidate for the leadership of the party or for the party's nomination in an electoral district is seen as one of the significant reasons for joining a party. In his study of Canadian parties' constituency associations, Carty (1991, 38) found clear evidence that the Liberal and Progressive Conservative parties' membership numbers fluctuated vastly between election years and non-election years, leading him to conclude that "when party elections are to be held—to nominate a candidate in an election, or select delegates for a leadership contest—membership takes on its meaning and worth, and individuals are mobilized for these contests with little concern for longer-term involvement or participation." This pattern did not hold for the NDP, which Carty found to have a more stable pattern of party membership.

In their study of members of the Reform Party in 1993, Clarke et al. (2000) found that collective incentives most commonly motivated party membership. When members were asked what was their most important reason for joining the party, the most frequent responses were concern with the deficit or economic problems (31 percent), concern with moral principles in government (29 percent), dissatisfaction with the then-governing Progressive Conservative Party (22 percent), concern that the province of Quebec was too powerful (17 percent), and a desire for individual freedom and less government (16 percent). A mere 2 percent of respondents cited material incentives, either business contacts or a desire to run for public office, as their most important reason, and that friends or family are party members. Respondents were not asked whether supporting a candidate for the party's nomination or leadership was a factor in their decision.

Recruitment

To what extent are individuals recruited into Canadian political parties, and to what extent do they take initiative to join the party? Table 22.2 below summarizes responses to the question "Who first asked you to join the _____ party?" It is clear that, at least among the long-term or core members of the five parties who responded to our survey, the majority were not recruited into party activity but rather took the initiative to join the party themselves. This pattern is all the more evident in the two newest parties—the Bloc and the Canadian Alliance—in which 68 percent and 71 percent of members, respectively, joined of their own initiative.

... at least among the long-term or core members of the five parties who responded to our survey, the majority were not recruited into party activity but rather took the initiative to join the party themselves.

Incentives to Membership

These patterns of recruitment suggest that conventional understanding of the importance of social networks and participation in leadership and nomination contests to joining Canadian political parties may be overstated and of limited salience in explaining membership in the

Table 22.2   Who First Asked the Member to Join the Party, Canada, 2000 (percentage of members)

	All parties	PC	Liberal	NDP	BQ	CA
No one; own initiative	59	59	47	51	68	71
A relative	11	14	14	11	7	7
A friend or neighbour	9	5	12	9	3	10
A candidate for party's nomination	6	8	10	6	5	2
A local party officer	6	5	6	8	8	5
A member of Parliament	2	2	4	1	3	1
A co-worker	2	1	2	4	1	1
A candidate for the party's leadership	2	3	2	1	2	1
A group or association	1	0	1	4	2	1
National party headquarters	1	0	0	1	2	0
Other	2	2	1	5	1	1

Source: "Study of Canadian Political Party Members" 2000.
Note: Columns may not add up to 100 because of rounding.

more ideologically oriented parties. To determine this with greater certainty, however, we need to examine party members' reasons for initially joining their party. Respondents were given a list of eight reasons for joining the party and were asked to rank each one as not at all important, somewhat important or very important. Responses were not mutually exclusive.

... the importance of social networks and participation in leadership and nomination contests to joining Canadian political parties may be overstated ...

As table 22.3 demonstrates, belief in the party's policies is the reason for joining given the greatest weight by party members. Fully 84 percent of respondents to the survey indicated that this reason was very important to them. Although important, support for a candidate for the party's leadership or nomination lagged far behind policy as a reason for initially joining the party. Of course, if we were to add the 45 percent of respondents who indicated that supporting a candidate for the local nomination was very important to the 36 percent of respondents who indicated that supporting an individual for the party's leadership was very important, this would

suggest that these personnel-related concerns were as important as belief in the party's policies. However, on closer examination we find that these are for the most part the same respondents: 72 percent of respondents who indicated that supporting a candidate for the leadership was a very important reason for joining the party also indicated that supporting a candidate for the nomination was very important. That belief in the party's policies outweighs personnel-related reasons for joining suggests that even though Canadian parties have recruited a substantial portion of their members through such routes, the individuals recruited for the most part feel some attraction to the party's ideological stance and are not merely joining in order to support an individual.

Contrary to expectations that a substantial portion of party members are recruited by friends or relatives, only 6 and 7 percent of respondents, respectively, indicated these as very important reasons. However, recruitment through a social network is related to support for a candidate for the nomination. Among respondents for whom recruitment by a friend was very important, 65 percent indicated that supporting a candidate for the nomination was also very important; similarly, among respondents for whom recruitment by a family member was very important, 60 percent indicated that supporting a candidate for the nomination was very important. To

Table 22.3   Reasons for Joining a Party, Canada, 2000 (percentage of members)[1]

	Not at all important	Somewhat important	Very important
I believe in the party's policies	3	14	84
To support a candidate for the local nomination	28	27	45
To support a candidate for the party's leadership	38	26	36
I wanted to influence party policy on a particular issue	44	37	19
A family member asked me to	81	12	7
A friend asked me to	81	13	6
I thought it would help my career	88	9	4
I thought it would help me get a government job	95	3	2

Source: "Study of Canadian Political Party Members" 2000.

Note: Columns may not add up to 100 because of rounding.

[1]The survey question was: "We are interested in knowing your reasons for originally joining the _____ party. Please indicate whether each of the following reasons was not at all important, somewhat important or very important to you."

the extent that recruitment through social networks occurs, then, it appears closely tied to recruitment for nomination campaigns.

Finally, the very low percentages of respondents indicating that they initially joined the party for material reasons—to help their career or get a government job—indicate that material incentives have very little power to attract individuals to Canadian political parties. This is not particularly surprising, given the relative absence of patronage or other such inducements available to Canadian parties.

... party membership in Canada is for the most part motivated by a sense of public service ... This signals a desire to influence public policy, which is precisely the public service that we expect political parties to perform.

In short, these findings support the notion that party membership in Canada is for the most part motivated by a sense of public service. Relatively few members join political parties in the hope of furthering their careers or getting a government job, whereas many are motivated by support for their party's policy stance. This signals a desire to influence public policy, which is precisely the public service that we expect political parties to perform.

ARE PARTY MEMBERS SATISFIED WITH THEIR ROLE?

◆ ◆ ◆

Members of Canadian political parties are largely dissatisfied with the role they are accorded in the development of party policy. As figure 22.3 shows, a majority of members of the five parties believe that members should have greater influence over party policy, while pollsters and advisers should have less. When given a choice between the statements "The party leader should have the freedom to set party policy" and "The leader should accept policy set by members," two-thirds of respondents chose the latter statement. While the results varied somewhat by party, a majority of members in each of the five parties favoured the idea that the leader should accept policy set by members. It is not surprising, then, that the vast majority of members agreed with statements to the effect that the party should do more to encourage local associations to discuss public policy, or that regular members should play a greater role in determining their party's national platform. In each of the five parties, including the populist Canadian Alliance, a sizable majority of members agreed with the latter statement.

The data presented in figures 22.3 and 22.4 suggest that party members are acutely aware that their traditional functions have been usurped by professionals. A majority of members of each party agree that these

Figure 22.3   Members' Views on Policy Development (Proportion Who Agree or Strongly Agree with the Statement), Canada, 2000 (percent)

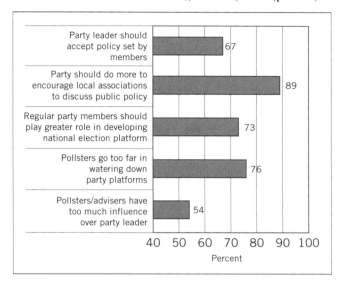

Source: "Study of Canadian Political Party Members" 2000.

Figure 22.4   Members' Perceptions of the Influence of Certain Groups, Canada, 2000

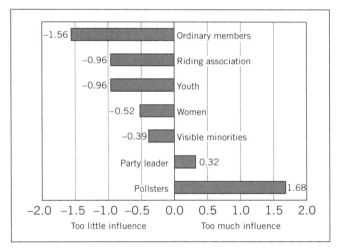

Source: "Study of Canadian Political Party Members" 2000.
Note: The differential is calculated for each respondent by measuring on a 7-point scale how much influence the respondent believes the group has, and then subtracting from that figure the score on a seven-point scale of how much influence the respondent believes the group should have. Negative numbers mean the respondent believes the group does not have enough influence and positive numbers mean the respondent believes the group has too much influence.

political professionals have too much influence over the party leader, and that this influence is used to water down the party's platform. Figure 22.4 demonstrates party members' perceptions of which groups lack influence and

which have too much influence. Party members perceive that ordinary members and riding associations are the most severely lacking in influence, while they believe that pollsters exert too much influence.

From this analysis, it is evident that members of Canadian political parties are far from content with their role in the party. Keeping in mind that the party members surveyed are those who renew their membership in non-election, nonleadership-contest years, the analysis leads us to believe that contemporary Canadian political parties are ill equipped to offer inducements to membership adequate to engage significant numbers of Canadians.

ENGAGING PARTY MEMBERS
◆ ◆ ◆

Our story to this point is one of political parties with few engaged members who are generally dissatisfied with their role in party life. In considering how our political parties might reinvigorate themselves, there are several points that are central to our investigation. The first is that while Canadians' satisfaction with their parties' performances can be judged to be only middling at best, they have not given up the belief that parties are central to successful democratic practice. When Canadians were asked to score the parties on a scale of 1 to 100, their mean ranking declined by almost 50 percent between 1968 and 2000. However, at the same time, 7 in 10 Canadians agree with the statement that "without parties, there can't be true democracy" (Blais and Gidengil 1991, 20).

Consistent with this, there is concrete, on-the-ground evidence that Canadians have not completely turned their backs on party politics. As discussed above, when parties offer grassroots voters a meaningful role in important decision-making, Canadians have shown a willingness to participate. This is evidenced by the dramatic increase in member recruitment during periods of candidate nomination and leadership selection. These personnel decisions have traditionally been left to the parties' members. Knowing that their participation determines the outcomes of these contests, thousands of Canadians who otherwise shun participation in political parties are enticed to join them. However, we also know that the large majority of these recruited members do not maintain an active presence in the party between personnel recruitment contests. We cannot know for certain why individuals drop out of active party life, but we do know that those who remain are generally dissatisfied with the decision-making role afforded them. Put simply, they see decision-making power between elections concentrated at the centre with little substantive role for grassroots members.

Too often, local party branches are ignored by the central offices and allowed to atrophy between elections. Indeed, the central offices themselves often suffer dramatic decreases in budget and staff between elections, reducing their ability to invigorate the party membership. The party in office dominates during these periods at the expense of input from the extraparliamentary membership. The elected party needs the membership to wage successful election campaigns and to support personal ambitions in intraparty contests but finds little use for them otherwise. As we have argued elsewhere, this is part of a trade-off in which the extraparliamentary members are given control over personnel recruitment in return for the elected party having near unchallenged authority in setting a policy direction (Carty, Cross and Young 2000, 115–6).

The elected party needs the membership to wage successful election campaigns and to support personal ambitions in intraparty contests but finds little use for them otherwise.

We suggest that if parties are to attract more Canadians as members and, more important, as ongoing participants in their affairs, they need to offer voters more extensive opportunities to influence party stances on questions of public policy. Along with providing voters with an incentive to participate in party affairs, this would provide real benefits to the parties themselves.

There are defensible reasons why Canada's traditional parties have not regularly provided their members with a meaningful role in determining party policy. The principal rationale reflects the brokerage practice in Canadian politics. This is the notion that the setting of public policy requires the accommodation of many different parochial (often regional) interests. Accompanying this has been a belief that only a small elite, representing these varied interests, can successfully make the compromises necessary in shaping these factionalized interests into a national policy (Noel 1977). Consistent with this,

party leaders, particularly when in government, have argued that their responsibility is to represent the interests of all voters and not solely those of their active supporters. Party leaders must necessarily balance party members' desire to affect party policy with considerations of brokerage, representation and electoral viability.

… the closer parties come to government, the more elite-concentrated their decision-making on policy issues becomes.

It is not surprising, then, that we observe that the closer parties come to government, the more elite-concentrated their decision-making on policy issues becomes. Parties far from government often position themselves as more participatory and democratic than their governing counterparts and, as proof of this, attempt to involve their active members in policy discussion and decision-making. The fledgling farmers' parties of the 1920s, occasionally the CCF and the NDP, and the Reform Party of the early 1990s are all examples of this. Similarly, former governing parties that find themselves mired in the opposition benches often try to reinvigorate themselves by promising their grassroots supporters a greater voice in rebuilding the party and setting its policy course. Unfortunately, these promises rarely last after the party comes close to, or achieves, power. The federal Liberals of the 1960s and 1970s and the Ontario New Democrats of the 1990s provide examples of these phenomena (Clarkson 1979; Cross 2004, 37–9). The participatory enthusiasm sparked by the Liberals' Kingston Conference and subsequently by the early days of Trudeaumania were quickly replaced with a disillusioned membership that once again felt isolated from important party decision-making. Similarly, the Ontario New Democratic Party under the leadership of Bob Rae faced strong criticism from its activist base when the party suddenly found itself in government and decreed, against long-standing party practice, that the parliamentary party (and thus the government) was not bound by the policy dictates of the extraparliamentary party. The result is that voters might be encouraged by perpetual opposition parties and wounded former governing parties to participate in policy debates, but should their preferred party get close to government, this participatory ethos is likely to evaporate. Once burned, voters are unlikely to come back for a second round of disappointment.

The position of the parties' leadership on this issue is not without merit. Successive prime ministers have been correct in asserting that once in government, they are there to serve all Canadians. And it is elected members who are accountable to voters, not the parties' activists. The data provided in the appendix to this paper, describing the socio-demographic makeup of party members, also speak against allowing them a direct role in the making of public policy. They are not representative of the total population. With few young people, disproportionately few women and in most parties a lack of regional and linguistic balance, members may not be well positioned to reflect the varied interests that need to be considered in making public policy. Of course, the parties' elected caucuses regularly reflect the same representational deficits. Nonetheless, the challenge for parties is to create a role for their supporters in policy study and development while not abdicating the responsibility of the parliamentary party to make final policy decisions. It is our view that these are not intractable positions; parties can create an environment in which their grassroots members are invited to contribute to policy study and development in a manner that assists, rather than threatens, the elected party's policy-making responsibilities.

Two democratic reform commissions have recommended that parties establish ongoing policy foundations for these purposes: the 1991 Royal Commission on Electoral Reform and Party Financing and the 2004 New Brunswick Commission on Legislative Democracy. These commissions found Canadian parties lacking both in the provision of participatory opportunities for their members in the development of party policy and in their capacity for ongoing study and development of policy options in aid of their legislative caucuses. Parties in many Western European democracies have established such foundations, allowing them to engage their grassroots supporters in the policy development process and to develop a series of policy alternatives for consideration by the party in elected office.

One reason why Canadian parties have resisted the creation of policy foundations is cost. Canada's extra-parliamentary parties, wholly focused on campaign efforts, have traditionally husbanded their resources for these electoral excursions and expanded few resources between campaigns. Parties are reluctant to divert funds to developing and maintaining a permanent policy structure if this is seen as taking away resources that might otherwise be available for campaign efforts. The

New Brunswick commission recognized this concern and included in its recommendations partial public funding for both the start-up and ongoing operations of party policy foundations. This is consistent with the practice in many of the European countries with party policy foundations.

At the federal level, the 2003 changes to the Canada Elections Act provide the parties with ongoing financial support between elections ($1.75 per vote on an annual basis). All of this public funding goes to the parties' central offices. The central parties also routinely claw back all, or a significant portion, of the public funding provided to constituency candidates. Thus, few if any of these taxpayers' dollars are used to support grassroots activity within the parties. There is no reason that Parliament could not require that a portion of these public subventions be directed toward a policy foundation. The tax credit currently available for contributions to federal parties might also be extended to cover additional contributions to policy foundations. Parties may well resist such initiatives, as their emphasis on electoral readiness encourages them to direct their financial resources accordingly. Moreover, parties have traditionally resisted such incursions by the state into their internal affairs. We argue, however, that requiring parties to engage in policy development is not unreasonable, given the extent of the public funds they are receiving. Many party insiders bemoan the decline of Canadian parties as generators of new policy ideas (see Fox 2005); regulations giving parties incentives to reverse this trend would arguably address such concerns.

It is our view that, in the long term, the establishment of vigorous party-policy foundations would not only help to address the concerns of voters about the lack of a meaningful role for them in party politics but also strengthen our parties and our democracy more broadly. At present, our parties have little capacity for generating new policy alternatives. The parliamentary parties are necessarily concerned with the immediate issues of the day, and the extraparliamentary parties have few resources for anything other than election preparation. The result is that our elected officials are largely dependent on other organizations for policy innovation. The Royal Commission on Electoral Reform and Party Financing captured the essence of this when it concluded: "The dilemma is that the core of the party organization is concerned primarily with elections; it is much less interested in discussing and analyzing political issues that are not connected directly to winning the next election, or in attempting to articulate the broader values of the party" (Royal Commission 1991, 292). Not surprisingly, then, voters interested in influencing public policy issues are not attracted to parties.

... in the long term, the establishment of vigorous party-policy foundations would not only help to address the concerns of voters about the lack of a meaningful role for them in party politics but also strengthen our parties and our democracy more broadly.

The cost to our democracy comes from the fact that parties, not interest groups or policy forums, are charged with brokering the various parochial concerns and forging national interests. If parties are absent in the field of policy study and development, this task is made all the harder. Their absence is filled by advocacy and interest groups that typically represent specific socio-demographic segments of our population and are not charged with finding policy alternatives that serve a national interest. The civil service also plays a role in developing government policy, but there is often little opportunity for ordinary citizens to involve themselves in these processes.

When the legislative parties become involved in policy issues, not only are they ill served by their concern with short-term electoral issues, they are hampered by the representational deficits found within all of the elected caucuses. Liberal caucuses regularly include few members from the Prairie provinces, just as Conservative caucuses have few members from Quebec; and all the parties' caucuses have a shortage of female and visible-minority members.

Party-policy foundations can help to address these concerns by serving as a vehicle for grassroots supporters and substantive experts to participate in the study and development of policy options within each party's broad ideological framework. Foundations can ensure that voices not found in a party's legislative caucus are heard in their work. In this sense, they can assist rather than detract from the accommodative work incumbent upon the national parties. Almost a century ago, the federal Liberal Party changed its method of

leadership selection at least partly out of concern that its Quebec-dominated caucus did not reflect the diversity of views that should be heard in the selection of their leader (Courtney 1995, 5). Accordingly, it opened up the process to include its extraparliamentary members from across the country. Our current parties would similarly benefit from an opening up of the policy development process to include their activists and invited experts from all parts of the Canadian community.

Well-functioning policy foundations would provide the legislative parties with a vehicle for the generation of new ideas and for longer-term planning than is currently possible. This might be particularly helpful in assisting parties in making the adjustment from opposition to government. Operating at some distance from the cut and thrust of daily political debate, foundations can take longer range perspective and can prepare policy options outside the constant glare of the media and political adversaries that are the reality for their legislative caucuses.

CONCLUSION
◆ ◆ ◆

Over the past century, political party membership in Canada has evolved from a route into the public service to a legitimate and important form of public service. A broad, active and representative membership base connects a political party to its social base of support and enables it to mobilize support between and during election campaigns. However, Canadian political parties have never been particularly robust membership organizations, and there is some evidence that they face a looming crisis in their ability to recruit members. To some extent, this inability is the product of broad social forces far beyond the control of the parties.

That said, parties are able to conduct their internal affairs in a manner that encourages individuals to join parties in order to engage in meaningful policy discussions and contribute in some small way to policy formulation. Knowing that policy interest motivates party membership in Canada, and that stalwart party members are not content with their circumscribed role in policy development within their party, we see clear potential for parties to involve their members more fully in policy discussions. In an era when Canada's federal political parties are funded largely by the public treasury, it is all the more important that they find ways to engage meaningfully with segments of Canadian society. Moreover, public funding can be structured in a manner that creates incentives for parties to speak directly with citizens on matters of public policy.

Our parties are often criticized for not presenting voters with competing detailed policy prescriptions. At least in part, this results from a situation in which no branch of the parties' organization is charged with the task of long-term policy study. The parliamentary parties are focused on the cut and thrust of daily politics, the party in central office is little more than an election preparation machine, and the party in the constituencies attracts members who are interested in studying policy but are denied any effective capacity to do so.

Policy foundations could benefit parties in several ways. First, they would provide an additional incentive for individuals to join political parties and maintain their membership. The evidence is clear that voters do not see participation in parties as an effective way of influencing public policy. Rather, they prefer activism in interest and advocacy groups, leaving the parties with an aging and often dispirited membership. Parties still rely on their grassroots members for activities such as local election organization and fundraising, so a reinvigorated base of grassroots supporters may well provide electoral dividends.

More important, however, the development of ongoing policy study capacity would better equip the parties to fulfill the responsibilities of the central role they play in Canadian politics. Parties are meant to provide a link between civil society and government. In a sense this is part of the public service role they are meant to play, and for which they are increasingly well funded from the public purse. Central to this task is the collection and brokering of policy interests from among competing groups of voters. Their ability to perform this task is compromised when voters do not engage with them in the policy realm. The establishment of policy foundations would provide an opportunity for parties to hear from civil society interests and policy experts in regions and from socio-demographic groups that are not included in their parliamentary caucuses. In doing so they would be better equipped for the accommodative role required of our national parties.

It is both our parties and the character of our democracy that suffer when parties are not fully engaged in the policy study enterprise. The solution is not to strengthen the policy capacity of the leaders' offices or of the Prime Minister's Office. While such an approach might enrich the policy offerings of the parties, it would do little to reinvigorate the connections between parties and citizens. We end then by recalling that while Canadians are largely dissatisfied with the operations of their political parties, they believe them to be key instruments of their democratic practice. Voters have not given up on parties. Let us hope that, at least in the realm of policy study, parties have not given up on voters.

Appendix   Demographic Profiles of Party Members Canada, 2000 (percent)*

	Total	Bloc	CA	Liberal	NDP	PC
Gender						
Male	62	64	68	53	54	67
Female	38	36	32	47	46	33
Age						
Over 65	46	37	59	33	40	53
Under 30	5	5	2	12	3	4
Education						
High school or less	28	33	35	23	26	26
College	16	15	24	11	17	13
University	36	35	28	41	31	38
Postgraduate	21	18	13	24	26	25
Family income						
<$20,000	9	14	9	9	10	6
>$100,000	15	11	13	19	10	21
Mother tongue						
English	71	0	88	61	83	87
French	19	99	1	28	4	6
Other	10	1	11	11	13	7
Ethnicity						
Born outside Canada	13	3	14	14	20	12

Source: "Study of Canadian Political Party Members," 2000.

Note: N = 3.872.

*Columns may not add up to 100 due to rounding.

Note

1. The Study of Canadian Political Party Members is a mail-back survey of randomly selected members of the five major Canadian political parties conducted from March to May 2000. The survey was mailed to a regionally stratified random sample drawn from the membership lists of the political parties. The regional sampling process varied by party. Where possible, a regional weighting variable was created. This was not possible for the Liberal Party or the Bloc Québécois. A total of 10,928 surveys were mailed to partisans, and 3,872 completed surveys were returned, yielding an overall response rate of 36 percent. All 3,872 surveys returned were usable. Results regarding rates of party activism in Quebec suggest that the Quebec sample was drawn from a list of activists, not members, so Quebec Liberals are excluded from all analysis of rates of activism to avoid overstating such rates. Membership in Canadian political parties fluctuates significantly over the course of an election cycle, so the timing of the survey is significant. Because the study was undertaken during a period when there was no election anticipated and no leadership contests underway, we expect that the members sampled are longer-term, more active members than would be captured had the survey been conducted when leadership or nomination contests were under way. The Canadian Alliance did have a leadership contest beginning in May 2000, but the list from which the sample was drawn was closed before the beginning of that leadership contest. This ensured that none of the members recruited by leadership candidates were included in the survey. The survey was funded by a Standard Research Grant from the Social Sciences and Humanities Research Council of Canada.

References

Blais, André, and Elisabeth Gidengil. 1991. *Making Representative Democracy Work: The Views of Canadians.* Toronto: Dundurn.

Carty, R. K. 1991. *Canadian Political Parties in the Constituencies.* Toronto: Dundurn.

———. 2002. "The politics of Tecumseh Corners: Canadian Political Parties as Franchise Organizations." *Canadian Journal of Political Science* 35: 723–45.

Carty, R. Kenneth, William Cross and Lisa Young. 2000. *Rebuilding Canadian Party Politics.* Vancouver: University of British Columbia Press.

Clarke, Harold D., Allan Kornberg, Faron Ellis, and Jon Rapkin. 2000. "Not for Fame or Fortune: A Note on Membership and Activity in the Canadian Reform Party." *Party Politics* 6 (1): 75–93.

Clarkson, Stephen. 1979. "Democracy in the Liberal Party: The Experiment with Citizen Participation under Pierre Trudeau." In *Party Politics in Canada,* 4th ed., edited by Hugh G. Thorburn. Scarborough, ON: Prentice-Hall.

Courtney, John. 1995. *Do Conventions Matter? Choosing National Party Leaders in Canada.* Montreal, Kingston: McGill-Queen's Press.

Cross, William. 2004. *Political Parties.* Vancouver: University of British Columbia Press.

Cross, William, and Lisa Young. 2002. "Policy Attitudes of Party members in Canada: Evidence of Ideological Politics?" *Canadian Journal of Political Science* 35 (4): 359–80.

———. 2004. "Contours of Party Membership in Canada." *Party Politics* 10 (40): 427–44.

Dalton, Russell J., and Martin P. Wattenberg. 2000. "Unthinkable Democracy: Political Change in Advanced Industrial Democracies." In *Parties without Partisan: Political Change in Advanced Industrial Democracies,* edited by Russell J. Dalton and Martin P. Wattenberg. New York: Oxford University Press, 3–18.

Fox, Graham. 2005. *Rethinking Political Parties.* Ottawa: Public Policy Forum, and Crossing Boundaries National Council.

Gallagher, Michael, and Michael Marsh. 2002. *Days of Blue Loyalty: The Politics of Membership of the Fine Gael Party.* Dublin: PSAI Press.

Heidar, Knut, and Jo Saglie. 2003. "Pre-Destined Parties? Organizational Change in Norwegian Political Parties." *Party Politics* 9 (2) 219–39.

Howe, Paul, and David Northrup. 2000. *Strengthening Canadian Democracy: The Views of Canadians.* Montreal: Institute for Research on Public Policy.

Katz, Richard, and Peter Mair. 1995. "Changing Models of Party Organization and Party Democracy: The Emergence of the Cartel Party." *Party Politics* 1 (1): 5–28.

Mair, Peter, and Ingrid van Biezen. 2001. "Party Membership in Twenty European Democracies. 1980–2000." *Party Politics* 7 (1): 7–21.

Noel, S. J. R. 1977. "Political Parties and Elite Accommodation: Interpretations of Canadian Federalism." In *Canadian Federalism: Myth or Reality.* 3rd ed., edited by J. Peter Meekison, Toronto: Methuen Press.

Norris, Pippa. 2002. *Democratix Phoenix: Political Activism Worldwide*. New York: Cambridge University Press.

Olson, Mancur. 1965. *The Logic of Collective Action*. Cambridge: Harvard University Press.

Royal Commission on Electoral Reform and Party Financing. 1991. *Report*. Ottawa: Supply and Services.

Scarrow, Susan E. 1999. "Parties and the Expansion of Direct Democracy: Who Benefits?" *Party Politics* 5 (3): 341–62.

———. 2000. "Parties without Members? Party Organizations in a Changing Electoral Environment." In *Parties without Partisans: Political Change in Advanced Industrial Democracies*, edited by Russell J. Dalton and Martin P. Wattenberg. New York: Oxford University Press, 79–101.

Seyd, Patrick. 1999. "New Parties/New Politics? A Case Study of the British Labor Party." *Party Politics* 5 (3): 383–405.

Seyd, Patrick, and Paul Whiteley. 1992. *Labour's Grass Roots: The Politics of Labour Party Membership*. Oxford: Clarendon.

van Biezen, Ingrid. 2004. "Political Parties in Public Utilities." *Party Politics* 10 (6): 701–22.

Ware, Alan. 1996. *Political Parties and Party Systems*. Oxford: Oxford University Press.

Whiteley, Paul, and Patrick Seyd. 2002. *High-Intensity Participation: The Dynamics of Party Activism in Britain*. Ann Arbor: University of Michigan Press.

Whiteley, Paul, Patrick Seyd, and Jeremy Richardson. 1994. *True Blues: The Politics of Conservative Party Membership*. Oxford: Clarendon.

Young, Lisa. 2000. *Feminists and Party Politics*. Vancouver. University of British Columbia Press.

Young, Lisa, and William Cross. 2002a. "Incentives to Membership in Canadian Political Parties." *Political Research Quarterly* 55 (3): 547–69.

———. 2002b. "The Rise of Plebiscitary Democracy in Canadian Political Parties." *Party Politics* 8 (6): 673–991.

Young, Lisa, Anthony Sayers, Harold Jansen, and Munroe Eagles. 2005. "Implications of State Funding for Party Organization." Paper presented at the annual meeting of the American Political Science Association, September 1–4, Washington, DC.

Terms and Concepts

mass-type parties
internal party democracy
cyclical party membership
plebiscitary democracy
chequebook members

patronage
social incentives
collective incentives
elected party
membership party

social networks
party professionalization
brokerage parties

Questions

1. Why has party membership fallen in Canada?
2. How can party members participate in party activities?
3. Why do people join political parties?
4. What functions do parties perform?
5. How do Cross and Young propose to increase membership in political parties?
6. If party members had more influence on party policies, what changes in party policies would we expect to see? Would the nature of Canadian politics change?

Unit 4 Annotated Bibliography

Bernier, Luc, Keith Browning, and Michael Howlett (eds). *Executive Styles in Canada: Cabinet Structure and Leadership Practices in Canadian Government.* Toronto: University of Toronto Press, 2005. This collection of essays explores Donald Savoie's "court government" thesis, namely, the domination of the political process by first ministers and their staffs. Case studies of provincial governments allow for interesting comparative analysis.

Carty, R. Kenneth, William Cross, and Lisa Young. *Rebuilding Canadian Party Politics.* Vancouver: UBC Press, 2000. This is an examination of the institutional (as opposed to the behavioural) side of Canadian political parties and how they fit in the broader Canadian political system.

Blakeney, Allan, and Sandford Borins. *Political Management in Canada.* Toronto: University of Toronto Press, 1998. These two collaborators blend wide-ranging political experience and theoretical expertise in their account of the mechanics of governance and administration.

Cardinal, Mario. *Breaking Point, Quebec/Canada: The 1995 Referendum.* Trans. Ferdinanda Van Gennip and Mark Stout. Montreal: Bayard, 2005. This is a detailed chronicle of the events and personalities associated with the 1995 Quebec referendum on independence from Canada. Cardinal suggests that the stunning closeness of the referendum result indicates this issue is not over.

Courtney, John, C. *Elections.* Vancouver: UBC Press, 2004. Courtney examines the development of the franchise and electoral institutions in Canada.

Cross, William. *Political Parties.* Vancouver: UBC Press, 2004. Cross examines the internal structure and operations of political parties in Canada as well as laws that affect them. He suggests that parties have evolved from private bodies to public institutions.

Docherty, David C. *Mr. Smith Goes to Ottawa: Life in the House of Commons.* Vancouver: UBC Press, 1997. This study of Canadian parliamentarians indicates that while MPs with new ideas can have influence, the institutional norms of parliamentary government, including party discipline, are hard to resist.

————. *Legislatures.* Vancouver: UBC Press, 2005. Docherty examines both the Canadian Parliament and provincial legislatures with a particular focus on their strengths and weaknesses as representative institutions.

Epp, Charles R. *The Rights Revolution: Lawyers, Activists and Supreme Courts in Comparative Perspective.* Chicago: University of Chicago Press, 1998. This is a study of the causes of the "rights revolution" in several countries, including Canada.

Erickson, Lynda. "Might More Women Make a Difference? Party and Ideology Among Canada's Parliamentary Candidates," *Canadian Journal of Political Science* 30 (1997): 663–88. Erickson examines whether gender affects policy preferences of Canadian politicians and what influence the gender gap has relative to party position.

Greene, Ian. *The Courts.* Vancouver: UBC Press, 2006. This is a thorough introduction to the court in Canada, covering institutional matters of appointment, independence, and administration. Greene also examines the courts' relationship to democratic principles in Canada.

Griffiths, Ann L., ed., *Handbook of Federal Countries, 2005.* Montreal and Kingston: McGill-Queen's University Press, 2005. Griffiths has created an excellent, accessible reference on federal countries around the world.

Hale, Geoffrey. *The Politics of Taxation in Canada.* Peterborough, ON: Broadview, 2002. This is a comprehensive, informative discussion of Canada's tax system.

Heard, Andrew. *Canadian Constitutional Conventions.* Toronto: Oxford University Press, 1991. Heard provides a comprehensive review of constitutional conventions and how they operate in Canada.

Joyal, Serge, ed. *Protecting Canadian Democracy: The Senate You Never Knew.* Montreal and Kingston: McGill–Queen's University Press, 2003. This collection of essays examines that much-maligned but poorly understood institution of Parliament. Readers will be surprised to learn about the importance of the Senate in Canadian politics.

Lawless, Jennifer L., and Richard L. Fox. *It Takes a Candidate: Why Women Don't Run for Office.* New York: Cambridge University Press, 2005. The authors explore why women in professions that normally furnish high numbers of political candidates are less likely to run for office than men.

LeDuc, Lawrence, Richard G. Niemi, and Pippa Norris, eds. *Comparing Democracies: Elections and Voting in Global Perspective.* Thousand Oaks, CA: Sage, 1996. This is an indispensable collection of research papers examining all aspects of electoral democracy in dozens of countries.

McKinnon, Janice. *Minding the Public Purse: The Fiscal Crisis, Political Trade-Offs, and Canada's Future.* Montreal and Kingston: McGill–Queen's University Press, 2003. McKinnon, former Saskatchewan finance minister in Roy Romanow's NDP government, writes about the challenges of that province's public debt, health care reform, and Canadian fiscal federalism.

McWhinney, Edward. *The Governor General and the Prime Ministers: The Making and Unmaking of Governments.* Vancouver: Ronsdale Press, 2005. McWhinney presents a contemporary account of the reserve powers of the governor general and explores possibilities for freeing this institution from its connection to the British Crown.

Moore, Christopher. *1867: How the Fathers Made a Deal*. Toronto: McClelland & Stewart, 1997. Moore takes a fresh look at the principles and compromises that went into the Confederation settlement. He shows that some current constitutional and political issues occupied Canadians from the beginning.

Reynolds, Andrew, ed. *The Architecture of Democracy: Constitutional Design, Conflict Management, and Democracy*. New York: Oxford University Press, 2002. This collection of essays surveys the institutional machinery necessary for contemporary democratic government.

Russell, Peter. *Constitutional Odyssey: Can Canadians Be a Sovereign People?* 3rd ed. Toronto: University of Toronto Press, 2004. Russell writes an excellent introduction to Canadian constitutional politics from Confederation to the 1998 *Quebec Secession Reference*.

Savoie, Donald. *Governing from the Centre: The Concentration of Political Power in Canadian Politics*. Toronto: University of Toronto Press, 1999. Savoie's study of the operation of the federal government indicates that the prime minister and the prime minister's office—not Cabinet or Parliament—is the heart of political power in Canada.

———. *Breaking the Bargain: Public Servants, Ministers, and Parliament*. Toronto: University of Toronto Press, 2003. Savoie is one of Canada's leading students of the executive function of government, and in this book examines the relationship between the political and administrative spheres in Canadian government.

Schneiderman, David. *The Quebec Decision*. Toronto: James Lorimer, 1999. This book contains the text of the historic *Secession Reference* opinion of the Supreme Court of Canada as well as a diverse collection of commentaries.

Smith, David E. *The Invisible Crown: The First Principle of Canadian Government*. Toronto: University of Toronto Press, 1995. Smith delivers a study of the continuing importance of the institution of the Crown (not to be confused with the royal family) for Canadian politics and government.

Smith, Jennifer. *Federalism*. Vancouver: UBC Press, 2004. Smith is one of Canada's foremost federalism scholars and provides here an assessment of the relationship between federalism and democracy in Canada.

Sunstein, Cass. *Designing Democracy: What Constitutions Do*. New York: Oxford University Press, 2001. This prominent American constitutional scholar describes what contemporary liberal democratic constitutions should and should not contain. Sunstein favours a particularly republican brand of liberalism, one that emphasizes the conditions that facilitate citizens' participation in their self-government.

Ware, Alan. *Political Parties and Party Systems*. Oxford: Oxford University Press, 1996. This is a comprehensive account of political parties and their institutional settings in developed democracies.

White, Graham. *Cabinets and First Ministers*. Vancouver: UBC Press, 2004. White engages one of the big questions of Canadian government: whether our parliamentary institutions create autocratic first ministers who dominate their cabinets and legislatures.

Young, Lisa, and Joanna Everitt. *Advocacy Groups*. Vancouver: UBC Press, 2004. The authors trace the activities of interest groups in Canadian politics and look at their internal operations, how they mobilize interests and citizens, and what success they enjoy.

Unit Five

Introduction: Contemporary Politics Abroad

◆ ◆ ◆

Readers of this collection will be most familiar with anglo-American liberal democracies. These regimes have well-educated, generally prosperous citizenries that benefit from the rule of law, stable political institutions, peaceful political succession, and efficient public bureaucracies that deliver services to their populations. The business of these regimes is ... well, business. They are market economies and much of political life is dedicated to debating ways to produce sustainable economic wealth. What may be surprising is how few regimes around the world conform to this familiar image.

Political scientists interested in the variety of contemporary regimes, political cultures, political institutions, political party systems, electoral arrangements, and economic and social policies are engaged in the study of comparative politics and government. They attempt to discern patterns between and among political regimes. For example, they may wonder if parliamentary systems generally produce political party systems in which only two main, competitive parties compete

for power at election time. They may ask what common political institutions allow some culturally divided countries to remain united and stable while others are plagued by secessionist movements. They may attempt to discern the conditions under which formerly Communist countries become stable, prosperous liberal democracies. They may debate whether Western-style democracy is compatible with Islamic or Confucian culture. Indeed, they will ask what it takes for a regime to be considered democratic at all.

The essays in this unit pursue these and similar questions. The first essay on the challenge of African development perhaps addresses the most fundamental issue: before there can be discussion of what kind of state is best, there must be the state itself, and so there must be conditions supporting "state-ness" itself. An impoverished population overseen by a state without any capacity to maintain order, build

© Iain Masterton/Alamy

Even the most insular regimes find themselves increasingly subject to international forces.

infrastructure, and protect the population from external threats is without hope. The lesson: focus initially not on political institutions but on the material conditions on the basis of which those institutions can operate.

Other essays generally address the conditions necessary for democracy. Some argue that a stable, functioning state is necessary to create the conditions for investment, growth, prosperity, and education; only a democratic state fits this bill. On the other hand, authoritarian regimes can provide the stability needed for economic growth, and that growth in turn may foster the development of a population with the education and expectations to demand democratic political change.

Also at issue in these debates is the role of history and culture in political change. If it is unthinkable for Canada eventually to become an Iranian-style Islamic republic, it is also unthinkable, or at least unrealistic, to imagine a Middle Eastern regime becoming a raucous, permissive, American-style commercial democratic republic. In like manner, it is naive to expect Russians to repudiate centuries of history in adopting Western-style liberalism—at least, any time soon. Stunning political change does occur; witness the surprising events of the fall of Communism in 1989 and the momentous attacks of 9/11. But deeper currents continue to flow.

Understanding African Poverty: Beyond the Washington Consensus to the Millennium Development Goals Approach

Gordon McCord, Jeffrey D. Sachs, and Wing Thye Woo

Editors' Note

An old adage in the international development movement is that if you give a man a fish, you feed him for a day. If you give a man a fishing rod, you feed him for a lifetime. The supply of the fishing rod is a necessary bit of physical capital that yields returns far beyond the cost of the initial investment. The rod (and presumably the training that comes with it) also means independence from the charity of others—colonialism, in the language of international political economy. The man can now live with dignity, not as a supplicant.

Notice what this adage assumes: that there are fish, that the fish can be caught from shore, that the means of economic independence are largely in place but for the provision of the fishing rod, and that corrupt government officials will not choke the man's opportunities with taxes, fees, permits, and other red tape designed to confiscate his newfound wealth.

When it comes to economic development in sub-Saharan Africa, such assumptions are not valid. The land is dry and difficult to cultivate. Markets for products are far away. Roads to markets are poor. The population lacks "human capital"—the skills and knowledge to compete in the global economy. Governments are often underresourced and corrupt; reliable public infrastructure is scarce. And most crucially, many are so poor that even if they had fishing rods, they would need to sell them to pay for the next day's meal.

A dominant development strategy of the 1980s was the "Washington Consensus." This battery of policy proposals assumed that governments were the problem and that free access to international markets was the solution. So countries were encouraged to produce commodities for sale on international markets. The policies failed. Many developed countries are highly protectionist and did not welcome the competition from the poorer nations. People in the poor countries starved because crops were grown for export, not domestic consumption. And the persistent problems posed by climate and political corruption exacted their toll.

The following article is co-authored by Jeffrey Sachs, whose *The End of Poverty*[1] has received wide acclaim. Sachs advances a bold proposal to lift Africa out of the "poverty trap"—that degree of extreme poverty that makes it impossible for people to save enough money from their labour to make the capital investments necessary to lift themselves out of poverty. The amount of assistance required from the developed countries is significant. Readers will wonder whether the developed countries have the will to advance the "Millennium Development Goals" the United Nations has set for the international community.[2]

---

1. Jeffrey D. Sachs, *The End of Poverty: Economic Possibilities for Our Time* (New York: Penguin, 2005).
2. For more information on the Goals, see www.un.org/millenniumgoals.

"Understanding African Poverty: Beyond the Washington Consensus to the Millennium Development Goals Approach" by Gordon McCord, Jeffrey D. Sachs and Wing Thye Woo from *Africa in the World Economy: The National, Regional and International Challenges* edited by Jan Joost Teunissen and Age Akkerman. Published by FONDAD, The Hague, 2005. Reprinted with permission.

THE MISPERCEPTIONS ABOUT AFRICAN POVERTY

◆ ◆ ◆

The era of structural adjustment, which can be dated approximately to the last two decades of the 20th century, was a failure for African economic development. Africa was the only major developing-country region with negative per capita growth during 1980 to 2000; its health conditions are by far the worst on the planet; its soaring population is exacerbating ecological stresses; and despite the policy-based development lending of structural adjustment, it remains mired in poverty and debt.

What went wrong? In the extreme interpretation of the Washington Consensus by its proponents, as well as by its critics, its unambiguous promise is that if a developing country were to implement conservative macroeconomic policies while expanding the role of the private market at the expense of the state, then it would achieve sustained high growth rates on its own. By extension, if a developing country is failing to grow, the problem must be either macroeconomic mismanagement or a hindering of the private market expansion in the country, usually attributed to corruption or more broadly "bad governance."

This first assumption—that Africa is suffering from a governance crisis—is unsatisfactory. Poorer countries systematically have poorer governance measures than richer countries, since good governance itself requires real resources. Regression analysis in Table 23.1 shows that Africa's governance, on average, is no worse than elsewhere after controlling for income levels. Using four different widely accepted measures of quality of governance, we estimate the effect of being a tropical African country after controlling for income, and find that for all four indicators, poor governance among developing countries is associated with having low income, and not with the dummy variable for Africa.

... good governance itself requires real resources.

This finding is not surprising, since—despite much rhetoric to the contrary—it is quite intuitive that good governance requires resources. For example, low-income country governments frequently need to raise civil service pay scales to make them comparable to the salaries offered by the private sector, international agencies, and development partners. Higher pay is needed to attract and retain highly qualified public sector workers and to reduce the incentives for corruption and moonlighting. Yet impoverished countries lack adequate domestic resources to make necessary investments in the physical infrastructure of the public administration to improve service delivery and reduce opportunities for corruption. Some examples include:

- Communication and information infrastructure for all levels of government, including computer and telecommunications services for government offices, public hospitals, land registries, schools, and other public institutions.

- Information systems to improve the speed, reliability, and accountability of public sector transactions and systems to share information across branches of government. India, for example, is working to put all land deeds into a national database, which citizens can access from anywhere in the country. This will eliminate the need for citizens to travel in order to request a copy of the deed to use as collateral in a loan.

- Modern technological capabilities for the customs bureau, to speed shipments, reduce smuggling, and control cross-border movements of illegal or dangerous goods.

- Modern technological capabilities for law enforcement, including national criminal databases, information systems to reduce response times, and adequate dissemination of information to local law enforcement.

- Electronic government procurement and logistical systems; for example, to ensure reliable access to essential medicines in government clinics and hospitals.

A second common assumption—that Africa grows slowly because of its poor governance—also rings hollow. Many parts of Africa are well governed, and yet remain trapped in poverty. Governance is a problem, but Africa's development challenges are much deeper. Even after controlling for governance (again using several different measures of governance quality), sub-Saharan African countries grew more slowly than other developing countries, by around 3 percentage points per year, as shown by the regression analysis in Table 23.2. Africa's crisis requires a deeper explanation than governance alone.

Table 23.1   Governance Quality and Income[a]

Independent Variable	Corruption Perceptions Index, 2003[b]	Index of Economic Freedom, 2001[c]	Average Kaufmann *et al* indicators, 2000[d]	Average ICRG indicators, 1982–1997[e]
Log (GDP pc PPP 2001)	**1.05** *(5.31)*	**−0.48** *(−4.75)*	**0.40** *(5.20)*	**0.45** *(4.00)*
Dummy variable for tropical sub-Saharan Africa	0.58 *(1.57)*	−0.27 *(−1.58)*	−0.05 *(−0.33)*	0.15 *(0.71)*
R-squared	0.40	0.27	0.42	0.29
N	67	82	92	73

Notes

[a] The sample consists of 92 countries worldwide, excluding high-income countries and former republics of the Soviet Union. All regressions are ordinary least squares and include a constant term (not reported). Numbers in parentheses are *t* statistics; coefficients within statistical significance at the 5 percent level are in bold.

[b] From Transparency International, this index relates to the degree of corruption in the country as perceived by businesspeople, academics, and risk analysts and ranges between 10 (highly clean) and 0 (highly corrupt).

[c] The index is published by the Heritage Foundation and the *Wall Street Journal* and ranges from 1 to 5, where 5 indicates the greatest government interference in the economy and the lesser economic freedom.

[d] Average of six World Bank governance indicators measured in units ranging from about −2.5 to 2.5, with higher values corresponding to better governance outcomes.

[e] Average of six governance indicators from the *PRS International Country Risk Guide,* with values ranging from 1 to 6, with higher values reflecting better governance.

[f] Refers to sample of 33 countries defined in Sachs et al. (2004).

Source: Authors' regressions using data from Kaufmann, Kraay, and Zoido-Lobatón (2002); PRS Group (2003); Kaufmann, Kraay, and Mastruzzi (2003); Miles, Feulner, and O'Grady (2004); Transparency International (2004); and Sachs et al. (2004).

Governance is a problem, but Africa's development challenges are much deeper.

Our explanation is that tropical Africa, even in well-governed parts, is stuck in a poverty trap, too poor to achieve robust, high levels of economic growth (and in many places, simply too poor to grow at all). More policy or governance reform, by itself, is not sufficient to overcome this trap. The fallacies of the Washington Consensus detailed in Woo (2004) certainly apply to the African case:

- While the expansion of the analytical sphere of the Washington Consensus from merely "get your prices right" to include "get your institutions right" is a quantum improvement in its understanding of the growth process, this second-generation Washington Consensus is still woefully incomplete in its prescriptions for the African countries. For example, the Washington Consensus preaches "free-trade regimes" while the successful East Asian growth experience featured extensive import tariffs and export subsidies.

- The Washington Consensus tends to deny the state its role in providing an important range of public goods, and does not acknowledge the importance of these public goods before "self-help" can work in Africa. The Washington Consensus is guilty of linear thinking on the complex growth phenomenon where certain prerequisites must be met before sustained growth is ensured.

- The Washington Consensus does not understand that the ultimate engine of growth in a predominantly private market economy is technological innovation, and that the state can play a role in facilitating this innovation.

- The Washington Consensus does not recognize the constraints that geography and ecology could set on the growth potential of a country. Having malaria and being landlocked seriously hamper foreign investment, regardless of the quality of governance.

Table 23.2 Governance and Africa's Economic Growth[a]

Independent Variables	(I)	(II)	(III)	(IV)	(V)
Tropical Sub-Saharan Africa Dummy[b]	−3.28 (−6.56)	−3.06 (−6.50)	−2.68 (−6.11)	−3.43 (−7.05)	−3.40 (−6.46)
Corruption Perceptions Index 2003	0.83				
Transparency International[c]	(5.23)				
2001 Index of Economic Freedom[d]		−0.96 (−2.75)			
2000 Average Kaufmann, Kraay			1.89		
Zoido-Lobatón indicators[e]			(5.91)		
1982–1997 Average ICRG Indicators[f]				1.56 (5.29)	
1982 Average ICRG Indicators[f]					0.68 (3.78)
Log (GDP pc PPP in 1980)	−2.07 (−7.02)	−1.65 (−6.06)	−1.75 (−7.07)	−2.00 (−7.01)	−1.82 (−5.84)
R-squared	0.58	0.46	0.59	0.59	0.54
N′	60	71	78	65	52

Notes

[a] The dependent variable is average annual growth of GDP per capita, 1980–2000. The sample consists of 92 countries worldwide, excluding high-income countries and former republics of the Soviet Union. All regressions are ordinary least squares and include a constant term (not reported). Numbers in parentheses are t-statistics; all coefficients reach statistical significance at the 1 percent level.

[b] Refers to sample of 33 countries defined in Sachs et al. (2004).

[c] From Transparency International, this index relates to the degree of corruption in the country as perceived by businesspeople, academics, and risk analysts and ranges between 10 (highly clean) and (highly corrupt).

[d] The index is published by the Heritage Foundation and the *Wall Street Journal* and ranges from 1 to 5, where 5 indicates the greatest government interference in the economy and the least economic freedom.

[e] Average of six World Bank governance indicators measured in units ranging from about −2.5 to 2.5, with higher values corresponding to better governance outcomes.

[f] Average of six governance indicators from the PRS International Country Risk Guide, with values ranging from 1 to 6, with higher values reflecting better governance.

Sources: Sachs et al. (2004). Regressions use data from Kaufmann, Kraay, and Zoido-Lobatón (2002); Miles, Feulner, and O'Grady (2004); PRS Group (2004), and Transparency International (2004).

... tropical Africa, even in well-governed parts, is stuck in a poverty trap, too poor to achieve robust, high levels of economic growth (and in many places, simply too poor to grow at all).

A better explanation of Africa's poverty trap would move beyond the limitations of the Washington Consensus to recognize that *before* privatization and market liberalization can unleash private sector-led economic growth in Africa, a massive amount of public investment in health, education, and infrastructure is required, which African countries cannot afford. Africa's poverty trap is the outcome of a complex web of many interactive factors, including structural conditions and sociopolitical history:[1]

- very high transport costs and small markets
- low-productivity agriculture
- very high disease burden
- a legacy of adverse geopolitics
- very slow diffusion of technology from abroad.

High Transport Costs and Small Markets

To a remarkable extent, Africans live in the interior of the continent and face enormous transport costs in shipping goods from coastal ports to where they live and work. These costs are much higher than in Asia. Moreover, the Sahara effectively cuts off sub-Saharan Africa from high-volume overland trade with Europe, its major high-income trading partner, adding to the high costs of transport. Problems of isolation are compounded by small market size. High-intensity modern trade in Africa can get started only with an extensive road system, which is expensive to build and maintain.

Low-Productivity Agriculture

Most Africans live in the subhumid or arid tropics, with few rivers to provide irrigation and a lack of the large alluvial plains, typical in much of South and East Asia, which permit cheap irrigation. As a result, Africa has the lowest share of food crops produced on irrigated land of any major region of the developing world. African agriculture also suffers from high transport cost of fertiliser, erratic rainfall, high rates of evapo-transportation due to high temperatures, and a secular decline in rainfall across the continent during the past 30 years, perhaps linked to long-term climate change. Finally, the new seed varieties that sparked the Green Revolution in Asia and Latin America are poorly suited to African farming conditions.

Very High Disease Burden

Africa carries a disease burden unique in the world. In recent years, the most prominent disease has been HIV/AIDS, wreaking economic and social catastrophe throughout the region. The spread of HIV is fuelling an epidemic of TB, which takes its heaviest toll among young productive adults. In some high-HIV-prevalence African countries, TB infection rates have quadrupled since the mid-1980s, placing overwhelming burdens on existing TB control programs. Africa is also home to numerous endemic tropical diseases, especially vector-borne diseases. Among these, malaria is by far the most consequential. Of the more than 1 million malaria-related deaths every year, it is estimated that 90 percent occur in sub-Saharan Africa, the great majority of them among young children.

A Legacy of Adverse Geopolitics

On top of the structural challenges, Africa has suffered brutally at the hands of European powers for almost five centuries, and the record with Arab powers has been little better. A massive slave trade helped undermine state formation and may have depopulated Africa's coastal regions. In the 19th century, the slave trade was replaced by direct colonial rule and a century of exploitation by European imperial powers, which left very little behind in education, health care, and physical infrastructure. Adding to the burden, during the Cold War politics of the late 20th century, many African countries found themselves battlegrounds in a global ideological struggle.

Very Slow Diffusion of Technology from Abroad

Africa has been the great laggard in technological advance, notably in agriculture and health. The uptake of technologies to prevent and treat major diseases, such as malaria, has been extremely slow. In agriculture, most of the developing world had a Green Revolution surge in crop yields in the 1970s–90s as a result of scientific breeding that produced "high-yielding varieties" combined with increased use of fertilisers and irrigation. The absence of a Green Revolution in Africa had a clear impact. Sub-Saharan Africa has the lowest cereal yield per hectare of any major region and was the only major region with a (slight) decline in food production per capita during 1980–2000.

Africa's extreme poverty leads to low national saving rates, which in turn lead to low or negative economic growth rates. Low domestic saving is not offset by high inflows of private foreign capital, for example, foreign direct investment, since Africa's poor infrastructure and weak human capital discourage private capital inflows. With very low domestic saving and low rates of market-based foreign capital inflows, there is little in Africa's current dynamics that promotes an escape from poverty. Something new is needed.

Africa's extreme poverty leads to low national saving rates, which in turn lead to low or negative economic growth rates.

THE WAY OUT OF THE POVERTY TRAP IN AFRICA: MDG-FOCUSED INVESTMENTS

◆ ◆ ◆

Sachs et al. (2004) and the United Nations Millennium Project (2005), an independent advisory project to Secretary-General Kofi Annan, argue that what is needed is a "big push" in public investments to produce a large "step" increase in Africa's underlying productivity, both rural and urban. Foreign donors will be critical to achieving this substantial "step" increase. In particular, well-governed African countries should be offered a big expansion in official development assistance (ODA) to enable them to achieve the Millennium Development Goals (MDGs), the internationally agreed targets for poverty reduction by the year 2015. The MDGs are useful intermediate targets in the process of helping Africa to break out of its poverty trap because they address the key areas in which major productivity improvement is both needed and achievable. We note with regret that the rich countries have repeatedly committed themselves to help Africa achieve these goals, with more funding if necessary, but some of them have yet to deliver fully on that promise.

... what is needed is a "big push" in public investments to produce a large "step" increase in Africa's underlying productivity, both rural and urban.

The UN Millennium Project's reports identify how a big push in key investments in social services, basic infrastructure, and environmental management could enable Africa to meet the MDGs, and how that, in turn, would help extricate Africa from the current development trap. This will require a comprehensive strategy for public investment in conjunction with improved governance. The Project has laid out an investment strategy focusing on *interventions*—defined broadly as the provision of goods, services and infrastructure—grouped into nine intervention areas:

1. Rural Development
2. Urban Development
3. Health
4. Education
5. Human Resources
6. Gender Equality
7. Science, Technology, and Innovation
8. Regional Integration Priorities
9. Public Sector Management Priorities.

Rural Development

The first investment area focuses on raising rural productivity, since three-quarters of Africa's poor live in rural areas. In particular, the investments in farm productivity will increase rural incomes and reduce chronic hunger, predominantly caused by insufficient agricultural productivity. A 21st-Century African Green Revolution is needed, and feasible, to help launch an environmentally sound doubling or more of agricultural productivity. Additional interventions in roads, transport services, electricity, cooking fuels, water supply, and sanitation all provide a basis for higher productive efficiency.

Urban Development

Throughout sub-Saharan Africa, the large cities do not have internationally competitive manufacturing or service-based industries. To generate such industries, an MDG–based urban strategy needs to focus on urban infrastructure and services (electricity, transport, water, sanitation, waste disposal, and so forth) and slum upgrading to attract foreign investment. Of course, the success of urban development and the establishment of viable export industries across Africa are contingent on improving access to rich countries' markets, particularly for apparel and light manufacturing, and the flexibility to use targeted industrial policies as needed. As populations are growing very rapidly across the continent, African countries must develop mutually reinforcing investment and urban development strategies that maximize job creation and prevent slum formation.

Health

Investments are needed to address Africa's extraordinary disease burden, widespread micronutrient deficiencies, and extremely high fertility rates by focusing on health, nutrition, and family planning. This package includes health-system-based interventions to improve child health and maternal health; prevent the transmission of and provide treatment for HIV/AIDS, TB, and malaria; improve nutrition; and provide reproductive health services. Halting the AIDS, malaria, and TB epidemics is critical.

Education

MDG–based strategies in Africa should aim for universal completion of primary education, and increased access to secondary and tertiary education. In designing this package of interventions, particular attention needs to be paid to increasing girls' completion rates through additional demand-side interventions, such as incentive payments to poor households to encourage them to keep their daughters in school.

Human Resources

To achieve the MDGs in Africa, significant investments in human resource development are needed urgently, since health, education, agricultural extension, and other critical social services cannot function without cadres of properly trained staff. Given the need to reach rural and often remote areas, we put great stress on scaling up the training of vast numbers of community workers in health, agriculture, and infrastructure, with training programs that are one year long. This process of scaled-up community-based training should start right away.

Gender Equality

As indicated above, all MDG–based investment programs for Africa should pay particular attention to promoting gender equality, both as a goal in itself and as a crucial input to achieving all the other MDGs. This includes ensuring full access to reproductive health rights and services, as well as guaranteeing equal property rights and access to work, backed by affirmative action to increase political representation. Of particular concern in many parts of sub-Saharan Africa are persistently high levels of violence against women and girls, which need to be confronted with public awareness, legislative and administrative changes, and strong enforcement.

... all MDG–based investment programs for Africa should pay particular attention to promoting gender equality, both as a goal in itself and as a crucial input to achieving all the other MDGs.

Science, Technology, and Innovation

An essential priority for African economic development is to mobilize science and technology. Tropical sub-Saharan Africa produces roughly one-twentieth of the average patents per capita in the rest of the developing world. And it has only 28 scientists and engineers per million population compared with 69 in South Asia, 76 in the Middle East, 273 in Latin America, and 903 in East Asia. We stress the need for increased investment in science, higher education, and research and development targeted at Africa's specific ecological challenges (food, disease, nutrition, construction, and energy).

Regional Integration Priorities

Regional integration is essential for Africa. It will raise the interest of potential foreign investors by increasing the scope of the market. It is also important in achieving scale economies in infrastructure networks, such as electricity grids, large-scale electricity generation, road transport, railroads, and telecommunications—and in eliciting increased R&D on problems specific to Africa's ecology but extending beyond any single country (e.g., public health, energy systems, and agriculture). Regional programs, such as those advanced by the New Partnership for Africa's Development (NEPAD), thus require greatly increased support.

Public Sector Management Priorities

Although governance in Africa is not systematically worse than that in other countries after controlling for income, many of the government systems are still weak on an absolute scale and require significant investments in public administration. Information management systems and investments in the training of public sector managers will undoubtedly be crucial. Addressing this issue should be closely linked to reversing and treating the AIDS pandemic, which is taking the lives of hundreds of thousands of civil servants throughout the continent.

IMPLEMENTING THE MDG STRATEGY: NATIONAL-LEVEL PROCESSES FOR SCALING UP
◆ ◆ ◆

To be aligned with the MDGs, the full intervention package must be converted into a country-level investment plan, one that works backward from the outcome targets to identify the infrastructure, human, and financial resources needed to meet the targets; this methodology is hence dubbed a "needs assessment" approach to the MDGs. The UN Millennium Project estimates the costs of the interventions for three African countries—Ghana, Tanzania, and Uganda—chosen for their high levels of extreme poverty, insufficient progress toward achieving the MDGs, and good governance relative to their level of income[. It] concludes that the financial costs required to meet the MDGs to be around $110 per capita. Of the $110, around $40 could be financed through increased domestic resources (both public and private), leaving a remainder of $70 that would need to be funded through ODA. The overall results suggest that, in order to reach the MDGs, these countries will require average annual ODA equivalent to at least 20 to 30 percent of GDP through to 2015.

The UN Millennium Project's core operational recommendation is that each developing country with extreme poverty should adopt and implement a national development strategy that is ambitious enough to achieve the MDGs. The country's international development partners—including bilateral donors, UN agencies, regional development banks, and the Bretton Woods institutions—should give all the technical and financial support needed to implement the country's strategy. In particular, ODA should be adequate to fill the financing needs, assuming that governance limitations are not the binding constraint, and assuming that the recipient countries are making their own reasonable efforts at domestic resource mobilization. For many low-income countries, such a policy-design mechanism already exists that allows governments to design a national strategy in collaboration with their development partners as well as with civil society and the private sector. This strategy is called the Poverty Reduction Strategy (PRS), which is the main country-level framework used jointly by the international development agencies and the national governments to focus their development efforts.

As the central country strategy document, however, poverty reduction strategies must be aligned with the MDGs (in countries where the Goals are already within reach, "MDG-plus" targets can be set). So far, most national strategies have not been ambitious enough to meet the MDGs, and have instead planned modest incremental expansions of social services and infrastructure, based on existing budgets and levels of donor aid. Instead, MDG–based poverty reduction strategies should present a bold, 10-year framework aimed at achieving the quantitative target set out in the MDGs. They should spell out a financial plan for making the necessary investments, then show what domestic resources can afford and how much will be needed from the donors. Although poverty reduction is primarily the responsibility of developing countries themselves, achieving the MDGs in the poorest countries—those that genuinely aspire to the MDG targets—will require significant increases in ODA to break the poverty trap. Importantly, the UN Millennium Project is not advocating new development processes or policy vehicles, only that the current processes be MDG oriented.

The core challenge of the MDGs lies in financing and implementing the interventions at scale—for two reasons. One is the sheer range of interventions that should be sequenced and integrated to reach the Goals. The second is the need for national scaling up to bring essential MDG–based investments to large proportions of the population by 2015. Scale-up needs to be carefully planned and overseen to ensure successful and sustainable implementation. The level of planning is much more complex than for any single project, and requires a working partnership between government, the private sector, NGOs, and civil society. In the past, scaling up has been immensely successful when governments are committed to doing it, communities are encouraged to participate in the process and implementation, and long-term predictable financing has been available.

A NEW NORTH–SOUTH COMPACT FOR ECONOMIC DEVELOPMENT

◆ ◆ ◆

A new framework for donor–African relations will be required to underpin the big investment push needed to meet the MDGs. The package of public investments proposed by the UN Millennium Project implies a significant increase in ODA transfers to Africa, perhaps a doubling or more. Donor–recipient mechanisms will be needed to translate large-scale aid flows into effective investments and poverty reduction. Where domestic governance is adequate (e.g., at or above the norm for countries at the given income level), aid processes should be guided by four core principles:

1. Policies should be aligned with the 2015 time horizon, with that MDG target date serving as the planning horizon for both recipient countries and donors.
2. The public investment program needs to be guided by bottom-up assessments of *needs* rather than *ex ante* budget constraints set by the donors.
3. Donor assistance needs to be harmonized and coordinated around budget support, particularly in countries where governance structures are not the limiting factor to accelerate progress toward the MDGs (only approximately 27 percent of net bilateral ODA to sub-Saharan Africa took the form of budget support in 2002).
4. Donor financing requires new notions of sustainability, including recognition that in some cases grant financing is the only way to pay for the investments and leave the recipient countries with viable public finances at the end of the process.

> *The public investment program needs to be guided by bottom-up assessments of needs rather than ex ante budget constraints set by the donors.*

In practical terms, African governments could implement these guiding principles through a three-stage process. First, each country would convene a planning team comprising government representatives, key stakeholders, and technical advisers—the bilateral and multilateral donors, UN specialized agencies, and civil society leaders—to conduct an MDG needs assessment. In the second step, the needs assessment would feed into a 10-year public investment and human resource strategy. The third step would be to construct the medium-term budget framework (e.g., for three to five years, as with the PRS), which would finance the first three to five years of the 10-year investment strategy. Government-led coordination will be crucial for not only crafting plans but also implementing them. As their part of the bargain, recipient governments will need to implement a clear and transparent system for monitoring and evaluating the implementation of plans, and building in regular milestones to monitor progress as well as checkpoints through which plans can be adjusted as necessary.

In developing an explicit MDG–based planning framework, increased ODA inflows will raise a number of structural macroeconomic issues. Countries must maintain their efforts to mobilize domestic revenue and foster domestic savings and investment in order to support long-term economic growth. With significant increases in ODA inflows, issues of Dutch disease will arise and need to be managed carefully. Finally, underlying this discussion of macroeconomic programming is the consideration of what to do if donor funds are not readily forthcoming to meet the needs of the MDG–based Poverty Reduction Strategies (PRSs). In that case, of course, the MDGs are unlikely to be met. The International Monetary Fund (IMF), however, should not simply urge a country to live within its means. The fund should present the technical case that the country could achieve the MDGs if given additional support, and should urge donor countries to expand the level of available support such that it is sufficient to enable any well-governed African country making the effort to achieve the MDGs.

In countries where governance is weak, the preceding framework will not apply, mainly because development aid allocated to poorly functioning governments can easily be squandered or even used to reinforce bad practices. The key is to understand the nature of the poor governance, and to take actions that make sense in the context. As mentioned previously, in some cases what is called poor governance actually derives from a lack of financial resources to carry out reasonable public functions. In other cases, the problems of governance are deeper. They may involve violent conflict, authoritarian rule, or corrupt and predatory practices by the state. When the problem is violent conflict, the role of aid needs to be focused in the first instance on peace making, peacekeeping, and humanitarian assistance. When the governance problem is entrenched despotic rule of some sort, large-scale aid transfers to the government are ill advised; aid to such governments should be limited and should instead be substantially allocated through nongovernmental organizations and international agencies.

> *... in some cases what is called poor governance actually derives from a lack of financial resources to carry out reasonable public functions. In other cases, the problems of governance are deeper.*

Sachs et al. (2004) have also compared the aid flows needed to achieve the MDGs (equivalent to 20 to 30 percent of recipient countries' GDP) with the benefits of increased international trade liberalization. Although trade reform is welcome and important, the paper outlines how it is certainly not sufficient to achieve the MDGs in tropical Africa. This is for two reasons. First, trade gains do not directly provide the targeted public investments needed in health, education, rural development, and other social sectors. Second, gains from trade liberalization are commodity specific and therefore country specific. Nonfoodstuff exporters, such as the cotton producers of West Africa, will enjoy significant benefits from trade liberalization with welfare benefits estimated at perhaps 2 percent of GDP. Meanwhile, net food-importing countries will in many instances be adversely affected by trade liberalization that increases global food prices.

After surveying the range of estimates from a number of studies, Sachs et al. (2004) concluded that:

Even if the Doha trade negotiations yield African countries the most optimistic outcomes, these countries' benefits will likely not exceed 1 or 2 percent of GDP per year. This level of welfare increase would amount to progress, but the economic benefits are at least an order of magnitude less than the level of resources required to achieve the MDGs in the poorest countries. So while the benefits of trade are real and non-trivial, they are not a substitute for sustained increases in ODA needed to fund the public investments required to attain the MDGs.

In considering the small population size of most African countries and the large number of landlocked countries, there is a critical need for deepening regional integration and investments in cross-country transport, energy, and communication infrastructure, as promoted by NEPAD. Not only does sub-Saharan Africa have extremely low per capita densities of rail and road infrastructure, but existing transport systems were largely designed under colonial rule to transport natural resources from the interior to the nearest port. As a result, cross-country transport connections within Africa tend to be extremely poor and are in urgent need of extension to reduce intraregional transport costs and promote cross-border trade.

In addition, many of Africa's challenges in agriculture, health, environment, or access to energy services require breakthroughs in science and technology. Examples of promising technologies that could help Africa achieve the MDGs include new vaccines or treatments against malaria and HIV/AIDS, improved varieties and cropping systems for predominantly rainfed and drought-prone agriculture, cost-effective information and communication technologies, and low-cost water treatment and purification systems. While private markets in developed countries are able to engage in development-stage scientific activities and, to a lesser extent, research-stage scientific activities, this is not the case in poor countries. Even though these market failures have been understood for some time, the international system has so far not responded adequately. Appropriate solutions could consist of global coordinating mechanisms based on one of the following models: (1) precommitment purchase agreements, (2) *ex post* prices, (3) public–private partnerships based on contractual terms that ensure free access to intellectual property rights generated through publicly funded research, and (4) direct financing of research.

... many of Africa's challenges in agriculture, health, environment, or access to energy services require breakthroughs in science and technology.

The UN Millennium Project's conservative bottom-up estimates suggest that the current level of ODA is a limiting factor for achieving the MDGs in the well-governed African countries and that those countries need an additional $40 or so per capita per year in development assistance. If we supposed that 620 million Africans were to receive that amount, it would add about $25 billion a year to the roughly $18 billion a year provided in 2002. If the increment were limited only to well-governed countries, the overall increase would be perhaps a bit more than half of the $25 billion a year, depending on where donors draw the line. The UN Millennium Project calculates that the total cost of supporting the MDG financing gap for every low-income country would be $73 billion in 2006, rising to $135 billion in 2015. In addition to these direct costs of investments in the Goals, there are added costs at the national and international level—in capacity-building expenditures of bilateral and multilateral agencies, outlays for science and technology, enhanced debt relief, and other areas. In total, the UN Millennium Project finds that costs of meeting the MDGs in all countries are in the order of $121 billion in 2006, rising to $189 billion in 2015, taking into account co-financed increases at the country level.

The bottom line is how small even these "large" numbers really are. In the Monterrey Consensus, and on many occasions both before and since, the rich world has committed to ODA of 0.7 percent of donor GNP. With a combined GNP of around $31 trillion, the donor countries of the OECD have in effect committed to donor flows on the order of $217 billion, compared with actual flows of around 0.25 percent of GNP, roughly $78 billion per year. Even the UN Millennium Project's estimate of $135 billion per year (this includes ODA for non-MDG purposes as well) would put the donor countries at around 0.44 percent of GNP (rising to $195 billion or 0.54 percent of GNP in 2015) far below the long-standing commitment.

> *... the world community should immediately start partnerships with well-governed African countries to help them to end their poverty trap once and for all.*

Large-scale aid is insufficient for ending the poverty trap, nor even warranted, when domestic governance is poor. ODA should be scaled up significantly only for countries that can help themselves. ODA numbers should not be picked out of the air, but instead based on true needs assessments on a country-by-country basis. The situation in much of Africa is sufficiently desperate and the potential benefits of increased donor-finance investment is sufficiently high, that the world community should immediately start partnerships with well-governed African countries to help them to [escape] their poverty trap once and for all.

ONE EXTREME IMPLICATION FROM THE FIXATION OF THE WASHINGTON CONSENSUS ON "INSTITUTIONS"

◆ ◆ ◆

"Bad governance" continues to be the lens through which the Washington Consensus interprets the failure of economic development in Africa. According to the investment banker and ex–World Bank official, Percy Mistry (2005), the annual $50 billion capital flight from Africa is evidence that

> Africa is failing to develop not because of a shortage of money. Rather, it suffers from a chronic inadequacy of human, social and institutional capital. Without such human, social and institutional capital (which is not the same as capacity building), development in Africa will not occur, no matter how much aid is thrown at it ... In any event, it is unlikely that the MDGs will be achieved in Africa by 2014 regardless of the amount of aid provided. The absorptive capacity does not exist to handle it." (p. 2, pp. 11–12)

While Mistry recognizes that Africa lacks the technical capacity to use aid most advantageously and to react fully to new economic opportunities (e.g., those created by globalization), he rejects aid-funded capacity building as the method to solve this "binding constraint on African development."[2] His answer is to import skill[ed] labour and put Africa under receivership: "The human capital that Africa needs will have to be sourced from around the world." Specifically, "the installation and embedding in Africa of human, social and institutional capital on a permanent basis" (p. 5) should occur as follows:

1. "African leaders and governments ... [should] pursue immigration policies as open as Africa's investment policies—something that no aid agency has suggested or required of African governments in the context of economic reform." (p. 6)
2. "To support civil administration[,] donors might consider establishing a permanent civil service for Africa. Such a service could adopt international (e.g., United Nations) standards of compensation and benefits to enable it to employ civil servants from around the world—with qualified Africans being given a clear preference—operating to international standards of probity, competence and efficiency." (p. 8)
3. "The international community could also create an international judicial service for Africa on lines similar to those suggested for civil servants. Such a judicial service could employ retired judges, advocates and attorneys from developed and developing countries or provide opportunities for serving lawyers in other countries to undertake rotational assignments in Africa under arrangements that provided continuity and quality control." (p. 8)
4. "The same could be done with an international law enforcement service for Africa whose remit would include regular policing as well as specialised law enforcement, such as narcotics trafficking, human trafficking, internal revenue, customs and excise. (pp. 8–9)

Mistry suggested that the last three "types of international services could be established and administered over the long term with oversight by agencies such as the Crown Agents who have experience in these particular areas of governance." Mistry, of course, realized that "[this] kind of thinking out of the box ... may, at first glance, smack of expatriate patronisation of the worst kind. It is worth asking, however, whether it is any worse than the condescension Africa now suffers from daily with micromanagement of African economic and political affairs from Washington D.C., London,

Paris and Brussels—a consequence of its chronic dependence on aid" (p. 9).

Clearly, Mistry's recommendations represent one extreme interpretation of "bad governance" in Africa, and it is most likely a minority view within the Washington Consensus camp. Bluntly put, Mistry is claiming that the "bad governance" is the outcome of Africans being incapable of governing themselves, at least up to this point, and that the moral thing for rich countries to do is to "recolonize" Africa for its own good. Building upon the fundamental assumption of the Washington Consensus that the engine of modern economic growth is the economic institutions that originated in Europe and North America, Mistry added the twist that in order for these institutions to work properly in Africa, qualified people from other countries will have to be in charge of these institutions—until the Africans are ready to take over.

The lucky truth for Africa is that Mistry is wrong in many of his claims, and in his prescriptions. To consider but a few examples on each front:

Facts

Mistry claimed that "the neosocialist wave that emerged in the latter half of the 1990s saw international development agencies being led by a new generation whose rhetorical commitment to social justice exceeded their capacity to learn from history" (p. 13). How could the neosocialists have usurped power at the World Bank and the IMF after the collapse of communism in Eastern Europe and the Soviet Union, after the highly successful reigns of Margaret Thatcher, Ronald Reagan, and Helmut Kohl, and the turn of China from in-your-face Communism to closet capitalism? Furthermore, the latter half of the 1990s were the high[-]point years of the institution-fixation type of Washington Consensus—which is why the IMF saw the Asian Financial Crisis as a crisis in crony capitalism.

Mistry also claimed that the ODA lobby and the neosocialists (naturally) have been using disinformation[3] successfully to secure "larger appropriations for aid budgets" (p. 13). Mistry is correct about the amount of aid only if we measure foreign aid in absolute numbers rather than as a proportion of donors' income or as aid per citizen in the recipient country—and we think that the ["]absolute numbers["] [approach] is the least defensible analytically. The data show that with the end of the Cold War, foreign aid had stagnated or declined as a proportion of GDP in most rich countries until the late 1990s. In the case of the United States, foreign aid rose markedly only after Osama bin Laden attacked the United States on September 11, 2001. Should we therefore be surprised that the African countries have generally not improved their performance in the 1990s in the face of reduction in ODA?

Prescriptions

Jumpstarting growth through inward immigration certainly worked for the lands of recent settlement like Australia, New Zealand, Canada, and the United States; but it is certainly not the mechanism that launched East Asian economic growth in the second half of the 20th century. Immigration in short is *not* a precondition for modern economic growth to take place. The fact is that ideas can travel from one country to another without permanent mass migration.

Capacity building, not mass migration, is the operative concept, and poor African countries cannot afford capacity building.

The problem is not that Africans are incapable of learning; the problem is that the typical poor African economy cannot even afford to educate everyone at the primary school level. Capacity building, not mass migration, is the operative concept, and poor African countries cannot afford capacity building.

Mistry pointed out that Botswana "has managed to attract immigrants of the required calibre" and he concluded that its "experience provides an example that the rest of Africa would do well to consider" (p. 7). Mistry neglected to mention that Botswana has rich diamond deposits and had a small population to begin with. The mining of natural resources afforded Botswana the ability to support a larger population at a new higher standard of living. If a landlocked semi-desert African country like Mali wishes to attract a massive inflow of foreign talents, the only way to do so would be to give high subsidies to the new immigrants. We do not see how Mali would be able to afford this policy—unless it expropriates the land of the existing residents and gives it to the new arriving residents, a common action by many colonial governments in the past. Since Mistry is surely not suggesting that African governments treat new citizens better than they treat existing citizens, his suggestion for immigration into Africa is a nonstarter for the poorest African countries. The usual phenomenon in migration is that many more people move from poor to rich countries than vice versa. Hence, Mistry's idea that there would be a large inward migration of skill[ed] labour into a poor landlocked semi-desert country if the country were to permit it (in addition to deregulating the economy into a neoclassical paradise) seems to us to be putting the cart before the horse.

Finally, among the many valid objections to why colonialism cannot, and should not, be the institution to initiate and sustain economic development in Africa, the most telling one is that is has been tried before on a massive scale before World War II, and it did not work most of the time. It is a sad sight indeed to see extreme proponents of the Washington Consensus like Mistry engaging in mental contortions about the causes of "bad governance" in order to avoid recognizing the existence of poverty traps.

SUMMING UP

◆ ◆ ◆

The Washington Consensus is an economic program focused myopically on short- and medium-term stabilization of output, prices, and the balance of payments, and not on long-run sustained growth, particularly in the poorest countries. This accountant's approach to economic management means that little attention is given to national specificities because accounting statements are the same everywhere in the world (even though the same outcomes might have been generated by different sets of factors). Why is there this accountant's mentality toward economic management?

... it needs to be re-emphasised that the causes of underdevelopment are many.

The answer [lies] in the institutional weaknesses of the international financial and development institutions, especially the World Bank and the IMF, and the need for root-and-branch reforms there. The recent negative experiences with the Eastern Europe and former Soviet Union economic transition and the Asian financial crisis show that bureaucratic inertia, operational convenience, and governance problems within the international financial and development institutions coalesced to produce the "one size-fits-all" type of policy packages. We have to change the incentives within existing international economic organizations, most importantly by making them goal oriented so that they design their programs specifically to meet the internationally agreed MDGs. They should help countries make financial plans to fund poverty reduction strategies that are ambitious enough to meet the Goals, and in countries where there is insufficient domestic and aid finance to make the necessary investments, the IMF and World Bank should request more funding from the donors. Our suggested role for the World Bank and the IMF are very different from their current role; we want them to transform themselves from being creditor institutions to become genuinely international institutions. These international financial and development institutions, and the international economy, would benefit greatly in the long run if the voting structure were altered to better represent developing countries, if an international bankruptcy court were created, and if the international financial and development institutions built into their programs policies regarding the tragedy of the global commons brought about by the trend of higher global economic growth.

In conclusion, it needs to be re-emphasised that the causes of underdevelopment are many. The reality is that countries differ in structure and in the international economic constraints they face; many combinations of different shocks produce similar readings on a number of economic indicators; and country characteristics and the international situation could change abruptly. A practice of differential diagnosis is needed to correctly identify what is causing a poverty trap or hindering economic growth in a particular country, and country-level plans need to be made accordingly. The international frameworks exist to do this correctly—the PRSP process brings together the developing country government, private sector, and civil society with the donors to design a strategy. The missing piece, however, has been the financing for strategies that are ambitious enough to break the poverty trap and meet the MDGs. The recent commitment of the European Union to reach the 0.7 percent of GNP target in ODA is a welcome step. Now Japan and the United States must pull their weight if the world is to hope of ending extreme poverty and achieving true security for us all.

Notes

1. See Sachs et al. (2004) for a formal model of some mechanisms that can create a poverty trap, e.g., the bad equilibrium in a multiple equilibrium world.
2. "Africa and the donor community ... can argue that Africa has the capacity to develop its own human, social and institutional capital organically—to cope with increasingly complex challenges of development in a globalising world. But such a choice will mean Africa and its donors continuing to explain for the next half century—as they have for the past four decades—why development still eludes Africa" (Mistry, 2005, p. 5).
3. Africa and the donor community are arguing "for more aid when they know (and acknowledge in camera) that it won't work ... [and they] pretend that money (particularly concessional aid) is the binding constraint" (Mistry, 2005, p. 5).

References

Kaufmann, Daniel, Aart Kraay, and Pablo Zoido-Lobatón, "Governance Matters II: Updated Indicators for 2000/01", World Bank Policy Research Working Paper 2772 (Washington D.C.: The World Bank, 2002).

Kaufmann, Daniel, A. Kraay, and M. Mastruzzi, "Governance Matters III: Governance Indicators for 1996–2002," World Bank Policy Research Working Paper 3106, (Washington D.C.: The World Bank, 2003).

Miles, Marc A., Edwin Feulner Jr., and Mary Anastasia O'Grady, 2004 Index of Economic Freedom, 10th Anniversary Edition of the Index of Economic Freedom by The Heritage Foundation and Wall Street Journal (Westminster, MA: Heritage Books, 2004).

Mistry, Percy, "Reasons for Sub-Saharan Africa's Development Deficit that the Commission for Africa Did Not Consider," African Affairs, Vol. 104, No. 417 (September 2005), pp. 665–78.

PRS Group, International Country Risk Guide Annual, (East Syracuse, NY: PRS Group, September 2003).

Sachs, Jeffrey D., John W. McArthur, Guido Schmidt-Traub, Margaret Kruk, Chandrika Bahadur, Michael Faye, and Gordon McCord, "Ending Africa's Poverty Trap," Brookings Papers on Economic Activity 1 (Washington, D.C.: The Brookings Institution, 2004).

Transparency International, Corruption Perceptions Index 2004 (London: Transparency International, October 2004).

United Nations Millennium Project, Investing in Development: A Practical Plan to Achieve the Millennium Development Goals (New York: Earthscan, 2005).

Woo, Wing Thye, "Serious Inadequacies of the Washington Consensus: Misunderstanding the Poor by the Brightest," in Jan Joost Teunissen and Age Akkerman (eds.), Diversity in Development: Reconsidering the Washington Consensus (The Hague: FONDAD, 2004).

Terms and Concepts

structural adjustment
Washington Consensus
governance
poverty trap

public investment
infrastructure
Millennium Development Goals
national savings rates

official development assistance
recolonization
capacity building

Questions

1. What are causes of poverty in tropical Africa?

2. What is the difference between poverty and extreme poverty?

3. How does governmental corruption discourage development? How does poverty encourage corruption?

4. Why are developed countries reluctant to transfer funds to the African countries on the scale the authors recommend?

5. The authors of this article are not socialists. They do not believe that the state can create economic growth. Yet they believe a strong state is essential to development. Explain.

6. Some argue that assistance to African countries should be accompanied by qualified administrators from the developed world to ensure that the assistance is properly invested. How do the authors respond to this proposal?

Ukraine's Orange Revolution:
Great Promise, Untimely Demise

Mikhail A. Molchanov

Editors' Note

Political change is often cast as "revolution." A revolution is a fundamental reordering of the principles of a regime. Revolution, for example, describes the change from monarchy to republican self-government, or from totalitarian dictatorship to liberal democracy. Such changes are not a matter of different personnel in office, or of having elections. Any dictator can rig an election. A revolution, in other words, is not a *coup d'etat*. What matters in a revolution is that the principles of the new regime permeate the great body of the people.

By this definition, references to "revolution" often say more about the hopes of their supporters than their actual political achievements. This is the essence of Mikhail

Molchanov's analysis of Ukraine's 2004 "Orange Revolution." Molchanov writes a case study in the complexities of democratization in the East European, post-Communist context.

A dozen years into post-Soviet independence, Ukrainians became frustrated with unfulfilled promises of democratic change. Donning orange scarves and toques, throngs of protesters took to the streets of Kiev in December 2004 and demanded an end to rigged presidential elections. The Orange Revolution was supposed to mark an irrevocable change from Soviet-style stagnation, corruption, and cronyism to Western-style, market-based liberal democracy. The Orange candidate, Viktor Yuschenko, won the Presidency. Expectations reached their zenith.

Those expectations were soon dashed. Yuschenko's reforms stalled, and old problems soon plagued the new government. Consequently, a number of questions arise: Did Yuschenko merely dupe the people? Did he succumb to the temptations of office? Did he lack the will to implement the elements of the Revolution? Is the office of president too weak to alter entrenched institutional incentives deeply rooted in a fatalistic political culture? Should the period of reform be measured in generations rather than months? These questions are all the more important in light of successes in post-Communist transition posted by several of Ukraine's neighbours.

◆ ◆ ◆

INTRODUCTION
◆ ◆ ◆

During the first round of Ukraine's presidential elections in 2004, observers suspected that substantial irregularities had occurred, but the election process carried on. The runoff elections on November 21 were characterized by massive fraud and indiscriminate use of the government machine to back

the candidate handpicked by the "party of power." All exit polls showed Viktor Yushchenko the winner. However, the Central Electoral Commission declared Viktor Yanukovych the winner. Immediately after that, opposition politicians called their supporters to the street. The Orange Revolution, so named after the colour worn by Yushchenko's supporters, became the largest nonviolent protest movement in modern Ukrainian history. The pressure from the streets and the criticism

---

Article prepared for this publication. © Nelson, 2008.

from the international community prompted the Supreme Court to annul the results of the second round and to call for a repeat runoff.

In the repeat elections, the candidate of the streets defeated the candidate of the establishment by 52 to 44 percent. On January 23, 2005, Yushchenko was sworn in as president of Ukraine. Informed observers thought the Orange Revolution secured Ukraine's return to the family of civilized nations of the West. Viktor Yushchenko's inauguration speech asserted, "Our place is in the European Union. My goal is, Ukraine in a United Europe."[1]

In the wake of the events of December 2004, the country appeared resolved to enact long-overdue democratic reforms. The victorious party claimed Ukraine was ready for EU membership, and only the authoritarian regime that the revolution toppled blocked Ukraine's accession bid. Yet, the EU had failed to respond in kind. Nine months later, the country's elite found itself in the throes of a deep political crisis. Ukraine's European bid was thwarted by accusations of corruption in the highest echelons of power. Like Leonid Kuchma before him, President Yushchenko seemed to be shying away from real reform at home, while maintaining the rhetoric of the European choice abroad. The Orange Revolution was stillborn. In order to understand why it failed to meet people's expectations, we need to address several long-standing problems of Ukraine's post-Communist transition. First, it is important to understand the roots of the Orange Revolution.

KUCHMAGATE

◆ ◆ ◆

In September 2000, Ukrainians were shocked by the abduction of Georgy Gongadze, the investigative journalist notorious for his relentless attacks on political corruption. Soon after, Gongadze's headless body was found in the woods not far from the national capital. On November 28, 2000, the leader of the Socialist Party of Ukraine, Oleksandr Moroz, accused Ukrainian President Leonid Kuchma of ordering Gongadze's abduction. It was intimated that the President was also involved in Gongadze's murder. As proof, Moroz submitted audiotapes that featured voices resembling those of the top members of the presidential administration, including the president himself, discussing what to do with the annoying Internet journalist. With respect to

Georgian-born Gongadze, Kuchma apparently ordered Minister of the Interior Yurii Kravchenko to "drive him out to Georgia, undress him, leave him without his pants," or find Chechens willing to abduct the reporter for ransom.

In early December, Ukrainian parliamentarians were shown a videotaped interview with a former security service officer Mykola Melnychenko (currently living in the United States), who claimed from his hiding place abroad that it was he who made the recordings revealed by Moroz. The Moroz and Melnychenko accusations prompted mass street protests, with up to 100,000 people demonstrating, engulfing the country in a political scandal of unprecedented magnitude. Protesters erected a tent camp in downtown Kiev to demand the president's resignation.

The government's reaction was predictable. President Kuchma angrily dismissed all accusations and sued Moroz for slander. According to the official version, the Gongadze case was concocted by foreign intelligence agencies with a vested interest in crippling Ukraine's independence. However, Western observers could not but notice that investigation of the case was stalled by the office of the prosecutor general. Pro-presidential factions in the parliament abstained from the vote to schedule a special hearing on the Gongadze case. Parliamentarians who brought a videotaped interview with Melnychenko from their fact-finding mission abroad were illegally searched in the Kiev airport. Their copies of the tape were confiscated, and then returned in a damaged state several days later.

In December 2000–January 2001, the Parliamentary Assembly of the Council of Europe (PACE) repeatedly criticized the conduct of investigation and expressed concern over prosecution, harassment, and aggression that Ukrainian journalists routinely faced. It had ample grounds for such an assessment. By the mid-1990s, media freedom in Ukraine had come under increased pressure from the government. Intimidation of the independent press gained momentum during the 1996–97 tenure of Prime Minister Pavlo Lazarenko—later indicted in the United States on charges of extortion and money laundering. By the time of the 1999 presidential election campaign the government's manipulation of the press included daily secret directives to the editors—the so-called *temnyky*—and taxation penalties and newspaper closures for misbehaviour. In the 10 months preceding Gongadze's disappearance, about 40 Ukrainian journalists were attacked and beaten, some of them severely. In 1999, Igor Bondar, director of a local television station in Odessa, was killed by attackers using automatic weapons. An editor of an Odessa daily, Yuly Mazur, was also murdered, presumably for exposing corruption in a local police department, in 2000. One year later, the director of an independent television company, Igor Aleksandrov, was beaten to death in Slavyansk, Donetsk *oblast'* (province). A letter of inquiry signed by 222 Ukrainian parliamentarians soon after Gongadze's abduction mentioned "dozens of cases … of death under suspicious circumstances, murders, beatings, hold-ups, blackmail and intimidation of the mass media personnel who criticized Leonid Kuchma … [and] exposed corrupt officials."[2]

According to data of the International Press Institute, 20 journalists have died because of their work in Ukraine since proclamation of the country's independence. Systematic and brutal suppression of freedom of speech had twice put Leonid Kuchma on the institute's list of the worst enemies of free press in the world.

Violations of press freedom were not all. Independent observers maintained that both presidential elections in 1999 and parliamentary elections in 2002 were rigged. The government did not hesitate to tap into the state budget funds, to use bureaucratic control and intimidation, and to apply outright pressure on voters in order to secure the compliant vote.

Systematic and brutal suppression of freedom of speech had twice put Leonid Kuchma on the institute's list of the worst enemies of free press in the world.

Market reform was sluggish, and those reforms that were implemented merely pushed the country away from the mainstream of law-based, transparent market practices. Both the government and the economy were run by the same small group of people, the "oligarchs," who dipped into the public purse as if it were their own. Under both the Kravchuk and Kuchma administrations, Ukraine's oligarchs effectively transformed Ukraine into a corrupt, developing country–like state. The national economy was turned into a shrinking trough for rent-seeking and thievish interests. Movement toward a free market economy was compromised by insider privatization according to which denationalized industries fell into the hands of oligarchic "clans" with intimate connections to the central and regional governments. Democracy was stifled by presidential authoritarianism,

which by the late 1990s was applied with increased capriciousness and with almost total disdain for the powers of parliament. The judiciary remained in the pocket of the executive. Kuchma's regime succeeded in parcelling out the state itself, and the state revenue flows in particular, to political supporters who ran departments of the government as their own private fiefdoms. Economic development—or the lack thereof—was determined by murky business deals and the relative power of rival gangs with intimate connections to the criminal underworld. Such was the context in which Ukraine's Orange Revolution unfolded.

Kuchma's regime succeeded in parcelling out the state itself, and the state revenue flows in particular, to political supporters who ran departments of the government as their own private fiefdoms.

THE ORANGE REVOLUTION
◆ ◆ ◆

The Orange Revolution started as a protest against the government's attempts to steal the results of the popular vote in the 2004 presidential elections. The election of a pro-European president seemed like Ukraine's best hope for democracy and eventual acceptance into the European family. However, few observers either in Ukraine or abroad doubted that Kuchma's regime would do everything in its power to prevent a democratic candidate from winning. Kuchma's hand-picked candidate, Viktor Yanukovych, had close personal ties with Ukraine's oligarchic clans and proved his personal loyalty to the outgoing president beyond any doubt. He was a member of the select group of the highly placed officials who ran roughshod over democratic opposition and independent media, twisted regional authorities' arms, and channelled state moneys into the private accounts of Kuchma's associates and family members. They worried that the victory of a democratic candidate would put an end to this brazen abuse of power. Thus, they harassed, marginalized, and attempted to intimidate the main opposition candidates, Viktor Yushchenko and Yulia Tymoshenko. These leading candidates of the democratic forces were denied fair access to the state-allocated funds for pre-election campaign publicity. Tymoshenko was temporarily jailed and Yushchenko allegedly poisoned. Their successes went unremarked in the media while their weaknesses were blown out of proportion. The stage was set for the three rounds of elections and the Orange Revolution that shook Ukraine and attracted the attention of international media.

Pro-democracy groups in Ukraine had long known that this battle might well be decisive. The choice was simple—either continue under the oligarchic regime à la Kuchma or attempt to rebuild the country on a firmer democratic footing. Electing a younger and seemingly less corrupt Yushchenko seemed like the best chance Ukraine had in years. However, democracy activists lacked funds and were denied free access to mass media, while their opponents shamelessly used the full weight of the so-called administrative resources. Faced with this uphill battle, pro-democratic groups and nongovernmental organizations (NGOs) increasingly sought financial and organizational support from Western-based NGOs and government agencies. Western embassies in Ukraine and such organizations as George Soros's International Renaissance Foundation, part of the billionaire's Soros Foundations network, provided such help, with the government of the United States alone reportedly spending about $65 million to provide communications, training, and direct financial support to the regime opponents. The International Renaissance Foundation had allocated $1,201,904 for "elections-related projects."[3]

These Western activities have raised questions about the limits of intervention in other countries' internal affairs, the appropriateness of the United States' official strategy to promote democracy worldwide, and the choice of means to implement it. While critics of Western involvement in the so-called "coloured revolutions" dismiss these events as wholly orchestrated and manipulated from abroad, supporters of such interventions point out that prodemocratic forces faced more powerful and institutionally entrenched opponents, that someone had to level the playing field to make genuine expressions of the popular will possible, and that foreign interventions in any event were relatively modest. External interventions in support of people's demand for just treatment by authorities can also be justified on moral grounds. Interventions of the opponents of democracy and freedom do not enjoy such justification.[4]

In the end, Western money did not cause people to resent their corrupt rulers; it merely helped the opposition channel that feeling into organized protest actions.

The Orange Revolution, even if facilitated by Western help, owes its success wholly to democratic-minded citizens of Ukraine. Because of that, it is crucial to understand how and why it has been stalled in its steps. Why did the Orange Revolution not spark internal reforms and a Western realignment? Why was such promise unfulfilled?

In the end, Western money did not cause people to resent their corrupt rulers; it merely helped the opposition channel that feeling into organized protest actions.

REFORMING THE ECONOMY
◆ ◆ ◆

Ukraine faced a complex post-Communist transition: from state-planned to market economy; from Communist dictatorship to electoral democracy; and from former Russian periphery to fully independent state ready to claim its rightful place among the historic sovereign nations of Europe. As each aspect of transition was hotly debated by political actors, economic reforms stalled. The first post-independence administration of Leonid Kravchuk tried to steer a middle course between the state regulation and the market economy. This ill-conceived policy resulted in hyperinflation of 1992–94, when the price of an average consumer basket of essential goods and services more than doubled in a month. In the meantime, as the state guarantees of employment and income supports evaporated, many people were left out in the cold.

While economic reforms stalled, a process of spontaneous privatization proceeded apace; former managers of the state-controlled factories and plants reasserted themselves as new owners of these same businesses, now ostensibly free from state tutelage. Kravchuk's successor Leonid Kuchma encouraged what often differed little from an open theft of the state resources, as long as the perpetrators would remain personally loyal and use at least some of the misappropriated resources to support his increasingly corrupt and incompetent regime.[5] The richest of these "new Ukrainians"—the oligarchs—exerted extraordinary influence on the government.[6] The idea of a special "Ukrainian way" in the economy flopped conspicuously, sending out waves of reform fatigue and cynicism throughout the society.

BUILDING THE DEMOCRATIC STATE

◆ ◆ ◆

Initially, Ukraine's democratic transition looked more promising than its economic transition. The Constitution of Ukraine was adopted on June 28, 1996, almost five years after the proclamation of independence and amidst intense political debate. The Constitution has been hailed by many as an important landmark on the road of democratic transformation of the country. It laid the foundation of a new political and legal system, containing many of the principles and mechanisms Westerners would recognize: rule of law, judicial review, separation of powers between the executive and legislative institutions, and transparent electoral machinery.

Initially, Ukraine's democratic transition looked more promising than its economic transition.

The country adopted a semi-presidential model of government similar to the French model. The Ukrainian parliament, the Verkhovna Rada, had been originally elected according to a majoritarian two-round system of elections. Later, a mixed-member system of representation was introduced. Under this system, half of the seats would go to the deputies who won the race in single-member districts, the other half allocated according to votes for party lists. A political party had to receive at least 3 percent of the national vote to send its candidates to the parliament. This constitutional provision, still in place, has effectively sent a number of smaller, single-issue or personality-driven parties into political oblivion and cleared the stage for bigger players. Constitutional amendments passed in 2006 changed the system once again. Now all 450 members of the Verkhovna Rada are elected by proportional representation, with the 3 percent threshold still in place.

While most of the post-Soviet states have adopted presidential or semi-presidential models of governance, with the head of the state nominating the prime minister and bearing ultimate responsibility for the work of the cabinet of ministers, Ukraine was never content with a weak or docile parliament. Even before the collapse of the USSR, the Verkhovna Rada could occasionally assert itself against the all-powerful executive. The Orange Revolution reopened the debate on the separation of powers, as democratically inclined parliamentarians struggled to erect effective barriers against power abuse by the president's offices. Leonid Kuchma was forced to negotiate with the parliamentary opposition. These talks prompted the Supreme Court's decision to annul results of the second round of the disputed presidential elections and cleared the stage for Viktor Yushchenko's victory. A significant part of the negotiated package dealt with the proposed constitutional reforms that would change the executive–legislative balance of power to the advantage of the parliament. This time, the outgoing president was all in favour of the enhanced checks on the powers of his successor. Ukraine took a big step down the road to a more accountable and constrained presidency.

Another aspect of the Ukrainian constitutional debate has to do with the rights of linguistic minorities. Ukraine's Constitution confirms that the Ukrainian citizenship is not defined by language or ethnicity, and all minorities that Ukraine had inherited from the former Soviet Union should enjoy full citizenship rights. In recognition of a unique character of Crimean society, which is numerically dominated by the Russians and the Crimean Tatars, the former Crimean *oblast'* was given the constitutional status of an autonomous republic. While the Ukrainian language has been proclaimed the sole official language of the state, certain linguistic rights of minorities, including, most importantly, the 11-million-strong Russian minority, were also entrenched.

However, some felt that those guarantees had been inadequate to start with, and were only half-heartedly implemented. Making Russian the second official Ukrainian language garnered substantial mass support in eastern and southern regions. It became one of the focal points in the ongoing constitutional debate and the rallying cry for several opposition groups, including the resurrected Communist Party of Ukraine. The language issue heated up prior to the 1994 presidential elections and during the Orange Revolution 10 years later, when Yanukovych tried to play the Russian language card against the candidate of the democratic forces, Viktor Yushchenko.

KNOCKING ON EUROPE'S DOOR

◆ ◆ ◆

Ukraine's foreign policy is largely determined by geography. Ukraine is located between Russia and several countries of the European Union. This has created a series of dilemmas. On the one hand, Russia—the former centre of the Communist world—still posed a threat of "reimperialization," or neoimperial reabsorption of its former borderlands. On the other hand, the collapse of the socialist "camp" meant that these newly liberalized countries were left standing on their own in a world in which earlier alliances and affiliations either no longer existed or were discredited. The desire to find a new community of interest was overwhelming. Finally, globalization exposed these newcomers to the discipline of world capitalist markets. The search for foreign investors, aid packages, loans, and subsidies began in earnest. The EU seemed to be an ideal trading partner. Since the early 1990s, Ukraine started reorienting itself toward Europe and the West and away from Russia and the Russian-led Commonwealth of Independent States.

Ukraine's foreign policy is largely determined by geography. Ukraine is located between Russia and several countries of the European Union.

Ukraine's determination to apply for EU membership dates back to 1993. Then, Ukraine attempted to emulate the strategy pioneered by the East Central Europeans and to secure a ticket to the affluent western club by distancing itself from Russia, Europe's perennial "other."[7] Kiev sought to capitalize on the country's well-advertised geostrategic location to secure some form of a privileged treatment from the West and eventually gain admission to NATO and the EU. This strategy seemed to work well with the United States. But Europe's embrace of Ukraine has been less than enthusiastic. In 1992, a decision to launch Programs of Technical Assistance to Ukraine was adopted. In 1992–95, the EU earmarked ECU236 million in technical assistance to Ukraine. For 1996–99, the volume of assistance was increased to ECU538 million. More funds had been committed by the European Bank for Reconstruction and Development (EBRD), and still more raised through the G7 group of the advanced industrialized countries, the International Monetary Fund, and the World Bank, all international institutions that tend to follow the American lead. However, as far as EU membership goes, Ukraine felt less than welcome, especially in comparison to its East Central European neighbours.

At first, the European countries' main concern with Ukraine was the transfer of its nuclear arms to Russia and the closure of the Chernobyl nuclear power plant. The question of Ukraine's prospective membership in the European Community was not seriously entertained. The Partnership and Cooperation Agreement that the EU offered to Kiev did not address the issue of future membership, carried no formal obligations, and was largely advisory in nature. Kiev was left with a feeling that European leaders consigned Ukraine to a limbo of unrequited dreams.

To gain a foothold in Europe, Ukraine had signed the Charter on Distinctive Partnership with NATO in 1997. The government had also adopted the State Program for Cooperation with NATO (1998), which proclaimed that Ukraine "inalienably belongs" with those Central and Eastern European countries that were well on their way to join the European Union in the near future. By implication, it also meant that Kiev no longer felt that Ukraine's primary affiliation should be with Russia and its kin, the other countries of the so-called post-Soviet space. Moreover, presidential decree no. 615 on Ukraine's integration into the European Union dictated that all departments of government in Ukraine should seek to follow European standards in their work.

The lack of reform in Ukraine contrasted sharply with progress in Slovenia, Hungary, Poland, the Czech Republic, the Baltic states, and, later, Bulgaria and Romania.

Easier said than done. The day-to-day work of the government remained bogged down in inefficient and frequently corrupt routines reminiscent of the Soviet period. Well into the new century, the promise of greater transparency and democratic accountability in the government fell far short of expectations. Thus, the European Union officials could not but notice a widening gap between mostly empty declarations of "European destiny" coming from Kiev and the illiberal practices of day-to-day governance that spoke louder than words. The lack of reform in Ukraine contrasted sharply with progress in Slovenia, Hungary, Poland, the Czech Republic, the Baltic states, and, later, Bulgaria and Romania. Because Kiev clearly put democratic reform on the back burner, Ukraine's potential associate membership in the EU has never been seriously considered. The European Commission refocused its attention on the issues of trade, technical assistance, and finance.

Throughout the 1990s, bilateral relations were dominated by EU concerns over Ukraine's alleged "dumping" of textiles, coal, and steel products. It took some time before Ukraine was given the status of a transitional economy, which marginally improved its terms of trade with European countries. EU technical assistance picked up some speed, too, although it had never reached levels comparable to the disbursement of funds to Poland, which, in less than a decade, received more than double the total of all EU aid to Ukraine. Antidumping measures were in full swing until October 2000, and had cost Ukraine millions of dollars. The EU did not grant Ukraine full market economy status until December 2005, a delay that significantly undermined Ukraine's terms of trade with Europe.

More recently, in response to repeated Ukrainian requests for EU membership, the focus of the European concerns over Ukraine shifted back from economic and environmental issues to political and legal concerns. The EU remains dismissive. EU Commissioner for Enlargement Günter Verheugen likened Ukraine's "irresponsible" bid for membership to an "argument that Mexico should be taken into the USA."[8]

Ukraine's European gambit will amount to little until the country proves itself sufficiently European in both political and economic terms.

Even as the Orange Revolution unfolded, EU External Relations Commissioner Benita Ferrero-Waldner merely offered Ukraine a place in the EU's "wider neighbourhood." The European neighbourhood policy, adopted by the European Commission in May 2004, has been specifically designed as a substitute for an association agreement. The European Commission Action plan for Ukraine aims "to hold out the prospect, not of membership but of gradual integration into certain EU policies (e.g., education, research, environment), to improve cooperation in fighting crime and in managing borders and population movements, and also to bring national laws gradually into line so that these countries can enjoy the benefits of the internal market."[9] Even as president-elect Yushchenko stressed, "We are the center of Europe,"[10] opinion in Brussels was that "now the journey is not for European Union membership."[11] Ukraine's European gambit will amount to little until the country proves itself sufficiently European in

both political and economic terms. Ukraine is still in the very early phases of this transition. The new Orange government's record over the course of the last few years has unfortunately confirmed Europe's skepticism about Ukraine's chances to join any time soon.

THE AFTERMATH OF THE ORANGE REVOLUTION

◆ ◆ ◆

Soon after the Orange Revolution, a new government, led by charismatic Yulia Tymoshenko, was formed. It featured a hodge-podge association of well-known politicians, including financial backers of the Revolution, ex-academics and pundits, and some relatively obscure loyalists selected from either the Yushchenko or Tymoshenko election teams. Some, like American-born justice minister Roman Zvarych, could not even produce university-level credentials that would qualify them for the job. Conflicts over portfolios and chains of command started at once. More often than not, these conflicts zeroed in on a stream of government revenue that this or that loyalist wanted to control. The corrupt privatization of the state-owned industry that Leonid Kuchma administered in his own and his cronies' interests was being reversed in the interests of the new power holders.

The Orange coalition unravelled before any long-promised reforms could be launched, let alone implemented. The immediate reasons for the fall of the Tymoshenko cabinet—the clash of personalities and mutual accusations of corruption between the Yushchenko and Tymoshenko lieutenants—were only surface manifestations of the deeper structural, institutional, and cultural causes that plagued the Orange government from the start. Chief among those has been the Orange elite's inability and unwillingness to part ways with the discredited legacy of the Kuchma regime in a way that would indicate a genuine commitment to building a law-based, transparent, open, and accountable state. This inability, in turn, can be attributed to the following interrelated factors.

First, the prevalent political culture in Ukraine, shaped by the years of authoritarianism, is not yet sufficiently conducive to the implementation of democratic norms in practice, even if the rhetoric of democracy abounds. Culturally, Ukraine still bears a burden of decades of Soviet communist influence—an influence, it must be said, embraced by many Ukrainians. Before that, Ukraine's elites struggled to find a niche in power structures dominated by foreign powers that ruled the land for centuries. Ukrainian nobles and hangers-on had adapted by pursuing their immediate personal and parochial interests at the cost to the country's national interests. This history has entrenched elitist contempt of the masses and bred certain patterns of behaviour that elevated an ability to ingratiate oneself with authorities. Those same patterns discouraged nonconformism and a proclivity to fight for one's personal and group rights. It contributed to regional and corporate fragmentation of Ukrainian society, which remains divided between the supporters of Russia in the east and detractors of Russia in the west, and the Ukrainian polity, which has been hostage to the competing interests of several oligarchic clans controlling the country's economy.

Culturally, Ukraine still bears a burden of decades of Soviet communist influence— an influence, it must be said, embraced by many Ukrainians.

Second, the reformers inherited a power machine that institutionalized corruption, nontransparency, and intimidation of political opponents. Rather than completely redoing the system, they have put this machine to their own uses.

Third, the "Orange" leaders were politically socialized and promoted inside the oligarchic Kuchma regime, which exerted a significant formative experience on their political behaviour. The learned modes of behaviour, which ensured political survival in the corrupt and lawless atmosphere of the 1990s, reasserted themselves with the "Orangists" now in supreme positions of power, thus undermining democratic ideals of the revolution.

Consequently, in the immediate aftermath of the Orange Revolution several regional politicians who supported the losing side in the election were arrested and temporarily jailed on sketchy charges. Thousands of local bureaucrats and officials of all ranks were dismissed for alleged involvement in election fraud, sometimes with little reason at all, to be replaced with Yushchenko supporters. The government embarked on a confused, costly, and legally dubious "reprivatization" campaign, confiscating business assets held by supporters of Viktor Yanukovych only to sell them into the hands of the new Orange elite. This property redistribution, guided almost

exclusively by political sympathies or antipathies of the government, panicked foreign investors and slowed Ukraine's economic growth from 12 percent to less than 3 percent in one year.

As the economy faltered, the government fell back on populism and boosted social spending in the absence of new streams of revenues. This triggered inflation and contributed to unemployment. To counter inflationary pressures, Tymoshenko resorted to interventionist policies reminiscent of the Soviet times. Ukraine's national currency was artificially strengthened against the U.S. dollar, while petroleum-selling companies were mandated to keep gas prices below the government-approved mark. By mid-2005, foreign governments doubted Ukraine's commitment to market reforms. Meanwhile, government members descended to mutual accusations of corruption and calumny. Cynicism only deepened when it was learned that the son of the "people's president" managed to register the Orange Revolution logos as the family's private trademarks. Against this background, the dismissal of Tymoshenko's cabinet and the split of the original Orange coalition was unsurprising.

Thus, the Orange Revolution left Ukraine with a weaker version of the Kuchma regime. No wonder so many took it with bitter disappointment. As Irina Bekeshkina, a sociologist, wrote on the *Ukrainska Pravda* website: "Explain to me what the difference is between privatization of political brands of the Orange Revolution by the current president and privatization of Kryvorizhstal (Ukraine's leading steel maker) by the previous president's son-in-law."[12]

... the Orange Revolution left Ukraine with a weaker version of the Kuchma regime.

Popular disappointment with the Orangists came to the fore in the March 2006 parliamentary elections, when one-third of the popular vote went to the Party of the Regions headed by the losing candidate of the presidential elections 2004, Viktor Yanukovych. The Yulia Tymoshenko bloc finished second, with 22 percent of the vote, while the president's Our Ukraine delivered no more than 14 percent. This rather humiliating result for the two Orange parties complicated their efforts to form a ruling coalition. The prolonged bickering over the distribution of the government posts revealed remaining mistrust among the leaders and their followers. Even more importantly, it sent a dire warning that a fight between the underachieving millionaires and the billionaires of the Kuchma era may well be continuing, even if the more politically successful of oligarchs are now wearing orange colours.[13]

CONCLUSION

◆ ◆ ◆

Contemporary Ukraine remains in the early stages of its post-Communist transition. It still has to build a functioning market economy and find its proper place in regional and global trade regimes. It has to find a national identity inclusive enough to appeal to the nation's numerous ethnic minorities. Most importantly, it ought to complete the democratic transition that the Revolution started.

The latter task is complicated by the institutional and cultural legacies of the Kuchma era, which saw extensive uses of the so-called administrative resources (executive decrees, law enforcement agencies, and tax police, among many) to bend opposition to the will of the establishment. Institutionally, as Dominique Arel argues, the central task that the new government and the Verkhovna Rada face is the "depoliticization of these 'punishing' state agencies and the establishment of real restraint in the application of executive power."[14]

The temptations of power abuse are many and hard to fight in an environment in which legal checks and balances against such abuse are barely noticeable, and the tradition of unquestioning subservience to authorities is strong and reinforced daily. Two years into the current presidency, legal reform is stalled, and efforts to bring transparency to the powers of the executive and administrative departments of the government are ineffective.

Nonetheless, Ukraine today is vastly different from the Ukrainian Soviet Socialist Republic of yesterday. It has achieved degrees of political and economic freedom that were simply unthinkable under Communism. It features numerous organizations of civil society that are at least partially independent from the state. It has developed a national, competitive political process, and made huge strides in developing a party system with recognizable profiles and distinguishable political platforms of the parties. It has developed and implemented an independent course in foreign policy, and has proven that its national sovereignty is irreversible. Last but not least, the Orange Revolution showed the world that Ukrainians would no longer tolerate a quasi-authoritarian rule that several other post-Soviet states still suffer. It is this experience of direct democracy that will most certainly outlive the Orange coalition itself, and ensure that Ukraine's subsequent governments will not get away with policies that systematically ignore the will of the people.

Notes

1. Viktor Yushchenko, Inaugural address of the President of Ukraine Viktor Yushchenko to the Ukrainian people on Independence Square, January 23, 2005. Retrieved March 16, 2007, from http://ww2.yuschenko.com.ua/eng/Press_centre/168/2167.

2. *Ukrayinska Pravda,* October 5, 2000.

3. Timothy Garton Ash, "The $65m Question: When, How—and Where—Should We Promote Democracy? *Guardian Weekly* (December 24, 2004), p. 13.

4. Michael McFaul, "What Democracy Assistance Is ... and Is Not," *Hoover Digest,* 1 (2005). Retrieved March 16, 2007, from www.hooverdigest.org/051/mcfaul.html.

5. Hans van Zon, "Political Culture and Neo-Patrimonialism Under Leonid Kuchma," *Problems of Post-Communism* 52.5 (2005), pp. 12–22.

6. Similar developments in Russia are well described in Chrystia Freeland, *Sale of the Century: Russia's Wild Ride from Communism to Capitalism* (Toronto: Doubleday, 2000). A well-documented description of the illegal and semi-legal tactics that the post-Communist tycoons used in making their riches can be found in Paul Klebnikov, *Godfather of the Kremlin: Boris Berezovsky and the looting of Russia* (New York: Harcourt, 2000).

7. Iver B. Neumann, *Uses of the Other: "The East" in European Identity Formation* (Minneapolis: University of Minnesota Press, 1999).

8. Reuters, November 25, 1999. Retrieved May 20, 2006, from www.reuters.com.

9. European Parliament, "The European Parliament's support for the 'Orange Revolution' in Ukraine is a step towards an ambitious Wider Europe—Neighbourhood policy" (September 7, 2005) Ref.: 20050819FCS00984. Retrieved November 15, 2006, from www.europarl.eu.int/news/public/focus_page.

10. Viktor Yushchenko, Inaugural address.
11. Jose Manuel Barroso, Transcript of Press Conference, Visit of Condoleezza Rice, Brussels (February 9, 2005) Ref.: SPEECH/05/84. Retrieved from http://europa.eu.int.
12. *Sydney Morning Herald,* "Orange Slice for Leader's Son" (August 6, 2005). Retrieved March 10, 2007, from www.smh.com.au/text/articles/2005/08/05/1123125905756.html.
13. Anders Åslund, "A Ukrainian Revolt—The Millionaires Against the Billionaires," *Taipei Times,* December 24, 2004, p. 9. Retrieved March 16, 2007, from www.taipeitimes.com/News/editorials/archives/2004/12/24/2003216538.
14. Dominique Arel, "Is the Orange Revolution Fading?" *Current History* Volume 104, Issue 684 (2005), p. 328.

Terms and Concepts

post-Communist transition
democratization
Kuchmagate
administrative resources

political culture
elitism
corruption
transparency

rent-seeking
quasi-authoritarianism
market economy

Questions

1. What was the Orange Revolution?
2. What caused it?
3. Molchanov suggests that Ukraine has been seeking to align itself with the Europe as opposed to Russia. What is at stake in this realignment?
4. Why did the Orange Revolution fail? What stands in the way of Ukrainian political and economic reform?
5. What will it take to produce lasting political and economic reform?
6. Does Molchanov's article contain any clues as to why Ukraine's post-Communist transition lags behind that of neighbouring countries?

Iraq and Democracy: The Lessons Learned

Larry Diamond

Editors' Note

Few doubt that the strategy the United States has employed to stabilize and democratize Iraq was poorly planned, underresourced, badly executed, and inadequately supported by the international community. More fundamentally, detractors point to the support the Americans gave Saddam Hussein decades ago to help counter what the United States considered a regional security threat emanating from neighbouring Iran. Many maintain that the Americans toppled Saddam's regime to gain an imperial foothold in the Middle East and guarantee the flow of oil from the region to U.S. consumers. Some say Bush the younger was merely finishing a job left undone by his father in 1991.

To these assessments should be added the following factors. Saddam Hussein's regime was a vicious, paranoid dictatorship that decimated the country's civil society, antagonized major religious groups, used biochemical agents on its own population, and fostered a personality cult around Saddam himself. It was the object of international criticism long before the United States planned a regime change.

Three main positions can be taken on the Iraqi occupation. The first is that the export of democracy by one state to another is wrong in principle. One state should not tell another how to order its domestic affairs, and it certainly should not use military power to change the other's regime. The problem with American policy in Iraq is not that it failed; the problem is that it was attempted. The second position is that democracy is in principle a better regime than dictatorship, and democratic regimes should be encouraged. The problem is that we do not know what encourages democratization, and that we should shy from the export of democracy for fear of making things worse. The third position is that democracy is the best available regime and that we can learn from experience and promote democratization prudently.

Larry Diamond is in the latter camp. He is an incisive critic of U.S. policy in Iraq but does not give up on the idea of democracy promotion or on Iraq's particular prospects. Like fellow political scientist Francis Fukuyama, Diamond believes that one important lesson is that democracy does not spontaneously spring up, like a daisy, after an oppressive regime is removed. It needs to be cultivated with patience and close attention to local conditions. Second, before there can be a democratic state, there must be a state. Third, before there can be an extensive state providing a range of services to its citizens, the state must be strong enough to deliver the essentials of government: order, enforcement of laws, and basic civil infrastructure.[1]

◆ ◆ ◆

Iraq is not yet lost. The December 2005 parliamentary elections—with their extraordinary voter turnout and their promise of more inclusive Sunni involvement in government—marked a turning point on the difficult path of stabilizing that tortured country. But Iraq is not yet won either, and it is important to understand why.

---

1. Francis Fukuyama, *State-Building: Governance and World Order in the 21st Century*. (Ithaca: Cornell University Press, 2004).

Whatever happens in the months and years to come, it is clear that in the two years following the toppling of Saddam Hussein's regime, the United States squandered its extraordinary military victory through a series of gross strategic mistakes, acts of ideological blindness, and a breathtaking failure to prepare military and politically for the postwar era. For the benefit of future policy making, it is vital that the United States learn the essential lessons for building democracy after conflicts that Iraq has taught.

WIN THE PEACE

◆ ◆ ◆

The first lesson of America's experience in Iraq is that the stabilization—not to mention democratization—of a state that has collapsed or been toppled through violent conflict is an intrinsically difficult and protracted process that requires a huge commitment from both internal and international actors. To generate and sustain this commitment, any effort at administration and reconstruction of the postconflict state must mobilize legitimacy, both internally in the postconflict country as well as internationally. It is therefore ill advised to go to war against a country for the specific purpose of democratizing it, or without compelling strategic reasons that muster broad international support.

… it is vital that the United States learn the essential lessons for building democracy after conflicts that Iraq has taught.

It was also a mistake to have gone to war largely alone. Washington can say that a coalition of some 30 countries joined the effort, but no sustained public opinion polling from any of these countries indicated that their publics supported what their governments were doing with the United States. In terms of international public opinion, the Iraq War was largely an American effort. As we have seen in Iraq, a war that lacks broad international sympathy and support depletes America's stock of "soft power" (and even over time its hard military power), creates a host of special postwar problems, and tends to weaken the international consensus behind democracy promotion as an endeavor.

It was unfortunate that the United States failed to correct its own international weakness and isolation in the postwar administration of Iraq. While it constructed a Coalition Provisional Authority (CPA) with the military and administrative participation of many countries (most prominently Britain), the occupation was in its design and structure overwhelmingly American. The Iraqis knew it. The United Nations—which was ready to work in close partnership with the United States as it had in Afghanistan but was largely spurned—knew it. And America's allies knew it. Clearly, the United States needed to do much more than it did in Iraq to generate legitimacy and trust.

A second and related lesson underscores what Washington knew before it went in, and what the Pentagon leadership ignored to the great misfortune of both Iraqis and the United States: that the United States needs to prepare in advance for a major commitment and resource it adequately. As James Dobbins and his colleagues noted in a 2003 RAND study, *America's Role in Nation-Building: From Germany to Iraq,* the typical successful experience involves an overwhelming commitment of force not so much for winning the war—which the United States could accomplish with the speed and maneuverability of Secretary of Defense Donald Rumsfeld's new military—but for winning the peace and securing it in the immediate aftermath of the war.

… what the world needs … is a sort of muscular gendarmerie.

From the day that Baghdad fell on April 9, 2003, it was clear that the United States did not have enough troops on the ground. It never had enough troops. Indeed, it never had enough of any kind of resource needed to secure the postwar era. Nor did it have the right mix of troops. It was missing, for example, enough military police. What it needed—what the world needs—is a sort of muscular gendarmerie. These would be well-armed and -trained mobile police that can be deployed in a situation like Baghdad and use nonlethal force to prevent the kind of massive looting of government institutions and public infrastructure that occurred in the war's aftermath. Even without this, senior Army officers had sought several hundred thousand troops—at least twice or even three times the number the United States had on the ground—to invade and then stabilize Iraq after the war. By a greater order of magnitude, the United States needed more military police, more civil-affairs officers, more armored vehicles, more helicopters, more body armor—more of everything.

Not only did the U.S. leadership fail from the beginning to deploy sufficient military resources to secure the country, to deter and face down potential spoilers, and to seal the borders to prevent Al Qaeda and other foreign jihadists from pouring in from Syria and Saudi Arabia—it also did not have in place enough resources for the civilian component of the postinvasion phase, including the capability to move civilians about the country while adequately protecting them. These failures led to a situation in which the United States could not effectively implement either the economic reconstruction plans or the political and civic reconstruction plans that it had for Iraq because it was so dangerous to move around.

... it also did not have in place enough resources for the civilian component of the postinvasion phase ...

Besides the need for sufficient legitimacy and resources, the experience in Iraq yields more specific lessons about building electoral systems that could aid Washington in the promotion of democracy in the next few years in the Arab world. Of course, if the United States were to become more active in this regard, as President Bush has committed it to doing, it will not confront the circumstances of a shattered state and a post-totalitarian landscape in the way it has in Iraq. Still, the American experiment in Iraq offers hands-on experience in several areas.

BUY TIME FOR POLITICS

◆ ◆ ◆

Building a level and pluralistic playing field is extremely important. The United States encountered in Iraq the "flattened landscape" that was found in the Soviet Union, Romania, and some of the other postcommunist countries after their ruling regimes fell. These nations had essentially no civil society or pluralistic array of political parties.

In the shadows of severe authoritarianism in the Muslim Middle East, the one type of political group that can mobilize outside the state's gaze and build support tends to involve some degree of radical Islamist ideology. If a country moves from a political vacuum very rapidly to elections, it will not have a level playing field because

of the overwhelming advantage of recently surfaced Islamist movements and parties, whose democratic credentials or commitments are at best ambiguous and at worst entirely absent. Moreover, in the absence of established political parties and civil society, the Islamist or authoritarian tendency will have a tremendous head start.

The United States encountered in Iraq the "flattened landscape" that was found in the Soviet Union, Romania, and some of the other postcommunist countries after their ruling regimes fell.

This creates concern about how to buy time and mobilize resources to try to level the political playing field. It is one of the issues that concerned the Coalition Provisional Authority, and it is one of the reasons why the CPA wanted to delay elections in Iraq. Unless there is time for different types of political parties, social movements, and civic organizations to develop—including groups that can project a more moderate, democratic, secular, or, at least, democratic Islamist orientation onto the political and electoral landscape—then the electoral arena will be dominated by a force that is not democratic.

Or it may become polarized, as it did in Iraq, along ethnic and identity lines. The January 2005 election, for all of its deeply moving character and successful elements, was largely an identity referendum. Ninety percent of the Kurds voted for the Kurdish list, more than 70 percent of the Shiites voted for the United Iraqi Alliance (a coalition of Shiite religious parties), and about 70 percent of the Sunnis did not vote.

Grand Ayatollah Ali a-Sistani, the most powerful Shiite leader, had demanded early direct elections for both a constituent assembly and a transitional parliament. Although the reasons why the United States resisted this were understandable, they were not based solely on the need for time to develop the administrative agenda and electoral framework. Washington was worried, frankly, that people who might not be committed to democracy and a liberal agenda would win—and win overwhelmingly. Yet because the American occupation was so badly lacking in legitimacy within Iraq (and internationally), authorities did not have the standing and trust that would have been required to delay elections very long without the Shiite south violently resisting.

As a result of the skillful mediation of the United Nations and its special envoy, Lakhdar Brahimi, a compromise was reached in February 2004 that delayed elections for a transitional national assembly until January 2005. This was about eight months longer than Sistani and the Shiite religious parties wanted to wait, but it was about two years earlier than might have been desirable and achievable if there had been from early in the postwar period a more broad-based, legitimate interim administration, of Iraqis, chosen by Iraqis.

There needs to be a strategy for democratization in the Arab world, and it needs to be serious in terms of having true democratization as the goal. It is not enough to engage in what Georgetown University's Daniel Brumberg and other specialists have called "tactical liberalization"—a game of hide-and-seek, back-and-forth, but never real, sustained movement toward democracy. At the same time, change should be gradual enough to give time for political parties to build their organizations, craft programs, and mobilize political support—points also made by a 2005 Council on Foreign Relations task force report on political change in the Arab world and the US role, *In Support of Arab Democracy*.

> There needs to be a strategy for democratization in the Arab world, and it needs to be serious in terms of having true democratization as the goal.

GO LOCAL FIRST

◆ ◆ ◆

In addition to how soon elections are held, it also matters where and in what order they are held. This is another lesson that the Iraqi postwar experience reinforces and sustains. It helps to have local elections first. The CPA was mistaken not to have gone ahead with local elections in many communities—local elections that different Iraqi communities were asking for, that many civilian and military CPA officials wanted to hold, and that Ambassador Paul Bremer and other officials in the CPA headquarters in Baghdad vetoed and prevented from happening.

Of course, critics argued that there was no electoral register, no voting infrastructure, no parties, no electoral law. There were serious obstacles. Yet the United

States could have used—and in a few cases local officials did in fact use—the records of household registration for Iraq's food-ration system and other practical means in order to register voters and allow them to cast ballots to choose local leaders. When local elections occur early, new actors emerge who have credibility and legitimacy, and who have roots in their community. This process of pushing forward local leaders, and encouraging them to garner support from within their own communities, tends to soften or deemphasize the major identity cleavages in a country. It could have exercised some brake on the political tendency of elections in a postconflict situation to become an identity referendum or a deeply ideological and symbolic process.

The United States and its allies should not, of course, apply what has been learned inflexibly and without reflecting on the local situation of a country that is emerging out of conflict or moving, hopefully, into democracy. But the lesson of Iraq regarding early local elections could also apply to a number of Arab nations where political openings are occurring, or where the people are at least appealing for them. Democratization in these countries might be more viable and sustainable if it proceeded with early emphasis on truly democratic and open local-level elections, where less is at stake.

> Democratization in these countries might be more viable and sustainable if it proceeded with early emphasis on truly democratic and open local-level elections, where less is at stake.

Power can thus be dispersed and a more pluralistic landscape can emerge without people feeling that their vital interests might be threatened. The practice of local political competition, and the need for victorious politicians and parties to deal with practical issues of local and municipal governance, might then generate the pragmatism in governance and the construction of mutual political trust and tolerance that could enable democratization to proceed more fully to higher levels of authority.

This points to yet another lesson of the Iraq experience: the importance of decentralized authority. If local and even mid-level provincial elections are going to be meaningful, power has to be devolved and resources provided to lower levels of government. Arab states historically have been extremely centralized. This was one of the problems of Iraq: it is one of the problems characteristic of virtually all of the world's petro-states. When people conduct politics only in a central political arena, this becomes conducive to the polarization of politics around larger identities. It is not conducive to a just distribution of resources or to a democratic approach to politics. If there is only one political arena at the central national level—and everything is at stake in that arena—then no one can afford to lose.

If, on the other hand, a large number of local elections take place, then Sunnis in Anbar province and Kurds in Kurdistan and Shiites in the city of Basra know that whatever happens in the center, they are going to be able to exercise some political power in their province. And if they receive some guaranteed share of the oil wealth to spend in their provinces and their communities, this takes some pressure off national-level politics. (We perhaps are beginning to see that the Sunnis, who have historically been the stronger advocates of a highly centralized fiscal and political system—since they controlled it—are waking up to the fact that decentralization can be useful to them. If the negotiations for a new constitution had not been so rushed, and if they had not adopted such a radical formula for regional power, which could potentially eviscerate the central government, the Sunnis might have gravitated more clearly to this understanding.)

PICK THE RIGHT SYSTEM

◆ ◆ ◆

The electoral system matters. Yet, partly because it seemed administratively easier to manage in the difficult circumstances of Iraq in late 2004 and January of 2005, the electoral system selected by a United Nations team was inappropriate for Iraq. The Iraqi interim government and the United States had invited in UN officials to help choose, train, and advise a new Iraqi electoral commission. Bremer and the CPA had insisted on having an independent electoral commission, even when many Iraqi political parties involved in the governing council wanted to relentlessly politicize and split up control of this body. This, too, is a lesson from Iraq. The electoral process requires popular confidence, and that comes from a neutral, professional electoral administration that is totally insulated from partisan politics.

The electoral system matters.

But the system chosen for the January elections was proportional representation in a single nationwide district, one that only a few other relatively small countries use (such as the Netherlands and, ironically, Israel). While proportional representation made sense for Iraq, the absence of any district basis for the system did not. No area of the country had any indication of what kind of minimum representation it would have in parliament. Since the Sunni areas had been the site of far greater violence and disruption, Sunnis feared that they would wind up being severely underrepresented in such a system, which accords seats to parties purely on the basis of national vote totals. This was one of the major reasons the Sunni Arab parties boycotted the January 2005 elections—a disastrous move for them, and for the country, since it intensified the polarization and violence.

Generally, proportional representation is useful in managing ethnic conflict and ensuring a just, inclusive result. But using only a single nationwide district leaves no possibility for local candidates, local identities, and local initiatives to emerge. And there is nothing that is more conducive to an election's becoming an identity referendum than a single national-list system in which voters hardly even know who the candidates are. They are literally just voting for a party and a symbol. In the case of Iraq, that meant most Shiites were simply voting for Sistani's picture on a poster.

If Iraq had adopted a system of smaller-scale multi-member districts based, for example, on the boundaries of the 18 provinces—something many of us who were within the CPA recommended for the first national elections—or even open-list systems under which people could look at the candidates and vote for individual candidates and rank them, that might have allowed local leaders to emerge and develop some constituencies. It could also have required elected officials to be responsible and accountable to local-level constituencies.

Fortunately, the provincial-list proportional representation system is precisely what Iraq adopted for the December 15 elections. This decision, which then assured a minimum number of seats for each province in the new parliament, played a major role in giving Sunni Arab parties confidence to participate vigorously in the elections. Although some Sunnis complained about the allocation of seats to their provinces (based on voter registration figures), their political and religious leaders urged full participation in the election, and even the diehard Saddamist and Al Qaeda terrorists largely refrained from the kind of violence and intimidation that suppressed the Sunni vote in January. As a result, Sunni voter participation soared on December 15, with ordinary Sunni voters now feeling the same pride and resolve in participating that other Iraqi communities had in January. The election itself was an unprecedented logistical and political success, with some 11 million Iraqis (over two-thirds of those registered) voting at more than 6,000 polling stations, and with only 18 reported attacks against polling sites (compared to about five times that in January). Even in the immediate aftermath of the balloting ... it was clear that the widespread and enthusiastic participation would ensure a much more representative parliament, and so at least the possibility of a more inclusive government. In the coming months, however, the stabilization of Iraq will depend to a great extent on whether the different political and sectarian groups are able to share power and fashion a more broadly acceptable constitutional bargain, particularly on federalism and the control of oil and gas resources.

DISARM THE MILITIAS
◆ ◆ ◆

Another lesson made obvious in Iraq is that any effort at post-conflict reconstruction must confront the problem of order. A country cannot build a democratic state unless it first has a state—a set of institutions of political authority that exercise a monopoly over the means of violence in a territory. If a democratic electoral process is to be successful and sustained to allow the emergence of a truly democratic system, attention must therefore be paid to the problem of armed force outside the control of the state. Armed groups controlled by political parties and political movements can use this private force to aggrandize their power, intimidate voters, and create an undemocratic playing field.

The CPA tried over many months to implement in essence a "DDR" plan—disarmament, demobilization, and reintegration of militias into the Iraqi economy and society. But the effort began too late. It lacked the force and legitimacy to be implemented effectively. And it was ultimately derailed by the twin insurgencies of the Falluja-based Sunni resistance and the Shiite fighters under Muqtada al-Sadr that erupted in April 2004, and then by the lack of enthusiasm for the disarmament

effort on the part of the Iraqi interim government that took power on June 28.

A country cannot build a democratic state unless it first has a state—a set of institutions of political authority that exercise a monopoly over the means of violence in a territory.

Iraq thus went into elections in January 2005 facing not only a virulent Sunni-based insurgency, but also increasingly muscular and ambitious Shiite militias on the streets as well. In the north was the country's most powerful Iraqi armed force, the Kurdish peshmerga, which had been extending the power and de facto borders of Kurdistan through force, even as it brought a degree of stability to the far north unknown in the rest of Iraq. The existence of these powerful, non-state militias could not help but affect the electoral environment.

To a degree that will take some time to fully assess, the mobilization of the militias did diminish the freedom and fairness of the December 15 elections. This was particularly so in the southern provinces, where militias associated with the Shiite religious parties of the United Iraqi Alliance intimidated and obstructed opposing political forces, attacked their headquarters, ripped down their campaign banners, and terrorized, assaulted, and assassinated a number of their candidates and campaign workers. The electoral misconduct was particularly brazen in Basra, where many police cars and government buildings displayed the electoral symbol of the Alliance, or the ballot number of its electoral list, 555, and where Iraqi police officers urged people to vote for the 555 list on election day (in open defiance of the electoral rules).

The militia problem is going to get considerably worse in future elections. Moreover, it is not just voting we must worry about. During the past year in particular, the militias of the Shiite Islamist parties and movements have used their high degree of organization and their coercive power to penetrate the police and the military. In the context of the provincial electoral victories that their parties and movements won in January 2005, they also have taken control of local governments and imposed harsh interpretations of sharia, or Islamic law. At the same time they have exacted vigilante vengeance against Sunnis believed involved with the insurgency or Hussein's regime.

A kind of Islamic state is emerging in the Shiite south. Although the Islamist parties—gathered together in the United Iraqi Alliance (still with the implicit blessing of Ayatollah Sistani)—did not do quite as well nationally in the December elections as they had in January, within the southern provinces they remain determined to consolidate their hold on power. For some time to come, there may be little that the United States can do to prevent the drift to Islamic rule in the southern provinces, except try to strengthen moderate and secular groups throughout Iraq, while standing up vigorously for basic principles of human rights and constitutionalism.

Meanwhile, the international community, the United States, the United Nations, the Europeans—everyone with a stake in a peaceful, stable Iraq, including, obviously, the Iraqi state itself—will need to confront the problem of very substantial armed force in the hands of private actors, political parties, and religious and social movements. These groups are bound to use that force in ways that will undermine democratic principles and processes if they are not demobilized.

> ... the international community ... will need to confront the problem of very substantial armed force in the hands of private actors, political parties, and religious and social movements.

Unfortunately, demobilizing them has never been more difficult, not only because many of their parties have won political power and legitimacy, but also because they have increasingly merged with the Iraqi state. A major test of Iraq's stability and viability in the coming months will be whether the units of the new Iraqi army and police are loyal to the state as a whole, or to the parties and movement from which they were recruited as militia fighters.

DEAL WITH THE INSURGENTS

◆ ◆ ◆

Even with the success of the December 15 elections, Iraq will not become a full democracy any time soon. There are simply too many groups on the ground, too powerful and too violent, that do not value or want a truly democratic order. Yet, with the prospect of a more legitimate and inclusive parliament and government, there is a chance for Iraq to turn away from the incremental descent into civil war and toward stabilization— if the insurgency can be significantly diminished.

Although the Iraqi armed forces are considerably larger, and more capable and spirited, than they were a year ago, there is still no prospect of defeating the insurgency through military means alone. Rather, turning the corner on the insurgency requires a political process that divides the more tactical elements of the insurgency—the Sunni tribal, political, and religious forces that have been seeking at least some share of power in the new order, and an end to the American occupation—from the diehard Al Qaeda and Saddamist elements.

In this respect, it is possible to see hopeful signs on the horizon. Despite their concerns and anxieties over the rise of targeted violence and assassinations against Sunnis, the Sunni parties and movements participated massively in the December elections and appear to have won a share of seats in much closer proportion to their share of the population than they did in January, when they boycotted the vote.

In November 2005, the Arab League gathered in Cairo to hold the broadest meeting yet of Iraqi political forces, including members of the transitional government and elements associated with the Sunni-based insurgency. They agreed on the principles of power-sharing and on the need to establish a timetable for American withdrawal. At the same time, the US ambassador in Iraq, Zalmay Khalilzad, has shown a flexibility, deftness, and interest in negotiation with insurgent elements that his predecessors lacked.

There are now three imperatives. First, power-sharing must be made to work so that all groups see that they can better secure their interests through peaceful participation in politics and government than through violence. Second, compromise must be achieved in the forthcoming process to review and amend the constitution adopted in October (over the bitter objections of the Sunni Arab communities, which voted overwhelmingly against it). In particular, the federal system must be revised to clearly establish central government control over future (as well as current) oil and gas production, and to rule out the creation of new governing regions, or at least to limit the number of provinces that can come together into a single region. This would remove one of the most alarming Sunni concerns, a Shiite super-region with control over most of the country's oil resources. And third, comprehensive negotiations are needed between the United States and the insurgents, involving as well the new Iraqi government and the mediation of the United Nations and the Arab League.

... power-sharing must be made to work so that all groups see that they can better secure their interests through peaceful participation in politics and government than through violence.

Through such negotiations, it may be possible to entrench power-sharing provisions and develop a mutu-

ally acceptable plan for American military withdrawal. This would lead many of the Sunni insurgent groups to suspend the violent struggle and to take visible public steps to discourage and delegitimate the continuation of the insurgency. With greater Sunni cooperation, it may also become possible to isolate, capture, kill, or expel the Al Qaeda fighters who have been responsible for the most destructive and destabilizing violence.

After nearly three years and a bitter cost in lives and treasure, the United States now has a real chance to help Iraq move toward stabilization. It will not be quick or easy, and real democracy may be years away. But compared with the tyranny of Hussein or the chaos since the invasion, stabilization would count as considerable progress. It would also improve long-term prospects for democratization efforts elsewhere in the region, if the bitter lessons learned in Iraq are heeded.

Terms and Concepts

stabilization
democratization
soft power

hard power
"muscular gendarmerie"
"flattened landscape"

identity referenda
proportional representation
national-list proportional representation

Questions

1. What factors led the United States to serious mistakes in its involvement in Iraq?

2. What is democratization? What changes to postauthoritarian regimes are necessary for democracy to flourish?

3. Do democracies have an interest in promoting democracies in other countries? Do they have the resolve to commit the resources to do so properly?

4. What is Diamond's argument for encouraging local democratic politics in Iraq?

5. Are the principles on which democratic regimes are based—human equality, the rule of law, the enforcement of civil liberties, adequate education to support democratic participation—merely Western ideas, or are they universal and properly applicable to all peoples?

China's Quest for Modernization

Wenran Jiang

Editors' Note

The Chinese political economy can be described as a type of Communist capitalism. North Americans have been brought up to think this is a contradiction in terms. But capitalism as an economic system is analytically distinct from the political regime in which it can operate. Economic freedom is distinct from political freedom. Some argue that capitalism and democracy are antithetical. Critics of capitalism argue that capitalism produces wealth but also inequality, the large portion of a society getting less than the wealthy minority. Capitalism's supporters claim that in a democratic regime, the majority would vote to expropriate the wealth of the minority, killing the incentives for the creation of wealth. If I cannot keep what I earn, I will not bother to earn it. Democratic majorities expropriating the wealth of the few might be acting against their own long-term interests, and for critics of democracy, this is an inherent flaw of democracy. To solve the problem, capitalist societies can at best be limited democracies.

Democracy must be limited by overarching constitutional rules. Rights of property must prevail over the rights of democratic majorities. Liberal constitutionalism is "Johnny sober preparing for Johnny drunk."

North Americans think Communist capitalism is a contradiction in terms because they oppose Communist statism and decentralized capitalist free markets. But the free market economies with which we are familiar are not the decentralized collections of myriad businesses operating in conditions of perfect competition we so often distinguish from Communist central planning. Business debates frequently revolve around the need to consolidate and merge business in order to reap economies of scale. Bigger seems to be better after all. This is an argument socialists have always made for state-owned enterprise. And businesspeople frequently ask for government assistance of various forms, whether a bailout when business is bad or regulations to protect them from international competitors. Thoughtful free-marketeers are the first to admit that businesspeople and the politicians who fawn over them are among the enemies of free markets.

Many argue that capitalist economies produce liberal democracies over time, especially in contemporary economic and technological conditions in which wealth creation requires sophisticated, well-educated workforces comfortable with information technologies. The kind of intellectual curiosity required to make an economy thrive is precisely what will make a workforce resist political authoritarianism. Will a Chinese businessperson keep his or her ears shut to liberal ideas when visiting Canada on business?

Chinese Communist capitalism combines the economic structures of the free market with the political machinery of an authoritarian, one-party state. There is every reason to doubt that this formula is sustainable. The real issue is the manner and pace of change to a more liberal, open society. Recent changes at the top of the Chinese Communist Party signal a cautious move toward political liberalism. While activists will remain impatient with the pace of change, China's caution may be the key to its success and it may make China one of the most successful examples of post-Communist transition to free markets and democratic stability. It is clear the fast-track model followed by Russia in the 1990s was a disaster.

In this essay, University of Alberta political scientist Wenran Jiang applies the literature on political and economic development to the Chinese case.

◆ ◆ ◆

Article prepared for this publication. © Nelson, 2008.

INTRODUCTION

◆ ◆ ◆

China has come a long way in its pursuit of modernization and great power status. Until just a few centuries ago, China had always been one of the most important nations on earth. But the rise of capitalism in the West and the global expansion of colonialism and imperialism challenged the traditional Chinese empire, interrupted its development process, and forced China into a semi-colonial status with different spheres of influence imposed by foreign powers.

After the establishment of the People's Republic of China (PRC) in 1949, it took another three decades for China to make the transition from revolution to a reform program that finally set the country on a path of rapid industrialization. By the turn of the century, China had become the most talked-about rising world power. It ranked as the world's fourth largest economy and the third largest trading nation, and possessed the largest foreign investment inflow and the largest foreign currency reserves of any country on the planet. China has been following a different model of political and economic change in contrast to the countries that used to follow a Soviet development strategy. Despite China's profound economic and social transformation, the political system remains unchanged, and the Chinese Communist Party (CCP) continues to retain power without organized opposition.

CHINA'S POLITICAL TRANSFORMATION

◆ ◆ ◆

"Chinese people have stood up," proclaimed China's new leader Mao Zedong to the rest of the world on October 1, 1949, the founding day of the People's Republic of China. Thus began the transition from decades of turmoil, civil war, foreign invasion, and revolution to establishing a new political, economic and social system that could maintain unification and stability, rebuild the economy, and set China on the road to modernization. In less than three decades, the Chinese Communist Party grew from only a small group of intellectuals to a political force that led a five million strong army and took over all of China through armed struggle. But the transition from revolution to putting China on the road to modernization took just as long. China's political transformation divides into three periods.[1]

Continuous Revolution 1949–78

When the CCP came to power as a governing party in 1949 amid high expectations from the public for a new political, economic and social environment, it faced the immediate task of making the transition from being an instrument of revolution to one of governing a country. The goals of revolution were to seize political power and gain national independence through armed struggle. The tasks of being a ruling party, in contrast, were to consolidate the power base, retain legitimacy, govern the country, maintain social order, rebuild the economy, and promote the welfare of the population. In the first three decades of the PRC history, the CCP's political activities were focused primarily on the following three areas.

The first was the consolidation of the new government's power base. In the early 1950s, the new government targeted various social elements that were identified as "anti-revolutionary" in a number of national political campaigns. Economically, the CCP pushed policies designed to get broad popular support and to fulfill its promises to the peasantry. The government carried out a forceful, violent land reform and redistribution movement in a country where more than 90 percent of the population lived in the rural areas. Socially, the government implemented a number of programs to eliminate "old vices," such as prostitution, drug addiction, and superstition, and tried to replace them with "new socialist values."

The second focus of the CCP in this period was the institutionalization of the one-party domination of the Chinese government and the country's political life. The PRC government resembled both a traditional Chinese pyramid structure of power concentration at the top and the Soviet government institutions of the 1950s. The centralized power arrangement in this period featured: 1) concentration of power at the center through different levels of government institutions in a pyramid structure from central to provincial to city to country to townships to villages; 2) central military control through a number of large military regions that crossed provincial borders; 3) administrative control through different departments in charge of specialized sectors of industry that was designed to further strengthen the centre-local mechanism; 4) the interlocking of CCP organizations with government institutions at all levels, which often meant that a party secretary was at the same time the administrative head of the government branch.

The third focus of the CCP in this period was the continuous mobilization of masses through nationwide political campaigns as means both to maintain the CCP legitimacy and to reshape society in accordance with Chairman Mao Zedong's vision. In this period, China's most permanent slogan was what Mao called the "continuous revolution." In the late 1950s, there was the "Anti-rightist Campaign;" in the early 1960s, there was the "Socialist Education Movement;" and from 1966–76, China was plunged into its most radical political movement, the "Great Proletarian Cultural Revolution." All these mobilizations were designed to ensure China's revolutionary status as Mao envisioned it, and to prevent China from "reverting to the capitalist road," a dangerous tendency in Mao's view.

However, these political movements and the nature of the political institutions, securing the CCP domination as they did, derailed China from making tangible economic progress at the same time, and thus brought new challenges to the legitimacy of the CCP. In this period, Chinese politics was radical, violent, divisive, and unpredictable. Mao Zedong exercised excessive power and control of the CCP, brutally purged all his real and perceived rivals, and finally pushed the entire country into the chaos of the Cultural Revolution.

... these political movements ... securing the CCP domination as they did, derailed China from making tangible economic progress ...

Limited Political Reform 1978–89

After Mao's death in 1976, it took a two-year internal power struggle at the highest levels to produce a successor. This is not surprising since Communist and dictatorial regimes have never had clear rules for transfer of political authority. Deng Xiaoping, earlier purged during the Cultural Revolution for his more pragmatic approaches to economic affairs, emerged the victor. Once in charge, Deng blamed past political campaigns for China's economic stagnation and the lack of improvement in people's living standards. Warning that China might be deprived of its "global citizenship" if it did nothing, Deng initiated bold economic reform programs aimed at achieving the "four modernizations" in China's

industry, agriculture, science and technology, and national defense. But how to deal with political reform or to determine the relationship between economic reform and political reform remained unclear in this period.

Unlike the many initiatives on the economic front, as we will discuss in the next section, there were only two limited changes on the political front, and these were largely designed to accommodate economic reforms.

First, there were limited periods of "openness" in freedom of expression and dissent. When Deng was struggling to defeat his opponents within the CCP, he called for open debates of critical issues based on what he called "practice as the sole criterion for establishing truth," implying that Mao's words should not provide the ultimate judgment on important issues, as some Mao loyalists insisted at the time. So in the late 1970s, there was a short period during which posters and unofficial publications were allowed to circulate, many of them harshly criticizing Mao, the past and current government policies, and the Chinese political system. There was an area in downtown Beijing where dissidents gathered regularly to debate and discuss critical issues facing Chinese politics. "Large Character Posters," articles written with Chinese brush on plain paper, were posted on the "Democracy Wall" in the same area. Deng at one point even praised these activities: "This is good development. People have democracy." But this came to an end shortly after Deng consolidated his own power base. Dissident gatherings were banned; political posters were forbidden; pro-democracy publications were shut down; and the "Democracy Wall" was demolished altogether. Throughout the 1980s, restrictions were sometimes tightened up and at other times relaxed, depending on how the CCP leadership perceived the overall environment and who specifically was in charge of the political reform agenda.

The second major political change in this period consisted of efforts to separate CCP party organizational posts from government positions. For many years, party secretaries occupied many government administrative posts and professional leading positions. But the problem was that the majority of the party leaders, although considered "red"—meaning loyal to the Communist course—had either little education or no professional training in what they were supposed to lead. As a result, politics took over everything, professionals were pushed aside, and this system became a major obstacle to effective management and the modernization efforts. So a reform of "separating the party from the administration" was launched in the 1980s in order to let the technocrats take over the government and professional leadership positions.

Neither of the above reforms posed any fundamental challenge to the CCP's domination of China's political life. But many still consider the 1980s a relatively open period for discussing political reforms, largely due to the fact that the CCP General Secretary Hu Yaobang and Premier Zhao Ziyang were more "liberal" and more tolerant during their time in power. Both were hand-picked by Deng Xiaoping and loyal to the course of the CCP; however, they were also relatively open-minded, surrounding themselves with younger and reform-oriented advisers. They were convinced that China, while pursuing economic reforms, must also carry out political reforms. They were willing to relax the CCP's control in many areas. They allowed debate about the future of China's political system. They were even willing to let students express their views through open demonstrations. However, the crackdown on the 1989 student movement ended expectations for speedy political reforms in China.

... many still consider the 1980s a relatively open period of time for discussing political reforms ...

New Authoritarianism 1989–

In the spring of 1989, hundreds of thousands of students and their supporters took to the street in Beijing and all major cities across China to demand more political openness, transparency, freedom of expression, and political reform. For over a month, students camped in Tiananmen Square in the heart of Beijing, and their idealistic cries for political reform were supported by many across China. But the CCP hardliners did not tolerate such an outburst of enthusiasm for long. The world watched with dismay as the Chinese authorities used force in and around Beijing's Tiananmen Square to crush the demonstrators and their aspirations. Since then, Chinese politics has been moving against global currents, namely the fall of Communism and the rise of democratization. In order to avoid another "Tiananmen Square," and to deal with the challenge posed by the fall of the Soviet Union, the new Chinese leadership centred on Jiang Zemin, who was chosen by Deng to head the CCP and who eventually became the PRC's President. He implemented three sets of policies to govern the post-Tiananmen China.

First, the Chinese government has used an iron fist to crush any political dissent it sees as threatening, in the name of stability and national security. Beijing has not tolerated independently established political parties that criticize the CCP, dissident organizations based abroad, or religious groups like Falun Gong that openly challenge CCP authority. Agitators have been arrested, charged with crimes of subversion and given long prison terms.

... the Chinese government has been using an iron first to crush any political dissent it sees as threatening ....

Second, the Chinese leadership has been trying to find a new political model in the wake of the collapse of the Communist system in the former USSR and Eastern Europe in the early 1990s. Based on the experiences of some East and Southeast Asian countries, such as South Korea, Taiwan and Singapore, some Chinese scholars and policy makers claim that a "new authoritarianism" would work in China. The main features of this new authoritarianism are to promote an open market economy while limiting political freedom; to maintain social stability in order to create an environment that allows the economy to grow at a high rate; and to strengthen state institutions to prepare for a gradual and orderly transition to a more pluralist political system in the future. Deng Xiaoping was reportedly in favor of such an approach when it was extensively debated in the late 1980s and early 1990s. And the Chinese state seems to have traveled along this path in the past decade.

Finally, the CCP has been trying to enlarge its organizational base and craft a more appealing ideological position. In late 2002 and early 2003, the Chinese leadership that came to power in the aftermath of the Tiananmen crackdown under Jiang Zemin handed power over to a new generation of leaders centered on President Hu Jintao and Premier Wen Jiabao.[2] Accompanying this transition was a major effort to reshape the CCP. Now the party is said to be representing all Chinese people's interests, thereby allowing people from all sectors to join the CCP. This is in sharp contrast to the last 50 years when only proletariats and their working class allies were qualified to be party members. China has also implemented village-level multi-candidate elections in the past decade and is experimenting [with the expansion of] more basic level elections to higher levels in the country-side and in the cities.[3]

These measures have worked only in a limited way to ease the growing tension between a rapidly changing society and the one-party state. Although the CCP remains the sole governing party and faces no credible opposition, it struggles to run the country the way it is now.[4] The party still interferes in the workings of government at all levels. Corruption of government and party officials is rampant and getting worse. The new leadership under Hu and Wen seems to be determined to root out corruption, as evidenced by major crackdowns, stricter measures, and the dismissal of Chen Liangyu, the party secretary of Shanghai and a member of the powerful Politburo. However, despite the tough "strike hard" campaigns carried out in recent years, the situation is getting worse.

Moreover, there is little sign of enthusiasm among the ordinary people for the CCP's new political study movements in recent years such as the "three represents" doctrine (claiming that the CCP represents the most advanced productive forces, the most developed culture, and the fundamental interests of the Chinese people), or the campaign to "preserve the progressiveness of the CCP." The People's Congress, China's legislature, remains a rubber-stamping body for the governing party; there are no plans to expand elections beyond the village and township levels.[5] Major flaws in China's political system were fully exposed in the outbreak of the severe acute respiratory syndrome (SARS) in spring 2003 when the government concealed the number of infected patients and forbade the press to report the bad news, leading to a major delay in fighting the disease worldwide.

... major flaws in China's political system were fully exposed in the outbreak of SARS when the government concealed the number of infected patients ...

In the process of consolidating his own power base, President Hu has placed greater emphasis on accountability, anti-corruption, efficiency of the bureaucracy, and making the country's income distribution more equitable. Meanwhile, he has also adopted a posture of tightened control over the media, the intellectuals, and the nation's political discourse in areas sensitive to the CCP legitimacy. Hu's ideological rigidity has been met with considerable resistance. Reform-minded party members, media,

and a growing number of Internet-based "netizens" have repeatedly challenged the authorities. They have pushed the envelope on freedom of speech, labour rights, and opened debates on issues considered by the CCP as taboos. The tension continues to intensify in a rapidly changing society with a one-party system that, despite all the reform measures, remains Leninist in nature.

The question is to what extent the CCP can continue to govern China without fundamentally changing its one party state status and implementing meaningful democratic reforms. To look for the answers to this question, we must now turn to the economic aspect of China's development experience.[6]

CHINA'S ECONOMIC TRANSFORMATION
◆ ◆ ◆

China's economic development in the past twenty years has been hailed by many as a new Asian miracle following Japan, South Korea, Taiwan, and other Southeast Asian countries that achieved a remarkably high rate of economic growth from the 1960s throughout the 1980s.[7] But China's modernization has been three decades in the making. We will examine China's economic development experience in the following two distinct periods.

From the Soviet Model to "Self-Reliance" 1949–78
When the People's Liberation Army marched into Beijing in 1949, the Chinese economy was totally devastated by decades of turmoil and war. Although the initial recovery policies were successful, the PRC leadership's desire to build a new economic system was heavily influenced by the Soviet Union. In the 1930s and 1940s, the Soviets supported the CCP in its armed struggle against the Japanese invasion and later civil war with the Nationalists. China also fought with the North Koreans against the United States in the Korean conflict of 1950–53. Given the new Cold War situation and the division of the world into two major ideological and military camps at the time, China decided to pursue a foreign policy of "leaning toward one side"—that is, to the Soviets in the 1950s. The USSR became the single largest aid provider to the new China; Soviet experts were dispatched to China as advisers; and many large projects were financed, designed, and built by the Soviet Union.

This commitment led Beijing to adapt wholesale a Soviet economic development model considered by many at the time as an alternative to the Western free market economy. With Soviet assistance, China's economic bureaucracy and other institutions were modelled on those of the USSR. China implemented a national five-year development plan like those in the Soviet Union. It began to build large-scale industrial projects for rapid industrialization. Private enterprises were converted, by both persuasion and force, to state-owned entities. A national movement of collectivization was carried out shortly after land reform to transform China's countryside into communes where individual peasants lost their autonomy and had to labour under a centrally assigned workload each year. And the whole country was subject to state command economic planning, from production to circulation to distribution to consumer price control.

.... the Great Leap Forward movement failed completely and was partially responsible for the three-year famine that followed ....

Although China would suffer [for] many years from such a rigid economic structure, it was not a simple duplicate of the Soviet model even in the 1950s. At the policy level, the Chinese leadership under Mao pursued a far more radical approach than the Soviet model was designed to accommodate. In line with the theme of "continuous revolution" discussed above, Mao believed that goals of economic construction could be accomplished by mobilizing the masses using a "people's war" method that was so successful in achieving revolutionary goals before 1949. Thus, the government launched the People's Commune movement for agricultural collectivization in the mid-1950s, the Great Leap Forward movement for targeting high output of iron and steel in the late 1950s, many large navigation and other construction projects using a "human-sea" method over the years, and the "learn from model work units" movements in industrial and agricultural sectors throughout the 1960s and 1970s. These costly mass mobilization projects proved to be either ineffective or counterproductive. For instance, the People's Commune system never worked to improve agricultural output or efficiency, and the Great Leap Forward movement failed completely and was partially responsible for the three-year famine that followed in the late 1950s and early 1960. An estimated 20–35 million people, mostly poor peasants, perished in this period, marking the darkest chapter in the PRC history.

Partly due to the failure of the Great Leap Forward and partly due to China's split with the Soviet Union in 1960 (when Moscow suddenly withdrew all its assistance and experts from China, leaving many large industrial projects half finished), China moved toward a development strategy of "self-reliance." Autarkic in nature, China relied on its internal resources for capital, material supply, innovation, industrial development, and welfare. The agriculture sector was further sacrificed for accumulating necessary funds to finance industrial and defense-related sectors because no external investment was available. As a result, agriculture and consumer manufacturing industry were subordinated to heavy industrialization demands of the government policy while most Chinese remained poor.

By the mid-1970s, the Chinese economy was in chaos due to the decade-long Cultural Revolution. Real incomes for most Chinese had stagnated for nearly twenty years. People were tired of the endless political movements, and demanded improved living standards. At the same time, China's East Asian neighbors had all excelled in economic growth and were in the middle of their modernization miracle. Reform was made possible by pragmatic leader Deng Xiaoping's ascent to power after Mao's death.

"Socialism with Chinese Characteristics" 1978–

Deng once said of economic development policies: "No matter if it's a white cat or a black cat, as long as it can catch mice, it's a good cat." Such was his pragmatism in an age of ideology and in a regime full of ideologues. Once firmly in charge, in the late 1970s, Deng initiated a bold economic reform program. Beijing was not sure where it was going, but the consensus was that it could not be worse than where China had been. As Deng put it: reform is like crossing the river by feeling the stones, step by step, and trying somewhere else if one place does not work.

"No matter if it's a white cat or a black cat, as long as it can catch mice, it's a good cat."

The first step of the reform programs began with the agricultural sector in rural China. Under the commune system, individual farmers did not own land; they worked for the communes rather than for themselves;

central government provided guidelines on what to produce; and the purchase prices for products were set below market price by the state. Thus, neither the peasants nor the communes had much incentive to work efficiently. The introduction of the "family responsibility system" was designed to change all of this. Under the new program, the commune system was virtually abolished overnight and land, although still collectively owned in name, was leased to individual households for extended periods. Product requirements by the state such as what to produce and how much to produce became general guidelines, not rigid specifications as before, and produce was purchased by the state at higher, more realistic prices. Farmers were also given the choice to sell their surplus to the free market, pocketing all profits—something not allowed under the previous system.

The rural reforms produced mixed results. Initially they were amazingly successful. There were visible improvements in most of China's countryside. From 1978–84, rural income grew 17 percent annually. But from the mid-1980s, rural income levels dropped substantially, and even declined in the late 1990s. This was partly due to a number of developments in both China and the world. First, the initial jump in productivity and income reached its peak around the mid-1980s. Second, urban reform sped up with urban income levels quickly surpassing those of rural areas. Third, the agriculture sector was not able to absorb the growing rural surplus population. Fourth, taxation by many local authorities increased the burden on peasants. Fifth, worldwide declines in food and basic commodity prices have made major Chinese agricultural products less profitable, and over-priced in the world market in comparison with Western products that enjoy government subsidies. Finally, China also committed unilateral tariff cuts to agricultural imports in the process of negotiating China's entry into the WTO in the early 21st century. Therefore, after the initial period of success, China's rural areas now face serious challenges posed by both its own growth and globalization.

The second major reform program was in the area of urban industries. This was essentially a process of dismantling the entire Soviet model. Privately owned enterprises were allowed to operate; the planning system of the command economy was gradually decentralized; supply and demand mechanisms were introduced to take over state-set prices for most commodities; foreign ownership, joint ventures and foreign direct investment were now allowed to enter the Chinese economy; deregulation was carried out at different stages to open the market; controls over consumer goods and wages were lifted; and non-profitable state-owned enterprises were either privatized or allowed to go bankrupt. By the late 1990s, a planned economy gave way to a market economy. None of these measures was implemented overnight. Many took months and years of debates, trials, experiments, and setbacks. And many of these measures are still in process today.

... by reforming the Soviet economic development model without causing the entire system to collapse, China succeeded where the rest of the Communist world failed.

These reform policies put China on a road of rapid industrialization, quadrupling its economic size in less than two decades, replacing its neighbours as *the* engine of growth in East Asia, becoming the fastest growing economy in the world, and, even more remarkably, lifting several hundreds of million people out of poverty within two decades. More importantly, by reforming the Soviet economic development model without causing the entire system to collapse, China succeeded where the rest of the Communist world failed.

China created its own post-Communist development path. But China's industrialization has also produced all the problems that are associated with rapid industrialization. Most of China's rivers are heavily polluted, and 16 of the 20 most polluted cities in the world are in China. China has problems with excessive [energy] consumption ..., using three times more energy than the global average in producing every unit of GDP. There are growing gaps between rural and urban areas, between the regions and within the regions, and between the rich and poor, with little indication of those gaps being narrowed in the near future. Social services are deteriorating: 80 percent of the population goes without medical insurance and 50 percent of the ill do not visit a doctor because they cannot afford the cost. Finally, China also suffers from rapid urbanization, increasing unemployment, rampant economic crimes, and corruption. These problems tend to increase the tension between society and the state, creating many potentially dangerous factors that may contribute to social instability.[8]

The third area of economic reform was China's relationship with the outside world. For decades, the Chinese economy was closed, with very limited international trade and no foreign firms or foreign investment in China. A reform of the late 1970s was to pursue an "open-door" policy. Envisioned initially as a way to attract foreign technology and investment to speed up Beijing's modernization programs, the opening led to China's broad engagement with the world, and to its integration into the world economy. Today, there are hundreds of thousands of foreign ventures and Chinese-foreign joint ventures in all sectors. After many years of tough negotiations, China finally joined the World Trade Organization in 2001.[9] Foreign investment in China has grown steadily, reaching an all-time high in 2002 when China overtook the United States as the largest destination for worldwide foreign direct investment.

The open-door policy and its domestic reform agenda have also affected the general direction of overall Chinese foreign policy. For decades, China was seen as a radical revolutionary Communist state, challenging the existing international order. Today, Chinese foreign policy is less confrontational, isolationist, and unilateral than it was in recent history.[10]

While increasing integration into the world economy has benefited China tremendously, globalization has also had negative effects. Many Chinese agricultural products are produced at a much higher cost than those subsidized in North America and Australia, forcing many farmers to abandon their land due to low market prices. Many state-owned enterprises are uncompetitive and were forced to lay off workers after China's entry into the WTO. All sectors of the Chinese economy are now feeling the heat, especially those that had long been shielded from competition from the world's largest multinational corporations.[11]

THE COST OF MODERNIZATION AND GROWING SOCIAL TENSIONS

◆ ◆ ◆

Today, China continues to fascinate the world with its high GDP growth, huge trading volumes, and surging consumption. Most figures out of Beijing look impressive, indicating that the Middle Kingdom is reclaiming its great power status at a speed faster than most forecasters anticipated. Yet evidence is mounting that the high-GDP-centred development paradigm is too costly to sustain. Rural, urban, and environment-related protest movements are moving from localized and isolated events to a widespread and serious social crisis.

... evidence is mounting that the high-GDP-centred development paradigm is too costly to sustain ...

Some may point to Beijing's new economic development figures as proof that China is doing fine: it has leaped over Italy, France, and Britain to become the fourth largest economy in the world; its economic structure seems to be more balanced with a much bigger service industry than previously reported; and China's foreign trade has been expanding so rapidly that its foreign reserves now exceed US$1 trillion. But other recent data, which have received less coverage, indicate a troublesome trend. In a rare disclosure of the enormous hidden cost of China's rapid economic development in 2005, the Chinese government acknowledged that "sudden public incidents" such as industrial accidents, social safety accidents, and natural disasters are responsible for over 1 million casualties and the loss of 6 percent of the country's GDP every year. China is now debating not only how the system can respond better to disasters but also if the current development paradigm can be sustained. According to a *People's Daily* online special, as many as 5.61 million various "public accidents" occurred in 2004 alone, causing the deaths of 210,000 people and injuring another 1.75 million; the direct economic loss was over 455 billion Chinese yuan (C$76 billion). It is estimated that the direct annual cost of such disasters for China is more than 650 billion yuan (C$108 billion) on average. To state the obvious: most of China's economic growth each year is simply cancelled out by the immediate sacrifice of human lives and long-term damage to the environment. China is no doubt one country that is seriously affected by natural disasters, which are large in volume, high in frequency, and severe in losses. The lives of more than 200 million people, or one-seventh of the Chinese population, are routinely disrupted by natural disturbances. Seventy percent of China's major cities, more than one-half of the Chinese population, and more than 75 percent of China's GDP are located in the eastern part of the country where climate, water, and earthquake disasters cause much damage every year. Even so, government figures put losses to Mother Nature at just over 100 billion yuan

(C\$17 billion) per year. That means the financial losses of some 550 billion yuan (C\$92 billion) every year are caused not by natural events but by human-generated accidents—a staggering number indeed. In the coal-mining sector, for example, China has the worst safety record in the world. From 2001 to 2004, according to the official *Xinhuanet,* accidents in China's coal mines took 6,282 lives every year on average—more than 17 people dying every day from coal mine accidents alone. There are more than 50 mine accidents annually, each resulting in more than 10 deaths; and in the past three years, five major coal mine accidents have each claimed more than 100 miners' lives. Moreover, estimates are that the real death toll per year may be close to 20,000 because many mine operators intentionally cover up the death numbers to escape responsibility.[12]

Worse yet, China's work safety authorities predict that for the foreseeable future China faces a severe challenge as more catastrophic accidents occur because the country's industrialization process has entered a high growth and high accident phase. At the current stage, China's economic development has produced an industrial structure that demands heavy resource and energy consumption, with coal [supplying] close to 70 percent of China's total energy needs. With China's shortage of energy and high world oil prices, the price of coal in the domestic market is also on the rise, which has resulted in a new boom for the coal mining industry. While large-scale industrial efforts are bound to bring a higher number of industrial accidents, the old heavy industrial infrastructure, built in the early decades of China's industrialization, has begun to age; and with little repair or renewal, this infrastructure is full of time bombs certain to cause more accidents.

Another set of numbers, as revealed by the *China Human Development Report 2005,* indicates that regional disparity is threatening the country's growth potential. Moreover, the widening urban–rural distribution gap has reached a dangerous level. Compiled by a group of Chinese researchers for the United Nations Development Program (UNDP), the report demonstrates that in all major categories of the Human Development Index (HDI)—from per capita income to life expectancy to literacy rate—regional imbalances are severe and growing. It concludes that China's Gini coefficient, a measurement of a country's income inequality, has increased by more than 50 percent in the past 20 years, with urban dwellers earning nearly four times what rural residents do. At 0.46, "China's Gini coefficient is lower than in some Latin American and African

countries, but its urban–rural income inequality is perhaps the highest in the world."

Annual increases in GDP make inequality only worse, and when systemic factors biased against the rural population are included, China's city-countryside income ratio is as high as 6:1. The result? People in richer cities enjoy a life expectancy of close to 80 years—the level of a middle-income country and 10 to 15 years longer than a farmer's life span in Tibet or other remote provinces. The UNDP report also shows that the inland regions lag in education, especially among the female population. Only two decades ago, China was one of the most equal societies on earth. Today, it ranks 90th in the UNDP's 131-nation HDI. It is ironic that while 250 million people have been lifted out of poverty in record time—a proud achievement that no one denies—China is also leading the world in creating one of the most unequal societies in history.

China's Gini coefficient is lower than in some Latin American and African countries, but its urban–rural income inequality is perhaps the highest in the world.

The Chinese government has repeatedly told the world that it needs social stability to develop its economy, and Beijing claims to value economic and social rights more than political rights. The question is whether China's traditional political control plus the new economic and social exclusion of the majority of its population can be accepted as a model of development by those who are now excluded from China's growing prosperity. Newly released reports from the Chinese government cite 87,000 incidents of "public order disturbances" last year, up 6.6 percent from the 74,000 figure in 2004; the number of events that "interfered with government functions" jumped 19 percent while protests seen as "disturbing social order" grew by 13 percent in 2005. Some say this is an alarming acknowledgment of the looming crisis in Chinese society that may soon tear China apart with unthinkable consequences. Others contend that the figure is not surprising and that it may not even be a new development; it reflects only that Beijing now allows more reporting of these protests, which have existed for a long time. The Chinese government even spins the story in its favour: letting the protests happen and informing the public about them is presented as evidence that the government is committed to greater democracy.

Despite differences in assessment, the emerging consensus is that various grassroots protests are increasing in number, are better organized, and often turn violent when local officials are seen as suppressing legitimate concerns. Indications are that such protest movements are gaining wider acceptance. Again, the UNDP report's survey of the Chinese public perception of income distribution gaps tells volumes about popular demand for social justice and potential support for radical actions: more than 80 percent of those surveyed believe that China's current income distribution is either "not so equitable" or "very inequitable."

Meanwhile, a recent global study by the Pew Global Attitude Project seems to contradict such pessimism. It shows that the Chinese are the happiest that they have been in recent years [(]in terms of improved living standards[)] and the most optimistic about their future. Seventy-two percent of Chinese, the highest among 16 countries polled, expressed satisfaction with national conditions. Although the survey acknowledges that the "sample is disproportionately urban and is not representative of the entire country," it does convey one important message that the pollsters failed to recognize: Chinese people have extremely high expectations for benefiting from the country's ongoing economic expansion, and if such high expectations are not met in the near future, their frustrations may turn to demands for equity and social justice.

Back in the 1950s–70s, most Chinese were very poor but relatively equal; consequently, social protests were rare and the Chinese Communist Party asserted control with little concern of large-scale grassroots unrest. Today's China, after more than two decades of reform, is [a] much more prosperous but ... very unequal society. Historical experiences show that when a country is embarking on rapid economic growth, social mobility accelerates and people's expectations for their own share of the prosperity increase. Yet at the same time, income distribution gaps widen and, with few exceptions, only a small portion of the population enjoys the benefits of the country's modernization drive. Such a paradoxical process often results in rising resentment among the populace and leads to large-scale protests for a more equitable distribution of wealth.

In other words, people may not rebel when they are poor but equal; they tend to rebel when they perceive that they are deprived of what they believe to be their fair share of the country's wealth. China today is at such a crossroad of unprecedented prosperity, [unmet] expectations ..., and growing frustrations with perceived social injustice.

> ... people ... tend to rebel when they perceive that they are deprived of what they believe to be their fair share of the country's wealth.

The current Chinese leadership headed by President Hu Jintao and Premier Wen Jiabao is keenly aware of the growing disparity and its serious consequences. After years of promoting Deng Xiaoping's famous call, "to get rich is glorious," the "harmonious society" seems to have become a central pillar of the Hu-Wen approach to easing China's social tensions. Despite a number of measures, ranging from investment in remote regions to elimination of agricultural taxes to "hard strikes" against corruption, social unrest is on the rise. With some of the recent bloody confrontations between peasants and local authorities, many wonder if a "tipping point" for a social crisis will arrive soon—a potentially explosive situation where large-scale upheavals shake the entire Chinese political, economic, and social establishment.

V. I. Lenin, mastermind of the Bolshevik Revolution in 1917, argued that three conditions must be present for a social crisis to generate revolutionary changes: first, the masses can no longer be governed; second, the ruling elite can no longer govern; and third, the social forces are fully mobilized under the leadership of a revolutionary party to overthrow the existing regime. By these standards, China is nowhere close to the "tipping point."

But it would be a profound mistake to take comfort from such abstract [analysis]. Lenin's first two conditions are increasingly apparent: widespread social protests are increasing, and the corruption of government and CCP party officials and the plight of ordinary citizens by local authorities have weakened the governance structure. These two conditions may well combine to produce a widespread belief that the majority of the population who are left behind are victims, not of their own failure to compete, but of corruption and exploitation of the masses by the privileged few. Such a belief would foster the conclusion that the only way to improve the life of the majority is to fundamentally change the existing social, economic, and political order.

This process of increasing dissatisfaction with the regime may well be accelerated if the inevitable economic slowdown in the coming years and natural, environmental, and other human-made disasters occur simultaneously. An externally imposed alternative political mechanism is unlikely (if possible at all) given China's tightly controlled conditions. But a crisis of governance is likely to trigger an internal split of the CCP ruling elite, with reform-oriented forces openly confronting hardliners who advocate total control by force. If history tells us anything about large-scale social turmoil, a total breakdown of Chinese society may not necessarily solve China's pressing problems. Therefore, the most challenging task for China and the world today is how to avoid such dangerous showdowns with reforms that effectively address the issues of income inequality, social injustice, and lack of democratization.

> ... a crisis of governance is likely to trigger an internal split of the CCP ruling elite ...

CONCLUSION

◆ ◆ ◆

Today's China is well on its way to reclaiming its great power status. In the past two and half decades, the Chinese economy has grown by nearly 10 percent annually. Based on the US dollar standard, China's GDP now ranks fourth in the world after the United States, Japan and Germany. But China is already the second largest economy after the United States in terms of purchasing power parity (PPP) standard. China has become the world's third largest trading nation, its largest auto market, and its second largest energy market. China also has the largest foreign currency reserves in the world. Many studies project that the Chinese economy will soon overtake Germany and Japan and by the middle of the century, it will surpass the US economy. Its military modernization is also moving forward quickly, making China a formidable regional military power. In fact, it is considered the only country in the world that could soon rival America's military hegemony.

At the same time, hiding behind the high growth figures and the striking skyscrapers in Beijing and Shanghai are the devastating damage to the environment, the high unemployment rate, the widening gap between the rich and poor, deteriorating government revenue, rampant corruption at all government levels, a collapsing health care system, increasing amounts of old and new crimes, dramatic jumps in widespread infectious diseases, and stagnating rural areas, as well as a general resentment toward growing social injustice and the unequal distribution of wealth.

To study China's development experience, including both its successes and failures, in the global context, we need to consider a number of important questions. First, is China's economic transition a species of the Asian economic miracle? If so, what does it have in common with its surrounding countries? Will China follow the pattern of transformation that occurred in South Korea and Taiwan? If so, then after a period of high economic growth, there will follow a process of political democratization. Or will China be able to maintain the current political economic arrangement and continue to move forward without liberal democratic political change?[13] Second, has China become a model of "post-Communist" development in comparison with other former Communist states? Why did the former Soviet Union and other Eastern European states fail in their efforts to reform, eventually collapsing while the Chinese Communist party not only survived the same process, but also transformed itself? Has the CCP "made it" so far, judged by what it has done, or is it a matter of time before the CCP will also fall?[14] Third, can China, as the most populous and one of the poorest countries on earth, be seen as a model of economic development in the global context? Does the Chinese experience have any universal significance that could be learned, and modeled by other developing countries? Or is China too unique and too big a country to be put in any regional, systemic or global context at all?

Notes

1. For a journalist's account of a changing China, see Nicholas D. Kristof and Sherly Wudunn, *China Wakes: The Struggle for the Soul of A Rising Power* (New York: Vintage Books, 1995).

2. For detailed studies of the new Chinese leadership, see Andrew J. Nathan and Bruce Gilley, *China's New Rulers: The Secret Files* (New York: New York Review of Books, 2002); and Cheng Li, *China's New Leaders* (Lanham, Maryland: Rowman & Littlefield Publishers, 2001).

3. To follow the Chinese official views on these issues, go to the following website: http://english.peopledaily.com.cn/home.shtml.

4. For more on the governance crisis in China, see Minshin Pei, "China's Governance Crisis, *Foreign Affairs,* Vol. 81, No. 5 (Sept./Oct. 2002): 96–109.

5. The most important NGO in China in promoting elections is the World and China Institute, and updated news, relevant activities, and analyses can be viewed at: www.world-china.org.

6. A good collection of articles on contemporary issues in China is Suzanne Ogden (ed.), *Global Studies: China* (10th ed.) Guilford, CT: Dushkin/McGraw-Hill, 2003).

7. For the praise for China's efforts in combating poverty, see United Nations Development Program, *2003 World Development Report.*

8. Some have proclaimed that, due to these problems, China will collapse soon. See Gordon G. Chang, *Coming Collapse of China* (New York: Random House, 2001).

9. On China's entry into WTO, see Supachai Panitchpakdi and Mark L. Clifford, *China and the WTO: Changing China, Changing World Trade* (Singapore: John Wiley & Sons, 2001).

10. But many argue that China's emergence as a world economic and military power may pose a threat. For a balance assessment of the China threat theory, see Herbert Yee and Ian Storey (eds.) *The China Threat: Perceptions, Myths, and Reality* (London: Routledge Curzon, 2002).

11. For some recent studies of China's integration with the world economy, see Nicholas R. Lardy, *Integrating China into the Global Economy* (Washington, D.C.: Brookings Institution, 2002); and David Cowhig, *Internationalizing China: Domestic Interests and Global Linkages* (Cornell: Cornell University Press, 2002).

12. "Eleven Killed In Latest China Coal Mine Disaster" *All Headline News* (July 24, 2006). Retrieved March 29, 2007, from www.allheadlinenews.com/articles/7004312617.

13. A further reference is Vera Simone, *The Asia Pacific: Political and Economic Development in a Global Context* (2nd ed.) (New York: Longman, 2001).

14. A classic comparative analysis of China's and the Soviet Union's reform experiences is Minshin Pei, *From Reform to Revolution: The Demise of Communism in China and the Soviet Union* (Cambridge, MA: Harvard University Press, 1994).

Terms and Concepts

Great Proletarian Cultural Revolution
Democracy Wall
new authoritarianism

Tiananmen Square
"Great Leap Forward"
Gini coefficient

Human Development Index
"socialism with Chinese
   characteristics"

Questions

1. What is the "new authoritarianism" and in what ways would China be an illustration of this ideology?

2. What is the relationship between political and economic liberalization? Is each essential to the other? Does one lead to the other?

3. What costs have accompanied China's remarkable economic progress in the last two decades? How do these costs compare to the benefits of economic progress?

4. What factors are likely to determine whether China's future development will be politically stable or politically explosive?

5. Western political leaders are frequently criticized for not applying pressure on China to pay more attention to human rights. On the other hand, when Stephen Harper did so during his first year in office, many criticized him for needlessly antagonizing the Chinese and jeopardizing our relations with that country. Do you believe that this kind of pressure from Western countries is productive or counterproductive in terms of moving China toward a greater respect for democratic and human rights?

Latin America's Left Turn

Jorge G. Castañeda

Editors' Note

Canadians understand the political "left" to be dedicated to the use of democratic processes to advance the interests of the poor and powerless. Its agenda is to redistribute wealth and other forms of social power to allow people to govern their lives on their own terms and to participate meaningfully in the government of their society.

The association of democracy and the left agenda makes sense. Democratic regimes enfranchise almost all adult citizens, and only a minority of them are wealthy and powerful. Democratic political processes should easily allow the relatively impoverished majority to command the levers of government and implement policies advancing the left's agenda.

But three problems come to mind. One is that elected leftist representatives of the people, like all politicians, may confuse their own interests with those of their constituents. Once in power, they may not deliver. The second problem is that the policies they implement may not actually serve the interests of the constituents, regardless of their intentions. The political left has always been good on the question of the distribution of wealth. Its critics argue that it has been less effective on the question of wealth genera- tion. A third problem is that influences external to a country may affect domestic pol- itics, making it difficult for elected politicians within a country to do anything about its fate. Just as bad is the opportunity available to local politicians to blame external actors for

the country's problems, whether the external actors are responsible or not.

These problems arise in the following article by author and former Mexican politician Jorge Castañeda. His subject is the ascendancy of leftist parties, movements, and leaders in Latin America. He indicates that there are many "lefts" and that two in particular are in contention in the region. One has come to terms with its excesses and failures and should inspire hope for the region's future. The other is a more volatile, authoritarian, populist version whose roots run deep in Latin American history and whose conse- quences for the region and for the left's political constituency and others may be damaging.

◆ ◆ ◆

A TALE OF TWO LEFTS

◆ ◆ ◆

Just over a decade ago, Latin America seemed poised to begin a virtuous cycle of economic progress and improved democratic governance, overseen by a growing number of centrist technocratic governments. In Mexico, President Carlos Salinas de Gortari, buttressed by the passage of the North American Free Trade Agreement, was ready for his handpicked successor to win the next presidential election. Former Finance Minister Fernando Henrique Cardoso was about to beat out the radical labor leader Luiz Inácio Lula da Silva for the presidency of Brazil. Argentine President Carlos Menem had pegged the peso to the dollar and put his populist Peronist legacy behind him. And at the invita- tion of President Bill Clinton, Latin American leaders were preparing to gather in Miami for the Summit of the Americas, signaling an almost unprecedented conver- gence between the southern and northern halves of the Western Hemisphere.

What a difference ten years can make. Although the region has just enjoyed its best two years of economic growth in a long time and real threats to democratic

Jorge G. Castañeda, "Latin America's Left Turn." Reprinted by permission of FOREIGN AFFAIRS, May/June 2006. Copyright 2006 by the Council on Foreign Relations, Inc.

rule are few and far between, the landscape today is transformed. Latin America is swerving left, and distinct backlashes are under way against the predominant trends of the last 15 years: free-market reforms, agreement with the United States on a number of issues, and the consolidation of representative democracy. This reaction is more politics than policy, and more nuanced than it may appear. But it is real.

Latin America is swerving left, and distinct backlashes are under way against the predominant trends of the last 15 years. ...

Starting with Hugo Chávez's victory in Venezuela eight years, a wave of leaders, parties, and movements generically labeled "leftist" have swept into power in one Latin American country after another. After Chavez, it was Lula and the Workers' Party in Brazil, then Nestor Kirchner in Argentina and Tabare Vasquez in Uruguay, and then [in 2006], Evo Morales in Bolivia. If the long shot Ollanta Humala wins the April presidential election in Peru and López Obrador wins in Mexico, it will seem as if a veritable left-wing tsunami has hit the region. Colombia and Central America are the only   exceptions, but even in Nicaragua, the possibility of a win by Sandinista leader Daniel Ortega cannot be dismissed.

... there is not one Latin American left today; there are two.

The rest of the world has begun to take note of this left-wing resurgence, with concern and often more than a little hysteria. But understanding the reasons behind these developments requires recognizing that there is not one Latin American left today; there are two. One is modern, open-minded, reformist, and internationalist, and it springs, paradoxically, from the hard-core left of the past. The other, born of the great tradition of Latin American populism, is nationalist, strident, and close-minded. The first is well aware of its past mistakes (as well as those of its erstwhile role models in Cuba and the Soviet Union) and has changed accordingly. The second, unfortunately, has not.

UTOPIA REDEFINED

◆ ◆ ◆

The reasons for Latin America's turn to the left are not hard to discern. Along with many other commentators and public intellectuals, I started detecting those reasons nearly fifteen years ago, and I recorded them in my book *Utopia Unarmed: The Latin American Left After the Cold War*, which made several points. The first was that the fall of the Soviet Union would help the Latin American left by removing its geopolitical stigma. Washington would no longer be able to accuse any left-of-center regime in the region of being a "Soviet beachhead" (as it had every such government since it fomented the overthrow of Jacobo Arbenz's administration in Guatemala in 1954); left-wing governments would no longer have to choose between the United States and the Soviet Union, because the latter had simply disappeared.

The second point was that regardless of the success or failure of economic reforms in the 1990s and the discrediting of traditional Latin American economic policies, Latin America's extreme inequality (Latin America is the world's most unequal region), poverty, and concentration of wealth, income, power, and opportunity meant that it would have to be governed from the left of center. The combination of inequality and democracy tends to cause a movement to the left everywhere. This was true in western Europe from the end of the nineteenth century until after World War II; it is true today in Latin America. The impoverished masses vote for the type of policies that, they hope, will make them less poor.

The combination of inequality and democracy tends to cause a movement to the left everywhere.

Third, the advent of widespread democratization and the consolidation of democratic elections as the only road to power would, sooner or later, lead to victories for the left—precisely because of the social, demographic, and ethnic configuration of the region. In other words, even without the other proximate causes, Latin America would almost certainly have tilted left.

This forecast became all the more certain once it became evident that the economic, social, and political reforms implemented in Latin America starting in the mid-1980s had not delivered on their promises. With the exception of Chile, which has been governed by a left-of-center coalition since 1989, the region has had singularly unimpressive economic growth rates. They remain well below those of the glory days of the region's development (1940–80) and also well below those of other developing nations—China, of course, but also India, Malaysia, Poland, and many others. Between 1940 and 1980, Brazil and Mexico, for example, averaged six percent growth per year; from 1980 to 2000, their growth rates were less than half that. Low growth rates have meant the persistence of dismal poverty, inequality, high unemployment, a lack of competitiveness, and poor infrastructure. Democracy, although welcomed and supported by broad swaths of Latin American societies, did little to eradicate the region's secular plagues: corruption, a weak or nonexistent rule of law, ineffective governance, and the concentration of power in the hands of a few. And despite hopes that relations with the United States would improve, they are worse today than at any other time in recent memory, including the 1960s (an era defined by conflicts over Cuba) and the 1980s (defined by the Central American wars and Ronald Reagan's "contras").

But many of us who rightly foretold the return of the left were at least partly wrong about the kind of left that would emerge. We thought—perhaps naively—that the aggiornamento of the left in Latin America would rapidly and neatly follow that of socialist parties in France and Spain and of New Labour in the United Kingdom. In a few cases, this occurred—Chile certainly, Brazil tenuously. But in many others, it did not.

One reason for our mistake was that the collapse of the Soviet Union did not bring about the collapse of its Latin American equivalent, Cuba, as many expected it would. Although the links and subordination of many left-wing parties to Havana have had few domestic electoral implications (and Washington has largely stopped caring anyway), the left's close ties to and emotional dependency on Fidel Castro became an almost insurmountable obstacle to its reconstruction on many issues. But the more fundamental explanation has to do with the roots of many of the movements that are now in power. Knowing where left-wing leaders and parties come from—in particular, which of the two strands of the left in Latin American history they are a part of—is critical to understanding who they are and where they are going.

ORIGINS OF THE SPECIES
◆ ◆ ◆

The left—defined as that current of thought, politics, and policy that stresses social improvements over macroeconomic orthodoxy, egalitarian distribution of wealth over its creation, sovereignty over international cooperation, democracy (at least when in opposition, if not necessarily once in power) over governmental effectiveness—has followed two different paths in Latin America. One left sprang up out of the Communist International and the Bolshevik Revolution and has followed a path similar to that of the left in the rest of the world. The Chilean, Uruguayan, Brazilian, Salvadoran, and, before Castro's revolution, Cuban Communist Parties, for example, obtained significant shares of the popular vote at one point or another, participated in "popular front" or "national unity" governments in the 1930s and 1940s, established a solid presence in organized labor, and exercised significant influence in academic and intellectual circles.

By the late 1950s and early 1960s, however, these parties had lost most of their prestige and combativeness. Their corruption, submission to Moscow, accommodation with sitting governments, and assimilation by local power elites had largely discredited them in the eyes of the young and the radical. But the Cuban Revolution brought new life to this train of the left. In time, groups descended from the old communist left fused with Havana-inspired guerrilla bands. There were certainly some tensions. Castro accused the leader of the Bolivian Communist Party of betraying Che Guevara and leading him to his death in Bolivia in 1967; the Uruguayan and Chilean Communist Parties (the region's strongest) never supported the local Castroist armed groups. Yet thanks to the passage of time, to Soviet and Cuban understanding, and to the sheer weight of repression generated by military coups across the hemisphere, the Castroists and Communists all came together—and they remain together today.

The origin of the other Latin American left is peculiarly Latin American. It arose out of the region's strange contribution to political science: good old-fashioned populism. Such populism has almost always been present almost everywhere in Latin America. It is frequently in power, or close to it. It claims as its founders historical icons of great mythical stature, from Peru's Victor Raúl Haya de la Torre and Columbia's Jorge Caitán (neither made it to office) to Mexico's Lázaro

Cárdenas and Brazil's Getúlio Vargas, both foundational figures in their countries' twentieth-century history, and to Argentina's Juan Perón and Ecuador's José Velasco Ibarra. The list is not exhaustive, but it is illustrative: many of these nations' founding-father equivalents were seen in their time and are still seen now as noble benefactors of the working class. They made their mark on their nations, and their followers continue to pay tribute to them. Among many of these countries' poor and dispossessed, they inspire respect, even adulation, to this day.

The other Latin American left ... arose out of the region's strange contribution to political science: good old-fashioned populism.

These populists are representative of a very different left—often virulently anticommunist, always authoritarian in one fashion or another, and much more interested in policy as an instrument for attaining and conserving power than in power as a tool for making policy. They did do things for the poor—Perón and Vargas mainly for the urban proletariat, Cárdenas for the Mexican peasantry—but they also created the corporatist structures that have since plagued the political systems, as well as the labor and peasant movements, in their countries. They nationalized large sectors of their countries' economies, extending well beyond the so-called commanding heights, by targeting everything in sight: oil (Cárdenas in Mexico), railroads (Perón in Argentina), steel (Vargas in Brazil), tin (Victor Paz Estenssoro in Bolivia), copper (Juan Velasco Alvarado in Peru). They tended to cut sweetheart deals with the budding local business sector, creating the proverbial crony capitalism that was decried much later. Their justifications for such steps were always superficially ideological (nationalism, economic development) but at bottom pragmatic: they needed money to give away but did not like taxes. They squared that circle by capturing natural-resource or monopoly rents, which allowed them to spend money on the descamisados, the "shirtless," without raising taxes on the middle class. When everything else fails, the thinking went, spend money.

The ideological corollary to this bizarre blend of inclusion of the excluded, macroeconomic folly, and political staying power (Perón was the dominant figure in

Argentine politics from 1943 through his death in 1974, the Cárdenas dynasty is more present than ever in Mexican politics) was virulent, strident nationalism. Perón was elected president in 1946 with the slogan "Braden or Perón" (Spruille Braden was then the U.S. ambassador to Buenos Aires). When Vargas committed suicide in 1954, he darkly insinuated that he was a victim of American imperialism. Such nationalism was more than rhetorical. In regimes whose domestic policy platform was strictly power-driven and pragmatic, it was the agenda.

These two subspecies of the Latin American left have always had an uneasy relationship. On occasion they have worked together, but at other times they have been at war, as when Perón returned from exile in June 1973 and promptly massacred a fair share of the Argentine radical left. In some countries, the populist left simply devoured the other one, although peacefully and rather graciously: in Mexico in the late 1980s, the tiny Communist Party disappeared, and former PRI (Institutional Revolutionary Party) members, such as Cuauhémoc Cárdenas, Porfirio Muñoz Ledo, and the current presidential front-runner, López Obrador, took over everything from its buildings and finances to its congressional representation and relations with Cuba to form the left-wing PRD (Party of the Democratic Revolution).

More recently, something funny has happened to both kinds of leftist movements on their way back to power. The communist, socialist, and Castroist left, with a few exceptions, has been able to reconstruct itself, thanks largely to an acknowledgment of its failures and those of its erstwhile models. Meanwhile, the populist left—with an approach to power that depends on giving away money, a deep attachment to the nationalist fervor of another era, and no real domestic agenda—has remained true to itself. The latter perseveres in its cult of the past: it waxes nostalgic about the glory days of Peronism, the Mexican Revolution, and, needless to say, Castro. The former, familiar with its own mistakes, defeats, and tragedies, and keenly aware of the failures of the Soviet Union and Cuba, has changed its colors.

CASTRO'S UNLIKELY HEIRS

When the reformed communist left has reached office in recent years, its economic policies have been remarkably similar to those of its immediate predecessors, and its respect for democracy has proved full-fledged and sincere. Old-school anti-Americanism has been tempered by years of exile, realism, and resignation.

The best examples of the reconstructed, formerly radical left are to be found in Chile, Uruguay, and to a slightly lesser extent, Brazil. This left emphasizes social policy—education, antipoverty programs, health care, housing—but within a more or less orthodox market framework. It usually attempts to deepen and broaden democratic institutions. On occasion, Latin American's age-old vices—corruption, a penchant for authoritarian rule—have led it astray. It disagrees with the United States frequently but rarely takes matters to the brink.

> When the reformed communist left has reached office in recent years, its economic policies have been remarkably similar to those of its immediate predecessors, and its respect for democracy has proved full-fledged and sincere.

In Chile, former President Ricardo Lagos and his successor, Michelle Bachelet, both come from the old Socialist Party (Lagos from its moderate wing, Bachelet from the less temperate faction). Their left-wing party has governed for 16 consecutive years, in a fruitful alliance with the Christian Democrats. This alliance has made Chile a true model for the region. Under its stewardship, the country has enjoyed high rates of economic growth; significant reductions in poverty; equally significant improvements in education, housing, and infrastructure; a slight drop in inequality; a deepening of democracy and the dismantling of Augusto Pinochet's political legacy; a settling of accounts (although not of scores) regarding human rights violations of the past; and, last but not at all least, a strong, mature relationship with the United States, including a free-trade agreement signed by George W. Bush and ratified by the U.S. Congress[,] and Washington's support for the Chilean candidate to head the Organization of American States. U.S.–Chilean ties have continued to prosper despite Chile's unambiguous opposition to the U.S. invasion of Iraq in the UN Security Council in 2003.

In Uruguay, Vázquez ran for president twice before finally winning a little more than a year ago. His coalition has always been the same: the old Uruguayan Communist Party, the Socialist Party, and many former Marxist Tupamaro guerrillas, who made history in the 1960s and 1970s by, among other things, kidnapping and executing CIA station chief Dan Mitrone in Montevideo in 1970, and being featured in Costa-Gavras' 1973 film *State of Siege*. There was reason to expect Vázquez to follow a radical line once elected—but history once again trumped ideology. Although Vázquez has restored Uruguay's relations with Cuba and every now and then rails against neoliberalism and Bush, he has also negotiated an investment-protection agreement with the United States, sent his finance minister to Washington to explore the possibility of forging a free-trade agreement, and stood up to the "antiglobalization, politically correct" groups in neighboring Argentina on the construction of two enormous wood-pulp mills in the Uruguay River estuary. He refused to attend Morales' inauguration as president of Bolivia and has threatened to veto a bill legalizing abortion if it gets to his desk. His government is, on substance if not on rhetoric, as economically orthodox as any other. And with good reason: a country of 3.5 million inhabitants with the lowest poverty rate and the least inequality in Latin America should not mess with its relative success.

Brazil is a different story, but not a diametrically opposed one. Even before his inauguration in 2003, Lula had indicated that he would follow most of his predecessor's macroeconomic policies and comply with the fiscal and monetary targets agreed on with the International Monetary Fund (IMF). He has done so, achieving impressive results in economic stability (Brazil continues to generate a hefty fiscal surplus every year), but GDP growth has been disappointing, as have employment levels and social indicators. Lula has tried to compensate for his macroeconomic orthodoxy with innovative social initiatives (particularly his "Zero Hunger" drive and land reform). At the end of the day, however, perhaps his most important achievement on this front will be the generalization of the Bolsa Familia (Family Fund) initiative, which was copied directly from the antipoverty program of Mexican Presidents Ernesto Zedillo and Vicente Fox. This is a successful, innovative welfare program, but as neoliberal and scantly revolutionary as one can get.

On foreign policy, Brazil, like just about every Latin American country, has had its run-ins with the Bush administration, over issues including trade, UN reform, and how to deal with Bolivia, Columbia, Cuba, and Venezuela. But perhaps the best metaphor for the current state of U.S.–Brazilian relations today was the scene in Brasilia last November, when Lula welcomed Bush at his home, while across the street demonstrators from his own party burned the U.S. president in effigy.

The Workers' Party which Lula founded in 1980 after a long metalworkers' strike in the industrial outskirts of São Paulo, has largely followed him on the road toward social democracy. Many of the more radical cadres of the party, or at least those with the most radical histories (such as José Genoino and José Dirceu), have become moderate reformist leaders, despite their pasts and their lingering emotional devotion to Cuba. (Lula shares this devotion, and yet it has not led him to subservience to Castro: when Lula visited Havana in 2004, Castro wanted to hold a mass rally at the Plaza de la Revolución; instead, Castro got a 24-hour in-and-out visit from the Brazilian president, with almost no public exposure.) Lula and many of his comrades are emblematic of the transformation of the old, radical, guerrilla-based, Castroist or communist left. Granted, the conversion is not complete: the corruption scandals that have rocked Brazil's government have more to do with a certain neglect of democratic practices than with any personal attempt at enrichment. Still, the direction in which Lula and his allies are moving is clear.

Overall, this makeover of the radical left is good for Latin America. Given the region's inequality, poverty, still-weak democratic tradition, and unfinished nation building, the reconstructed left offers precisely what is needed for good governance in the region. If Chile is any example, this left's path is the way out of poverty, authoritarian rule, and, eventually, inequality. This left is also a viable, sensitive, and sensible alternative to the other left—the one that speaks loudly but carries a very small social stick.

POPULISM REDUX
◆ ◆ ◆

The leftist leaders who have arisen from a populist, nationalist past with few ideological underpinnings—Chávez with his military background, Kirchner with his Peronist roots, Morales with his coca-leaf growers' militancy and agitprop, López Obrador with his origins in the PRI—have proved much less responsive to modernizing influences. For them, rhetoric is more important than substance, and the fact of power is more important than its responsible exercise. The despair of poor constituencies is a tool rather than a challenge, and taunting the United States trumps promoting their countries' real interests in the world. The difference is obvious: Chávez is not Castro; he is Perón with oil. Morales is not an indigenous Che; he is a skillful and irresponsible populist. López Obrador is neither Lula nor Chávez; he comes straight from the PRI of Luis Echeverria, Mexico's president from 1970 to 1976, from which he learned how to be a cash-dispensing, authoritarian-inclined populist. Kirchner is a true-blue Peronist, and proud of it.

The despair of poor constituencies is a tool rather than a challenge, and taunting the United States trumps promoting their countries' real interests in the world.

For all these leaders, economic performance, democratic values, programmatic achievements, and good relations with the United States are not imperatives but bothersome constraints that miss the real point. They are more intent on maintaining popularity at any cost, picking as many fights as possible with Washington, and getting as much control as they can over sources of revenue, including oil, gas, and suspended foreign-debt payments.

Argentina's Kirchner is a classic (although somewhat ambiguous) case. Formerly the governor of a small province at the end of the world, he was elected in the midst of a monumental economic crisis and has managed to bring his country out of it quite effectively. Inflation has been relatively controlled, growth is back, and interest rates have fallen. Kirchner also renegotiated Argentina's huge foreign debt skillfully, if perhaps a bit too boldly. He has gone further than his predecessors in settling past grievances, particularly regarding the "dirty war" that the military and his Peronist colleagues waged in the 1970s. He has become a darling of the left and seems to be on a roll, with approval ratings of over 70 percent.

But despite the left-wing company he keeps, Kirchner is at his core a die-hard Peronist, much more interested in bashing his creditors and the IMF than in devising social policy, in combating the Free Trade Agreement of the Americas (FTAA) than in strengthening Mercosur, in cuddling up to Morales, Castro, and

Chávez than in lowering the cost of importing gas from Bolivia. No one knows exactly what will happen when Argentina's commodity boom busts or when the country is forced to return to capital markets for fresh funds. Nor does anyone really know what Kirchner intends to do when his economic recovery runs out of steam. But it seems certain that the Peronist chromosomes in the country's DNA will remain dominant: Kirchner will hand out money, expropriate whatever is needed and available, and lash out at the United States and the IMF on every possible occasion. At the same time, he will worry little about the number of Argentines living under the poverty line and be as chummy with Chávez as he can.

Chávez is doing much the same in Venezuela. He is leading the fight against the FTAA, which is going nowhere anyway. He is making life increasing miserable for foreign—above all American—companies. He is supporting, one way or the other, left-wing groups and leaders in many neighbouring countries. He has established a strategic alliance with Havana that includes the presence of nearly 20,000 Cuban teachers, doctors, and cadres in Venezuela. He is flirting with Iran and Argentina on nuclear-technology issues. Most of all, he is attempting, with some success, to split the hemisphere into two camps: one pro-Chávez, one pro-American.

At the same time, Chávez is driving his country into the ground. A tragicomic symbol of this was the collapse of the highway from Caracas to the Malquetía airport a few months ago because of lack of maintenance. Venezuela's poverty figures and human development indices have deteriorated since 1999, when Chávez took office. A simple comparison with Mexico—which has not exactly thrived in recent years—shows how badly Venezuela is faring. Over the past seven years, Mexico's economy grew by 17.5 percent, while Venezuela's failed to grow at all. From 1997 to 2003, Mexico's per capita GDP rose by 9.5 percent, while Venezuela's shrank by 45 percent. From 1998 to 2005, the Mexican peso lost 16 percent of its value, while the value of the Venezuelan bolivar dropped by 292 percent. Between 1998 and 2004, the number of Mexican households living in extreme poverty decreased by 49 percent, while the number of Venezuelan households in extreme poverty rose by 4.5 percent. In 2005, Mexico's inflation rate was estimated at 3.3 percent, the lowest in years, while Venezuela's was 16 percent.

Although Chávez does very little for the poor of his own country (among whom he remains popular),

he is doing much more for other countries: giving oil to Cuba and other Caribbean states, buying Argentina's debt, allegedly financing political campaigns in Bolivia and Peru and perhaps Mexico. He also frequently picks fights with Fox and Bush and is buying arms from Spain and Russia. This is about as close to traditional Latin American populism as one can get—and as far from a modern and socially minded left as one can be.

> What will prove most damaging is that the populist left loves power more than democracy, and it will fight to keep it at great cost.

The populist left leaders who are waiting in the wings look likely to deliver much the same. Morales in Bolivia has already made it to power. López Obrador in Mexico was close in 2006. Such leaders will follow the footsteps of Chávez and Kirchner, because they have the same roots and share the same creed. Still, they will tread the same path. Morales and Humala have both said that they will attempt either to renationalize their countries' natural resources (gas, oil, copper, water) or renegotiate the terms under which foreign companies extract them. López Obrador stated that he would not allow private investment in PEMEX, Mexico's state-owned oil company, or in the national electric power company. He has given away money right and left in Mexico City, financing his magnanimity with debt and federal tax revenues. Morales has deftly played on his indigenous origins to ingratiate himself with the majority of his country's population, to whom he is promising everything but giving very little. Morales and Humala have received at least rhetorical support from Chávez, and Morales' first trip abroad was to Havana, his second to Caracas. Humala, a retired lieutenant colonel in the Peruvian army, has confessed to being an admirer of the Venezuelan president. Like Chávez, he started his political career with a failed coup, in his case against Alberto Fujimori in 2000. López Obrador's deputy, certain to be the next Mayor of Mexico City, has openly declared his admiration for Chávez and Castro, despite having been a high-level official under Salinas.

What will prove most damaging is that the populist left loves power more than democracy, and it will fight to keep it at great cost. Its disregard for democracy and the rule of law is legendary. Often using democratic means, it has often sought to concentrate its power through new constitutions, take control of the media and the legislative and judicial branches of government, and perpetuate its rule by using electoral reforms, nepotism, and the suspension of constitutional guarantees. Chávez is the best example of this left, but certainly not the only one: López Obrador has already committed himself to "cleaning up" Mexico's Supreme Court and central bank and opposes any autonomy for the country's infant regulatory agencies.

This populist left had traditionally been disastrous for Latin America, and there is no reason to suppose it will stop being so in the future. As in the past, its rule will lead to inflation, greater poverty and inequality, and confrontation with Washington. It also threatens to roll back the region's most important achievement of recent years: the establishment of democratic rule and respect for human rights.

RIGHT LEFT, WRONG LEFT

◆ ◆ ◆

Distinguishing between these two broad left-wing currents is the best basis for serious policy, from Washington, Brussels, Mexico City, or anywhere else. There is not a tremendous amount Washington or any other government can actually do to alter the current course of events in Latin America. The Bush administration could make some difference by delivering on its promises to incumbents in the region (on matters such as immigration and trade), thereby supporting continuity without interfering in the electoral process; in South American nations where there is a strong European presence, countries such as France and Spain could help by pointing out that certain policies and attitudes have certain consequences.

But there is a much bolder course, a more statesmanlike approach, that would foster a "right left" instead of working to subvert any left's resurgence. This strategy would involve actively and substantively supporting the right left when it is in power: signing free-trade agreements with Chile, taking Brazil seriously as a trade interlocutor, engaging these nations' governments on issues involving third countries (such as Colombia, Cuba, and Venezuela), and bringing their leaders and public intellectuals into the field. The right left should be able to show not only that there are no penalties for being what it is, but also that it can deliver concrete benefits.

The international community should also clarify what it expects from the "wrong left," given that it exists and that attempts to displace it would be not only morally unacceptable but also pragmatically ineffective. The first point to emphasize is that Latin American governments of any persuasion must abide by their countries' commitments regarding human rights and democracy. The region has built up an incipient scaffolding on these matters over recent years, and any backsliding, for whatever reason or purpose, should be met by a rebuke from the international community. The second point to stress is that all governments must continue to comply with the multilateral effort to build a new international legal order, one that addresses, among other things, the environment, indigenous people's rights, international criminal jurisdiction (despite Washington's continued rejection of the International Criminal Court and its pressure on several Latin American governments to do the same), nuclear nonproliferation, World Trade Organization rules and norms, regional agreements, and the fight against corruption, drug trafficking, and terrorism, consensually defined. Europe and the United States have enormous leverage in many of these countries. They should use it.

Finally, Washington and other governments should avoid the mistakes of the past. Some fights are simply not worth fighting: If Morales wants to squabble with Chile over access to the sea, with Argentina over the price of gas, with Peru over border issues and indigenous ancestry, stand aside. If, for whatever reason, López Obrador wants to build a bullet train from Mexico City to the U.S. border, live and let live. If Chávez really wants to acquire nuclear technology from Argentina, let him, as long as he does it under International Atomic Energy Agency supervision and safeguards. Under no circumstances should anyone accept the division of the hemisphere into two camps— for the United States, against the United States— because under such a split, the Americans themselves always lose out. Such a division happened over Cuba in the 1960s and over Central America in the 1980s. Now that the Cold War is over, it should never happen again. So instead of arguing over whether to welcome or bemoan the advent of the left in Latin America, it would be wiser to separate the sensible from the irresponsible and to support the former and contain the latter. If done right, this would go a long way toward helping the region finally find its bearings and, as Gabriel Garcia Márquez might put it, end its hundreds of years of solitude.

Terms and Concepts

populism	left	reconstructed left
Castroism	radical left	
nationalism	populist left	

Questions

1. What are the causes of the left's ascendancy in Latin America?

2. How is the "left" defined in Latin America?

3. What explains the return of the populist left?

4. What does the Latin American populist left suggest about flaws or limitations of democratic regimes?

5. What characteristics or traits of a citizenry allow the populist left to flourish?

6. Castañeda proposes a statesmanlike means of encouraging the "right left." What is his proposal?

Unit 5 Annotated Bibliography

Akeya Agbando, George, and Yakubu Saaka, eds. *Issues and Trends in Contemporary African Politics: Stability, Development, and Democratization*. New York: Peter Lang, 2003. This collection by African scholars addresses subjects related to political change on the continent.

Ash, Timothy Garton. *In Europe's Name: Germany and the Divided Continent*. New York: Random House, 1993. Even when a former Communist state is fully and voluntarily absorbed by the strongest economy in Europe, adjustment to the changes is problematic.

Ayittey, George B. N. *Africa Unchained: The Blueprint for Africa's Future*. New York: Palgrave, 2005. Reflecting Africans' growing frustration with political corruption, Ayittey argues that Africa's problems lie mainly at home and not so much with the external forces that are often blamed for Africa's underdevelopment. He advocates return to the traditions of indigenous governance and small-scale rural economy as a remedy for Africa's many woes.

Beissinger, Mark R., and Crawford Young (eds.). *Beyond State Crisis?: Post-Colonial Africa and Post-Soviet Eurasia in Comparative Perspective*. Washington, D.C.: Woodrow Wilson Center Press, 2002. Comparing state crises across two continents, this volume offers both in-depth focus on specific countries and problems, and useful generalizations regarding similarities and differences between the Eurasian and African experiences. It examines state effectiveness, state breakdown, and violence in Africa and Eurasia.

Carter, Jimmy. *Palestine: Peace not Apartheid*. New York: Simon & Schuster, 2006. Former U.S. President Carter makes a strong argument for peace and recognition of the Palestinian aspirations for a state in the Middle East. The book summarizes the history of the Israeli–Palestinian conflict, the role of American diplomacy to resolve it, and the position of such neighbouring states as Lebanon and Syria.

Chabal, Patrick, and Jean-Pascal Daloz. *Africa Works: Disorder as Political Instrument*. Bloomington: Indiana University Press, 1999. This work by two leading scholars examines the political uses of disorder in sustaining regimes and enriching individual rulers.

Chaliand, Gerard, and Jean-Pierre Rageau. *The Penguin Atlas of Diasporas*. New York: Viking Press, 1995. If you want to know who moved where and when, this is the study to consult.

Cohen, Lenard J. *Broken Bonds: Yugoslavia's Disintegration and Balkan Politics in Transition* (2nd ed.) Boulder, CO: Westview Press, 1995. This book provides essential, detailed information on the crisis leading up to the war.

Constable, Pamela, and Arturo Valenzuela. *A Nation of Enemies: Chile under Pinochet*. New York: W. W. Norton, 1991. This book is a leading history of the Pinochet era.

Current History. This monthly publication features accessible articles on world affairs by leading specialists. It typically features the Middle East in January, Latin America in February, Europe in March, India and South Asia in April, Africa in May, China and East Asia in September, and Russia in October.

Dickson, Bruce J. *Red Capitalists in China: The Party, Private Entrepreneurs, and Prospects for Political Change*. Cambridge, UK; New York: Cambridge University Press, 2003. Viewing the evolving relationship between the Chinese Communist Party and private entrepreneurs, this book examines the rise of the so-called "red capitalists." Dickson argues that China's entrepreneurs are willing partners with the state, not an autonomous force in opposition to the state.

Hesli, Vicki L. *Governments and Politics in Russia and the Post-Soviet Region*. Boston, New York: Houghton Mifflin Company, 2006. This is a comprehensive history of the Soviet system, the Russian Federation, as well as post-Soviet Lithuania, Ukraine, Georgia, and Uzbekistan. The author compares these states to each other and surveys a range of themes, from elections and party politics and the relations between the states and societies to public policy issues that these countries face in their transition from Communism.

Malia, Martin E. *Russia under Western Eyes: From the Bronze Horseman to the Lenin Mausoleum*. Cambridge: Belknap Press, 1999. Malia delivers a penetrating analysis of Western views of changes in Russia.

Manion, Melanie. *Corruption by Design: Building Clean Government in Mainland China and Hong Kong*. Cambridge, MA: Harvard University Press, 2004. Manion uses two case studies to learn what can be done elsewhere to reduce political and economic corruption. She argues that proper institutional design, rigorous enforcement, and thorough education are all part of an effective policy.

Peerenboom, Randall P. *China Modernizes: Threat to the West or Model for the Rest?* Oxford; New York: Oxford University Press, 2007. The author suggests that China may well show the world a concrete alternative model of successful development. China's continued economic growth is paving the way for subsequent democratization and governmental accountability.

Rashid, Ahmed. *Jihad: The Rise of Militant Islam in Central Asia*. New Haven: Yale University Press, 2002. Rashid prepares an excellent reflection on historical background and more contemporary sources of the rise of militant Islamist movements in the lands of the former Soviet Union.

Regalado, Roberto. *Latin America at the Crossroads: Domination, Crisis, Social Struggle and Political Alternatives for the Left*. New York: Ocean Press, 2006. Cuban intellectual Regalado looks at recent political and economic changes in Latin America and addresses reasons for the sharply critical view of the United States by many countries of the continent.

Reno, William. *Warlord Politics and African States*. Boulder, CO: Lynne Rienner, 1998. This book explores the phenomenon of failed states and privatized political violence in Africa.

Rose-Ackerman, Susan. *Corruption and Government: Causes, Consequences, and Reform*. New York: Cambridge University Press, 1999. This is an authoritative investigation into political corruption around the world and what can be done about it.

Sachs, Jeffrey. *The End of Poverty: Economic Possibilities for Our Time*. New York: Penguin, 2005. Sachs writes a wide-ranging plea for increased international aid to lift sub-Saharan Africa permanently out of the poverty trap.

Shipler, David K. *Arab and Jew: Wounded Spirits in a Promised Land* (rev. ed.). New York: Penguin, 2002. Shipler examines the history and politics of one of the most intractable conflicts in world politics. His book is the product of long interviews with Israelis and Palestinians representing all shades of opinion on how to reconcile the needs for land, security, identity, and peace in the Middle East.

van de Walle, Nicolas. *African Economies and the Politics of Permanent Crisis, 1979–1999*. New York: Cambridge University Press, 2001. This analysis argues that the dynamics of African political structures are the primary factor in the continent's economic collapse.

Zakaria, Fareed. *The Future of Freedom: Illiberal Democracy at Home and Abroad*. New York: W. W. Norton, 2003. Zakaria, editor of *Newsweek International*, assesses a worldwide trend, under the cover of democratic regimes, toward either outright dictatorship or a "simple-minded populism" (even in the United States) at the expense of liberal freedoms. He argues that liberal economies precede democratic political systems.